ECONOMICS
FOR
EVERYBODY

THIRD EDITION
REVISED

GERSON ANTELL / WALTER HARRIS

AMSCO SCHOOL PUBLICATIONS, INC.
315 Hudson Street / New York, N.Y. 10013

AUTHORS:

Gerson Antell, former Curriculum Coordinator, Junior Achievement, and former Assistant Principal for Social Studies, Hillcrest High School, New York City, is coauthor of *Economics: Institutions and Analysis* and *Current Issues in American Democracy*.

Walter Harris, former Principal at Sheepshead Bay High School, New York City, and former Director of Education, The Kolburne School, New Marlboro, MA, is coauthor of *Economics: Institutions and Analysis* and *Current Issues in American Democracy*.

CONSULTANT:

Carol J. Gómez, Former Assistant Principal (Supv.) for Social Studies, New York City School System; New York City Social Studies Supervisors' Association Executive Board.

Text and Cover Design: Merrill Haber

Compositor: Nesbitt Graphics, Inc.

Text Illustrations: Nesbitt Graphics, Inc.

Cover Photos: Image Copyright © Digital Vision; Eyewire

Please visit our Web site at:
www.amscopub.com

When ordering this book, please specify either **R 7530 P** *or* ECONOMICS FOR EVERYBODY, THIRD EDITION.

ISBN: 978-1-56765-640-4
NYC Item: 56765-640-3

2   3   4   5   6   10   09   08   07

PREFACE

You may have asked yourself several questions as you opened this book: First, what is economics? Second, why is economics for everybody? What does this strange-sounding subject have to do with me and my life, plans, and goals?

Economics has been called the study of how individuals and groups earn their living. All right, you say, but there are some 300 million people in the United States today. They do not all earn a living, do they? Some are too young, some are in school, and some are retired—do you mean everybody? Yes, we do, because each person, in some way, contributes to the economy of the United States.

In our first unit, we explain the roles of consumers and producers in economic life. We explore the basic questions that every nation's economy, or economic system, must answer. We show how money, goods, and services flow to and from different groups. We explain what money is and why it has value. Subsequent units explore in depth the role of consumers, workers, businesses, and governments. After that, we turn to the global economy and see how other nations earn their living. Finally, we look at some of the most pressing issues and problems that the United States faces today.

Each chapter opens with a preview telling what the chapter is about. This section also contains a list of questions that the chapter will answer. These questions reappear as chapter subheads in the text. You will also find many photographs, tables, and graphs in the text. The photographs were chosen to show typical scenes or events that are discussed. The captions to the photos often ask questions for thought and understanding. The graphs and tables make it easy to understand the quantities and time spans that are discussed in the text.

We have included many topical readings in the chapters. Some will enhance your understanding of the text. Others present controversial problems in economics. While some are devoted to more personal topics, others concentrate on topics of general interest.

In your study of economics, you will encounter many words that are new to you. At the beginning of each chapter, we have provided a list of Key Terms. These are the new words and phrases that are introduced and explained in the chapter. These words are also defined at the back of the book, in the Glossary.

End-of-chapter summaries review important ideas and information. Looking Ahead sections tell briefly about the next chapter or unit. You will see how well you understood what you read when you answer the questions at the end of each chapter. Activities and questions for thought help you apply the principles you have learned. If you want to review the meaning of a term, you can either look it up in the Glossary or check the Index for the page on which it is explained.

The First and Second editions of *Economics for Everybody* had always been known for an emphasis on consumer education. The Third Edition goes even further in introducing students to additional basic concepts of personal finance, such as financial planning.

Another major concept—entrepreneurship—has also been emphasized in the Third Edition of the text. New features in Chapter 21 and elsewhere concentrate on problems and prospects of going into business for oneself. For the Third Edition, all of the statistics, graphs, and tables have been updated, as well as many of the photographs. More emphasis on using the Internet for economic research has been added.

We hope that your understanding of your own life, of the lives of your family and friends, and of the economy of the United States is enriched by your study of this book. And now, welcome to economics—it is for everybody.

GERSON ANTELL

WALTER HARRIS

CONTENTS

Unit *1*

WHAT IS ECONOMICS ALL ABOUT?

Goods: Sneakers of many sizes and styles satisfy different wants and needs.

We all have many wants and needs, but no one can have everything. This is the first lesson of economics. In Chapter 1, you will learn that *resources*—the things that are needed to satisfy these needs and wants—are always limited. In economics, the limit on resources is called *scarcity*. Because of scarcity, individuals and societies must make *trade-offs*. That is, in order to have one thing, they must give up something else.

Societies organize *economic systems* to produce and distribute goods and services. Different nations and groups have different kinds of economic systems. These are discussed in Chapter 2. All economic systems must answer three questions: (1) What should be produced? (2) How should it be produced? and (3) Who should receive what is produced? Chapter 3 tells how the United States economic system answers these questions.

In Chapter 4, you will learn about the *demand* for and the *supply* of goods and services. Demand and supply set prices and determine how resources will be used. Chapter 5 describes what money is and how it meets society's needs. You will also find out about the role of banks. Chapter 6 explains what happens when the value of money changes.

CHAPTER *1*
Making Choices

Think of some of the thousands of things that you can buy in American stores, online, and by mail order. Here are some examples.

radio	compact disks	dictionary
jeans	sneakers	personal computer
television set	camcorder	ten-speed bicycle

Many businesses have decided to spend millions, even billions, of dollars to produce these items and thousands more for you and others. Why did the merchants choose to open stores in your community to sell these items? Why did customers decide to buy them?

Each of these questions involves an important choice, or decision. And every day of the year, people all across our country—and in every country of the world—make such decisions as buyers and sellers, workers and business owners. Their collective decisions make up a nation's economic system. *Economics* is the study of why people make one choice rather than another when buying and selling, spending and saving. Economics explains how businesses are formed to satisfy different wants and needs. Your decisions every time you walk into a store, movie theater, restaurant, or bank are part of the study of economics.

Without realizing it, you have already made hundreds of economic decisions. In your lifetime, you will make thousands more, including choosing a career, getting an education, accepting a job, forming a business, and saving, investing, borrowing, and lending money. The main purpose of this book is to give you the knowledge that you will need to evaluate choices and make sound decisions. Let us begin to acquire that knowledge by asking several questions:

- What are goods and services?
- What are economic resources?
- Why must we make economic choices?
- What is the cost of every choice?
- What do economists do?

WHAT ARE GOODS AND SERVICES?

In your study of economics, you will discover many new words and phrases. This is not surprising. Almost every activity has its own vocabulary. Two of the most important words in economics are *goods* and *services*.

Goods are things that can be seen or touched. Some examples of goods are the compact disks, sneakers, and bicycles that were listed at the beginning of this chapter.

Services are useful work that cannot be seen or touched. The salesperson who rents or sells you a DVD is performing a service. So, too, is the individual who keeps track of a business's records and files. Services have value, just as goods do. The care of a

Services: Haircuts are useful work that can be seen and understood.

doctor when you are sick, a haircut, and a ride on a bus are all things of value. Although they cannot be touched, they fill our needs.

Goods and services must be made, or produced. Businesses offer both goods and services for sale. They have *value* because they satisfy people's needs and wants. The business owners, managers, and workers who made the disks, sneakers, and bicycles are called *producers*. The doctor, barber, and bus driver are also producers. They are producing services. The users of the goods and services are called *consumers*. When you buy a CD or visit a doctor's office, you are a consumer.

WHAT ARE ECONOMIC RESOURCES?

Economic resources are the things that go into the making of goods and services. There are three kinds: *natural resources, human resources*, and *capital resources*.

Natural Resources

The things provided by the world around us are natural resources. Air and water; minerals such as iron ore, gold, and quartz; coal and gas; vegetable products such as trees, plants, grains, and fruits—all are natural resources. Without natural resources, there could be no goods of any kind. Natural resources appear plentiful. Yet no nation has an unlimited supply of them.

Natural Resources: This managed pine forest is an example of a natural resource that can be harvested and renewed over time. Can you name a natural resource that, once used, cannot be renewed?

Human Resources: Skilled people are needed to plan, operate, and service the complex machinery and technology of today's world.

Human Resources

The people who put everything together to make goods and services are human resources. These individuals are the producers we mentioned earlier. How much a nation can produce depends to a large extent upon the abilities of its people. Consider a compact disk that you may have bought recently, or a visit to a doctor's office. You are probably aware of the education and training needed to become a doctor or nurse. But a music recording is also the product of many people's talents and skills. A nation of educated and highly skilled people is able to produce more, earn more, and live better, than a nation whose people have little training and few skills.

Capital Resources

The machines, tools, and buildings used in the production of goods and services are capital resources. A nation's wealth is often measured in terms of the capital it possesses. The United States is rich and powerful today in part because it has more abundant capital resources than most other nations. With this capital, the United States produces more goods and services than any other

Capital Resources: In factories such as this chemical plant, natural resources are used to manufacture finished products. What role do people play in using capital resources?

nation. The bus that brings you to school and the paved streets and highways of your town or city are forms of capital. So, too, are the trucks and trains carrying goods across the country.

Entrepreneurship

The process of bringing together the three factors of production (natural, human, and capital resources) is called *entrepreneurship*. The individual who organizes a business and assumes the risks and rewards (profits) is called an *entrepreneur*. The entrepreneur introduces new products and methods of production and new ways of running the business. The entrepreneur invests time and money in a business in the hope of earning a profit.

WHY MUST WE MAKE ECONOMIC CHOICES?

We have said that economics is about the decisions all of us must make as producers and consumers. Why do we always have to make a choice between either this or that? Why can we not have everything we want? Economists try to answer this question by discussing *scarcity*.

Scarcity

Scarcity means that there is not enough of everything to go around. Consumers everywhere want more goods and services than their nations' economies can possibly produce. We have said that all natural resources are limited in supply. There are limits to the number of doctors, farmers, engineers, factory workers, and other human resources that a nation can supply. And capital resources are also limited. Since *all* resources are limited in supply, the kinds and quantities of goods and services that can be produced are limited. Therefore, decisions must be made how best to use the natural resources, workers, and capital that are available.

You have faced the problem of scarcity and the need to make choices. Perhaps you earned $2,500 this past summer. What did you do with the money? Did you spend it all as you got it, or did you save some of it for expenses during the year? For certain, you could not buy everything you wanted and still have money to spend later. You had to make economic choices.

What we said about one person's need to make choices is true for all individuals and families. It is also true for businesses. Even the largest companies in the United States must make choices. A company worth many billions of dollars does not simply replace its machinery every time a new or improved process comes along. The company's managers have to think of the costs of buying new equipment and retraining its workers. After all, the company might do many other things with its money. It could launch a new advertising campaign, for example, or start a research program. Both are costly activities. But just as you could not spend your summer earnings *and* still save the money for later use, the company will also have to choose from among the things it would like to have. The combination it selects depends upon what best suits its purposes.

Even the United States government must make choices. It cannot afford to do everything that it wants. Although the government would like to spend more on ending poverty, cleaning up the environment, maintaining national defense, and building schools, roads, and hospitals, it just cannot afford to do all these things at the same time. The government must often make a *trade-off*, or choice, such as between $1 billion more for defense or $1 billion more for education.

Yes, you—as well as every consumer, business, and government—must make choices. Together we make up a *society* (the group, community, or nation to which we belong). Scarcity forces us, as a society, to make choices. Society must decide (1) what goods and services to produce, (2) how these goods and services will be produced, and, finally, (3) who should receive these goods

No one can have everything. Individuals, businesses, and governments must make trade-offs and pay an opportunity cost each time they make a decision. Well, then, how does a thoughtful person make a sound decision? Whether the decision involves an economic choice or any other choice, the process is the same. We should take the following steps:

1. Get the facts.
2. Consider the choices, or alternatives, open to us.
3. Keep our goals and objectives in mind.
4. Estimate the short-term and long-term results of each alternative.
5. Make our decision.

Given the same facts, will two individuals reach the same decision? Possibly not, because each person's objectives may be different. Economists, who spend their lives studying economic activity, do not always agree on what action to take in dealing with various economic problems. Let us consider a real economic problem—that of unemployment among teenagers. Economists can recognize the facts and may even agree on the choices. They know *what is*. But they do not always agree on *what ought to be*.

We may reach different conclusions as facts (or conditions) change. At one time, people accepted as fact that the world was flat and that a sailing ship could fall off the end of the flat world. If, indeed, the world were flat, it seemed logical to conclude that a ship sailing in any one direction would reach the end of

the world and fall off. Today, we know that the world is *not* flat. It is a sphere (ball). One need not fear sailing off the end of the world. The "facts" (at least what were thought to be facts) changed, and so our conclusions based on those facts changed. (A fact is not the same as an opinion. A fact can be proven true or false. An opinion is more like a feeling or a guess that something is true but cannot be proven to be true.)

When discussing teenagers and unemployment, there are several important facts to consider. Nearly one out of every seven teenagers is unemployed and looking for work. Unemployment among minority teenagers can be more than double this figure. Teenagers without jobs may never have the chance to develop the work habits and skills of the adult world. Some teenagers have already turned to illegal ways to get money.

Let us consider two ways to solve the teenage unemployment problem: (1) Lower the *minimum wage* for teenagers. The minimum wage is the lowest amount of money that an employer may legally pay a worker for each hour of work. In 2002, the federal minimum wage was $5.15 an hour. (2) Spend more money on education and training for teenagers.

To reach a conclusion, we must examine the arguments for and against each alternative. You may have other suggestions as well. The following table presents arguments for and against each proposal.

If you were asked to make a choice in this case, what would you recommend? Keeping in mind your goals and objectives, do you think that increased spending for education is more important than increased spending for other purposes? Do you think that lowering the minimum wage for teenagers would create more jobs? If you favor *both* a lower minimum wage *and* more education and training, which would you suggest be tried first?

Two Proposed Ways to Solve Teenage Unemployment

Proposal	Pro	Con
1. Lower the minimum wage for teenage workers.	It would cost employers less to hire teenagers. Firms would be encouraged to hire more young people and to create jobs for them.	No new jobs would be created. Hiring more teenagers would mean more adults would be unemployed. This would be worse than teenage unemployment.
2. Spend more money on education and job training for teenagers.	Trained young people are more likely to find jobs than those who are poorly educated.	Spending on education and job training is very costly. Huge sums are already being spent on education. Better teaching, higher standards, and more parental involvement are needed, not more money.

and services. Every society—past, present, and future—in every part of the world must answer these same *What? How?* and *Who?* questions, but they answer them in the different ways. Our way of doing things and our values are not the same as those of people living in, say, Saudi Arabia. Moreover, how we do things changes over time. Had you been living in the United States 100 years ago, your whole lifestyle and way of thinking would most likely be different than it is today. How different societies answer the three basic questions and how societies change their answers to the three questions is discussed in the next chapter.

WHAT IS THE COST OF EVERY CHOICE?

Making a choice—any choice, always has some cost. For example, suppose that you saved $1,300 from the $2,500 you earned last summer. With that money, you would like to buy both an digital camcorder and a multimedia computer with a fast modem. But when you go shopping, you discover that $1,300 is not enough to buy both. The computer that you want (not including the monitor and printer) costs $599. The camcorder that you want costs

$1,099. The total is $1,698. Since you are $398 short, you must make a choice, or trade-off. You may purchase one, but you will have to give up the other.

The large company that decides to spend $1 million on advertising rather than on research has also made a trade-off. It has given up the chance to discover new products in order to try to attract new customers.

The U.S. government might give up the opportunity to spend $1 billion on education when it chooses instead to spend this money on building highways or for national defense.

Opportunity Cost

The term used to describe the choices made by people, businesses, and government is *opportunity cost*. It means that by spending a certain amount on A, we are giving up the opportunity to have B. Every time a person, a business, or a government makes an economic choice, there is a cost in addition to the actual price. The cost of the camcorder is $1,099, that is true. But the cost is greater than that. From an economist's point of view, the price of the camcorder also includes an opportunity cost—another item you might have bought with the same money. Every time you make an economic choice, there is an opportunity cost to you in terms of what you had to give up, or trade off, in order to get whatever you selected.

WHAT DO ECONOMISTS DO?

Economists are professionals who study the workings of our economic system and all that goes on within it. Broadly speaking, economists are concerned with how the goods and services we want are produced and distributed among us. For example, suppose that the President were to ask Congress to approve an appropriation for an advanced missile defense system. Congress might be concerned how spending money for missiles will affect other government programs and the economy as a whole. Economists will gather data related to this problem, analyze that data, and identify problems that might arise among the choices available to Congress. Hopefully, the economists will be able to suggest solutions to those problems.

Economists often agree on the data and the problem, or what we call the "what is." But they will often disagree on "what ought to be." The economist may state that the country cannot afford both the President's missile program and all the other proposed government programs and stay within its budget. In this illustration, the economist is presenting a description of what is.

If the economist suggested, however, that an increase in spending is or is not wise, the economist would be discussing the world as the economist thinks it should be. In this instance, the economist would be making a value judgment. Economists, like everybody else, have sets of values that often influence how they view economic problems.

Like other professionals, economists often specialize in their work. Some look at the individual elements of the economy. Other economists focus on the big picture, or the economy as a whole.

Microeconomics

Some problems involve the effects of economic forces upon individual parts of the economy, such as business firms, households, and workers. For example, what will happen to a firm's sales if it increased its prices to make up for wage increases? Such studies are called *microeconomics*.

Macroeconomics

Some problems involve the impact of changes on the economy as a whole rather than on an individual part. For example, what will be the effect of an increase in federal spending on consumer spending and the federal budget? *Macroeconomics* is the name given to such studies.

--- **SUMMARY** ---

The choices that people make every day as buyers, sellers, workers, and business owners are the concern of economics. Economics is an area of study that tries to find out why and how people make one choice rather than another. It is concerned with people as producers and consumers of goods and services.

Goods are objects of value that can be seen and felt. Services also have value but cannot be seen or felt. Producers are the people who make the goods and services, and consumers are those who buy them.

Economic resources—including natural, human, and capital ones—are the things that go into the making of goods and services. These resources are limited in supply, or scarce. Entrepreneurs bring these resources together.

Choices have to be made as to how resources are to be used. There is an additional cost to every choice that is made—an opportunity cost. This cost equals the value of the goods or services we give up in order to have something else.

One should use critical thinking skills *before* making any decision. This means that we should gather our facts and consider alternatives *before* reaching a conclusion. If the facts change or conditions change, we should be prepared to reexamine our conclusions and, if necessary, revise our conclusions.

Economists are professionals who study the ways an economy allocates its resources. The economist studies cause-and-effect relationships involving economic forces. Microeconomics is the study of the effects of decisions by individuals and firms on various parts of the economy. Macroeconomics is the study of the effects of changes on the economy as a whole.

LOOKING AHEAD

You have learned that because of economic scarcity, people cannot have everything they want. An individual, a business firm, and a nation must make choices. How are these choices made? How do different societies (nations) answer the three basic What? How? and Who? questions? In our next chapter, we will discuss how different nations of our world have organized different economic systems in order to answer these basic questions.

EXERCISES

✔**Matching** Match each term in Column A with its definition in Column B.

Column A	Column B
1. economics	*a.* go into making goods and services
2. goods	*b.* one good or service given up in order to get another
3. services	
4. producers	*c.* business owners, managers, and workers
5. consumers	*d.* things of value that cannot be seen or touched
6. resources	*e.* the study of the choices people make as producers and consumers
7. scarcity	
8. opportunity cost	*f.* things of value that can be seen and touched
	g. those who buy or use goods and services
	h. limited supply of goods and services

✔**Multiple Choice** Choose the letter of the item that best completes the statement or answers the question.

1. The main idea of this chapter is that (a) only poor people and governments must make economic choices (b) all people, businesses, and governments must make choices (c) it is easy to make economic choices (d) it does not cost anything to make a choice.

2. Which one of the following is an example of an economic good? (a) visit to a dentist (b) pair of sneakers (c) lesson taught by your teacher (d) ride on a bus.

3. Which one of the following is an example of an economic service? (a) haircut (b) camcorder (c) DVD (d) pair of scissors.

4. Which one of the following is an example of a consumer? (a) doctor treating a patient (b) recording artist (c) person buying a pair of jeans (d) worker in an auto plant.

5. Which one of the following groups of names contains only capital resources? (a) trees, water, iron ore (b) workers, business owners, managers (c) machines, tools, factories (d) nature, people, services.

6. A good or service has value because it (a) costs money (b) satisfies a human want or need (c) is sold in stores (d) is abundant in nature.

7. The reason scarcity exists is that (a) people want more goods and services than can be produced (b) some people are wealthy while others are poor (c) there is plenty of everything for everyone (d) individuals and governments do not make the right choices.

8. What is the opportunity cost to a nation that chooses to spend another $1 billion on a defense project rather than on an education program? (a) $2 billion (b) the cost of the defense project (c) the $1 billion education program (d) no cost.

9. Suppose that you are given a problem to solve and four ways to solve your problem. Which one of the following choices is an example of critical thinking? (a) Doing what your "gut feeling" tells you is best. (b) Doing whatever your friends do. (c) Checking your facts and alternatives before making a decision. (d) Getting as many opinions as possible and choosing whatever the majority has selected.

✔**Interpreting a Cartoon** Study the cartoon below and then answer the questions that follow.

"One of these would pay for a hundred new schools."

1. What would be a good title for this cartoon?

2. Who is the person in the cartoon?

3. Explain the meaning of the caption.

4. What is the trade-off or opportunity cost that is paid by the person in the cartoon?

✔*Reading for Critical Thinking*

Read the selection below and then tell whether the statements that follow are true (**T**) or false (**F**) based on the reading. If there is not enough information in the selection to answer true or false, answer **NI**.

Decisions! Decisions! With so many things to choose from, how do we decide which is the best choice? Economic decision-making should be based on a careful evaluation of the choices open to us. This means that we must (1) know the facts, (2) have goals or objectives in mind, and (3) understand the possible consequences of each of our alternatives (choices).

Remember, because of scarcity, we must make trade-offs in deciding how to use our resources. These trade-offs are the opportunity cost to us. So, if we decide to do A rather than B, the trade-off or opportunity cost to us is not being able to do B. Consider the problem that two high school seniors have.

Mary and Lillian are classmates. They work at Tip-Top Cleaners after school. Their boss, Mr. Barron, wants them to work full time after graduation. He has offered each of them $200 for a 35-hour week, plus various paid benefits, including health insurance and a vacation.

Mary has accepted Mr. Barron's offer—to work full time. She knows that to continue her schooling for two years would cost her family $10,000 per year. This expense would mean a lot of sacrifice for them. In addition, there would be an opportunity cost—the salary she would lose by not working. For two years, this cost would come to $20,800, before taxes.

Lillian has turned down Mr. Barron's offer. She wants to learn word processing. She has decided to continue her schooling at the local community college for two more years. Lillian is basing her decision on the long-term consequences of her actions. At first, or in the short term, it will be more expensive to go to college than to continue working. Lillian will earn nothing for two years. And her family will pay her tuition and living expenses while she attends college. But Lillian expects that over a period of years her earnings in word processing will be greater than her earnings at Tip-Top Cleaners.

1. A good title for this reading is "Making a Choice."

2. Not all people are required to make a trade-off when reaching an economic decision.

3. A trade-off is another way of describing an opportunity cost.

4. Mary plans to open her own business after a few years.

5. The total cost to Lillian of continuing her education for two years is the cost of tuition and other living expenses.

6. Mary will be financially better off as a result of her decision in the short term, but Lillian is likely to earn more in the long term.

7. Lillian had career objectives in mind when making her decision.

8. The reading suggests that a person who faces making a similar decision should follow Lillian's example.

CHAPTER 2
Types of Economic Systems

Key Terms

economic system	free enterprise	class struggle
what, how, who	capitalism	five-year plan
traditional system	means of production	exploit
market system	mixed economy	Gosplan
competitor	proletariat	quota
command system	communism	commune
		privatize

Ms. Perry teaches economics classes at Columbia High School. She asked her class to produce a good or service that they would sell. As an incentive, Ms. Perry said that the class could keep all of the money they might earn from their business venture.

The following are some of the ideas put forward in Ms. Perry's second period class:

Joe: "In ceramics class we made clocks. We had clock molds and we poured plaster into them. After the plaster hardened, we painted the clocks and fired them in the kiln. When finished, we attached a quartz movement in each that the teacher had bought for us. I'll bet we could sell them easily for $20 each."

Marie: "I was in that class, too. I made a cute ceramic cat and painted it white with green eyes. I think ceramic figures would sell better than clocks."

Tom: "Ceramic clocks and figures are too complicated. Who will do what? Why can't we run a service business? We could advertise to mow lawns, baby-sit, and things like that. People are always looking for help and willing to pay for it."

Sally: "Where will we get the money to start our business? Who will we sell our product or service to?"

In this class, Ms. Perry's students had to make some important decisions: What to produce (a good or a service); How to produce (method of manufacturing clocks or ceramic figures or performing various services); and Who will get whatever the class produced.

Decisions such as these are made every day. *What? How? Who?* These are three basic questions of economics. All groups must answer them, from small entrepreneurs (such as members of the class) to powerful nations. After studying this chapter, you will know why they must be answered. You will also know:

- What are economic systems?
- What do all economic systems have in common?
- What happens when an economic system fails?

WHAT ARE ECONOMIC SYSTEMS?

An *economic system* is the term used to describe how a nation is organized for production, that is, whether it has a *traditional, market,* or *command* economy. The terms traditional, market, or command are used by economists to describe economic systems. It is important to keep in mind that classifying nations' economies in this way is just a convenient tool for examining how economic systems work. It does not give us a complete and accurate picture of how any real society works. The three economic systems we will describe are only *models,* simplified pictures of reality. In the real world, no modern economic system completely fits any of the models. By examining the models, however, we get a better understanding of the economic systems as they really exist.

Traditional Economic System

A *traditional economic system* is one in which people's economic roles are the same as those of their parents and grandparents. Societies that produce goods and services in traditional ways are found today in some parts of South America, Asia, and Africa. There, people living in an agricultural village still plant and harvest their own food on their own land. And the ways they produce food, clothing, and shelter are almost exactly the same as those used in the past. Tradition decides what these people do for a living and how their work is performed. Today, no country has a traditional economic system. Only parts of countries follow this system.

Market Economic System

A *market economic system,* or *capitalism,* is one in which a nation's economic decisions are the result of individual decisions by

Traditional Economic System: These Peruvian farmers follow centuries-old ways of planting and harvesting their crops.

buyers and sellers in the marketplace. Market systems are also known as *free enterprise systems.* The United States has a market, or free enterprise, economic system. When you finish school, you may go to work where you choose, if a job is open and you are hired. You are also free to go into business on your own. Suppose that you decide to open a business. You will risk the money that you have saved or borrowed in the hope that you will be successful. The price that you charge for your goods or services will be influenced by the prices charged by your *competitors* (other businesses selling the same items or services). The success that you have will depend on the demand by consumers for your goods. You may do extremely well. But if people do not want what you are selling, you will go out of business.

Command Economic System

In a *command economic system,* the main decision maker is the government. No person may independently decide to open and run a business. The government decides what goods and services are to be produced and owns the places where the production takes place. The government sells these goods and services and decides how the talents and skills of its workers are to be used.

WHAT DO ALL ECONOMIC SYSTEMS HAVE IN COMMON?

In Chapter 1, you learned that all societies have limited economic resources. Since there is not enough of everything to go

Market Economic System: In the U.S. free enterprise system, anyone can open a business and sell goods and services for a profit.

around, each society has to make choices about how it will use these scarce resources. These choices may be expressed as questions:

1. What goods and services should be produced?
2. How should the goods and services be produced?
3. Who will receive the goods and services that are produced?
4. Who owns the means of production in economic systems?

All economic systems—traditional, market, and command— must answer these questions. But each type of economic system answers the what, how, and who questions in different ways.

The Question of What

A business firm that employs 100 workers could, in theory, produce anything it chooses: baseball gloves, carpets, or automobiles. But the firm cannot produce all of these things at once. Instead, the firm must concentrate on making one or two products and give up other possibilities. In a traditional system, habit or custom decides what will be produced. In a market system, the *what* question is decided by individuals or companies seeking opportunities

Government-Directed Command Economy: Under the Soviet Union's command economy, government planners decided what goods would be produced, at what quantities, and for whom. This government-owned factory produced steel.

for profit. In a command economic system, the *what* question is decided by the government.

For example, let us assume that all three economic systems produce carpets. First, consider a traditional economic system. In a traditional society, carpets will have been produced for years on end. Regardless of changes in prices or the demands of the market, the traditional society would continue to produce carpets. People today produce carpets in virtually the exact same way as "they have always been produced." Changes in price or demand for carpets would not necessarily cause this traditional community to stop producing carpets and start producing some other product.

In a market system, if it appears to be profitable to produce carpets, some individuals or companies will do so. Some will stop producing carpets when it becomes apparent that it is not profitable for them to do so. Similarly, firms will produce baseball gloves or automobiles—or most anything else—should they believe they could make a profit producing that product. In Chapter 4, you will learn how the decision-making process determines what to produce in a market economy.

In a command system, a government office would tell factory managers whether they should produce gloves, carpets, or automobiles. The government would also say how many of each workers would be expected to produce and what prices should be charged.

The Question of How

Let us suppose that the owners of a business firm decide to produce baseball gloves. How should these gloves be produced? Should each of the workers individually make one glove at a time by hand? Or should a factory be built and equipped with machinery for making the separate parts of the glove—back, front, stuffing, and lacing? Moreover, how should each worker be compensated?

All economic systems must find a way of answering the *how* question. In a traditional system, a glove will be made in the same way it has been made for generations. In a market system, the factory owner will decide how a glove will be produced. In a command system, the *how* question will be decided by the government.

The Question of for Whom

Who shall receive the goods and services that are finally produced? Since there is never enough of everything to go around, this is an important problem facing all economic systems. Should the consumers be those who need or deserve the goods and services most, as decided by the government? Should only those who received these goods and services in the past continue to do so? Or shall the consumers be the people who have enough money to buy the goods and services?

In a traditional economic system, a family group works as a unit. Family members usually receive most of whatever the group produces. However, in some traditional societies (for example, during the historical period known as feudalism), it was customary to give a portion of the family's production to a feudal or tribal chief. The family's share of their society's output remained about the same generation after generation. Few traditional societies exist today.

In a market system (the United States, for example), you get the goods and services you want *and can pay for.* You may want many things, but you do not get the things you cannot pay for. Those who have a lot of money will be able to buy lots of goods and services. Individuals with little money will be able to buy fewer goods and services. Thus, in a market system, the *who* question is answered largely in terms of how much money a person or family has.

Finally, in a command economic system, a government agency may decide *who* gets certain goods and services. Central authorities decide where and how goods and services are to be distributed. In theory in the Soviet Union, each person produced according to his ability and received according to his needs. But that was only in theory and not in reality!

Again we must point out that no modern economy fully fits the models we have just described. In the U.S. market economy, for example, the government regulates businesses in order to protect consumers. In the Soviet Union, with its command economy, some elite individuals had more money than most and were able to get the goods and services they wanted. Meanwhile, the vast majority of the people were often forced to do with much less.

Who Owns the Means of Production in Economic Systems?

We have classified economic systems according to the way they answer three basic questions of what, how, and who. It is helpful also to discuss a fourth question, "Who owns the means of production?" An economy's *means of production* are its factories, farms, shops, office buildings, mines, and machinery. The means of production are used to produce other goods and services. Generally speaking, in a free enterprise economic system, individuals own the means of production. In a command economic system, the government usually owns the means of production. In a traditional economic system, means of production are usually owned by families, or the heads of families.

Mixed Economic Systems

No country today has an economic system that is either 100 percent free market or 100 percent command. The U.S. system most closely represents a free market economy. The Communist economic systems of Cuba (in Latin America) and North Korea (in Asia) are closest to our description of command economies. China has a command economy, but it has slowly been introducing elements of a market economy. All countries today have mixed economic systems or *mixed economies*, with some free enterprise and some government ownership.

Figure 2.1. Market, Mixed, and Command Economies Compared

Market Economy	Mixed Economy	Command Economy
Private Ownership of Means of Production	Public and Private Ownership of Means of Production	Public Ownership of Means of Production
Decisions by consumers and businesses determine economic activity.	Decisions by consumers and businesses and by government determine economic activity.	Decisions by government determine economic activity.

WHAT HAPPENS WHEN AN ECONOMIC SYSTEM FAILS?

In 1848, Karl Marx and his friend Friedrich Engels wrote the *Communist Manifesto*. In it, they claimed that a *class struggle* had always existed between a ruling class and the lower classes. The Roman Catholic Church and the nobility made up the ruling classes during the Middle Ages (500 to 1500 C.E.) in Europe. The peasants and middle class were the ones being dominated then. In the 1800s, however, the middle class became the ruling class in Europe as a result of the Industrial Revolution. Marx said that in the mid-1800s this middle class was *exploiting* (taking advantage of) those who worked for a wage—the *proletariat* (workers). He believed that discontent among the working class would unite workers and that they would rise up and overthrow the capitalists and establish a classless society called *communism*.

Since there would be only one class—the working class—there would no longer be a class struggle and, therefore, no need for a government. The state, said Marx, would "wither away." All workers would work to the best to their abilities and be paid according to their needs.

Marx believed that the Communist state would start out as a dictatorship in order to build the Communist society and to fight off its capitalist neighbors. He predicted that eventually workers in every country would overthrow their capitalist ruling class and that all nations would become Communist.

Communism in Russia

In 1917, two revolutions took place in Russia. In the second one, the Russian Communist party under V.I. Lenin seized control. This group created the first Communist state, Soviet Russia

Soviet Union: Moscow shoppers lined up at food stores in the 1980s. Not much was available on that day, or on most days, so long lines were common long before shops opened.

(to be enlarged in 1922 as the Soviet Union). Its economy soon became a prime example of a command economy.

Special Role of the Government

The Soviet state owned almost all the means of production and distribution (including factories, mines, farms, and stores). It determined how the basic questions of WHAT, HOW, and WHO would be answered. Moreover, because the Communist party was the only legal political party, it exercised ultimate power over the government. Thus, the Communists decided what the general economic goals for the coming years would be. These goals were written down in formal plans for the coming years.

1. Five-Year Plans. When Joseph Stalin rose to power in the Soviet Union in the mid-1920s, he found himself at the head of an industrially backward nation. In an attempt to modernize the Soviet economy as rapidly as possible, Stalin instituted a series of *five-year plans*. Each plan was a detailed statement of the nation's production goals for the next five years. The plans applied to all aspects of the economy, including industry, agriculture, trades, and the professions. For example, the government expected lawyers to handle their quota of cases, taxi drivers to log so many miles, and barbers to perform a minimum number of haircuts.

The five-year plans not only set forth production goals but also tried to assign the resources necessary to achieve them. If, for example, Soviet leaders determined that steel production should be increased, the plan provided for the construction of additional steel production facilities and allocated the raw materials and labor needed to meet the goal. With exception of the war years 1939–1945, five-year plans or their equivalent (there was one seven-year plan) were in force from 1928 to the end of the Soviet era in 1991.

2. Deciding WHAT to Produce. The Soviet agency responsible for preparing and administering the central economic plan was the State Planning Committee, or *Gosplan.* After consulting with the various economic ministries and industries, Gosplan prepared production *quotas* (targets) for each of the country's 350,000 business enterprises.

The managers then estimated the quantities of raw materials and the amount of labor they would need to meet their quotas. The managers' requests were sent back to Gosplan. Since the managers' requests rarely matched the available resources, Gosplan had to modify many of its quotas and reassign tasks among the enterprises until a final plan was achieved. The plan, which was binding on all Soviet enterprises, set forth target quotas for sales, costs, profits, and productivity increases for the coming year.

3. Deciding HOW Goods Were to Be Produced. The responsibility for carrying out the annual plan rested with the managers of the local factories, farms, stores, and offices. They hired and fired workers, purchased machinery and equipment, and made the everyday decisions necessary to running a business. But, unlike capitalist entrepreneurs (whose primary motivation is to earn profits), the Soviet managers' goal was to conduct their "businesses" in ways that would meet their quotas.

4. Deciding WHO Was to Receive the Goods and Services. Since the government controlled nearly all of the nation's output, it could reward some people by allowing them to purchase goods and services unavailable to most others. For example, while the government controlled rents so that almost everyone could afford housing, there simply were not enough apartments to go around. Nevertheless, good housing was made available for certain categories of workers who were deemed essential by the government, such as Olympic athletes, scientists, and high party officials. Similarly, these privileged people were able to obtain scarce items in stores set aside for their exclusive use.

The Spread of Communism Elsewhere

After World War II (1939–1945), the Soviet Union expanded its influence and helped set up Communist political systems and economies in Eastern Europe. In 1949, China also had a Communist Revolution and soon set up a command economy. North Korea, North Vietnam, and Cuba also became Communist in the mid-1900s.

1. Communism in China. Mao Zedong and the Chinese Communist party came to power in China in 1949. In the 1950s, it nationalized industries and created five-year plans for its national economy. The government soon owned all factories, stores, and means of transportation.

Farming was done on *communes* of 2,000 to 4,000 people. Residents of the communes were organized military style in shared living quarters and mess halls. Everyone worked at assigned tasks and received wages. Private farms were abolished, as were village markets. The Central Planning Committee of the Chinese government in Beijing told the people on the commune what to grow, how much to grow, and how to grow it. Housing was assigned, and essential coupons for food and clothing made it impossible for anyone to leave the commune or dormitory assigned to them. Furthermore, party officials controlled when people could get married and who could have children. Like the Soviet Union, the government was a dictatorship controlled by the Communist party.

2. Reform Movement in China. In 1978, Mao died, and the Communist system in China slowly began to change. Leadership of the Communist party fell to Deng Xiaoping, who introduced some capitalist changes in the economy. But the dictatorship remained.

In 1979, Chinese agriculture was reformed to allow individual households and groups of households to lease land from the state for a specified number of years. During that time, the renters would have to pay taxes and fulfill planned production quotas. The goods produced to meet those quotas would have to be sold to the state at set prices. But after meeting these obligations, rural households would be free to produce what they could. Furthermore, farmers could sell surplus products on the free market at whatever price they could get. These rural reforms were very successful. Chinese farm output and farmers' standard of living increased greatly.

Also under Deng, the government encouraged private ownership of light and medium industries, such as the manufacturing of toys, textiles, garments, shoes, and consumer electronics. Many state factories were *privatized* (made privately owned) by selling shares of ownership to the public. The five-year plans continued, but the state's share of the nation's economy gradually declined.

Chinese High Technology: Factory workers assemble telephone equipment in newly industrializing China. How do you think working conditions compare to those in Western nations?

China gave priority to increasing overseas trade and to attracting foreign investments in Chinese factories and other businesses.

Privatization in China has been a great success. Output of goods and services quadrupled between 1978 and 2005. However, economic growth has caused problems, such as unemployment and pollution.

In 1978, there was virtually no unemployment in China. The state owned the means of production. The employment market changed as many private factories and other businesses opened. This prompted millions of farm workers to move to cities in search of jobs. But jobs for that many workers did not exist; thus unemployment rose.

Pollution has been another consequence, as rapid growth causes massive energy consumption. The least expensive fuel in China is coal, but coal is a major pollutant. China now has 16 of the top 20 most polluted cities in the world.

The Fall of the Soviet Union

From 1917 to 1991, the Communist party governed the Soviet Union. The Soviet government spent a large part of its resources building heavy industry and a strong military. Shortly following the end of World War II, the Soviet Union became one of the two most powerful nations in the world (the other being the United States). But in 1991, the Soviet empire collapsed. Why? Perhaps it was because a command economy is inefficient. By allowing planners rather than supply and demand to determine what goods and

Understanding Economics

EASTERN EUROPE AFTER COMMUNISM

The contrast between life in Poland, Hungary, and the Czech Republic today and what it was under communism is startling. Gone are the secret police, prisons filled with political opponents of the regime, and censorship. Gone are the central planners. Consumer choice, rather than government planners, guide business people as they decide what to produce and how much. Gone, too, are food shortages, ration coupons, drab clothing, and poorly made Soviet goods. Today, Western-European and Japanese cars make their way through traffic. Cellular phones are commonplace. Young people are well dressed in the latest international fashions. Restaurants are filled. There is freedom to travel to and from these countries. In fact, tourism is a major industry. U.S. visitors to

Warsaw, Budapest, and Prague find the experience not much different from trips to other major European capitals.

Professionals and businesspeople in the free-market economies enjoy a lifestyle similar to their counterparts in the West. Were you to visit Prague (or Budapest or Warsaw) and talk to a student there, you would find that the two of you have much in common. You might stop at a McDonalds or a pizza stand. You could share the latest CDs or DVDs. Your new friend would most likely own a digital phone, computer, and TV set. Most amazing to a Czech student is the thought that his or her parents did *not* have these luxuries, and that ration coupons, police informers, and daily propaganda ever existed in their country.

Questions for Understanding

1. What evidence in this reading suggests that these Eastern European countries are free market economies?

2. The opportunity cost to the command economies of allocating resources to producing heavy machinery and war materials was the cost of not having sufficient resources to produce consumer goods with those resources. According to the reading, how has this changed in these Eastern European countries today?

3. Can you conclude from the reading that a free market economy is more efficient than a command economy? Why or why not?

services were to be produced, the Soviet economy was overwhelmed with products for which there were no buyers and with shortages of products that were in great demand. Because the Soviet Union spent so much on the military and heavy industry, it could not spend enough on producing consumer goods. Though the demand for consumer goods was great, they were in short supply.

Prices of basic commodities were deliberately kept low—but the shelves were empty. People had to wait on long lines for scarce goods. If they were lucky and had political connections, they could get what they wanted. Those who could afford it were able to buy on the unofficial, illegal market. Here, goods were often available—but at prices much higher than the official prices for goods sold at government stores.

Most young people in Russia were happy to see the Soviet system collapse in 1991. Many of the older generation were not. Under Communism, they had enjoyed job security and government-supported housing, education, and medical care. When they were too old or ill to work, the government had taken care of them. Vacations had been paid for by the government. In the Russian market economy, these things became very expensive.

SUMMARY

All nations and peoples have developed economic systems in order to answer the basic economic questions. These questions are: *What* should be produced, *how* should it be produced and distributed, and *who* should receive the finished goods and services? A fourth question asks, Who will own the means of production?

In a traditional economic system, these basic questions are answered according to custom. Things are done in the same ways they have been done for a long time.

A free enterprise, market system relies upon independent decisions of millions of consumers and privately owned businesses. The means of production are owned mainly by private individuals and firms.

In a command system, the what, how and who questions are mainly decided by some central authority. The means of production are owned mostly by the government.

The command system has been a failure. Nations that had command systems have moved or are moving closer to market economies.

Almost all of today's economies are mixed with some elements of tradition, command, and free market.

LOOKING AHEAD

In the next chapter, we will take a close look at the U.S. economic system. As you read about this system, you will learn more about how it answers the fundamental questions of what, how, and who. You will learn why it is often described as a mixed economy. We will also look at the goals of the U.S. system.

───────────────────────── **EXERCISES** ─────────────────────────

✔**Matching** Match each term in Column A with its definition in Column B.

Column A

1. mixed economy

2. Gosplan

3. means of production

4. economic system

5. what, how, who

6. traditional economic system

7. market economic system

8. command economic system

Column B

a. an economic system in which economic decisions are made by the government

b. an economic system in which people's roles are the same as those of their parents

c. an economic system with some free enterprise and some government ownership

d. the state planning committee in the former Soviet Union

e. the way a group organizes itself for production

f. an economic system where decisions result from buyers' and sellers' actions

g. basic economic questions that all societies must answer

h. an economy's capital goods, which are used to produce other goods and services

✔**Multiple Choice** Choose the letter of the item that best completes the statement or answers the question.

1. The main idea of this chapter is that (a) a market economic system is the best economic system (b) there are different types of economic systems (c) people should not criticize the economic system of their own country (d) there is one global economic system.

2. Which *one* of the following questions does this chapter help you to answer? (a) What do all economic systems have in common? (b) What do Chinese leaders think of the United States? (c) Should people give up their traditions? (d) How shall I earn my living?

3. Which statement is an opinion rather than a fact? (a) Private individuals own most of the factories in the United States. (b) All societies must answer the what, how, and who questions. (c) Societies answer the what, how, and who questions in different ways. (d) The most important economic goal in the United States at the present time is to end poverty.

4. Which of the following is most likely to happen in a market economic system? (a) Storekeepers will try to give customers what they want. (b) Most stores will be owned by the government. (c) The price of goods and services will be set by the government.

(d) Young people will take on the occupation of their parents when they grow up.

5. Which of the following is most likely to happen in a command economic system? (a) Storekeepers will try to give customers what they want. (b) A central authority will determine what will be produced and at what price. (c) There will be many different brands of each type of merchandise. (d) Businesses will spend a lot of money advertising their products.

6. Which of the following best explains why every society must find ways to answer the what, how, and who questions? (a) It helps the government to make plans for the future. (b) The law requires it. (c) There is not enough of everything to go around. (d) People in business need that information.

7. Generally speaking, the means of production in a free enterprise economy are (a) owned by individuals (b) owned by the government (c) the consumer goods that the economy produces (d) the way it decides who, how, and what to produce.

8. The fall of the Soviet Union in 1991 led to (a) the rise of dictatorships in Western Europe (b) greater economic and political freedom among the nations of Eastern Europe (c) more nations in Eastern Europe turning towards a Communist economic system (d) the spread of communism among the nations in Africa, Asia, and Latin America.

9. Communists no longer rule (a) China (b) Russia (c) Cuba (d) North Korea.

10. China in the 21st century (a) refuses to introduce any elements of a free market (b) discourages overseas trade and investment (c) prohibits private ownership of all factories (d) allows foreign companies to do business and own factories in China.

✔ Critical-Thinking Questions

Review the dialogue in the opening to this chapter. Suppose that you are a student in Ms. Perry's economics class. You are asked to participate in a discussion of the issues that were raised in that class.

1. Explain why you would favor either Joe's, Marie's, or Tom's idea for a business venture.

2. How would you answer Sally's question, "Where will we get the money to start our business? Who will we sell our product or service to?"

3. Why might you describe the activity proposed in Ms. Perry's class an example of a market economic system in action rather than either a traditional or command system?

CHAPTER 3

The United States Free Enterprise System

The U.S. economy is basically a free enterprise system. As you learned in Chapter 2, free enterprise means that everybody has the right to start up and operate a legal business—to buy and sell goods and services for the purpose of earning money. With some restrictions, each person may run a business as he or she sees fit.

Suppose that you have a good working knowledge about personal computers. And you think you can teach new owners how to get the most out of their computers. There are dozens of people in your community who might pay $20 or even $30 an hour for your services. So you place this small ad in your local newspaper:

> **HOUSEBREAK YOUR COMPUTER**
> Computer specialist will train your new computer
> to obey your every command.
> - Reasonable rates
> - Inquire 800–1000

The phone rings and you make your first appointment. You are in business! By your decisions, you have already demonstrated some knowledge of the U.S. economic system.

You may recall from Chapter 2 that every nation in the world has its own economic system for satisfying people's needs. Now we will discuss how the U.S. economic system does this.

After reading this chapter, you will be able to answer the following questions about the U.S. free enterprise economic system:

- How does the U.S. free enterprise system operate?
- How does the U.S. free enterprise system answer the basic economic questions of what, how, and who?
- Why is the U.S. system called a mixed market economy?

HOW DOES THE U.S. FREE ENTERPRISE SYSTEM OPERATE?

The U.S. economic system of free enterprise operates according to six main principles: the freedom to choose our employment and form businesses, the right to private property, the profit motive, competition, consumer sovereignty, and the rule of law.

Freedom to Choose Our Employment and Form Businesses

In this country, the decision as to which field of employment to go into is basically yours alone to make. So too is a decision to form a business. And after setting up a business, you will decide what fees to charge and what hours to work. Certain laws prohibit you from cheating or harming your customers or other people. And you have to keep accurate financial records and pay taxes. But, in general, you will be left alone to run your business as you see fit.

Right to Private Property

Private property is a piece of land, building, vehicle, or other things owned by an individual, a family, or a group. It differs from *public property*, such as the city hall, a park, or a highway, all of which are owned by a government. In the U.S. economic system, people's right to buy and sell private property is guaranteed by law. People must use the property in safe and reasonable ways, of course. In setting up computer systems for your customers, for example, you do not have the right to interfere with the electrical, telephone, or computer systems of other people.

Free Enterprise: Directory of businesses in a mall. Can you tell what types of businesses are represented here?

Profit Motive

The main reason why you or any enterprising person organises a business is to make a *profit*. You do this by earning more money than you spend. The amount of money left over after subtracting your business expenses from your business income is known as your profit. In the free enterprise system, business firms try hard to keep costs down and increase their income from sales. The better they succeed at this, the higher are their profits. Economists describe the desire by business owners to earn the greatest profits as the *profit motive*.

Competition

Just as you are free to start a computer business, so is everyone else. The rivalry between sellers in the same field for consumers' dollars is called *competition*. If your business is profitable, it is likely that others will enter the same business hoping to be as successful as you are. They will be competing with you for the same customers. To win a share of the computer business, other sellers may try to offer more and better services, or services at lower prices. Because of the pressure of competition, business firms must constantly try to provide the best services and create the best products at the lowest possible prices.

Consumer Sovereignty

In the end, it is the customers, or consumers, who determine whether any business succeeds or fails. In the U.S. free enterprise economy, consumers are said to have *sovereignty*—the power or freedom to have final say. Consumers are free to spend their money for Product X or for Product Y. If they prefer Y over X, then the company making X may lose money, go out of business, or decide to manufacture something else (perhaps Product Z). Thus, how consumers choose to spend their dollars causes business firms of all kinds to produce certain goods and services and not others.

Rule of Law

Our economic system works because it operates within the framework of a government of laws, not of individuals. No one is above the law. No officer of government can use authority unless and except as the U.S. Constitution or the laws of Congress and the 50 states permits. Both small business firms and large companies enjoy the same full protection of the law. Thus, individuals

Consumer Sovereignty: The wants and needs of consumers determine what kinds of goods are carried in markets. What other factors help determine what is available in your local supermarket?

and businesses can conclude contracts concerning their employment or business deals, with the expectation that the legal system will back up these contracts.

HOW DOES THE U.S. FREE ENTERPRISE SYSTEM ANSWER THE BASIC ECONOMIC QUESTIONS OF WHAT, HOW, AND FOR WHOM?

When you want to buy something—anything at all—why is it almost always available to you, at a certain price? Why do drugstores almost never run out of soap, toothpaste, and aspirin? Why do supermarkets always seem to have fresh supplies of dairy products, meats, vegetables, and fruits? Whether you are shopping for a simple pen or a complicated computer, why are you certain to have a wide variety of choices?

In short, how does it happen that the many goods and services you want as a consumer are actually produced and sold by various businesses? To answer this question, we will use the felt-tipped pen business as an example of how free enterprise works to provide consumers with a steady supply of useful goods.

Free Enterprise: Consuming and Producing

Let us suppose that last week the stationery stores in your community sold an unusually large number of felt-tipped pens. As a result, stores all over town ran out of these pens. If you were a store owner, what would you do? You would probably order more pens from your suppliers. Why? Because if you did not, you would lose sales, and your income might decline.

Now let us suppose that stores all over the country started running out of felt-tipped pens. From Maine to California, storekeepers (also called *retailers*) start demanding more pens from their suppliers. People who supply goods to retailers are called *wholesalers*. As pen sales increase, the wholesalers order more pens from the pen factories. The factories in turn order from other business firms more of the raw materials that go into the making of felt-tipped pens. The desire to beat out the competition and increase profits makes the pen producers try to eliminate shortages wherever they exist.

But suppose that the opposite is happening. Large quantities of felt-tipped pens sit unsold on dealers' shelves. Will the pen manufacturers continue to make pens that consumers do not want? It is not likely that they will. Instead of the expansion process described above, a contraction occurs. (1) Retailers buy *fewer* pens

**Figure 3.1 Flow of Goods From Manufacturers to
Wholesalers to Retailers to Consumers**

| Manufacturers | Wholesalers | Retailers | Consumers |

from their suppliers. (2) Wholesalers *reduce* the size of their orders from the pen factories. (3) Factories produce *fewer* felt-tipped pens. (4) Retailers may lower the prices of pens in order to clear out unsold stocks.

So we see how the producers and sellers of felt-tipped pens need constantly to adjust output to consumers' needs. Consumers buy pens as they need them. Storekeepers, by ordering additional

Pens for Sale: What may happen to the price of pens when consumers buy fewer than before, and retailers have many unsold pens in stock? Who else is affected when consumers buy fewer goods?

Personal Economics

FACES BEHIND FAMOUS BRAND NAMES

Did you know that many of our brand-name products are the names of real people? Ford, Chrysler, and Chevrolet were individual auto manufacturers. Many, if not most of the brand names in the cosmetics and high fashion fields are also the names of real people—Mary Kay, Chanel, Estee Lauder, Calvin Klein, Donna Karan, Armani. Other products named after their inventors or manufacturers include Levi's (denims), Campbell's and Hunt's (canned soups and vegetables), and Hershey's (chocolates).

Some of those who started a business of their own were no older than you. Teenager Sara Lee Lubin, the daughter of a Chicago baker, had the idea of mass producing a cake that would be "better than Grandma's."

Many successful products were first introduced for reasons other than the profit motive. Dr. Thomas Welch, a New Jersey dentist, opposed the use of wine in church communion services. He came up with a substitute product, "Dr. Welch's Unfermented Wine" (grape juice). Charles Hires tried unsuccessfully to sell Hires' Herb Tea as a substitute for alcohol to Pennsylvania coal miners. He had better luck when he changed the name of his product to Hires' Root Beer. The graham cracker, a whole wheat product, was named after the Reverend Sylvester Graham, who preached against consuming meat, alcohol, and white flour.

Health and diet needs led Will Kellogg to invent corn flakes, an easily digestible food, while working in his brother's Battle Creek hospital. Charles W. Post, a cowboy and patient of Kellogg's, developed other cereal products as well as a coffee substitute called Postum, made from grains and molasses.

So, as you can see, if you have an idea, go ahead and try it. That is what free enterprise is all about.

or fewer pens, make the needs of consumers known to wholesale suppliers. Wholesalers pass the word along to the manufacturers. They, in turn, notify their suppliers—and so on down the line.

Now let us return to the question raised at the beginning of this section. How does the U.S. system of free enterprise answer the basic economic questions of what, how, and who? It does so in the following ways:

1. What Goods and Services Will Be Produced? The number of pens—or any other good—produced is determined by (1) the buyers who are willing to pay the price at which the goods are being sold, and (2) the sellers who are willing to manufacture and sell the goods at that price. (We will discuss buyers' demand for goods and sellers' supplying of goods in Chapter 4.)

2. *How Will the Goods and Services Be Produced?* The people who manufactured and sold the pens had to answer a lot of questions, such as: Should we purchase new equipment for manufacturing the pens? What are the costs and availability of natural resources? What kind of advertising and promotion should we use? Their decisions were influenced mostly by their desire to beat the competition and to make a profit.

3. *Who Should Receive the Goods and Services That Are Produced?* In our free enterprise system, the consumers who are both willing and able to pay the price may have all the pens—and other goods— they want. But those who think the price is too high, and those who cannot afford to pay the price, will just have to do without new pens and other goods.

WHY IS THE U.S. SYSTEM A MIXED MARKET ECONOMY?

The U.S. economic system is a market economy. But in the United States, market forces alone do not decide how all goods and services will be produced. Federal, state, and local governments have an important role in the production of goods and services. We call a system where both the free market and government play roles in deciding what and how to produce a *mixed market economy* or, simply, a *mixed economy.*

Governments on the local, state, and national level produce many of the services we use. For example, each public schools in the United States receives funds from local, state, and federal governments. Your town, village, or city funds the police department and, very often, the fire department. The roads you walk, bicycle, or drive on are built and maintained by local, state, and/or federal funding. The postal system and national defense network are services provided by the federal government. Privately owned businesses, however, produce schoolbooks, road-building materials, fire trucks, police cars, aircraft, and other equipment and materials that governments buy and use.

In these situations, resources that otherwise might have been used to produce goods and services for private use were used for the production of goods and services for public use. Suppose, for example, that the federal government decided it was important to build another fighter plane. With money it has received from private individuals and business firms through taxation, it is able to do so. If that tax money were left in the hands of private individuals and business firms, the money, materials, and labor that goes into building the fighter plane might have been used to build a factory or an office building instead.

As illustrated above, in the U.S. mixed economy, government does get directly involved with the free market to influence *what* goods and services private individuals and businesses will produce.

The Federal Reserve Board, a federal agency, largely determines interest rates in the United States. This is important because high interest rates tend to lower production. For example, high interest rates may discourage people from buying new homes. Builders, therefore, will produce fewer new homes. By contrast, low interest rates tend to encourage greater production. They will encourage people to buy new homes. If that happens, builders will produce more new homes.

Government also influences *how* goods and services will be produced. Local, state, and federal laws regulate business activity in many ways. Business firms often complain of the excessive govern-

Understanding Economics
GROSS DOMESTIC PRODUCT

GDP 2006 = $13.2 trillion
Consumer Spending = $9.3 trillion (70.5%); Business Spending = $2.2 trillion (16.7%); Government Spending = $2.5 trillion (18.9%); Net Exports = (−)$.763 trillion (−6.1%).

Some economists like to think of the U.S. economy as a giant business or company. Like many business firms, this company produces both goods and services. But unlike ordinary businesses, the U.S. economy creates all of the goods and services that the nation produces.

The total money value of the goods and services produced by a nation's economy in one year is called its *gross domestic product,* or *GDP.* In 2006, the GDP of the United States was $13.2 trillion ($13,200,000,000,000).

The GDP is purchased by the economy's "customers." These are U.S. consumers, business firms, and governments, as well as buyers in other countries. Economists measure the size of the GDP by totalling the amount of money spent by each of these groups.

Consumers are people like you, your family, and friends who buy goods and

services for their own use. Consumer spending amounted to $9.3 trillion in 2006.

Business spending is also called *investment.* Businesses invest in capital resources, such as factories, machinery, and tools, which are used to produce goods and services. In 2006, investment accounted for $2.2 trillion of the GDP.

In 2006, government spending for goods and services on the federal, state, and local levels totalled $2.5 trillion.

Foreigners purchased $1.466 trillion worth of goods and services from the U.S. economic system in 2006. But Americans purchased $2.229 trillion worth of goods and services from foreign business firms. The difference of $763 billion was deducted from the total spending in the United States in order to arrive at the GDP for that year of $13.2 trillion.

ment regulations they must contend with. Among these are: requiring a permit or license to do business; inspecting restaurants and food and drug production; regulating imports and exports; regulating minimum wages and hours; setting a minimum age for working, drinking alcoholic beverages, buying tobacco products, driving motor vehicles; and taxing incomes, purchases, and property. Business firms say that the endless forms they must fill out to meet government regulations are time consuming, costly, and often unnecessary.

Government plays an important role in deciding the *who* question in the United States. Taxes at all levels of government take income from individuals and corporations. Individuals and corporations, therefore, have fewer dollars to spend as they wish. Government then decides how it will spend the tax dollars it receives. Some tax dollars will be used to help individuals in need. These individuals will have more money to spend on goods and services. In these instances, government, rather than the market, is deciding who is to receive the goods and services society produces.

The role of government in the U.S. economy is discussed in greater detail in Unit V.

The Circular Flow of the U.S. Economy

As you learned in the discussion of gross domestic product, the nation's mixed market economy consists of three major sectors, or parts. These are households, businesses, and government.

A *household* is one or more people occupying the same dwelling unit (such as a house, an apartment, or a mobile home). All of us live in households. Figure 3.2 on the next page shows the relationship between the nation's households and businesses. As you can see, people (that is, households) rely on businesses in two ways. First, people can earn incomes by selling their services to businesses. Second, people get goods and services from businesses.

The illustration also shows that businesses rely upon households to (1) provide the resources—labor, land, management, and capital—needed to produce goods and services, and (2) buy their goods and services.

Now you can see why the illustration is called a *circular flow chart*. The money that businesses pay out (in wages, rent, interest, and dividends) returns when people (households) pay for goods and services. Similarly, the land, labor, management, and capital resources that households sell to businesses create goods and services that are bought by households.

As you probably know, there are three levels of government in the United States. These are the federal government in Washington,

Figure 3.2 Circular Flow Between Households and Businesses

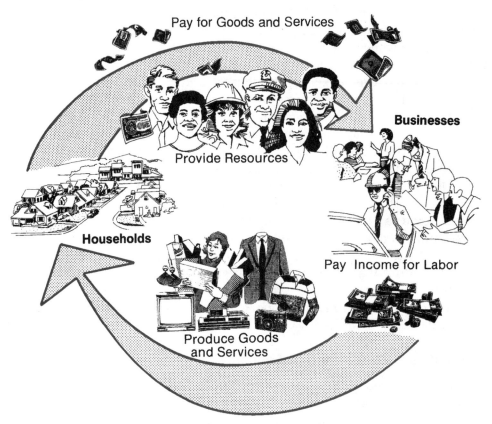

D.C., the governments of the 50 states, and the thousands of local governments across the nation. The relationship between these governments and households, and between governments and businesses, is much like that between households and businesses.

In the second illustration, you can see that households rely on governments in two ways: First, households receive services such as police and fire protection, roads, and schools from governments. Second, households can earn income by selling their services to governments.

Figure 3.3 also shows that governments rely upon households in two ways: (1) Households provide the labor and other resources that governments need to produce goods and services. (2) Households provide income to governments through the payment of taxes.

The relationship between governments and businesses is shown in Figure 3.4 on page 46.

As you can see, governments rely on businesses in two ways: (1) Businesses provide governments with goods and services. (2) Businesses pay taxes to governments. Meanwhile, businesses also look to governments to (1) buy their goods and services, and (2) provide them with necessary services.

Figure 3.3 Circular Flow Between Households and Governments

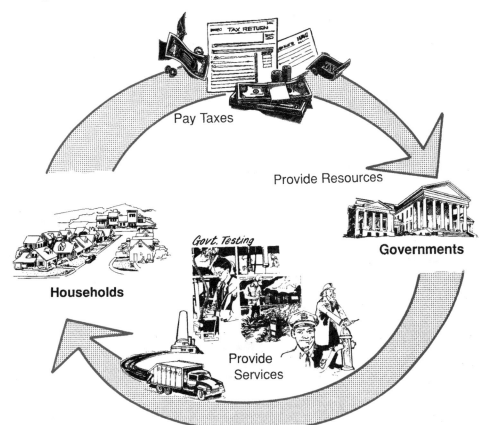

Now that you have seen how each one of the three sectors of the U.S. economy relates to the other two, you will be able to understand the "big picture." This is shown in Figure 3.5 as the circular flow of the U.S. economy.

As you examine the diagram on page 47, think about the following questions. Where do you fit in the circular flow? What might happen to the U.S. economy if one part of the circular flow were to change? For example, what might happen if household spending increased, or if business production declined?

Goals of the Mixed U.S. Economy

If you were to ask Americans what they want their nation's economic system to provide, they might mention the following goals: growth, stability, security, justice, freedom, and economic efficiency.

1. Economic Growth. An increase in the nation's output of goods and services (its GDP) is a sign of economic growth. Naturally, Americans would like to live better today than they did in past years. And they want to live even better in the future. This

Figure 3.4 Circular Flow Between Governments and Businesses

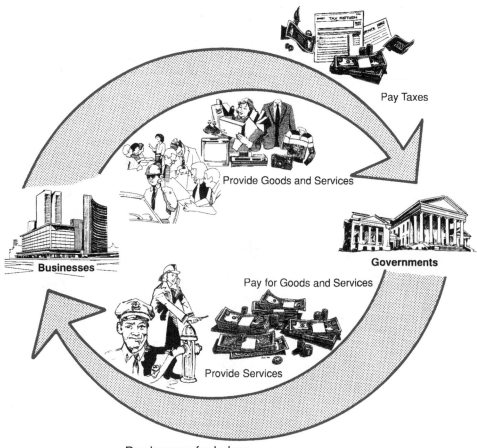

Pay Taxes

Provide Goods and Services

Businesses

Governments

Pay for Goods and Services

Provide Services

Pay Income for Labor

will be possible only if the nation produces more, so that more goods and services are made available for all. In other words, we want to improve their *standard of living*. Economists define standard of living as the quantity and quality of goods and services available to an individual or society. It will be possible to improve our nation's standard of living only if the nation produces more per capita (economic growth). In this way, more goods and services would be made available for all. We will have more to say about economic growth in the final unit of this book.

2. Economic Stability. In the past, the United States has gone through cycles of economic good times followed by periods of economic bad times. Americans want to eliminate the bad times, make sure that everyone who wants a job has one, and keep a steady output of goods and services. And Americans want to know that their savings will not be made worthless by rising prices in the future. (Inflation is discussed in Chapter 6.)

3. *Economic Security.* Americans want to be sure that even in hard times—or when they are unemployed—they will not suffer too much.

4. *Economic Justice.* Americans believe that their economic system should offer equal opportunity and reward based on what a person does regardless of race, sex, age, religion, or national origin. In addition, the system should provide all Americans with a "fair share" of the nation's output of goods and services. Americans do not agree, however, as to what a "fair share" should be.

5. *Economic Freedom.* A number of rights or freedoms are involved here. Workers have the right to accept or refuse jobs. Everyone has the right to own property, form a business, and attempt to make a profit. Individuals have the freedom to spend or save their money as they wish and to own or dispose of the goods that they buy.

6. *Economic Efficiency.* As we have said, it takes human and natural resources to produce goods and services. But these re-

Figure 3.5 Circular Flow of the U.S. Economy

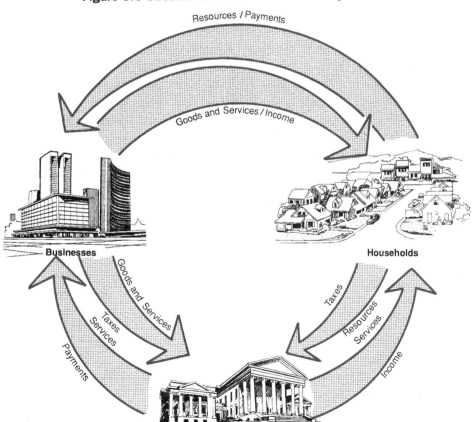

sources are limited in supply. An efficient economic system strives to do the most with what resources are available. It strives to get its citizens the greatest output of goods and services from the input of human and natural resources.

7. Invisible Hand. In a pure free enterprise system, things work out without government officials interfering with the process. Instead, an "invisible hand" is said to guide a free enterprise economy. The 18th-century economist Adam Smith also used the term "self interest" to mean that guiding hand. An example of an "invisible hand" guiding economic activities would be a storekeeper who sold pens. The store owner did not have to be told by a government agency to order more pens when her stock was running out. The storekeeper did so because it was in her self-interest. So, too, self-interest prompted a producer to make the pens and a supplier to sell them to the storekeeper.

Meeting the Nation's Goals

The U.S. economic system has been able to achieve many of these basic goals for most of its people. At the same time, it has maintained personal and political freedom. Many Americans believe that they have these freedoms only because they have prevented government from gaining too much economic control in their lives. As long as economic power (in the form of individual ownership and free enterprise) is widespread, political power will not fall into the hands of a few people.

The production of goods and services in the United States is greater than the production of any other nation in the world. As a result of our nation's continuing economic growth, nearly 94 percent of U.S. families have at least one telephone, 69 percent have air conditioners, 83 percent have central heating, and almost all have television sets. The average home has two rooms per person and at least one car per family.

The quality of the goods and services produced is also high. More important, Americans are healthier and live longer today than Americans did in the past. Heart disease and stroke deaths have declined. Measles and mumps have almost been wiped out.

Scarcity has not been eliminated, however. To do so is impossible because economic resources are always limited. Nor have all the American people shared equally in the country's rising living standards. However, inequalities based upon race, sex, religion, and national origin have been greatly reduced. Other factors, such as the amount of education a person has received, now often play a more important part in determining family income.

SUMMARY

In this chapter we learned about the U.S. economic system of free enterprise. Free enterprise rests upon six principles: freedom to choose one's way of earning a living (including starting a business), private property, the profit motive, competition, consumer sovereignty, and the rule of law.

Like every economic system, free enterprise must provide a means to answer three basic questions: what goods and services to produce, how to produce them, and who shall receive them. In our market economy, the answers are largely the result of the decisions of individual buyers and sellers.

The U.S. economic system is actually a mixed market economy. The market alone does not make all the decisions about what will or will not be produced. Federal, state, and local governments are major buyers and sellers of goods and services. These governments may also regulate market activity.

The goals of the U.S. economic system are growth, stability, security, justice, freedom, and economic efficiency. The U.S. economy produces more goods and services than any other nation. It has succeeded in meeting many, but not all, of its goals.

LOOKING AHEAD

The principal reason why buyers and sellers behave the way they do can be summed up in one word: *price*. Why is this so? And why do prices rise and fall? What effect does the behavior of buyers and sellers have on prices? The answers to these questions may be found in the laws of supply and demand. They will be the focus of our next chapter.

EXERCISES

✔**Multiple Choice** Choose the letter of the item that best completes the statement or answers the question.

1. A major idea of this chapter is that (a) government should not interfere with free enterprise (b) the U.S. economy is basically a free enterprise system (c) the manufacture and sale of felt-tipped pens is profitable (d) consumer goods are always plentiful in a free enterprise system.

2. Another major idea of this chapter is that (a) it pays to sell felt-tipped pens (b) anyone may start a business in a free enterprise economic system (c) factories produce whatever they please (d) a free enterprise system is run by the government.

3. In a free enterprise system, both buyers and sellers decide (a) what goods and services should be produced (b) how goods and services should be produced (c) who should receive the goods and services that are produced (d) why goods and services are produced.

4. What role do profits play in the felt-tipped-pen industry example in the chapter? (a) Profits have no role in the example. (b) Profits result in high prices for pens. (c) Profits discourage people from entering the pen industry. (d) Profits encourage sellers to produce the number of pens that buyers want.

5. The U.S. economic system is best described as one with (a) no role for government (b) the government controlling all (c) mostly free enterprise, but some role for government (d) pure competition in all industries.

6. In the U.S. economic system, consumer sovereignty means that (a) the customers decide whether any business succeeds or fails (b) consumers are not free to spend their money as they wish (c) business firms, and not consumers, have the final power (d) companies may choose to manufacture things consumers do not want.

7. Which of the following best describes business competition? (a) your right to enter into a business (b) the right of others to enter the same business as you do (c) your reason for entering the business (d) the equipment used in operating your business.

8. Suppose that there are too many felt-tipped pens on retailers' shelves. Which of the following is likely to take place? (a) Retailers will buy more pens from their suppliers. (b) Wholesalers will increase orders from manufacturers. (c) Pen sales will increase. (d) Factories will produce fewer pens.

✔ **Matching** Match each term in Column A with its definition in Column B.

Column A	Column B
1. capitalism	a. businesses that sell to local storekeepers
2. free enterprise	b. the total value of the goods and services produced by a country in one year
3. profit motive	
4. competition	c. the lands, buildings, or goods owned by individuals or businesses
5. private property	
6. retailers	d. the lands, buildings, or goods controlled or operated by federal, state, or local governments
7. wholesalers	
8. public property	e. the right of individuals to enter into legal businesses and operate them as they see fit
9. gross domestic product (GDP)	
10. invisible hand	f. the effort to outperform other businesses
	g. a system of private ownership of raw materials, factories, and equipment
	h. the desire to earn a surplus
	i. storekeepers who sell directly to consumers
	j. Adam Smith's view on how a nation's economic resources can be efficiently allocated

✔ *Developing Economic Skills*

Use the information you have learned in this chapter and study the illustration below. Then answer the questions that follow.

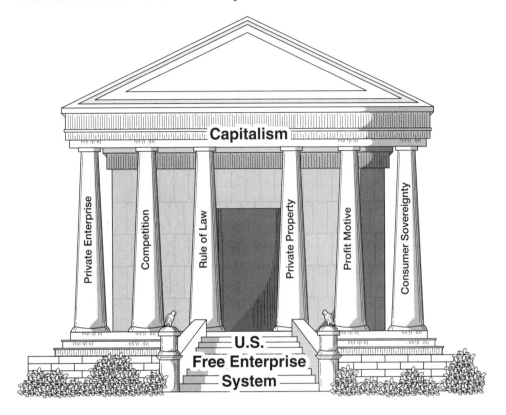

1. What is a good title for this illustration?

2. What evidence is given in the drawing that justifies calling the U.S. economic system a free enterprise system?

3. What are the six main principles of the U.S. free enterprise system that are shown in the drawing?

4. What information would you add to indicate that the United States has a mixed market economy?

✔ *Using the Internet*

For the latest GDP statistics, check out the Website of the federal government's Bureau of Economic Analysis, at <<www.bea.doc.gov>>.

CHAPTER 4
Demand and Supply

A helicopter hovers above the streets of your community. Suddenly, fluttering down from its open hatch, are thousands of slips of paper. You pick up a handful of them and discover that they are $20 bills, $50 bills, even $100 bills. You look up, amazed and speechless. The sky is now raining money from the hatches of a fleet of helicopters.

Everybody is out in the streets scrambling for the falling bills. People stuff their pockets and purses. Some fill up the trunks of their cars or collect the money using wastepaper baskets and shopping carts. You and your neighbors soon become rich.

But your community is not alone in its good fortune. Radio and television news programs report that other helicopters have dumped trillions of dollars over most of the major cities in the country. Almost every American, it seems, has become wealthy overnight.

The next day, millions of rich Americans cannot wait to spend their bundles and baskets of cash. But as they crowd into stores, they are again astonished. What has happened to the price of everything? The cheapest TV set is now selling for $33,350. A candy bar is priced at $150 and a cheeseburger at $950. People are angry and bewildered. Apparently, as the supply of money went up, its value went down.

If everyone suddenly had a lot of money, do you think the money would have the same value it had when only a small number of people had a lot?

You and the other unhappy millionaires have been disappointed by the operation of two major economic laws. These are the Law of Demand and the Law of Supply. How these laws operate in a free enterprise system is the subject of this chapter. In this chapter, you will find out the answers to these questions:

- What are the Laws of Demand and Supply?
- What is market price?
- How do changes in the demand for or supply of a product affect its price?
- Why are prices important in a market economy?

WHAT ARE THE LAWS OF DEMAND AND SUPPLY?

Before we buy anything, we usually ask ourselves two questions: "Do I want this item?" and "Am I willing to pay the price?"

Suppose you see a pair of jeans that you like selling for $75. You are not willing to pay that price. If the same jeans were selling for

$40, however, you would be willing to buy a pair. And if the price were $15, you would buy two pairs. Economists say that at $75 your demand for jeans is 0 (zero), at $40 it is 1, and at $15, it is 2.

Law of Demand

To an economist, *demand* is the amount of an item that buyers are willing and able to purchase at any and all prices. Normally, demand is greater at a lower price than at a higher one. Take the case of last spring's chocolate chip cookie sale at North High. To raise money for its class picnic, the junior class at North High decided to sell chocolate chip cookies baked by its class members. As a first step, the class conducted a survey among the students. The class wanted to determine (1) how much students were willing to pay for chocolate chip cookies, and (2) how many cookies could be sold at specific prices. This is what the survey revealed:

Demand for Chocolate Chip Cookies

At a price of	Students will buy
$.70	100 cookies
.60	200 "
.50	400 "
.40	700 "
.30	1,100 "
.20	1,600 "
.10	2,300 "

As you can see, the number of cookies that the students said they were willing to buy increased as the price decreased. Indeed, at a price of 10 cents, more cookies will be sold than there are students in the school! At that price, some students are willing to buy two or more cookies. Others who normally would not buy cookies might buy them when the price is so low.

What is true of chocolate chip cookies is also true of other things: *More of an item will be purchased at a lower price than at a higher price.* This idea is so important that economists have refined it into the *Law of Demand*. This law states that the quantity of items demanded increases and decreases in the opposite direction from changes in price.

Why does demand change in the opposite direction from price changes? One reason is that at a lower price people can afford to buy more of an item than they can at a higher price.

A second reason is that at lower prices people tend to buy things as a substitute for something else. So, for example, at 60 cents for two cookies, some students in the junior class might have decided to buy the cookies instead of a candy bar. At a price of $1.40 for two cookies, however, many students would substitute a candy bar for the cookies.

We know that fewer items will be bought at a higher price than at a lower price. But will the quantity demanded decrease by the same amount for all goods and services? For example, how much more milk will you buy if the price is greatly reduced? 5 percent more? 10 percent more? Probably not much more milk, because you can drink only so much milk. Moreover, it is considered to be relatively inexpensive to begin with. In addition, you cannot buy a lot of milk and stockpile it. It will turn sour. On the other hand, will you buy less milk if the price is increased? Probably not, if the increase is not too great. Most people consider milk to be a necessity and will continue to buy it as its price increases.

Now let us look at another product—steaks, which are normally much more expensive than milk. Many people would consider steak to be a luxury because of its cost. If the price of steak declines significantly, people who normally would not buy steak would grab the opportunity. And some people with a freezer would stockpile it.

Elasticity of demand is the percentage change in the quantity of goods or services demanded resulting from a 1-percent change in price. If a small percentage change in price (up or down) causes a great increase or decrease in the amount of the product demanded, we say that the demand for this product is *elastic*. On the other hand, if a small change in price has little effect on the quantity of a product demanded, we say that the product has an *inelastic* demand.

If we were to make a chart as to what happens when we lower or raise prices for steaks and milk, it might look something like this:

Demand for Steaks and Milk

	Price	Units Sold	Total Revenue
Steaks	$5.00	60	$300.00
	2.50	175	437.50
Milk	$1.20	200	$240.00
	.60	350	210.00

According to the chart, lowering the price of steaks increased the quantity of steaks sold from 60 to 175. Total revenue also increased from $300 to $437.50. The demand for steaks in this example is elastic because a decrease in price resulted in an increase in revenue and an increase in price resulted in a decrease in total revenue.

Lowering the price of milk, however, did not result in an increase in revenue. Just the reverse happened. Lowering the price from $1.20 to $.60 reduced revenue by $30. Increasing the price of milk from $.60 to $1.20 would increase total revenue by $30. Therefore, the demand for milk is inelastic because a decrease in price results in a decrease in total revenue and an increase in price results in an increase in total revenue.

What difference does it make if demand is elastic or inelastic? It makes a great deal of difference. Suppose, for example, that you are making decisions for a large manufacturer of computers. Does it make sense to increase the price of your computers from $500 to $1,000? No, because the demand for your product is elastic. Therefore, your total revenue would be less if you raised your price to $1,000. The reverse is also true. It might pay you to lower your price from $1,000 to $500. A milk producer, on the other hand, knows that the demand for milk is inelastic. An increase in the price of milk would increase total revenue whereas a decrease in the price of milk would reduce total revenue.

Law of Supply

We have seen that the price of a product will affect the number of units that people are willing and able to buy—its demand. Price will also affect the supply of an item. In economics, *supply* is the quantity of a good or service that is offered for sale at all prices.

Let us return to the cookie sale at North High. The organizers of the sale have a plan by which individual student bakers will be paid 20 percent of the selling price of their cookies. So, for example, a student whose cookies sell for a total of $100 will receive $20. The problem now is to find out how many cookies will be offered for sale at the prices listed in the earlier survey.

The results of this survey, which give the sale planners a picture of the supply of chocolate chip cookies available to North High, are as follows:

Supply of Chocolate Chip Cookies

At a price of	Sellers will offer
$.70	2,000 cookies
.60	1,800 "
.50	1,600 "
.40	1,400 "
.30	1,100 "
.20	700 "
.10	100 "

As you can see, the student bakers are willing to provide many more cookies at the higher prices than at the lower prices. What is true for chocolate chip cookies applies to most other things. *More of an item will be offered for sale at a higher price than at a lower price.* Economists explain this as the *Law of Supply*. This law states that supply increases as prices increase, and decreases as prices decrease.

There are two reasons why the quantity of items offered for sale at higher prices will be greater than the quantity offered at lower ones. The first reason is that those already in a business will try to increase production as a way of increasing their profits. Suppose that the price of tomatoes shot up from 85 cents to $10 a pound. What then? Many farmers who usually grew other hot-house vegetables would give them up in order to grow tomatoes.

The second reason why the quantity offered at a higher price will be greater is that other people will be attracted into the business. They believe that at the higher price they too will be able to earn a profit. Why, at $10 a pound, *you* might even take up growing tomatoes.

Supply, like demand, is subject to elasticity. Some commodities react to price changes more than others do. If a change in price brings about a large percentage change in supply, the supply is said to be elastic. If a change in price produces a small change in supply, the supply is said to be inelastic. Manufactured goods tend to be elastic. On the other hand, products from farms (such as wheat, corn, or milk) tend to be inelastic. Automobile manufacturers can more easily increase their output than can dairy farmers. They can, for example, add an additional shift of workers at one or more plants. Farmers, by contrast, cannot easily add to their herds of cows. Any one cow will produce only so much milk. Suppose prices rose for both automobiles and milk products. Of the two groups of producers, automobile manufacturers and dairy farmers, which could increase the supply of their products the most? The answer, of course, is automobile manufacturers.

WHAT IS MARKET PRICE?

Thus far, we have described what buyers and sellers are willing to do at a variety of prices. But at what price will cookie sales actually take place? Before answering that question, let us combine the results of our surveys of demand and supply.

From the table on the next page, we see that at a price of 30 cents, demand is exactly equal to supply. At that price, the student buyers will buy and the student sellers will sell 1,100 cookies. Economists call 30 cents the *market price* of cookies.

Demand and Supply of Chocolate Chip Cookies

Students will buy	At a price of	Sellers will offer
100 cookies	$.70 each	2,000 cookies
200 "	.60 "	1,800 "
400 "	.50 "	1,600 "
700 "	.40 "	1,400 "
1,100 "	**.30** "	**1,100** "
1,600 "	.20 "	700 "
2,300 "	.10 "	100 "

HOW DO CHANGES IN THE DEMAND FOR OR SUPPLY OF A PRODUCT AFFECT ITS PRICE?

We have been talking about the effect of price on demand and supply. But price is not the only factor affecting the demand or supply of an item. When, for whatever reason, the demand for or the supply of a product increases or decreases, the change will affect the price of the item.

Changes in Demand

Have you ever noticed what happens to the prices of Christmas cards and decorations after December 25? Prices drop. They are usually much lower than they were just before the holiday. Much the same sort of thing happens to the prices of winter clothing in the spring and the current year's automobiles in the late fall. The demand for holiday decorations, winter clothing, and cars is seasonal. It changes as the seasons of the year change. When spring comes, people no longer need or want winter clothing as much as they once did. Merchants therefore reduce prices to sell out their remaining stocks. Similarly, new-model automobiles usually make their appearance early in the fall. For example, 2004 models appear in the fall of 2003. Since new-car buyers generally prefer these "next-year" models, the demand for the current year's models is lower. Automobile dealers generally reduce the prices of their unsold cars as a way of clearing them out.

When the demand for something increases, prices rise. On Mother's Day, millions of people want to buy flowers for their mothers. The cost of flowers is higher on this day than on any other day of the year. Florists raise their prices because of the increase in demand.

To summarize, changes in demand also affect the price at which goods will be bought and sold. If the demand for an item *in-*

Seasonal Demand: If more items are offered for sale at a lower price than at a higher price, what will happen to the number sold?

creases, the price at which it will be sold will also increase. But if the demand for an item *decreases*, its price will also decrease.

Changes in Supply

Have you ever compared the summer prices of fresh fruits and vegetables with their winter prices? Fruits and vegetables are more plentiful during the warm growing months, and they cost less. During the winter the opposite is true. Fresh fruits and vegetables are less plentiful, and they cost more.

Here is how changes in the supply of an item will affect its price. If the number of items available for sale at a particular price (the supply) *increases*, the price will fall. But if the supply of items *decreases*, the price will rise.

WHY ARE PRICES IMPORTANT IN A MARKET ECONOMY?

Prices are key ingredients in our economy because they make things happen. If buyers want to own some items badly enough, they will pay more for them. When sellers want to sell some items badly enough, they will lower their prices. Prices play such an important role in economic life that the United States is often described as a *price-directed market economy*. Let us see why.

1. Act as Signals to Buyers and Sellers. One of the things that prices do is carry information to buyers and sellers. When prices are low enough, they send a "buy" signal to buyers (consumers), who can now afford the things they want. When prices are high enough, they send a "sell" signal to sellers (retailers), who can now earn a greater profit at the new price.

2. Encourage Efficient Production. Prices encourage businesspeople to produce their goods at the lowest possible cost. The less it costs to produce an item, the more likely it is that its producers will earn a profit.

Firms that are efficient will produce more goods with fewer or less expensive raw materials than firms that are inefficient. Producers strive for *efficiency* as a way of increasing their profits. While these efforts are in the best interests of the sellers, all of us may benefit because we are provided with the things we want at lower costs.

3. Determine Who Will Receive the Things Produced. Finally, prices help determine who will receive the economy's output of goods and services. The price that a worker receives for doing a job is called a *wage* or salary. The amount of this wage or salary determines how much the worker has to spend. What the worker can buy with those wages will depend, in turn, upon the prices of the goods and services that the worker would like to own.

Graphing Demand, Supply, and Market Price

We can use graphs to illustrate and study the demand for and supply of a particular product. Returning to our chocolate chip cookie surveys as an example, we would graph demand as shown in Figure 4.1.

Line D is a *demand curve*. The demand curve slopes downward from left to right. At a price of 70 cents, the students would buy 100 chocolate chip cookies. At a price of 40 cents, they would buy 700 cookies. At 30 cents, they would buy 1,100 cookies. And at a price of only 10 cents, 2,300 cookies would be sold. This bears out the Law of Demand because it shows that more will be purchased at a lower price than a higher one.

Now let us see what the supply curve looks like. In Figure 4.2, line S is a *supply curve*, which slopes upward from left to right. It shows that more cookies would be offered for sale at a higher price than a lower one.

As you can see, at a price of 70 cents, 2,000 cookies would be offered for sale. At the price of 30 cents, 1,100 would be offered.

Figure 4.1 Demand for Chocolate Chip Cookies

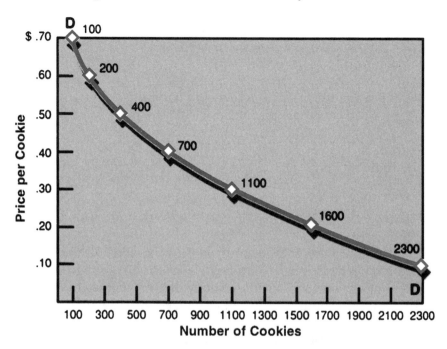

Figure 4.2 Supply of Chocolate Chip Cookies

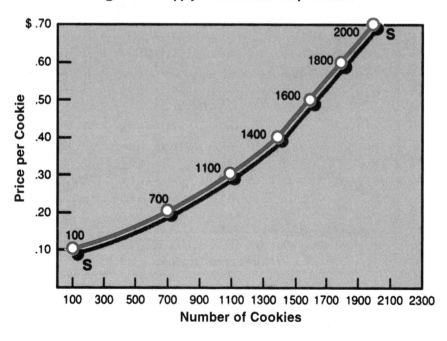

But at 10 cents, sellers would offer only 100 cookies for sale. This bears out the Law of Supply. Now let us see what happens when we combine the results, in Figure 4.3.

The market price is the point at which the supply curve and the demand curve *intersect* (cross). At point *M*, 1,100 cookies would be offered and sold at 30 cents each. To put it another way, *market price is the price at which supply and demand are equal.*

Why is 30 cents the market price? If the price were lower, say 20 cents, buyers would want 1,600 cookies. But sellers would offer only 700. In that event, possible buyers who are willing to spend more than 20 cents would offer more money for the item. This would bring in the sellers who are willing to sell at 30 cents (but not 20 cents). Meanwhile, seeing that they can unload cookies at 30 cents, sellers would turn down the offers of 20 cents in favor of the higher price.

At 40 cents, the same kind of thing would happen. Sellers would offer more cookies than buyers would be willing to take. In their competition to sell their cookies, sellers willing to accept 30 cents for their cookies would sell to buyers willing to pay the price.

Figure 4.3 Demand for and Supply of Chocolate Chip Cookies

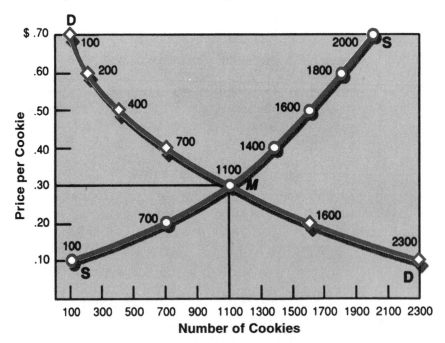

Graphs can also be used to study the effect of changes in supply or demand. An increase in demand is shown in Figure 4.4.

Figure 4.4 Increase in Demand for Chocolate Chip Cookies

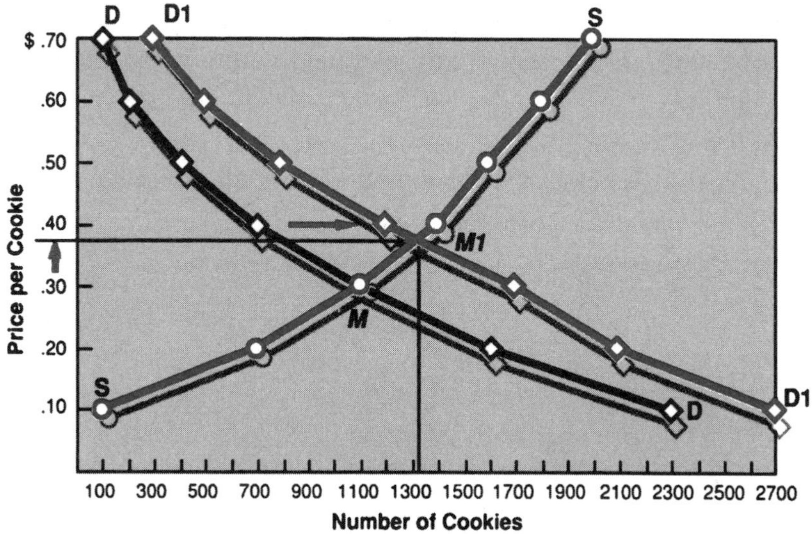

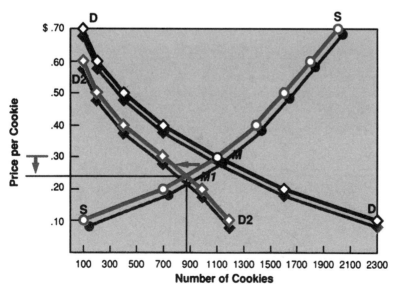

A decrease in demand is shown in Figure 4.5.

Figure 4.5 Decrease in Demand for Chocolate Chip Cookies

As you can see, when demand increases, so too does the market price. When demand decreases, the price falls.

Similarly, we can illustrate the effect of an increase in supply in Figure 4.6. As you can see, when supply increases, price decreases.

But when there is a decrease in supply, there is an increase in price. In Figure 4.7, we see that a change in supply has the opposite effect on market price.

Figure 4.6 Increase in Supply of Chocolate Chip Cookies

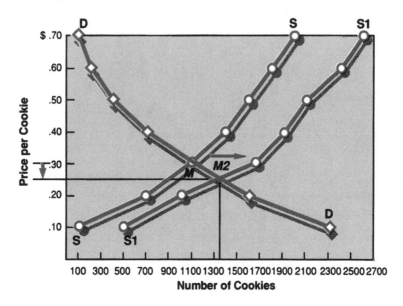

Figure 4.7 Decrease in Supply of Chocolate Chip Cookies

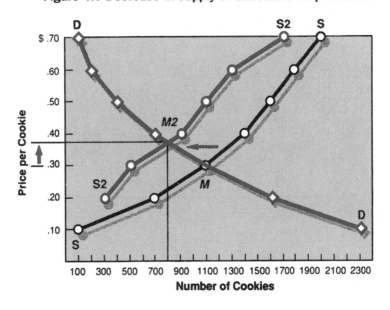

The graphs that we have been analyzing of cookie sales represent a study of one small segment of the economy—a single firm or, perhaps, a single industry. Here the economist is concerned with consumer demand for a particular product—cookies in our example—or the price per unit that a firm may charge for a specific quantity of its output of milk or computers. Economists refer to such studies as *microeconomics* because the focus is on a small, or micro, section of the economy.

Economists also analyze the impact of supply and demand on the economy as a whole or from what they call a *macroeconomic* perspective. How, for example, would an increase in the price of petroleum affect the entire economy? Petroleum is needed to run factories, and as fuel in homes, trucks, and airplanes. Will prices rise in industries that use petroleum and petroleum products, and, if so, by how much? How, then, will the resulting increases affect the general level of income, prices, and output of goods in our economy? The difference between micro- and macroeconomics is like considering the batting average of a single member of a baseball team (micro) with an analysis of how the team as a whole performed throughout the season.

SUMMARY

Demand refers to the number of items that buyers would be willing to buy at any and all possible prices. The Law of Demand tells us that demand varies in the opposite direction with price. That is, more items will be bought at a lower price than at a higher one.

Supply is the quantity of a product that would be offered for sale at all possible prices. The Law of Supply states that supply varies in the same direction as price. That is, more items will be offered for sale at a higher price than at a lower price.

The market price is the price at which supply and demand are equal. The market price will remain unchanged as long as supply and demand remains unchanged. If there is an increase in demand or a decrease in supply, the market price will increase. If the opposite occurs—that is, if demand decreases or supply increases—the market price will decrease.

Prices help determine which goods and services will be produced and which will not. Prices also determine who will be able to enjoy goods and services, because only those who can afford to pay will be able to buy them.

LOOKING AHEAD

Supply, demand, and the price system would be meaningless were it not for the dollars and cents in which they are expressed. In the following chapter, we will be taking a look at the things that people in other times and places have used as "money," and at the present-day U.S. system of money and banking.

─────────────── **EXERCISES** ───────────────

✔**Matching** Match each term in Column A with its definition in Column B.

Column A
1. demand
2. Law of Demand
3. supply
4. Law of Supply
5. market price
6. wage

Column B
a. the quantity of a good or service that is offered for sale
b. states that supply increases as prices increase, and decreases as prices decrease
c. the amount of an item that buyers are willing and able to purchase at any price
d. states that the quantity of items demanded increases and decreases in the opposite direction from changes in price
e. the hourly price that a worker receives for doing a job
f. the price at which supply and demand are equal

✔**Multiple Choice** Choose the letter of the item that best completes the statement or answers the question.

1. The main idea of this chapter is that (a) supply always equals demand (b) supply and demand help determine market price (c) demand never changes (d) market price never changes.

2. Indoor ice skating has become very popular, and the rinks have raised their admission prices. The price increase is a result of (a) an increase in supply (b) a decrease in supply (c) an increase in demand (d) a decrease in demand.

3. At a price of $2 a pound, buyers will take 2,000 pounds of beef, and at a price of $4 they will take 1,500 pounds. These facts illustrate (a) market price (b) the Law of Demand (c) the Law of Supply (d) all of the above.

4. At a price of $2 a pound, sellers will offer 800 pounds of beef, and at a price of $4 a pound they will offer 1,200 pounds of beef. This illustrates (a) market price (b) the Law of Demand (c) the Law of Supply (d) all of the above.

5. The prices charged for fruits and vegetables are lower in the warm summer months than in the cold winter months because (a) people prefer fruits and vegetables when it is warm (b) fruits and vegetables are in greater supply during warm months (c) all items cost more in winter months (d) people go away during summer months.

6. Which statement is true of supply and demand curves? (a) They move in the same direction. (b) They never meet. (c) They must meet at one point. (d) They slope upward, from right to left.

✔ What Will Happen . . . ?

In the questions that follow, something will happen to the supply of, the demand for, or the price of a particular good or service. See if you can tell what it is.

1. What will happen to the price of catfish if the government announces it has discovered that "an ounce of catfish a day will keep the doctor away"? Why?

2. What will happen to the price of catfish if the government announces that the first statement was a terrible mistake—in fact, "even less than a pound brings the doctor around"? Why?

3. What will happen to the price of toothpaste if, because of a shortage of tubes, the supply of toothpaste is cut in half? Why?

4. What will happen to the amount of lamb chops bought if the price is tripled? Why?

5. What will happen to the amount of chicken bought if the price is cut in half? Why?

6. What will happen to the number of red-white-and-blue shoes produced if it is found that the average person is willing to pay as much as $500 a pair for such fashionable footwear? Why?

7. What will happen to the price of diamonds if it is found that they can be made in your school's chemistry lab? Why?

8. What will happen to the price of bicycles if the President of the United States recommends that everyone bicycle to school or work to help cut down on air pollution? Why?

9. What will happen to the number of CD players that people are willing to buy if the price is cut in half? Why?

10. What will happen if, in the middle of a July heat wave, a store announces that electric heaters, normally priced at $85 and up, are on sale for $14.95? Why?

✔ *Graphing Supply and Demand*

Price	$16	14	12	10	8	6	4	2
Quantity	6	10	16	24	30	40	50	80

1. Construct a curve based on the data given above. You may use graph paper for more precise plotting of points.

2. Is this a demand or a supply curve?

3. Why does the curve slope downward?

4. On the same graph, construct another curve using the following data:

Price	$16	14	12	10	8	6	4
Quantity	48	44	40	36	30	20	10

5. Does this curve represent supply or demand?

6. Why does this curve slope upward?

7. What is the market price?

8. Why cannot the market price be $16?

CHAPTER 5

Money and Banks

Key Terms

money
barter
medium of
   exchange
monetary unit
currency
checking account
check
credit union
Federal Deposit
   Insurance
   Corporation

withdrawal
traveler's check
bank
depositor
interest
commercial bank
savings and loan
   association
mutual savings
   bank
cancelled check
deposit

Federal Reserve
   System
endorsement
reserves
electronic funds
   transfer (EFT)
automatic teller
   machine (ATM)
debit card
borrow
endorse

We all know what *money* is. Or do we? You will probably be surprised as you read a list of items that, somewhere and sometime, have served as money. For example, each of the following has been used as money:

In Ancient China: bronze knives and farm tools
In the Mayan civilization of Central America: cacao beans
In the African empire of Mali: salt chunks
Among the people of the Pacific islands of Yap: stone discs
Among the Native Americans of the Pacific Coast: fishhooks
In French Canada, around the year 1700: playing cards
In the English colonies of North America: beaver pelts, musket balls, nails, and beads
Among soldiers in prison camps during World War II: cigarettes.

You know that if you tried to pay for groceries at your local supermarket with playing cards, beads, fishhooks, furs, or stone discs, you might get a few laughs. But you certainly would not get the groceries. You could, however, pay for them with paper.

Now, is that not odd? Why is paper accepted as money? Why are beads not accepted? How do we store and save our money for future use? In short:

- What is money?
- What does money do?
- What types of money do we use?
- How are banks involved with the supply of money?
- What is modern banking like?

You will learn the answer to these questions in this chapter.

WHAT IS MONEY?

Money can be anything—yes, *anything*—that most people are willing to accept in payment for goods or services. Several centuries ago, North American colonists used beaver pelts, musket balls, nails, and beads to make purchases and to pay their debts. And other colonists were willing to accept those items in payment. The colonists' acceptance of beaver pelts and beads was what made these goods money. Something similar might happen today.

Money in Another Culture: People of the Pacific Islands of Yap once considered huge stone discs such as these to be money. What objects in your everyday life might acquire similar value?

Suppose the U.S. government announced that from now on beads would have to be accepted in payment for all debts. If the American people agreed, then beads would become a form of money in the United States.

WHAT DOES MONEY DO?

All modern societies use money. With money, people can easily trade goods and services with one another. That is, money promotes trade. It does so in three ways: Money provides a medium of exchange, a way of calculating value, and a method of saving.

Medium of Exchange

Suppose our society did not use money. If Jones wanted something you owned, how could Jones obtain it? Perhaps Jones might steal it. But could a society continue to exist in which people had to steal from one another? No, probably not. The only reasonable solution is a system in which people exchange a good or service that they have for another that they want or need. This system is called *barter*. But barter presents many problems. Suppose you had a coat that you wanted to swap for a pair of shoes with Jones. What would you do if Jones did not want your coat? Pay for the shoes with money. Or suppose the coat was worth more than the shoes. How would Jones make up the difference? With money, of course.

By using money, you do not run into the problems of bartering goods and services. If you have a coat to sell and want to buy a pair of shoes, you need only find a buyer for your coat. You can then use the money you receive to buy a pair of shoes. Money has enabled you to exchange, or trade, your coat for shoes. Since a medium is something that enables another thing to take place, we can say that money provides a *medium of exchange.*

Measure of Value

Let us return to our barter economy, where money does not exist. A farmer has a cow to sell. What is its price? That would depend upon what someone else has to trade. Suppose it is hay. How much hay is equal to one cow? Things are much easier in a money economy. In this system, the worth or value of anything can be expressed in terms of its price in the *monetary unit* of a country. The monetary unit of the United States is, of course, the dollar. Canada, too, has dollars, while Switzerland has francs, and Mexico has pesos.

Method of Saving

Money can be set aside and saved. Today, a couple can set aside a certain amount of their weekly paychecks until they have saved enough for a down payment on a house. But if the couple lived in a barter economy and made their living by growing vegetables, saving for a house would be very difficult. How would they go about saving their vegetables? Who, for example, would accept them after they had rotted?

Of course, even money can lose value over time. When that happens, as it does during periods of inflation, the prices of most goods and services increase. You will learn more about the changing value of money in Chapter 6.

WHAT TYPES OF MONEY DO WE USE?

Let us see what kinds of money you are carrying today. Take a look. What do you see? There may be some pennies, nickels, dimes, quarters, and what do you know—a dollar coin. This must be a good day. You may also have a $1 bill, a $5 bill, and a $20 bill. Now, what is that you are holding in your hand—a check? Someone gave you a check for $20 as a birthday present? Fine. Now, let us see. Should we put it with the rest of the money? We should. Why? You are absolutely right. Checks are another form of money. Let us review the reasons.

We said earlier that anything generally accepted in payment for goods and services is money. Since checks are usually accepted in payment, they also are a form of money. The principal kinds of money in use in the United States are *paper money, coins,* and *checks.*

Currency and Coins

The paper money issued by the federal government is the nation's *currency.* This currency has value because the government says it is worth something *and* because people are willing to trust the government. We accept this value even though the paper in a $20 bill is worth but a fraction of a cent. And the metal in the quarter, dime, and nickel coins is also worth very little, less than the face value of the coins.

Checks

Paper money and coins account for less than half of the nation's money supply. Because currency can be lost or stolen, most money

Different Kinds of Paper Money, top to bottom: $2 New York banknote from the 19th century; $100 Confederate note, 1862; 1 million German Mark note, 1923—actually worth almost nothing (to learn why, see page 92); $1 Massachusetts note from the 18th century—the hole was punched when the note was cashed.

is kept on deposit in *checking accounts* at banks. People who have deposited their money in checking accounts spend it by writing checks. A *check* is a written order directing a bank to pay a specified sum from one person's account to another person or to a business.

Figure 5.1 American Express Traveler's Check

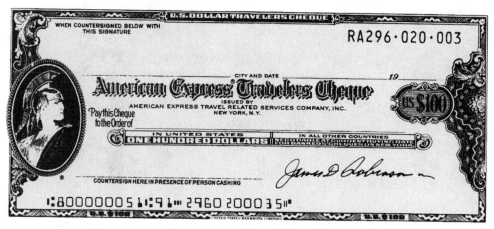

Traveler's Checks

Travelers know that it is often difficult to use their personal checks in places where they are not known. But most people do not want to carry a lot of cash on vacations or business trips because it can easily be lost or stolen. One solution to this problem is to use *traveler's checks*. Most large banks sell these checks. Traveler's checks are widely accepted as payment in the United States and other countries. The U.S. government considers traveler's checks to be money.

The table shows the kinds and amounts of money in circulation in a recent year.

United States Money Supply, 2007
(in billions)

Checking accounts	$621.4
Currency and coin	751.2
Traveler's checks	6.7
Total	$ 1,379.3

THE BUSINESS OF BANKING

Have you visited a bank lately? Did you notice what its customers were doing? In all likelihood, most were there to either add money to their accounts by making *deposits* or taking funds out as *withdrawals*. Others may have visited the bank to *borrow* money. Bank loans help people buy homes and motor vehicles, start businesses, expand farms, or do other things that require money.

Banks Exist in a Variety of Forms

Commercial banks take deposits and make loans to individuals and businesses. *Savings and loan associations (S&Ls)* and *mutual savings banks* take deposits and make loans primarily for buying homes. *Credit unions* provide loans for its members. Since commercial banks, S&Ls, and credit unions all accept deposits, they are also known as *depository institutions*. But most people think of them as banks, and that is what we will be calling them.

Banks Are Businesses That Sell Financial Services

Like all privately owned businesses, banks need to earn profits in order to operate. They do this by charging money for the loans, credit cards, checking accounts, and other services they provide.

Where do banks get the money to lend? They get it from their *depositors*, the people who open accounts. Depositors entrust their money to banks because of the safety they provide, and the *interest* earned on most accounts. Among other things, the *Federal Deposit Insurance Corporation (FDIC)* guarantees the safety of bank accounts. The FDIC insures bank accounts in amounts up to $100,000.

Banks draw upon their depositors' savings to make loans. Banks pay their depositors *interest*. Interest earned on savings accounts varies from year to year. Those who borrow pay interest on their loans to the lending banks. Naturally, the interest charged on loans is higher than the interest that banks pay their depositors. The difference between the amount that banks charge for their loans and the amount paid to depositors pays expenses and adds to bank profits. For example, a bank may pay 2.5 percent interest on savings accounts while charging 8 percent for car loans.

In recent years, banks have begun to sell insurance, as well as stocks and bonds. (These subjects are discussed in Chapters 13 and 23.)

Checking Accounts

Of all the services provided by banks, checking accounts are the most popular. When you write a check, you are instructing your bank to transfer a specific amount of money from your checking account to another individual or organization. You can also write a check just to convert some money in your account into cash.

Checks are safer to carry than cash. You know that if you lose your cash, there is a good chance that you will never see it again. But if you lose your checkbook, no one else will be able to use it. Another advantage of checks is their convenience. Think, for

Personal Economics

WRITING AND ENDORSING A CHECK

Martha Nieves has a checking account in the First National Bank of Peoria, Illinois. Today, March 1, is the day the rent is payable to her landlord, the Yardley Realty Company. She will write a check for $582.70 to pay the rent. Here is the blank check she will use.

```
  Martha Nieves (1)                                          (3) 812
                              (2) _____          20 ____

  (4) Pay to                                            (5)
      the Order of _____ $ _____

  (6) _____ Dollars


  (7) First National Bank                   (8)
      of Peoria, Illinois                        _____
                                        (3)
  (9) ⑆0210⑆0008⑈17320545⑆ 0812
```

1. First National Bank has printed Martha Nieves's name on her check.

2. This is where the date is entered.

3. This is the number of Martha's check.

4. Following the words "Pay to the Order of" is written the name of the individual or organization to whom the check is made out.

5. The amount of the check follows the $ sign. Many people write the number of cents as a fraction of 100. Thus, $582 70/100.

6. Here the amount of money is written out. Once again, most people list the cents as a fraction of 100.

Thus, $582.70 could be written as "Five hundred eighty-two and 70/100," followed by a line to the word "Dollars," if space remained.

7. The name of the bank is printed on the check.

8. The person writing the check (Martha Nieves) signs here.

9. These are the code numbers that identify Martha Nieves's account and bank. These numbers can be read by an electronic data-processing machine. It automatically sorts out the checks that each person who has a checking account has written, and then it adds up the sums of money.

Martha Nieves (1)

(2) _____ *March, 1* _____ 20 _*02*_

(3) **812**

(4) **Pay to the Order of** _*Yardley Realty Company*_ (5) $ _*582 70/100*_

(6) _*Five hundred eighty-two and* _____ 70/100_ **Dollars**

(7) **First National Bank of Peoria, Illinois**

(8) _____ *Martha Nieves* _____

(3)

(9) ⑈:0210⋯0008⑈:17320545⋯⑈ 0812

Martha Nieves's check to Yardley Realty is shown above.

Suppose that Martha Nieves had carried the $582.70 rent money in cash in her purse and then the purse had been lost or stolen. She would have been out the money. But if Martha had lost the rent check, all she would have had to do was notify the bank to stop payment on it. No money would have been lost. She could then have paid her rent by writing a new check.

Endorsing a Check

After receiving Martha's check, Yardley Realty will either cash it or deposit it in a bank account. In either case, Yardley's bookkeepers will have to endorse the check by stamping the company's name on the back. The *endorsement* looks like this:

YARDLEY REALTY COMPANY

When you endorse a check that has been made out to you, you give someone else the right to cash it. Until that happens, no one else but you has the right to the money. This is one reason why checks are so widely used as money.

It is easy to endorse a check that is made out to you. All you must do is sign your name on the back of the check. If you are going to deposit this check to your account and send it through the mail, it is safer to add the following:

Your name
For deposit only
to account number
_____

A check endorsed in this way can be deposited only into your bank account. No one can claim to be you or that you endorsed the check over to them.

Banks ask their checking account customers to use deposit tickets. On these tickets are printed the customer's name, address, and account number. The customer fills in the amount of the cash and/or checks being deposited and includes the ticket with the deposit.

Balancing the Checkbook: Why is it important to keep accurate records of all checking deposits and payments?

example, of how much easier it is to mail someone a check for $39.95 than it would be to send that amount in cash.

Those who receive checks need to *endorse* them (by signing their name on the back of the check) before they can deposit or convert them to cash. Eventually, the endorsed checks are stamped by the bank and returned to the owner of the checking account as *cancelled checks.* Another reason for the popularity of checking accounts is that cancelled checks are proof that a bill has been paid. Because they are so safe and convenient, checks are widely used to pay for expensive purchases and to transfer money.

Because of their safety and convenience, checking accounts are the largest component of the money supply. But banks must have cash available when people need it. One way that people obtain needed cash is by cashing a check at their bank. In that way, they exchange their deposited money for cash. When they are holding more cash than they need, people can deposit some of it in their bank account.

The public needs more currency at certain special times of the year. During the winter holiday season, spring and summer vacations, and when schools reopen, people often withdraw more cash from their bank accounts than they are putting in. During the rest of the year, currency tends to flow back into bank deposits.

The Federal Reserve System

By now, you may be wondering where the banks get the currency that they give to people who cash checks. In 1913, the U.S.

Congress created the *Federal Reserve System*. This agency (often called the "Fed") operates 12 Federal Reserve Banks in this country. Each of these banks supervises the banking activities in one of the nation's Federal Reserve districts.

One of the tasks that Congress assigned to the Federal Reserve was to meet the nation's need for cash. The Fed is able to put currency into the hands of the nation's banks when they need it, and take it back when they do not need it. Here is how the Fed does this:

A bank maintains an account with the Federal Reserve Bank in its district in much the same way that a person holds an account at a local bank. When a local bank needs cash, it simply withdraws the money from its account at the Fed. When a bank has more cash than it needs, it redeposits the money with the Fed. In an emergency, when a bank needs more money than it has in its account at the Fed, the bank can borrow the money it needs from the Fed. The bank will then pay interest to the Fed for this borrowed money.

The 12 Federal Reserve Banks get their supplies of paper currency from the Bureau of Engraving and Printing in Washington, D.C. Coins come from the Bureau of the Mint in Denver and Philadelphia. (A map of the Federal Reserve System appears on page 458.)

How Commercial Banks Create Money

Having read this far, perhaps you believe that only the government can create money. This is not the case. A great deal of the

Banks and Businesspeople: Owners of small businesses such as this one often depend on banks for short-term loans. What happens to the nation's money supply when banks loan money to their customers?

money in circulation is created by commercial banks. Commercial banks often make loans to businesses. When a business firm borrows a sum of money, the bank places it on deposit in the firm's checking account. The business withdraws the money as it needs it.

Take the case of Harry and Sylvia Girard, the owners of the Girard Jewelry Company. In October, they borrowed $15,000 from the Safety First National Bank to buy watches and jewelry to sell during the holiday season. The $15,000 was deposited in their checking account at the bank. As the various shipments of merchandise were received, the Girards wrote out checks in payment of the bills. After January 1, they repaid the loan with the money they had earned from the sale of the jewelry.

In this example, a very interesting event occurred. The country's money supply was increased by $15,000 for a short time, and the government had nothing to do with it. This money was not taken away from anyone—therefore, *the bank created $15,000.* Commercial banks all over the country do this every day: They create checkbook money by granting loans. Of course, as loans are repaid, money is taken out of circulation. Thus, the Girards' checking account balance was reduced by $15,000 when they repaid their loan.

Since banks earn profits by lending money, it follows that the more they have to lend, the greater their profits will be.

"Now, wait a minute," you say. "Do you mean to tell me that the bank will take the money I deposited for safekeeping and lend it to someone I don't even know?"

That is correct. Of course, before it makes a loan the bank does what it can to determine that the business or individual who borrows will be able to pay the money back.

"But how will I and others like me be able to get our money back when we want it if the bank has loaned it out?"

That is easy. Although on any given day some depositors will make withdrawals, other depositors will make deposits. In fact, on most days the amount of deposits will more than offset withdrawals. Furthermore, banks cannot lend all the money they have on deposit. They must always keep part of this amount on hand in case there is a heavy run of withdrawals at a particular time. The sum kept on hand is known as the banks' *reserves*. The portion of their total deposits that they must keep on reserve at any one time is determined by the Federal Reserve Board.

Suppose that a bank has $1 million in deposits, and the federal government has said that all banks must keep 20 percent of their deposits on hand as a reserve. How much of its $1 million in deposits could the bank lend out? If you said $800,000, you were absolutely right. The reason is that 20 percent of $1 million is

$200,000. This amount must be set aside in the bank's reserves. The balance of the $1 million, or $800,000, may be given out in loans. But the process does not stop there. If the full $800,000 loaned out is redeposited and the bank keeps 20 percent ($160,000) as a reserve, $640,000 can be loaned out.

There is a limit to the amount of money a bank may create because there is a limit to the amount of money it may lend. Remember, a bank must keep some money—reserves—on hand to meet the demands of its depositors. This is shown in the table.

How a Bank Creates Money Through Loans

Bank	Deposits	Required Reserves	Loans
Safety First	$1,000,000	$200,000	$800,000
National Bank	800,000	160,000	640,000
	640,000	128,000	512,000
	512,000	102,400	409,600
	409,600	81,920	327,680
Sum of remaining bank activities	1,638,400	327,680	1,310,720
Total	$5,000,000	$1,000,000	$4,000,000

As you can see in the table, an initial deposit of $1 million made it possible to loan out $4 million. In our example, the reserve ratio was 20 percent. It should be clear that if the reserve ratio were greater than 20 percent, less than $4 million could have been loaned out. If the reserve ratio were less than 20 percent, banks could have created more than $4 million through loans.

WHAT IS MODERN BANKING LIKE?

The electronic revolution that has brought us computers and video games has also brought about major changes in the way people bank and pay for the things that they buy.

Automated Teller Machines

Previously when one went to a bank to make a deposit or withdrawal, one usually dealt with a teller. With an *automated teller machine (ATM)*, it is possible to make bank deposits and withdrawals without talking to a teller or any other person, and without having to write a check or withdrawal slip. These machines are activated simply by inserting a special plastic card into the

Automatic Teller Machine (ATM): How can customers protect themselves from robberies when withdrawing money from an ATM?

machine and keying in one's private code, usually a four- to six-digit number.

Electronic Funds Transfer

When people deposit checks at their banks, it normally takes a few days for the amounts to be credited to their account. Depositors cannot withdraw and spend those amounts until their account is credited. Using an *electronic funds transfer* (*EFT*) system, however, accounts can be credited immediately. The ETF system uses computers and automated equipment to do this. Consequently, depositors can spend their money on the same day that they put the money into their accounts. This is one of the advantages EFT offers over the system of checks.

Still another way in which EFT has been replacing the use of checks has been in the way that people pay their bills. New electronic systems link either telephones or home computers to special bank accounts. By keying instructions into their telephones or computers, subscribers are able to pay bills in an instant.

Recent improvements in personal computers and the Internet have made it possible for people to do much of their banking at home. Several banks around the country offer software packages that enable their customers to use their personal computers and the Internet to write checks, pay bills, check their account balances, and even apply for loans.

SUMMARY

Money is anything that people will accept in exchange for goods and services. Money serves as a medium of exchange, a way of calculating prices, and a way of saving. We use currency (paper and coins) and checks as money. Banks receive money from and lend money to businesses and individuals. The Federal Reserve System provides banks with their day-to-day currency needs. The Treasury Department prints currency and coins money.

Checks make up a large part of our money supply because they are easier and safer to use than cash. In order to write a check, you must have a checking account at a bank. The check should be filled out completely and accurately. If you wish to cash a check, you must endorse it properly.

Electronic funds transfer uses computer technology. It has become an increasingly important means of making and receiving payments. The Internet has made it possible for people to do much of their banking at home, using a computer.

LOOKING AHEAD

Like everything else, the value of money may vary from one time to another. When this happens, the prices of goods and services will either rise or fall. The next chapter explores some of the reasons why the value of money changes, and how these fluctuations affect us all.

EXERCISES

✔**Multiple Choice** Choose the letter of the item that best completes the statement or answers the question.

1. A main idea of this chapter is that (a) our economy can function without money (b) money serves as a medium of exchange, a way of calculating value, and a method of saving (c) cash is a better way of making payments than electronic funds transfer (d) checks are always a better way of making payments than cash.

2. Under which of the following circumstances would beads be considered money? (a) You said they were money. (b) They were very valuable. (c) You could buy something with them anywhere in the United States. (d) They were very rare.

3. In a barter economy, (a) people exchange goods and services for the things they want (b) people rely exclusively on checks for money (c) people save, buy, and exchange more easily than in a money economy (d) paper money is printed by the government.

4. Suppose that you melted down $100 in quarters. What would be the value of the metal? (a) equal to its weight in gold (b) much more than $100 (c) much less than $100 (d) exactly $100.

5. Why are traveler's checks considered a form of money? (a) Anyone can buy them. (b) They are widely accepted in payment for goods and services. (c) They are easy to use. (d) They can be replaced if stolen or lost.

6. Electronic funds transfer (a) involves making and receiving payments via computers and other automated means (b) is the amount of demand deposits held at banks (c) is a payment procedure involving the use of checks (d) involves the transfer of funds from the Federal Reserve to member banks.

7. Which one of the following people is the *endorser* of a check? The one who (a) writes his or her name on the back of the check (b) originally wrote the check (c) makes payment on the check (d) printed the check.

8. Your local bank finds itself running short of the $1, $5, and $10 bills it will need to take care of its customers' needs. Where is it most likely to go to stock up on this currency? (a) the U.S. Treasury Department (b) a neighboring bank (c) the Bureau of the Mint (d) the Federal Reserve Bank of its district.

✔**Matching** Match each term in Column A with its definition in Column B.

Column A	Column B
1. barter	a. the use of computers to receive and make payments
2. money	
3. currency	b. the standard unit of value of a country's currency
4. monetary unit	c. a person who places money in an account in a bank for safety and earnings
5. depositor	
6. Bureau of the Mint	d. anything generally accepted in payment for goods and services
7. electronic funds transfer (EFT)	e. paper money
	f. a system in which people exchange goods or services
8. Federal Reserve System	g. an organization that regulates the nation's banks and its money supply
	h. an organization that manufactures U.S. coins

✔ *Writing and Endorsing Checks*

1. Suppose that you have a checking account at the Bank of Industry. Your phone bill for $21.82 is now due. The phone company is the Central City Telephone Company. Using today's date, your own name, and the blank check shown below as your guide, prepare a check in payment. (Do not write in your book. Instead, make a copy of this blank check either by hand or by using a photocopying machine.)

Your Name	**752**
	_____ 20 ____
Pay to the Order of _____	$ _____
_____ **Dollars**	
Bank of Industry Centerville, MO	_____
17320545··020101000081: 0752	

2. Now let us suppose that you have received a $20 check as a birth-day gift. You want to deposit this check to your savings account at the Security Federal Savings Bank. Your account number is 5972506. List the steps involved in your endorsement of the check.

✔ *Using the Internet*

Visit the Website of a major banking company to find out what the bank provides to its customers. Possible sites include:

<<www.bankofamerica.com>>
<<www.chase.com>>
<<www.citigroup.com>>
<<www.db.com>>

To learn more about money, visit the U.S. Mint's Website at <<http://www.usmint.gov>> and the Bureau of Engraving and Printing's Website at <<http://www.moneyfactory.com>>.

CHAPTER 6

The Value of Money Might Increase or Decrease

Key Terms

value	Consumer Price	demand-pull
inflation	Index	cost-push
purchasing power	index number	monetary policy
deflation	base period	inflationary spiral

You may have heard people complain, "A dollar just isn't worth a dollar anymore." They do not mean that you cannot get 100 cents for each one of your dollar bills. A dollar is still worth 100 cents in any combination of quarters, dimes, nickels, and pennies. But this dollar has lost *value*—it cannot buy as much as it once did.

Look at the illustration of the three dollars on page 87. Each dollar has a face value of 100 cents. Yet the 1970 dollar is two-and-a-half times the size of the 1985 dollar, and it is six times the size of today's dollar. The shrinking dollar means that since 1970 the value of a dollar has fallen considerably. In 1970, one dollar bought over six times the amount of goods and services that one dollar buys today.

After reading this chapter, you will have a better understanding of the dollar and how its changing value affects you. You will also be able to answer the following questions:

- What is inflation?
- Why are we concerned about inflation?
- What causes inflation?

WHAT IS INFLATION?

Inflation is a rise in the prices of most goods and services. When prices rise, you cannot buy as much with your dollar in one year as you bought in an earlier year. That is why it is said that during periods of inflation the *purchasing power*, or value, of the dollar is falling.

Deflation is the opposite of inflation. During periods of deflation, prices *fall*. Deflation, however, rarely occurs. For that reason, we will focus our attention on inflation.

The purchasing power of the dollar is measured by the *Consumer Price Index (CPI)*. This index compares the prices of 400 commonly bought goods and services in one year with their prices in an earlier year. These goods and services include food, shelter, clothing, transportation, medical care, fuel oil, gas and electricity, and

Figure 6.1 Decreasing Value of the Dollar Since 1970

1970

1985

Today

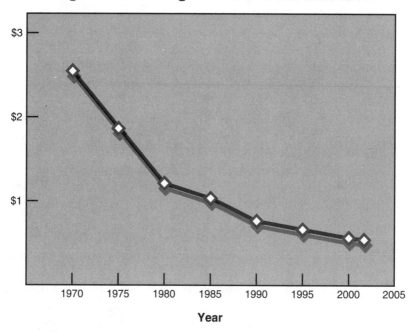

Figure 6.2 Purchasing Power of the Dollar Since 1970

telephone service. The prices of the items in the CPI are checked monthly by the U.S. government. The CPI tells us how much a dollar can buy compared to an earlier year, or years. (See the feature "The Consumer Price Index and Index Numbers," on page 90.)

WHY ARE WE CONCERNED ABOUT INFLATION?

Effects of Inflation: Who Is Hurt

Inflation hurts some people more than others *at first*. If inflation lasts long enough, it is likely to hurt us *all*. Let us see how and why.

1. Retired People. Many retired people live on incomes from private pensions, bonds, and Social Security. Private pension incomes are *fixed*—they are not likely to increase very much from one year to the next. Similarly, the income paid in the form of dividends on bonds remains constant. When prices suddenly increase, as they do during inflation, the elderly and others living on fixed incomes are unable to buy as much with their money as they could in the past. For them, inflation often means having to cut down on necessities such as food or heating fuel. By law, Social Security payments increase when there is a large increase in the Cost of Living Index. Thus, Social Security income keeps up with inflation.

2. People With Savings. People who put all their extra cash into savings accounts may find that because of inflation, their money is worth less after a period of years than when they deposited it. Suppose that a couple deposited $1,000 in a savings account in 1970. Remember from the opening of this chapter that the dollar has less than a sixth of its 1970 purchasing power. Today, it takes over $6,000 to buy what their $1,000 could buy. Thus, unless the interest on their savings added $5,000 to their original deposit, their money has less value now than when they deposited it.

3. People With Low Incomes. Those who earn low wages are hurt by inflation. These individuals have little enough to spend to begin with. Low-income people face increasing problems as prices rise. Prices generally rise faster than their incomes. As food, clothing, and housing cost more, the poor are forced to make do with fewer necessities.

Effects of Inflation: Who May Benefit

Inflation may benefit some people, however. Let us see how and why.

1. People Who Owe Money. Those who borrow money before the start of an inflationary period may benefit from it. They can

How do you think the adult answered the youngster's question?

"How can the dollar inflate and shrink at the same time?"

From the Wall Street Journal. *Permission, Cartoon Features Syndicate.*

Understanding Economics

THE CONSUMER PRICE INDEX AND INDEX NUMBERS

The Consumer Price Index (CPI) is a measure of the change in the prices of about 400 items of food, clothing, shelter, and health care that U.S. consumers use on a daily basis. The prices in one period can then be compared with the prices of the same items in an earlier period. The measure of one year's prices as compared with another year's is expressed as an index number.

Index numbers allow us to see how parts of the economy are behaving from year to year. These numbers may also be used to measure changes in almost any area that can be expressed in numbers.

The accompanying table lists the CPI for selected years since 1970. The line "1982–1984 = 100" tells us that 1982–1984 is the period to which consumer prices in the other years are being compared. We call 1982–1984 the *base period*. The index number of a base period is always 100.

To determine the percentage change from the base, find the difference between the index number and the base. Remember that the base is always 100. For example, if the index number for a year is 130, there has been a 30 percent *increase* over the base (130 minus 100 equals +30). If an index number stands at 82, it represents an 18 percent *decrease* from the base (82 minus 100 equals −18).

**Consumer Price Index Since 1970
(1982–1984 = 100)**

Year	Index Number
1970	38.8
1980	82.4
1982–84	100.0
1985	107.6
1990	130.7
1995	152.4
1997	160.5
2005	193.3

From looking at the table, what can you say about prices in 2005 as compared to 1982–84? Prices were 93 percent higher than in the earlier period. Why? Because the CPI in 2005 was 93 points higher than in 1982–1984.

Figure 6.3 shows the Consumer Price Index as a graph.

Questions for Thought

1. What is the Consumer Price Index?
2. What is an index number?
3. What is a base period?
4. Compare consumer prices in 2005 to those in 1980 and 1970.

repay their loans with dollars that are worth less than when they took out the loans.

For example, in 1970 the dollar had more than twice the purchasing power of the 1980 dollar (see the table above). Someone who borrowed $5,000 in 1970 would have been able to repay the loan (plus pay interest charges) in 1980 with dollars that were

Figure 6.3 Consumer Price Index Since 1970

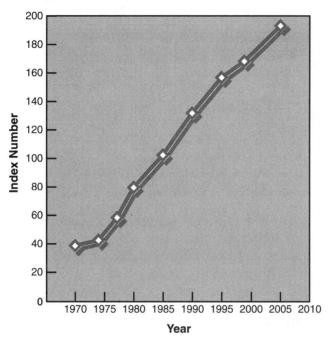

worth only $2,500. Needless to say, the lender would have been harmed by the inflation, just as the borrower benefited.

2. People Who Own Real Estate. People who own homes or other properties are likely to find that their value has increased during a time of inflation. For example, a home purchased for $75,000 in 1975 might sell for over $400,000 today.

Although some people may benefit for a time from inflation, in the long run it hurts us all. For example, banks and other lenders know that the value of the money they lend will be diminished by inflation. By way of protecting themselves, banks and other lenders will raise interest rates when inflation seems likely to occur.

Let us suppose, for example, that the Second City Bank of Centerport is charging 9 percent interest per year on personal loans. But the bank anticipates that inflation will add 10 percent to the cost of living each year for the next few years. Since the managers of the bank do not want to lose money on their loans, they will add the cost of inflation to their interest charges. Borrowers will now have to pay a much higher interest rate on their loans. Thus, Second City decides to increase its interest charges

Inflation and the Home: How does inflation affect people who want to sell their homes? How are potential home buyers affected by inflation?

on personal loans to 14 percent. Now people who would have borrowed money at 9 percent might not be able (or want) to do so.

Businesspeople are also hurt by high interest rates because they add to the costs of running a business. The businesses may not be able to pass these increased costs on to their customers. Moreover, sales of high-priced items may decline as fewer people are able to borrow the money they need to buy the goods that businesses sell.

As for people whose homes and other property have increased in value because of inflation, some will discover that the gain is only on paper. The family whose $80,000 home is now valued at $120,000 might be delighted with the gain. But if they want to move to another community, they might discover that it costs $120,000 or more to buy a similar home there.

Inflation and a Nation's Economy

In extreme cases, inflation can become so bad that prices simply "run away." Perhaps the most notorious "runaway inflation" took place in Germany after World War I (1914–1918). In 1913, just before the war began, one U.S. dollar was worth about four German marks. By 1923, it took about 4,000,000,000,000 (4 *trillion*) marks to buy one dollar. Or, to put it another way: In 1913, all the mortgages in Germany added up to 10 billion marks, but in 1923, 10 billion marks was equal to only a single U.S. penny. Pictures in newspapers showed people pushing a wheelbarrow on the way to market to buy a single bottle of milk. Why the wheelbarrow? To carry the money needed to pay for the milk.

In the mid-1990s, a number of nations experienced high rates of inflation. While these rates were not as serious as the German inflation of 1923, they did represent a problem.

Inflation in Germany in the 1920s: During the period of *hyper*(super)*inflation*, paper money was burned for fuel or used as wallpaper. During such a circumstance, what happened to the value of the money that people had deposited in savings accounts?

WHAT CAUSES INFLATION?

Why are there times when prices are generally rising? Most of the reasons fall into one or two categories: rising demand or increasing costs.

Demand-Pull: Rising Demand

One reason for inflation is rising demand. People become *willing and able to pay higher prices* for the goods and services they want. As demand increases, so too do prices. And when the general level of prices increases, inflation results.

Inflation that results from rising demand is called *demand-pull inflation*. This means that the demand of buyers is pulling the prices of goods and services to higher and higher levels.

Economists describe demand-pull inflation as "too much money chasing too few goods." This is another way of saying that there are not enough goods and services available to satisfy the demand for them *at current prices*. In the United States, the late 1940s were a time of demand-pull inflation. During World War II

Understanding Economics

LIVING WITH INFLATION IN TURKEY

In modern-day Turkey, inflation has been an everyday fact of life. Inci Behar has just received her monthly paycheck: 415 million! No, Inci is not a millionaire. She lives in Istanbul, Turkey, where she works in the office of a large insurance company. The 415 million Turkish liras she is paid are equal to about 600 U.S. dollars. When she can afford it, Inci loves to visit the nearby McDonald's. Her favorite dish is the Big Mac. In 2001, a Big Mac sold for 2 million liras. When she was born in 1975, one could have bought an entire restaurant for 2 million liras.

Since the 1970s, inflation has been eating away at the Turkish lira. Between 1975 (the year Inci was born) and 2001, prices in Turkey increased by an average of *70 percent per year*! That increase meant that something that cost 2 liras in 1975 would have increased to 3.4 liras in 1976, 5.8 in 1977, and 9.8 liras in 1978. By the year 2001, it took more than 2 *million* Turkish liras to buy something that was selling for just 2 liras in 1975.

In December 2004, it took 1.3 million Turkish liras to buy one U.S. dollar. In January 2005, Turkey replaced the lira with *new liras* at the rate of 1 new lira for 1 million old liras. As a result, it then took 1.3 Turkish liras to buy $1. Why do you think the government took that step?

Inflation in Turkey, 1994–2003
(Annual percentage change in Consumer Prices)

1994	106.3
1995	88.1
1996	80.3
1997	85.7
2001	54.4
2003	25.3

1. Inci Behar had been putting a portion of her salary in an account at her local bank. One of the things she had been saving for was a trip to the United States. "I wonder if this inflation will have any effect on my vacation plans," she thought. (a) How might the inflation in Turkey make it difficult for Inci to visit the United States? (b) Is there anything Inci might do to protect her vacation plans?

2. Imagine that you are living in Turkey. How would you expect to be affected by its double-digit (10 percent or more) inflation rate?

3. In February 2001, it took 686,000 Turkish liras to buy one U.S. dollar. Compare this to the rate of exchange today. What does this information tell you about the success or failure of Turkey's efforts to control inflation?

(1941–1945), Americans had not been able to purchase many consumer items, such as clothing, appliances, and cars. Factories had been too busy making items for defense (such as guns, tanks, planes, and ships). After the war ended, consumer goods were once again available. As a result, people went on buying sprees, and prices quickly rose.

The U.S. economy was troubled by inflation during the 1970s. Most economists believe that the inflation had been caused partly by demand-pull factors. Government spending to fight the war in Viet Nam helped to create jobs and increase the production of military hardware. But the output of civilian goods and services did not keep pace with rising incomes. Then, with "too much money chasing too few goods," prices rose.

In Chapter 30, we will describe how the Federal Reserve System (Fed) uses monetary policy to control demand-pull inflation. As you will see, the Fed can decrease the money supply when prices are rising because "too much money is chasing too few goods." When, on the other hand, more money is needed to keep prices from falling, the Fed can increase the money supply. The Fed's use of its ability to regulate the money supply to benefit the economy is known as *monetary policy*.

Cost-Push: Increasing Costs

The increasing costs of doing business are a second reason for inflation. When the owners of your local grocery store discover that they have to pay more for the goods they sell, they raise their prices. If costs rise for other grocery stores and businesses around the country, they too will raise their prices. Other costs can rise too, such as raw materials, taxes, and insurance.

As workers find that they have to pay more for the things they want, they will seek wage increases to make up for the rising prices. Unions often refer to increased living costs to justify their demands for higher wages.

If workers win wage increases, businesses will often raise their prices. But the upward spiral does not end there. With still higher prices to pay, workers again ask for higher wages. These recurring events have been called an *inflationary spiral*. In an inflationary spiral, costs push up prices. For that reason, the spiral is often described as *cost-push inflation*.

Inflation has not been a serious problem in the United States since the 1970s. The reasons for this can be found in the nation's record-breaking output of goods and services and actions taken by the Federal Reserve System to regulate prices. We will be describing those steps in Chapter 30.

SUMMARY

Inflation occurs when there is a general rise in the prices of most goods and services. We are concerned because inflation can harm many people as well as the entire economy of a nation. Rising prices hurt people whose income does not increase as rapidly as the rate of inflation. This includes savers, lenders, and persons living on fixed or low incomes. Inflation may benefit people whose income rises faster than the inflation rate. Borrowers and homeowners sometimes benefit from inflation.

Inflation is measured in terms of the general level of prices. The Consumer Price Index is one tool used by the government to measure changes in price levels.

Two explanations for inflation are demand-pull and cost-push. Demand-pull inflation results when too many dollars are chasing too few goods. Demand (or spending) is greater than the economy's ability to produce the things necessary to satisfy that demand at current prices. Cost-push inflation results when businesses raise their prices in response to higher labor costs, and workers demand higher wages in response to higher prices. Both cost-push and demand-pull have been thought to be responsible for our most recent inflationary periods.

LOOKING AHEAD

The U.S. economy has been compared to a show in which there are three players: government, businesses, and consumers. The following unit looks at the role played by consumers in the U.S. economy. We also see why it is said that in a free enterprise system consumers are sovereign.

EXERCISES

✔**Matching** Match each term in Column A with its definition in Column B.

Column A	Column B
1. inflation	a. a time that has an index number of 100
2. purchasing power	b. a type of inflation in which prices are pushed up by costs
3. Consumer Price Index	c. a type of inflation in which "too much money is chasing too few goods"
4. base period	d. a rise in the prices of most goods and services
5. demand-pull	e. measures the changes in the prices of commonly bought goods and services from one year to another
6. cost-push	f. how much a set amount of money can buy

✔**Multiple Choice** Choose the letter of the item that best completes the statement or answers the question.

1. An increase in the prices of most goods and services is called (a) inflation (b) deflation (c) purchasing power (d) savings.

2. Inflation may hurt retired people because they (a) own stocks (b) often live on fixed incomes (c) have part-time jobs (d) own their own businesses.

3. Bonnie Plata deposited $1,000 in her savings account. Two years later, she withdrew her money, which totaled $1,100 with the 5 percent interest the bank paid her per year. During that time, the cost of living increased by 15 percent. Which of the following best describes what had happened to Bonnie's money? (*Hint*: Compare Bonnie's interest for two years with the inflation rate for that period of time.) (a) Her deposit was worth more when she withdrew it than when she first made it. (b) She was able to buy more with her money after two years. (c) The value of money had increased over the two years. (d) The $1,000 Bonnie deposited was worth more than the $1,100 she withdrew.

4. Runaway inflation can lead to (a) the collapse of the economy (b) lower prices (c) a higher standard of living (d) the growth of democracy.

5. If the Consumer Price Index is 140, prices since the base year have (a) decreased by 40 percent (b) increased by 140 percent (c) increased by 40 percent (d) remained the same.

6. Suppose the Consumer Price Index increased by 50 percent over a five-year period. What effect would this have on the standard of living of a family whose income over the same period had increased from $40,000 to $60,000? (*Hint*: What percentage is the increase from $40,000 to $60,000?) (a) The family's standard of living would have improved because of the $20,000 increase in income. (b) The family's standard of living would have remained about the same. (c) The family would have lost purchasing power because prices had risen faster than its income. (d) None of these is correct.

✔*Developing Skills in Economics*

1. Look at the table on page 90. It shows the Consumer Price Index during the years since 1970. What has been the trend of prices over the period shown? (A trend is the general direction in which something moves.)

2. Read the following selection and then answer the questions that follow:

In 1970, a young man received a $1,000 inheritance, which he promptly buried in an airtight container in the backyard. At the end of 2000, he dug it up. When he told his son, who was studying economics at the time, what he had done, his son said, "That's just great, Dad. You buried $1,000 and dug up about $175."

a. Explain what the young man meant by this statement.

b. Give a few examples of things the father might have done with the $1,000 to preserve, or to increase, its value over the years. (See Chapter 11 for a discussion of the choices available to him.)

✔ *Inflation Hits the Supermarket*

The table below shows what happened to the average prices for 18 popular food items for selected years between 1979 and 2000. The figures are based upon surveys conducted by the federal government in cities across the country. Study the table and answer the questions that follow.

Average Prices of Popular Foods, 1979, 1986, and 2000

Product	Unit	1979	1986	2000
Round steak	pound	$1.99	$3.39	$3.91
Pork chops (center cut)	pound	1.89	2.99	2.55
Hamburger	pound	1.59	1.69	3.45
Frankfurters	pound	1.49	1.19	3.29
Chicken (frying)	pound	.45	2.94	1.61
Eggs (grade A large)	dozen	1.00	1.35	1.55
Milk	quart	.58	.69	.93
Ice cream	1/2 gallon	1.75	3.75	8.78
Butter	pound	1.98	2.45	3.00
Sugar	5 pounds	1.29	2.36	2.84
Coffee	pound	2.67	4.09	4.43
White bread	pound	.71	.94	1.49
Apples	pound	.33	1.09	1.50
Cornflakes	12 oz.	.59	1.26	2.52
Oranges	dozen	1.41	4.00	5.13
Potatoes	pound	.16	.34	.51
Lettuce	head	.69	1.09	1.49
Tomatoes	pound	.69	1.09	2.00

1. With the exception of two items, all of the products listed in the table increased in price from 1986 to 2000. What were those items?

2. "The purchasing power was about twice as much in 1979 as it was in 2000." Explain the statement.

3. Identify and explain at least one reason for the relative *increase* in the prices of some foods from 1979 to 2000.

To bring the survey up to date, visit your local supermarket and find today's prices for each item.

✔ **Studying Inflation and Its Consequences**

Purchasing Power of the Dollar Since 1940
(Annual Average as Measured by Consumer Prices)

1940	7.12	1985	0.93
1945	5.53	1990	0.77
1950	4.15	1995	0.66
1955	3.73	1996	0.64
1960	3.37	1997	0.62
1965	3.17	1998	0.61
1970	2.57	1999	0.60
1975	1.86	2002	0.56
1980	1.22	2005	0.52

When he was still alive, Frank Johnson's Great Grandpa owned a plumbing and heating business. In 1940, Great Grandpa's earnings were $5,000. Frank now owns the business. In 2002, Frank's earnings totaled $55,000.

"I don't get it," said Frank, "I earn much more than Great Grandpa ever did, but some people say his money was *worth more* than mine. Seems to me, a dollar is a dollar. And besides, I live much better than he did back in 1940!"

1. How could it be said that Great Grandpa's $5,000 was worth more than Frank's $55,000?

2. What made Frank think that he lived better than his Great Grand-father?

✔ **Using the Internet**

To convert current dollar prices from any year since 1800 to their constant dollar equivalents, see the: (1) copyrighted table *Consumer Price Index Conversion Factors* at: <<http://www.oregonstate.edu/Dept/pol_sci/fac/sahr/sahr.htm>>, or (2) the Bureau of Labor Statistics Website at: <<http://www.bls.gov/opub/mlr/curlabst.htm>>. To find prices for selected supermarket items in recent years, see <<http://www.census.gov/prod/www/statistical-abstract-us.html>>.

Unit 2

SPENDING, SAVING, AND INVESTING: THE ROLE OF CONSUMERS

Consumers: Why is it important to review our choices before making a purchase?

Everyone who buys goods and services is a consumer. Therefore, the habits, tastes, wants, and needs of consumers are all-important in a market economy. Chapter 7 shows that the decisions we make each day as consumers determine what goods and services the U.S. economy will produce. Chapter 8 discusses how sellers try to influence consumers, and what effects these efforts may have.

Chapter 9 introduces the topic of getting the most for your money when shopping for food and health-care products. Chapter 10 tells how government agencies and private organizations protect consumers' rights. Ways of practicing wise money management by saving and investing are discussed in Chapter 11. In Chapter 12, we see how to use consumer credit wisely. Private insurance and financial protection plans are covered in Chapter 13. Government social insurance programs are treated in Chapter 14. Chapter 15 concludes the unit with a discussion of budgeting and financial planning.

CHAPTER 7

Consumers in a Market Economy

Susan Rodriguez, 17, a high school senior from Phoenix, Arizona, offers to type other students' papers for a fee of $2.50 a page. She uses most of the money she earns to pay for weekly tennis lessons.

Ernie Matthews, 14, a freshman from Muncie, Indiana, has an afternoon dog-walking route. With tips, he averages $75 a week. Ernie is putting some of his earnings aside each week to purchase a moped when he reaches the age of 16.

Sally Eng, 18, a senior from Corona, New York, works at a hospital after school and on weekends. She earns $8.25 an hour. Sally pays for all of her school expenses, cosmetics, and clothing.

Teenagers account for much of the spending that is done in the United States. Some researchers estimate that the nation's millions of teenagers spend more than $90 billion yearly. When computed on an hourly basis, this huge sum amounts to spending more than $10 million an hour!

Every teenager is a *consumer*. We are all consumers. We use up, or consume goods and services every day of our lives. Each time you spend money, *consumption* is taking place. Whenever you eat, drink, or use up something, consumption is taking place.

The consumer plays a very important role in the U.S. market economy. As you read this chapter, you will better understand this role. You will learn the answers to the following questions:

- How do different consumers spend their money?
- How does consumer demand affect the nation's economy?

HOW DO DIFFERENT CONSUMERS SPEND THEIR MONEY?

In some ways, all consumers are alike. We buy to satisfy *needs*, such as for food, clothing, and shelter. In other ways, all consumers are different. They have individual tastes and wants, values and beliefs. Tim Hagstrom satisfies his hunger with cheeseburgers, while Molly Edwards enjoys a cottage cheese salad for lunch. A young child cannot buy an automobile, and an adult does not need a tricycle. People who live in warm climates do not wear heavy woolen clothing. Members of certain religious groups do not eat some kinds of foods.

No two individuals spend money in exactly the same way. Nevertheless, we can see some general patterns of spending for different age groups as well as for all age groups.

Spending Patterns According to Age Group

1. Youth (Birth–12 Years Old). Adults do much of the spending for this preteen group. Even in this age group, however, children as they mature are allowed to make more and more of their own spending decisions. Thus, an infant will not make any spending decisions, whereas a 12-year-old will have much to say about spending. Spending by this group will usually be for food and recreation.

2. Young People (13–19 Years Old). Young people in their teenage years total about 29 million consumers. They spend tens of billions of dollars each year. Most of this spending goes for such things as food, clothing, books and other school supplies, CDs and tapes, recreation, carfare, and personal necessities.

Teenagers influence the spending of their parents as well. Most young people have some say about what clothes they wear and what foods they prefer at family meals. Their advice is sought before the family buys such things as a new automobile, a television set, and other recreational appliances for the home.

3. Singles (20s–40s). Single people who live alone or with roommates spend a major part of their income on rent, food, and entertainment. The rental and personal expenses for this group are usually quite high. If they live with a parent or parents, they have fewer expenses for food, rent, and furnishings, and have more money to spend on other items, such as education, cars, and travel.

4. Young Couples and Single Parents. The major expenses of young couples and single parents include rent or mortgage payments, household expenses, the cost of home furnishings, the cost

Teenagers' Interests (from top left, facing page, clockwise): attending a sporting event and a musical performance; buying clothes; socializing with friends; competing in sports; exercising and studying; listening to and collecting compact disks. In what ways are these teenagers consumers? What goods or services (or both) are being consumed?

of food, and car payments and upkeep. If they have young children, the medical care, clothing, education, and child care are also major expenses. A larger apartment or house becomes necessary and adds to expenses.

As couples and single parents reach their 30s and 40s, their incomes usually increase. But so too do their expenses. If high school or college students are part of the household, the needs of these members of the family are major items.

The spending patterns change as people grow older and when their children leave home. More money is available to spend on personal items and vacations. Weddings, other family occasions, and gifts to the children and grandchildren involve additional spending for this group. More thought is given to saving and investing for retirement.

5. Mature Adults. When people pass the age of 50, they usually take a more careful approach to spending. These individuals have reached close to the maximum amount that they will earn. There is greater concern with saving and investing for the future and with spending to make life easier. This group might spend more, for example, on a more expensive apartment or house, car, clothes, meals at restaurants, and travel.

6. Retirees. Sixty-five used to be a standard age for retirement. Now some people who have necessary funds put away are retiring earlier, while others find it necessary to continue working past age 65. As one gets older, out-of-pocket medical expenses may increase. Retirees generally spend less on clothing than before, but more on travel. Those retirees from the Northern states who retire to the Southeast and the Southwest may find that certain home expenses, such as heating, are reduced.

Factors That Affect Spending by All Age Groups

People of different ages are likely to have different wants and needs. Therefore, they spend their money differently. There are, however, some spending practices that are common to all age groups. While many factors determine how much we spend and what we buy, economists often cite the following as most important: income, expectations, the influence of those around us, and advertising. Advertising will be discussed separately in our next chapter.

1. Size of Income. First and most important in determining how much people spend and what they buy is the size of their incomes. As you might expect, people with high incomes spend more than people with low or moderate incomes. They also spend their money differently. People with low incomes must spend the bulk of their incomes to buy those goods and services that they need to exist. These items are called *necessities*. By contrast, people with high incomes use a larger share of their incomes to buy those items that add to their enjoyment. These items are called *luxuries*.

2. Future Expectations. People often decide to spend—or not to spend—on the basis of what they think the future has in store for them. Suppose that you want to buy a car. If you learn that you may soon lose your job, you may hold off making the purchase. On the other hand, if you expect to earn more money soon, you probably will go ahead with your purchase. The price of the car will also affect your purchasing decision. If you think the price of the car is going to fall soon, you will hold off buying it. But if you think the price is going to rise soon, you may buy now as a way of beating the price increase.

3. Social Influences. Two terms or phrases are often used to describe certain consumer spending patterns. Spending on high-priced items that is done to impress other people is called *conspicuous consumption*. When people spend as a way of staying on the same social level as their friends and neighbors, their actions are called *keeping up with the Joneses.*

Do you know someone who has bought an expensive car or expensive clothing and prominently displays their purchase? Why do you think that person made the purchase? To impress others with the wearer's spending powers. This is an example of conspicuous consumption.

Do you feel pressured to "keep up" with your friends and neighbors? Do you buy and wear the "right" clothes and the styles that the most attractive and popular people have? Do you spend money that you would rather save just so that you are not left out of your group's activities? If you do these things, then you are trying to keep up with the Joneses. The Joneses, of course, are not real people. That name is used to stand for your friends or for the family or persons living next door.

You may have heard it said that we are a *materialistic* society. Usually this expression is used in a negative way. Those who say that we are a materialistic nation believe that we spend too much on *nonessential* goods and services (those we do not need). Furthermore, they say that we emphasize consumption well beyond our basic needs.

All modern societies are materialistic. But not all societies are able to produce goods and services to meet basic needs, much less to go beyond those needs. Critics, however, claim that most Americans buy foolishly and wastefully. According to these critics, we should consume goods and services only after asking ourselves the following questions:

- Do I need it?
- Can I get along without it?
- Is it worth the time and effort I spent/will spend to earn the money to pay for it?

The above is good advice. But only you can make the decision as to what you need, what you can get along without, and whether or not the spending was worth it to you. Your spending decisions should be made intelligently.

People in the United States consume a good percentage (roughly 30 percent) of the world's resources. But our spending is not necessarily bad. Our productive economy has made it possible for us to support many cultural, spiritual, and humanitarian activities at home and around the world. It is important to realize that we consume more than other nations because we produce more and can afford to buy more than other nations. Generally speaking, the more an individual or nation has, the more that individual or nation will spend and consume. Spending has fueled the U.S. economy as well as the global economy. Keep in mind that the whole purpose of producing goods and services is to satisfy the needs and wants of people. People spend money to satisfy their wants and needs.

HOW DOES CONSUMER DEMAND AFFECT THE NATION'S ECONOMY?

Consumer sovereignty, first discussed in Chapter 3, is one of the major principles of the U.S. free enterprise system. Decisions as to how consumers choose to spend their dollars cause businesses of all kinds to produce certain goods and services but not others. *Producers* supply the goods and services that are consumed in our market economy.

Goods and Services

Each time you buy something, you are voting for what you want. Suppose that you decide to buy a recording on a compact disk or any other format. If you choose country over hip hop or hard rock, you are voting for more country music recordings. Your vote, together with the votes of other consumers, is "counted" by the recording's producers. This "count" is made in dollar sales. Often producers do not know who casts these votes. You may be male or female, of any age, race, or nationality. Each dollar cast has the same vote. Of course, the more money you have to spend, the more votes you can cast. One reason why consumer demand is important, then, is that it helps determine what goods and services will be produced in our market economy.

Prices

A second reason why consumer demand is important is that consumer spending influences prices. As we discussed in Chapter 4, the price of any product depends upon the supply of and the demand for that product. Consumer spending is an important part of total demand.

Suppose that consumers start spending more for homes. What will happen? This increase in demand will cause the price of homes to rise.

Imagine that consumers begin to pass up products made with cane sugar and choose those made with other sweeteners instead. What will happen? The price of cane sugar will fall. We can conclude that in most cases when consumer demand is strong, prices will be high. When consumer demand is weak, prices will be low.

Business and Employment

A third reason why consumer demand is important is that this demand affects business and employment. Consider the story of the Kings' new house. Jeff and Lisa King got married in June. Before they did, they decided to buy a house in a new development 20 miles from their jobs. Dozens of new homes were being built there in an area that only a short while before had been farmland.

Jeff and Lisa did not have the $145,000 in cash that their new home cost. Like many other couples, they were able to borrow the money from a local bank. They had to make a down payment and sign an agreement to make set monthly payments for a number of years.

The Kings loved watching the carpenters, bricklayers, plumbers, and electricians building their new house. Miles of telephone wires, sewage lines, and electric wiring went into their house and the other homes in the development. Lisa and Jeff watched with

Building New Homes: How would an increase in the demand for new homes affect housing prices? What would a decrease in demand for homes do to prices?

satisfaction as new stores and a shopping center went up in what once was a potato field. Roads were built connecting the new homes with the main highway. A school, churches, and a library were also soon to be built.

Let us review the story of the Kings' purchase of a new house for a moment. Their demand, as well as the demand of many others for new homes in this development, resulted in an increase in employment and business activity. Real estate firms sold the land and the houses to the Kings and others. Construction firms hired the workers to build the houses. Other firms contracted to clear the land, transport materials to the site, pour the concrete for the foundations, and install electrical and telephone cables. Later, teachers will be hired for the school, librarians for the library, and salespeople for the stores. Supervisors and maintenance workers will also be needed.

Just as an increase in consumer demand causes increases in business activity and employment, the opposite is also true. A decrease in consumer demand will cause a decrease in both business activity and employment. If fewer consumers demand new homes, there will be less need for firms and workers to do the jobs described above.

Consumer Spending and the Economy

Consumer demand is important for a fourth reason. Consumers buy the largest share of all the goods and services that the nation's economy produces. Suppose that we add up all the spending done by each business firm in the United States. Then we combine this amount with the spending done by every town, village, city, state, and even the federal government. We will still find that the total is *less* than the spending done by American consumers. This fact is shown in Figure 7.1.

As you examine the illustration of total spending in the United States, you will see how important consumer spending is to the nation's economy. Almost 66 percent of all the money spent for the goods and services purchased in the United States in year 2005 were spent by consumers. This fact ties in with what we have said about the importance of consumer sovereignty, the influence of consumer spending on prices, and the impact of this spending on business and employment. Yes indeed, the consumer is a very important person in the U.S. economic system.

Figure 7.1 Consumer, Government, and Business Spending, 2005

Business
$2.1 trillion
16.3%

Government
$2.3 trillion
17.8%

Consumers
$8.5 trillion
65.9%

SUMMARY

We are all consumers, but we do not all spend in exactly the same way. There are some general patterns of spending that seem to be typical of different age groups. There are also common factors that affect the spending by all age groups. People with higher incomes spend more. They also buy differently from people with lower incomes. Future expectations, conspicuous consumption, and the desire to keep up with others all affect consumer spending.

Consumer demand affects the U.S. free enterprise economy. Consumer spending informs producers what consumers want and helps determine what goods and services our economy will produce. Consumer demand also has an impact on prices, business activity, and employment. Consumers buy the largest share of the goods and services produced in the U.S. economy.

LOOKING AHEAD

The importance of the consumer and consumer spending is well known to producers. Producers also know what influences consumers to buy various products and services. The next chapter discusses how sellers try to convince consumers to want the goods and services they have to offer.

EXERCISES

✔ **Multiple Choice** Choose the letter of the item that best completes the statement or answers the question.

1. A main idea of this chapter is that (a) consumer spending is important for the U.S. economy (b) consumers have little to choose from (c) young people are not consumers (d) all consumers spend in the same way.

2. Olga bought a tie for Dad in Parsons' Department Store. In this example, who is the consumer? (a) Olga (b) the salesperson (c) the tiemaker (d) the owner of the store.

3. After the last bell rang, Bob left school, bought some ice cream, rode the bus home, and telephoned Jane. Which of the items that Bob used is a good? (a) bus ride (b) telephone call (c) ice cream (d) education.

4. In some ways, all consumers are alike. This is because all consumers (a) have similar tastes and wants (b) share the same religious beliefs (c) are of the same age (d) buy to satisfy their needs.

5. Which of the following is likely to *decrease* when consumer spending increases? (a) prices (b) business activity (c) unemployment (d) production.

6. Which of the following is the most important factor in determining how much a consumer will spend? (a) age (b) size of income (c) religion (d) marital status.

7. Buying which of the following is an example of conspicuous consumption? (a) school supplies (b) lunch (c) tickets to a dance (d) expensive clothes or car.

8. Under which circumstance would you be most likely to buy an item that you want *now*, rather than wait for a later time? You expect that soon (a) prices will rise (b) prices will fall (c) you will lose your job (d) a better product will be coming on the market.

9. What is most likely to happen to the pattern of consumer spending as family income increases? (a) Spending for necessities decreases. (b) The proportion of family income spent on necessities increases. (c) The proportion of family income spent on luxuries increases. (d) Spending for luxuries decreases.

10. Which of the following purchases most of the nation's output of goods and services? (a) business firms (b) consumers (c) state and local governments (d) the federal government.

✔**Matching** Match each term in Column A with its definition in Column B.

Column A	Column B
1. consumer	*a.* those things that satisfy people's needs and wants
2. producer	
3. consumption	*b.* excessive spending done to impress others
4. consumer "vote"	*c.* an individual who buys or uses up goods or services for his or her own use
5. goods and services	
6. conspicuous consumption	*d.* the spending to stay on the same social level as one's friends and neighbors
7. "keeping up with the Joneses"	*e.* something that takes place when individuals buy or use goods or services
8. necessities	*f.* someone who makes goods or supplies services
9. luxuries	
	g. goods and services that add to our enjoyment of life
	h. something that occurs when a consumer buys a particular good or service
	i. the goods and services we need to exist

✔ *Skills/Analysis: Interpreting a Pie Chart*

Study the information in the pie chart "Consumer, Government, and Business Spending," on page 111, and then answer the questions below.

1. What was the total dollar value of spending by consumers, businesses, and government?

2. Of that total, how much was spent by consumers?

3. Of that total, how much was spent by government?

4. What percent of total spending was consumer spending?

5. If we add up the total of the percent spending by consumers, government, and businesses, how much does it come to?

6. Which represents a greater portion of spending—business or government spending?

CHAPTER 8

Selling and Advertising to Consumers

Key Terms

personal selling	half-truth	mail-order buying
advertising	pressure tactic	e-buying
media	bait-and-switch	e-commerce
packaging	door-to-door sales	Better Business
public relations	bandwagon	Bureau
appeal to vanity	brand loyalty	Federal Trade
exaggeration	testimonial	Commission

Have you ever noticed that some folks will order a bottle of water in a restaurant for $4.00 rather than drink water from the tap at no additional charge? Is it because bottled water is tastier or healthier than water from the tap? Or is there some other explanation? Why do some athletes wear sneakers or T-shirts with a noticeable "swoosh" logo? Do you know which sneaker this logo represents? What is "the breakfast of champions"? Do "champions" truly eat a certain brand of cereal? How many of the following names and slogans can you connect with a particular product: *Drivers Wanted, The Energizer Bunny, Ronald McDonald, the Kentucky Colonel, Like a Rock,* and *Windows*?

By now you realize that some names, slogans, and logos (a company's emblem or trademark) are very familiar to you. You also know that star athletes are paid lots of money to wear the logo of a particular manufacturer. Why? The answer is very simple. Advertising works. Consumers remember the products and services that they have seen advertised.

The ads for soft drinks, fast foods, and home remedies that you see and read cost each of the producers of these products many millions of dollars each year. Why do businesses spend so much money on advertising? To sell products and services, of course.

Business firms want to increase their profits. In order to do so, they try to increase sales. But first, businesses must create a demand for whatever they have to sell. That is where advertising comes in. The principal purpose of advertising is to increase sales by creating a demand for the products that are advertised.

This chapter explores the role of selling and advertising in the U.S. economy. After reading this chapter, you will be able to answer the following questions:

- How do sales techniques create demand?
- How can advertising inform—and misinform?
- What are the pros and cons of advertising?
- Who protects consumers against false or misleading advertising?

HOW DO SALES TECHNIQUES CREATE DEMAND?

As a nation, we must either consume all that we produce or sell whatever is left over to other countries. If we do not do either, we are in trouble. The idea, then, is to get people to buy. Creating consumer demand becomes more and more important as our nation increases its ability to produce goods and services. The nation's factories are designed and equipped to produce vast quantities of products.

There are three basic ways of selling to consumers. First, businesses can deal directly with consumers. This is called *personal selling*. The second method of reaching consumers is through *advertising*. This method makes use of the *media*—radio, newspapers, magazines, television, billboards, and, most recently, the Internet—to reach a wide audience. The third selling method is the *packaging* of a product. Companies have found that the color, shape, or design of a package often influences sales. All three selling methods are frequently used together. They are used on all consumers.

Some companies spend millions of dollars on a fourth way of selling to consumers—*public relations*. They will sponsor Little League teams, contribute to various community activities, add their names as sponsors for a variety of art and theater programs, and contribute money, products, and their own personnel to community projects. Perhaps companies are truly interested in the communities and the activities that they support. Just as likely, a company knows that developing good public relations is an asset when selling their product or service. Would you want to buy from a company that nobody likes? Of course not. So good public relations makes for good dollars and "sense."

Window Shopping: Stores exhibit goods for sale in window displays. How can window shopping help this consumer decide whether or not to make a purchase?

Techniques to Create Demand

A number of techniques are used to create consumer demand. Many are quite helpful to consumers. Others, of course, are used solely to get consumers' money. You will find examples of both as you come in contact with personal selling, advertising, and packaging.

1. Appeals to Reason, Needs, and Interests. Some legitimate techniques for creating demand are appeals made to your sense of what is reasonable or practical. Salespersons will often take the time to explain to you the advantages and disadvantages of items that you are considering. A compact car might be sufficient for your needs and cost a lot less to buy and maintain than a larger car or a S.U.V. Clothing sales clerks might suggest certain materials because they are comfortable and easy to care for or cooler to wear. They might suggest certain colors and designs that are flattering to you. Remember, most salespersons want you to be satisfied and return to the store.

Many businesses and salespeople will direct their appeal to your basic needs for food and security. Stores and restaurants let consumers know about food that they offer for sale. Banks advertise the importance of saving and investing. Insurance agents advise people about purchasing various kinds of insurance protection.

Appeals are also made to satisfy your interests. Since many teenagers are interested in music and/or sports, businesses will try to connect these interests to the products they are selling.

But there are also sales techniques that attempt to deceive us. These include appeals to vanity, exaggerations or half-truths, pressure tactics, and bait-and-switch tactics. Let us explain each technique.

2. Appeals to Vanity. Watch out for the fast talker. Have you ever gone into a store where a salesperson, who never saw you before, became one of your best friends right away? Sure you have. The jacket, dress, or coat you tried on was just right for you. It made you look great, the salesperson claimed. If you did not like it, of course, the next item you looked at became the one for you. This salesperson was appealing to your vanity.

3. Exaggerations or Half-Truths. Watch out for claims or suggestions that a product is going to make a major or permanent change in your health, happiness, or lifestyle. Very few items by themselves are capable of doing all that advertisers often suggest they can. Or a product may be presented as the newest, most powerful, sleekest, and most economical of its kind on the market. In these cases, advertisers are usually taking one fact about a product and building a series of *exaggerations* or *half-truths* around it.

4. Pressure Tactics. The salesperson who uses pressure tactics tells you that the item you are interested in is on special for a very limited time only. You have to buy right away. Or the salesperson

"This CD player costs less than players selling for twice as much."

How might a statement that is obviously true mislead some consumers?
© *The New Yorker Collection 1989* Robert Weber from cartoonbank.com.

does not let up even though you are not interested. You may be made to feel stupid or even threatened if you do not buy. Tourists visiting a foreign country often complain of being subjected to pressure tactics.

5. Bait-and-Switch Tactics. Using a cheap product in order to sell a more expensive one is called *bait-and-switch* (to hook you, just as bait is used to catch fish). Bait-and-switch selling is done both in store and home sales. In bait-and-switch store selling, the customer who arrives at the store to buy an advertised low-priced special finds that the product is either "sold out" or poorly made. The salesperson then explains that the store does have a product just like the one that was advertised. The only catch is that this item costs more than the advertised special. The store is betting that a good number of customers will be enticed by the phony, low-priced "special." Then the store could switch them to the higher-priced item, which it wanted to sell them in the first place.

Bait-and-switch is also used in *door-to-door sales*—those to people at home. A consumer answers an ad offering a home product or service, such as a burglar alarm or a fire alarm system with installation, at a very low price. When a salesperson arrives, it turns out that the product was not at all what the consumer expected. At this point, the salesperson just happens to have a better product on hand—a more expensive one, of course. Do you think that the consumer was expected to buy the cheaper product or service advertised? Of course not.

HOW CAN ADVERTISING INFORM—AND MISINFORM?

Through advertising, businesses tell consumers what products are available. Advertising may also give the consumer reasons to buy a particular product. Suppose that you are interested in purchasing a television set. Before visiting several stores selling this product, you might examine the advertisements of several major manufacturers. You will save time at the store because you will already have a better idea of the features of each set. At the store, you can concentrate on those sets with the features that interest you. The ads might even call to your attention certain features that you might not have thought about. Ads that give retail prices will help you decide whether you are able to afford the item.

Advertising to Create Demand

Salespeople employ the direct, one-to-one approach in creating demand. Advertisers, however, have to depend upon an indirect approach—through messages on radio and television, in newspapers and magazines, and even on handbills given to consumers on the street. The purpose of advertising is to do just what the sales-person tries to do: sell goods or services. The advertiser will try to make the consumer want something whether or not it is really needed. The advertiser is creating a demand for a product.

Just as there are sales techniques to watch out for, be on the lookout for a variety of common advertising techniques. For example, even though young children do not buy products, advertisers will direct their appeals to children. The advertisers know that these youngsters will tell their parents that they want certain products.

1. Appeals to Emotions. Probably the most effective appeal to young people and adults is the appeal to their emotions. Two basic feelings are love and fear. So, advertisers appeal to or play on these emotions in trying to sell their products. Sales of personal care products, for example, reach into the billions of dollars each year. Their advertising may say that since dating is very important, you have to smell sweet, hide any skin blemishes, keep your teeth white, and do your hair just right. The ads show how a particular product will help make you attractive and popular. Do these products work? It is certainly questionable that they will do for you all that the ads lead you to hope for.

Ads that promise to increase your personal attractiveness if you use a product are very common. Almost any product can use this appeal. The ads may tell you that you will be better looking if you wear, eat, chew, drink, or use any one of hundreds of different items.

2. Desire to Conform. Advertisers appeal to our desire to conform. This technique is known as the *bandwagon approach*. Look around your classroom. Notice your classmates' hairstyles and clothing. Chances are that students have more things in common with one another than they care to admit. Most of us are afraid of being "left out," of not being in style. So the advertisers say: "Don't be left out—get on the bandwagon! Buy the same goods and services that your friends and classmates do." In addition, advertisers appeal to consumers' desire for good health and prestige.

3. Brand Names. Like other consumers, young adults are influenced by brand names. Advertisers try to get teenagers familiar with a particular brand in the hope that, in later years, they will stick to this brand. The advertisers are trying to develop *brand loyalty*. Therefore, commercials are repeated over and over again on radio and television. We soon get to know them by heart. Slick advertising slogans will pop into our minds as we reach for a product.

Some advertisers use written or spoken endorsements of products by sports or entertainment stars. Consumers begin to associate

Comparing Features and Prices of Different Brands: In addition to judging products by their visual appeal, this consumer is checking prices and manufacturers' guarantees of their products.

a product or service with the famous person that they see in the ads. This advertising technique is called the *testimonial*.

4. Getting Something for Nothing. Advertisers know that we would all like to get something for nothing. So you will see ads offering two-for-the-price-of-one sales. Banks and department stores sometimes offer new accounts a "free" gift. There is nothing wrong with buying sales items or accepting gifts when opening a new account. In fact, it is often wise to do so, provided you want and need the product offered. However, it is also wise to be on the alert that "there is no free lunch"—it is rare that you will get something for nothing.

Beyond the Retail Store

In addition to traditional retail stores, shoppers have a number of other ways to shop for the things they want.

Companies spend millions sending out catalogs that fill the mailboxes of consumers. The products that the company has to offer for sale are illustrated and described, and the prices listed. Consumers may then order products, if they wish, directly from the catalog by either mailing in an order form or by phoning the company on a toll-free number. *Mail-order buying* is a convenient way for many consumers because it enables them to shop without leaving their home. They avoid traffic jams, searching for parking spaces, and pushing through crowds.

Veritime Dress Quartz

The Dress Quartz is slim and elegant on the outside, and a precision Veritime inside. Wear it proudly. It is one of 15 golden-finish timepieces in the exciting new Veritime Style collection. $89.95, suggested retail price.

What appeals do the illustration and advertisement copy make? Which group of buyers do you think this ad is meant to attract?

Another way to shop directly from home requires using a computer. Today, almost anything from almost anywhere in the world can be bought while sitting at home at a computer. It is possible to pay bills, bank, save, invest, and buy automobiles, flowers, life insurance, food, clothes, books, music, and many more items over the Internet. Buying and selling over the Internet is called *e-commerce*. Currently, total online sales are not nearly as great as the sales from the other sources previously mentioned.

Marketers like using the Internet. It enables them to track who visits a site and who makes a purchase through a site. Analyzing the data gained enables the merchant to determine among which group of consumers the market for their product is greatest. With this knowledge, the marketer can determine with some accuracy where it would be most profitable to advertise and where it would be least likely to expect sales. From the consumers' view, the information gathered might be considered an invasion of privacy. The consumer may not want different companies knowing what they like, what they buy, and where and how they make their purchases.

Personal Economics

SHOULD YOU SHOP ONLINE?

If you have not shopped online, you probably will some day. Some of the pros and cons of this *e-buying* are shown below.

Greenfield Online Survey

Reasons for Shopping Online		Reasons for Not Shopping Online	
Save time	60%	Shipping charges	51%
Avoid crowds	47%	Cannot see/touch items	44%
Find the lowest price	46%	Cannot return items easily	32%
Buy hard-to-find items	35%	Worried about credit card safety	24%
Better selection	29%	Cannot ask questions	23%
More product information	22%	Takes too long to load screen	16%
Easier to ship	15%	Worried about delivery time	15%
Good gift ideas	14%	Enjoy shopping offline	10%

SOURCE: *PEW INTERNET AND AMERICAN LIFE PROJECT*, <<http://www.pewinternet.org>>.

According to the survey, most consumers shop online because they believe that it saves time. But avoiding crowds and finding the lowest price are also very important reasons given. Shipping charges seems to be a major reason why others do not shop online. So too is the fact that it is difficult to see items and impossible to touch them online. It may surprise you that the least important reason given for not shopping online is that these consumers enjoy shopping offline.

Not included in the survey, but very significant, is the fact that many people buy online to avoid paying state and local sales taxes. Legally the consumer is supposed to report such transactions and pay the taxes. In reality, however, few consumers do so.

WHAT ARE THE PROS AND CONS OF ADVERTISING?

You are probably wondering at this point whether advertising is good or bad for consumers. Actually, it may be a little of both. To help you decide for yourself, some of the advantages and disadvantages of advertising are listed below.

Advantages of Advertising

1. Gives Information. Consumers learn about new products and find out more about products already on the market.

2. Saves Time. Advertising tells what products are available and where they are sold. Consumers can shop and compare prices without leaving home.

3. Stimulate Demand. Demand increases sales, makes possible the production of large quantities of goods, and keeps employment high.

4. Stimulates Competition. Manufacturers have to keep on their toes because consumers know about the different brands and new products that are being offered, and their prices.

5. Lowers Manufacturing Costs. The demand created by advertising may result in large-scale manufacturing. With this process, manufacturers may produce goods at low costs. Lower costs may also mean lower prices for consumers. (The advantages of large-scale manufacturing are discussed in Chapter 24.)

6. Provides Entertainment. In most cases, advertising pays the costs of presenting entertainment on radio, television, and the Internet. Athletic events, election returns, quiz shows, and many of your favorite programs are presented "free" (or at low cost) to you because of advertising. Advertising provides the major source of income for magazines, newspapers, radio, and television. Without the income from advertising, the cost of purchasing most media services would be too expensive for the average consumer.

Disadvantages of Advertising

Since the main purpose of advertising is to sell goods, the advertiser is not always concerned about the best interests of the consumer. Here are some of the drawbacks of advertising.

1. May Mislead the Public. Ads sometimes mislead the public into thinking they are getting something that is not really being offered. Since some advertising is deliberately tricky, it is cheating the public. It is relatively easy to make viewers think that they are seeing something on television that is not really happening at all, such as actors dressed as doctors promoting health-care products.

2. Encourages Impulse Buying. Consumers often buy on impulse, without planning ahead. Because of this, they often buy what they do not need. Or they choose according to brand names and, thus, do not get the best buy for their money.

3. Raises Selling Prices of Goods or Services. It costs money to advertise. Consumers pay for television programs every time they buy a product that they had seen advertised. The cost of advertising a product or service is added to its cost to consumers.

4. May Influence the Media. Big advertisers can control the press, radio, and television by refusing to advertise in newspapers or on networks with whose editorial policy they disagree. This can force some newspapers and magazines (or networks) to print (or broadcast) only the news and editorials that the advertisers wish.

WHO PROTECTS CONSUMERS AGAINST FALSE OR MISLEADING ADVERTISING?

Advertising has been used at times to mislead and even deceive consumers. For that reason, a number of safeguards (protections) have been developed. These safeguards fall into three categories: (1) those that are imposed (set) by businesses; (2) those that are imposed by government; (3) those that are set by private (nonprofit) organizations and consumer groups. The first two safeguards are discussed below. The third method is discussed in Chapter 10.

Businesses Regulate Advertising

There are a number of ways in which businesses try to regulate advertising. These ways include company policies, trade and media associations, and Better Business Bureaus.

1. Company Policies. Many firms realize that they ought to be the first line of defense against false or misleading advertising. People in business know that a good reputation is one of their most valuable assets. Few want to risk ruining their reputation with advertising that the public may see as faulty. For that reason, many firms have policies designed to prevent the publication of advertising that strays far from the truth.

2. Trade and Media Associations. Trade associations are groups of companies in the same industry. These associations often prepare advertising guidelines, or statements of policy, which they ask their members to observe. Similarly, newspapers, radio and television stations, and magazines have formed media groups that set forth advertising guidelines designed to protect consumers.

3. Better Business Bureaus. Like trade associations, *Better Business Bureaus* are sponsored by private industry. About 150 BBBs are located in communities across the country. The primary purpose of the bureaus is to promote honest advertising and ethical business practices.

Consumers who feel that they have been misled or cheated by a false advertisement or business practice can bring the matter to their local Better Business Bureau. The organization will investigate the complaint. If it finds that the ad was indeed misleading, it will ask the firm to stop its unethical practice.

Governments Regulate Advertising

Advertising is regulated by the federal government and most states. The purpose of this regulation is to protect the public from the effects of false or misleading ads. Congress has given the *Federal Trade Commission* (*FTC*) the primary responsibility for enforcing federal laws affecting advertising. The FTC maintains a toll-free consumer fraud complaint line, 1-877-FTC-HELP. You may call this number if you believe that you have been misled or cheated as a result of misleading advertising.

States regulate advertising, too. Within state executive branches are consumer protection boards and consumer affairs offices. These agencies are involved in monitoring advertising by correspondence schools, vocational-training programs, and professionals who are subject to state licensing.

Billboards: To what extent does government regulate where billboards can be placed and what products cannot be advertised on them?

Understanding Economics

THE FEDERAL TRADE COMMISSION (FTC) REGULATES ADVERTISING

Health care and health-care products are important consumer concerns. We want to look good, feel good, and be pain-free as quickly as possible. We read ads, watch television, and turn to the Internet in our search of health information. Can we simply trust what we read, see, and hear from advertisers? Not entirely. We sometimes have to turn to the FTC to check the claims of advertisers.

There was a time when the makers of pain-relief medicines claimed that their products contained the "ingredient that doctors recommend most." The ingredient was aspirin. Why was aspirin not mentioned by name? Perhaps if people knew that the most important ingredient was aspirin, they would stop buying a widely advertised product and buy plain aspirin. In 1983, the FTC directed the drug manufacturers and their advertising firms to say that these products contain aspirin.

Today, many consumers search for health information on the Internet. Some Internet ads and Websites, though, use deceptive promotions to peddle products. They may promise cures without any scientific proofs. By using these products, consumers may take unnecessary health risks and delay treatment. To address this problem, the FTC instituted "Operation Cure All," challenging the marketing and selling of unproven and dangerous products on the Internet. The following examples are just two cases settled by the FTC in 2001.

Western Botanicals, Inc., manufactured and marketed a variety of products containing the herbal ingredient comfrey. The company claimed that their products were beneficial in the treatment of bronchial diseases, gastritis, duodenal ulcers, colitis, rheumatism, arthritis, osteoporosis, multiple sclerosis, and other conditions. The company advertised that their products were safe when taken internally or applied to open wounds. The FTC argued that comfrey products are not safe when taken internally or applied to an open wound. Furthermore, the FTC said, there was no scientific proof that the products would do as claimed. The company agreed to include on their product label and in their advertising a warning, "for external use only," and to stop making unproven health claims.

ADHD is a behavioral disorder which affects an estimated 2.5 million school-aged children in the United States. ADHD can severely affect a child's attention span and scholastic performance, family relationships, and social behavior. Natural Organics, Inc., doing business as "Nature's Plus," markets Pedi-Active A.D.D. In their advertisements, brochures, informational letters, and Website, the company made a number of claims. It claimed that Pedi-Active A.D.D. would treat or reduce ADHD or its symptoms, including inattention and poor school performance. After settling with the FTC, the company agreed that they would no longer claim that Pedi-Active A.D.D. would improve the attention span or scholastic performance or treat or mitigate ADHD in children unless they have scientific evidence to substantiate those claims.

Advertising and You

As a consumer, you are going to be confronted by advertisements just about every day of your life. Most of these ads will be honest. The messages that they carry will probably not try to cheat or deceive you. The ads may, however, try to sell you things that you may not need. The important thing to remember is that businesses and government can do just so much to protect you. You have the principal responsibility for dealing with advertising directed at you. You must decide whether the claims made by the advertiser describe something that you really need or want. How well you can do this will directly affect how much you will be able to get for your money.

SUMMARY

The principal purpose of advertising is to increase sales by creating demand for the products that are advertised. Three techniques for creating demand include personal selling, advertising, and packaging.

Consumers should be aware of deceptive sales techniques, such as appeals to vanity, exaggerations and half-truths, pressure tactics, and bait-and-switch tactics. Ads can inform as well as misinform. Ads will appeal to one's desire to conform. Testimonials of famous persons are used to promote products.

Advertising has been praised. It provides product information, stimulates competition among businesses, and leads to lower manufacturing costs. Advertisers pay for radio and television programs and are a major source of income for newspapers, magazines, and the Internet. Advertising is itself a highly profitable business that employs thousands of people.

Advertising has been criticized. It may provide information that is either of little value or misleading. Advertising may lead to higher prices, enable the advertisers to dominate the media, and reduce competition.

Industry and government provide a number of safeguards to protect the public from deceptive or misleading advertising. But it is up to each individual consumer to approach advertising with caution.

LOOKING AHEAD

How well people live—the amount of goods and services they can buy—depends on two things: their income and how well that income is spent. The next chapter focuses on some of the things that people can do to s-t-r-e-t-c-h their dollars so as to get more out of their money.

—————————————— **EXERCISES** ——————————————

✔**Matching** Match each term in Column A with its definition in Column B.

Column A	Column B
1. advertising	*a.* a method of selling directly to consumers
2. personal selling	*b.* advertising that uses a famous person to sell a product
3. packaging	
4. creating demand	*c.* offering a cheap item for sale when the real purpose is to sell a more expensive item instead
5. bait-and-switch	
6. testimonial	*d.* doing things the way one's friends do them
7. pressure tactic	*e.* urging the consumer to buy right away before the price rises
8. bandwagon	
	f. the use of newspapers, magazines, radio, and television to interest consumers in a product
	g. boxing or wrapping a product so as to make it appeal to consumers
	h. getting consumers to want something that they did not want before

✔**Multiple Choice** Choose the letter of the item that best completes the statement or answers the question.

1. The main idea of this chapter is that advertising is (a) good (b) bad (c) not really necessary in a modern economy (d) an industry whose purpose is to create a demand for products.

2. Imagine that you are a businessperson wishing to sell a product. Which of the following techniques for creating demand for your product would most likely reach the greatest number of consumers? (a) personal selling (b) advertising (c) packaging (d) public relations.

3. Which statement is true, according to this chapter? (a) All salespeople are dishonest. (b) Advertising can inform consumers. (c) It is wrong to try to create demand. (d) Do not believe any advertising.

4. The main purpose of advertising is to (a) sell goods (b) educate consumers (c) entertain consumers (d) fool consumers.

5. Which one of the following is an advantage of advertising for consumers? Advertising (a) may mislead the public (b) encourages impulse buying (c) raises prices (d) gives information.

6. Which one of the following is a disadvantage of advertising for consumers? Advertising (a) saves time (b) stimulates demand (c) may mislead buyers (d) stimulates competition.

7. According to this chapter, the consumer (a) never sees false and misleading advertising (b) can rely upon the honesty of producers and sellers (c) is fully protected by federal and state regulations (d) must approach advertising with caution.

✔ *Understanding an Advertisement*

Study the ad on page 122 and then answer the following questions.

1. What product is being offered for sale?

2. What information about this product is given in this ad?

3. To what audience or age group do you think this ad is being directed?

4. What sales techniques or appeals are being used in this ad?

5. Why do you think that this is or is not a good ad?

6. How would you make this ad more appealing to teenagers?

✔ *Using the Internet*

1. Log on to *three* of the following sites on the Internet: (1) <<http://ebay.com>> (2) <<http://amazon.com>> (3) <<http://barnesandnoble.com>> (4) <<http://cnn.com>> (5) <<http://msn.com>>. For each site you visit, report on it to your class by answering the following questions:

   A. What information is provided concerning products offered for sale?

   B. How clear is this information?

   C. How useful to you is the information?

   D. Why would you or would you not buy from the site?

2. The Better Business Bureau maintains a Website: <<http://www.BBB.com>>. Here you will find more information about the BBB's activities. You may also use this site to contact the BBB to make a complaint or to find out more information about a business in your local area.

3. The Federal Trade Commission maintains a Website: <<http//www.ftc.gov>>. Here you can find a wealth of information about the FTC as well as its cases involving misleading advertising and consumer fraud.

CHAPTER 9

Getting the Most for Your Money

How can you get the most for your money? The students in an economics class wanted to know the answer to this question. They tried the following project.

Each student in the class received an imaginary $25. With this "money," each student was to go to local stores to "window shop" for a specific list of products. Students were asked to write down what each item had cost. Several days later, the class met and compared results. Sheila Sharpe found that she would have $.54 in change if she had bought every item on the list. But Joe Friendly found that $25 would not be enough for him to buy all of the products on the list. On the next page, is a sample of the items Sheila and Joe "bought" and the prices each "paid."

Sheila would have spent 25 percent less than Joe for the same items. Why were the results so different? Joe told the class that he shopped at only one store: Thriftmark. He bragged that he "bought only the best." Sheila said that she too selected quality items. But when she shopped, she went to several stores to compare prices. Sheila also remembered what she had learned in economics class about the advantages of advertising. Before going to stores, she looked at the store ads in the newspaper. She also cut out special discount coupons.

Comparison of Prices in a Classroom Buying Exercise

Item	Price Sheila Paid	Price Joe Paid
Ground beef (chuck, lb.)	$ 1.99	$ 2.29
Chicken (whole breast, lb.)	1.24 (sale)	1.89
Salmon steak (fresh, lb.)	3.99	5.99
Orange juice (64 oz.)	1.68 (store brand)	1.89
Cereal (1lb., 8oz.)	3.29 (store brand)	4.19
White bread (22 oz. loaf)	.99 (sale)	1.99
Milk (one qt.)	.86	.90
Butter (1 lb., sweet)	3.50	3.69
Eggs (one dozen)	1.19	1.39
Aspirin (100 tablets)	5.79 (store brand)	6.49
Total	$24.46	$30.71

The class agreed that there is a lot to know about shopping. Read on to find out how you can get the most for your money. After completing this chapter, you will be able to answer the following questions:

- What is the best way to shop for food and household items?
- How should you shop for health-care products?
- Why should consumers be cautious shoppers?
- What four words should guide your shopping?

WHAT IS THE BEST WAY TO SHOP FOR FOOD AND HOUSEHOLD ITEMS?

In the family budget, the biggest single expense that you can do something about is the cost of food and household items. If you own or rent a home, your monthly payments (mortgage or rent) are *fixed*: they stay the same. Your household expenses, however, are normally not fixed. A smart shopper can reduce these costs, or get more without spending more money. Let us follow Betty Sharpe, Sheila's mother, as she does her shopping.

Plan Ahead and Compare Prices

Betty Sharpe is a smart grocery shopper. She reads store ads in a local daily newspaper. Then she prepares menus for family meals for the week based on sales and specials. She always shops with a written list. This week, Ace Supermarket had lower prices than Thriftmark on most of the food items that her family needed and liked. An exception was milk, which was cheaper at Thrift-mark. But Mrs. Sharpe figured that it would cost her more in fuel to drive to more than one supermarket than she could save by buying the milk at the lower price. So she shopped only at Ace.

Her shopping list included items that were on special sale. For example, pork was on sale, so Mrs. Sharpe decided to serve her family pork instead of beef. She bought large quantities of specially priced goods that could be stored easily, such as canned goods. She compared prices and quantities of several brands of household products. She did not buy much cake or bread, even when these items were on sale. Cake and bread became stale or spoil quickly if not frozen. And after having been frozen, baked good rarely taste as good as when they are fresh.

Unlike Betty Sharpe, there are shoppers who seem hypnotized by all the products they see in the supermarket. They walk up and down the aisles, scanning the shelves and picking out items that attract them. These people are doing *impulse buying* (purchasing without a plan or goal). If they had prepared shopping lists in advance, they would not have selected many of the products that ended up in their carts. Think of the money they would have saved if they had bought only what was on their shopping lists!

Comparing Brands: Why do smart shoppers check the prices and the quantities of competing brands of household items before choosing one?

Let us summarize what Mrs. Sharpe did before she went to the market. She checked newspaper advertisements and compared prices of similar products at different stores. This action is called *comparison shopping*. She planned her purchases and prepared a shopping list at home. Mrs. Sharpe bought where she could get the best buys, took advantage of sales, and used store and manufacturers' coupons to lower her food costs.

Use Unit Pricing

But, you may well ask, did Mrs. Sharpe get the best-quality products? Joe Friendly, you will recall, said that he "bought only the best." He thought that he got what he paid for. Well, Mrs. Sharpe did buy the best. Product X is still product X even if it is bought on sale or at a store where prices are lower, or if the cost is lower as a result of a coupon special.

Mrs. Sharpe also saves money because she takes advantage of *unit pricing* when she shops. Large size, family size, economy size—what do they mean? Which detergent is the better buy: 29 ounces at $2.79, or 34 ounces at $3.65? Do you need a pocket calculator to figure this out? To make your choice easier, stores in some communities are now required by law to display unit pricing. Next to the price of the product appears the unit price, which tells you the price per unit of weight or volume. (See Figure 9.1.)

Which is the better buy: Brand X or Brand Y?

Figure 9.1 Unit Pricing for Soap Powder

Brand Y is the better buy because it costs less per ounce than Brand X. Unit pricing gives the consumer an easy way to compare prices on the basis of standard weights and measures.

Buy Store Brands

Sheila Sharpe and Joe Friendly both insist that they bought only quality products, yet Sheila paid less for many of these products. If you look carefully at the sample of the items both students selected, you will notice that Sheila listed some *store-brand* products (orange juice, cereal, and aspirin), while Joe listed only *name-brand* products. Are the lesser-known store brands as good as well-known name-brand products? Read on and then you judge for yourself.

Check Grades and Ingredients

The next time you walk into a supermarket, do the following:

1. Look for cartons of eggs. Check the seal stamped on them.
2. Look for packages of butter. Look for the word "Grade" on them.

What do these grades mean? They are standards of quality established by the U.S. Department of Agriculture (USDA). Eggs, canned goods, and frozen foods are inspected periodically by USDA officers if the producer agrees to use the grading system.

There is no difference, once opened, between a white egg and a brown egg of the same grade and size. If the brown egg is cheaper, buy it. After all, you do not eat the shell. Butter graded AA is top quality. This is true whether that butter is a store brand, a name brand, or a little-known brand.

The best-quality meat is graded *Prime*. Meat stamped *Choice* is just below Prime in quality, but the difference is mostly a

Figure 9.2 Food Grade Labels

matter of *marbling* (fat distribution) and taste. Choice meats are just as nourishing as Prime—and a lot cheaper.

Read the labels of products that you are considering buying. The label will indicate a food product's grade, if it is graded. Labels for most products must list the *ingredients*. For food products of the same grade or containing the same ingredients, you may be fairly sure that they are of equal *nutritional* (health) *value*. The store-brand product may be cheaper. Which should you buy?

Many people will argue, and rightly so, that if you are satisfied with a particular name-brand product, stick with it. (Buying a particular product over a long period of time is called *brand loyalty*.) You know the product and feel comfortable with it. It has proven satisfactory over the years. You like it, and it works for you. You do not know that you will have the same satisfaction with store brands and lesser-known brands. Of course, you could experiment with other brands and products. You may find the "new" brand quite satisfactory.

Personal Economics

READING A NUTRITION FACTS LABEL

The label on a can of peas, a box of cereal, a quart of milk, and, in fact, on most food products provides valuable information that will help you get the best diet and the most for your money. The *nutrition facts label* (or nutritional label) advises you of the following facts:

1. How much of the product the package contains—in ounces, grams, or liters—and the number of servings in the package.

2. How many calories and nutrients are provided by one serving, including the number of calories from fat, and the grams of fat, cholesterol, sodium, carbohydrates, protein, vitamins, and fiber.

3. The percentages of recommended daily values of fat, cholesterol, sodium, total carbohydrates, and

fiber that the food contains, based on a diet of 2,000 calories.

4. The ingredients in the package: food, water, sugar, salt, and any additives or preservatives.

Although some people believe that we live to eat, the fact is that we must first eat to live. Throughout our lives, we all need the same nutrients, but the amounts vary, depending on our age, sex, build, and daily activities. Developing and maintaining good eating habits, along with getting proper rest and exercise, is an important way to staying healthy.

Experts believe that many Americans eat foods containing too much saturated fat, cholesterol, and sodium. Doctors also warn about the number of calories we consume and a lack of sufficient fiber in our diets. That is why the nutritional label

Figure 9.3 Nutrition Facts Label for Canned Peas

Nutrition Facts

Serving Size 1/2 cup (125g)
Servings Per Container About 3.5

Amount Per Serving

Calories 70   Calories from Fat 5

	%Daily Value*
Total Fat 0.5g	**1%**
Saturated Fat 0g	**0%**
Cholesterol 0mg	**0%**
Sodium 390mg	**16%**
Total Carbohydrate 11g	**4%**
Dietary Fiber 2g	**8%**
Sugars 5g	
Protein 4g	

Vitamin A 10%	•	Vitamin C 10%
Calcium 0%	•	Iron 6%

Quality Guarantee
Our products are 100% guaranteed. If you have any comments or questions regarding Price Chopper Brand products, please call 1-800-666-7667.

* Percent Daily Values are based on a 2,000 calorie diet. Your daily values may be higher or lower depending on your calorie needs:

		Calories:	2,000	2,500
Total Fat	Less Than		65g	80g
Saturated Fat	Less Than		20g	25g
Cholesterol	Less Than		300mg	300mg
Sodium	Less Than		2,400mg	2,400mg
Total Carbohydrate			300g	375g
Dietary Fiber			25g	30g

Calories per gram:
Fat 9 • Carbohydrate 4 • Protein 4

INGREDIENTS: PEAS, WATER, SUGAR, AND SALT.

DISTRIBUTED BY
THE PRICE CHOPPER, INC. SCHENECTADY, NY 12301

provides us with this information so that as consumers we can make intelligent choices in our food purchases.

Examine the label of the can of peas shown in Figure 9.3. This can has about 3½ servings, based on a serving size of one-half cup (125 grams) per person. You also learn that by eating one serving of peas you will consume 70 calories, 5 calories of which are from fat. The total fat content is very low (0.5 gram), and there is no saturated fat or cholesterol in a serving. There are 4 grams of protein. Note, however, that the sodium content is high (390 mg.), some 16 percent of the daily requirements. At 11 grams, total carbohydrates are 4 percent of daily values; at 2 grams, dietary fiber is 8 percent. One serving provides 10 percent of vitamin A, 10 percent of vitamin C, 6 percent of iron, but no B vitamins or calcium.

On all food labels, the ingredients are listed in order according to the quantity of that ingredient found in the product. The ingredient found in the greatest quantity is listed first. In the canned peas, the main ingredient is peas. Next is water, followed by sugar and salt.

How does this label help you get the most for your money? You can compare this product with other brands of the same food and with other foods and vegetables. First, if the nutritional facts for each are the same, you can purchase whichever costs least. You will know that you are getting the same nutritional value for less money. Second, you can compare the list of ingredients of this brand with others and tell which gives better value in terms of the ingredients. If the ingredients are the same, then the cheaper product is probably the better buy. Some brands, however, may be preferable regardless of price. They may have less sodium, fat, or sugar. They may have more minerals (such as potassium) or vitamins (such as B, D, and E) essential to your particular dietary needs.

Finally, and most important of all, reading and understanding nutritional labels help you to provide a proper diet for yourself and your family. Variety and balance are keys to a healthy diet.

Filling a Prescription: Wise consumers take only the drugs that are pre-scribed for their specific conditions by their doctors.

HOW SHOULD YOU SHOP FOR HEALTH-CARE PRODUCTS?

Consumers spend a lot of money for nationally advertised health-care products. These include vitamin and mineral supplements, drugs, and products for the hair and skin. The simplest rule for saving money when shopping for health-care products is to buy only what you need. Many of the products purchased for health care are practically useless. They do not always accomplish whatever it is consumers are led to believe they will do. For example, as we grow older, we go through a natural process of aging. No pills, creams, lotions, or diets can reverse this process.

Vitamins and Minerals

Consumers can purchase vitamins and minerals at local stores, by mail order, or on the Internet. Relatively few consumers, however, really know what vitamins and minerals they need—or if they need to take supplements to their regular diet. Taking more of some vitamins than your body needs can be dangerous. If you have a health problem or want to ask questions about health-care products, the cheapest and safest approach is to go to your family doctor for advice.

Drugs

Pam is studying to be a doctor. She knows that abusing drugs can be dangerous or fatal. Taking certain drugs for "kicks" or to carry you through a difficult problem can only bring on pain. Pam has seen many young people who thought that they could handle drugs and then wound up in the hospital dead or near death. She has also seen children carried in on stretchers after having swallowed a drug that should have been kept out of their reach. Pam knows that many people have had allergic reactions to certain drugs.

A *prescription drug* is one that is prepared and sold only on a doctor's order. A doctor knows each patient's age, height, weight, general health, and needs. Therefore, a doctor's prescription (order) is written for a particular patient. Another person has different needs and should not use the same prescription unless the doctor says it is all right to do so. You should not try to be your own doctor.

You do not need a prescription to buy any of the drugs offered for sale on pharmacy and supermarket shelves. Nevertheless, take an *over-the-counter drug* only when you must. Follow the directions on the label. As the label always warns, if the condition persists, see a doctor.

As we have noted, you can save money by buying only those health-care products that you need. You can save more money by comparing prices much as you would for food. The prices of drugs vary greatly. The price of a particular product may be lower at one place of business than at another.

Name Brands and Generics

Sheila paid $5.79 for a bottle of 100 aspirin tablets, while Joe paid $6.49 for the same quantity. Sheila bought the store brand, while Joe bought a name brand. Aspirin is aspirin, no matter which brand you buy. Yet aspirin sold under various brand names sells at different prices.

It is cheaper to buy drugs under their *generic* (chemical) name than under a brand name. For example, a frequently prescribed drug sold at a pharmacy for $11.50 under its generic name. The same pharmacy, however, charged $30 for this product when sold under a brand name.

According to the federal government's *Food and Drug Administration (FDA)*, there is no difference between a generic drug and a brand-name drug if their chemical formulas are the same. The FDA tests and approves drugs that may be legally sold in this country. Many pharmacies post prices of prescription drugs. Compare these prices. However, if you feel safer and have greater confidence in a particular brand, stay with it. You may believe that one product is of better quality and works more consistently. If you do believe that this is so, your peace of mind may be worth the extra money.

WHY SHOULD CONSUMERS BE CAUTIOUS SHOPPERS?

The wise consumer is always a cautious shopper. Remember, your best protection is to buy from someone you know and trust. Otherwise, you may not be getting the most for your money. Here are just a few examples of the ways in which consumers have been cheated and how you can avoid the same fate.

Unsolicited Goods by Mail

You do not have to pay for something *unsolicited*—that you receive in the mail but did not order. You can keep it, give it away, or throw it away. You do not have to return it. Do not feel sorry for the sender, who is counting on getting your sympathy. Buy the product only if you want it, need it, and consider it a good buy.

Internet Ads

If you ever browse the Internet, you will notice that part of your screen is often covered by ads. You are probably not interested in seeing these ads, but you have no choice. It is all too easy to click on one or more of these ads and be convinced by the presentations to buy things that you do not need. However, think twice about clicking on Internet ads.

If you have access to an e-mail account, you might receive a lot of *spam* (unsolicited, unwanted Internet mail). Many e-mail users consider spam messages the most annoying aspect of having an e-mail account. These messages are sent to you by people, organizations, or companies you do not know. They probably do not know you either. Somehow they have obtained your e-mail address. Most likely you do not want their mail. Most Web browsers allow you to block and filter some of this spam mail. But sometimes, no matter how many unwanted messages you remove, more keep coming. Think twice before opening the messages and responding to them.

Telephone and Door-to-Door Promotions

How many times have you answered the telephone and the voice on the other end has tried to sell you a subscription, asked for a donation, or wanted to speak to an adult about some product

Cautious consumers reject "come-ons" and deals that are too good to be true. How do you and your family act when faced with similar situations?

or service? Door-to-door salespeople try to do the same thing. Many of these people and their promotions are honest. But, then again, many are not. That is why it pays to be cautious.

Merchandise sold door-to-door or by phone order is often over-priced and of poor quality. Think it over before you buy. Compare the prices with those for similar merchandise at local stores. Avoid impulse buying, just as you would at the supermarket. Check the seller's identification and ask for references. If you decide to buy, pay by check made out to the company, not to the individual selling you the product.

Cure-Alls

The list of ailments or problems that some companies claim that their products can cure is a mile long. These products can be labeled *cure-alls*. Stay away from health lectures in small hotel halls unless the lecture is sponsored by a reputable health concern. Often, these so-called lectures are nothing more than sales promotions for a particular product or cure. Be sceptical about ads for cure-alls on the Internet. Your best bet is to see a doctor whenever you have a health problem.

Easy-Money Deals

Closely tied to health-care sales are various *easy-money deals*. You start out buying the products of a company, and you are soon recruited to become one of its agents. You, in turn, are to recruit others and receive a commission on their sales. Or you are asked to refer a friend to the company, and if that friend buys, you will get money or a gift.

Remember, you do not get something for nothing. The cost of the product being sold is increased by all the "free gifts" or commissions that are paid out.

Big-Ticket Items

Many people today use the Internet for comparison shopping of electronic products and other big-ticket items. You can check out what other consumers have to say about a product before you buy it. Various products are rated by a reviewer, sometimes a professional but often a consumer just like you. At some sites, you may add your own comments to the reviews. Often, there are links to other sites and buyers' guides that review the same product. One of the great advantages of comparison shopping using the Internet is that you can get opinions from people all over the world who use, and then rate, a product that interests you without leaving your own home! Several product-rating sites on the Internet include: <<http://www.epinions.com>>; <<http://ratings.net>>; and <<http://www.consumerreview.com>>. Log on to one of these sites and select a product that you might consider buying. See how your choice compares with the opinions of other consumers who have rated this product.

Shopping for a used car can be fun. It can also be a hassle and, if you are not cautious, very expensive. Know the seller of the car and be sure of the guarantees you are promised. If you are buying from a dealer, read your contract before signing. If possible, ask your mechanic to look the car over first. The cautious consumer buys from a well-established, reputable dealer. Many states have *lemon laws* that do provide some protection. These laws require the dealer to tell you what is wrong with the car before you make the purchase. Usually, you will receive a written guarantee of from 30 to 90 days on some parts of the car. If something goes wrong with the car, you may then return it for repair to the dealer as stated in your contract. Of course, if something does go wrong with the car, it is not easy to prove that the dealer knew about the problem before selling the vehicle. That is why it is often better to pay a reliable dealer a little more than you would pay a private seller you do not know.

WHAT FOUR WORDS SHOULD GUIDE YOUR SHOPPING?

At the beginning of this chapter, the question was asked, "How can you get the most for your money?" The members of Sheila Sharpe's economics class thought about all that had been discussed in this chapter. They looked over their notes and the information that had been placed on the chalkboard. Mr. Abel, their teacher, suggested that four words should guide their shopping. He then wrote the following words on the chalkboard: *Know—Plan—Read—Save.*

Before You Buy

1. **Know**
   - What you want.
   - What you can afford to spend.

2. **Plan**
   - Make a list of things to buy.
   - Do not buy on impulse.
   - Compare prices and brands.
   - Shop around. Try different stores and different neighborhoods.
   - Buy only what you can use or store safely.

Before We Buy: *Know* what we want and can afford; *plan* by making a list; *read* labels, ads, and contracts; and *save* by watching for sales.

3. **Read**

- Labels, tags, guarantees.
- Advertising.
- Contracts or sales agreements.

4. **Save**

- Watch for sales, specials, clearances, coupons.
- Borrowing costs money. If you do borrow, shop around for the best credit rates and most favorable terms.

SUMMARY

In the family budget, food is the biggest single expense that can be controlled. The smart food shopper plans ahead, compares prices, and does not buy on impulse. In order to make intelligent comparisons, the food shopper should understand unit pricing. The shopper should also understand food grading and how to read labels. Then the shopper can decide whether to buy store-brand, name-brand, or generic products.

Care must be taken when buying health-care products, particularly drugs. It is best to follow the advice of a doctor. There are prescription drugs that are dispensed by doctors and over-the-counter drugs, which may be sold to anyone. In either case, the shopper should understand that drugs may be purchased under their generic names or by their brand names. Comparing the two and comparing prices at different pharmacies can save money.

You can purchase items over the Internet. Perhaps more important, though, you can research on the Internet goods and services that you wish to buy, finding out what consumer organizations and other consumers think of these goods and services.

Caution is advised for all shoppers. The four words to guide the smart shopper are Know, Plan, Read, and Save.

LOOKING AHEAD

Even the wise consumer needs help. You cannot possibly know enough about all the goods and services you are asked to buy. You need protection from dishonest sellers. You also need information to enable you to choose wisely from among the many products and services offered for sale. In the next chapter, you will learn how the government and private agencies provide help for the consumer.

EXERCISES

✔ **Multiple Choice** Choose the letter of the item that best completes the statement or answers the question.

1. The main idea of this chapter is that (a) we get what we pay for when we shop (b) prices are the same wherever we shop (c) we waste time and money when we shop around (d) it pays to plan ahead and shop around.

2. The wise consumer *does not* (a) read labels carefully (b) buy on impulse (c) make a shopping list (d) shop around.

3. Jones sees two brands of canned peaches on the supermarket shelves. Both brands are the same weight, and both are Grade A Fancy. One is cheaper than the other. The cheaper brand is (a) a better buy (b) of poorer quality (c) not as healthful (d) packed in lighter syrup.

4. Four packages of the same product in the supermarket carry unit prices as follows. Which one is the cheapest? (a) 15 cents an ounce

(b) 2 ounces for 31 cents (c) 1 ounce for 17 cents (d) 1/2 ounce for 8 cents.

5. In family budgeting, the most costly, single category that you can control is (a) rent (b) clothing (c) food (d) medical expenses.

6. Lemon laws have to do with (a) unsolicited goods (b) door-to-door sales (c) food products (d) used-car sales.

7. An over-the-counter drug (a) is harmless (b) should be used only as directed (c) needs a doctor's prescription (d) can be taken at any time one chooses.

8. Which statement is generally true of drug prices? (a) The price of a drug will be the same whether it is sold under its generic name or its brand name. (b) The prices of prescription drugs are the same wherever you shop for drugs. (c) Drug prices may vary greatly, so it pays to shop for drugs as you would shop for groceries. (d) The prices of over-the-counter drugs are set by the manufacturer.

9. After shopping for fish fillets at several markets, you have noted that the package labels indicate the net weight, price per pound, total cost, and product type (such as fish fillets). Which item probably tells you which market is giving the best buy? (a) net weight (b) price per pound (c) total cost (d) product type.

✔**Matching** Match each term in Column A with its definition in Column B.

Column A	Column B
1. Know, Plan, Read, Save	a. the government agency that sets food standards
2. comparison shopping	b. the highest-quality meat grade
3. U.S. Department of Agriculture	c. purchasing goods without advance planning
4. Prime	d. the government agency that tests and approves drugs
5. unit pricing	e. wise buying practices to get the most for our money
6. prescription drug	f. checking prices for the same products at two or more stores
7. brand name	g. the chemical name of a drug
8. generic name	h. stating a product's price by its weight or volume
9. impulse buying	i. a drug dispensed only on a doctor's orders
10. U.S. Food and Drug Administration	j. the name given to a product by its manufacturer

✔ *Developing Skills as a Consumer: Shop and Compare*

1. Go to three different food markets or grocery stores. Jot down the prices charged at each for the same brands of your favorite cereal, cheese or other dairy product, or canned fruit. Prepare a chart like the one shown below:

	Store #1		Store #2		Store #3	
Brand Name	Price	Weight	Price	Weight	Price	Weight

2. Which brand was cheapest? Which store sold this brand?

3. Does this example illustrate the advantage of unit pricing? Explain your answer.

✔ *Using the Internet*

1. There are many sites on the Internet that can help you find out more about health topics and health-care products. For health topics, you might begin by checking out the Website of the Department of Health and Human Services at <<http://healthfinder.gov/>> or the FDA Website at <<http://www. fda.gov>>. For comparing health-care products, try the Consumers Union's Website, <<http://www.consumersunion.org>>. Most of the major platforms, such as MSN, Yahoo, and CNN, have health Websites such as <<http://WebMD.com>>.

2. If you are interested in learning about fuel-efficient cars, the Department of Energy and the Environmental Protection Agency can help at: <<http://www.fueleconomy.gov/feg/>>.

3. The following Websites offer advice and ideas for the wise consumer: <<http://www.italladdsup.org>> and <<http://www.chicagofed.org/consumer_information/index.cfm>>.

CHAPTER *10*
Consumers' Rights

Do consumers have rights? Today the answer is yes, of course they do. Why should consumers not have rights? After all, our rights as citizens are protected and guaranteed by the federal Bill of Rights. Well, not so long ago, consumers took their chances every time they made a purchase, borrowed money, or even deposited money at a local bank. The nation had relatively few laws that recognized or protected consumers' rights. Now, laws recognize that consumers have the right to be safe, to be informed, to choose, and to be heard.

It is said that an ounce of prevention is worth a pound of cure. In earlier chapters, we learned how to be wise consumers. We learned how much wiser it is to take steps and avoid problems before they occur. However, even if you have taken all the wise precautions, you—as a consumer—may still have problems. If you are a consumer with a problem, do you know where to go for help?

After reading this chapter, you will have a better understanding of the rights of consumers. In addition, you will be able to answer the following questions:

- What laws can help consumers borrow, invest, and save?
- How are consumers protected and kept informed?
- What services are offered by state and local agencies?
- How can consumers get reliable information?
- How can consumers get help for their problems?
- What help is offered by business and professional organizations?
- What are the responsibilities of consumers?

WHAT LAWS CAN HELP CONSUMERS BORROW, INVEST, AND SAVE?

Louise Johnson saw an ad that urged "Buy Now, Pay Later." So she signed a *sales contract* to buy a $500 stereo color television set on the installment plan from an appliance store. She made regular payments until she realized that she had paid over $500. Then she stopped making payments. But she recently received a letter notifying her that she owes $109.50 more. Furthermore, the letter warns that her employer may be asked to *garnish* (deduct from her wages) $15 a week until the full amount is paid.

There is a possibility that the federal government's Truth-in-Lending Act (1968) has been violated. This federal law requires the *lender* (the appliance store) to tell the *borrower* (Louise Johnson) exactly how much it will cost to borrow, including all extra charges. The law also limits the amount that the lender may have garnished. States and cities now have *consumer-protection agencies* that will help people who have been given inaccurate information about loan costs.

Investors also can get help from government agencies. Take the case of Paul Plunge. One morning, he received a call from a woman who introduced herself as a securities dealer for a large stock brokerage firm. Paul was told that he could make a lot of money by buying the stock of a new company that had created a self-chilling beverage can. He had to act fast to get in on the chance to make huge profits. Thus, Paul invested $5,000 in this stock.

But it turned out that the stock was "phony." Scores of *small investors* (people who invest small amounts of money) like Paul were cheated in this scheme. And several large investors lost over $1 million each.

The *Securities and Exchange Commission (SEC)* is the federal agency that took action to help Paul and the other investors. It found that the company did not have a self-cooling container ready for mass manufacture. The SEC charged the company with

"And to think if I hadn't been home having dinner I might have missed this wonderful investment opportunity."

What should this couple do before investing their money?
© *The New Yorker Collection 1989* James Stevenson from cartoonbank.com.

taking money illegally from the investors. The SEC obtained a court order to seize the assets of the company and its officers. An agreement was reached whereby the brokerage firm that pushed the sale of the stock and the company supposedly manufacturing self-chilling containers, would return most, but not all, of the money of those who invested in the stock. Not all investors are so lucky. Sometimes cases of this sort drag on for years. Sometimes the brokerage house and/or the manufacturer may not be financially able to pay refunds to investors taken in by such schemes. The lesson to be learned is that even with government protection, the wise investor is a careful investor. How true is the motto, "Let the buyer beware!"

In addition to protecting people's investments, the federal government also protects people's savings. Mrs. Phillips had warned her newlywed granddaughter, Jodi, not to deposit all of her wedding gift money in a bank. Mrs. Phillips told how she had lost all of her savings some decades earlier when the Home Bank of Nevada had failed. But Jodi does not have to worry. The *Federal*

Deposit Insurance Corporation (FDIC), created in 1933, insures savings deposits up to a maximum of $100,000 per depositor. This means that if one has over $100,000 in a bank, the amount over $100,000 is not insured. Almost every bank in the country is a member of the FDIC or a similar government-protected insurance program. Should a bank fail for any reason, its depositors' money is still protected. In addition to savings accounts, the FDIC insures checking deposits, deposits in NOW accounts, Christmas Club accounts, certificates of deposit (CDs), cashiers' checks, and money orders. It does not insure mutual funds, stocks, and bonds.

HOW ARE CONSUMERS PROTECTED AND KEPT INFORMED?

A large supermarket chain was ordered to stop adding chemicals to ground meat to color it. A red color made the meat look fresher than it really was. In another action, an entire shipment of shellfish was taken off the market after it was found to be contaminated. The shellfish had been taken from waters polluted by sewage. In these and other cases, the Food and Drug Administration (FDA) was the federal agency that sought to protect consumers from unsafe foods.

In the past, consumers could not always know what was inside an attractively packaged product. Therefore, the *Truth-in-Packaging and Labeling Act* (1966) required that packages of most products be clearly labeled. Quantities must be stated in ounces or grams, making it easier for consumers to compare brands. Which is heavier: a package weighing 1 pound, 5 ounces or one weighing 19 ounces? Now labels must give the weight as 21 ounces and 19 ounces, respectively. It is now easier to compare the two packages.

As we said in Chapter 9, labels must indicate ingredients in order of the amounts contained. Labels must also provide consumers with important nutritional information.

Federal Agencies

There are more than 50 federal agencies that provide some form of protection and information to consumers. One of them, the *Consumer Product Safety Commission*, monitors the safety of over 15,000 kinds of consumer products. It is this Commission that recalls products deemed to be unsafe, such as clothing items that may easily catch fire, electric appliances that might produce shock, and baby carriages and toys that are potentially dangerous.

Federal Protection for Consumers: U.S. Department of Agriculture inspectors examine and grade beef. How do inspection and grading maintain food quality?

1. The Food and Drug Administration (FDA). This agency protects consumers against dangerous foods, drugs, and cosmetics. One area of its concern is the presence of cancer-causing substances in these products. The FDA has banned the use of Red Dye Number 2 in foods because it is believed to cause cancer.

2. The U.S. Department of Agriculture (USDA). This agency, first discussed in Chapter 9, inspects and grades meats and regulates the grading of fruits and vegetables as well as eggs, frozen foods, and canned products.

3. The Federal Trade Commission (FTC). This agency, first discussed in Chapter 8, combats false and misleading advertising. The FTC, for example, forced manufacturers to stop advertising "little liver pills" that did not have any liver in them. It stopped advertisements for "wool" sweaters that were only part wool, and hundreds of other false claims.

WHAT SERVICES ARE OFFERED BY STATE AND LOCAL AGENCIES?

State and local agencies also work for consumers. Your state department of agriculture and your local department of health or markets will handle many of your complaints. These local agencies check weights and measures in stores and supermarkets.

They watch over the dating of milk and other dairy products, inspect sanitary conditions in restaurants, check the labeling of frozen and processed meat products, and perform countless other similar services to protect consumers. Some states have a department or office of consumer affairs to help protect consumers.

State agencies license hundreds of professional and service occupations, including doctors, nurses, beauticians, lawyers, accountants, and auto repair workers. Some localities license restaurants and auto repair shops. While a license does not guarantee full protection, it does allow local governments to set minimum standards. Firms and professionals who fail to meet those standards may lose their licenses, receive fines, or be forced out of business.

For reasons of economy, a bus company wanted to stop late-night runs on a certain route. But this route happened to be the only public transportation to a large hospital. Without late-night buses, many nurses and other night-shift employees would have been stranded. The state's *Public Service Commission* ordered the company to continue making the late-night trips.

State Protection for Consumers: An expert from a state agricultural department examines plants to determine why a crop failed. How does this activity help consumers?

State and local agencies are concerned with the public's well-being in other ways as well. Health departments inspect public beaches and pools. Movie theaters, video shops, and bookstores are regulated to prevent the showing or sale of pornography to young people.

HOW CAN CONSUMERS GET RELIABLE INFORMATION?

In addition to government agencies, many private organizations specialize in consumer services. Some organizations provide assistance in organizing consumer groups. Others develop educational programs for consumers. Consumers' Research, Inc., was the first independent, nonprofit national organization devoted to testing and rating products. The results of their findings are published in their magazine *Consumers' Research*. Another, and perhaps better-known, nonprofit testing organization is Consumers Union. Its widely read magazine *Consumer Reports* is frequently used by consumers as they check products they may wish to buy. Neither of these publications carry advertising. When a product is tested and rated by one of these organizations, consumers may be sure that they are being given an honest opinion of the product by experts. Both Consumers' Research and Consumers Union maintain Websites, which may require a fee to download material.

Soap manufacturers make all sorts of claims and promises about their particular brand of soap. One claims to leave your skin

Private Protection for Consumers: Employees of Consumers Union prepare brands of peanut butter for testing. Are you influenced by brand ratings? Why or why not?

Consumer Decision: If she had purchased a moderately priced CD player, this consumer could have been able to afford more CDs. What economic principle was at work here?

"silky smooth." Another promises to give you "a healthy clean." And yet another advertises that their soap will give you "an energy rush." Some soaps are promoted as being healthy for your skin because they contain vitamin E, aloe, chamomile, and other botanicals or antibacterial agents. Of course, there are extra charges for these ingredients. But are they worth the additional price? To answer that question, Consumers Union tested 14 different bars of soap. Its experts found no meaningful differences in terms of how well different soap bars rinsed off or how the skin felt later. They found that the ingredients vitamin E, aloe, and other botanicals were present in such small amounts as to be insignificant. If you buy soaps containing glycerine to attract moisture to your skin, keep in mind that glycerine does not stay on the skin—it rinses off!

Not all soaps lather equally, especially if you have hard water. Soaps made with synthetic detergents will lather better than ones made with pure soap. But a better lather will not make you cleaner. Consumers Union tests showed very little difference in lather among the various brands of soap in soft water.

Finally, different brands offer various fragrances, including fruity, floral, citrus, spicy, and herbal scents. So what do the experts recommend? They say that you should pick a fragrance that you like, and then shop for the lowest-price soap having that scent.

Of course, Consumers Union does not only test soaps. They test all sorts of products from automobiles to lawn tractors, electric juicers to computers, and from garden supplies to kitchen supplies. Should you buy what they recommend? Well, that is up to you. It is important that you get all the information about a product from as many reliable sources as possible before you make your purchase. If at all possible, ask others who have used the product that you are interested in what they think about it.

HOW CAN CONSUMERS GET HELP FOR THEIR PROBLEMS?

Lila Hunt was unhappy with her new car. It burned oil so fast that Lila had to add a quart every 700 miles. Each time she complained to the dealer from whom she bought the car, she seemed to get the runaround. Usually, she was told to wait because the car was still "breaking in."

Lila "surfs" the Internet frequently. So she sat down at her computer to see what information was available on the Internet to help her with her car problem. Lila clicked on *Search*, typed in "consumer complaints," and a list of Websites related to consumer complaints came up. Lila clicked on one of these, ActionLine, at <<http://www.consumeradvocate.net>>. She learned that this site offers consumers assistance in resolving consumer issues when the consumer, working alone, does not seem to be getting satisfaction in resolving a complaint.

The site listed such categories as household products and appliances, pesticides, and computers. Lila selected the category *Autos, Trucks, and Motorcycles*. She then filled in a form on her computer screen. Lila typed in her name and address, the make and model of her vehicle, where she bought it, what was wrong with it, and the unsatisfactory response she had received from the dealer. The agency to which Lila's complaint was referred then contacted the dealer as well as the automaker. The complaint brought prompt action from both. Now, Lila's car runs well, and the repairs did not cost her a cent.

There are many ways to find professional help for consumer problems, of course. Lila might have called her local government's department of consumer affairs or the Better Business Bureau. Newspapers and television stations often feature stories about government agencies and community action groups that assist consumers.

Consumers are fighting back. All over the country, consumer groups have been organized to press for consumer-protection laws. Some radio and television stations broadcast consumer complaints. Local newspapers often have consumer-action hot lines and will come to the aid of readers who have consumer problems. Many groups advise consumers and help them resolve complaints.

WHAT HELP IS OFFERED BY BUSINESS AND PROFESSIONAL ORGANIZATIONS?

Many national associations of business and professional people are interested in helping consumers get a fair deal. Some of the leading ones are discussed in this section.

Suppose that Billy Gao buys a digital camcorder and finds there is something wrong with it. What should he do? The first thing he should do is take it back to the store. But what if the manager claims that Billy broke it and refuses to exchange it or refund Billy's money?

If this is the line Billy gets, he can write a formal letter of complaint to the store. Next, he can complain to the local Better Business Bureau. (Discussed in Chapter 8.) Someone at the Bureau will check out Billy's claim. If Billy is right, the Bureau will press the store to straighten out the matter. Suppose that the store still does not cooperate. Billy could take his case to a *small claims court*. This court is a place where people who believe that they are owed a small amount of money (in the hundreds of dollars) may appear before a judge to state their case. There is little paperwork, fees are low, and a lawyer's services are not required. The Bureau may testify for Billy. The Bureau will also advise other consumers of the store's lack of cooperation.

Before buying any costly item, you might call the Better Business Bureau. It is listed in your local telephone directory. To the person who answers, give the name of the firm you want to buy from and ask if any complaints have been lodged against the firm.

Business Associations

Many industries are organized into associations. Very often these *business associations* have set up ways of informing and protecting the consumer. The American Insurance Association (representing over 370 property and casualty insurance companies), the Textile Manufacturers Institute (representing textile firms producing more than 80 percent of domestic textiles), and the American Gas Association are just a few examples of such groups. If you are interested in buying a gas appliance, for example, you might ask the American Gas Association to send you information about natural gas, fact sheets on residential gas appliances, and the latest updates on standards used in the industry. Bear in mind, however, that while these organizations may be good sources of information, their main function is to act on behalf of the producers they represent. The organizations' interests are not always the same as the interests of the consumer.

Personal Economics

WRITING A LETTER OF COMPLAINT

Do not be afraid to complain if you believe that you were unfairly treated as a consumer. Even the largest companies have a top-ranking officer who will take an interest in your problem and try to settle your complaint.

Most of the time, all you need to do is return the defective merchandise or discuss your complaint with the store manager or the person who waited on you. But if this does not work, make a formal complaint in writing.

Your letter of complaint need not be long. In fact, keep it brief and to the point. All you need are three paragraphs that do the following:

1. Describe the item purchased. State what you bought, its model number (or name) and serial number, and the date and place of purchase.

2. State the problem. State your complaint and what you have tried to do about it. Include the names of

Figure 10.1 Letter of Complaint

```
                              Your Address
                              City, State, Zip Code
                              Date




Appropriate Person
Company Name
Street Address
City, State, Zip Code

Dear  (Appropriate Person):

I recently purchased a (name of product or service
including model number).  I made this purchase at
(place, date, and other important details of the
transaction).

Unfortunately, (the product or service) has not per-
formed satisfactorily because (state the problem).
Therefore, I would like you to (state the specific
action you want, such as "return my deposit" or "take
back my purchase in exchange for undamaged goods").
Enclosed are copies (do not send originals) of my
records of this transaction.

I am looking forward to your reply and to a prompt
resolution of this matter.  Please contact me at the
above address or by phone at (your telephone number).

                              Sincerely,

                              Your Name
```

the store personnel you have spoken to about the problem.

3. Ask for satisfaction. State what you want done. Then indicate in your letter what further action you might take. Allow a reasonable time before taking further action.

You should enclose copies, *not the originals,* of all receipts and documents (such as the manufacturer's warranty). Keep, the originals and a copy of your letter for your own file. Your finished letter of complaint should look something like the letter on page 158.

Professional Associations

Many professionals—such as doctors, dentists, accountants, and lawyers—have associations of their own. The American Medical Association (AMA), the American Dental Association (ADA), and the American Bar Association (ABA) are examples of *professional associations.* These groups have found that even if only a few of their members are dishonest, the entire profession is hurt. Therefore, they try to keep the standards of their professions as high as possible. And by doing so, they are helping consumers who use the services of their members. These professional associations often sponsor activities to promote improvements in their professions. The ABA, for example, will offer recommendations to the governor of a state considering appointing a judge to a state court. The ADA will give its stamp of approval to some brands of toothpaste, indicating that the product is beneficial in fighting tooth decay. Similarly, the AMA may approve (or disapprove) a medical procedure.

Testing Organizations

Look at the bottles in your medicine cabinet. Pick up the cord on your living room lamp. Check your air-conditioning unit. In each case, you should find—stamped or attached to the item—a mark or label of a *testing organization.* Drugs and vitamins that have been tested and approved by the *United States Pharmacopoeia* will carry the *USP* mark. Electrical equipment that has been tested for fire and shock hazards by the *Underwriters Laboratories* will carry the *UL* label.

WHAT ARE THE RESPONSIBILITIES OF CONSUMERS?

In this chapter, we have discussed the rights of consumers. But with rights go responsibilities as well. Just as we have the right to expect sellers to deal honestly and fairly with consumers, so too should consumers deal honestly with sellers.

Personal Economics

READING ENERGYGUIDE LABELS

Appliance manufacturers are required to display energy-cost information on all new refrigerator-freezers, freezers, dishwashers, water heaters, clothes washers, room air conditioners, central air conditioners, heat pumps, furnaces, and boilers. The information, in the form of *EnergyGuide labels*, allows the consumer to compare the energy costs of competing products. These bright yellow labels with black lettering must be clearly visible.

The manufacturer, model number, type of appliance, and capacity are listed at the top of the label. The line-scale in the middle of the label shows how that particular model compares in energy efficiency with other models of comparable size and type.

The most efficient models of refrigerators, freezers, water heaters, dishwashers, and clothes washers will show energy consumption at or near the left-hand end of the scale, close to the words "Uses

Figure 10.2
EnergyGuide Label for a Refrigerator-Freezer

Estimated average yearly energy cost of this model ($91)

Estimated lowest and highest yearly energy costs of competing models ($68, $132)

Energy cost of this model per year, based on various utility rates

(Name of Corporation)
Refrigerator-Freezer — Model(s) AH503, AH504, AH507
Capacity: 23 Cubic Feet — Type of Defrost: Full Automatic

ENERGYGUIDE

Estimates on the scale are based on a national average electric rate of 4.97¢ per kilowatt hour.

Only models with 22.5 to 24.4 cubic feet are compared in the scale.

$91

Model with lowest energy cost		Model with highest energy cost
$68	THIS ▼ MODEL	**$132**
▼	Estimated yearly energy cost	▼

Your cost will vary depending on your local energy rate and how you use the product. This energy cost is based on U.S. Government standard tests.

How much will this model cost you to run yearly?

		Yearly cost
		Estimated yearly $ cost shown below
Cost per kilowatt hour	2¢	$44
	4¢	$88
	6¢	$132
	8¢	$176
	10¢	$220
	12¢	$264

Ask your salesperson or local utility for the energy rate (cost per kilowatt hour) in your area.

Important Removal of this label before consumer purchase is a violation of federal law (42 U.S.C. 6302)

(Part No. 371026)

Least Energy." Near the bottom of the label will be an estimate of the unit's estimated annual operating costs.

The EnergyGuide label for room air conditioners, central air conditioners, heat pumps, furnaces, and boilers gives the unit's *energy-efficiency rating* (*EER*) rather than its energy consumption. The EER may range anywhere between 5 and 11. The higher the number, the more efficient the air conditioner and the lower its operating cost.

EnergyGuide labels are not required on kitchen ranges, microwave ovens, clothes dryers, portable space heaters, and lights. Some appliances, such as television sets and computer monitors, display the Energy Star symbol to indicate that the model is energy efficient.

Using EnergyGuide labels can help you save money. Often, it is cheaper in the long run to buy a more expensive product if it is energy efficient. Suppose that you are considering two refrigerator-freezers. Model A costs $900, while Model B costs $700. The EnergyGuide labels show that Model A (Figure 10.2) costs $91 yearly to operate, while Model B costs $120. Which is the better buy?

Although Model B costs $200 less to buy, its yearly operating cost is $29 higher than Model A's. Dividing the difference in the purchase price ($200) by the difference in yearly operating costs ($29) tells you that it will take seven years for the energy-efficient model to cancel out the difference in the original purchase price. A refrigerator lasts for about 15 years. Over this period of time, you will save $232 if you purchase the more expensive model.

A major problem many businesses face is that some people walk out of a store with merchandise that they have not paid for. *Shoplifting* (theft of merchandise) is a crime punishable by law. Businesses have attempted to prevent thefts by hiring security personnel and by attaching to products devices that will sound an alarm if they are not removed before they are taken from the store. The loss of sales, as well as the cost of trying to prevent more thefts, raises the cost of doing business. This cost is passed on to other consumers because merchants must raise their prices to recover their losses.

Another major problem arises from the false claims that some consumers make about products and services. Some consumers falsely claim that a product has injured them. As a result, businesses and professional people have to pay very high insurance premiums to protect themselves against these claims. In addition, legal fees must also be paid. Once more, the expensive insurance and legal costs add to the cost of doing business. These added costs are also passed on to the consumer in the form of higher prices for goods and services. Of course, consumers have a right to make claims if a product or service is defective. False claims, however, hurt all of us.

SUMMARY

Consumers have rights. These rights are protected by federal laws and enforced by federal agencies. State and local laws and agencies also help consumers. Consumers can obtain information from government agencies and private organizations. They can obtain help from local community action groups. National business associations and professional groups try to maintain high standards for their members. These associations provide consumers with information and will, if necessary, support consumer complaints against members.

Consumer complaints may be oral or in the form of a letter. Consumers can seek further help from government agencies, private associations, and business and professional organizations.

National organizations place their seal of approval on items such as electrical appliances and medicines. Consumers Union publishes unbiased reports about consumer products in its monthly magazine and online. EnergyGuide labels on many major appliances assist consumers in choosing the most energy-efficient products.

With rights also go responsibilities. Consumers should deal honestly with sellers. Dishonest consumers force sellers to pass along their added costs to the rest of us.

LOOKING AHEAD

In this chapter, we have discussed how best to buy wisely. In the next chapter, we will discuss where we put the money we want to save or invest. We will find out that we have many choices, some riskier than others.

EXERCISES

✔**Matching** Match each term in Column A with its definition in Column B.

Column A
1. Truth-in-Lending Act
2. Truth-in-Packaging and Labeling Act
3. Securities and Exchange Commission
4. Federal Deposit Insurance Corporation
5. Federal Trade Commission
6. Public Service Commission

Column B
a. a government agency that insures deposits in banks
b. a federal government agency that regulates securities transactions
c. a government agency that protects consumers against false and misleading advertising
d. an organization that tests and approves drugs and vitamins
e. an organization of leading businesspeople that encourages fair business

7. EnergyGuide label
8. Consumers Union
9. Better Business Bureau
10. U.S. Pharmacopoeia
11. UL

practices

f. a state agency that regulates public transportation

g. requires that borrowers be told the total cost of borrowing money

h. a label indicating the product has been tested for fire and shock hazards

i. an organization that publishes its tests and ratings of consumer products

j. requires that labels clearly state quantities and list ingredients in order of amounts

k. a label, required on major appliances, that tells a unit's yearly operating costs or its operating efficiency

✔ Understanding *What You Have Read*

Base your answers on what you have read in this chapter. On a separate sheet of paper, write **T** if the statement is true. If the statement is false, write **F** and explain why it is incorrect.

1. Only the federal government helps consumers.

2. There is no guarantee on the safety of your savings deposit.

3. You should be able to tell by their order on the label the relative amounts of each vegetable in a can of mixed vegetables.

4. Lenders must tell borrowers the exact cost of borrowing money.

5. Drugs carrying the label *USP* are manufactured by the United States Pharmacopoeia.

6. A magazine such as *Consumer Reports* always favors the products it reports on and rates.

7. If you think that you have been cheated by a merchant or professional, you may complain or seek help from many different sources.

8. Consumers as well as business firms have a responsibility to be honest.

✔ Buying *a Major Appliance*

Imagine that you are interested in buying a refrigerator-freezer. You checked the EnergyGuide label of three different models having similar features but selling at different prices. Complete the arithmetic necessary to determine which model would be cheapest in the long run.

Manu- facturer	Model Number	EnergyGuide Estimated Yearly Operating × Cost	Average Years of = Service	Estimated Energy + Cost	Purchase = Price	Total Cost
AOK Co.	2755	$70	15	( )	$850	( )
EEZ Co.	4086	$82	15	( )	$790	( )
IBY Co.	5420	$90	15	( )	$775	( )

Which model will be cheapest to run for 15 years?

✔ Writing a Letter of Complaint

You purchased a shirt or blouse at Hegeman's Department Store. After wearing it once, you washed it, following the washing instructions. Then you let it dry, as directed. To your surprise and alarm, the colors ran. When you returned the garment to Hegeman's, the clerk told you that it was the store's policy not to accept merchandise that had been worn.

1. Write a letter, following the model letter on page 158.

2. Assume that you are not satisfied with the response to your letter. Explain how you can get help in resolving your complaint.

✔ Using the Internet

1. The federal government supplies a wealth of information to consumers online at various Websites.

   - Consumer World is a good place to start, at <<http://www.consumerworld.org>>. This Website lists other sources to get information for almost any product or service.
   - The Federal Consumer Information Center (located in Pueblo, Colorado) at <<http://www.pueblo.gsa.gov>> suggests consumer information available from the government in such formats as pamphlets, books, audio tapes, or online.
   - If you are interested in services to protect consumers, check out the Consumer Product Safety Commission's Website at <<http://www.cpsc.gov/indexmain.htm>>. Among other information, the site has lists of products that have been recalled.
   - And do not miss the FTC Website at <<http://www.ftc.gov>>.

2. State governments, like the federal agencies, maintain consumer protection Websites. You will find them listed at the previously mentioned Consumer World Website.

3. Among the many private, nonprofit organizations on the Web are Consumer Reports Online at <<http://www.consumerreports.com>> and ActionLine at <<http://www.consumeradvocate.net>>.

CHAPTER 11
Saving and Investing

Back in 1887, Charlie Johnson decided to strike out on his own. Like many others in those days, Charlie headed west and started farming. Charlie's farm had a creek with crystal-clear water running through the south end. Joe and Clementine Parks owned the farm just to the north. "Dig yourself a well, Charlie," Joe and Clementine would say every time they met Charlie. And Charlie would reply every time, "Sure thing. I'll do it first chance I get." But he did not dig the well. Charlie thought he would always have that good creek water. The summer of 1889 was a scorcher, however. No rain fell, and the creek dried up. Charlie was hot and thirsty, and his crops did not grow. An old proverb urges, "Dig a well *before* you are thirsty." It is too bad that Charlie never took that advice to heart.

Proverbs are catchy sayings that contain a piece of wisdom or advice. "Dig a well *before* you are thirsty" suggests that the way to meet tomorrow's problems is by planning for them today. A century ago, planning for a farmer meant digging a well and planting crops in ways to control soil erosion. Times have changed, but the principle is still the same. Nowadays most people prepare for the future by saving and investing.

"Dig a well *before* you are thirsty": How does this proverb apply to saving and preparing for the future?

After reading this chapter, you will be able to answer the following questions:

- Why do people save and invest?
- Where do people save and invest?
- How do you shop for ways to save and invest?

WHY DO PEOPLE SAVE AND INVEST?

If you were to ask people why they save, they would give you one or all of the following reasons: for emergencies, to buy costly things, for income, and for the future.

1. For a "Rainy Day." One of the most important reasons for saving is to provide for the unexpected. None of us knows when an accident, illness, or other emergency will strike. But we can set aside funds to prepare us to deal with one if it does come.

2. To Buy Expensive Things. Many of the goods that we most want to own—a 12-speed bike, a DVD player, a leather jacket— are expensive. The only way that many young people can pay for these things is to set aside money in some form of savings until they have the full amount.

3. For Additional Income. Money you are not using can earn more money for you. Just suppose that you had a secret spot to hide your savings, and a ferocious animal to guard it. Would it make sense to put your savings there? Certainly not. Hidden money is idle money. It earns nothing. One of the principal reasons why people put their money into saving accounts, CDs, bonds, and stocks is to earn the *interest* and/or *dividends* that these accounts pay. Dividends are the shares of a company's profits that are distributed to stockholders. Income in the form of dividends and interest can really add up over the years. How compound interest can increase one's savings is shown on pages 173–174.

4. For Retirement. Most people want to be able to stop working when they reach a certain age. The best way for workers to insure that they can retire comfortably is to put money regularly into a fund that they will be able to draw upon later.

WHAT ARE SAVINGS AND INVESTMENTS?

Most people do not immediately spend all of their income. They usually set aside some amount for use at a later time. Income that is not spent is called *savings*. People often use their savings to buy property that they believe will increase in value. This activity is called *investing*. The properties that people purchase with the savings that they expect will increase in value are called *investments*. Stocks, bonds, and mutual funds are some popular investments that you will learn about in this chapter.

WHERE DO PEOPLE SAVE AND INVEST?

Savings Institutions

Many people keep their savings in one or more *savings institutions*. Commercial banks, savings and loan associations, mutual savings banks, and credit unions all hold money for safekeeping. Much of the money that people deposit in these savings institutions is insured by the federal government.

Savings institutions offer a number of different kinds of savings plans. The following is a summary of what these are and how they differ.

1. Passbook Savings Accounts and Statement Savings Accounts. *Passbook* and *statement savings accounts* earn the lowest rates of interest. They are offered primarily by mutual savings banks and savings and loan associations. Depositors receive either a passbook or a monthly statement that records their deposits, withdrawals, fees, interest, and balance. Money can be withdrawn at any time.

2. Interest-Bearing Checking Accounts. NOW *accounts* entitle depositors to write checks against the balance in their accounts. Unlike regular checking accounts, which do not pay interest, NOW accounts do pay a small rate of interest. NOW stands for Negotiable Order of Withdrawal.

3. Money Market Savings Accounts. Money market savings accounts pay a higher rate of interest than passbook accounts. Withdrawals can be made at any time. Many banks permit depositors to write checks against the balance in their accounts. Money market accounts often require that a minimum sum of money be kept on deposit at all times.

4. Certificates of Deposit. Certificates of deposit (CDs) offer the highest rates of interest paid by savings institutions. That is the good news. The bad news is that CDs require a minimum investment, usually of $500. Moreover, depositors must agree to keep their money in the account for a fixed period of time, running anywhere from a few months to ten years or more.

5. Credit Union Savings Accounts. A *credit union* is a kind of bank owned by a group of people who have something in common. They may be members of the same labor union, church, or club, or employees of a particular firm. Credit unions offer their members a variety of insured savings plans. These plans pay interest rates similar to those of savings and loan associations and banks.

U.S. Savings Bonds

Many young adults find that buying government savings bonds is both safe and easy. A U.S. *savings bond* is a safe investment because it is a contract showing that money has been loaned to the Treasury of the United States. Thus, these bonds are backed by the full faith and credit of the U.S. government. It is easy because the bonds can be purchased at a bank or through Treasury Direct on the Internet at <<www.savingsbonds.gov/>>.

There are three different types of U.S. savings bonds: the I Bond, the Series EE Bond, and the Series HH Bond. I Bonds and Series EE Bonds may be purchased in paper form or electronically through Treasury Direct. Both I Bonds and Series EE Bonds are sold in eight denominations: $50, $75, $100, $200, $500, $1,000,

$5,000, and $10,000. Series HH Bonds are sold in four denominations: $500, $1,000, $5,000, and $10,000. Series HH Bonds are issued only in paper form.

The I Bond. The I Bond is purchased at full face value. For example, you pay $100 for a $100 bond. From the date you purchased your bond, interest is accumulated monthly and compounded every six months. What makes the I Bond attractive to investors is that the interest rate consists of two parts: a fixed rate and an inflation adjustment. The fixed rate, which is set at the time of purchase, remains the same for the life of an I Bond. The inflation adjustment is updated every six months based on the Consumer Price Index. This protects your earnings from inflation. There is no guaranteed level of earnings with the I Bond.

The Series EE Bonds. Paper EE Bonds are issued at a 50 percent discount from face value, and electronic EE Bonds are issued at face value. Like I Bonds, Series EE Bonds earn a fixed rate of interest for the life of a 30-year bond. Also as with I Bonds, Series EE Bonds accrue interest monthly and are compounded semiannually. Unlike the I Bond, the Treasury guarantees that a Series EE Bond will double in value after 20 years. If the value does not double with the set fixed rate after 20 years, the Treasury will make a one-time adjustment at the time of original maturity to make up the difference. Interest is paid when the bond is redeemed. There is no inflation adjustment for these bonds.

The Series HH Bonds. Unlike the I Bond and Series EE Bond, the Series HH Bond does not increase in value. Every six months, holders of such bonds receive an interest payment by direct deposit to the bondholder's checking or savings account. Series HH Bonds are redeemed at their face value. These bonds reach final maturity and stop earning interest 20 years from their issue date. The interest rate is set when originally purchased, and then at 10 years from the issue date. Series HH Bonds may be redeemed at face value when held at least 6 months past date of issue.

U.S. savings bonds are very desirable for investors because:

- Savings bonds are safe investments. Both principal and interest are guaranteed by the U.S. government.
- Savings bonds can be replaced free of charge if lost, stolen, mutilated, or destroyed.
- They can be bought without paying a fee and cashed any time after 12 months.
- They are exempt from state and local income taxes.
- If the bond is used for qualified education expenses, it becomes eligible for tax benefits upon redemption.

U.S. Series EE Savings Bond: This bond was purchased for $100. Upon maturity, it will be worth $200. How do consumers prepare for future wants and needs with such purchases?

U.S. savings bonds have some drawbacks:

- There is a three-month interest penalty applied to I, EE, and HH bonds redeemed during the first five years.
- Other types of investments may offer a higher return.

Money Market Funds

When people, businesses, and governments borrow money, they must give the lenders signed *notes*. A borrower's note, or IOU, states when the amount borrowed is to be returned and how much interest the borrowers will pay. The notes of major borrowers such as the federal government, banks, and big businesses are bought and sold in what is called the *money market*. Money market notes pay a higher rate of interest than passbook accounts.

The average person cannot afford to buy money market notes because they sell for amounts of $10,000 and above. A *money market fund*, however, can afford to purchase these notes. This fund is a corporation that uses the money of many people who have small amounts to invest to buy money market instruments. In this way, people with as little as $500 to invest may share in the kind of earnings that would not otherwise have been available to them.

Stocks, Bonds, and Mutual Funds

In Chapter 23, we will describe how large corporations raise money by selling their stocks and bonds to the public. Some people will put a portion of their savings into corporate stocks and bonds. *Stocks* represent shares of ownership in a corporation. This means that stockholders are part owners of a corporation. *Bonds* are a kind of IOU. The corporation promises to return the bondholder's money at a certain date in the future. Just as the purchasers of U.S. savings bonds are loaning money to the government, those who buy corporate bonds are loaning money to businesses.

People who put their savings into corporate stocks and bonds should know that they risk losing some or all of their money. To lessen the risk, many people with small savings buy shares in corporations called *mutual funds*. These funds are discussed in Chapter 23.

HOW DO YOU SHOP FOR WAYS TO SAVE AND INVEST?

If you want to buy a new jacket or coat, you will probably spend some time shopping before you actually make your purchase. It makes just as much sense to shop for a way to save or invest your money. But what should you look for when shopping for a way to save or invest?

Safety

Some forms of savings are more secure than others. You might think that the cookie jar is a great place to hide cash, and maybe it is. But then again, maybe it is not. After all, if you can get to it without too much difficulty, so too can a burglar. Savings accounts in banks, savings and loan associations, and credit unions are insured by the federal government up to $100,000. Similarly, U.S. savings bonds and other types of government bonds are as safe as the government that guarantees them.

By contrast, the stocks and bonds that corporations issue are no safer than the companies that issue them. It is quite possible, therefore, to lose part or all of the savings that one invests in stocks and bonds.

Personal Economics

THE POWER OF COMPOUND INTEREST

There is a mighty force working behind most of the forms of savings described in this chapter. It is called *compound interest.* This is the interest that is earned on your savings and on the interest that you previously earned.

Suppose, for example, that your Aunt Dorothy gave you a $1,000 check for your 15th birthday. You put the $1,000 in a seven-year certificate of deposit (CD) that was paying 6 percent per year. Let us see how compound interest would work in this example.

At the end of the first year, your account would be credited with $60 in interest (because $1,000 × .06 = $60). This would give you a new balance of $1,060 (because $1,000 + $60 = $1,060).

At the end of the second year, the 6 percent would be *compounded.* That is, your account would be credited with $63.60 in interest instead of the $60 that it received the previous year (because $1,060 × .06 = $63.60). This would give you a new balance of $1,123.60 (because $1,060 + $63.60 = $1,123.60).

By the end of the third year, the account would be worth $1,191.02 because of the addition of $67.42 in interest ($1,123.60 × .06 = $67.42). This process would continue until the end of the seventh year, when the CD would come due. By that time, the $1,000 would have increased to $1,503.63.

The more time that you give it, the more powerful compound interest becomes. Suppose, for example, that you decided to leave Aunt Dorothy's $1,000 gift in the bank until you reached the age of 65. Suppose, too, that during those 50 years the deposit continued to compound at 6 percent per year. By the time you reached the age of 65, the original $1,000 would have grown to $18,420.14!

1. ***Figuring It Out Using Arithmetic.***
   How long will it take for money earning compound interest to double? A simple formula called "the rule of 72" can help you determine that. Simply divide the number 72 by the interest rate and read the result in years.

   For example: Suppose you deposited $200 at 6 percent interest. 72 ÷ 6 = 12. It would therefore take 12 years for the $200 deposit to double.

2. ***Figuring It Out With a Calculator.***
   Compound interest can be computed on a calculator or computer. First, express the interest rate as a decimal. Then add 1 to the interest rate; multiply this figure by the *principal* (the amount on deposit); and hit the (=) sign once for each year to be compounded.

For example: Suppose that you want to calculate the balance after five years of a deposit of $200 in an account that pays 7 percent in compound interest. This is entered in your calculator as follows:

.07 + 1 = 1.07
1.07 × 200 =
=
=
=
= 280.51

Or suppose the deposit is $650, earning 8½ percent (.085) interest for four years. The total value of the account at the end of that time could be computed by your calculator as follows:

.085 + 1 = 1.085
1.085 × 650 =
=
=
= 900.81

The final readout of $900.81 is the correct balance.

Rate of Return

People who take your money for safekeeping do so in order to use it to make more money. They do this by either lending it to others or by investing it themselves. For that reason, they are willing to pay you to leave your money with them. The money that is paid to those with savings accounts is called either interest or dividends. The amount of interest paid for the use of other people's money depends upon the *interest rate*.

The interest rate is expressed as a percentage of the amount deposited (in the case of a bank account) or invested. So, for example, if you keep $100 on deposit in an account that pays 6 percent interest, it will earn $6 in interest in the course of one year. Technically, mutual savings banks are owned by their depositors. Therefore, the return that people with accounts in mutual savings banks receive is called a "dividend" rather than "interest."

The interest rate that banks will pay you for your savings varies with economic conditions and the length of time that you are willing to let them hold the money. In 1981, for example, banks were offering their depositors interest rates ranging from 5½ percent to 16 percent, depending on the type of account that they opened. Twenty years later, however, the rates were much lower.

People who use their savings to invest in stocks may receive dividends. These dividends represent a share of a corporation's profits. The size of the dividend will depend upon how much the corporation earned in a given year.

Access to Savings

The ease with which one can turn savings into cash is described as *liquidity*. Some banks offer automated teller services that can process deposits and withdrawals 24 hours a day, seven days a week. Savings accounts that allow depositors to write checks are also highly liquid. How important is liquidity? That will depend upon the goals of your savings program. Savings that have been set aside for emergencies ought to be easy to turn into cash. Savings that you expect to accumulate for a long time (to pay for college or to buy a car) need not be so liquid.

Pension Plans, 401(k) Plans, and IRAs

Many businesses and government agencies require that their employees contribute a portion of their income into a *pension plan,* which will give them monthly income when they retire. Employers usually contribute to such a plan also. This kind of pension has two important advantages. The first advantage is that it is a kind of forced savings, because payments into the pension fund are deducted from the employees' regular wages. This is especially helpful to those who find it difficult, if not impossible, to save on their own. The second advantage is that contributors do not have to pay income taxes on the interest and dividends their money earns while it is held in the pension plan.

The federal government has authorized several methods to allow individuals to accumulate funds for retirement. An *individual retirement account (IRA)* can be set up by individuals with earned income. An individual has many investment options with an IRA.

With drive-in banking, customers have quick access to their accounts. What might be some disadvantages of this method of banking?

Individual Retirement Accounts (IRAs): What are some advantages of IRAs that the bank lists in its offering to customers?

In fact, any one or combination of savings and investment vehicles previously discussed may make up an IRA.

For their employees, some firms have *401(k) plans* in addition to or instead of a pension plan. In a typical 401(k) plan, both the employer and the employee put in a set amount of money into the plan each pay period. The employee's contribution is automatically deducted from the pay check. The employee is able to make some choices on how to invest the retirement money. Income put in these plans is tax deferred. This means that employees do not have to pay taxes on the money until they withdraw it. Thus, the income can grow and grow, and will not be taxed until after the employee is retired (and presumably has less income and is in a lower tax bracket). Moreover, taxes are levied only on the amount withdrawn from the 401(k) plan each year. Funds remaining in the plan continue to accumulate tax-deferred income.

SUMMARY

In this chapter, we learned about saving and investing. Anything not spent out of income is called savings. The use of savings to purchase property in the expectation that it will increase in value is called investing. People save to have money for a crisis, to buy costly things, to have additional income, and to enable them to retire.

The most popular ways to save are savings accounts, U.S. savings bonds, money market funds, 401(k) plans, and IRAs. People who invest their savings are likely to put them into stocks, bonds, and mutual funds.

It pays to shop for ways to save or to invest one's savings. When looking for ways to save or invest, consider these factors: relative safety, the rate of return, and liquidity.

─────────────── **LOOKING AHEAD** ───────────────

Sometimes it is not possible to wait until we have saved enough to buy the things we need or want. In those instances, people often turn to credit. Credit, or borrowing, enables people to purchase and use the things they want now and pay for them in the future. The following chapter explains why credit can be costly, and why it is important for all of us to know something about credit before we borrow.

─────────────── **EXERCISES** ───────────────

✔ **Matching** Match each term in Column A with its definition in Column B.

Column A	Column B
1. credit union	*a.* ease of withdrawal
2. IRA	*b.* a share of ownership
3. bond	*c.* a type of bank owned by its members
4. stock	*d.* a share of profits
5. dividend	*e.* a kind of checking account
6. liquidity	*f.* a certificate of deposit
7. NOW account	*g.* a retirement account
8. CD	*h.* a promise to pay

✔ **Multiple Choice** Choose the letter of the item that best completes the statement or answers the question.

1. Which of the following has the highest level of risk? (a) savings account (b) U.S. savings bond (c) corporate stock (d) credit union savings account.

2. Saving "for a rainy day" means saving (a) for a new roof for one's home (b) for retirement (c) for a college education (d) to meet unexpected expenses.

3. Stockholders are (a) part owners of a corporation (b) creditors of a corporation (c) those who deposit money in commercial banks (d) all of the above.

4. Which of the following pays the highest rate of return? (a) a 5.7 percent certificate of deposit (b) a $1,000 bond that pays $59 per year (c) a savings account that pays 3.25 percent interest (d) a money market account that pays 3.05 percent interest.

5. Which is the most liquid form of savings? (a) a savings account (b) an IRA (c) a money market account (d) a certificate of deposit.

6. Why are banks willing to pay you interest on your deposits? (a) They use your money to earn money. (b) The law requires that banks pay their depositors interest. (c) They like you. (d) All of the above.

7. Which of the following is true of mutual funds? (a) They invest the funds of their stockholders. (b) They spread the risk of investing among many securities. (c) Earnings are distributed to stockholders in accordance with the number of shares each owns. (d) All of the above.

8. Lila Lewis works for the Accabonac Fish Company. Last year the company formed the Accabonac Union, or as they call it, "AU." AU offers interest-paying accounts to Accabonac employees. It also offers them low-cost loans. AU is (a) a bank (b) a mutual fund (c) a credit union (d) a labor union.

✔ *Application Questions*

1. If you now, or will soon, earn extra money, do you plan to save or invest any of it? Explain why you would or would not do so.

2. Savings institutions offer different kinds of savings plans. Explain which plan you might choose and why you would choose this method of savings.

✔ *Using the Internet*

1. Information about U.S. government securities are available at: <<http://www.publicdebt.treas.gov/bpd/bpdhome.htm>>.

2. You probably have many questions you would like to ask before investing your money. To help you and other investors, the Securities and Exchange Commission makes available a number of publications. You may request them over the Internet at <<http://www.sec.gov>>, by phoning 1-800-SEC-0330, or by writing to the U.S. Securities and Exchange Commission at 450 5th Street, NW, Washington, DC, 20549. Also check <<http://financialplan.about.com/>>.

3. To help you better understand what you need to know about saving and investing to meet long-term goals, take a "Reality Check" offered without charge at: <<http//www.jumpstartcoalition.org>>.

CHAPTER *12*

Using Consumer Credit Wisely

🔑 *Key Terms*

credit	repossess	annual per-
charge account	personal loan	centage rate
credit line	secured loan	(APR)
interest rate	unsecured loan	collateral
unpaid balance	debit card	creditor
installment plan	ATM card	credit history
down payment	finance charge	

Maybe you can help Peter and May Wang solve their family's Friday-night problem. They have only one television set for a family that consists of themselves, their three children, and Mrs. Wang's mother. Many a night, there is a quarrel about who gets to watch what program. The Wangs agree that buying another TV set might be a solution. A local discount store is offering a 32-inch stereo TV set, with universal remote and sleep timer, for $399. This is 25 percent off the standard price.

But the Wangs cannot afford to pay $399 out of their bank account. It is not in their monthly budget. Should they get the TV set anyway by purchasing it on *credit*—by buying it now and paying for it later? Or should they buy a cheaper black-and-white set, for which they do have the cash?

You will be able to offer good advice to the Wangs after reading this chapter. As you read, look for the answers to these questions:

- What is consumer credit?
- What are the more common forms of consumer credit?
- How can you shop for credit?
- What are the advantages and the disadvantages of buying on credit?
- How do you get and keep a good credit rating?

WHAT IS CONSUMER CREDIT?

Once upon a time, if you did not have cash in your pocket or deposited in a bank, you went without. Today, you can buy almost anything you want without having the money to pay for it. And many people do, using credit.

Credit is a form of borrowing. If the Wangs purchase a TV set on credit, they are receiving merchandise for which they promise to pay at a later date. In other words, they "buy now, pay later."

The Wangs may be allowed to pay the amount owed in a series of payments, or *installments*. One plan, for example, would be to pay $7.68 a week for 52 weeks. Another plan would be to pay the amount of purchase ($399) plus a percentage charge in a lump sum at the end of two months.

How is it possible for consumers to buy without money? It is *not* possible. When consumers use credit, it may seem that they are getting something for nothing. But the fact is that consumers are using someone else's money to make their purchases. Consumers will have to repay the loan. And they will have to pay the store or the bank or the credit card company something extra for the use of its money. This extra charge is called *interest*. (Recall what we said earlier about earning interest on one's savings. Interest is the payment for use of someone else's money.)

The Wangs realize that if they buy the $399 TV set on credit, it will cost them more than $399. Can you figure out how much more it will cost the Wangs to buy on credit than to pay cash? (*Hint:*

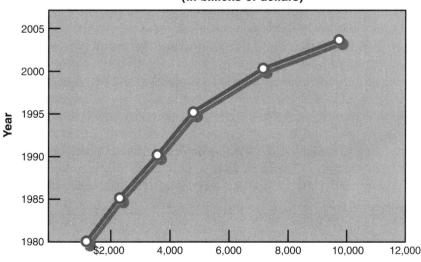

**Figure 12.1 Household Debt Outstanding Since 1980
(in billions of dollars)**

Assume the interest charged on this purchase is 18 percent a year. Two months is one-sixth of a year; one-sixth of 18 percent equals 3 percent, or .03. Multiply $399 by .03 to find the interest the Wangs will have to pay.)

Consumer credit is most widely used in buying homes. But over one-fifth of all credit is for payments for consumer goods and services. Consumer credit outstanding (unpaid) equals more than 21.5 percent of Americans' after-tax income. Figure 12.1 on page 179 shows how household debt outstanding has increased since 1980.

WHAT ARE THE MORE COMMON FORMS OF CONSUMER CREDIT?

Consumer credit is available in any or all of the following forms: charge accounts, installment plans, personal loans, and credit cards.

Charge Accounts

Bill Adair purchased a shirt and tie at Dunham's Department Store. "How would you like to pay for that, sir?" asked the salesperson. "Charge it, please. Here's my card." Bill replied. The clerk took the store's charge card and entered the sale in the computer.

Dunham's Department Store offers *charge accounts* to qualified customers. Charge accounts enable people to buy merchandise without having to pay cash. Instead, customers are billed once a month for their purchases. Dunham's has probably given Bill Adair a *credit line*—the maximum amount he may owe at any one time. Bill may charge more purchases at any time as long as he does not go above the credit line. A credit application from Dunham's Department Store is shown on page 188.

A monthly *interest rate* is quoted to charge account customers. Usually, this is about 1 or 1½ percent a month on the *unpaid balance*—the amount the customer owes. When Bill receives his monthly statement from Dunham's, it will show the purchases he made last month and their costs. If Bill soon pays the total amount he owes for these purchases, no interest charges will be added. In other words, Bill will be paying the same for his charge purchases as cash customers would. But if Bill does not soon pay all of the amount due, he will have to pay an interest charge on the unpaid balance. About one-third of all charge account customers pay their monthly bills in full when they are due. They do not pay the extra monthly charge.

Installment Plans

Installment plans are a common form of consumer credit. These plans enable buyers to use and enjoy merchandise in exchange for a promise to pay for it at regular intervals over a period of time.

> **Own This DVD Player! Only $50 Down,
> and Pay Just $10 a Week . . .**

This advertisement is offering to sell a DVD player on the installment plan. The *down payment* would be $50, while weekly installments would be $10. Many consumers would be attracted by such an offer because it would enable them to buy something that they could not otherwise afford.

If you are thinking of buying something on the installment plan, there are two things that you should know before you buy. First, you will not legally own the goods until you have finished paying for them. This means that if you fail to keep up with your installment payments, the seller can *repossess* (take back) the merchandise.

Second, additional charges to cover the interest rate and service costs will be added to the selling price. For that reason, goods purchased on the installment plan cost more than if they had been bought for cash. Usually, they cost much more.

Personal Loans

Banks, finance companies, credit unions, and certain other financial organizations lend money to qualified consumers. In exchange for their credit, lenders charge interest on their loans. These *personal loans* may be either secured or unsecured. A *secured loan* is one in which the borrower pledges *collateral* (something of value, such as a bank account, a car, or stock certificates) in case the loan is not repaid. *Unsecured loans* are those that are given without any collateral. Naturally, lenders must have confidence in borrowers who receive unsecured loans.

Credit Cards

In recent years, there has been an increase in the use of credit cards—and the trend is growing! These little plastic cards (also called "plastic money") are accepted at stores, hotels, restaurants, and airlines—in fact, by businesses of all kinds all over the world. Credit cards enable consumers to make purchases simply by signing charge slips. Credit cards, like charge accounts, have maximum credit lines depending on each cardholder's income and credit rating.

While credit cards are convenient for shoppers, they can be costly.

1. Annual fees. Consumers pay a price for using credit cards. Some credit card companies charge their customers an annual fee, while others do not.

2. Late charges. If you do not make a monthly payment by a certain date, you will be charged a late fee. You can also be charged if you make a partial payment that is below a stated minimum.

3. Interest rates. Credit cardholders who do not pay the full amount of their monthly purchases are charged interest on the unpaid balance. Interest charges vary from bank to bank that issues the cards. Therefore, if you are going to use a credit card, choose one with the lowest interest charges.

Shop for a credit card much as you would shop for anything else you might buy. No matter what credit card you may use, remember it is cheaper to pay the entire balance when due so as to avoid having to pay a credit charge.

Credit Card Buying: If consumers pay their credit bills in full within a certain time, their credit card company will not charge them interest.

Personal Economics

CREDIT CARDS, DEBIT CARDS, AND ATM CARDS

Some people confuse the following with credit cards. Do you?

1. **Debit Cards.** Debit cards are like paperless checks. This is because a debit card purchase is deducted from the cardholder's checking (or savings) account at the bank that issued the card. Debit cards, unlike credit cards, *are not credit instruments*. From the moment they are used to make a purchase, the buyer's bank balance is reduced by the amount of the purchase.

2. **ATM Cards.** As discussed in Chapter 5, an ATM card enables a cardholder to withdraw money from an individual's checking or savings account at ATM machines all over the world. ATM machines are located in shopping malls, movie theaters, tourist rest stops, and at many other locations. The costs for this service are greater at a non-bank ATM machine as well as at a bank ATM other than that of the bank that issued the card.

HOW CAN YOU SHOP FOR CREDIT?

Anyone thinking of buying on credit should shop around for the best terms. The law requires that those who offer credit to consumers must provide information about the finance charge and the annual percentage rate (APR). This information is valuable because it will help you to shop for the best credit deal.

The *finance charge* is the total amount that you will have to pay for the use of credit. It includes such things as interest charges, fees to investigate the borrower's past use of credit, and anything else the seller might add to the retail price of your purchase.

The *annual percentage rate (APR)* is the percentage cost of the credit on a yearly basis. In this way, the borrower can easily see whether the cost of credit is high or low. For example:

Pat Hayes has been shopping for a car. She found just what she wanted at Clinton Motors for $14,500. Pat estimated that she could afford to make a $3,500 down payment. Now, she needs an $11,000 loan in order to buy the car.

The Clinton Motors salesperson said that Clinton could arrange to finance the loan for four years. So too did the First National Bank. The Hill Savings and Loan Association also offered to lend Pat the money. But it wanted to be repaid in three years.

All three lenders provided information about their finance charges and annual percentage rates. Pat summarized this information in a table, as follows:

Credit Choices on an $11,000 Loan

Lender	APR	Length	Month/Payment	Finance Charge	Total Paid
CM	8.50%	4 yrs.	$271.30	$2,022.39	$13,022.39
FN	8.25%	4 yrs.	269.83	1,952.08	12,952.08
HS	7.75%	3 yrs.	345.97	1,352.44	12,352.44

Which plan should Pat choose? The lowest-costing plan is offered by Hill Savings and Loan, whose finance charges amount to $1,352.44. This figure would bring the total cost (after Pat repaid the $11,000 loan) to $12,352.44.

Pat could, however, lower her monthly costs by financing the car purchase at First National. Since First National would give Pat an extra year to pay, her monthly payments would be only $269.83 as compared to $345.97 at Hill. It would make little sense for Pat to finance her car purchase at Clinton Motors. To do so would cost her nearly $670 more than at Hill and $70 more than at First National.

We can reach several conclusions about APRs and credit costs based on what we have just read: First, when two loans are for the same length of time, the better loan is the one with the lower APR. Second, when the APRs for two loans are the same, but the length of the loan period differs, monthly payments are smaller for the longer loan period. But the total cost of this loan is greater.

WHAT ARE THE ADVANTAGES AND DISADVANTAGES OF BUYING ON CREDIT?

There was a time when people were fearful of buying on credit. They thought that it almost always led to trouble. "Neither a borrower nor a lender be," they would say. But borrowing can be either good or bad, depending on how it is used.

Credit is now part of the American way of life. You should know both the advantages and the disadvantages of using credit before you borrow.

Advantages of Consumer Credit

Credit enables consumers to do the following:

1. Buy and Enjoy Things Now. Were it not for credit, most people would have to save for many years before they could afford

What should consumers do before signing up for loans and other credit deals?

to buy a new home. In the same way, credit helps consumers to buy automobiles, home furnishings, computers, and any number of other costly items.

2. Deal With Financial Emergencies. The loss of a job, long illnesses, and emergencies can lead to piles of unpaid bills and added worries. At such times, a loan is often just the thing a family needs to help ease its problems.

3. Make Purchases Without Carrying Cash. Using credit cards, consumers are able to shop, go on vacation, and eat at restaurants without carrying cash. Credit cards and charge accounts have become popular means of purchasing many goods and services.

4. Save Money. The TV set that the Wangs want is on sale at $399. This is 25 percent below the regular price of $532 ($532 × .25 = $133; $532 − $133 = $399). Even adding on the cost of credit, the Wangs could save money by buying the TV set now, while it is on sale. (This assumes that the same model set will not be on sale when the Wangs would have had time to save $399.)

5. Help the U.S. Economy to Grow and Prosper. Credit increases sales. It enables consumers who could not or would not use cash to make purchases. Increased sales add to business profits and can lead to the expansion of a business. When businesses expand, they often hire new employees, add new floor space, buy more raw materials, and advertise more.

Personal Economics

SHOULD YOU BORROW?

There is no one answer for everybody. Each person's financial situation is different. Before you borrow, you should ask yourself:

1. Could I instead save a certain amount from each paycheck and later on pay cash for the item I want?

2. Is having the item now worth the extra cost?

3. Can I handle this much debt?

Then examine your financial situation. Ask yourself these questions:

1. How much is left from your yearly salary after you meet all your expenses and put money into your savings? Do not go into debt larger than this amount.

2. Can you easily meet the payments on what you owe now? If not, do not add to your burden.

3. How much do you now have saved? If it is not enough to meet payments in case of illness or sudden loss of job, do not add to your troubles.

4. Will your present income remain steady? If you expect to earn more in the future, you can handle a bigger debt. If you think you might earn less, you should spend and borrow less, not more.

If you do borrow:

1. Shop around for the best credit deal.

2. Read your contract before signing it.

3. Learn what will happen if you cannot meet your payments.

4. Make as large a down payment as possible.

5. Pay off the loan as soon as you can.

Disadvantages of Consumer Credit

Credit has a number of disadvantages. A credit purchase:

1. Costs More Than Cash Purchases. A credit purchase includes the cost of the cash purchase *plus* the additional interest charges.

2. Leaves Consumers With Less Money to Spend on Other Items. This follows from the first disadvantage listed. With a given income, you have to make a trade-off. If you are spending more on item A, then you have less to spend on item B.

3. Encourages Consumers to Spend Beyond Their Means. Easy credit lures some consumers into spending more than they can afford. As their monthly loans charges mount, these consumers find it increasingly difficult to meet payments. Finally, these buyers fall so far behind in payments that lenders repossess their goods. For many, this means the loss of the furniture, car, appliances, and other purchases already partly paid for.

4. May Hurt the Nation's Economy. As easy credit lures consumers into increased spending, higher prices and interest rates throughout the economy may result. As demand increases, the prices for most goods and services will also increase. So, too, will interest rates increase with an increased demand for borrowing. (Recall what we said about demand-pull inflation in Chapter 6.)

HOW DO YOU GET AND KEEP A GOOD CREDIT RATING?

People in the business of making loans want to lend as much money as they can. That is how they earn their living. However, they could not stay in business very long if too many borrowers failed to make their payments on time. Therefore, creditors will refuse loans to people who may not live up to their obligations.

What Creditors Look For

Creditors (those who lend money) judge those coming to them for loans by the "three C's." These are: capacity, collateral, and character.

1. Capacity. This term refers to your ability to meet payments on time. Creditors want to know enough about your job, income, and expenses to satisfy themselves that you will be able to meet the loan payments.

2. Collateral. Creditors want to know that if something happens to your income, you will still be able to repay the loan. For that reason, they will ask you about your *collateral*—property that can be pledged to protect the interests of the lender.

3. Character. Some lenders regard character as the most important of the three C's. It refers to your willingness to repay your debts. For that reason, they will check your *credit history*—the record of how well you have kept up on paying your bills.

A sample credit application is shown on the next page. The application asks questions about you, your work, and other charge accounts and bank accounts. By signing the application, you will authorize the lender to check your credit history. From the information you give on your application and from a check of your credit history, the lender determines how well you meet the three C's.

Figure 12.2 Credit Application

CREDIT APPLICATION

DUNHAM'S DEPARTMENT STORE

ABOUT YOU

Name	First	Middle	Last		Date of Birth	Mo.	Day	Year
Name Address	Street No.	City, Town	State	Zip	Years There		Own ☐ Rent ☐	
Home Phone	(Area Code)	Monthly Rental or Mortgage Payment		Social Security No.				
Previous Address	Street No.	City, Town	State	Zip		Years There		
Name of Close Relative	Name	Address City	State	Zip	Relative's (Area Code) Phone			
Present Employer	Name of Company			Your Position				
Business Address	Street No.	City	State	Zip	Business (Area Code) Phone			

YOUR CAPACITY

Annual Salary		Years There		Other Income		
Previous Employer					Years There	

YOUR CREDIT HISTORY (CHARACTER) AND COLLATERAL

American Express ☐ Visa ☐ Mastercard ☐	Account No.	Exact Name of Account
Savings Bank	Account No.	Address of Bank
Checking Bank	Account No.	Address of Bank
Loan Reference		

I hereby certify that all statements made are true and complete and submitted for the purpose of obtaining credit. I authorize you to check my credit and employment history.

Signature _____

Date _____

SUMMARY

Consumer credit is a form of borrowing. Consumers use it to help make purchases. The most common sources of consumer credit are charge accounts, installment plans, personal loans, and credit cards. Before you use credit, shop around for the best terms. In doing so, compare finance charges and annual percentage rates.

There are several advantages to consumer credit. It enables people to enjoy things now that they would otherwise have to wait to buy. Credit can help people deal with emergencies. Credit may help people save money. Credit can also help the nation's economy to grow.

There are several disadvantages to consumer credit. Credit purchases can be more costly than buying with cash. Buying on credit leaves one with less money to spend on other things. Credit also may lure people into spending more than they can reasonably afford.

It is important to pay all your bills on time. Doing so will help you to get and keep a good credit rating. Remember that creditors will judge how good a credit risk you are on the basis of the "three C's" of capacity, collateral, and character.

─────────────── **LOOKING AHEAD** ───────────────

Another important item in the family budget or personal budget is insurance. The following chapter discusses how we can use insurance to protect ourselves, our families, and our property.

─────────────── **EXERCISES** ───────────────

✔️ **Matching** Match each term in Column A with its definition in Column B.

Column A	**Column B**
1. credit	a. capacity, collateral, character
2. APR	b. a portion of the cost of goods that the buyer pays at the time of purchase
3. contract	
4. finance charge	c. an agreement by which a consumer is allowed to pay off the purchase in a series of weekly or monthly payments.
5. installment plan	
6. down payment	d. the amount that is owed after a payment is made on a loan
7. unpaid balance	
8. "three C's" of credit	e. a uniform way of telling the consumer what the yearly interest rate on a loan is
9. collateral	f. the advance of money with a promise to repay at a future date
	g. something of value, pledged to protect the interest of the lender
	h. a binding agreement between two or more persons
	i. the total dollar cost of borrowing

✔️ **Multiple Choice** Choose the letter of the item that best completes the statement or answers the question.

1. The main idea of this chapter is that credit is (a) good (b) bad (c) either good or bad (d) unnecessary.

2. Credit has (a) made savings unnecessary (b) made money unnecessary (c) had little impact on the U.S. economy (d) become a part of the American way of life.

3. An advantage of buying on credit is that credit (a) enables consumers to enjoy things that they could otherwise not afford (b) causes people to go deeper into debt (c) has caused interest rates to fall (d) stimulates impulse buying.

4. A disadvantage of buying on credit is that credit (a) helps people deal with financial emergencies (b) reduces the need to carry large sums of cash (c) usually costs less than paying cash (d) may cause consumers to spend beyond their means.

5. If you must borrow, it is wise to (a) borrow from the business where the purchase is made (b) shop for the best deal (c) put as little money down as possible (d) spread out repaying the loan over a long period.

6. Which statement is incorrect? (a) It is cheapest to borrow where the APR is lowest. (b) It is always cheapest to pay cash. (c) The cost of credit is the same everywhere. (d) The cost of borrowing increases as the time period for repayment is lengthened.

7. What will happen if a family extends the time period for repaying a loan with an APR of 8.5 percent from two to three years? (a) The APR will rise to 9.5 percent. (b) The monthly payments will be reduced. (c) The finance charges will be reduced. (d) The total cost of the loan will remain unchanged.

8. When lenders speak of "capacity," they are referring to the borrower's (a) ability to repay the loan (b) savings, investments, or other property (c) previous credit history (d) other credit charges.

9. Which method of repaying a $250 loan would be cheapest overall? (a) $28 a month for 12 months (b) $7 a week for 52 weeks (c) $26 a month for 24 months (d) $75 down payment and $20 a month for 12 months.

✔**Preparing a Retail Installment Credit Contract** Read the selection below and then answer the questions that follow.

Ricardo Gomez wanted to buy a digital video disk player. It cost $800, but he had only $200 in cash. The salesperson said that Ricardo could make a $200 down payment for the player and pay $600 on the installment plan.

Ricardo signed a paper, and a week later the player was delivered to his house. Beginning in June, Ricardo made 12 monthly payments of $63, due on the 10th of each month, to the Friendly Finance Company. A credit service charge of $12 had been added to his bill.

Ricardo was late twice in making payments. He was billed $2.50 extra each time. Once the finance company told Ricardo that if he did not make a payment soon, they would repossess the set. Ricardo borrowed $65.50 ($63 plus $2.50 for the late charge) from his mother-in-law and made the payment.

Here is a retail installment credit contract Ricardo might have signed.

Retail Installment Credit Contract

Terms:

_____

1. Cash Selling Price $ _____

2. Cash Down Payment $ _____

3. Balance of Cash Sales Price $ _____
   (No. 1 less No. 2)

4. Credit Service Charge $ _____

5. Total Balance $ _____
   (Total of items 3 and 4)

6. Buyer agrees to pay this balance at the office of the Seller or such place as the Seller may designate, in _____ install-ments of $_____ each, commencing _____, _____, and on the same day of each successive month thereafter. A late charge of $2.50 shall be added for pay-ments in arrears seven days from this date.

7. Total Due $ _____

1. What do we call the $200 Ricardo paid when he ordered the player?

2. What do we call the paper that Ricardo signed?

3. How much did Ricardo actually pay for the player?

   (a) Multiply $ 63.00   Monthly payments

                    × 12   Number of payments

                    $ In payments

   (b) Add   + $200.00   Down payment

                 +   12.00   Credit service charge

                 +   5.00   Late fees

4. How much more did it cost Ricardo to buy on time than if he had paid cash? Subtract the $800 cash price from the total of what Ricardo actually paid for the set.

✔ *Understanding a Cartoon*

Examine the cartoon on page 185 and then answer the questions below. Base your answers only on the information in the cartoon. On a separate sheet of paper, write **T** if the statement is true, **F** if the statement is false, and **NS** if there is not sufficient information given to answer true or false.

1. The bank is eager to lend money to consumers.

2. Interest rates on car loans at this bank have gone down.

3. This bank is advertising borrowing (credit) in much the same way as clothing stores advertise clothing.

4. The interest rates at this bank are the lowest in town.

5. These consumers have shopped around for the lowest interest rates for loans.

6. This bank offers free gifts to its customers.

7. Consumers would be better off doing business elsewhere.

✔ *Using the Internet*

You can learn more about credit and credit cards at the Website <<http://www.studentcredit.com/learn.htm>>. Of particular interest is a section on credit card vocabulary. Also see how to determine how much credit you can afford, the difference between an account balance and minimum payment on a credit card monthly statement, and where and how to find out what information credit bureaus have compiled on you.

CHAPTER *13*

Insurance and Financial Protection

🔑 *Key Terms*		
risk	straight-life	motor vehicle
insurance	insurance	insurance
policy	20-payment life	no-fault
policyholder	insurance	insurance
beneficiary	health insurance	homeowner's
premium	major medical	insurance
insurance claim	insurance	renter's
insurance agent	property	insurance
lawsuit	insurance	extended
term life	liability	coverage
insurance	insurance	cash value

Tricia Johnson smashed her car into a new sports car last Saturday night. The driver of the sports car is suing Tricia for $150,000 for personal injury and property damage.

Because their house was badly damaged in a fire, the Marshes are temporarily living with relatives. A short circuit in the wiring of their home had started an electrical fire. Luckily, no one was hurt.

Everyone was shocked when they heard about Ed Jones. Imagine, only 43 and dead from a sudden heart attack. Arlene Jones and the two girls still cannot believe it. The funeral is Friday.

What will happen to Tricia Johnson? She does not have $150,000—or even $20,000. What can the Marshes do? Their house was still not paid for, and they have so many other bills. With Ed Jones gone, what will happen to Arlene and the children? Her salary will not cover all of the family's monthly expenses.

As you read this chapter, it will become clear to you that the answers to these questions depend upon whether the people we have mentioned are insured, upon the kind of insurance they have, and upon the amount of their insurance. You will also be able to answer the following questions:

- How may insurance provide financial protection?
- What kind of insurance do you need?
- How can you insure your life, your health, and your property?

HOW MAY INSURANCE PROVIDE FINANCIAL PROTECTION?

Insurance and Risk-Sharing

You may frequently hear people say, "Your life and property are precious—protect them." Well, how *do* you protect your life and property? Each day of our lives, at work or at play, we face all sorts of *risks*—chances that we may suffer some harm or loss. Tricia and the Marshes suffered damage to or loss of their property. Ed Jones lost his life. We may lose our health and then need money for doctors' bills, medicines, and hospital expenses. When we grow old, we may lose our ability to work and earn a living.

This is where insurance comes in. Insurance cannot prevent from happening any of the events just mentioned. But it can help us meet the financial burdens that follow. *Insurance* is a way of protecting ourselves and others against money losses. Tricia cannot possibly pay $150,000. And the Marshes do not have the money to pay for repairs on their house. Fortunately, Tricia and the Marshes are insured. They will not have to pay out of their own pockets for the damages and the expenses they incurred. Their insurance will cover all, or part, of their losses.

Insurance is a cooperative, risk-sharing plan. In buying insurance, many people join together to share the risk of losses. Each insured person thus avoids becoming responsible for a big financial burden if he or she should have a loss. Millions of drivers, such as Tricia, and homeowners, such as the Marshes, pay a small sum of money regularly to an *insurance company*, a risk-sharing group.

Not everyone who puts money into an insurance plan is going to be in an auto accident or lose a home in a fire. We buy motor vehicle insurance, but we may never have an accident. And we buy fire insurance for our home, but we may never have a fire. The insurance company may never have to dip into its "pool" of money to pay for our losses because we may never have any losses. Thus, insurance is like an umbrella. While an umbrella protects us when it rains, insurance protects individuals when a financial loss occurs.

Accidents and Unexpected Losses: How do these pictures show the need for insurance to cover accidents and unexpected losses in people's lives?

Obtaining Insurance

When individuals obtain insurance, they sign a contract called a *policy*. The buyer is called the *policyholder*. Life insurance policies have *beneficiaries*, the people who are to be paid in the event of a policyholder's death. With homeowner's or renter's insurance, the policyholder is the person to be paid in case of a fire or other damage to a home. With motor vehicle policies, the insurance company may agree to pay other persons not named in the policy to cover losses described in the policy. Such was the situation when Tricia had her auto accident.

The insurance company's promise to pay upon loss is given in return for the policyholder's agreement to pay a *premium* to the company. A premium is the amount of money that goes into the "pool" that we mentioned earlier. The sum is agreed to in advance, and it is usually paid in installments, either on a yearly or a quarterly basis. Then, if the insured persons are in an accident or have a fire or other loss, they file an *insurance claim* with the company. The claim states the loss, damage, or injury that occurred.

WHAT KIND OF INSURANCE DO YOU NEED?

Insurance is part of good money management. You buy insurance to fit your own individual needs. You do not need motor vehi-

Insurance is like an umbrella that shelters people from unforeseen, unexpected, or inevitable changes.

Personal and Family Insurance: These people are reviewing their insurance needs with their insurance agent. How do our insurance needs change over time?

cle insurance if you do not own a motor vehicle. A young, single person has different insurance needs from a person who supports a family. The insurance needs of a young couple will also differ from the needs of an older couple. For example, as we grow older, our medical expenses often increase. Thus, we may need more health insurance to prepare for that possibility. The following table lists common risks that consumers face and the insurance programs that are designed to reduce the financial losses that may result.

People Reduce Financial Losses Through Insurance

Risk	Type of Insurance
Loss of life	Life insurance; Mortgage insurance
Accident; Illness	Accident insurance; Health insurance
Loss of job	Unemployment insurance
Old age	Social Security; Life insurance
Auto accident	Motor vehicle insurance
Fire; Theft	Homeowner's or renter's insurance; Fire and theft insurance
Lawsuit	Liability insurance

Insurance policies are fairly complicated. That is why you might buy insurance through an *insurance agent*. This person will usually select the company from which you will buy your insurance policy.

Sometimes it is less costly to buy insurance directly from an insurance company by answering advertisements in the mail, in newspapers and magazines, or elsewhere. Today, more and more consumers are using the Internet to learn about insurance companies and to compare and contrast costs and benefits of various policies. There are a number of Websites that conveniently provide all of the necessary information. Some Websites will help you search many different insurance companies to find a policy at, they claim, the lowest cost.

Buying insurance over the Internet should be approached the same way as you would buy any other product. Check several sites. Suppose a site recommends a policy that is sold by Company X. Do you know anything about that company? Probably not. But you can find out information about the financial status of Company X through one of several organizations that rate and analyze insurance companies. Among these are Moody's, AM Best, and the Fitch's Insurance Group. You may also contact your State Insurance Department. Ask them about the insurance company that is offering to sell you a policy. Remember that your policy is only as good as the company that has issued it.

For almost every possible risk we face in life, there is insurance that we can buy to reduce the money losses that we may incur. Remember, insurance does not do away with the risks we face. It only reduces the dollar cost to us resulting from losses or *lawsuits* (legal actions in court).

HOW CAN YOU INSURE YOUR LIFE, YOUR HEALTH, AND YOUR PROPERTY?

There are three basic types of insurance that you will want to know about. They are (1) life, (2) health, and (3) property and liability insurance.

Life Insurance

The main purpose of *life insurance* is financial protection for the policy's beneficiary (or beneficiaries). The policy provides for a specified amount of payment to the beneficiary upon the insured's death.

Life insurance may also be a means of forced savings. During each year that the policyholder pays premiums, the policy increases in *cash value*. The policyholder may borrow against this cash value or cancel the policy and receive a cash settlement. For example, the cash value of a $50,000 policy may be $997.60 after five years, $3,939.60 after ten years, and $8,575 after fifteen years.

There are two basic forms of life insurance: (1) term, and (2) straight-life.

1. *Term.* *Term insurance* is limited to a specific number of years, usually five. But a term policy can be renewed at a higher premium after the end of each term. Term insurance does not have a cash-in value. It is an ideal plan for someone who wants the maximum amount of life protection at the minimum cost over a limited period of time.

2. *Straight-Life.* *Straight-life insurance* costs more than term, but it also offers much more. It provides a forced saving by building a cash value. You can borrow against this cash value or allow it to accumulate. At some point, you may decide that you no longer need or want this life insurance. Then you can cash in your policy—receive its cash value. That is the "forced saving" part of straight-life insurance. Some people prefer buying term insurance instead (it is cheaper) and then investing on their own the difference between the two types of policies.

Straight-life insurance can offer another advantage over term insurance. You can select a policy whose premiums will cost the same each year for as long as you hold it.

Insurance companies also offer many variations of term and straight life. You can, for example, purchase a *20-payment life* policy. You make payments for 20 years, stop paying premiums, and continue to be insured for the remainder of your life. Or you can buy *decreasing-term life* insurance, paying the same premium each year but having the amount for which you are insured decline each year. Another option you have is to use the dividends that your policy pays each year to reduce your annual premium payments. As you can see, buying insurance is complicated—not something to be done casually.

Study the table and graph on page 200. The table shows the annual premium rates for three different $100,000 life insurance policies. Figure 13.1 indicates the dollar cash value for each type of insurance after the first year of the policy.

Let us suppose that Ed Jones had bought life insurance at age 40—three years prior to his unexpected heart attack and death. Ed could have bought a $100,000 five-year term policy for just $108 per year. But its price would go up every five years. The same amount of insurance in a straight-life policy would have cost $590 a year. Its price would *not* increase as he got older. If Ed had purchased a straight-life policy at a younger age—say at age 25— he would have had to pay only $206 per year.

Figure 13.1 Dollar Value of Three Types of Insurance

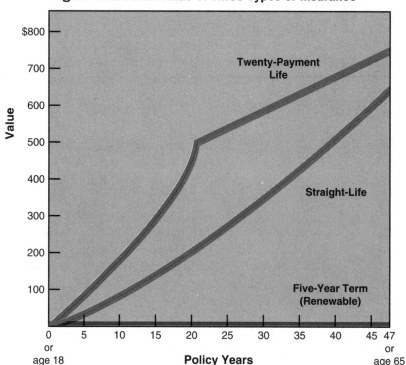

Sample Annual Costs per $100,000 Life Insurance Policies for a Male, Non-Smoker*

Taken at Age	Five-Year Term (renewable, convertible)	Straight-Life	20-Payment Life
Under 30	$36	$206	$406
30–34	54	309	510
35–39	84	481	590
40–44	108	590	800
45–50	156	722	N/A

Life insurance rates are higher for smokers than nonsmokers and lower for females than males. It is important to shop for insurance, as rates for similar policies vary among insurance companies and change from year to year. Rates shown are for comparative purposes only.

Because term insurance is at first so much cheaper than other types of life insurance, many young parents buy term to give themselves maximum protection while their children are growing up. Then they might drop the policy when the children are older and have moved out of the house.

Another reason for buying term insurance is to guarantee that mortgage payments will be made on an insured person's home in case of death, disability, or inability to make payments.

Suppose that Jack Stevens buys a home when he is 35 years old. Jack obtains a $100,000 mortgage from his bank for a 30-year period. The table on page 200 shows that buying a term policy at age 35 could cost Jack $84 a year to guarantee his $100,000 mortgage. When Jack is 50 years old, he will have paid off a big part of this mortgage. Perhaps he will still owe $50,000. A term policy when Jack is 50 would cost $78 (one-half of $156) a year for the $50,000 that he would still owe on the mortgage.

Jack's bank might offer him a decreasing-term life insurance policy. Jack would pay the same premium each year. But over the years, the amount of insurance would decrease as he paid off the mortgage.

Here are two questions to ask yourself when buying life insurance:

First, how much money will your family need to get along without you? Remember that you may have savings, investments, other insurance, and pension benefits. These will provide for some of your family's needs when you are gone. Life insurance can supply the rest.

Second, how much money can you afford to set aside each month to buy life insurance? Teenagers usually do not have much, if any, money with which to buy life insurance. And they may not need it, yet. Sometimes, parents start life insurance programs for their children. The parents continue making payments until the children become adults and can afford to take over the payments on their own. In fact, though, most people do not buy life insurance until they are married or have children.

Health Insurance

There are basically two types of *health insurance*. The first pays for various medical expenses. The second gives protection against loss of income while the insured is unable to work.

Ed Jones had a heart attack and died. But not all heart attacks are fatal. Had Ed lived, his medical expenses over the years would have been substantial. In addition, he would have had to remain out of work for several months. The following forms of health insurance protection would have reduced Ed's financial burden if he had lived:

Hospital covers many of the hospital costs such as room and board; drugs and medication taken in the hospital; general nursing care; use of operating room; and laboratory tests.

Surgical covers all or part of the surgeon's fee for operations, if needed.

Medical pays for doctor's services—other than surgery—in the hospital, at home, or in a doctor's office.

Major medical pays for all of the above once an established minimum has been reached. If Ed's medical bills were $10,000 and the rest of his policy paid up to $7,000, major medical insurance would have paid most of the remaining $3,000.

Loss of income pays monthly benefits to offset the loss of wages or other earnings because of extended illness or disability.

Today, many individuals and families have health insurance coverage through their workplace. Plans vary from one workplace to another. How much the worker contributes to the cost of the policy (if anything) will also vary. In most cases, however, the employee contributes a portion and the employer and/or union contributes the remainder of the cost.

Property and Liability Insurance

Property insurance provides financial protection against loss or damage to the insured person's property. Property, as you know, refers to something someone owns. We usually think of property as a tangible good such as a car, house, or piece of land.

Liability insurance provides financial protection to the insured for damages or injuries to other persons or damage to their property. It is a must today—for your home and your motor vehicle. A *liability* is a debt that must be paid. Liability insurance is very important to an owner or renter of a house or an apartment. For example, suppose a guest slips on the floor of your kitchen, or a worker falls off a ladder. You may be responsible for paying medical expenses and even loss of income to the injured party. Motor vehicle insurance and homeowner's insurance are the two most common types of property and liability insurance.

1. *Motor Vehicle Insurance.* Tricia Johnson's motor vehicle insurance provided the following coverage:

Bodily injury liability applies if Tricia's car injures or kills someone, whether that person was riding in her car or not.

Property damage liability applies when one auto damages another—as Tricia's car damaged the sports car. Tricia is also covered should her car damage other property such as a lamppost, fence, or storefront. Damage to Tricia's car is not covered under this category.

Collision applies to any damage caused to Tricia's car. Tricia's car sustained damage as a result of colliding with another car. Her collision coverage applies even if her vehicle hits another object or is damaged.

Medical covers medical bills that Tricia and members of her family might have incurred if they were injured while riding in her car. They are also covered while riding in someone else's car, or if they are struck by a car while walking. Anyone hurt while in Tricia's car is similarly covered.

Uninsured motorists coverage also protects Tricia and members of her immediate family. But here the protection is to cover cases in which an uninsured motorist or a hit-and-run driver is legally liable for the damages caused. An injured person is unlikely to collect damage from an uninsured motorist or a hit-and-run driver.

Comprehensive coverage protects Tricia from financial losses if her car is damaged as a result of fire, theft, glass breakage, falling objects, riot, or hitting an animal.

Many states (but not all) have *no-fault insurance* laws. These laws provide that each person's medical and hospital expenses will be paid by one's own insurance company *no matter who was responsible* for the accident. Sometimes, loss of income is also covered.

2. Homeowner's or Renter's Insurance. The Marshes' property is protected by a package policy called a *homeowner's policy.*

Aftermath of an Earthquake: Houses wrecked by a severe earthquake in San Francisco. Do you think that insurance against such natural disasters is included in a typical homeowner's insurance policy?

Each year, the Marshes pay a single premium that insures their property against a wide variety of perils, including fire, theft, and personal liability.

A standard fire insurance policy protects the insured for damages to the home and its contents resulting from fire and lightning only. *Extended coverage* broadens the policy to include damage from wind, hail, smoke, explosion, riot, vehicles, and falling aircraft. The losses to the Marshes' property that resulted from the electrical fire will be paid by the insurance company.

The Marshes are also covered for losses due to burglary or theft. In addition, should a visitor to their new home slip or fall and suffer injury, *personal liability* coverage will pay for any legal costs and for damages assessed against them up to the limits set by their policy.

People who rent apartments or houses can also purchase insurance for all the just-mentioned potential losses. This policy is called *renter's insurance.* Many renters, however, do not. Perhaps they think that the policies of the owners of the buildings will cover them. In many cases, they do not.

SUMMARY

Insurance is a way of protecting yourself and others against financial losses that result from illness, accident, death, fire, theft, and many other risks. While insurance does not prevent loss, it provides financial help when a loss occurs.

Insurance should be bought to fit the needs of the individual or family. There are three basic types of insurance—life, health, and property and personal liability insurance. Life insurance may be purchased solely for the protection of beneficiaries in case of death. It can also serve as a means of forced savings. Health insurance is a type of coverage that pays benefits in case of illness or injury. Property insurance provides financial protection against losses due to damages to the insured person's or family's property. Liability insurance protects against claims by others against the insured.

LOOKING AHEAD

In this chapter, we have discussed types of insurance that consumers may choose to buy. In some instances, an employer or union will provide some kinds of health and life insurance for workers. In addition to these forms of coverage, most of us will be covered by government insurance programs such as Social Security. These programs are discussed in the following chapter.

━━━━━━━━━━━━━━━━━━━ **EXERCISES** ━━━━━━━━━━━━━━━━━━

✔**Matching** Match each term in Column A with its definition in Column B.

Column A	Column B
1. insurance	*a.* covers losses due to windstorms, riots, or
2. risks	plane crashes
3. beneficiary	*b.* pays all or parts of hospital and medical bills
4. premium	*c.* automobile insurance that requires the insur-
5. cash value	ance company to pay damages no matter
6. policy	who was responsible
7. no-fault insur-	*d.* the chances that we may suffer harm or loss
ance	*e.* a way of protecting ourselves and others
8. personal liabil-	against financial loss
ity insurance	*f.* person who receives insurance money in the
9. extended cover-	event of the policyholder's death
age	*g.* the contract between the insured and the in-
10. health insurance	surance company
	h. a sum of money paid periodically to the insur-
	ance company
	i. the dollar value of a life insurance policy if
	turned in or used to borrow from
	j. provides protection against claims arising
	from injury on a homeowner's property

✔**Multiple Choice** Choose the letter of the item that best completes the statement or answers the question.

1. The main idea of this chapter is that insurance is (a) too expensive (b) a protection against financial loss (c) unnecessary (d) a guarantee against risks.

2. The person who buys an insurance policy in his or her own name is called the (a) agent (b) beneficiary (c) premium (d) policyholder.

3. Owning an accident insurance policy reduces the (a) costs involved in an accident (b) chances of having an accident (c) need for safety devices (d) financial losses to the insured resulting from an accident.

4. The least expensive $100,000 life insurance that a person can buy is called (a) term insurance (b) straight-life (c) major medical (d) 20-payment life.

5. According to the graph on page 200, the cash value of a straight-life policy purchased by an 18-year-old after 20 years is (a) $100 (b) $200 (c) $500 (d) $1,000.

6. According to the table on page 200, the premium for a $100,000 five-year term policy taken at age 18 is (a) $36 (b) $54 (c) $206 (d) $406.

7. Automobile insurance is an example of which kind of insurance? (a) life insurance (b) health insurance (c) travel insurance (d) property and liability insurance.

8. Which of the following insurance policies provides a means of saving as well as financial protection? (a) term (b) straight-life (c) motor vehicle (d) homeowner's.

✔**Thinking About Insurance** Can you explain each of the following?

1. Why it is less expensive for an 18-year-old to buy life insurance than it is for a 40-year-old. Why it is less expensive for a 40-year-old to buy motor vehicle insurance than it is for an 18-year-old.

2. Why some people prefer term insurance even though it does not have any cash-in value. Why other people prefer straight-life insurance even though it is more expensive than term.

3. Why it pays to buy fire insurance for your home even though you may never have a fire. Why a healthy person still needs health insurance.

4. Why it is important for homeowners, those who rent, and owners of motor vehicles to have liability insurance.

✔*Using the Internet*

The following Websites will help you to determine the costs of various types of insurance:
<<http://www.allquotesinsurance.com>>
<<http://www.budgetlife.com>>
<<http://www.insuranceanywhere.com>>
<<http://www.insurance.com>>
<<http://www.insweb.com>>
<<http://www.IntelliQuote.com>>
<<http://www.quotesmith.com>>

For checking up on insurance companies, go to one of the following Websites:
<<http://ambest.com>>
<<http://www.moodys.com>>
<<http://www.standardandpoors.com>>

CHAPTER 14
Social Insurance

In the previous chapter, we learned how insurance helps people to protect themselves, their families, and their property against certain risks. But most people cannot afford, or are unable to buy, all of the insurance they need to cover every risk. This is why nearly every country in the world today provides some kind of insurance to protect its citizens. Having a *Social Security* number proves that you are enrolled in the United States social insurance system.

In this chapter, you will learn more about the nation's social insurance programs. When you have finished your reading, you will be able to answer the following questions:

- Why should you apply for a Social Security number?
- What benefits are provided by Social Security programs?
- How do social insurance and private insurance programs work together?

WHY SHOULD YOU APPLY FOR A SOCIAL SECURITY NUMBER?

There are a number of very good reasons for obtaining your own Social Security number. Here are some of them.

Once you have enrolled in the Social Security program, you and your dependents will be entitled to receive its benefits. Consider the following story.

Sue Warwick and Frank McFee were high school sweethearts. Just about a year after their graduation from high school, they married. Both worked for two years, and then Sue gave birth to a girl. Three years later, she gave birth to a boy. The Warwick-McFees were a happy family. Frank had a good job, and they had two lovely children—a boy and a girl. Then tragedy struck. Frank was killed in an automobile accident. He had just turned 25 years old.

At the time of his death, Frank was earning $2,500 a month. He had not earned enough *work credits* to be fully insured under Social Security. As you work and pay taxes, you earn Social Security "credits" up to a maximum of four credits a year. Most people need 40 credits, that is, at least ten years of work, to qualify for benefits. Frank had been working and paying Social Security taxes even while he was in high school but he had not earned 40 credits by the time of his death. Fortunately for Frank's family, though, people who die need to have accumulated fewer than 40 credits for their families to be eligible for survivor's benefits. Frank had enough credits for this. Thus, Frank's wife and children will receive $1,874 a month in benefits— about 75 percent of Frank's monthly earnings.

Most employers require that you provide them with your Social Security number even if the job that you have is only a part-time one.

You will also need a Social Security number in order to open a bank account in your own name. This is true whether you open an account yourself or someone else opens one for you.

Most health, accident, and life insurance policies require that beneficiaries—those who are to receive benefits—be identified by their Social Security numbers.

Many high schools require Social Security numbers as a means of identifying their students.

Recently, the federal government revised its income tax laws. Taxpayers must now list on their federal income tax returns the Social Security numbers of all persons—including children five years and older—who are claimed as dependents.

Applying for a Social Security Number

You can apply for a Social Security number and card at any Social Security office. You can also apply in person or by mail. Applica-

Landmark Social Security Act: In 1935, President Franklin D. Roosevelt signed the Social Security Act into law. It was the first U.S. act to provide income insurance for Americans.

tions are available on the Internet at <<http://www.ssa.gov>>. Once you have a Social Security number, it is yours for life. Your Social Security number represents an insurance policy, and it is all yours.

The Social Security Act of 1935

In 1935, the United States was in the middle of the Great Depression. It was the worst economic setback in U.S. history. In the 1930s, businesses failed in record numbers, and unemployment rose to all-time highs. In response, Congress in 1935 passed the Social Security Act. The law's purpose was to help several groups of people who were in need of economic assistance. Since its passage, the Social Security Act has been expanded several times. One or more of its programs now protects almost everyone in the United States.

The Social Security Act relies upon two strategies to help the public in time of need. One of these is social insurance. The other is public welfare.

1. Social Insurance. Any form of insurance that is provided by the government is known as *social insurance*. Both the people who are covered by social insurance and their employers contribute to the cost of the program. If someone is self-employed, that person has to pay the whole cost of the insurance.

2. Public Welfare. Some government programs aid people in need who, for whatever reason, are not covered by the insurance programs of the Social Security Act. These programs are classified as *public welfare*. The purpose of this chapter is to focus on social insurance programs. In Chapter 38, we will discuss public welfare programs.

WHAT BENEFITS ARE PROVIDED BY SOCIAL SECURITY PROGRAMS?

Social Security benefits are paid to people who have contributed to the programs during their working years (or to their dependents). These programs provide the following benefits.

1. Pensions and medical care are provided for the elderly and the disabled.
2. Monthly payments are made to the widows and children of workers who have died or have become disabled.
3. Under the unemployment insurance program, benefits are paid to workers who have lost their jobs.
4. Benefits are paid to people who are unable to work because of illness or accident.

Let us take a closer look at the insurance programs associated with Social Security.

Old Age, Survivors, Disability, and Health Insurance (OASDHI)

1. Retired Workers. A monthly pension is provided for workers 62 years of age and older who have retired from their jobs. Max Milton has been working since he was 17. Now that he is going to turn 66, he has decided to retire. Max will receive a monthly pension retirement benefit of $1,342 from the Social Security Administration. In addition, Max and his wife, Irene, have an IRA (discussed in Chapter 11) and a savings account. When added together, these funds will provide Max and Irene with a comfortable retirement.

2. Survivors. A monthly pension is provided for the survivors of deceased workers (widows and widowers and children under

Benefits of Social Insurance
Millions of Americans—retired
persons, children, and those with
special needs—are aided by
government social insurance
programs.

Figure 14.1 Medicare Card

age 18). At the time of his retirement, Max Milton and his wife were in good health. Nevertheless, it was reassuring for him to know that his wife would continue to receive a portion of his Social Security benefits if he were to die before her.

3. Disabled Workers. A monthly disability check is provided for disabled workers and their dependents. There are no age restrictions on disability insurance. All members of the Social Security system are eligible for these benefits if they have worked for certain minimum periods of time. But the disability must have existed for at least a year before the person is eligible.

4. Health Insurance. Medicare provides hospital and medical care benefits to people age 65 or older and to disabled persons under 65 years of age already covered by Social Security.

Jane Cooper, age 67, was told by her doctor that she needs an operation. Jane and her husband, Fred, have both been retired for several years and receive Social Security retirement checks. Their employers' medical plans had stopped when Jane and Fred retired.

Jane Cooper can have her operation. Medicare *hospital insurance* begins at age 65, even for workers who do not retire. Most, if not all, of Jane's hospital bills will be paid by Medicare.

In addition, the Coopers signed up for another of Medicare's benefits: *medical insurance.* In exchange for a small monthly payment, or premium, medical insurance helps pay bills for doctors' services and other medical needs. Jane Cooper's doctor has agreed to accept Medicare payments as payment in full for services.

Unemployment Insurance

The *unemployment insurance* program pays benefits to workers who have lost their jobs. Although the federal government created the program, it is now run by the states. Employers, who contribute a percentage of their payroll to the state-operated fund, pay the cost of the program.

The amount and duration of unemployment benefits vary from state to state and year to year. In a recent year, the average weekly benefit was $262, with payments made for 13 weeks.

When the Three-Star Plywood Company laid off 25 percent of its workforce, Barbara Henderson lost her job. Barbara is willing to return to work whenever she can find a job. In the meantime, she needs money for everyday family expenses.

Barbara went to her state unemployment office and reported that she was out of a job and looking for work. Until she finds another position, Barbara will receive $215 a week for a maximum of 26 weeks.

Workers' Compensation and Disability Benefits

Most states require employers to insure their workers for *workers' compensation*. If a worker is injured, in any way disabled, or killed because of a work-connected accident, the worker or the worker's family may be entitled to benefits. Workers' compensation benefits are paid only to those who are injured in accidents that happen *on the job*. Consequently, some states also require that employers provide disability benefits. The disability insurance program pays cash benefits to workers who are disabled by off-the-job accidents or illnesses. Workers receive these payments for a limited period of time.

State Unemployment Office: People looking for work check listings of jobs in their fields.

HOW DO SOCIAL INSURANCE AND PRIVATE INSURANCE WORK TOGETHER?

Social Security and all the other social insurance programs were never meant to replace personal savings and private insurance. In many instances, however, social insurance is the only protection people have against loss of income caused by unemployment, disability, sickness, and old age. Taken together, social insurance, savings, and private insurance can provide a *complete* approach to financial planning for most families. This is illustrated in the table below:

Private and Government Insurance Programs

Problem or Condition	Private Programs	Government Programs
Unemployment	Savings	Unemployment insurance
Old Age	Savings; Insurance; IRA; Pension; 401(k) plan	Social Security pensions
Death	Life insurance; Savings	Social Security survivors' benefits
Illness	Health insurance; Savings	Medicare; Public hospitals and clinics
Disability	Insurance; Savings	Social Security; Workers' compensation; Disability benefits

Understanding Economics

THE SOCIAL SECURITY SYSTEM IN CRISIS?

Figure 14.2 Social Security Card

The Social Security Trust Fund is a "pay-as-you-go" system. The money that goes into the fund is used to pay for the benefits received. At this time, the payroll tax money going into the fund is greater than the benefits that are currently owed. However, as the number of retirees grows relative to the number of workers who contribute to the fund, it is feared that outflows from the trust fund will eventually be greater than inflows into the trust fund.

In 2005, for each Social Security recipient there were 3.2 workers contributing to the system. As the U.S. population ages, it is estimated that by the year 2030 there will only be 2.1 workers contributing money into the fund for each recipient. At this point, then, the Social Security System may go broke. Can anything be done to save the system?

There are any number of proposals to reform the system. Each is highly controversial.

1. Increase the age at which retirees can collect full benefits. (This is already being done. The age is gradually being raised from 65 to 67. Some people want the age to be increased still further.)

2. Decrease the annual cost-of-living increase. It now is tied to the inflation rate.

3. Increase Social Security tax rates on high-income workers, raise the ceiling on wages to be taxed, and cut benefits for high-income retirees.

4. *Privatize* Social Security. This proposal is the most controversial. Basically the idea is to let workers divert all or part of their payroll tax into individual accounts. The worker could then pick among investments such as stocks and mutual funds, the income from which will go into the individual's account. The assumption is that the stock market and other investments will provide a better return than the current system, which relies on interest from federal bonds. Each individual investor, not the government, would choose a private financial service firm to make her or his investments.

Those in Favor of Privatization Say:

1. The system, if it continues in its present direction, will eventually run out of money and, therefore, must be changed anyway.

2. According to its proponents, including President George W. Bush, workers will have more money available to them upon retirement than under the present system.

3. Initially, less money will be going into the Social Security Trust Fund as dollars are diverted into individual accounts. Eventually, though, everyone will be enrolled fully in the individual accounts program. There will no longer be a need for the "Old Age" in the federal Old Age, Survivors, Disability, and Health Insurance program. The present pay-as-you-go plan would be replaced by a system of individual accounts. This would lead to an "ownership society" in which every worker has a stake in society.

4. A modification of the privatization proposal is to have the federal government invest some Social Security funds in the stock market rather than just in federal bonds (as they do now). Many state employee pension funds are already invested in the private stock and bond markets. Members of these state pension programs may choose whether they want their investments entirely in stocks or bonds, or some combination of both. The decision as to which stocks or bonds to purchase, however, is made by a professional group under the supervision of the state pension fund managers.

Critics of Privatization Say:

1. Privatization is risky, and the worker bears the burden of risk. The stock market is uncertain. Stocks can go down as well as up. There is no guarantee that private accounts will earn more than the present system. The worker's contribution is based upon earnings, but the ultimate benefit would depend upon investment returns. The worker would bear the risk of shortfalls in returns in his or her individual account. The result might be a reduced pension. The Social Security pension plan was designed to diffuse risk among all workers and across generations. Its benefit formula is fixed. The only risk is that elected officials may change benefits or required contributions.

2. Less money would be going into the Social Security Trust Fund as dollars are directed into individual accounts. Money diverted from the Trust Fund would increase the fund's future shortfall for paying retirees. This gap would have to be made up by having the government either borrow to fill the gap, increase interest on the government debt, or increase taxes.

3. Administrative expenses for maintaining the individual accounts would be high and would be passed on to individual enrolees, thereby reducing the returns to each individual account.

4. The greatest beneficiaries of privatization would be the financial enterprises selling products for individual accounts.

SUMMARY

The Social Security system provides retirement benefits for persons 62 years and older, health and hospital care (Medicare) for persons 65 and older, and survivors' benefits and disability benefits for people of any age. State programs insure workers against loss of income due to unemployment or disability. Social Security was designed to work with private insurance and savings programs. There is concern that the Social Security System will eventually be paying out more in benefits than it receives in payroll taxes. Proposals to change the present Social Security System are controversial.

LOOKING AHEAD

The word "economy" comes from an ancient Greek word that means the management of a household's income and spending. So managing one's income has been a problem that people have faced since ancient times. In our next chapter, you will see that managing your income is something that you can learn to do.

---------------------------- **EXERCISES** ----------------------------

✔**Matching** Match each term in Column A with its definition in Column B.

Column A	**Column B**
1. social insurance	*a.* a program that pays cash benefits to persons who are injured or disabled by a job-related accident
2. Social Security	
3. unemployment insurance	
	b. a program that pays cash benefits to people who cannot work because of illness or an accident that occurred off the job
4. workers' compensation	
5. disability insurance	*c.* a program that pays monthly pensions to persons 62 years old and over who no longer work
6. Medicare	*d.* a program that provides hospital and medical benefits to elderly and disabled persons
7. survivors' insurance	*e.* any form of insurance provided by a government
8. retirement insurance	*f.* the United States social insurance program
	g. a program that provides cash payments to widows and widowers and children of deceased workers
	h. a program that provides cash benefits for a limited time to people who have lost their jobs

✔*Understanding a Salary and Deductions Statement*

Below is an employee's statement of salary and deductions, such as you might receive with your paycheck at the end of a pay period. Examine the statement and then answer the questions that follow.

Employee's Statement of Salary and Deductions

Soc. Sec. No.	Regular	Overtime	Rate	Gross Pay
095–27–2360	40 hrs.	5 hrs.	$6.00 (R) 9.00 (OT)	$285.00

FICA	FWT	SWT	MED
$17.67	$38.25	$12.80	$4.13

Union Dues	U.S. Savings Bonds	Pension	Net Pay
$ 4.20	$ 5.00	$7.50	$195.45

Notes: FICA is the deduction for Social Security. FWT is the deduction for federal withholding tax. SWT is the deduction for state withholding tax. MED is the deduction for Medicare.

1. How many hours did this employee work during the pay period?

2. If the employee earned $240 for regular time and a total of $285 for the entire week, how much was earned for overtime? What was the hourly overtime rate?

3. What was the employee's actual take-home pay this week?

4. What was the total amount deducted from this employee's paycheck?

5. How much of the employee's payroll deductions went for savings and insurance programs? Explain how you figured your answer.

6. How much of the employee's payroll deductions went for taxes? Explain how you figured your answer.

7. How much was deducted for Social Security (FICA)?

✔ *Understanding What You Have Read*

Base your answers on what you have read in this chapter. On a separate sheet of paper, write **T** if the statement is true. If the statement is false, write **F** and explain why it is incorrect.

1. A young person has no need for a Social Security number.

2. A Social Security number is needed to open a bank account.

3. Two or more people often have the same Social Security number.

4. The Social Security program provides monthly pensions for retired workers.

5. Medical benefits are not provided under Social Security.

6. Unemployment insurance is provided for those workers who are laid off from their jobs.

✔ *Using the Internet*

1. The Social Security Administration has an Internet site <<http://www.ssa.gov/>>. At this site, you can compute your estimated Social Security benefits as well as learn much more about the Social Security System.

2. You can learn more about Medicare benefits on the Internet site <<http://www.medicare.gov/>>.

3. You should also know that health insurance is provided for children through the Children's Health Insurance Program (CHIP). CHIP maintains a Website <<http://www.insurekidsnow.gov/>> that provides state-specific information on who is eligible and how to enroll children in this program.

15

Personal Finance: Making the Most of Your Money

Key Terms

financial plan	fixed expense	surplus
short-term goal	variable expense	balanced budget
long-term goal	deficit	money manager
budget	income	

    Three friends collect weekly paychecks from their after-school jobs. But for reasons they cannot quite understand, all three often run short.

    Lisa Perrotti loves to shop—especially for new clothes. There have been times, she will tell you, when she has spent every cent of her paycheck on the day that she got it. She has a lot of trouble making it from one payday to the next.

    Like Lisa, Jack Edwards rarely has spending money. He has been hiding about half of his pay in a box hidden away in his closet. When he has enough set aside, he will buy a car. Meanwhile, he has been unable to afford many of the pleasures his friends enjoy. But he does spend a lot of time visiting used car lots. "It doesn't cost anything to look and dream," he says.

    Unlike her friends Lisa and Jack, Flora Millin always seems to have money with her. But Flora has neglected to save money for any big-ticket items. For example, she will not be able to afford the trip to the Grand Canyon that she so much wanted to take after graduation.

    Lisa, Jack, and Flora would have had fewer problems if they had done a little planning about saving and spending their money. This chapter will introduce you to the elements of financial planning. It will also show you how to prepare a plan of your own. Of course, you do not have to be a teenager to benefit from financial planning. Once learned, the principles described in this chapter will apply long after you have left high school.

After reading this chapter, you will be able to explain what a financial plan is. You will also be able to:

- Define your financial goals.
- Prepare a budget.
- Explain the value of setting aside savings regularly.
- Explain why career planning, investments, insurance, and credit are also part of financial planning.

WHAT IS A FINANCIAL PLAN?

A *financial plan* is a kind of road map of your financial future. It shows you how to achieve your financial goals. By following the steps described below, you should be able to tailor a plan especially suited to your needs. These are:

1. Define those personal goals that will cost money.

2. Determine the cost of achieving these goals and a plan for obtaining the necessary money.

3. Prepare a budget.

4. Set aside savings.

5. Invest wisely.

6. Buy necessary insurance.

7. Shop wisely and use credit wisely.

HOW DOES ONE DEFINE FINANCIAL GOALS?

You may have heard the saying, "If you don't know where you want to go, you won't know how to get there." The same applies to financial planning.

Setting personal goals involves identifying what it is that you would like to do in the future—in both the long term and the short term. Most of your goals will probably involve spending money, such as, "What would I like to acquire with my money this year? in the years to come?" Goal-setting gives you targets to shoot at. It is part of your financial plan.

Part-Time Jobs: An after-school or a weekend job is often a teenager's major source of income. What are some other advantages of having a part-time job? How might holding a job during the school year be difficult for a student?

Short-Term Goals

Short-term goals are those that you would like to achieve in a year or less. Would you like to vacation out of town, buy an expensive item of clothing, or purchase a piece of electronic equipment? If you could save the money that you would need to pay for these things in a year or less, we would call them *short-term goals*.

Long-Term Goals

Goals that will take you more than a year to achieve are *long-term goals*. An automobile of your own and going to a post-secondary school are the kinds of long-term goals that high school students might be thinking about. As you grow older and leave high school, some of those former "long-term goals" become the short-term variety.

As you grow older and your lifestyle changes, new goals will come forward. It is then that some people begin to think about getting married, setting up a home, and having children. Then later, as the life cycle proceeds, the long-term goals of middle age will need to be attended to. Here your financial plan may include funds to care for elderly family members, money for insurance to protect your family against risks, money to pay for your children's education, and funds for your own retirement.

Like those earlier long-term goals, it will take careful planning and years of saving and investment to achieve them.

In thinking about your goals, it is useful to set time limits. While you are at it, you might also want to draw up a "goals worksheet" to help you see what it would take to achieve them.

Goals Worksheet

Short-Term Goals	Cost	Completion Date	Saving From Income Needed per Month
Example: Vacation*	$1,200	12 months	$100

Long-Term Goals	Cost	Completion Date	Savings Needed per Month
Example: Used car **	$3,000	36 months	$83.33

If your goal is to take a vacation in 12 months that will cost $1,200, you will need to save $100 per month.

**If your goal is to buy a used car for as much as $3,000 in three years, you will need to save $83.33 per month. You may be able to borrow the money and pay off the loan in monthly installments. But this method will cost you more because you will have the added cost of interest payments.*

Identifying your goals is an important first step in the process of financial planning. It is time now to move on to creating a plan to achieve them.

HOW DOES ONE PREPARE A BUDGET?

A *budget* is a financial plan that summarizes income and expenditures over a period of time.

While the period of time covered by a personal budget might be as little as a week or as long as a year, most are planned on a monthly basis. Creating a budget gives you an idea of where you stand financially. It tells you what your overall income is. It shows your total expenses. After creating a budget, you will know how much you can save or how much you will be going in debt each month.

Budgeting need not be a complicated process. Indeed, by following simple steps, you will be able to prepare a monthly budget of your own.

Determine One's Financial Situation

As a first step in preparing a budget, write down every purchase you make and everything you earn in the course of a month. Then organize the results in a "budget worksheet." Recording your income and expenses in this way will help you to (1) see if you are living beyond your means, (2) find problem areas, and (3) know how much you can set aside in savings.

The budget process is illustrated in the example on the next page, as Dana Smith prepares a budget worksheet.

Review and Revise the Budget Worksheet

In completing a budget worksheet, Dana discovered a problem. She has a *deficit*. Her total expenses are greater than her total income. She was either spending too much or earning too little. If she continues in this way month after month, she will not be able to save money. And without saving money, she cannot achieve many of her goals.

Let us review Dana's budget worksheet.

1. Current Monthly Income. If one has a job, a portion of this person's wages is usually deducted to pay things like taxes, health benefits, and other obligations. As you can learn from Dana's budget worksheet, $55 in withholding taxes was deducted from Dana's monthly salary. You should familiarize yourself with what is being deducted from your wages, and why. This is important because it

Personal Economics

PREPARING A MONTHLY BUDGET

Dana Smith, a high school senior, recorded in a notebook every dollar she received and spent during the month of January. The following is a summary of the entries in Dana's notebook:

- Part-time job at a fast-food restaurant: income $590; minus $55 deducted for Social Security, Medicare, unemployment compensation, and income taxes
- Monthly allowance: $100
- Monthly payment on a loan from parents: $48
- Restaurants: $105
- Skiing, 4 days @ $50 per day: $200
- Haircuts: $30
- Computer Club membership dues: $10
- Bus fare to job: $45
- Movies, arcade, and other entertainment expenses: $110
- American Red Cross: $20
- Daily newspaper and magazine subscriptions: $30
- Computer programs: $95

Dana entered the data in a budget worksheet, as follows:

Budget Worksheet for the Month of January

Current Monthly Income

Wages/Salary	$ 590.00
less withholding:	$ 55.00
(=) Net wages	$ 535.00
(+) Other (monthly allowance)	$ 100.00
(=) Total income	$ 635.00

Current Monthly Expenses	**Fixed**		**Variable**
Club dues	$ 10.00	Entertainment	$ 110.00
Haircuts	$ 30.00	Charity	$ 20.00
Carfare	$ 45.00	Restaurants (7 times)	$ 105.00
Subscriptions	$ 30.00	Vacation (4 ski trips)	$ 200.00
Other (loan)	$ 48.00	Other (computer programs)	$ 95.00
Total fixed	$163.00	Total variable	$ 530.00
		= Total Monthly Expenses	$ 693.00

Financial Summary

Total Income	$ 635.00
(−) Total Expenses	$ 693.00

(=) Surplus or Deficit * $ 58.00 deficit

* If spending is less than income, the difference is a surplus. If the opposite is true, it is a deficit.

may be possible to reduce the withholding for income taxes. This amount depends on your earnings, and the number of exemptions you claim. In many instances, young workers can increase their take-home pay by claiming the one exemption to which they are entitled. Fifty-five dollars was deducted from Dana's wages because Dana had not claimed any exemptions. If, instead, Dana had claimed one exemption, only $19 would have been withheld rather than $55.

2. *Current Monthly Expenses*. The money spent last month is summarized under the category of "Current Monthly Expenses." Some expenses, like carfare, rent, and payments on a loan recur every month. These are listed under the category of *fixed expenses*. Others may vary from one month to the other. These are *variable expenses*. It is the variable expenses one should work at reducing if one wants to save money for future purchases.

3. *Financial Summary*. This section will tell you whether your budget is balanced, showing a surplus, or running a deficit. A *deficit* budget is one in which spending is greater than income. In order to spend more than one earns, it is necessary to make up the difference out of either savings or credit. A variety of credit alternatives are discussed in Chapter 12.

A *balanced budget* is one in which income equals spending. A *surplus* occurs whenever spending is less than the income. In such a budget, the difference between the income and the the amount spent is the surplus. Surpluses may be set aside in some form of savings or investment. A discussion of savings and investment alternatives is found in Chapter 11.

In reviewing your worksheet, you will want to look for ways to eliminate deficits and increase the size of your surpluses. This is especially important if you want to achieve those short-term and long-term goals that you identified earlier on. In this illustration, Dana Smith had a budget deficit of $58. Note: In this example, Dana can have a budget surplus by reducing the number of ski trips to three and restaurant visits to six, while keeping all other expenditures at the same level.

Trade-Offs, Opportunity Costs, and Financial Goals

Let us say that you have recently received $100.00. Also assume that one of your goals is to add to your savings, while another is to spend $100 on clothing. If you put the money in an account that pays 5 percent interest, you would have $105.00 at the end of the year. If instead you spent the $100 on clothing, you would not have the $105. But you would have some new things to wear. Which will you choose, the savings deposit or the clothing?

It is your choice, but whichever you choose will involve a trade-off. If you decide to buy clothing, you will be trading it off against a deposit to your savings account. If you deposit the money in a savings account, you will be trading it off against buying the clothing.

Every trade-off has a cost. The cost is the opportunity that was lost when one choice was made over another. Economists refer to these as opportunity costs. If you chose to spend your $100 on clothing, the opportunity cost of that decision by the year's end would be $105. If you chose to save the $100, the opportunity cost would be the dollar value of the satisfaction you would have received from owning the new clothing.

You have set your goals, estimated your fixed and variable expenses, identified savings targets, and prepared a budget. Now it is time to put your plan to work. Give your budget a few months to see how things work out. Were you able to save as much as you planned? If not, look over those variable expenses and see where you might be able to cut back.

Try, too, to be a smart shopper. In Chapter 9, we described a number of things you can do to get more for your money.

WHAT IS THE VALUE OF SETTING ASIDE SAVINGS?

It is difficult to set aside money that you could spend now in order to save it for some time in the future. But difficult as it may be, savings are the key to meeting your financial goals. By way of making it easier to postpone spending, many authorities advise that you treat savings as a fixed expense. One way to do that is to

Family Budget Planning: Each person in a family makes his or her needs felt when the family sits down to plan its budget. Which needs must be budgeted for first?

Figure 15.1 Household Expenses for an Average Family

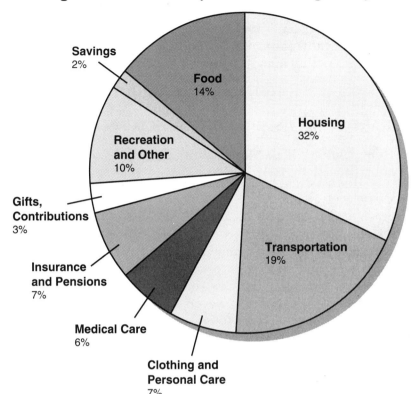

write yourself a check or deposit a specific amount to your savings account at the beginning of each month. It is a good habit to acquire, but it will take a little effort.

In Chapter 11, we saw that because of the effect of compound interest, savings can grow well beyond the amount set aside. This is illustrated in the table below.

Effect of Compound Interest on Deposit of $100 a Month

Interest Rate	Year 5	Year 10	Year 15	Year 20	Year 25
4%	$ 6,630	$14,725	$24,609	$36,677	$51,413
5%	6,801	15,528	26,729	41,103	59,551
6%	6,977	16,388	29,082	46,204	69,299
7%	7,159	17,308	31,696	52,093	81,007
8%	7,348	18,295	34,604	58,902	94,769
9%	7,542	19,351	37,841	66,789	118,779

How long will it take for your savings to double? Apply the *"Rule of 72"* Take the interest you are earning on your money and divide that number into 72. The result is roughly the number of years it will take your *principal*—the money you started out with—to double.

As illustrated by the table above, the greater the interest rate, the greater will be the effect of compounding on one's savings deposit. For that reason, it pays to shop around for the most advantageous place to deposit your savings. Savings alternatives such as savings accounts, money market funds, and government bonds were described in Chapter 11.

WHAT ARE OTHER ASPECTS OF FINANCIAL PLANNING?

Investing: Making Your Money Work For You

Some financial goals take a long time to achieve. A post-high school education, marriage, and a home of your own are but a few of the things that you may want to start saving for well in advance of the fact. But putting all your savings in a savings account will probably not generate enough money for you to reach those goals. For those purposes, you may want to consider investing in financial vehicles such as savings bonds, mutual funds, and other securities. They will help your money grow even more over the long term.

Many of the options open to investors were described in Chapter 11. We would remind you, however, that not all investments will make money. And some are very risky. So remember, *caveat emptor* ("buyer beware").

Choosing and Preparing For a Career

There was a time when a high school diploma and a willingness to work were all that most people needed to find a job and start a career. Not so anymore. In today's job market, employers expect both a good education and some extra preparation in the way of job knowledge and skills.

Like getting the most for your money, it takes a certain amount of "shopping around" and effort to make a wise career choice. It is good to know beforehand (1) which career fields offer the best opportunities, and (2) how you can acquire the skills that businesses and organizations in that field want from their employees.

For starters, you might want to read Chapter 16. It has many fine suggestions on how to go about choosing a career.

Managing Risk With and Without Insurance

"Risk management" involves identifying what risks you and your family are exposed to and what you can do to manage them. "Risks" include things like loss of life, accident, illnesses, damage to property, and personal liability.

Once you have identified the risks, you should try to eliminate or reduce them. Things like better door locks can reduce the risk of burglary. A healthful diet can reduce the risk of illnesses. But some risks simply cannot be avoided or controlled. They can, however, be transferred to a third party by purchasing insurance.

As described in Chapter 13, insurance enables many people and institutions in similar circumstances to share the cost of specific risks. Good financial planning calls for the budgeting of some money for buying insurance.

Shopping Smart and Paying Smart

You will often get more for your money if you pay cash whenever possible. Interest charges for loans and credit purchases add to the cost of your purchases. Of course, for certain major purchases, you may need to borrow money.

Using Credit Cards, Charge Cards, ATM Cards, and Debit Cards

1. Credit Cards. Sooner or later, you will probably want to apply for a credit card. Using credit cards is a convenient way to buy goods and services. Here again, it pays to shop carefully. There is a wide range of annual fees, interest rates, late fee charges, and other fees that can make it very costly to use a credit card.

MasterCard, Visa, and Discover are "revolving-credit" cards. You can charge up to a certain limit. As long as you pay a minimum amount each month, you can continue to use the card. If you pay in full and on time each month, then there will be no interest charge. Because of interest charges, it can be very costly if all you pay is the minimum amount due. The best rule is to charge only what you can afford to pay in full by the end of every month.

2. Charge Cards. American Express and Diners Club are considered *charge cards*. They require that the entire balance be paid each month. Although they charge no interest, they do require an annual fee.

3. Debit Cards and ATM Cards. A *debit card* looks like a credit card, but works like a check. When you make a purchase, your bank account is charged for that amount. Since the payment for a purchase is drawn from your account, debit cards do not incur interest charges.

Like debit cards, *ATM (Automated Teller Machine) cards* withdraw money from your bank account when you use them. But unlike using a debit card in a store, you receive cash, which you can spend as you wish.

Chapter 12 has a more extensive discussion of consumer credit.

─────────────────── **SUMMARY** ───────────────────

Planning is the essential ingredient if we are to get the most out of our income. For that reason, everyone should have some kind of financial plan. The steps in preparing a financial plan are as follows:

1. Identify your long-term and short-term financial goals so as to have a target to aim at as you prepare your plans.

2. Prepare a budget, a plan for spending and saving one's income over a particular period of time. Budgets are personal and should be adjusted according to changing needs and conditions.

3. Set aside savings. One key to meeting financial goals lies in one's ability to save. For that reason, a provision for savings needs to be included in every budget.

4. Good career planning and investing strategies, proper use of credit, and buying insurance are also part of financial planning.

5. Give your budget time to prove itself. If adjustments are necessary, make them.

─────────────────── **LOOKING AHEAD** ───────────────────

In this unit, we have discussed how best to manage our money. We learned how to buy wisely, budget, save, borrow, and invest our money. But now it is time to learn about getting a job and earning the money that we have learned to manage. In the next unit, we will also discuss occupations, career planning, and organized labor in the United States.

─────────────────── **EXERCISES** ───────────────────

✔ Matching Match each term in Column A with its definition in Column B.

Column A
1. budget
2. balanced budget
3. short-term goal

Column B
a. something to strive for in the distant future
b. a situation whereby one's income is greater than one's expenses

4. long-term goal   *c.* something to strive for in the near future

5. surplus   *d.* a plan for one's expenses and income

6. income   *e.* spending that does not change from month to month

7. principal

8. financial planning   *f.* writing down one's financial goals and means to achieve them

9. fixed expenses

10. variable expenses   *g.* money that you originally put in a savings account

   h. spending that is not the same each week or month

   i. money received from any source

   j. a plan in which expenses are equal to income

✔ **Multiple Choice** Choose the letter of the item that best completes the statement or answers the question.

1. According to the chapter, (a) a budget is a plan for managing money (b) not every family needs a budget (c) budgets are very complicated (d) everyone could use the same standard budget.

2. Budgets are valuable for (a) rich families only (b) middle-income families only (c) poor families only (d) all families.

3. As a first step in financial planning, one should (a) define those personal goals that will cost money (b) borrow enough money to pay all the expenses you are likely to incur (c) track your income and expenses for one month and then use the results to prepare a budget (d) shop wisely and use credit wisely.

4. Budgets should be (a) followed very strictly (b) flexible (c) unchanging (d) complicated.

5. Putting first things first in a budget means that (a) your needs and wants are equally important (b) whatever comes to your mind first is usually the most important thing (c) even the smallest expenses are included (d) you must first plan obtaining money and spending for those things that are most important to you.

6. Which *one* of the following items is classified as a fixed expense in a typical student's budget during the school year? (a) saving for a car (b) snacks (c) dating expenses (d) car fare to school.

7. Which *one* of the following items is part of estimated income? (a) savings (b) school supplies (c) earnings (d) lunches.

8. Wise money management (a) helps you to make the most of the money that you have (b) reduces the need for bank accounts (c) makes saving unnecessary (d) results in an increase in your allowance or wages.

9. The price tag on both the West Coast and the Hippity Hop CDs was $14. Although Lonnie would have loved to buy both, they were too expensive. After much thought, Lonnie purchased the Hippity Hop recording. What was the opportunity cost of Lonnie's decision? (a) $14 (b) the West Coast CD (c) $28 (d) the Hippity Hop CD.

✔ *Questions for Thought and Discussion*

1. The opening section of the chapter described financial problems faced by Lisa, Jack, and Flora. Lisa and Jack would like to have had more money in their pockets between paydays. Flora wanted to travel to the Grand Canyon. If they had asked for your opinion, what advice would you have given *each* to help them achieve those goals?

2. What does the following statement have to do with preparing a personal budget? "If you don't know where you want to go, you won't know how to get there."

✔ *Using the Internet*

To learn more about financial planning, visit the following Websites: <<http://www.finpipe.com>>; <<http://www.jumpstartcoalition.com>>; and <<http://www.nice.emich.edu>>.

✔ *Preparing a Monthly Budget Worksheet*

On a separate sheet of paper, prepare a "Monthly Budget Worksheet" like the one below. Then for the next month, enter everything you receive in income and pay out in expenses.

My Monthly Budget Worksheet

Current Monthly Income

Wages/Salary	$ _____	
Less:		
Taxes $ _____		
Other $ _____		
Total deductions	$ _____	
Net wages	$ _____	
Allowance	$ _____	
Other	$ _____	
Total income		$ _____

Current Monthly Expenses

Fixed		Variable	
Club dues	$ _____	Entertainment	$ _____
Haircuts/ Cosmetics	$ _____	Charity	$ _____
Carfare	$ _____	Restaurants	$ _____
Newspapers/ Publications	$ _____	Vacation	$ _____
Automobile	$ _____	Automobile	$ _____
Other	$ _____	Other	$ _____
Other	$ _____		
Total fixed expenses	$ _____	Total variable expenses	$ _____
		Total monthly expenses	$ _____

Financial Summary

Total Income	$ _____
(−) Total expenses	$ _____
(=) Surplus or deficit	$ _____

Unit 3

WORKING: THE ROLE OF LABOR

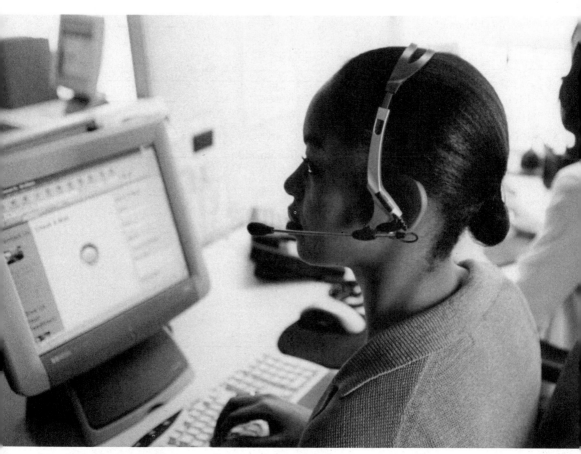

In recent decades, the percentage of women in the workforce has increased steadily.

When we began this study of economics, we discussed the need to make choices throughout our lives. One of the most important of these choices is treated in Chapter 16: how to begin deciding on a career. Next, in Chapter 17, you will receive practical advice on looking for a job and applying for one that interests you. In addition, you will also learn how to prepare for a job interview. You are aware from talking to family and friends that not all jobs pay the same wages. Chapter 18 discusses how our skills, talents, and training affect our earnings.

Labor unions are important in our market economy. They directly affect the jobs and wages of millions of Americans. Unions also influence prices and production. In Chapter 19, you will learn about the growth of organized labor in this country, the laws affecting unions, and the present-day problems that unions and their members face. Chapter 20 explains how a contract is negotiated between an employer and the union representing the firm's workers.

CHAPTER *16*
Choosing a Career

Key Terms

career	blue-collar worker	vocational
labor force	service worker	preference test
migrant worker	farm worker	talent
illegal alien	goods-producing	skill
occupation	industry	on-the-job
occupational	service industry	training
cluster	job outlook	apprenticeship
white-collar	high-tech industry	program
worker	earnings	

The conversation was quite lively at Pete's table in the school cafeteria. "Pete, what do you want to do after you graduate?" asked Joey. "I don't know," replied Pete. "But whatever I do, I want to make a lot of money at it."

Suppose that you were talking with Pete and Joey. Do you know the kind of work you will eventually be doing to earn a living? Ask your classmates this question. You may be surprised at the different replies you will get. But that is fine. Our nation's economy needs people to do thousands of different kinds of work.

Do you have to decide now which *career* (area of work) will be right for you? You may have been thinking about a career in one of many fields, such as business, medicine, sports, construction, or entertainment. Is a firm goal necessary now? Perhaps not. But you should begin to prepare yourself so that you will be ready to make your choice within the next few years. Whatever area of work you do choose, you will want to know the likelihood of finding steady employment with a promising future.

After you have read this chapter, you will have a better understanding of the relation between your career interests and job opportunities. You will learn the answers to the following questions:

- What is the labor force and how is it changing?
- What will affect your choice of occupation?
- How do you prepare for the career of your choice?

WHAT IS THE LABOR FORCE AND HOW IS IT CHANGING?

As soon as you take some action to find a job, you have entered what is commonly called the job market, or the world of work. Economists would say that you are now part of the *labor force*. In the United States, all persons 16 years of age and older who are either working or looking for work are part of the labor force. The labor force therefore includes people who have jobs as well as some who do not.

Changes in the Labor Force

The U.S. labor force has been changing rapidly in recent years. Some of the most significant changes in the number, age, and sex of workers are described below.

1. Number of Workers. The size of the labor force has increased. In 1960, the total population of the United States was 180 million people. Of this total, 75 million people were in the labor force. By 2007, the population had increased 67 percent, to 301 million people, and the labor force had grown 104 percent, to 153 million people. As the population grew, the U.S. economy also expanded, so more jobs were available for more people.

2. Age of Workers. Although the labor force could include everyone 16 years old and older, not all 16-year-olds immediately enter the labor force. Instead, many people between the ages of 16 and 24 are choosing to stay in school. Also, many people over 55 are taking advantage of retirement possibilities, and the number of retirees is likely to increase. Thus, the 25-to-54-year-old age group will increase greatly as a percentage of the total labor force.

3. Sex of Workers. A striking change in the labor force since the 1960s has been the increasing employment of women. In 1960, fewer than 40 percent of women 16 years of age and older were in the labor force. Now, however, almost 60 percent of women over 16 are part of it. Moreover, their participation in the labor force is expected to increase even more. Almost half (about 46 percent) of today's workers are women. Women still are scarce in certain occupations such as the construction industry, where they make up

Figure 16.1 Working-Age Population, Labor Force, and Employment of Women Since 1960

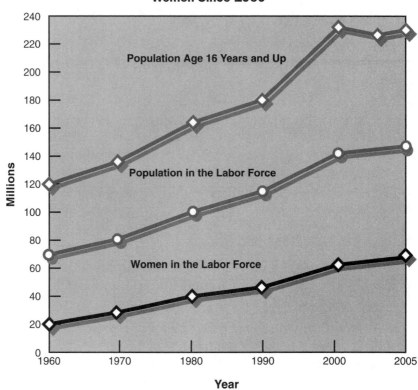

only about 10 percent of the workforce of that industry. Some construction firms are trying to attract more female employees.

4. Immigrants, Migrant Workers, and Illegal Aliens. An immigrant is an individual who comes to this country from another. The United States is a nation of immigrants. Therefore, the labor force in this country has always consisted of large numbers of immigrants. They play important roles in the economy, some bringing valuable skills with them. Immigration laws, however, have long limited the number of immigrants allowed in. The labor force also includes many illegal aliens. An *illegal alien* is a person who enters the country without the permission of the government or who enters with permission to stay a limited period of time and remains in this country beyond that time.

Our labor force also contains *migrant workers.* Although the word "migrant" sounds something like "immigrant," the two words have different meanings. A migrant worker is someone who goes from place to place in search of employment. Migrant workers

Professional Occupations: What skills and interests might be required of a person who teaches a group of students from different backgrounds?

may or may not be U.S. citizens. They may be legal or illegal aliens. Migrant workers generally work at agricultural jobs that are seasonal. These workers might pick grapes during the grape-growing season, and then move elsewhere to harvest other fruits or vegetables. After the harvests are over in one part of the country, they might move on to another area to work, or they may return home. Many migrant workers are from Mexico and other Latin American countries. Other migrant workers have come to the United States from Asia, Africa, and Eastern Europe.

Occupations Defined

One's *occupation* is what one does to earn a living. The U.S. Department of Labor defines an occupation as a group of jobs or job clusters in which workers perform similar tasks, duties, or activities at similar skill levels. The Department of Labor and the Census Bureau prepare lists of *occupational clusters*. These lists of occupational clusters change from time to time. For example, before there were computers, there was no cluster that would include computer engineers. Within each cluster there is a wide range of jobs, including just about every job currently available. The following table shows some of today's major occupational clusters, with the number of people employed in each one.

U.S. Department of Labor Occupational Clusters

Occupational Cluster	Examples	Number Employed
Management, Professional, and Related occupations	engineers, doctors, chief executives, scientists	43,397,641
Service occupations	bank teller, insurance agent	19,675,399
Sales and Office occupations	salesperson, merchandiser	34,728,951
Farming, Fishing, and Forestry occupations	farm manager, fruit picker, farm owner, migrant worker, fisherperson	965,156
Construction, Extraction, and Maintenance occupations	boilermaker, miner, roofer, and carpenter	12,340,953
Production, Transportation, and Material Moving occupations	assemblers, truck driver, bus driver, sailor	9,121,617

Types of Occupations

The occupations at which Americans earn their living have changed greatly during the past 40 years—and occupations will continue to change. One way to study these changes is to compare what has happened to white-collar, blue-collar, service, and farm workers.

White-collar workers are people in the professional, technical, managerial, and sales categories. The term "white collar" originated many years ago when men wore white shirts and women wore white blouses on these jobs.

Blue-collar workers are employed in the textile mills, steel and auto plants, transportation, heavy machinery, and machine tool industries. At one time, these workers wore sturdy work clothes made of blue denim. Thus, they acquired the name blue-collar workers.

People in *service occupations* include government workers, hospital employees, fire fighters, building service workers, and hotel and restaurant workers.

Farm occupations include farmers as well as farm managers and laborers.

Changes in Occupations

White-collar and service workers account for increasingly larger percentages of the total labor force. The percentage of workers in blue-collar manufacturing jobs has declined in recent decades, as shown in Figure 16.2. The number of farming, fishing, and forestry workers is less than half what it was 30 years earlier.

Figure 16.2 Employment in Goods and Services Industries Since 1960

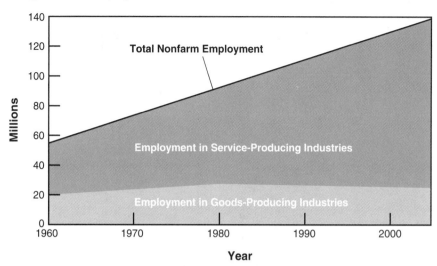

The following factors help to explain why these changes have occurred:

1. Where Goods and Services Are Produced. The shirt, blouse, or sneakers that you wear was, most likely, manufactured in Asia or Latin America. At one time these, and many other such items, were manufactured largely in the United States. But now there is less of a demand here for blue-collar workers in industries making shirts, blouses, or sneakers. On the other hand, there is a greater demand than previously for white-collar workers to market, sell, finance and insure foreign products sold in the United States.

High-Technology Occupation: Web page designers and other kinds of computer programmers need special training.

Service Occupation: A ticketing agent for a large bus company studies seat availability on a monitor.

2. The Aging of Our Society. People are living longer today. As people live longer, there is a greater need for facilities and personnel to care for this aging population. Furthermore, the number of years people are retired have also increased, on average. The need for workers to service retirement communities and leisure activities has increased to meet this growing need. Thus, there is a greater demand for health-care workers—doctors, nurses, medical assistants, social workers, and office and support staff. These are mostly white-collar jobs.

3. How Goods Are Produced. More shifts are expected in job opportunities in the future because of technological innovations. Computers and computer-driven equipment has become part of everyday business and manufacturing. More workers are needed in computer industries to develop, manufacture, and service their complex equipment. On the other hand, the government projects that the number of U.S. workers in *goods-producing industries* such as mining and manufacturing will decline or remain constant. Machines, computers, and robots are now doing many of the jobs in these industries.

But the number of workers in finance, retail trade, and other *services industries* will increase greatly. Figure 16.3 shows the *job*

Figure 16.3 The Ten Occupations With the Largest Job Growth, 1998–2008

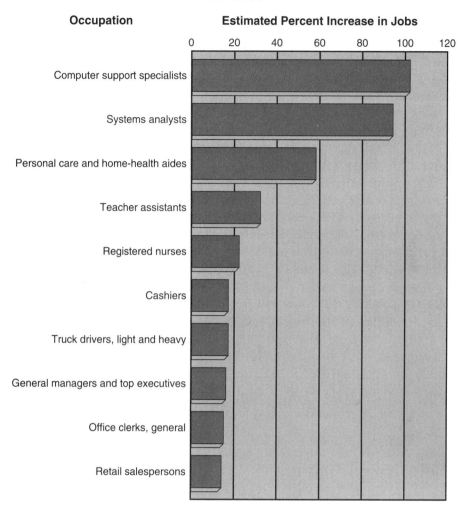

outlook (the chances of getting work in a specific occupation at some future time) in a number of occupations in various goods and services industries.

Total employment is expected to increase by 20.3 million jobs over the 1998–2008 period, a 14 percent increase. Occupations that require more education and training generally are projected to grow the fastest. Job opportunities are expected to decline rapidly in textiles, farming, and certain operator and assembly occupations. On the other hand, many more workers will be needed in computer-related, travel, and health-care occupations.

Growing Demand for Workers With More Education

One sign that a nation's economy is healthy is that a good number of its occupations are growing and flourishing. Many new occupations have been created in the United States in recent decades. Some of these involve designing, programming, operating, and servicing the new machines and computers. These are the *high-tech* (high-technology) *industries.* You may want to prepare yourself now for one of the better-paying jobs in a field where workers will be in demand in the future. Preparation will probably require an education.

The evidence is quite clear that education pays off. Unemployment rates for high school dropouts are higher than for high school graduates. And even when dropouts are working, they will earn, on the average, only about three-quarters as much as high school graduates. College graduates will earn almost three times as much as high school dropouts. Moreover, workers over age 25 with a high school diploma or better increased from 66 percent of the workers of that age in 1980 to 82 percent in 2000. Those with college degrees also increased, from 16 percent to 24 percent, during this period. So when you are ready to begin working, you will be competing against better-educated people than those who had previously made up the labor force. Yes, it is true that there are those who have been very successful despite the fact that they have not completed college (such as Bill Gates of Microsoft) or ever attended college. But their numbers are few. Why chance it? Get an education!

Unemployment Rate and Median Earnings by Educational Level*

Unemployment Rate in 2003 (Percent)	Education Attained	Median Weekly Earnings in 2003
1.7	Professional degree	$1,307
2.1	Doctorate	1,349
2.9	Master's degree	1,064
3.3	Bachelor's degree	900
4.0	Associate degree	672
5.2	Some college, no degree	622
5.5	High school graduate	554
8.8	Less than a high school diploma	396

*year-round, full-time workers, age 25 and older

Your chances of finding a job—if you are well prepared—is very good. According to the Bureau of Labor Statistics, there will be a strong demand for workers from the time you graduate from high school or post-secondary school, until at least 2025. About 60 million of the so-called "baby boomers" (those born between 1946 and 1964) will be reaching retirement age. Occupations with large numbers of older workers (for example, secondary school teachers) and fast-growing fields (such as computer engineering) will need replacement workers to fill the empty slots. You can fill one of those slots.

WHAT WILL AFFECT YOUR CHOICE OF OCCUPATION?

Once you enter the labor force, you are going to spend about half of your waking hours going to, returning from, or working on the job. The kind of job you have will determine how much you will earn. Your *earnings* (income) will determine the kind of life you can lead during your leisure time. So it is important to start thinking about choosing an occupation. Chances are that, sooner or later, you will be looking for full-time work.

Let us do some thinking together and consider what forces will influence your decision about a future job.

Factors That May Limit Your Choices

1. Availability of Jobs. The job that you want may or may not be there when you want it, for three reasons. First, the types of jobs in the labor force are changing, as you have seen. Second, some jobs are only seasonal. For example, stores hire additional workers before Christmas and release them soon afterward. Ski instructors and lifeguards usually work at these jobs only a part of the year. Third, it is easier to get work when the country is enjoying good business times than when business conditions are bad.

2. Location. Some jobs are available only in certain areas. For example, the movie and television industries are located mainly in California and New York. Mining is carried out mostly in the Appalachian region and the West. If you live in areas where such jobs are available, you may be tempted to enter these industries. If you want a job in an industry that is not located near you, you must be willing to move to the area where such jobs are available.

3. Discrimination. Job discrimination because of race, ethnic background, age, or sex is illegal. Nevertheless, discrimination has affected many people now in the labor force. In the past, minorities and women have had fewer chances of becoming managers and executives. Fortunately, discrimination is slowly becoming less of an obstacle in determining what people do for a living. Minorities and women occupy leading roles in all aspects of our

Figure 16.4 Influences on Your Choice of Occupation

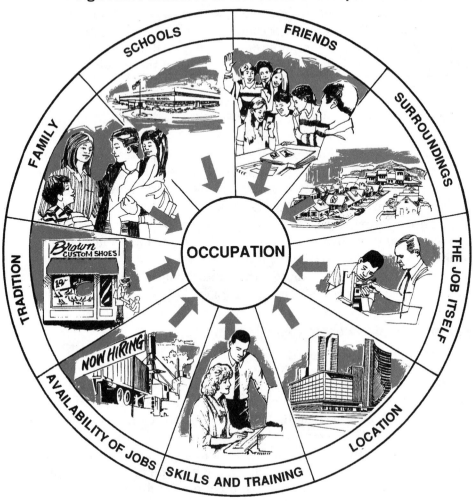

society. There are numerous examples of this today in government, industry, sports, entertainment, and communications.

Factors That May Enlarge Your Choices

Perhaps the best advice ever given to someone thinking about choosing a career comes from a Greek writer who lived long ago: "Know yourself." To know yourself, you must know your goals, interests, and abilities.

1. Goals. Thinking for a while about your goals will probably help you identify them. What do you want most out of your career? Is it money? prestige? working with people? helping people? A recent survey of high school seniors suggests that being successful at the kind of work they do is more important than making a lot of money.

2. Interests. Begin to explore your interests. Do you like to work with your hands? Or is math more interesting to you than shop? You are more likely to succeed at an occupation if you enjoy and are interested in your work. But suppose, like many high school students, you do not know what your interests are. What then? Here are some things you can do to identify these interests.

Talk to your school guidance counselor. She or he may recommend a local counseling service that can help you identify your interests. A counselor may also suggest that you take a *vocational preference test*. This test asks a number of questions about your likes and dislikes. There are no right or wrong answers. A counselor can study your answers and suggest careers that you are likely to find interesting.

A sample of just a small part of such a vocational preference test is given below. For each activity on the test, students are asked to choose one of the following replies: (1) I have a strong interest in the task described. (2) I am somewhat interested in what is described. (3) I have no idea whether or not I am interested. (4) I have little interest in what is described. (5) I have a strong dislike for what is described.

Vocational Preference Test

1. Answering telephones, giving and taking messages for others
2. Taking apart engines, clocks, or motors
3. Using a computer
4. Using a ruler, micrometer, or other measuring devices
5. Looking up facts to prove a point in an argument
6. Visiting homes when people are in need or in some kind of trouble
7. Working with children or teenagers
8. Drawing cartoons or painting pictures
9. Writing for the school newspaper
10. Organizing or becoming a leader in a school club
11. Performing experiments with chemicals; studying plants or animals
12. Taking part in school plays

Continue to explore your interests. Visit stores, factories, offices, technological and industrial exhibits, and museums. Learn what people do for a living and whether these activities interest you.

Find a part-time job or volunteer for work in a field that interests you.

Read a variety of magazines specializing in career areas. Almost every industry, trade, profession, and craft has one or more trade journals. These magazines can give you an inside view of many occupations.

Talk to people about their occupations. Most people enjoy talking about their work. By learning what it is about their work that interests them, you may discover something about your own interests.

Check the *Occupational Outlook Handbook*, published by the U.S. Bureau of Labor Statistics. It is available in many libraries and on the Internet.

3. Abilities. Guidance specialists tell us that our abilities come from two sources: our *talents* and our *skills*. Talents are those abilities that we seem to come by almost naturally—they are a part of us. Skills are those abilities that we develop through training or study. In most instances, it would be wise to develop skills that are related to our talents.

PREPARING FOR THE CAREER OF YOUR CHOICE

Whatever the career of your choice may be, there is a certain amount of knowledge and skills that you will need in order to succeed. X-ray technicians must learn to operate X-ray equipment. Secretaries must learn to type and use computers and other office machines. Factory workers must be able to operate the machinery and equipment associated with their jobs.

The amount of training necessary varies from one occupation to another. For that reason, you will have to ask yourself how much time and effort you are willing to put in toward preparing for a career. After graduating from high school, will you spend another six months, a year, or more for additional training?

Private schooling can be quite costly. You and your family will have to think about how much you would be willing and able to invest in your education. Before making your decision, speak to your school counselors. These people are familiar with the problems of young people. They will help you seek financial assistance if your family is unable to pay for your education.

Whatever career path you follow, your first goal should be to complete high school. But what should high school graduates do next?

In working toward a career, high school graduates have at least three paths open to them, as Figure 16.5 shows. Which one will they choose? Which would you choose?

High school graduates could take the first path and enroll in school. Junior colleges and community colleges offer two-year programs leading to an associate degree. Many of these programs are in career areas. Four-year colleges prepare students for bachelor's degrees in a variety of academic or professional subjects. Speak to your school's college adviser about college programs.

Figure 16.5 Three Career Paths After High School

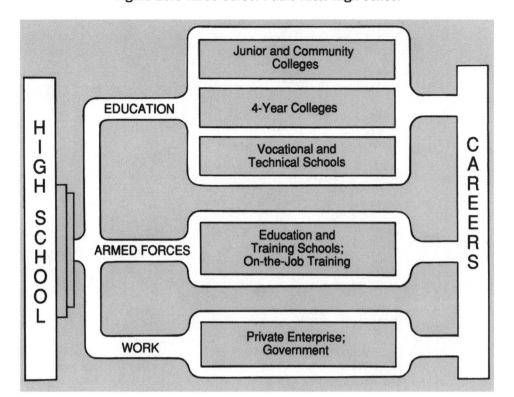

Vocational and technical schools specialize in teaching their students specific job skills. Students who complete their programs receive certificates as evidence of their achievements. There are literally hundreds of skills that are taught by all of the vocational-training schools in this country. The time required to complete these courses varies considerably. For example, you may take an eight-week course in driving a tractor-trailer, a half-year (26-week) course in heating and plumbing, or a one-year (52-week) course in watchmaking and repairs.

The second path, the armed forces, provides another career road. Some of the training programs offered by the armed services are in occupations that can be followed later, when you return to civilian life. Or you may decide that you enjoy the service so much that you make it your lifetime career. In addition, armed forces personnel are entitled to benefits that help to pay the cost of further education and training after their discharge from active service.

The third path takes high school graduates directly into the world of work. There they will learn first-hand about occupations and sharpen their skills by actually working at a job. They will learn from other, more experienced workers. In some instances,

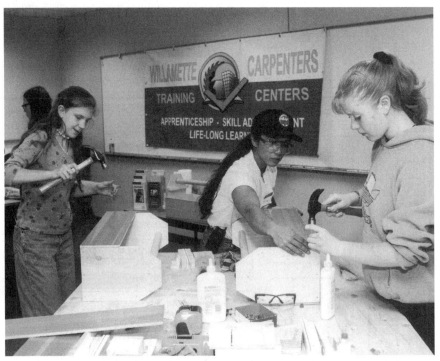

Apprenticeship System: Master carpenter explains a technical detail to an apprentice in a union apprenticeship program. Skilled crafts jobs are often learned directly from an experienced person.

their employers will hold *on-the-job training* classes. Of course, the new workers might still take evening courses, which, in a way, will bring them back to the first path.

Apprenticeship programs provide more formal kinds of on-the-job learning experiences. Sometimes they are sponsored by unions. Apprentices learn their trade by helping experienced workers and taking directions from them.

Finally, you may choose to follow one path for a certain period and then switch to another.

SUMMARY

The labor force in the United States is made up of all those 16 years of age or older who are working or looking for work. As the population of the United States has grown, so too has the labor force. The makeup of the labor force has been changing. More women have become workers. The 25-to-54-year-olds of both sexes are an increasing percentage of the total workforce. White-collar workers and service workers are increasing as a percentage of the labor force, while blue-collar workers and farm workers are decreasing.

You should begin now to prepare for an occupation or career. Jobs of the future will demand more and more education. People with more education tend to earn more money. Know your goals, interests, and abilities. Your guidance counselor may be able to help you in this area. Then get the education and training needed for the occupation of your choice. Plan your courses while you are still in high school, and finish high school. You will continue to develop skills when you enter a trade or technical school, a two- or four-year college, the armed forces, or the world of work.

LOOKING AHEAD

Choosing a career is a first step in preparing for your future in the world of work. In the next chapter, we will learn how to go about finding a job.

EXERCISES

✔**Matching** Match each term in Column A with its definition in Column B.

Column A
1. labor force
2. occupation
3. white-collar worker
4. blue-collar worker
5. service worker industry
6. on-the-job training
7. vocational preference test
8. talents and skills
9. career

Column B
a. businesses and organizations such as banks and insurance companies
b. the sources of our abilities
c. learning a job by working at the job
d. a field or area in which one works
e. the total of all those working or looking for work
f. a way of finding out what careers one may be interested in
g. a factory employee or mechanic
h. the type of work a person does for a living
i. a clerical worker or a professional employee

✔**Multiple Choice** Choose the letter of the item that best completes the statement or answers the question.

1. As soon as you take some action to find a job, you (a) become a blue-collar worker (b) are a white-collar worker (c) enter the labor force (d) have chosen a career.

2. A striking change in the labor force since the 1960s has been the (a) increasing employment of women (b) declining importance of the 25–54-year-old age group (c) increasing share of men in the civilian workforce (d) increase in the employment of farm workers.

3. White-collar workers and service workers are becoming an increasingly larger percentage of the workforce. The reason is that (a) these jobs pay more than others (b) white-collar jobs require little education or training (c) the way that goods and services are produced has changed (d) farm work is unpleasant.

4. There is a growing demand for workers with (a) increased strength (b) more education (c) mechanical skills (d) little education and training.

5. Average yearly earnings are generally highest for (a) high school dropouts (b) high school graduates (c) elementary school graduates (d) college graduates.

6. Which of the following may *enlarge* your choice of occupation? (a) your parents' wishes (b) location of jobs (c) where you grow up (d) your interests and abilities.

7. The main idea of this chapter is that you should (a) accept the first job that you are offered (b) choose a career and prepare yourself for it (c) leave school early (d) go for technical training.

8. Which of the following occupations is expected to have the greatest *percentage* job increase during the period 1998–2008? (a) office clerks (b) computer support specialists (c) systems analysts (d) retail sales.

9. The labor force in the United States is made up of (a) the total population of the United States (b) all those people who are 16 years of age or older (c) all those 16 years of age or older who are working or looking for work (d) all males between the ages of 16 and 65.

10. According to the table on page 244, as an individual's education increases, the chances are that there will be (a) greater unemployment and lower earnings (b) lower earnings but less likelihood of unemployment (c) greater earnings and lower unemployment (d) greater earnings and higher risk of unemployment.

✔ *Critical-Thinking Questions*

Study Figure 16.4, "Influences on Your Choice of Occupation." There are nine forces that influence most individuals' career choice.

1. Compare and discuss how three of the nine influences listed have affected or will affect your personal choice of a career.

2. Most of us take pride in our friends, family, and surroundings. Why have these three influences been accused, in some cases, of being a burden rather than a help when choosing a career?

3. Why is it important to "know yourself," that is, your goals, interests, and abilities, when deciding on a lifetime career?

✔ *Using the Internet*

The following are sources of information you might use to find the information on population shifts, job opportunities, and occupations that are most likely to need more workers.

1. <<http://factfinder.census.gov>>

2. <<http://stats.bls.gov>>

3. <<http://armedforcescareers.com>>

4. <<http://bls.gov/oco/home.htm>>

CHAPTER *17*
Finding a Job

Imagine that you are in charge of hiring new workers for a bank in your community. Your records department needs a word processing trainee. You call the vocational counselor at Central High School and ask to have the job posted. A day later, the counselor calls and makes appointments for two graduating seniors to see you. Here are descriptions of the two students.

Elizabeth is pleasant, neat, and well-groomed. She wears clothes that are in style but not unusual. She arrives on time. Elizabeth gives you her printed *résumé* (summary of her background). Her *career goal*, the résumé says, is to be an executive secretary. While at school, she did secretarial work for the assistant principal for business education. During her past two summer vacations, she worked for the Ace Manufacturing Company. Her job required her to do some letters and memos, but mostly she did filing and answered calls from customers.

Bob arrives a few minutes late. He is wearing designer jeans, an open shirt, and sneakers. Bob does not have a résumé, but you quickly realize that he is bright. You ask him to prepare a sample letter, and you are impressed by his speed and accuracy. Bob admits that he does not want to make banking a career. But he adds that he would be willing to give the job a try.

Which student would you hire for the job? Why?

Finding and holding a job takes some knowledge and skill. This chapter discusses how to find and hold a job. After you read this chapter, you should be able to answer the following questions:

- What job is right for you?
- How can you find a job in your chosen occupation?
- How can you win an employer's confidence?

WHAT JOB IS RIGHT FOR YOU?

Elizabeth is a more skillful job seeker than Bob. She comes to the interview prepared. And she has a goal in mind—she wants to be an executive secretary. Bob, like many high school seniors, still has not decided on a career or occupation. He should review Chapter 16 to obtain some ideas on this topic.

A job is not the same as an occupation. A *job* is any kind of paid employment at some task. It may or may not be related to one's occupation. An occupation is a long-term pursuit. It is your job day after day, for many years to come. In our example, Elizabeth needs more education or training to qualify for the occupation of her choice. The job at the bank, if she gets it, will be one step in the direction of getting the training she needs. Turn back to page 249. Figure 16.5 shows three career paths open to the high school graduate. Elizabeth chose the path that enters the world of work. She will gain work experience and build a reputation as a good worker. Elizabeth hopes that her supervisors will recognize her abilities and give her additional on-the-job training. She also intends to take evening courses to improve her skills.

Now what about you? Your first job will, most likely, not be the only one you ever have. Like Elizabeth, you should think of the first job you get as part of a big picture. This job, and any other you might get in the future, should help you to fill in different parts of that picture. In time, you will be ready for bigger, more responsible jobs.

HOW CAN YOU FIND A JOB IN YOUR CHOSEN OCCUPATION?

Finding a job is like selling a product. Just as a company will launch a campaign to sell its products, you will need a job campaign to sell *you*. To do so, you will have to know (1) where to go for information about jobs, (2) how to apply for a job, and (3) how to interview for a job.

This is how you might put your job campaign together.

Sources of Job Information

There are many sources of information about current job openings, including people, places, print sources, and the Internet. Be sure to investigate all of them.

1. **People**

   - High school guidance counselor.
   - Friends and relatives.
   - Teachers, particularly business or trade teachers.

2. **Places**

   - School job-placement center.
   - Private employment agencies. These services charge a fee, which may be paid either by the person who gets the job or by the employer. Employment agencies often place help-wanted ads in local newspapers.
   - State employment offices. These government agencies do not charge fees for their work in filling jobs. They may provide aptitude tests and job-counseling services.
   - Armed forces recruitment offices. These offices provide information for those interested in military service and careers.
   - Company personnel departments. Many large companies have personnel departments where you may talk to someone about applying for a job. It is usually best to write or call for an appointment. But a "help-wanted" sign outside a store, an office building, or a factory is an invitation to walk in and apply for a job.

3. **Books and Newspapers**

   - *Occupational Outlook Handbook*. This U.S. government publication describes some 250 occupations. For each one, it tells the nature of the work, working conditions, requirements for the job, number of jobs and where they are, typical salaries, and the *job outlook*, or chances of finding work.
   - Advertisements in local newspapers. In the *classified section* of your local newspaper, you will find *help-wanted ads* (job advertisements). (See the feature on pages 257–258.)
   - Civil service announcements. Listings of jobs and civil service examinations for jobs at local, state, and federal levels appear in special newspapers such as *The Chief—Civil Service Leader*. Ask your school or community librarian for copies.

Personal Economics

READING THE CLASSIFIED ADS

Figure 17.1 Help-Wanted Advertisements

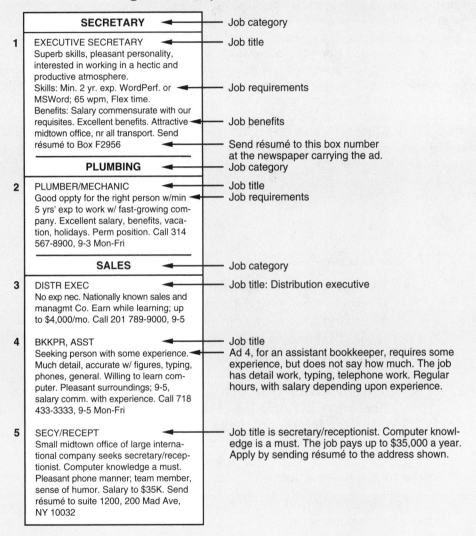

In help-wanted advertisements, jobs are often grouped together under the field or profession they cover, such as *advertising, banking,* or *engineering.* Categories are often listed in alphabetical order, so that "advertising" would appear before "banking."

Each category may have a number of different jobs listed. Under "advertising," you may find such job titles as *copywriters, production assistants,* and *secretaries.* Secretaries may also appear under the field of "banking." There will probably be a separate category called "secretaries." All sorts of secretarial jobs might be listed under this category, including legal secretary.

Study the examples of help-wanted ads in Figure 17.1. In each ad, find out what kind of job is being offered, its requirements, how much it pays, and how a person may apply. Note that abbreviations are used to save space in most ads.

When you read the want ads, you can learn to eliminate those jobs that you do not want or for which you are unqualified. Thus, if you want a full-time (F/T) job, do not even read an ad that advertises a part-time (P/T) job. Similarly, if you can-

not type, avoid jobs that require being able to type a certain number of words per minute (wpm).

Examine the third ad carefully. It may be one you wish to avoid. The pay may sound good, but the ad does not really tell you how much you will earn. It says "up to $4,000 per mo.," which could mean that you might earn a lot less per month. The ad also says that no experience is needed and you earn while learning. The job might really involve door-to-door selling or telemarketing (trying to make sales by telephone). Your pay for this kind of work usually depends on the amount of selling you do. Income is not guaranteed.

4. **The Internet**

- The Internet is a wonderful tool for searching for a job. There are a number of Internet search engines to choose from. Your browser has provision for you to search for all kinds of information. You can enter "job search" in the space of your browser where it says, "SEARCH".
- You could go directly to "Career Job Search—Guide to Internet Job Search" at <<http//:www.e-careercenter.com>>. Here you will find a list of various job-search sites, hints on using the Internet to make your job search more effective, instructions on how to prepare a résumé, and much more.

How to Apply for a Job

Let us assume that the want ad for a secretary-receptionist on page 257 appeals to you. What is your next step? The ad asks that you send in your résumé. On page 260 is a sample letter you might write in applying for this position.

Your Résumé

A résumé, as you know, is a written summary of a person's background. Your résumé should list (1) your career objective, (2) your education, (3) your work experience, (4) personal facts, and

(5) your *references*, that is, the names, addresses, and phone numbers of people who know you and can tell an employer about your skills and character. (Make sure that you have asked these people if you may use them as references!) You may send your résumé to a potential employer along with a request for a personal interview. In this way, you are able to reach many more employers than would be possible if you first tried to see each one in person.

A good résumé lets the employer know many things about you. The employer can then decide whether it would be worthwhile to ask you to come in for an interview. This saves both of you time that might otherwise be wasted.

Keep in mind that your résumé is a picture of *you*. Keep it neat and simple, and above all truthful. Show that you are a responsible person willing and able to do the job that is called for.

How do you write a résumé? One page is all you need to list the following:

1. Your full name, address, and phone number.

2. Your educational background, including school(s) attended and the graduation date(s), diploma(s) received, and major subject(s).

3. Your employment history: employer(s') names and address(es), your job(s), dates of employment. The usual practice is to list your current job *first* and your first job *last*.

Preparing a Résumé: What are the most important items to include in a student's résumé?

Potential employers are interested mainly in what you are doing or have done most recently.

4. Some personal facts: your occupational goal, hobbies, awards you have won, special interests.

5. Other information: licenses held, special skills.

6. References: Give the names and addresses of people who will attest to your aptitudes and abilities; or state that these references will be given on request.

Figure 17.2 Reply to a Help-Wanted Advertisement

```
                              Your house number, street, apt. no.

                              Your town, state, zip code

                              Today's date


Suite 1200

200 Madison Avenue

New York, NY 10032


Dear Sir or Madam:

     In answer to your advertisement in the Tribune for

a secretary/receptionist, I would like to submit the

following information:

     In June, I will be graduating from Central High School,

where I have majored in business education.  I can type 85

wpm and operate a word processor.  I believe that the busi-

ness skills courses I have taken will enable me to perform

the duties of the job advertised.

     I have enclosed a copy of my résumé and will be avail-

able for an interview at your earliest convenience.  I can

be reached at the above address or by phone at (give your

phone number).

                         Sincerely yours,

                         (Sign your name and then

                          type your name beneath the

                          signature.)
```

Figure 17.3 Résumé Prepared by a Student Seeking a Full-Time Job

Résumé

Robert Simon
Address (include zip code)
Phone (include area code)

OBJECTIVE: Word processing trainee position

EDUCATION

Attending Central High School, Center City, (state and zip)
Grade: 12. Expect to graduate in June
Major: Business education
Subjects taken: accounting, bookkeeping, computer programming,
          English, social studies, and word processing

WORK EXPERIENCE

September 2001–present: Center City Supermarket, Main Street,
     Center City (state and zip)
   Job: Part-time assistant (after school, on Saturday, and during
     vacations)
   Duties: Maintain stock and replace inventory, receive cash, check
     register, bag merchandise

July–August 2000, 2001: Lakewood Camp, Lake Elsinore, California
   Job: Counselor and waterfront specialist
   Duties: Worked with 12-year-old boys; taught swimming, boating,
     and canoeing

October 2000–June 2001: Served as part-time secretary to Mr. James
     Macaffery, Assistant Principal, Business Education, Central High
     School. Used word processor and copier, filed, took telephone
     messages.

EXTRACURRICULAR ACTIVITIES

Teams: baseball team, swimming team, won award for swimming
Clubs: computer club, Future Business Leaders, Boy Scouts

REFERENCES on request.

You will recall that Bob appeared at the interview for a job at
the bank without a résumé. Figure 17.3 is a résumé that Bob
might have prepared and submitted to the personnel director.

Summer Job Interview: What kinds of questions would an interviewer ask a high school student seeking a summer job?

How to Interview for a Job

Now let us get back to your job search. Suppose that an ad for an administrative assistant appealed to you. You wrote your letter of application and enclosed your résumé.

Good news! Your letter of application and résumé have interested the employer. You received a call to go for an *employment interview*. The interview is probably the toughest part of your job campaign. You are face to face with the person who is going to decide whether you will get the job. You will have only about 15 minutes to make a good impression. You have to do it right the first time. Here are a few suggestions:

1.   Arrive at the interview a few minutes early, but not too early.
2.   Your appearance is important. Be clean and neat. Dress conservatively.
3.   Be prepared to answer questions about yourself.
4.   Bring a copy of your résumé with you even though you have already sent one to the firm.
5.   Smile. Give a firm handshake. Introduce yourself to the interviewer.

6. Be polite and keep calm. Above all, do not argue with the interviewer.

7. Avoid nervous habits such as finger tapping, looking around the room or at your watch, squirming in your seat, and gum chewing.

8. Answer questions to the point. Take your time but do not mumble. Leave your troubles at home. Do not be too aggressive.

9. Above all, leave the impression that you want the job, that you can do the job, and that you will fit in with this company.

Very often, *even before* the interview, you will be asked to fill out a *job application*. By examining the model application form on page 264, you can see that this will include much of the information on your résumé. It is important, however, that you fill out this job application form neatly and carefully for company records, the employment agency, or the personnel interviewer.

"*Any qualifications other than being very comfortable with yourself?*"

Is a person's self-assured manner enough to get a job? What else might be as important? More important?

© *The New Yorker Collection 1990* Bernard Shoenbaum from cartoonbank.com. All rights reserved.

Figure 17.4 Job Application Form

Application for Employment
The Law Prohibits Discrimination Because of Race, Religion, Ethnic Origin, Age, or Sex

Name _____
| Last | First | Middle |

Present Address _____
| Street | City | County | State | Zip Code |

Telephone Number _____
| Area Code | Number |

Permanent Address _____
| Street | City | County | State | Zip Code |

Telephone Number _____ Email Address _____
| Area Code | Number |

Position Objective   Check one (√):   ☐ Permanent   ☐ Part Time   ☐ Temporary   ☐ Summer

Please describe your work interest _____

Salary required $_____ per _____ When could you be available to begin work? _____

Would you relocate? ☐ Yes ☐ No Geographic Locations Preferred: 1. _____

2. _____

Do you object to shift work? ☐ Yes ☐ No   Overtime work? ☐ Yes ☐ No

Rotational work schedule? ☐ Yes ☐ No   Work schedule other than Monday through Friday? ☐ Yes ☐ No

Education

Type of School	Name and Location of School	Dates Attended				Graduated		Type of Diploma or Degree	Major and Minor Fields of Study	Academic Standing	
		From		To						Grade Average	Out of Possible
		Mo.	Yr.	Mo.	Yr.	No	Yes				
High School (Last Attended)											
All Vocational Schools, Technical Institutes, and Junior Colleges											
Other Training— Include Military Schools and Equivalency Diplomas											

Employment Experience

Company Name			Type of Business		Company Address	
Starting Date		Leaving Date		Starting Base Salary per Year	Final Base Salary per Year	Starting Position Title	Present or Last Position Title
Mo.	Yr.	Mo.	Yr.				

Name of Supervisor _____   Supervisor's Position Title _____

Explain reason for leaving. _____

Please describe your duties and responsibilities. _____

References

Name	Position	Company	Address

Please give us permission to contact these references by signing your name below.

_____   _____
Name   Date

HOW CAN YOU WIN AN EMPLOYER'S CONFIDENCE?

Thousands of young people enter the job market every year. Because of their youth and inexperience, they often make mistakes at employment interviews. Perhaps this is because young people fail to understand the viewpoint of the employer. When hiring a new worker, the employer is taking some risks. Therefore, the employer wants to make sure that the employee will be reliable. If you want a good job and expect to keep it, be honest with your employer. You may be found out if you are bluffing, and then you will be the loser.

An employer wants to know how interested you are in the job. Convince the employer that you can do the work and that you really want a chance to prove it. Employers expect you to ask questions at the interview and, of course, later on if you get the job. You may want to ask:

What will my job duties be?
What hours will I work?
How much will I earn?
Will there be job training?
Are there opportunities for advancement?

After your interview, say thank you! Let the interviewer know that you appreciated the time given to you. Give a firm handshake and leave.

Following Up

After a few days, follow up by writing or calling to say thank you again for the interview. This is the time to let the firm know that you are still interested in the job.

After You Are Hired

Well, congratulations! You came through the job interview with flying colors and you have been hired. Keep in mind that you are building a career. As you gain experience from this job, you will be able to advance to one with greater responsibilities and rewards. Here are some good traits that employers look for in employees.

1. **Personal**

   loyal, conscientious, honest, pleasant, friendly, cheerful, patient, tolerant, courteous.

On the Job: After being hired, workers must show that they are willing and able to learn and perform their jobs. How can they start to do these things?

2. **Job Performance**

    concern for quality of work, accurate, efficient, speedy, orderly, careful, alert, perceptive, thorough, well organized, dependable, punctual, reliable.

3. **Attitudes**

    ambitious, independent, show initiative, adaptable, resourceful, cooperative, emotionally stable, use good judgment, poised, dedicated to the business, respectful of supervisors, able to get along with others, willing to work hard, accept criticism, and learn from mistakes.

    If you have to miss work, or arrive at work late, notify your employer as soon as possible and be sure that you have a good and legitimate excuse. A reputation for being reliable is one of your greatest assets. Do not do anything to tarnish your good image.

SUMMARY

The job that is right for you is the job that will help you to achieve your career goal. You can learn from each job, gain work experience, and prepare yourself to advance to another job.

To find a job, develop a job campaign. Know the people, places, and publications that can help you. Understanding how to read the help-wanted ads in local newspapers and on the Internet will help you know which jobs to pursue and which jobs to avoid.

You may apply for a job by writing a letter of application and enclosing a résumé. The résumé is a summary of your education, work experience, and background. Prior to your job interview, you will probably be asked to fill out a job application, which will require much of the same information. You should show the employer that you want the job, can do the job, and that you are personable and reliable.

Once you get a job, you should do everything possible to hold on to it and advance. You are gaining work experience and building a reputation. Employers want workers who are conscientious, reliable, hard-working, on time, courteous, friendly, and willing to accept criticism.

LOOKING AHEAD

Having been successful in finding a job, you may now be wondering why some jobs pay more than others. We will discuss this fascinating question in the following chapter.

EXERCISES

✔**Matching** Match each term in Column A with its definition in Column B.

Column A
1. résumé
2. career goal
3. reference
4. *Occupational Outlook Handbook*
5. employment interview
6. classified ads
7. work habits

Column B
a. a section of a newspaper containing help-wanted and other advertisements
b. a sourcebook about different jobs
c. a person's pattern of behavior on the job
d. a face-to-face meeting with a possible employer or a company representative
e. someone who knows you and will attest to your aptitudes and abilities
f. a written summary of your work experience, education, and interests
g. an occupation a person wishes to follow as a life's work

✔**Multiple Choice** Choose the letter of the item that best completes the statement or answers the question.

1. The main idea of this chapter is that (a) you should not change jobs (b) a job search takes knowledge and skill (c) an employer does not

take a risk when hiring a new worker (d) the first job you get after graduation will be your career.

2. In help-wanted advertisements, jobs are often arranged (a) alphabetically under the field they cover, such as advertising or banking (b) according to how much they pay (c) with the jobs considered to be the most important listed first (d) by geographic area, such as Alabama or Delaware.

3. Which of the following should be your first step in your job campaign? (a) go for an interview (b) write your résumé (c) investigate sources of information about job openings (d) send a letter of application to a firm that might need workers.

4. Which of the following abbreviations found in a want ad tells you one of the skill requirements for the job? (a) $23K (b) P/T (c) Sec'y (d) 80 wpm.

5. Which of the following people is most likely to win an employer's confidence? A worker who is (a) grumpy and impatient (b) slow, careless, and disorganized (c) ambitious and shows initiative (d) unwilling to admit mistakes.

6. Which statement is true? (a) It is easy for a high school graduate to find a high-paying job. (b) Before hiring a new worker, employers rarely ask for references. (c) A job interview lasts only about 15 minutes, so it is unimportant. (d) Selling yourself to an employer is an important part of job hunting.

7. Which of the following statements is false? (a) A résumé is a brief autobiography. (b) There are very few sources of information about current job openings available to young people. (c) Finding a job is like selling a product. (d) A want ad tells you about a job opening, skills required, salary, and how to apply.

✔ *Writing a Letter of Application*

If you make a mistake in writing a letter to a friend, the results are not serious. When writing to a possible employer, however, one mistake could be your last. You may never get the chance to meet the employer. In the following exercise, imagine that you are applying for a job at Quality Clothes, Inc. Using your own job interests and personal qualifications, copy and complete the model letter of application on the next page.

✔ Reading Help-Wanted Ads Using the information given in the help-wanted ads on page 257, answer the following questions.

1. In ad 2, how many years' experience are needed as a minimum requirement for the job as plumber?

Figure 17.5 Model Letter of Application

```
                                        (Address)
                                        (Date)


Mr. Roger Stone, Office Manager
Quality Clothes, Inc.
1417 South First Street
Boston, Massachusetts  02107

Dear Mr. Stone:
      _____, my Secretarial Studies teacher, has told
me that a vacancy exists in your secretarial staff for
the summer months.  Please consider me an applicant for
this position.
      I am _____ years old and a student in the _____
class at _____ High School.  I have taken the _____
course of study.  I have had classes in _____, _____,
_____, _____, _____ and _____.  I can do word processing
at the rate of _____ words a minute.
      During the past year, I have worked for _____,
located at _____, in the capacity of _____.  I believe that
my interest in secretarial work makes me especially suited
for the full-time summer position with your company.  I plan
to continue my studies in the fall.
      I have permission to give you the following references:
            _____, Teacher
            _____, High School
            _____
            _____

            _____, Office Supervisor
            _____
            _____
            _____

      May I have a personal interview at your convenience?
My telephone number is _____.

                              Very truly yours,

                              (Signature)
                              (Typed name)
```

2. How fast must you be able to type in order to get the job of executive secretary?

3. Which ads require sending a résumé?

4. In ad 5, what is the salary being offered for a secretary-receptionist?

5. Where would you send your résumé if you were interested in the job as executive secretary?

CHAPTER *18*

Some Jobs Pay More Than Others

Key Terms

median	annual salary	worker mobility
wages in kind	gross pay	social attitude
piecework	take-home pay	equivalent pay
productivity	output	comparable worth

Mark was sitting in the students' lounge. Noticing a discarded newspaper, he picked it up and turned to the sports section. His eyes lit up as he read that his favorite basketball player had just signed a three-year contract at a salary of $1.5 million per year. "Wow!" Mark said aloud. For years, Mark has dreamed about becoming a basketball star and earning lots of money.

Sherry was impressed. Her goal is to become a world-class long-distance runner. But Sherry knows that, no matter how good she might become, she will never earn as much as star basketball players.

Joe entered the discussion. "Let's be realistic," he said. "None of us is likely to make *that* kind of money." Joe plans to become an air conditioning systems service specialist. He added, "Maybe I won't make millions, but I'm pretty sure I'll earn a lot more than you guys."

Sherry also knows that the odds against her becoming a successful professional athlete are enormous. So she has been taking business courses in high school and has developed excellent computer skills. Mark believes that if he does not make it in basketball, he can stay with the sporting goods store where he now works after school and between practice sessions.

Which of our three friends do you think will have the highest earnings in his or her career? Can you explain why some jobs pay more than others? We hope you will be able to do so after reading this chapter. You will learn the answers to the following questions:

- How do wages vary by occupation?
- How do the market forces of demand and supply affect wages?
- What other forces affect wages?

HOW DO WAGES VARY BY OCCUPATION?

Different jobs pay different amounts. Most of us know that wages vary, and we take it for granted. Proof that persons with certain jobs earn far more money than others is given in the table below.

Let us study the table carefully. Note that the *median* weekly earnings of a worker in an occupation in the construction trades was $604. The median figure means that half of the people in this occupation earned $604 or more per week and half earned less. Median income is a good way to compare earnings among different occupations. For example, you can see that handlers, equipment cleaners, helpers, and laborers had median weekly earnings of $443, while that for mechanics and repairers was $704 per week.

Median Weekly Earnings of Men and Women, by Occupation, 2004

Occupation or Category	Both sexes	Men	Women
Total, 16 years and over	$638	$ 713	$573
Executive, administrative, and managerial	965	1,158	812
Professional specialty	883	1,049	767
Technicians and related support	852	1,005	741
Sales occupations	604	747	464
Administrative support, including clerical	635	587	522
Service occupations	411	476	374
Mechanics and repairers	704	707	611
Construction trades	604	606	504
Transportation and material moving occupations	520	549	410
Handlers, equipment cleaners, helpers, and laborers	443	457	402
Farm workers	356	367	322

Which group in the table had the highest median weekly earnings? That is right: male executives, administrators, and managers ($1,158). Which groups of those listed earned the lowest wages? Women in service occupations earned $374 per week. Female farm workers earned $322 a week. The difference in median weekly wages between the highest- and the lowest-paid workers in the table was $836. On the basis of this evidence, we can conclude that:

- wages do vary greatly by occupation.
- wages also vary by sex. In nearly all occupations, women earned an average of 10 to 40 percent less than men for doing the same or similar work. (Discussed further on page 278.)

HOW DO DEMAND AND SUPPLY AFFECT WAGES?

We have shown that wages vary considerably from job to job. Why is this so? The reasons are not always obvious. For example, both Mark and Sherry hope to become top athletes. If both are successful, Mark will probably earn the higher salary. Track events are fairly popular, but basketball is one of our favorite national sports. Competition for jobs on major league basketball teams is fierce. Fans pay millions of dollars a year to attend games, and they also watch their favorite teams on television. Top basketball players, therefore, are in greater demand than top long-distance runners. Thus, because the demand for basketball games is greater than the demand for track events, basketball players earn more than track stars. Price rises as demand increases, as you learned in Chapter 4. In this case, price represents the wages paid to the athletes.

Factors Affecting the Demand for Labor

Let us go back to our friends in the students' lounge. Joe has learned from his study of careers that there are many jobs available for air conditioning systems service specialists. He thinks that he can earn at least $400 a week to start. Actually, the demand for people with the skills that Joe plans to acquire at a wage of $400 per week depends upon (1) the demand for the goods or services they produce, and (2) the workers' productivity.

1. Demand for Goods and Services. Many businesses today have heating, cooling, and ventilating systems. Therefore, people who install and service these systems are in demand. As more systems go into use, the demand for people with these skills will increase. Similarly, as more people own automobiles, the demand for workers to build, service, and repair automobiles will increase. We can thus see that the demand for goods influences the demand for workers to produce and service them. If the demand for goods increases, the demand for workers to produce and service them will increase. If the demand for the goods decreases, however, fewer workers will be needed.

Personal Economics

HOW WORKERS ARE PAID

There are different ways an employer may pay wages. Most of the time, wages are paid in money—in dollars and cents. But wages may also be in the form of meals, merchandise, and even rent. If you work in a restaurant, you may receive "free" meals. The meals are not really free. You have received what economists call *wages in kind*. Of course, in addition to meals, you will also receive money wages.

Money wages can be paid in different ways. One method of work and payment is called *piecework*. Some farm workers receive a payment for each bushel of fruits or vegetables they pick. Some factory workers receive a certain amount for each piece of work they complete. Piece-workers are paid only for the actual quantity of work that they do. Employers who pay workers on a piecework basis believe that this method increases *productivity* (how much one worker produces in a given time). The faster employees work, the more money they earn.

Many workers in blue-collar jobs are paid wages on an hourly basis. Other workers earn a weekly salary and are expected to work 35 to 40 hours each week. Professionals and government employees are usually paid weekly. An *annual* (yearly) *salary* of $30,000 can be broken down into weekly earnings of $576.92 before taxes.

If you have a job now, you already know that there is a difference between your gross pay and what you actually receive. *Gross pay* is the total before any deductions are made. Assume that you earn $9,285 a year, or $178.56 per week. This amount is your gross pay. You will not find $178.56 in your weekly pay envelope, however. From your gross pay your employer must deduct federal income, Social Security, and Medicare taxes, health insurance charges, and possibly a pension contribution and union dues. If these weekly deductions add up to $32.80, you take home $145.76. Gross pay minus deductions equals *take-home pay*. (Deductions are discussed further in "Preparing an EZ Tax Return" on page 412.)

2. Productivity. The term productivity, as we said, tells how much one worker can produce in a given time. This production is called the worker's *output*. The greater the worker's output and the higher the value of the output, the more an employer can afford to pay the worker.

Because of productivity, wages will be different for workers in different occupations. A specialist in a technical field may add $750 a day to a firm's income. But a restaurant worker behind a fast-food counter may add only $125 a day to a firm's income. It stands to reason that the specialist will earn more than the unskilled worker. Thus, in the table on page 271, the median weekly income of women in professional specialties was $763, while the median weekly income of women doing sales work was $441.

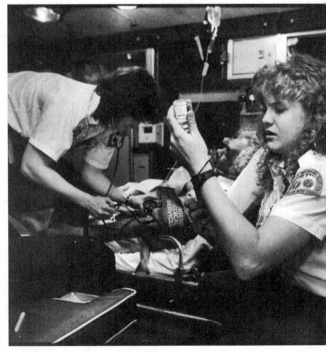

Different Jobs Pay Different Wages (from top left, facing page, clockwise): Aircraft engineer and factory manager; department store executive; bricklayers; computer operator; systems analyst; lathe operator; paramedics; counterperson. Which two of these people (or pairs) shown here probably earn the highest salaries? Why? Which two probably earn the lowest salaries? Why?

Factors Affecting the Supply of Labor

Demand is but one of the market forces affecting wage levels. A second important market force is the *supply of labor*. This term refers to the number of workers who would be willing and able to take a job at all wage levels. The Law of Supply applies to labor in two ways:

- All other things being equal, more people will take a job at a higher wage than at a lower wage.
- An increase in the supply of workers will push wages down.

What, then, are the factors affecting the number of workers who are willing and able to perform a job?

The number of workers available depends on several factors: the wages, the talents and skills required, the attractiveness of the job, and workers' willingness to move where the jobs are.

1. Wages Offered. More people are willing to work at a particular job for a high wage than for a low wage. For example, what do you think would happen if employers who had offered $5.15 per hour raised wages to $8 per hour? More people would be willing to work at the higher wage. If wages were raised even more, people might leave their current jobs for the higher-paying ones. Similarly, if wages in an industry fall, workers there will move to higher-paying jobs in other industries. The level of wages, then, is one factor affecting the supply of labor.

2. Talents and Skills Required. Only a small number of people may have the talents and skills needed for certain jobs. No matter how well the job pays, few people can be top athletes. And it takes time and study to learn nursing, computer programming, or accounting. Not everyone is willing or able to make the effort or pay the high costs to get this training. Professions such as medicine and law require years of training beyond high school.

3. Attractiveness of the Job. People often choose jobs because they enjoy the work. Money is not the only reason Joe wants to become an air conditioning systems specialist. Joe likes the activities and surroundings of this kind of work. Other people prefer working outdoors. Still others prefer staying in offices. Some people like solitary work. Others prefer to work with people.

4. Mobility. The willingness of people to move to where the jobs are is described as *worker mobility*. Many people do not want to leave families, friends, and familiar neighborhoods unless they absolutely have to. Raising wages slightly might not attract work-ers to move from a different area or state. The supply of workers is affected by their mobility, or lack of it.

WHAT OTHER FORCES AFFECT WAGES?

While the market forces of supply and demand are the major factors explaining why some jobs pay more than others, they are not the only ones. In some instances, other forces influence why some jobs pay more than others. Among these factors are labor unions, laws, social attitudes, and education.

Labor Unions

When union negotiators and an employer's representatives sit down to discuss wages, the outcome often depends on the strength of each side. If the union workers can afford a long strike and the company cannot, the workers will probably win higher wages than they would if the company had been stronger. Wages for union workers are likely to be higher than wages for nonunionized work-ers in the same occupations. Of course, businesses must make profits in order to survive. This requirement places a limit on how much they can pay in wages. But if wages are too low, workers will look for better-paying jobs elsewhere. (Unions are discussed in Chapters 19 and 20.)

Government Laws

The laws of the federal government and the states affect wages.

1. Minimum Wage Laws. Federal law sets a *minimum wage*. (In 2007, the federal minimum wage was $5.15 an hour.) An em-ployer must pay the minimum wage even though a worker may be willing to work for less. States (and cities) can have higher mini-mums than what the federal law calls for.

2. Child Labor Laws. Other laws tend to push up wages be-cause they reduce the supply of potential workers. For example, laws prohibit the employment of children in many industries. And states have education laws that require young people to remain in school until they reach a certain age.

3. Unemployment Insurance Laws. State unemployment in-surance laws enable some workers to receive income while they are unemployed. Unemployment insurance enables these workers to hold off taking lower-paying jobs while they are looking for jobs that pay what they had previously earned.

Most economists conclude that as a result of government laws such as those just described, wages are higher than they would be if wages were determined by market forces alone.

Social Attitudes

People's beliefs about themselves and other members of society are called their *social attitudes*. For example, one social attitude of the past was that a man should be the "breadwinner" of the family and, therefore, should earn more than a woman. Another social attitude may be prejudiced beliefs about a group of people. All social attitudes are learned. They are taught by parents to their children and by one friend to another. Some social attitudes are harmful. Since social attitudes can be taught, it makes sense to teach good attitudes and to unlearn harmful ones.

Prejudice is a harmful social attitude. It can lead to discrimination. In employment, discrimination is evident when one group is favored over another in hiring, salary, or promotion for reasons that have nothing to do with the workers' performance on the job. Workers' wages should be based upon what the workers do, not who the workers are. Federal and state laws prohibit discrimination based upon race, sex, age, physical disability, sexual orientation, or national origin. Still, discrimination exists and affects what jobs pay. On average, women and members of minorities earn less than white males.

Women doing the same work as men generally do not earn *equivalent* (equal) *pay*. Women often earn less. In 2001, for example, the median weekly earnings of women in all occupations was $517, while men earned $683, some 25 percent more. In addition, the ratio of women to men was highest in certain low-paying service occupations and lowest in high-paying executive, administrative, and managerial occupations.

As a result of discriminatory attitudes, women in the United States traditionally went into different occupations than men. For the most part, the occupations that women dominated paid less. Was this fair? Many people thought not. They suggested that pay for these occupations should be based on *comparable worth*. According to this concept, pay for traditionally female occupations would be based on the requirements for the job. Suppose, for example, the education and training for a secretary's job (which women dominate) are of similar difficulty and length as the education and training for a carpenter's job (which men dominate). If that were so, then the jobs should pay the same.

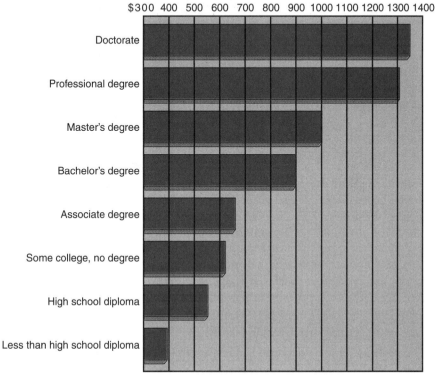

Education

Stay in school! Evidence shows that people who have completed many years of school earn more than those who have completed only a few. (See the graph below.) When you combine going to school with learning a skill that is in demand, you are in a good position to earn a decent wage. Since there are few people available with the education and training needed for some jobs, these jobs will pay more than others. Remember how supply and demand affect wages.

More and more workers are better educated. In 1960, 41 percent of workers had high school diplomas and 8 percent had college degrees. In 2000, however, the percentage of workers with high school diplomas jumped to 84. And those with college degrees increased to 26. Because more women and minority workers are better educated today than they were over 40 years ago, they too are able to earn more.

Figure 18.1 Median Weekly Earnings, by Highest Educational Attainment

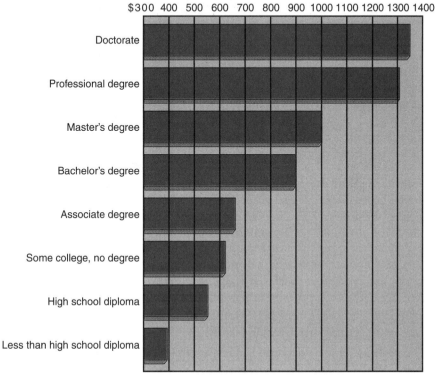

SUMMARY

Some jobs pay more than others. The market forces of supply and demand explain why wage differences exist. Wages will be highest in occupations where the demand for a worker's services is greatest and the supply of such workers is smallest. The demand for a worker is influenced by the demand for the product or service with which the worker is involved. The supply of workers is influenced by the skill, training, and education needed, the attractiveness of the job, and whether workers are willing to accept jobs in certain areas.

Other forces also influence wages. These include the influence of labor unions, government laws, social attitudes, and education. These forces affect either the supply of or the demand for workers.

It pays to stay in school. Generally, a better-educated person earns more than one with less education.

LOOKING AHEAD

In the next chapter, you will learn about organized labor—that is, unions—in this country. You will find out why labor unions were formed, the difficulties early unions faced, and the present status of unions.

EXERCISES

✔**Matching** Match each term in Column A with its definition in Column B.

Column A	Column B
1. wages	*a.* a worker's output in a given time
2. gross pay	*b.* the lowest legal hourly pay a worker may receive
3. take-home pay	*c.* the ways in which people think about others, especially about those different from them
4. productivity	
5. worker mobility	*d.* the money or other compensation an employer pays for a person's labor per hour
6. social attitudes	
7. piecework	*e.* the wages a worker receives after deductions are made
8. minimum wage	
	f. work paid for at a set rate per unit
	g. the willingness of workers to move to where the jobs are
	h. the total wages a worker earns before deductions are made

✔**Multiple Choice** Choose the letter of the item that best completes the statement or answers the question.

1. A worker who does not pay for the meals provided by an employer is receiving (a) gross pay (b) tips (c) money wages (d) wages in kind.

2. John gets paid $5.15 an hour for delivering supermarket orders. John's earnings are called (a) piecework (b) hourly wages (c) annual salary (d) wages in kind.

3. Mary earns $400 a week but finds only $325 in her weekly pay envelope. The $325 is Mary's (a) gross pay (b) take-home pay (c) hourly pay (d) minimum wage.

4. Earnings are not the same for all workers because (a) all people are almost exactly alike (b) all jobs are about the same (c) it is not legal to pay every worker the same wage (d) not all people and all jobs are alike.

5. The lowest wage that an employer may pay a worker (a) is the minimum wage (b) depends upon the skill of the worker (c) depends upon whether the worker is a man or a woman (d) depends upon the worker's race and ethnic background.

6. Members of some minority groups often receive lower wages than the national average because (a) minority workers are not speedy workers (b) minority workers usually belong to unions (c) job discrimination exists against members of some minority groups (d) this is the law.

7. The main idea of this chapter is that (a) wages are not the same for all workers (b) wages should be the same for all workers (c) discrimination is against the law (d) wages are the same for everybody.

8. The concept of comparable worth suggests that (a) all workers should receive the same pay for the same number of hours worked (b) men and women should receive the same pay if they do the same work (c) men and women should work at the same occupations (d) pay for occupations that generally employ women should be based on jobs generally employing men and having similar requirements.

✔ Essay Question

Discuss how *each* of the following factors can affect how much a worker is paid: (a) supply and demand for workers, (b) education, (c) labor unions, and (d) government laws.

✔ Using the Internet

To learn more about wages, hours, and employment by occupations, age, and gender go to either <<http://www.bls.gov>> or <<http://factfinder.census.gov>>.

CHAPTER *19*

Organized Labor

Have you ever felt that you would like to go to the principal of your school and complain about a thing or two? The chances are that, even if you wanted to, you were afraid to do so. Perhaps you felt that all alone you would be in too weak a position to get anywhere.

If your school has a student organization, you can let this group—which represents you—do the talking for you. When you start working at a job, you may face the same problem. Instead of the principal, you will have to face your boss or another supervisor with your complaint. If your place of work has a *labor union* (an organization that represents workers' interests on the job), the union can do the talking for you.

In the United States, some 15.4 million persons (about one out of every ten workers, not counting self-employed persons) belong to labor unions. They are members of the *organized labor movement*. Large numbers of workers in the auto, trucking, shipping, and steel industries belong to unions. So too do many teachers and office workers. Naturally, unions are important. You have already learned that unions can influence wages and jobs. Unions can also influence working conditions and prices. Therefore, you should know more about them. After reading this chapter, you will be able to answer the following questions:

- What have been the reasons that workers organized labor unions?
- How did national labor unions organize and grow?
- What laws have affected unions' growth?
- What recent developments have affected organized labor?

WHAT HAVE BEEN THE REASONS FOR ORGANIZING LABOR UNIONS?

Higher Wages and Better Working Conditions

The main reasons that workers organized labor unions have been to get higher wages and better working conditions. Why did workers begin to create and join unions a century ago? To answer this question, we will describe what happened to several workers in industries before they had unions.

1. A Miner's Story: Kulpont, Pennsylvania, 1902. Jimmy Travis was a miner, just as his dad had been before him. Jimmy had worked the mines of Pennsylvania since 1882, when he was just 12 years old. His big hope was that his three sons would never have to go into the mines. The oldest boy was ten in 1902.

Jimmy's day started at five o'clock in the morning. After breakfast, he walked to the mine shaft. His wife, Sue, had given up trying to clean the clothes Jimmy wore in the mines. They were black with coal dust.

The mine was dark, damp, and dangerous. A few timbers held up the sides where hunks of coal had been chopped out. The walls could have caved in at any minute. If that did not happen, the coal dust could ignite and explode. Anyway, miner's asthma, often called the black lung disease, was bound to get you if you breathed air full of coal dust year after year.

What did Jimmy have to show for his years of working in the mines? He did not get a vacation, sick pay, or a pension. Had Jimmy died in a mining accident, his family would have received nothing.

The owners of the mines, factories, and mills were, for the most part, against labor unions. For one thing, it was a matter of dollars and cents. Unions led to higher wages. If wages went up, the owners feared their profits might go down. Health and safety measures, medical care, and income security all cost money. Moreover, in the early 1900s, many of the mine owners believed that

Figure 19.1 Union Membership and the Total Labor Force Since 1900

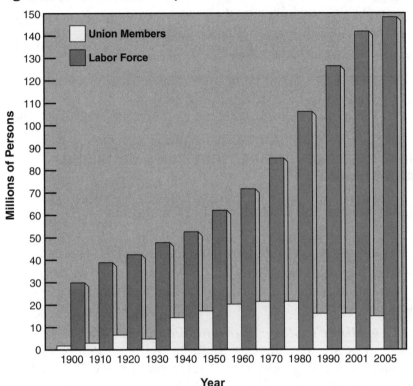

unions were dangerous to the free enterprise system. They considered unions to be examples of *collectivism*—a kind of communism—and an evil foreign influence in this country. The owners believed that a worker should act as an individual, not as part of a group (such as a union).

The mine, factory, and mill owners were rich and powerful people. They often owned all the workers' homes and the stores in the small mining towns and mill towns. The owners could influence local and state legislators. During conflicts with workers, they could get the local police and state troopers to support them by claiming that police support was needed to protect the rights of property.

In 1902, Jimmy Travis and some other miners in his town tried to organize a union. When the company found out, the bosses told them to stop organizing or else they would lose their jobs and homes. Jimmy and his fellow miners had no choice but to stop.

2. A Lumberjack's Story: Portland, Oregon, 1910. One day in Chicago in the year 1910, Sam Bisbee read a poster: "Men Wanted in Lumber Camps! High Wages! Steady Work! Come West!" So Sam went west, to Portland, Oregon.

A lot of men answered this ad. When they got to Oregon, they found that wages in the lumber camps were low. And living costs were high. Furthermore, there was work for only four months, after which many of the men were laid off. Most of them then went on the road looking for more work.

After Sam was laid off, he stayed in the area and joined a union of lumberjacks. The union men protested the conditions in the camps. They planned to ask the timber company for decent wages and steady work. But one day, sheriff's deputies came into the work camp with clubs swinging. Sam and the other union men were rounded up, branded *agitators*, and thrown into jail. "Agitator" was a word often used to describe a *union organizer*. It meant "troublemaker." The next day, Sam was told to leave town—or else. He left fast.

HOW DID NATIONAL LABOR UNIONS ORGANIZE AND GROW?

Early Unions—Small and Secret

Labor unions in this country date back to colonial times. Workers joined those early unions because then, as now, they wanted higher wages and better working conditions. But the early unions were small, often secret organizations. Workers knew that their employers would punish them if they found out about the unions.

American workers faced a new challenge in the decades after the Civil War ended in 1865. The United States then was becoming a great manufacturing nation. New industries such as iron and steel, lumber, mining, and oil were developing. Railroads were being built to transport goods and raw materials across the country. Large businesses had great wealth and power. To combat these giant businesses, workers began to realize that they would have to band together on a nationwide scale. The growth of labor unions since 1900 is shown in Figure 19.1.

Solidarity

In 1915, Ralph Chapin, a poet who was a member of a labor organization called the International Workers of the World (IWW), wrote a song expressing why workers needed unions. Chapin called his song "Solidarity Forever." (*Solidarity* means sticking together.) This song says that the worker harvested the crops, built the cities, dug the mines, and put down thousands of miles of railroad tracks. Without the muscle and brain of the worker, not a single wheel could turn. Yet, the song tells us, the worker's position in the midst of all these wonders is pretty bad. There is no force on earth more feeble than that of one worker. The answer to the worker's problem, therefore, is "Solidarity Forever." There is no force mightier than workers who are united, "for the union makes us strong," says the song.

Knights of Labor

The Knights of Labor was organized in 1869 by Uriah S. Stephens. All workers could join this union no matter what kind of work they did. All members living in the same area were also members of the same local chapter of the union. Under the leadership of Terrence Powderly, membership in the Knights grew to over 700,000 by 1886. Then, after some strikes had failed, the organization rapidly declined.

American Federation of Labor

In 1886, Samuel Gompers, the leader of the Cigar Makers Union, organized the *American Federation of Labor (AFL)*. It was an association of *craft unions*. Membership in each union was restricted to skilled workers in one particular craft, or trade. Thus, if you were a plumber, you belonged to the union of plumbers. If you were a carpenter, you belonged to the union of carpenters.

As many industries in the United States grew larger, they hired more and more workers who had no skills. Since the AFL accepted only skilled workers, the unskilled workers in these huge industries could not belong to an AFL union.

John L. Lewis Forms the CIO

In 1935, John L. Lewis, leader of the United Mine Workers, got his union to split away from the AFL. Several years later, Lewis formed the *Congress of Industrial Organizations (CIO)*. The CIO was different from the AFL. The CIO organized an entire industry. Every worker in that industry could belong to one union. It did not matter if the workers were skilled or unskilled. It did not matter what job they performed. As long as they were in the same industry, they could belong to the same union. This type of union is called an *industrial union*. The CIO was an association of industrial unions.

1. The CIO Shows Its Strength. In January 1937, newspaper headlines told of workers at General Motors plants "sitting down" on the job. They sat at their workstations throughout the factories. No one worked. *Life* magazine's picture of workers sitting down on the job was seen all over the country.

The police were sent in to remove the striking workers. As the police rushed through the doors, they were met by flying coffee mugs, door hinges, soda pop bottles, and anything else workers could pick up and throw. John L. Lewis was quickly called to a meeting with the president of General Motors. The auto company agreed to recognize the United Auto Workers as the union that would bargain for the autoworkers. The CIO was on its way.

2. Growth and Merger. CIO membership grew from four million workers in the late 1930s to nearly six million in the mid-1950s. (AFL membership also made strong gains in this period.) By the 1950s, the differences between the AFL and the CIO were less clearcut than they had been a generation earlier. A large percentage of AFL members also belonged to industrial unions. In 1955, the two large unions, with similar membership and economic goals, agreed to merge. They formed the AFL-CIO, with some 16 million members. Later, the Teamsters Union separated from the AFL-CIO to form its own independent union with over two million members.

Right to Bargain: In 1937, unionized GM workers celebrated their victory. The company recognized their union, and it agreed to bargain with the union for a contract.

WHAT LAWS HAVE AFFECTED UNIONS' GROWTH?

Laws affecting unions have changed over the years. There have been three major periods. (1) Before 1933, the government was antiunion; (2) during the New Deal and World War II (1933–1945), the government favored unions; and (3) since 1946, laws have been fairly evenly balanced.

Laws Against Unions (Before 1933)

The antiunion attitude of the government prior to the New Deal was seen in the way the federal courts interpreted the law and in the use of federal troops or state militia during a strike.

In the early 1900s, there were some very serious strikes. U.S. army soldiers or state militia (armed troops) were sometimes called out to remove strikers from a plant. Employers then brought in *strikebreakers* (nonunion workers hired during a strike) to work in the plant and crush the strike.

In the Danbury Hatters strike of 1903, a federal court used the Sherman Antitrust Act of 1890 against the striking union. The Sherman Act stated that activities in "restraint of trade" (that stopped businesses from operating freely) were illegal. The union was forced by the court to pay triple damages to the hat company for losses resulting from the strike of hatmakers. It was not until 1914, with the passage of the Clayton Antitrust Act, that Congress said labor unions could not be prosecuted (as big businesses were) under the terms of the Sherman Act.

Before 1932, an employer could easily get an *injunction* (court order) directing a union to stop striking or picketing. Then the Norris-LaGuardia Act of 1932 made injunctions more difficult to obtain.

Laws Favoring Unions (1933–1945)

The cards had been "stacked" against labor. Government laws and court actions had been unfair to workers. Therefore, many people felt that the cards had to be reshuffled, and a "New Deal" of the cards made. Three major laws that were passed during the New Deal period in the 1930s directly affected workers. The *Wagner Act* was of particular concern to unions. The *Wages and Hours Act* and the *Social Security Act* affected most workers, whether or not they belonged to a union.

1. The Wagner Act, 1935. The Wagner Act gave workers the right to form or join any union of their own choice, and the right to strike. Employers were required to bargain with the union chosen by the majority of the workers. (Bargaining between employers and unions is the subject of the following chapter.) The act also prohibited certain "unfair labor practices" by management. The *National Labor Relations Board* (*NLRB*) was created to enforce the Wagner Act. The NLRB holds elections in which the workers in a company decide whether they want a union to represent them, and if so, which one.

2. The Wages and Hours Act, 1938. This law established a minimum wage of 25 cents per hour and a maximum workweek of 40 hours for industrial workers. Workers were to receive overtime pay at the rate of one-and-a-half times their hourly pay. Child labor was restricted.

This federal law applied only to businesses engaged in *interstate commerce* (business in two or more states). Most states passed similar laws affecting businesses engaged in commerce within the state. The minimum wage has been raised many times over the years. In 2002, it was $5.15 per hour.

3. The Social Security Act, 1935. There are three phases to the Social Security program: (1) benefits to cover the risks of old age, death, dependency (of children), disability, and blindness; (2) medical care for the aged (added in 1965); and (3) unemployment benefits. These are all discussed in Chapter 14.

The Trend Toward Balance (1946–Present)

The prolabor attitude of government during the New Deal and World War II was an important reason why union membership grew from about 3 million in 1933 to over 12 million persons in 1945. In that later year, unions represented one-third of the non-farm workers in this country. With the growth in membership, union power also grew. After World War II, however, the public attitude toward labor unions began to change. The public became fed up with the rising prices and strikes of the postwar era. The public felt that the Wagner Act had been one-sided, favoring labor. Labor was no longer seen as the underdog, and the employer was no longer always seen as wrong. In addition, many people thought that Communists were gaining control of some unions. In this atmosphere, Congress passed the *Taft-Hartley Act* and the *Landrum-Griffin Act*.

1. Taft-Hartley Act, 1947. The Wagner Act had said that certain management practices were unfair to labor. It had not mentioned union practices that were unfair to management. The Taft-Hartley Act amended the Wagner Act and set up standards of conduct for both unions and management. These were the major provisions of the act:

a. Unions were required to give notice before striking. If a strike threatened the national interest, the President could request an injunction to delay the strike for 80 days, during which time negotiations could take place.

b. Unions were required to bargain with employers (in much the same way that the Wagner Act required that employers bargain with unions).

c. Unfair labor practices by unions were listed and prohibited.

d. Unions could be sued and held legally responsible for the actions of their members.

e. Some boycotts and certain kinds of strikes were declared illegal.

f. Financial contributions to political campaigns were forbidden.

g. The *closed shop*, which required that all employees be union members before they could be hired, was declared illegal. The *union shop*, which required all employees to become union members within a certain period of time after they had been hired, was permitted. However, the act gave the states the right to pass laws about unions. A *right-to-work law* prohibits the union shop in that state and permits workers there to hold jobs without joining a union.

2. Landrum-Griffin Act, 1959. As a result of Senate investigations during the 1950s, *racketeering* (criminal activities) and

Collective Bargaining: Company and union negotiators shake hands to show that agreement has been reached on a new contract. In this case, the company is Amtrak—the national passenger railroad. It is represented by its Chairman, Tom Downs, on the left. On the right is Jedd Dodd, Chairman of the Brotherhood of Maintenance of Way Employees. In the center is Rodney Slater, former U.S. Transportation Secretary.

undemocratic practices in some labor unions were disclosed. The Landrum-Griffin Act was passed to force unions to open their financial records to the public. Another major purpose of the act was to protect union members' rights and to make it easier for members to participate in union activities. Other provisions of the law were designed to curb racketeering and eliminate corrupt practices within unions.

3. Labor Legislation Update, 1959–Present. No major labor laws have been passed by Congress since the Landrum-Griffin Act. Instead, many of the problems regarding labor-management relations have been handled either by the National Labor Relations Board or the courts. The lack of new legislation may be the result of the changing nature of labor unions and a decline both in union power and the ability of labor and management to work out their problems in peaceful ways.

UNIONS IN DECLINE

Membership is the most serious problem facing unions today. Figure 19.3 on page 294 shows that the percentage of workers belonging to unions has been declining since the 1960s. Union memberships in the construction, manufacturing, and transportation industries have had sharp declines. However, the number of unionized government employees (as well as their percentages belonging to unions) has risen. Economists suggest the following as reasons for this decline.

In the 19th and early 20th centuries, it was the blue-collar workers in the major U.S. industries who joined unions. Blue-collar employment has fallen, however. Today, there are fewer jobs in the iron and steel plants, textile mills, auto plants, and on the railroads than there were a generation ago. With fewer jobs in these industries, there are also fewer union members.

The decline in union strength has been caused by changes in U.S. industries and by competition from other lands. These factors are discussed below.

Changing Methods of Production

A major reason for declining union strength has been the trend toward using modern, automated equipment and scientific know-how to produce more goods with fewer workers. Modern industries need fewer mechanics but more technicians, computer operators, and office workers. As a result of these *technological changes*, there has been a decline in blue-collar employment and an increase in white-collar and service employment, where unions have been traditionally weak.

Personal Economics

JOINING A UNION?

Whether or not you join a union depends upon (1) where you live, (2) the kind of work you do, and (3) the labor-management contract, if any, of the place where you work.

1. Where You Live. You are more likely to join a union if you live in the Middle Atlantic, Northeast, North Central, and Pacific states than in the Southeast, South Central, or Southwest states. California (2.3 million), New York (2.0 million), and Illinois (1.0 million) have the greatest number of union members. More than half (54 percent) of the 16 million union members in the United States live in seven states. Southern cities, such as Atlanta, Dallas, Houston, tend to have low percentages of workers in unions. In contrast, Northern cities, such as Chicago, Philadelphia, and New York, tend to have high percentages of workers in unions.

2. Work You Do. Many union members are in manufacturing, transportation, construction, mining, and crafts jobs. White-collar workers (except for government workers) represent but a small per-

Figure 19.2 Union Membership by Industry

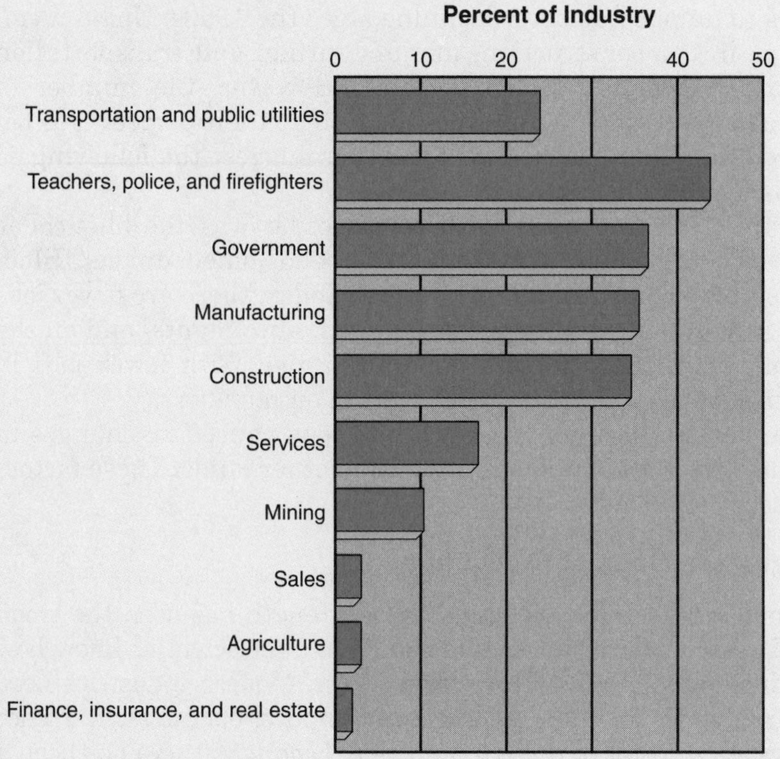

Percent of Industry

Industry	Percent
Transportation and public utilities	~33
Teachers, police, and firefighters	~45
Government	~40
Manufacturing	~40
Construction	~40
Services	~14
Mining	~20
Sales	~4
Agriculture	~4
Finance, insurance, and real estate	~4

centage of total union membership. Business owners, executives, and most supervisors and professional people do not join unions. In transportation and public utilities industries, about 24 percent of the workers are union members. In the finance and insurance industries, about 2 percent of the workers belong to unions. Government workers, however, are the largest group (36 percent) of unionized workers. Local government workers (teachers, police, and firefighters) have the highest unionization rate—42 percent.

As to be expected, full-time workers are more than twice as likely as part-time workers to be union members.

Since most women workers are in white-collar or service jobs, or in professional or technical jobs, they have not joined unions in the same numbers as men. Thus, two out of every three union members are men. Another reason why more men than women belong to unions is that there are more male than female workers in the labor force. Also, some unions have discriminated against women.

3. Union Shop Clause. In some firms, unions have been able to include a union shop clause in their contract with the employer. This means that all non-management workers must join the union within a given number of days, usually 30 to 60, after starting work. If you go to work in a union shop, you must join the union. A firm that does not require a worker to join a union is called an *open shop*. Some contracts that unions have signed with employers provide for an *agency shop*. If you work in an agency shop, you are not required to join the union representing workers in that shop. You are required, though, to pay union dues whether or not you are a union member. About 1.7 million workers are represented at their workplace by a union even though they are not union members themselves.

Technology may cause another problem for unions. Highly automated machinery can very often be run by fewer workers than was formerly the case. In the event of a strike, management can often hold onto its position because it can keep operating with a few nonunion managerial employees. Highly automated industries such as telecommunications depend more on electronics and computers than they do on human workers. As a result, in recent years strikes by telephone workers have been broken because management personnel kept telephone lines open.

Foreign Competition

At one time, U.S. industries sold their manufactured goods all over the world. There were few—if any—competitors. Today, there is strong competition. Steel is made in Asia, Europe, and South America. Textiles and shoes often come from countries in Asia, and autos are made in China, Western Europe, and South America.

Foreign competition has hurt union strength in at least three ways. (1) Industries that have lost sales to foreign companies now

**Figure 19.3 Union Membership as a Percent of
Total Labor Force Since 1900**

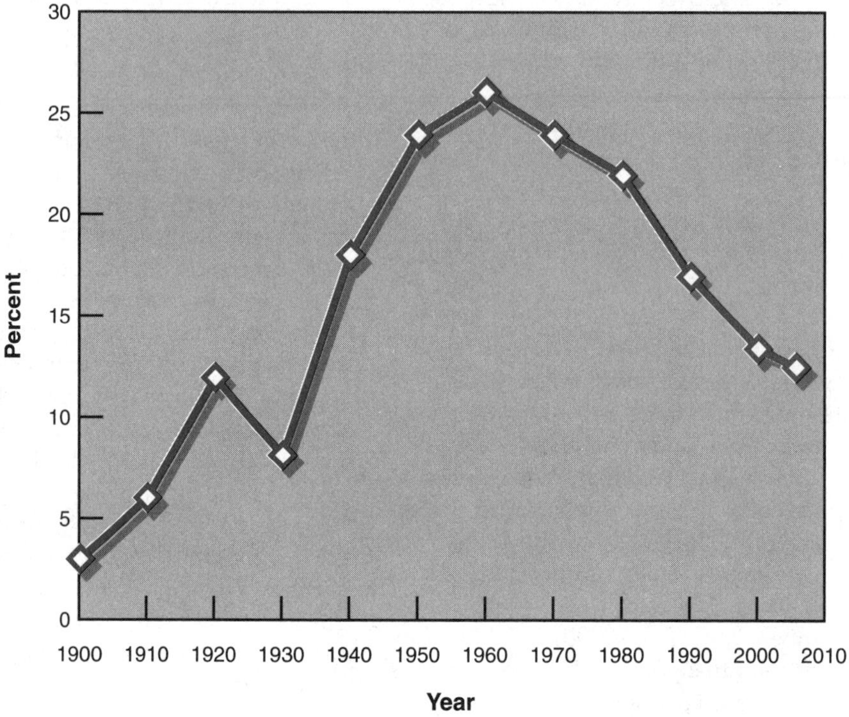

employ fewer workers, and, thus, fewer union members. This is true in the steel, textile, and auto industries. (2) Foreign workers usually earn less than U.S. workers for doing similar tasks. As a result, it costs foreign producers less to manufacture something because labor costs are lower overseas. Unions in the United States, therefore, often reduce their own wage demands in their dealings with manufacturers of steel, textiles, and autos. (3) Many U.S. firms have built plants in other countries.

Move to Less Expensive Areas

To reduce wage costs and to meet the competition of foreign firms that have lower labor costs, many U.S. firms once located in the Northeast and Midwest have relocated to the South and the Southwest. U.S. firms have also relocated to countries in Latin America, Africa, and Asia where wages are lower.

Very often, a U.S. firm will obtain parts from overseas sources, including subsidiaries of the U.S. company in a foreign land. In addition, some clerical services of a U.S. company may be contracted out to a foreign company or subsidiary in order to lower operating costs. For example, a U.S.-based information concern has some of its clerical work done in Ghana, West Africa. Workers there are paid only 80 cents an hour plus benefits. This is low by U.S. standards, but it is much greater than the minimum wage of 80 cents *a day* in Ghana.

Unions have not been as successful in organizing workers in the South, the Southwest, and in foreign countries as they have been in the North. In addition, companies having difficulties with unions simply move away or set up operations where unions are weak. As a result, unions lose members.

The United Auto Workers (UAW) has never organized a foreign-owned assembly plant in the United States. But the number of such plants has been increasing, mostly in the South. General Motors, Ford, and Chrysler plants are unionized. Their foreign competitors, such as Nissan, Toyota, Honda, BMW and Mercedes-Benz, operate nonunion assembly plants. They discourage unionization by paying the same wages as the U.S. automakers—$45,000 to $100,000 a year (including overtime pay). These nonunion plants, though, do not offer the same generous health insurance and other benefits that U.S. automakers provide.

The fastest growing sectors of the economy, such as hotels, child care, finance, retail trade and airlines, have added millions of new jobs. However, only one out of twenty workers in those sectors is a union member. By contrast, in industries with the greatest job losses, such as autos and steel, four-fifths of the 2.1 million jobs lost belonged to union members.

Poor Image of Labor Unions

Charges of illegal activities in some unions have been made since the 1950s. The public still regards some labor unions with suspicion and mistrust.

Perhaps of equal importance is the fact that labor leaders today often lack the spark of the early leaders: Powderly, Gompers, and Lewis. Today, union leaders are very much like the business executives with whom they deal. They manage huge union pension funds and sometimes invest them in the very corporations for which their members work. Some union leaders even serve on companies' boards of directors.

Proposals for Organized Labor in the 21st Century

Many people believe the economic changes that we have just discussed will be permanent ones. Old-fashioned industrial America will never return, they say. But a wide difference of opinion has developed within the AFL-CIO on the strategies needed to deal with the problem of declining union membership. In July 2005, two of the nation's largest unions, the Teamsters, with 1.3 million members, and the Service Employees International Union (SEIU), with 1.7 million members, resigned from the AFL-CIO. They were later joined by the United Food and Commercial Workers and Unite Here—a union of hotel, restaurant, and garment workers. This union shake-up has been as dramatic a change as when the CIO organized workers in the auto and steel industries and separated from the AF of L during the 1930s.

The break-away unions, led by James Hoffa of the Teamsters and Andrew Stern of the SEIU, differ from those of AFL-CIO president John J. Sweeney on ways to stop the decline in union membership.

- *The Use of Union Funds.* The Teamsters, SEIU, and unions allied with them have been responsible for more than half of the new members brought into the AFL-CIO in the period 1995–2005. They have accomplished this feat through very aggressive membership drives. Therefore, Hoffa and Stern want unions to allot 50 percent of their AFL-CIO dues to organizing efforts. In addition, they want the federation to allocate $70 million of member union contributions to the federation, mostly in the form of rebates back to the member unions and the remainder in organizing campaigns. Sweeney, on the other hand, offered to spend $22.5 million on rebates and organizing campaigns. He asked that all affiliates dedicate 30 percent of their own budgets to recruitment. Sweeney believes that union money can be used more effectively in political campaigns. Sweeney argues that the decline in union membership results from unfavorable laws in Washington, such as those that encourage overseas outsourcing of jobs. Therefore, he concludes, unions must work harder to get out the vote on behalf of politicians more favorable to labor. Hoffa and Stern disagree. They argue that the focus should be on the long-term development of the labor movement which, they say, can be achieved only by being more aggressive in recruitment drives for more union members.
- *Structure and Role of the Federation.* Andrew Stern argues that small unions do not have the financial strength or the labor power to fight against modern, global corporations. Stern asserts that the AFL-CIO currently lacks the authority or the will to order union mergers and to dismiss union

leaders who do not measure up to organizing goals. Sweeney, on the other hand, rejects the idea that the federation has the authority to order unions to merge or to fire union officials because their union fails to meet a recruitment quota.

Since the break-up, Sweeney has agreed to changes designed to strengthen organizing and to provide more money for such efforts.

Will the labor split weaken or strengthen unionism in the United States? Will it weaken the political power of unions? It is much too early to tell. Most people, however, do agree that labor unions must change to meet the challenge of a changing, global economy. Some suggestions include:

1. *Organize New Workers.* In order to organize new workers, unions must organize in the expanding occupations, such as those involving computers and telecommunications, and in white-collar and service industries. In recent years, unions have successfully organized public employees. Public employees make up almost 40 percent of total union membership. Union spending on hiring, training, and sending labor organizers to all parts of the United States has increased considerably under the leadership of John J. Sweeney, who became AFL-CIO president in 1995.

The Union of Needletrades, Industrial and Textile Employees is actively seeking to organize workers in the laundry industry. Physicians, about 35,000 or 5 percent of the total, have been signing up with unions that have little or nothing to do with the medical profession. Some doctors, angry with health maintenance organizations (HMOs), have joined unions for greater bargaining strength. The American Medical Association, long opposed to doctors joining unions, has changed its policy and has set up a unit to conduct collective bargaining.

2. *Changed Attitude Toward Illegal Immigrants.* Unions have traditionally been opposed to firms hiring illegal immigrants. In fact, unions have strongly supported laws to restrict immigration to the United States. Immigrants, particularly "illegals," work for lower wages than union workers and, say the unions, take jobs away from U.S. workers. President George W. Bush, meeting with President Vicente Fox of Mexico, discussed a guest-worker program with Mexico. This would allow Mexican workers to accept employment in the United States on a year-to-year basis. The AFL-CIO opposes the guest-worker plan. Instead, the union leadership is pushing to obtain legal status and citizenship for illegal foreigners

Organizing New Workers: In the 1960s, Dolores Huerta helped Cesar Chavez lead California farmworkers in a successful drive for recognition of their union. She is now Secretary-Treasurer of the United Farm Workers.

working in this country. The union hopes, of course, to get as many of these workers to join the union as possible.

3. Union Mergers. Some unions today may not have the financial strength needed for successful organizational drives or the ability to withstand long strikes. U.S. labor unions are merging with one another in order to strengthen their power at the bargaining table. Some big mergers include the Communications Workers of America combining first with the National Association of Broadcast Employees and Technicians and then with the Newspaper Guild. The International Ladies' Garment Workers Union combined with the Amalgamated Clothing and Textile Workers' Union to become the Union of Needletrades, Industrial and Textile Employees.

SUMMARY

Unions were organized to improve wages and working conditions for their members. Union leaders recognized that a worker acting alone could not bargain successfully with an employer. With a union, a worker can gain benefits, including improvements in wages, hours, working conditions, job security, and promotions.

Early unions faced difficulties in organizing workers. At first, unions did not have much support from the public or the government. Employers did not want unions to organize their businesses.

National labor organizations developed after the Civil War as the United States rapidly industrialized. From 1869 to 1886, the Knights of Labor dominated national unions. The American Federation of Labor organized along craft lines and held power beginning in 1886. In the late 1930s, the Congress of Industrial Organizations, which organized all the workers in certain large manufacturing industries, was created. The two rival union organizations merged as the AFL-CIO in 1955.

Laws were generally unfavorable to unions prior to the beginning of the New Deal. Then came a period of legislation favoring unions, which lasted until 1939. After 1945, legislation was passed reducing some of the powers of unions. Attempts were made to make unions more democratic and honest. No major labor legislation has been passed since 1959.

Declining union strength is the most serious problem facing organized labor today. Unions have suffered also from changing technology, increasing foreign competition, the movement of firms to nonunion areas, and a poor image of labor leaders.

Unions may regain their strength by organizing more aggressively (especially in the occupations that are growing) and shifting emphasis from wage issues to improving labor-management relations, increasing productivity, and retraining workers to perform new jobs.

LOOKING AHEAD

The following chapter discusses how representatives from unions and employers try to agree on wages, hours, and working conditions. We will find out what happens when they cannot reach an agreement.

EXERCISES

✔**Multiple Choice** Choose the letter of the item that best completes the statement or answers the question.

1. What happened as more and more industries became assembly-line, mass-production industries? (a) Craft unions grew. (b) Industrial unions grew. (c) Fewer unskilled workers were needed. (d) Workers quit unions.

2. The main idea of this chapter is that labor unions in the United States are organized to (a) prevent new technology from being introduced (b) create labor unrest and make conditions difficult for employers (c) improve workers' wages and working conditions (d) raise the productivity of the average worker.

3. Which is an example of a craft union? (a) bricklayers, masons, and plasterers' union (b) textile workers' union (c) mine workers' union (d) automobile workers' union.

4. Today, the AFL and the CIO are (a) merged (b) apart and un-friendly (c) separate but friendly (d) no longer in existence.

5. Labor legislation was most favorable to labor unions during the period (a) 1960–present (b) 1945–1959 (c) 1933–1945 (d) 1865–1933.

6. Which of the following acts favored U.S. labor unions the most? (a) Sherman Antitrust Act (b) Wagner Act (c) Taft-Hartley Act (d) Landrum-Griffin Act.

7. The Wagner Act (a) established a national program of social security (b) gave workers the right to join unions and bargain collectively (c) set heavy fines for unions conducting strikes (d) set a minimum wage and maximum workweek for industrial workers.

8. The Wages and Hours Act (a) gave workers the right to choose their hours of work (b) gave workers the right to strike (c) set a minimum wage and maximum workweek for industrial workers (d) forced unions to pay employers for time lost in strikes.

9. All of the following were leaders of major labor unions *except* (a) Uriah S. Stephens (b) Ralph Chapin (c) Samuel Gompers (d) John L. Lewis.

✔**Matching** Match each term in Column A with its definition in Column B.

Column A	Column B
1. union	*a.* an association of both skilled and unskilled workers who work in one particular industry
2. agitator	
3. solidarity	*b.* originally, a union of many different kinds of craft unions
4. Knights of Labor	
5. Congress of Industrial Organizations	*c.* an association of skilled workers, such as carpenters
	d. a term meaning "sticking together"
6. American Federation of Labor	*e.* the name applied to an early union organizer who was considered a troublemaker by employers
7. technological change	
	f. a term referring to all unions and the workers who belong to them
8. craft union	
9. industrial union	*g.* an organization that represents workers' interests on the job
10. organized labor	
	h. one of the first national labor unions in the United States
	i. the trend toward using modern, automated equipment and scientific know-how to produce goods and services
	j. originally, an association of industrial unions

✔**Understanding a Graph** Study the graphs on pages 284 and 294 and then answer the questions below.

1. What was the size of the labor force in 1960, 1970, and 2005?

2. How many workers were union members in 1960, 1970, and 2005?

3. What happened to the size of the labor force during the period 1960 to 2005?

4. What happened to the size of union membership during the period 1960 to 2005?

5. What percentage of the labor force belonged to unions in 1960?

6. What percentage of the labor force belonged to unions in 2005?

✔*Critical-Thinking Questions*

1. Imagine that the UAW has chosen you to organize workers at a foreign-owned automobile assembly plant in the South. How do you think each of the following would react to your efforts? (a) the workers (b) the company (c) local businesses

2. Discuss three arguments you would offer to encourage workers to join your union.

3. Organized labor has traditionally shunned illegal immigrants and has erected sanctions against employers who hire undocumented workers. (a) Why would organized labor be opposed to illegal immigrants and undocumented workers? (b) Why did organized labor change its policy and is now pushing to obtain legal status and citizenship for foreign laborers living in the United States?

4. The AFL-CIO suffered a drastic change when the Teamsters and Service Employees International Union withdrew from the organization. (a) Explain the two major differences in the positions between Sweeney (of the AFL-CIO) and Hoffa and Stern (of the break-away group). (b) Explain why you agree or disagree with Sweeney that political action is the most effective way to deal with declining union membership.

CHAPTER 20
Collective Bargaining

Key Terms

collective bargaining	fact-finding board	jurisdictional strike
union contract	mediation	scab
fringe benefit	arbitration	yellow-dog contract
seniority	strike	blacklist
grievance	picketing	two-tier wage system
shop steward	boycott	
check-off	primary boycott	
bargaining power	slowdown	secondary boycott
sweetheart contract	job action	
	lockout	

The workers at the Hi-Lite Manufacturing Company are upset and worried. They have asked the company for a 15-percent wage increase over three years and changes in working conditions at the plant. But the company has refused to make any changes in its operations and has offered a 6-percent wage increase.

By what means will the differences between the demands of the workers and the offer of management at Hi-Lite be settled? The answer is *collective bargaining* (a series of meetings between representatives of the union and those of the company). But this answer raises two questions that will be discussed in this chapter. These questions are:

- What happens during collective bargaining?
- What happens when collective bargaining fails?

WHAT HAPPENS DURING COLLECTIVE BARGAINING?

The backbone of labor-management relations is the process of collective bargaining. The union bargains for, or speaks for, the workers that it represents. Representatives of the union and the company (employer) sit down at a conference table and discuss each issue until they reach an agreement. More than 90 percent of all *union contracts* (the written agreements between the employer and representatives of the union) are drawn up solely on the basis of such discussions. Union contracts usually run for two or three years.

The Basic Aims of Unions

Labor unions have many goals. The major ones are higher wages, shorter hours, fringe benefits, job security, and a grievance machinery. These goals are reflected in the union contract.

1. Wages and Hours. The union contract will state the pay for the jobs done and the hours of work. Of course, unions seek higher wages for their members each year. Often the contract will tie in workers' wages to the cost of living so that wages will rise if the cost of living increases. Unions often insist that workers should also share in a company's increased profits, if any. Unions say that large profits justify wage increases.

The contract may have provisions to keep the wage level of their members equal to or higher than wages paid to workers performing similar or identical jobs in other companies. Unions have been successful in reducing the number of hours worked each day as well as the number of days of the workweek.

2. Fringe Benefits. In addition to wages and hours, there will be provision for *fringe benefits*, that is, benefits not directly connected with wages or hours worked. Among these are such items as coffee breaks, the number of paid holidays, vacation time, health insurance, and the pension program for employees.

3. Job Security. Job security is important to most workers. The union contract protects workers from being fired without a valid reason. If there is not enough work and employees must be laid off, *seniority* (ranking workers according to how long they have been on the job) rules determine who will be laid off first. The last worker hired will be the first one laid off. Workers will be rehired according to seniority too. Moreover, many job promotions are based upon seniority. The worker with the most seniority has to be considered first when a job opening occurs in the shop.

4. Grievance Machinery. A method of working out *grievances* (workers' complaints that management has violated the union contracts) will be stated in the union contract. If a worker has a disagreement with a supervisor or boss, the worker will be able to resolve it with the help of the shop steward or union representative.

The *shop steward* is an employee of the company who has been chosen by the workers to uphold their rights and see that the union contract is fairly enforced. The *union representative* is usually a full-time employee of the union who performs a similar function.

5. Union Dues. Many union contracts provide for dues *check-off*. This means that union dues are taken directly from the workers' wages by the employer and given to the union. The workers never see this money. Unions like the check-off because it is hard for unions to collect from individual union members.

6. Other Matters. The union would like the contract to provide for a union shop, a workplace where every nonmanagment employee is required to join the union. In states that have laws prohibiting union shops, the union will try to have an agency shop. In an agency shop, all employees must pay union dues, even those employees who are not union members.

Union Bargaining Power

Generally, how favorable a contract the union will get for its members depends upon a number of factors. If the union is strong and management is weak, the union is likely to get better terms than if the opposite is true. The *bargaining power* of the union depends on a number of factors.

1. The Extent to Which the Industry Is Organized. If the workers in every firm in an industry belong to the union, the union is more powerful. Otherwise, employers in the industry can easily hire nonunion workers.

2. The Power of the Company Within the Industry. In some industries, such as automobiles, a few business firms control most of the production and prices. These firms can easily agree to higher wages and pass on the increased labor costs to consumers in the form of higher prices.

3. The Proportion of Wages to Total Production Costs. In some industries, such as electrical power production and oil refining, labor costs are a relatively small part of the costs of production. Union members in these industries find it fairly easy to obtain a wage increase because the increase will not have a serious effect on total costs. However, unionized employees of a company where labor costs make up a sizable proportion of total costs may find that a wage increase is more difficult to get.

4. Perishability of a Product or Service. If the producers in an industry can store their products—such as steel—they may be

On Strike: Transit workers in a large city use union workers' strongest weapon to fight for higher wages. Are strikes by public employees fair to citizens? What do workers lose when they go out on strike?

able to resist a strike threat and reduce the union's bargaining power. But producers whose products quickly decay, rot, or lose value—such as fresh foods—may find that the union is very strong.

5. Need for a Product or Service. Some strikes can cause hardship for many people who depend on a good or service. The threat of a strike by public transportation workers, for example, will increase their union's bargaining power.

6. Number of Unionized Workers in the Company. Suppose that a company has two plants in two different states. Also suppose that one plant is unionized and the other is not. If there is a strike by union members, the company can shift its production to the nonunionized plant. This situation is one reason why unions favor bargaining for all workers in a company at one time rather than bargaining just for workers in one locality.

7. Skill in Bargaining. Often the ability of the negotiators determines the outcome of the bargaining. If labor's negotiating team is more skillful than management's team, the union may win a better contract.

8. Other Factors. Sometimes strange things happen during collective bargaining. The media might come out either for or against the union. The influence of the President, a governor, or a mayor might be brought to bear on the union, management, or both. Sometimes, unknown to the union members, a crooked labor leader might sign a contract favorable to management in return for money or favors. This is called a *sweetheart contract*.

WHAT HAPPENS WHEN NEGOTIATIONS FAIL?

Nine times out of ten, union contracts are worked out through negotiations. Sometimes, however, negotiations break down. When this happens, either a third party is called for or there is labor-management conflict.

Third-Party Intervention

There are three recognized procedures to follow when negotiations fail. These methods are known as fact-finding, mediation, and arbitration.

1. Fact-Finding. Both parties might ask for a *fact-finding board*. The board studies the problems, issues a report, and sometimes recommends solutions. The board's recommendations are not binding (they do not have to be accepted by the parties).

2. Mediation. In *mediation*, a third party called a mediator enters the scene to help bring the two parties together. As in fact-finding, the mediator's proposals or suggestions are not binding on either party.

3. Arbitration. Both parties must agree beforehand to arbitration. In *arbitration*, a third party (called an arbitrator) makes a decision that is binding on both sides. They both must follow the decision. Arbitration is rarely used in negotiating a labor contract. It is more frequently used to handle a grievance about an existing contract.

Labor-Management Conflict: Tactics of Unions

Sometimes, of course, both collective bargaining and the help of a third party fail. Then unions, management, or both may use more dramatic methods. Unions and employers use a number of tactics to get what they want.

The legal methods used by labor include strikes, picketing, boycotts, slowdowns, and public relations.

1. Strikes. The *strike* is labor's most powerful weapon. In a strike, workers refuse to work. Production stops, and the employer loses income. Of course, the strikers also lose wages. But strikers hope to make up their losses by winning the strike and receiving higher wages and better benefits.

2. Picketing. You have probably seen workers walking up and down in front of a manufacturing plant or business. They may have been carrying signs that said, "Strike!" This action is called *picketing*. One purpose of picketing is to discourage other workers from going to work. Another purpose is to urge the public not to deal with the employer being struck.

3. Boycotts. The refusal of consumers to buy from a company whose workers are on strike is called a *boycott*. Workers on strike often organize a boycott of their employer's goods or services. If the union applies the pressure only to the company being struck, it is called a *primary boycott*.

4. Slowdowns. In a *slowdown,* workers deliberately reduce their output or refuse to do part of their usual routine. (This tactic is sometimes called a *job action.*) Since the workers are not on strike, they still draw their pay.

5. Public Relations. Unions advertise, publish newspapers and magazines, create Websites, and provide speakers to present labor's view on labor-management conflicts.

Unions may not legally use force to get agreement to their demands. Moreover, *jurisdictional strikes*—strikes between two or more unions over which one will represent the workers on a

Picketing for Rights: Hotel workers picket to protest alleged anti-union attitudes and activities by management. Do you think such picketing is effective?

particular job—are illegal. So too are *secondary boycotts,* which occur when a union asks consumers not to do business with a company that is doing business with a company that is on strike.

Labor-Management Conflict: Tactics of Management

There are many legal methods that employers can use against unions.

1. Injunctions. An *injunction* is an order issued by a court prohibiting a certain action. An employer may seek an injunction if it believes that the union has broken a law. In a labor dispute, the injunction might order the union to stop picketing.

2. Lockouts. In a *lockout,* management shuts down a plant where there is or might be a strike. If management can afford the shutdown better than the union members who are put out of work, it may force the union to come to terms. In recent decades, some lockouts have been followed by the company's moving the plant to a region of the country where unions are weaker.

3. Strikebreaking. Sometimes, nonunion workers are hired to replace the union workers who are on strike, a tactic called *strikebreaking.* The union term for a strikebreaker is a *scab.*

4. Public Relations. During a labor-management dispute, the company may buy time on radio and television, place ads in newspapers, and set up a Website to present its point of view to the public.

5. Two-Tier Wage System. In recent years, a major issue in collective bargaining has been the *two-tier wage system.* In such a system, new employees are paid lower starting wages than senior employees had been. For example, in many airline contracts, a new flight attendant receives 20–30 percent less than what new flight attendants had received under earlier contracts.

The two-tier wage system is gaining popularity with management as a way of reducing labor costs. But unions oppose the system. They argue that it pits worker against worker. It also encourages management to find reasons to get rid of higher-wage employees and to replace them with lower-paid ones.

6. Part-Time Employees. Another technique used by management to reduce wage costs is to hire part-time employees. Many firms, especially fast-food chains and supermarkets, hire part-time workers at lower wages and with few if any of the benefits (health coverage, pension, paid vacation) that are enjoyed by full-time workers.

Furthermore, companies that need additional help can save money by using part-time workers instead of paying overtime to full-time workers. (Overtime is usually 1.5 times regular pay.) For example, instead of paying six full-time workers four hours each in overtime (6 workers $\times$ 4 hours = 24 hours. 24 hours $\times$ $1\frac{1}{2}$ = 36 hours' overtime pay), one part-time worker can be hired to work the 24 hours. This saves the company the equivalent of 12 hours of regular pay.

Yellow-dog contracts and blacklists are management tactics that have been forbidden by federal laws. Under a *yellow-dog contract*, workers have to sign agreements swearing they were not union members and agreeing not to join unions. Then if they did join, they could be fired or sued by the company. The yellow-dog contracts were outlawed by the Norris-La Guardia Act of 1932. The *blacklist* is a list of union organizers that is circulated among employers in an industry. People on the list are kept from getting jobs in that industry. The Wagner Act of 1935 declared the blacklist an unfair labor practice, and it has been illegal ever since.

Effects of Strikes

Unions do not have as much power as they once had. At one time, unions were easily able to shut down companies and cripple parts of the nation's economy by calling a strike. They are still sometimes able to do this, but they do so less frequently. In long, drawn-out strikes in recent years, workers in copper mines, paper-making plants, and telecommunications were replaced and company operations continued. Sometimes, neither side wins a long strike. Eastern Airlines, for example, went into bankruptcy after a machinists' strike.

On the other hand, a strike by 185,000 United Parcel Service (UPS) workers in 1997 was successful. The strikers, members of the powerful Teamsters Union, shut down delivery of packages all across the United States. Thousands of UPS customers, from individuals and small businesses to huge mail order companies, were affected. Many reluctantly began looking for alternative ways to get their packages delivered. Public sympathy was with the strikers, who were demanding higher wages, full-time jobs for part-time workers, and preservation of the union pension fund. Many UPS customers refused to cross the union's picket lines, and the company had difficulty getting workers to replace the strikers. Fearing loss of a significant share of the market if the strike continued, the company agreed on key issues. The union, however, yielded to the company's demand for a five-year contract rather than a more common three-year one.

Understanding Economics

PUBLIC EMPLOYEES' RIGHT TO STRIKE

The federal government and most state governments prohibit strikes by their employees. In spite of these laws, however, government employees have gone out on strike. Postal workers, schoolteachers, air traffic controllers, firefighters, police officers, sanitation workers—all have defied the law and have struck. Should they be allowed to strike? The arguments pro and con are given below.

CON	PRO
1. Strikes by public employees are like a rebellion against the government's authority.	1. Public employees generally respect the government and laws, but a strike is their only way of getting concessions.
2. Strikes by public employees threaten public safety, health, and order. For example, if police or firefighters strike, who will protect people and put out fires? Strikes by sanitation workers could result in a health hazard.	2. Most strikes by public employees are no more dangerous to the public than strikes by workers in private industry. If you do not get your mail, for example, it is only an inconvenience.
3. Unlike private industry, governments usually do not charge money for their services. Thus, governments often cannot finance a wage increase by raising the price of a particular service.	3. Most government income is from taxes. Therefore, wage increases for public employees may come in part from new or higher taxes. Most people do not want to pay higher taxes, but they will do so in order to settle a strike.

SUMMARY

Collective bargaining is the negotiations between a union and an employer in order to agree to a contract covering the workers in the employer's business. The ability of either union or employer to get what it wants depends upon many factors. Among these is the extent to which the industry is organized, the power of the company within the industry, the proportion of wages to total costs, the perishability and/or need for the product or service, and the bargaining skills of each side. When negotiations fail, a third party may be introduced in an effort to reach a settlement without a strike.

Unions and management have used many tactics to get what they want. Strikes are often not as effective as they once were because of the ability of employers to replace striking workers with nonunion workers. Strikes have been effective when the general public is affected. Millions of union jobs have been lost in recent years.

LOOKING AHEAD

This chapter concludes our unit on labor. In the next chapter, we begin the study of business in the United States. We will find out how the majority of U.S. business firms are organized.

EXERCISES

✔**Matching** Match each term in Column A with its definition in Column B.

Column A
1. union contract
2. collective bargaining
3. grievance
4. injunction
5. fact-finding
6. mediation
7. arbitration
8. lockout
9. strike
10. strikebreaking

Column B

a. a court order to stop a certain action (e.g., picketing)

b. an attempt by a third party to settle a dispute between labor and management

c. the act of hiring nonunion workers to replace union workers who are on strike

d. negotiations by company management and union representatives about terms of the union contract

e. a formal complaint by a union member that a term of the union contract has been violated

f. a binding decision by a third party in a labor-management dispute

g. a refusal by workers to work

h. something that sets forth pay of workers, hours of work, holidays, vacations, paid insurance, pensions

i. a study of the issues in a labor-management dispute by a board interested in solving the dispute

j. the shutting down of a business to keep union workers out of the workplace

✔**Multiple Choice** Choose the letter of the item that best completes the statement or answers the question.

1. The negotiations between union and management in order to reach agreement on a contract is called (a) lockout (b) grievance (c) strikebreaking (d) collective bargaining.

2. A main idea of this chapter is that collective bargaining (a) rarely works (b) works 90 percent of the time (c) gives unions an advantage over management (d) gives management an advantage over unions.

3. A situation in which workers refuse to work is known as a(n) (a) boycott (b) lockout (c) injunction (d) strike.

4. Which tactic might be used by union workers against management? (a) picketing (b) blacklisting (c) lockout (d) injunction.

5. Which tactic might be used by management against union workers? (a) strike (b) lockout (c) slowdown (d) job action.

6. A two-tier wage system favors (a) new employees (b) unions (c) nonunion employees (d) management.

7. An employee is required to pay union dues even if not a member of a union if the contract provides for (a) a union shop (b) an open shop (c) an agency shop (d) check-off.

8. An example of a fringe benefit in a union contract is a provision for (a) health insurance (b) a 35-hour workweek (c) grievance machinery (d) yearly pay increases.

✔ Understanding *What You Have Read*

Indicate on a separate sheet of paper whether each of the following statements is true (**T**) or false (**F**). If a statement is neither true nor false but an opinion, write **O**.

1. Workers should refuse jobs in companies that do not have union contracts.

2. Ever since collective bargaining first began, relations between workers and employers have been peaceful.

3. The union speaks for the workers at a collective-bargaining session.

4. The union and the employer are equally matched at all collective-bargaining sessions.

5. Most labor contracts are arrived at by collective bargaining only.

6. It is illegal for workers in private industry to strike.

7. Mediation is binding on all parties.

8. In a long strike, it would be easier for a producer of steel to hold out against union demands than it would be for a producer of lettuce to do so.

9. Public employees should not be allowed to strike.

10. Blacklists are illegal.

✔ *Reading for Greater Understanding*

Read the following three paragraphs and then answer the questions that follow.

You are probably familiar with the woolen baseball caps worn by the Major League teams. For many years, a factory in Derby, New York, produced these caps. Then in June 2001, 300 workers set up a picket line at the New Era Cap Company located in Derby. Why did the workers strike? The union said it was because they rejected New Era's proposal to cut wages for most of the workers unless they speeded up production. The union argued that speeding up production would increase an already high rate of repetitive-stress injuries at the factory. Furthermore, in 1988 New Era had transferred production of its top-of-the-line Major League caps to nonunion plants in Alabama. According to the union, the transfer of production to Alabama had occurred because the workers at the Derby factory in 1987 had joined a union—the Communications Workers of America.

New Era management rejected the union's claims. New Era said that it had to cut costs because it was a small company that had to compete with giants like Reebok and Nike, who have low-wage plants in Asia. They said, for example, that New Era paid $10 an hour, while producers in China paid 15 to 20 cents an hour. It cost $2.80 to produce a cap at the Derby plant, while only $1.10 at New Era's Alabama plant. The New Era plant was continuing to operate using replacement workers for those on strike.

A nationwide student group came to the support of the union. They accused New Era of having a high injury rate and sought to punish the workers for joining a union by cutting wages and transferring production to the South. In addition to the college group, the giant AFL-CIO came to the support of the Derby union and urged its 13 million members to boycott New Era products. New Era management, however, argued that a boycott would shift consumer purchases to caps made in China and other countries where wages are low and working conditions are a lot worse than at New Era. This would destroy the New Era company, the one remaining large domestic cap company in the United States.

1. Why were the workers at the New Era plant dissatisfied?

2. What happened when collective bargaining broke down?

3. What tactics did the union use?

4. What tactics did the company use?

5. Which side would you have supported and why?

Unit *4*

PRODUCING: THE ROLE OF BUSINESS

Producers sell their goods and services to all who are willing and able to buy them.
This shopkeeper sells Italian food products.

In a free-market economy, most of the decisions about what will be produced and how it will be produced are made by private businesses. As you may have guessed, privately owned businesses do not just appear. Some individual or group of individuals have to create them. The person or persons who start a business are known as *entrepreneurs.*

Entrepreneurs play an important role in the U.S. economy. They acquire materials, employ workers, promote sales and do whatever else it takes to organize a business and keep it operating. But creating a business requires the outlay of time, money, effort, and a lot of risk. Studies show that 24 percent of new ventures fail in their very first year, while 52 percent are out of business by the end of their second year. By the sixth year, 63 percent of start-ups will have bitten the dust.

Despite the risk of failure, there is no shortage of people willing to start new enterprises. In a recent year, for example, 155,000 new businesses were launched. That same year, some 72,000 firms failed.

Why do they do it? Why do people risk time, effort, and money to start new businesses? To some, the idea of being "one's own boss" and not having to be responsible to others outweighs the risk of failure. Others see starting a new business as an opportunity to put an idea that they have been thinking about into practice. Of course, many (if not most) who venture into entrepreneurship do so in the hope of earning lots of money. They are mindful of the experience of people like Michael Dell, Steve Jobs, and Bill Gates—people who formed their own companies and became billionaires while still in their 30s. With role models like these, it is little wonder that so many are willing to risk all in the hope of succeeding where others have failed.

How individuals, spurred by the desire to make a profit, organize their businesses is discussed in Chapter 21. There you will learn about two forms of business organization, the sole proprietorship and the partnership. In Chapter 22, you will find out how corporations are organized and why the corporate form is especially well suited to large businesses. Next, in Chapter 23, you will learn about the buying and selling of corporate stocks and bonds.

In Chapter 24, you will learn how the mass production of goods has made the U.S. economy great. Chapter 25 considers the advantages and disadvantages that occur when firms combine rather than remain independent competitors. Chapter 26 discusses how the government promotes and regulates competition.

CHAPTER *21*

The Sole Proprietorship and the Partnership

For a number of years, George Lee had been thinking about owning his own business. When he was in high school, George opened a savings account at a local bank. He was preparing for the day when he would open his own company and be his own boss.

After graduation, George got a job with a company that operated a chain of retail stores that sold computers and computer supplies. Over the next four years, he learned the retail computer business from the inside. Although he had started as a stockroom clerk, he soon advanced to sales. After two years with the firm, he became an assistant manager of one store. All the while, he continued to set money aside in anticipation of the day when he would open his own business.

George was not alone in wanting to own a business of his own. There are now well over 20 million small businesses in the United States. And that number keeps growing. Government statistics tell us, for example, that every week some 3,000 new businesses are begun. Not all of them succeed, though. Indeed, every year the number of failing businesses reaches into the tens of thousands.

In this chapter, you will study businesses and their role in the U.S. economy. When you have finished reading the chapter, you should be able to answer the following questions:

- Why do people go into business for themselves?
- Why are most businesses sole proprietorships?
- Why do some businesses organize as partnerships?

WHY DO PEOPLE GO INTO BUSINESS FOR THEMSELVES?

Although George Lee liked his job as assistant manager of a computer store, he still looked forward to the day when he could start a business of his own. It thrilled him to think of being his own boss, of trying out new ideas, and, if things worked out well, of earning great profits.

The day finally came when George felt that he had saved enough money to go ahead with his plans. He found an empty store for rent in a nearby shopping center. He then went to his local bank to see if he could borrow the additional funds he would need to start operations. He discussed his plans with Ms. Hamilton, the bank's loan officer. She thought that George's idea sounded very promising. She asked him to write a *business plan* that she could present to the bank's loan committee. Before lending money to a business of any size, banks and other investors usually ask for a formal business plan. Business plans describe the following:

- Nature of the business and the business's goals.
- *Marketing* plans, including the location and type of market the company expects to reach, the potential demand for its product or service, and how the company plans to advertise and price its product or service.
- What is the competition and what advantages the new company may have over the competition.
- Planned ways of operating the business.
- Planned key personnel, including who will run the business and what are their skills, training, and experience.
- Types of business insurance that will be purchased.
- Projected financial data, including the amount of money needed to start the business, a monthly budget for the first year of operation, a cash flow statement, an income statement, and a balance sheet.

A few days later, Ms. Hamilton called George to tell him that the bank would lend him several thousand dollars. Based on Ms. Hamilton's recommendation and his business plan, the bank felt confident that George's store would be a success and that he would be able to repay the loan out of his earnings.

Using the bank loan and the money he had saved, George was able to furnish his store and buy the computer equipment and supplies that he planned to sell. In the language of economics, George was an entrepreneur. George Lee called his store Byteland. It was an instant success. Everyone liked the rock-bottom prices and excellent service that George provided. But he had to work very hard. He opened the store at 9 A.M. every morning and remained there until closing at 6 P.M. every night. He was salesperson, bookkeeper, stock clerk, and janitor. Because there was no one to relieve him, he even had to eat his lunch in the store.

In time, the store's success enabled George to hire an assistant to help him with sales. But it was still his business. For that reason, George felt that he had to keep a close eye on things. After all, if the customers stopped coming in, George would no longer be able to pay the rent or keep up with bank payments.

As sales increased, George looked for ways to expand his operations. One idea that he had was to sell his merchandise also by mail order. By advertising his computers and supplies in certain national magazines, George reasoned, he could greatly increase his sales. More sales would lead to more profits.

Profits are what remain out of income after a business has paid all its costs of doing business. These costs are its *expenses*. When George worked for the computer store, the company paid him a wage. As you have learned, wages are the hourly rewards paid to workers for their labor. After George started his own business, he began to look to profits as the main reward for his efforts.

A mail-order business requires national advertising and catalogs. But George could not pay for them without another loan. Unfortunately, the bankers insisted that they could not lend him any more money until he paid off his first loan. Besides, George was not sure that he could handle more work even if he got the loan. He decided to forget about mail order for the time being.

WHY ARE MOST BUSINESSES SOLE PROPRIETORSHIPS?

Byteland was a *sole proprietorship*—a business owned and run by one individual. (The owner is called the *proprietor*.) The proprietorship is the most common form of business in the United States.

Advantages of the Sole Proprietorship

Those who choose to organize their businesses as sole proprietorships do so for several reasons:

1. Ease of Operation. George chose to form his company as a sole proprietorship because it is the easiest and least expensive kind of business organization to create. Although requirements vary from one state to another, in most instances entrepreneurs can obtain the licenses or permits required to operate a business without outside help.

Other kinds of businesses frequently require the services of a lawyer, an accountant, or both before they can be set up or closed down.

2. Potential Profits. The owner of a sole proprietorship can do whatever he or she wishes with the profits. Let us suppose that George Lee sold $150,000 worth of merchandise last year. This amount was his income from doing business. Suppose, too, that it cost George $25,000 to rent and operate his store and pay taxes, $15,000 to pay the bank loan, $7,000 for his assistant, and $60,000 to buy the merchandise that he sold. How much profit would he have made? $43,000. Why? Because income (of $150,000), minus expenses (of $107,000) equals profits ($43,000).

Sole Proprietorship: What advantages may the owner expect from running a store by himself? What problems may he face?

Personal Economics

SHOULD YOU GO INTO BUSINESS FOR YOURSELF?

Figure 21.1 Factors Affecting Your Decision About Starting a Business

SHOULD YOU GO INTO BUSINESS FOR YOURSELF?

Your own background	Other people	Opportunities for business growth

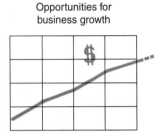

Education Experience Hobbies

A. The illustration above appeared in a U.S. government publication. Its purpose was to help people who were thinking of starting their own business. Study the illustration. Explain the meaning of each of the three parts of the illustration by answering these questions:

1. What does your background have to do with your selection of a business to start?

2. Why are the following factors included under a person's background: (a) education (b) experience (c) hobbies?

3. Why should other people affect a person's choice of business?

4. What is meant by "opportunities for business growth"? How should this factor influence a person's choice of business?

B. If you have ever thought that you might like to own a business, you should look at the following checklist. You should be able to answer these seven questions in detail before you actually take the plunge. As you read them, ask yourself these questions: (a) What is the meaning of each of these items? (b) Why was each item included? How is it important?

Checklist

1. What business should you choose? In what business have you had previous experience? Do you have special technical skills, such as those needed by a pharmacist, a plumber, an electrician, or an air conditioning service person?

2. What are your chances for success? What are conditions like in the line of business you are thinking of entering?

3. How much capital will you need to operate the business? (*Capital* in this case refers to money.)

4. Where can you get the money? Will your own savings be adequate, or will you have to borrow?

5. Where should you locate? Should you open your business near your source of materials, near your source of labor, or near your customers?

6. What records should you be prepared to keep? Are you going to keep the records yourself? Hire a bookkeeper? Have an outsider come in periodically?

7. Will you keep up to date? How do you plan to keep up with changes in your trade?

3. "You're the Boss." For many people, the most attractive feature of the sole proprietorship is the opportunity it offers for independence. Proprietors are their own bosses. They can set their own hours and assume risks that they would not be able to take if they worked for someone else.

Disadvantages of the Sole Proprietorship

The sole proprietorship carries with it a number of disadvantages, however. Foremost of these are limited life, limited funds, limited abilities, and unlimited liability.

1. Limited Life. A proprietorship can last only as long as the person who owns it. George Lee's business would come to an end on the day he died. While his heirs might be able to continue the business, doing so could involve a legally complicated procedure. For that reason, proprietorships are said to have *limited life.*

2. Limited Funds. We have seen that George Lee wanted to expand into the mail-order computer business. But he was unable to do so. He did not have the necessary funds, and the bank was unwilling to lend him more money. One of the reasons for the bank's reluctance to lend George more money has to do with the limited life of the sole proprietorship. If George were to die, who would pay his debts? This, then, is another shortcoming of the proprietorship. Funds are limited to the amount that proprietors themselves are able to raise.

3. Limited Abilities. There are just so many skills and talents that one person can possess. No one, including a sole proprietor, is an expert at everything. But the sole proprietor is just that: the only owner of a business. All too frequently a business suffers as the proprietor tries to solve problems about which she or he knows little or nothing.

4. *Unlimited Liability.* A proprietorship has *unlimited liability*. Its owner can be held personally *liable* (legally responsible) for all the debts of the business. If Byteland fails, George Lee's home and all his savings and investments could be seized to pay what he owes to his creditors.

Limited life, limited funds, limited abilities, and unlimited liability explain why many people hesitate to go into business for themselves. But there are other forms of business organization that overcome some or all of these handicaps. These are the partnership and the corporation.

To illustrate, let us return to our story of George Lee and his company, Byteland.

One day, George met Dolores Ramon, a former high school classmate. Dolores said that she had spent the years since graduation working in the electronic toy department of a mail-order house. She was now thinking about investing her savings in a business.

This information gave George an idea. "Why not team up?" he asked Dolores. After all, Byteland was doing quite well and would do even better if it could move into mail order. With her *capital* (money) and experience, the business would have just what it needed to expand. Moreover, the two could share the responsibility for running the business. This would take a lot of the load off George. The suggestion sounded great to Dolores. She went on to describe some of the ideas she had about mail order and how they could be used to expand sales.

WHY DO SOME BUSINESSES ORGANIZE AS PARTNERSHIPS?

George was glad that he had thought of asking Dolores to go into business with him in Byteland. They formed a *partnership*—a business owned by two or more persons. As a first step in forming a partnership, the two had a lawyer prepare a *contract* (legal agreement) for them. Under its terms, Dolores Ramon agreed to invest $40,000 in the business. In exchange, she was to be made an equal partner. This meant that both she and George would split their profits (or losses) on a 50–50 basis. The new firm would also be known as Byteland.

George and Dolores rented warehouse space and published a catalog. Because they had more money to spend on merchandise than George alone had had, the partners were able to buy in larger quantities and at lower prices. Lower wholesale prices enabled them to lower their own prices and to raise sales. They also hired a part-time clerk to work during peak hours in the store and a full-time worker to assist in the warehouse. Dolores spent most of her time looking

Understanding Economics

SUCCESSFUL ENTREPRENEURS

More and more Americans find the idea of owning a business of their own to be an attractive one. But with only a third of all newly opened businesses lasting more than five years, one has to ask these questions before going into business for oneself, "Why do I want to do this?" and "What does it take to succeed?"

As for the reasons for risking time and financial loss by opening a business, most people will mention things like:

"There is real satisfaction in being your own boss and watching something that you created, prosper, and grow."

"There is a certain amount of power, influence, and respect from others that goes with owning your own business."

What does it take to succeed in business? While opinions differ, most authorities agree that to be a success requires the right combination of:

- training and experience
- careful planning
- adequate financing

It is beyond the scope of this book to discuss in detail how each of the above ingredients contributes to business success. What follows, however, are brief biographies of three successful entrepreneurs. Each of them started with an idea, some would say a "dream," that ultimately became a reality. As you read the biographies, think about how these entrepreneurs became successful.

Muriel Siebert

Her father's illness compelled Muriel Siebert to abandon college and the accounting career for which she had been preparing. In 1954, with only $500, she drove from Cleveland, Ohio, in quest of a job in New York City. Although jobs then were scarce, her persistence paid off: she was hired by a brokerage firm as a trainee.

Siebert's accounting skills and her ability to analyze financial statements attracted new clients. As her reputation grew, she moved to other firms. Each new job increased her responsibilities and salary.

She learned to deal with the problem of being a woman in a predominantly man's world. "I changed jobs three times because they were paying a man more than

I was making for the same job." Once, she had to walk up the stairs to attend a board meeting because the club at which the meeting was being held would not take women in their elevator.

By 1967, Siebert thought it time to launch her own brokerage firm. But before she could trade stocks and bonds, she needed to have a seat on the New York Stock Exchange. No woman had ever owned her own brokerage firm or held a seat on this exchange. No woman, that is, until 1967, when the forces resisting her finally agreed to sell her a seat. Muriel Siebert & Co., the first brokerage firm owned by a woman, was open for business. By 2001, her firm earned $32 million in revenues.

Robert L. Johnson

Robert L. Johnson was born in Hickory, Mississippi, in 1946, the ninth of ten children. His family soon moved to Illinois. Robert Johnson graduated from the University of Illinois and moved on to earn a Master's degree from Princeton University. After Princeton, Johnson landed a job as a lobbyist for the National Cable Television Association (NCTA).

Johnson had long felt that television could be used to promote black-owned businesses and media. He would do this by producing television programs especially targeted to African-American viewers. Convinced that his idea had merit, Johnson turned to the problem of finding the money necessary to turn the dream into reality. As a first step, he applied for and received a bank loan of $15,000. Then through a combination of effort, timing, and luck, Johnson was able to enlist the support of NCTA and other leading firms in the cable television industry to provide the necessary satellite space and additional financing.

Johnson named the new venture Black Entertainment Television (BET). At 11 P.M. on January 11, 1980, BET officially aired its first program. It became the largest black-owned broadcasting company on cable TV. Ten years later, BET was reaching 25 million homes. In 2000, Johnson sold BET to Viacom for nearly $3 billion, making him the nation's first African-American billionaire. Johnson agreed to remain with the company as its Chairman.

James Chu

James Chu was born and raised in Taiwan, where he later entered the business world by selling Chinese-English dictionaries and English instruction tapes. In 1986, he accepted an offer to run U.S. operations for a Taiwanese computer keyboard manufacturer. Although that job

specialized in selling *computer peripherals* (equipment that can be connected to a computer).

As his organization grew, Chu saw a need for high-performance, competitively priced color monitors. In 1990, he gave his company a new name, ViewSonic, and launched a colorful advertising campaign featuring three Australian finches as the logo for his new monitors. Apparently the finches were a big hit, for ViewSonic soon became the world's fastest-growing brand of monitors.

Chu's achievements earned him many honors including the Ernst & Young "Entrepreneur Of The Year," in 1994, and *TransPacific Magazine's* "Top Under 40 Asian American Entrepreneur," in 1996. At the time, one magazine writer said that "... Chu may be the most successful immigrant in American history." His success has continued. In 2001, for example, with Chu serving as ViewSonic's President and CEO, the company received the top award in display technology.

did not work out, Chu was able to use the contacts he had made to start his own company in the United States, in 1987. It

after the mail-order end of the business. George concentrated on the retail store. They met several times a week to "discuss problems."

Advantages of the Partnership

George and Dolores's experiences tell us something about the advantages of the partnership form of business. We can summarize the advantages as more money for the business and the knowledge and experience of two people instead of one.

1. More Money (Capital) Available. Because there is more than one owner in a partnership, there is more than one source of money. In the case of Byteland, Dolores Ramon brought an additional $40,000 into the business. Also, banks are more willing to lend money to partnerships than to proprietorships. This fact is true because the loan is guaranteed not only by one person, but by each and every partner.

2. "Two Heads Are Better Than One." When she came into the business, Dolores Ramon brought special skills and experience with her. She made it easier for Byteland to enter the mail-order business. Moreover, Dolores and George were able to "put their heads together" to discuss and solve their business problems. (This situation is what people mean when they say that "two heads are better than one." When George had operated the business as a sole proprietorship, he had to solve all problems by himself.)

Disadvantages of the Partnership

There are a number of disadvantages to a partnership. The most important of these are its unlimited liability, limited life and resources, and the problems that arise when partners disagree.

1. Unlimited Liability. Each and every partner in a business may be held liable for its debts. No matter how many partners a business has, any one of them can be responsible for paying off what it owes. For this reason, there is no limit to the amount of money that a partner may lose. Why? Because there is no limit to

Partnership: Sharing business responsibilities lightens the job of these partners. What problems may they face?

Personal Economics

WHAT'S WHAT? TRY SWOT

Every now and then, entrepreneurs need to step back and examine their business to see how things are going. In doing so, they will be looking for answers to questions like: "Where are we now?"; "Where do we want to be in the near and distant future?"; and "How do we get there from here?" While there are any number of ways to assess a business, one method that has become popular in recent years is known as *SWOT analysis*.

SWOT provides entrepreneurs with a framework to organize and develop business strategies. The elements of SWOT are:

Strengths
Weaknesses
Opportunities
Threats

Typically, an entrepreneur or a management team will investigate each element of the business using the SWOT formula of strengths, weaknesses, opportunities, and threats. Upon completion of the study, steps may be taken to use the firm's strengths and opportunities while reducing its weaknesses and threats.

SWOT in Action

Leslie Prentiss and Dana Bird, owners of Happy Trails Bike Company, have decided to use a SWOT analysis study of their business operations. After consulting with customers, suppliers, and employees, Prentiss discovered the following:

1. Everyone agreed that Happy Trails's location—across the street from a major park with miles of bike paths—was ideal for bicycle rentals.

2. The company had to defend itself from lawsuits by rental customers who had injured themselves in falls.

3. While Happy Trails's bikes are in good condition, most lack gears, even though the bike paths are hilly in places.

4. A number of customers left after being told that the business had no "bicycles built for two" available for rent. They were, however, available for sale on a "special order" basis.

5. Many customers have said that they enjoyed cycling so much that they would like to buy a bike of their own. Others were heard to say that they would especially like to buy from Happy Trails because the staff ". . . seemed to know a lot about bikes."

6. Shoppers entering the store to look at bicycles and equipment often leave without having spoken to any employee.

7. A number of prospective rental and new-bike customers wanted to take their young children with them on the bike trail. But since Happy Trails did not have the necessary equipment (e.g., trail-a-bikes, and jogging strollers), they took their business elsewhere.

8. A number of customers said that they liked the friendly service they had received.

9. Bicycles in need of repair were quickly restored to service. As a result, the business never lost a rental because of unavailable bikes.

Prentiss and Bird entered their findings in a table similar to the following one.

Positive		Negative
Strengths	:	**W**eaknesses
	:	
	:	
Opportunities	:	**T**hreats

1. On a separate sheet of paper, prepare a chart like the one shown. Then enter the information obtained in Prentiss's study.

2. Using the information contained in the SWOT analysis, identify and explain two things that Happy Trails might do to expand its business and increase profits.

the amount that the firm may lose. Thus we see that in a partnership, as in a sole proprietorship, there is unlimited liability.

2. Limited Life. A partnership is legally ended when one of the partners dies. While it is possible to continue the business by forming a new partnership, to do so can present legal problems.

3. Limited Funds. As in the case with the sole proprietorship, the amount of money the partnership can raise is limited. This limit depends upon the personal resources of the partners, plus whatever money they can borrow.

4. Partners May Disagree. It has been said that a partnership is often a "very unsteady ship to sail." Sometimes, partners will have such serious disagreements that they can no longer function as a team. When this happens, it can easily bring the business to an end.

Byteland Grows Larger

Business at Dolores and George's Byteland grew quickly. The partners soon began to talk about opening several additional stores.

"Before you open any more stores, you ought to think about incorporating," Jed Frank, their lawyer, recommended.

"Jed, do you think Byteland is big enough for us to form a corporation?" asked Dolores.

"Yes, Dolores," Jed replied. "As a matter of fact, your business does not have to be very large in order to incorporate. And it would make a lot of sense for you to form a corporation."

"Well, then," George Lee chimed in, "why don't the three of us meet tomorrow morning so that you can tell us about these advantages?"

SUMMARY

In this chapter, we learned that people go into business for themselves in the hopes of directing their own financial destinies and earning profits. We also learned that the sole proprietorship is the most common form of business organization. Proprietorships are popular because they are easy and inexpensive to form. But sole proprietorships can raise only limited amounts of money. And the total burden of responsibility of running the business is on the owner.

As compared to a sole proprietorship, a partnership provides the advantages of additional capital and the sharing of the responsibilities of ownership. But both the proprietorship and the partnership have limited life, limited capital, and unlimited liability. It is because of these disadvantages that many business firms are organized as corporations.

LOOKING AHEAD

George, Dolores, and Jed agreed to meet the next day to discuss the possibility of converting Byteland into a corporation. We will read about the results of that meeting in the following chapter. As we do, we will also learn about the advantages and disadvantages of incorporating and the reasons why all large businesses are corporations.

EXERCISES

✔**Matching** Match each term in Column A with its definition in Column B.

Column A	Column B
1. sole proprietorship	a. personal responsibility for all the debts of a company
2. partnership	
3. unlimited liability	b. another word for "money"
4. capital	c. the money earned by an individual or a firm
5. contract	d. a business owned by one person
6. income	e. a business owned by two or more persons
7. expenses	f. the risk that a business will close upon the death of an owner
8. profits	
9. limited life	g. what is left out of income after expenses are paid
	h. the costs of doing business
	i. a legally binding agreement

✔ **Multiple Choice** Choose the letter of the item that best completes the statement or answers the question.

1. Which one of the following is *not* an advantage of a sole proprietorship? (a) The proprietor may keep all the profits. (b) The proprietor can lose only a limited amount of money. (c) The proprietor is his or her own boss. (d) There is no limit to the amount of money one may make.

2. A sole proprietorship has limited capital. This means that (a) only a limited number of machines and factories are available for proprietorships (b) the amount of money that a proprietorship can raise is limited (c) there is no limit to the amount of money one can lose in a proprietorship (d) two heads are better than one.

3. A sole proprietorship is a business organization that (a) has only one owner (b) has only two or three owners (c) is very small (d) does not have to pay taxes.

4. The term "profits" refers to (a) the total income received by a business (b) all the expenses of running a business (c) the total of all the income and expenses (d) anything left out of income after expenses have been deducted.

5. Both the sole proprietorship and the partnership have unlimited liability. (a) This is an advantage of both forms of business organization. (b) This means that there is no limit to the amount of money a proprietor or partner may lose. (c) This means that there is no limit to the amount of money a proprietor or partner may make. (d) This means that there is no limit to the things a proprietor or partner may be expected to do in running a business.

✔ *Imagine Applying for a Loan*

Imagine that you are planning to open a small store where you intend to sell candy, magazines, newspapers, toys, and stationery. You have several thousand dollars saved up. You plan to add to your savings by getting a loan from your local bank. When you go for your loan, the banker gives you a form to complete. It asks some detailed questions about your business plans. Some of these questions are listed below. How would you answer them if you really were in this situation? Why do you suppose a bank might ask questions like these?

1. What kind of business do you plan to operate?

2. Why do you want to open this business?

3. What three problems do you expect to be most troublesome? Explain briefly.

4. What made you select the location for your business?

✔ *Imagine Setting Up a Partnership*

Peter Brimar and Paul Hanno have been friends since high school. Now that they have completed their training at a local trade school, they have decided to go into the food-catering business together as partners. Peter has $20,000 in savings that he will be able to put into the business. Paul has $10,000. The partners agree that they will both draw weekly salaries of $500 from the business. In addition, they agree that, if there are any profits remaining at the end of the year, Peter will get two-thirds, while Paul will get one-third.

In order to avoid any misunderstanding, they put this agreement in writing and both partners signed it.

1. Why do you suppose partners usually put their agreements in writing?

2. Why did the partners agree that Peter Brimar would get two-thirds of the profits, while Paul Hanno only one-third?

3. Suppose that Brimar and Hanno have asked you to draw up the partnership agreement for them. On a separate sheet of paper, write out an agreement that both partners can sign. All the details described above should be included.

4. At the end of the first year, the partners had $48,000 in profits to share. (This was in addition to the salaries they had already drawn.) How much did each partner receive?

5. At the end of the second year, the partnership came to an end. The partners had $10,000 in debts. Peter Brimar had no more money in the bank, but Paul Hanno had saved up $15,000 during that time. How was the $10,000 paid off?

✔ *Using the Internet*

For practical advice on how to start your own business, visit the Website of the U.S. government's Small Business Administration, at <<http://www.sba.gov/starting/>>. If you want to prepare your own business plan, go to <<http://biztech.nfte.com/>>.

CHAPTER 22

The Corporation

Key Terms

corporation	corporate income	open corporation
charter	tax	board of
stock certificate	not-for-profit	directors
share of stock	corporation	proxy
stockholder	government-	officers
limited liability	owned	franchise
unlimited life	corporation	franchisor
double taxation	cooperative	franchisee
S corporation	closed corporation	

The partnership of Ramon and Lee was doing very well. It was doing so well, indeed, that the partners, Dolores Ramon and George Lee, decided to open several more Byteland stores. It was then that their attorney, Jed Frank, suggested that they form a corporation.

"But I thought that all corporations were multimillion-dollar businesses," said George.

"It's true, of course, that all large business firms are corporations," Mr. Frank replied. "But, as a matter of fact, most corporations are small businesses just like yours."

As you read this chapter, you will learn what Mr. Frank meant by his last statement. You will also learn the answers to the following questions:

- What is a corporation?
- What are some of the advantages and disadvantages of corporations?
- Who owns, controls, and manages large corporations?

WHAT IS A CORPORATION?

Dolores Ramon, George Lee, and Jed Frank sat around a table in Byteland's office. They met to discuss the possibility of transforming Byteland from a partnership to a corporation.

Mr. Frank continued the meeting by saying, "I think you will find these illustrations to be of interest." The illustrations he showed them looked like the ones in Figure 22.1.

"When you look at the pie chart 'Percent of Total Number of Firms,'" Mr. Frank asked, "what strikes you?"

"I see that about 73 percent of all business organizations are sole proprietorships," said George.

Figure 22.1 Proprietorships, Partnerships, and Corporations: Number and Receipts

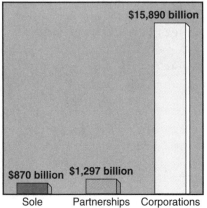

Number of Businesses

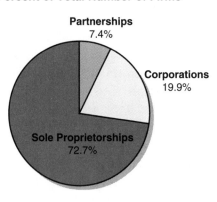

Percent of Total Number of Firms

Receipts

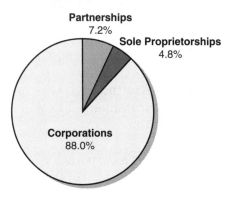

Receipts as a Percent of Total Business Income

"That's right," Dolores chimed in, "but look at the 'Receipts' pie chart. It shows that corporations account for 88 percent of all business receipts."

"I bet I know what that tells us," George said. "Jed, are all of the biggest businesses in the country corporations?"

"That's correct," their lawyer said. "And here's another fact about corporations: About 85 percent of all corporations are *small* businesses. Let me tell you why."

"Great," said Dolores. "Why don't you begin by telling us what a corporation is?"

"I'd be glad to," Mr. Frank replied. "A *corporation* is a business that is licensed by a state or the federal government as a legal individual. The license is called a *charter*. Ownership of the corporation is represented by *stock certificates*, or, as they are more commonly called, *shares of stock*. The people who own these shares of stock are known as *stockholders*."

So, for example, if Byteland were to incorporate with 1,000 shares of stock, both Ramon and Lee (each of whom owns half of the business) would receive 500 shares each. If, at a later date, Ramon or Lee sold 100 shares to someone else, that person would own a 10 percent interest in the business (because 100 shares is 10 percent of 1,000 shares).

WHAT ARE SOME OF THE ADVANTAGES AND DISADVANTAGES OF CORPORATIONS?

Advantages of Corporations

Corporations have advantages over the sole proprietorship and the partnership forms of business that we discussed in Chapter 21. The three most important advantages are limited liability, unlimited life, and easy transfer of ownership.

1. Limited Liability. There is no limit to the amount of money you might lose as a proprietor or partner. Were the business to shut down, partnership law allows any one of the partners to be held responsible for all the company's debts.

But such is not the case with a corporation. It has *limited liability*. This is because a corporation, in the eyes of the law, "has a life of its own." This phrase means that, if the corporation owes money to someone, only the business is responsible for the debt, not the people who own it. For example:

Lance Lotte invested $5,000 in a partnership. A year later, the partnership in which Lance had invested went out of business. The money that Lance had invested in the partnership was all he had in the world. All, that is, except for a savings account amounting to $15,000 that he was planning to use to help send his daughter, Lana, to college.

At the time that it folded, the firm was in debt for a total of $15,000. Naturally, those to whom the business owed the $15,000 wanted to be repaid. But none of the partners had any money. None, that is, except Lance. Since the business was a partnership, the law allowed the creditors to regain their $15,000 from him. Lana had to make other plans for her future.

But suppose, instead, that the business in which Lance Lotte invested was a corporation. In that case, no individual could be held responsible for the $15,000 debt. The most that Lance could have lost would have been his original $5,000 investment. Lana could have gone to college.

2. Unlimited Life. The life of a sole proprietorship and a partnership is limited. The law requires that these businesses be brought to an end upon the death or retirement of any of their owners. When this happens, a sole proprietorship and partnership, if they are to continue, must go through a complicated legal process in which new owners are substituted for the old ones. A corporation does not have this problem. It has *unlimited life.* When stockholders die, their shares simply become part of their estates and are passed along to their heirs. For that reason, corporations can (in theory at least) live forever.

3. Easy Transfer of Ownership. Selling a sole proprietorship or partnership can be a very complicated and expensive process. The sale requires the services of lawyers and accountants. But shares of stock in a corporation can be sold merely by signing them over to a new owner.

Disadvantages of Corporations

Not all businesses are corporations. Indeed, as you saw earlier, the most popular form of business organization is the sole proprietorship. Corporations have the disadvantages of being costly and complicated to set up, and their owners are subject to double taxation.

1. Costly and Complicated to Set Up. The reason why there are so many more sole proprietorships than corporations is that proprietorships are easier and less costly to set up. In order to organize as a corporation, a firm must first get permission from the state or federal government. This is a complicated and costly procedure that usually requires the assistance of a lawyer.

Understanding Economics
OTHER FORMS OF BUSINESS OWNERSHIP

Most businesses can be classified as sole proprietorships, partnerships, or corporations. There are, however, special types of corporations and other business organizations that operate in special situations. You may be familiar with some of them. They include government-owned corporations, S-corporations, not-for-profit corporations, and cooperatives.

1. Government-Owned Corporations. Corporations owned by federal, state, or local governments fall into this category. *Government-owned corporations* are usually created to provide a product or service that the private sector is unwilling or unable to offer. The United States Postal Service, National Aeronautics and Space Administration (NASA), Federal Deposit Insurance Corporation (FDIC), and any number of metropolitan public transit authorities are examples of government-owned corporations.

2. S-Corporations. Think of the "S" in *S-corporations* as standing for "small" because S-corporations were especially designed to benefit smaller businesses. S-corporations enable firms that qualify as "small" to enjoy the advantages of corporate ownership while avoiding many of the disadvantages. Like regular corporations, S-corporations have the advantage of limited liability. But unlike regular corporations, they do not have to pay corporate income taxes. Thus, they avoid the disadvantage of double taxation, which is associated with regular corporations.

3. Not-for-Profit Corporations. *Not-for-profit* (also called nonprofit) *corporations* are organized to provide an educational, religious, or other nonbusiness service rather than to earn a profit. Not-for-profit corporations do not sell stock. Most importantly, because they earn no profits, not-for-profit corporations pay no income taxes.

4. Cooperatives. A *cooperative* is a business owned by members using its services. People benefit from membership in cooperatives because the organization can perform more effectively than individuals acting alone.

Do you know someone who lives in a co-op (another word for cooperative)? If you do, they can tell you that the multiple dwelling in which they live is owned by the families who live there. But cooperative housing is but one type of cooperative.

Consumer cooperatives are retail businesses owned by its members. Members share in its profits and/or purchase goods or services at lower cost.

Producer cooperatives manufacture or grow the products they sell on behalf of their members. Producer co-ops are most often found in agriculture. Ocean Spray Cranberries, Inc., which controls over 70 percent of the cranberry market, is a 900-member producer cooperative.

2. Double Taxation. In the eyes of the law, the corporation is a person. Just as people pay income taxes, so do coporations. In fact, they are taxed twice.

The profits of most corporations are subject to *corporate income taxes*. These taxes are levied by the government. (They are not levied on partnerships or proprietorships.) After the corporate tax is paid, part or all of what remains out of a corporation's profits may be paid out to the stockholders. These profits, or *dividends*, as they are called, are then subject to personal income taxes. Thus, the stockholders are said to be subject to "double taxation," first, when the corporation's profits are taxed, and second, when the stockholders' dividends are taxed at income tax time.

After Jed Frank had finished telling Dolores and George the advantages and disadvantages of corporations, Dolores exclaimed, "You've convinced me. Let's incorporate."

"Absolutely," George agreed. "How soon can we get going on forming a corporation?" Acting on Ramon and Lee's instructions, Jed Frank applied for and received permission in the form of a charter that transformed Byteland from a partnership to a corporation. From now on, the company would be known as Byteland, Inc.

WHO OWNS, CONTROLS, AND MANAGES LARGE CORPORATIONS?

Byteland, Inc., is a small, *closed corporation*. This type of corporation is one whose stock is not for sale to the general public. Indeed, in Byteland's case, all its stock is owned by just two people: Dolores and George.

But some businesses are *open corporations*. Anyone can purchase the stock of these corporations. As you can see in the table on page 339, the number of stockholders in some of the nation's largest open corporations reaches into the hundreds of thousands. And, in one instance, it reaches 2.3 million.

But how can 2.3 million owners of stock manage a business? Where does the money come from to operate such a large enterprise? The pages that follow will answer these questions.

Board of Directors

Stockholders in large corporations elect representatives to oversee business operations and look after their interests. These representatives are known as *directors*. Together, they make up the corporation's *board of directors*.

Electing the directors of a corporation is different from political elections. Americans select their government representatives on the basis of "one person, one vote." That phrase means that one citizen's vote is as important as another's. But this is not the case in

Shareholders in Widely Held U.S. Corporations

Corporation	Number of Shareholders
AT&T	2,300,000
Procter & Gamble	1,426,000
Verizon	1,100,000
Walt Disney	1,001,000
IBM	662,000
General Electric	660,000
Exxon Mobil	659,000
Coca-Cola	366,000
Wal-Mart	329,000
Merck	216,000

an election for a corporation's board of directors. In corporate elections, stockholders have one vote for every share of stock they own. Let us suppose, for example, that the J Corporation consists of 175 shares of stock. Jack owns 50 shares of stock in the corporation, Jill owns 25 shares, and Jean owns 100 shares. In an election for the chairperson of the board of directors of the corporation, Jack and Jill vote for Jill. Jean votes for herself. Who won the election?

If you said "Jean," you would be absolutely right. Her ballot counted for 100 votes, while the shares of stock of Jack and Jill add up to only 75 votes.

Since most stockholders have other responsibilities, and since corporate meetings may be held hundreds or even thousands of miles from their homes, few stockholders attend annual meetings of their corporations. Instead, stockholders in giant corporations give their voting rights to others. They do this by signing a form known as a *proxy*. In most instances, the holders of proxies can vote as if the stock were their own. For that reason, the boards of directors of large corporations generally ask their stockholders to give them their proxies whenever they announce a stockholders' meeting.

Officers

Directors are not usually involved in the day-to-day operations of their corporations. These are the concerns of the firms' *officers*: the president, secretary, treasurer, and vice presidents. (See Figure 22.2 on page 340.) Boards of directors, however, will be involved with questions directly affecting the stockholders, such as:

"How much of this year's profits should be distributed to the stockholders (as dividends)?" and "Should the corporation sell more of its stock to the public?"

Technically speaking, those who own a corporation are its stockholders. But as we have seen, those who control a corporation are the members of its board of directors. As a practical matter, therefore, in giant corporations ownership and control are quite separate.

Of course, the directors are responsible to the stockholders who elected them to office. But stockholders rarely take an active interest in those who represent them. Most will either ignore the annual meeting or give their proxies to the existing board. For that reason, most boards continue to serve for long periods of time. Occasionally, however, the news media report on the struggle for control of a particular corporation. This often leads to proxy fights in which competing groups ask stockholders to give them the right to cast their ballots.

Some people feel that it is a terrible thing that most stockholders in large corporations have lost control of their business to the small group of "insiders" sitting on their boards. Apparently, most stockholders feel otherwise. They would argue that only specially trained persons of considerable talent have the ability to run today's giant corporations. The stockholders' principal interest seems to be in sharing in the profits and growth of the companies rather than in controlling business operations.

Figure 22.2 Organization Chart of a Typical Manufacturing Corporation

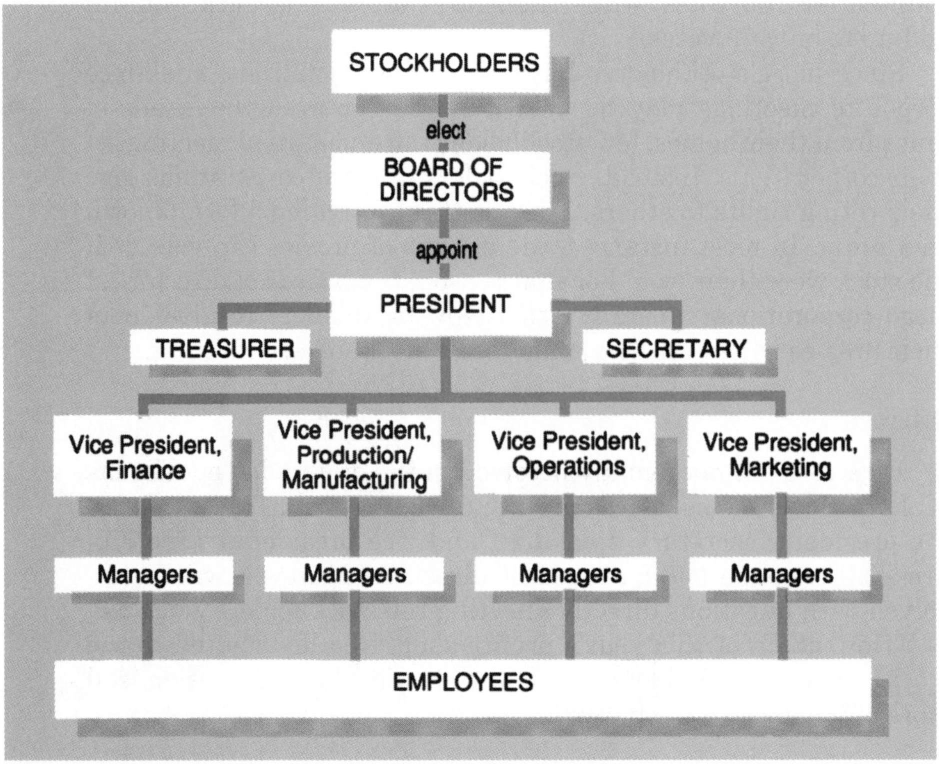

Understanding Economics

THE FRANCHISE ALTERNATIVE

"I'm tired of working for other people, I'd love to own a business of my own—be my own boss, keep all the profits, and build up something for the future."

"Have you thought about buying a franchise?"

"No, tell me about it."

Franchises are individually owned businesses that are licensed to operate as if they were part of a larger chain of outlets or stores. Those who sell franchises are known as *franchisors*. Those who buy and operate franchises are the *franchisees*.

Advantages of Franchises

Those who buy franchises do so because it enables them to operate a business of their own with: (1) limited capital, (2) a recognized name and advertising, (3) a tested way of doing business, and (4) less risk.

1. Start a Business With Limited Capital. One of the most difficult problems facing small businesses is lack of money. It takes money to start an operation, and it takes money to keep it going. Eventually, entrepreneurs expect that income generated by the business will be enough to cover expenses and generate a profit. But until that time comes, a business must rely on its own sources of funds.

Franchisors have a good idea of how much money is needed to start and operate one of their businesses. They also have the resources necessary to secure loans and other financing for qualified franchisees.

2. Name Recognition and Advertising. Franchises often have nationally recognized names like McDonalds, Meineke, and Avis. While an independent fast-food stand cannot afford national advertising, Wendy's and Burger King can. This advertising pretty well guarantees that even newly opened franchises will have customers waiting.

3. A Proven Way of Doing Business. Those who buy franchises know that the business has worked many times before. When problems arise, the franchisees can look to the franchisor for help in solving them.

4. Less Risk. According to the U.S. Department of Commerce, better than 90 percent of all franchises make it through their fifth year. This is much higher than the national average for other types of businesses.

Disadvantages of Franchises

Franchises are not without their disadvantages. Most notable of these are the following:

1. Restrictions on Freedom of Ownership. Unlike privately owned businesses in which the entrepreneur is his/her "own boss," franchisors have a great deal of control how the business will operate. They can, for example, prescribe how employees should dress, set the hours of operation, decorate the facility according to their standards, and require that franchisees purchase equipment and supplies from them.

2. High Costs. Costs of operating a franchise may be higher than a privately owned business. One reason for this is that the cost of equipment and supplies furnished by franchisors is often more costly than similar items purchased elsewhere. In addition, franchisees are usually required to pay an annual fee to the franchisor for the privilege of owning the franchise.

3. Success Often Depends on the Reputation of Others. Mistakes, or improper business practices by one franchisee can reflect badly on all the others.

4. Competition From Franchisor. Even success can cause problems. In some instances, franchisees have been so successful that the franchisor opened its own outlet in the same neighborhood.

Franchise Start-Up Costs

Franchise	Nature of Business	Minimum Start-Up Investment
Radio Shack	Retail electronics stores	$ 50,000
Dunkin' Donuts	Food/quick-service bakery products/donuts	$200,000
Meineke	Discount muffler and brake repair services	$ 50,000
Sir Speedy	Printing, copying, digital networking	$125,000
Blockbuster	Retail video rental and sales	$200,000

SUMMARY

A corporation is a business organization recognized by government as a legal individual and owned by its stockholders. As compared to the sole proprietorship and partnership forms, the corporation offers the following advantages: limited liability, unlimited life, and ease of transfer to a new owner. The greatest disadvantages of the corporation are that it is costly to organize and it may be subject to double taxation.

Stockholders in large corporations elect boards of directors to represent them in controlling the corporation. Stockholders have one vote for every share of stock they own.

Responsibility for the day-to-day operation of large corporations is in the hands of the officers and their staffs. In this way, ownership is separated from management in large corporations.

---------------------------- **LOOKING AHEAD** ----------------------------

How do corporations raise money? How do individuals buy shares of stock? The answers to these questions are contained in the following chapter. As you read, you will also be introduced to the world of high finance. You will learn about the role of the stock market and about the speculators and investors who trade there.

---------------------------- **EXERCISES** ----------------------------

✔**Matching** Match each term in Column A with its definition in Column B.

Column A	**Column B**
1. corporation	*a.* a document that authorizes another to vote one's stock
2. stockholder	
3. charter	*b.* the people who control corporations
4. S corporation	*c.* a business licensed by a government as an individual and owned by its stockholders
5. proxy	
6. board of directors	*d.* a form of corporation for a small business
7. limited liability	*e.* an individually owned business licensed to operate as if it were part of a chain
8. double taxation	
9. franchise	*f.* a problem faced by corporations
10. cooperative	*g.* an owner of a corporation
	h. the principal advantage of the corporation
	i. a state-issued license to incorporate
	j. business owned by its members

✔**Multiple Choice** Choose the letter of the item that best completes the statement or answers the question.

1. A corporation is (a) the same thing as a very large partnership (b) always owned by two people (c) always larger than a sole proprietorship or a partnership (d) licensed by a state or federal government and owned by those holding shares of its stock.

2. A corporation has limited liability. This means that there is (a) no limit to the amount of money the corporation may lose (b) no limit to the amount of money an individual stockholder may lose (c) a limit to the amount of money the corporation may lose (d) a limit to the amount of money an individual stockholder may lose.

3. One advantage of the corporation over other forms of business organization is that ownership is easily transferred. The reason is that (a) there are more corporations than any other kind of business (b) ownership is transferred through the sale of stock (c) all one needs to do to sell one's stock is to turn the matter over to one's

attorney (d) most people know someone who would be willing to buy shares in a corporation.

4. Compared to sole proprietorships and partnerships, corporations are (a) more likely to be controlled by their owners (b) subject to fewer taxes (c) usually smaller (d) more expensive to form.

5. The major responsibility of the board of directors in a large corporation is to (a) take care of the day-to-day problems of running the business (b) look after the well-being of the employees (c) look after the interests of the stockholders (d) direct the purchase of supplies and equipment.

6. A small corporation is totally owned by five stockholders: Smith, Diaz, Chin, Blue, and Fink. Smith owns 100 shares of stock; Diaz owns 200; Chin owns 600; Blue owns 150; and Fink owns 100. Both Chin and Blue want to run the business. In the election for chairman of the board of directors, Chin voted for himself; everyone else (including Blue) voted for Blue. Who won? (a) Chin (b) Blue (c) Fink (d) It was a tie.

7. The ownership and the control of a large corporation may be separate. This means that (a) all the stockholders live a long distance from the company's offices (b) persons who own stock in the corporation are not permitted by law to run it (c) persons who serve as officers are not permitted to receive dividends (d) only a small percentage of the stockholders may be elected to the board of directors.

✔ **Understanding Charts and Graphs** Study Figure 22.1 on page 334 and then answer the questions below.

1. How many sole proprietorships, partnerships, and corporations are there in the United States?

2. What percentage of the total are sole proprietorships? partnerships? corporations?

3. What are the total receipts of all U.S. businesses?

4. Of that total, what percentage was made up of sole proprietorships? of partnerships?

5. Why do you suppose that there are more sole proprietorships in the United States than any other kind of business organization?

CHAPTER *23*

Buying and Selling Stocks and Bonds

Key Terms

securities	stockbroker	speculator
common stock	stock exchange	bull
capital gain	Securities and	bear
preferred stock	Exchange	mutual fund
corporate bond	Commission	investor
investment bank		

> "And now, turning to Wall Street, traders were bullish as stocks moved sharply higher in a day of quiet trading. . . ."
>
> "The bears were out in force today as stock averages turned downward. Bond prices rose. . . ."

Every day millions of Americans pick up their newspapers, turn on their television sets, or check the Internet in order to keep up with their investments in stocks and bonds. Perhaps you have read or seen some of these reports and have wanted to learn more about the subject. In this chapter, we will be taking a look at how stocks and bonds are sold. We will learn why corporations sell stocks and bonds, how they reach the general public, and the reasons why people buy them.

When you have finished reading the chapter, you will be able to answer the following questions:

- How do corporations obtain funds?
- What is a stock exchange?
- Why do people buy corporate stocks?
- What are mutual funds?
- How is the public protected in the sale of securities?

HOW DO CORPORATIONS OBTAIN FUNDS?

Your garden may be the most beautiful in the neighborhood. But unless your garden receives its regular supply of water, sunlight, and fertilizer, it will wither and die. A business, like a garden, needs nourishment in order to thrive and grow. It needs *capital*, or money. Money is needed to pay for the day-to-day expenses of running a company. Money is also needed to buy replacements for worn-out machinery, tools, and other equipment. A growing business will also have to have money to pay for new factories, machinery, and offices.

You learned in the previous chapters of this unit that sole proprietorships and partnerships depend upon the money that their owners bring to their businesses. Proprietors and partners may also borrow money from outside sources such as banks to help finance their operations. Banks lend money to businesses in exchange for interest payments (as discussed in Chapter 5). These loans are usually made for short periods of time—a year or less.

Figure 23.1 Sources of Corporate Funds

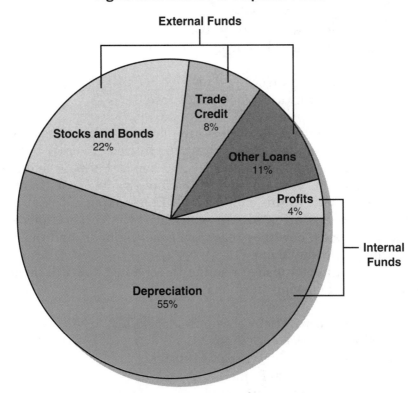

External Funds

Stocks and Bonds
22%

Trade Credit
8%

Other Loans
11%

Profits
4%

Internal Funds

Depreciation
55%

Corporations, like sole proprietorships and partnerships, obtain the money they need for growth from both internal sources and external ones. (See Figure 23.1.) *Internal funds* are those earned by the corporation in the course of business. These funds are mostly used to pay the corporation's expenses.

One of a corporation's most important items of expense is *depreciation*. This expense is the money that a corporation sets aside to replace its old or out-of-date equipment.

Whatever sums remain after business expenses are paid represent profits, as you have learned. A corporation does not have to distribute all of its profits to its shareholders. Profits that are not paid out are an important source of business funds.

External funds are those that come from individuals and institutions outside the corporation. Bank loans and mortgages are external funds. So, too, are *trade credit* (delays in payment that firms grant to business customers) and corporate securities such as stocks and bonds.

Sale of Corporate Securities

One factor that sets the corporation apart from the sole proprietorship and the partnership is the legal right of a corporation to sell its *securities*. This term is another name for its stocks and bonds. Stocks represent ownership in corporations. Bonds represent loans to corporations.

1. Stocks. Most corporate securities are held as *common stock.* Owners of common stock are entitled to vote in the selection of the corporation's board of directors and to receive a percentage of the profits, if any, of the corporation. The money paid to stockholders from a corporation's profits is called a *dividend.*

Corporations often issue *preferred stock* in addition to common stock. Holders of a company's preferred stock are entitled to a fixed dividend whenever the corporation's board of directors decides to pay it. Holders of common stock do not receive dividends until the holders of preferred stock have been paid. If a corporation is dissolved and all its assets are sold for cash, the creditors will be paid first. The holders of preferred stock and the holders of common stock, in that order, will receive their share of whatever is left. Usually, the holders of preferred stock do not vote to elect the company's board of directors.

Although the sale of stock accounts for only 5–10 percent of *new* corporate financing, it is the method that attracts the most attention from the public. One reason, of course, is that so many

Common Stock of the Ford Motor Company: Corporate stocks are sold by brokers who are members of stock exchanges.

people own stocks. In a recent year, for example, some 20 percent of U.S. families had investments in corporate stocks. And millions more had invested indirectly when they purchased life insurance policies and shares of mutual funds, or had money in pension funds. The people who manage these businesses invest the public's money in corporate stocks. All told, some 49 percent of U.S. families have directly or indirectly invested in securities. Some, having purchased individual shares in their name, own the stock *directly*. Others are said to own shares *indirectly*. They did this by investing in mutual funds and/or retirement accounts that invested some or all of their funds in stocks.

2. Bonds. When the public buys *corporate bonds*, it is lending money to the corporations that issue them. These bonds represent a debt. They also are promises from the corporation to pay a fixed rate of interest for a certain number of years. For example, a 20-year, $5,000 bond may pay an 8 percent rate of interest. The bond-holder receives $400 interest each year. When the bond "matures" in 20 years, the bondholder is entitled to $5,000, or the *face value* of the bond. Corporations are legally obligated to pay interest on bonds. Failure to do so can put them out of business by forcing them into bankruptcy.

WHAT IS A STOCK EXCHANGE?

Corporations that want to raise money by selling shares of stock usually do so by going to a special kind of institution known as an *investment bank*. Investment banks are businesses that help corporations sell their stocks to the public. These banks buy entire issues of stocks from corporations. The banks hope to earn profits by selling these corporate stocks to the public, often through stockbrokers.

At this point, the corporation has raised money through the sale of its securities. The public holds shares of stock in the corporation. From this time forward, income from the sale of stock will go to the individuals who own the stock, *not the corporation.*

Let us consider the case of the Miracle Flashlight Company. Good-quality products and its slogan, "If it works, it's a Miracle," have made the Miracle brand a success. Malcolm Blue, president of the company, and chairperson of the board of directors, has concluded that the firm needs to raise $100 million. This money will be used to build a new plant, purchase modern machinery, and hire more workers.

After meeting with a group of investment bankers, Mr. Blue decided that Miracle could raise the $100 million through the sale of stock. The board has approved Blue's plan. Miracle would sell 4 million shares of stock at $25 a share to the investment banks.

New York Stock Exchange: On the trading floor of the exchange, brokers buy and sell stocks for their customers. Individuals, corporations, public institutions, and private groups may own shares of the same company.

Bond Traders: The bonds issued by corporations, states and localities, and utilities are sold by investment-bond specialists.

That would give Miracle its $100 million (4 million $\times$ $25 = $100 million). For their part, the investment banks planned to resell the stock to the public for slightly more than $25 a share, thereby making a profit on each of the 4 million shares.

Once it has received its money from the investment banks, Miracle Flashlight is no longer involved in the purchase or sale of its stock. From that time on, those who own the stock and wish to sell it and those who wish to buy it will have to deal with *stock-brokers*. These people work for brokerage firms (such as Merrill Lynch and Shearson Lehman Hutton) that buy and sell shares of stock for their customers on stock exchanges.

Finding a buyer for shares of stock could be a problem were it not for the nation's *stock exchanges*. Stock exchanges are market-places in which the stocks of certain corporations can be bought and sold. Buyers and sellers of stocks and bonds send their orders to the "floor" of these exchanges, where the transactions take place. The largest of these floor-based exchanges are the *New York Stock Exchange* (*NYSE*) and the *American Stock Exchange* (*AMEX*), both located in New York City. Several smaller stock exchanges are located in other cities around the nation, including Philadelphia, Chicago, and Los Angeles. Stock exchanges are also located in major cities abroad—for example, London, Paris, and Tokyo.

Stocks not listed on any exchanges are traded in the over-the-counter-market (OTC). Unlike the NYSE, where securities are traded on the floor of the exchange, OTC stocks are traded over a vast telecommunications network. The network, known as the *National Association of Securities Dealers Automatic Quotations*, or *NASDAQ*, is composed of thousands of brokerage firms. While most of the 5,000 or more companies traded on the NASDAQ are small firms, it also trades the securities of some of America's best-known technology firms such as Microsoft, Intel, and Apple.

The exchanges provide a place where stockbrokers can get together to trade on behalf of their customers. The prices at which trades take place are the results of auctions. Buyers announce the price they are willing to pay, sellers state the price they are willing to take for their stocks. When the two agree on a price, a transaction is made. Stock prices are directly affected by the laws of supply and demand (discussed in Chapter 4). If the demand for a particular stock were to increase, the price of the stock would rise. But if the supply of the stock were to increase, the price would be likely to fall.

With millions of people buying shares of stock every year, we might next ask the question, "Why do people buy corporate stocks?"

WHY DO PEOPLE BUY CORPORATE STOCKS?

People who buy stocks do so for a variety of reasons. The major reasons are: for yearly income; for investment, and for speculation.

Yearly Income (Dividends)

Many people who buy stocks do so primarily to receive income, or dividends. *Dividends* are the portion of a corporation's profits that are distributed to its stockholders. If a company paid its stockholders $1 per share in dividends, a person who owned 100 shares of stock received $100 in dividends during the year.

The size of a company's dividends depends primarily on its success in earning profits. For this reason, people who buy stocks know that there is no guarantee that they will receive the same dividend, or any at all, from one year to the next.

Investment

The value of a share of stock often changes from one day to the next. When shares of stock increase in value, there is said to be "growth in the value of its capital." There are many reasons why a company and its stock will become more valuable. Perhaps its

Figure 23.2 Number of Corporate Stockholders Since 1975

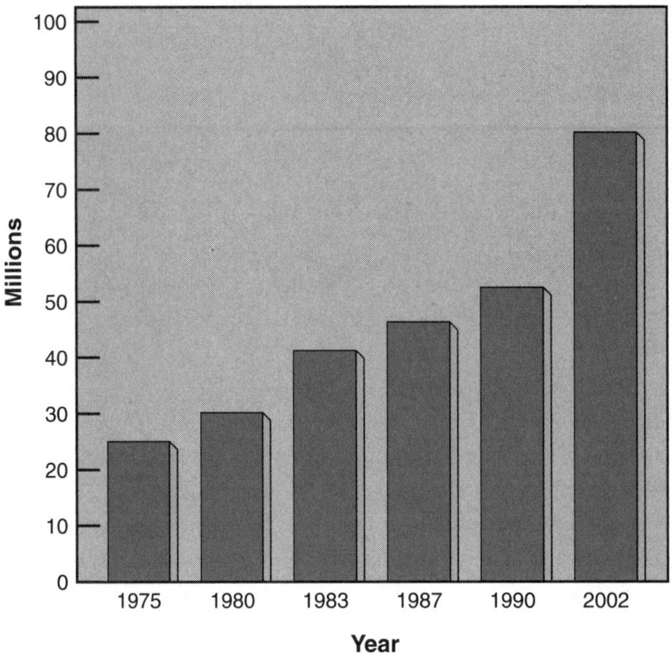

profits have been increasing. Or it may have developed a new manufacturing process, and the prospects for future earnings look particularly good. In fact, anything that makes the company seem more attractive will cause the price of its stock to rise. Owners of the stock will then be able to sell their shares at a profit. This profit is called a *capital gain*.

People who buy stocks in the hope that their value will increase over the long term can be either investors or speculators. The term *investors* describes people who buy securities with the intention of holding them for the long term. They do this as a way of: (1) earning dividend or interest income, or (2) profiting from the possible rise in value of the securities over the long term.

Speculation

The term *speculators* refers to those who hope to profit by correctly predicting short-term fluctuations in the value of stocks and bonds. We have seen that the price of a stock may rise or fall from day to day. (It may also stay the same.) If people *knew* which way the price of a stock was going to go before it happened, they could easily profit from the knowledge. While no one can predict future

Figure 23.3 Newspaper Stock Exchange Listing
(Disney Corporation highlighted)

52-Week High	52-Week Low	Stock	Div	Yld %	PE Ratio	Sales 100s	High	Low	Last	Chg.
18.78	11.88	Dial	.16	1.0	dd	5228	16.55	16.15	16.27	−0.26
45.65	22.83	DiaOffs	.50	,1.9	36	7692	26.70	26.01	26.03	−0.76
43.55	25.75	Diebold	.64	1.6	33	3201	39.95	39.20	39.47	−0.36
22.50	12.06	Dillards	.16	1.0	dd	5408	16.05	15.56	15.86	−0.24
21.79	14.81	Dillard38	1.88	10.1	...	208	18.74	17.76	18.59	+0.59
11.61	4.81	Dimon	.36	5.0	10	400	7.25	7.15	7.24	−0.01
34.80	**15.50ᵥ**	**Disney**	**.21**	**1.0**	**dd**	**68522**	**21.50**	**0.01**	**20.50**	**−0.98**
17.63	10.10	Dist&Srv	.25 e	2.1	...	1366	12.05	11.88	11.92	−0.28
26.00	10.04	DrReddy n	.10 p	...	...	994	19.98	19.71	19.80	−0.03
27.65	14.60	Dole	.40	1.5	cc	938	26.37	25.80	25.83	−0.43
24.05	10.50	DollarG	.13	0.9	27	37736	15.23	14.10	14.75	+0.72
25.78	8.40	DollarTh	...	...	11	621	15.69	15.30	15.30	−0.15
25.40	24.56	DmCNG pf	1.95	7.7	...	959	25.40	25.10	25.35	...
69.99	55.13	DomRes	2.58	4.3	18	11475	60.53	59.51	59.63	+0.13
66.56	55.50	DmRes04	4.75	8.0	...	1205	60.14	58.75	59.50	+0.40
25.05	15.70	DmRsBW	3.21 e	16.1	q	72	20.00	19.88	19.91	+0.06
10.74	6.80	Domtar g	.14	...	...	120	9.69	9.46	9.46	−0.13
40.35	24.45	Donldson	.30	0.9	20	2034	34.36	33.60	33.70	−0.20
31.90	24.30	DonlleyRR	.96	3.2	27	2540	30.75	29.80	29.93	−0.58
16.20	12.55	Donnelly	.40	3.1	14	92	12.90	12.75	12.85	−0.05
8.00	1.06	DotHill	...	...	dd	204	2.35	2.25	2.27	−0.07
43.55	**26.40**	**Dover**	**.50**	**1.5**	**7**	**5460**	**35.42**	**34.05**	**34.05**	**−1.45**
17.00	10.38	DoverD	.18	1.4	16	208	13.55	13.30	13.30	−0.15
39.67	**25.06ᵥ**	**DowChm**	**1.34 f**	**5.5**	**dd**	**237138**	**26.15**	**23.66**	**24.55**	**−1.90**

Reading from left to right, the listing presents the following information: 52-week high and low prices ($34.80 and $15.50). Company name. Dividend: Dollar amount of the company's per-share earnings paid to shareholders ($.21). Yield: Per-share dividend divided by per-share stock price, expressed as a percentage (1.0). Price-earnings ratio: Compares the stock's current market price to the company's earnings per share of stock (dd means that there was a loss, so the percentage could not be calculated). Sales volume: Number of shares bought and sold on the previous day, in hundreds (6,852,200 shares). Prices paid for the stock during the previous day: highest, lowest, and closing ($21.50, $0.01, $20.50). Net change: Difference between the past two days' closing prices ($.98).

events with absolute certainty, speculators feel they can make some pretty good guesses. When they are correct in their predictions, speculators profit. When they are wrong, they lose money.

Every business day, millions upon millions of shares of stock are bought and sold at the nation's stock exchanges. When a sale takes place, the price and number of shares traded are instantly recorded and reported in brokerage houses and on wire services around the world. Stock prices and transactions are published daily in major newspapers around the world and are available almost instantly on many Internet sites.

Speculators hope to profit by correctly predicting whether a stock will rise or fall in value. Those who predict a rise in the price of a stock are known as *bulls*. To be "bullish" on something is to be optimistic about its future. Speculators who expect the price of a stock to fall are called *bears*. To be "bearish," therefore, is to be pessimistic about the future.

Understanding Economics

SPECULATORS AND THE STOCK MARKET

Marjorie Morris, Clarence Berens, Harry Wong, and Sylvia Finn do not know one another, but they have a number of things in common. Each thought that they could profit by buying the stock of companies in the electronics industry, and selling them after they had gone up in value. Each made their buy on March 24, 2000, and held on to their stock for about a year.

DATE: March 24, 2000

Buyer	Stock	Number of Shares Purchased	Price Per Share	Total Cost
Morris	Microsoft	70	$111.69	$7,818.30
Berens	Cisco Systems	100	79.38	7,938.00
Finn	Intel	100	69.53	6,953.00
Wong	Yahoo	40	194.00	7,760.00

On March 29, 2001, each of the speculators sold their shares at a substantial loss. Here is how it happened.

Starting in January of 1997, stocks issued by electronics and Internet-related companies (popularly described as the "dot-coms") began a run-up in prices that looked to many speculators like it would never end. Despite warnings that stock prices never increase forever, people like Morris, Berens, Wong, and Finn kept buying those securities, and prices continued their advance. "Look at those stocks climb," they said. "We will make a fortune!"

Alas, there was no fortune to be made because early on in 2001 the long predicted collapse of the electronics and dot-com stocks began. In the course of that decline, the four speculators saw their potential profits disappear. Meanwhile, the collapse of electronics stocks came as a terrible blow to investors across the United States and overseas. As the value of their investments fell, panicky stockholders ordered their brokers to sell. Our four speculators did the same. On March 29, 2001, Morris, Berens, Wong, and Finn sold the stocks they had purchased only a year earlier. The results of their sales are summarized in the table below:

DATE: March 29, 2001

Buyer	Stock	Number of Shares Sold	Price Per Share	Total Received
Morris	Microsoft	70	$55.38	$3,876.60
Berens	Cisco Systems	100	15.25	1,525.00
Finn	Intel	100	28.56	2,856.00
Wong	Yahoo	40	15.00	600.00

In less than one month's time, Morris had lost $3,941.70; Berens, $6,413; Finn, $4,097; and Wong, a whopping $7,160! Millions of other investors also lost money in the stock market that month.

The reasons why the electronics industry stocks collapsed when they did may never be known. Whatever the reasons, the events stand as a stark reminder for those who thought it possible for stock prices to rise indefinitely. The fact is that the only thing certain about stock prices is that they will *fluctuate*. Sometimes they will rise, and sometimes they will fall. For that reason, investors and speculators alike need to be prepared for the unexpected, which may occur at any time.

© *The New Yorker Collection 1997 Roz Chast from cartoonbank.com.*
Optimistic bulls expect stock prices to rise, while pessimistic bears expect them to fall.

WHAT ARE MUTUAL FUNDS?

Although the advice given above about investing is good, few people have the knowledge, time, or money to follow the advice. But there is a method for people of average means to invest in stocks and bonds while limiting their risks. For millions of investors, the method is to invest in *mutual funds*.

A mutual fund is a company that invests on behalf of its shareholders. People purchase shares of the mutual fund, and the company pools the money of all these people. The company invests the pooled money in a variety of securities, including stocks, corporate bonds, and government bonds. Income earned by a fund is distributed to the shareholders in accordance with the number of shares they own.

Advantages of Mutual Funds

1. Professional Management. The employees of a mutual fund are trained to study financial information, economic trends, and political developments. Few investors have the time or expertise to do this.

2. Diversification. To reduce the risks of ownership, mutual funds invest in a wide variety of stocks and bonds.

3. Liquidity. A mutual fund investment can be turned into cash quickly and easily.

Figure 23.4 Household Ownership of Mutual Funds Since 1980 (percent and number of U.S. households)

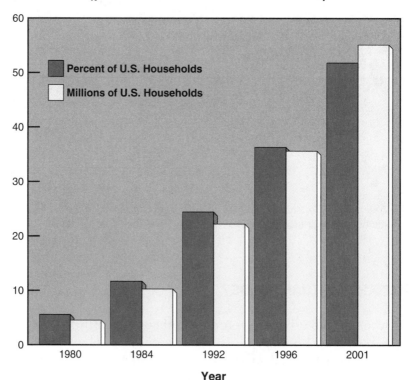

Personal Economics

SOME ADVICE TO WOULD-BE INVESTORS

Are you thinking about investing in corporate stocks or bonds? Then consider the following advice:

1. Investigate before you invest. Know something about the business in which you plan to invest: its finances, history, and future outlook. Get the advice of an expert.

2. Do not "put all your eggs in one basket." You can reduce your risks by *diversifying* (investing your money in a number of companies rather than in just one or two). You can further diversify by putting your money in different kinds of stocks or in both stocks and bonds.

3. Keep checking your investments. Nothing is forever! Even the best of corporations will at times perform poorly. Keep an eye on your investments, and switch to new ones when necessary.

Disadvantages of Mutual Funds

Mutual funds are not free from risk, however. If stocks in general are doing poorly, so too will most mutual funds. Generally, funds that invest in government securities carry less risk than ones that invest in corporate stocks. In addition, many different companies sell mutual funds. Some of these companies are better managed than others. So, even when investing in mutual funds, investigate before you invest.

HOW IS THE PUBLIC PROTECTED IN THE SALE OF SECURITIES?

The federal government has taken steps to protect those who invest in corporate stocks and bonds. In the 1930s, it established the *Securities and Exchange Commission (SEC)* to regulate the sale of securities. The SEC also tries to make it easier for the public to get the information that it needs to make intelligent decisions about investments. The SEC does *not*, however, offer advice on the worth of any particular stock or bond. The decision to buy or sell is left to each individual investor.

In 1970, Congress took another step to protect investors by creating the *Securities Investor Protection Corporation (SIPC)*. Like the Federal Deposit Insurance Corporation (FDIC), which insures bank accounts, the SIPC insures the cash and securities in customer accounts in the event that a brokerage firm were to fail.

State governments also regulate securities, specifically those that are not subject to federal regulation.

Each of the major exchanges also acts as a self-regulator. An exchange establishes rules for trading and will penalize or expel a member who fails to follow its rules. An exchange does not guarantee the safety of any investment traded. Nor does it take responsibility for the advice given to an investor by any of its members.

What does this mean for you, your family, and your friends? It means that if you are thinking of buying securities or mutual funds, you would be wise to be careful. Remember, you can easily lose part, or all, of your investment.

SUMMARY

Corporations pay for their operations from their earnings or from money raised from outside sources. Outside sources include loans and the sale of stocks and bonds. Lenders are paid interest for the use of their money. Stockholders receive a share of the company's profits in the form of dividends. Stock exchanges make it possible for millions of shares of stocks and bonds to change hands daily.

People invest in corporate stocks to receive dividends, to acquire capital gains, and to speculate.

Mutual fund companies pool large sums of money that they invest on behalf of their customers. In this way, the mutual funds offer the advantages of professional management and diversification to investors of modest means.

The federal Securities and Exchange Commission regulates the purchase and sale of stocks and bonds. The primary function of the SEC is to see to it that the public is given accurate and honest information about the corporations whose securities are offered for sale. Another federal agency, the Securities Investor Protection Corporation, protects the investing public by insuring the contents of their brokerage accounts.

LOOKING AHEAD

The following chapter looks at one of the major reasons for the size and wealth of the U.S. economy: mass production. This term refers to the ability of businesses to manufacture large quantities of goods at low cost and to sell them at a profit.

---————— **EXERCISES** —————---

✔**Matching** Match each term in Column A with its definition in Column B.

Column A	Column B
1. investment bank	a. the agency that regulates the sale of stocks and bonds
2. stock	b. any investment based on one's hope to profit from its short-term rise or fall in value
3. stock exchange	
4. bond	c. a business that sells new issues of stocks and bonds to brokers
5. capital gain	
6. dividend	d. one who buys and sells stocks for investors
7. speculation	e. a place where publicly traded securities are bought and sold
8. bull	
9. bear	f. one who expects the price of stock to rise
10. mutual fund	g. an increase in the value of a share of stock
11. stockbroker	h. one who expects the price of stock to fall
12. Securities and Exchange Commission	i. a pool of funds invested in a variety of stocks
	j. a share of ownership in a corporation
	k. a debt of the company that issues it
	l. a payment by a company to its stockholders

✔**Multiple Choice** Choose the letter of the item that best completes the statement or answers the question.

1. Recently, XYZ Corporation, one of the nation's largest corporations, sold several million shares of its stock to the public. How was the stock sold? (a) by mail-order catalog (b) by one or more investment banks (c) over the counter at the corporation's many stores and offices (d) all of the above.

2. A year after all its stock was sold, investors are still busily buying and selling shares of XYZ stock. Who receives the money from these sales? (a) the individual owners of XYZ who choose to sell their stock (b) the XYZ Corporation (c) the managers of the XYZ Corporation (d) the stock exchange that handles the sales.

3. Alvin Atwell is buying shares of stock in a retailing corporation because he is convinced that the price of its stock is going to rise very soon. Alvin is a (a) "bear" (b) pessimist (c) careful investor (d) "bull."

4. Millicent Marcus owns 100 shares of the Blue Sea Fishing Company of Portland, Maine. At the end of the year, Blue Sea declares a $1.50 dividend. How will this declaration affect Millicent? (a) Each share of stock will increase in value by $1.50. (b) She will receive a check for $150. (c) She will receive a check for $1.50. (d) It will have no effect at all on Millicent because she lives in Oregon.

5. The Securities and Exchange Commission (a) regulates the amount of money and credit in circulation (b) supervises the coining of money (c) regulates the sale of stocks and bonds (d) guarantees home mortgages.

6. Stock dividends (a) must be paid to stockholders every year (b) are paid to those who lend the corporation money (c) represent shares of profits and are paid to stockholders (d) are not taxable.

7. Which of the following is true of corporate bonds? (a) They represent a debt of the corporation. (b) They pay bondholders a fixed rate of interest. (c) They promise to repay bondholders a specified amount after a fixed period of time. (d) All of the above.

✔ **Developing Skills in Economics** Study the graphs on pages 352 and 356 and then answer the questions below.

1. How many people owned shares of corporate stock in 1975? in 1987? in 2002?

2. What has been the trend in corporate stock ownership over the period shown? (*Trend* refers to the general course or direction in which something is moving.)

3. What reasons can you suggest for this trend in corporate stock ownership?

4. How many households owned shares in mutual funds in 1980? in 1992? in 2001?

5. What was the trend in mutual fund share ownership in the period shown?

6. What reasons can you suggest for the trend in mutual fund ownership?

✔ *Using the Internet*

The following Websites will provide further information about investing:

1. *The Stock Market Game* at <<http://www.smgww.org>>. Sponsored by the securities industry, *The Stock Market Game* enables participants to discover the risks and rewards involved in decision-making, the sources and uses of capital, and other related economic concepts.

2. The SEC's Office of Investor Education and Assistance Website can take you to many valuable resources on the Internet. You will find it at: <<http://www.sec.gov/investor/students.shtml>>.

CHAPTER 24
Mass Production

Back in George Washington's day, in the 1700s, muskets were manufactured one at a time by gunsmiths. Each trigger, hammer, and gun barrel had to be made by hand. Thus, each musket had parts that were slightly different from other muskets. The handcrafted method of making muskets came to an end in the early 1800s.

Inventor Eli Whitney (1765–1825) was under contract to make 10,000 muskets for the U.S. Army. But Whitney spent so much of his time designing machines and tools to produce the gun parts that for several years he delivered nothing. Finally, the day came when he was able to pack a box with enough parts to make ten muskets and go to Washington, D.C. There Whitney invited a group of government officials to assemble the parts into ten finished weapons. The officials were puzzled.

"How will we know which trigger fits into which barrel?" one asked.

"It doesn't matter," Whitney explained. "You see, all the parts are *interchangeable*. Each trigger, for example, is exactly the same as every other one. Try it. You will see that all ten guns will go together very easily."

Sure enough, the government officials soon discovered that it did not matter which gun part they started with. All the different parts went together quite easily. In a short time, the ten guns were assembled.

In this chapter, you will learn how all U.S. industries benefited from this method of production. You will also find out the answers to the following questions:

- What is mass production?
- Why does mass production depend upon specialization, the division of labor, and automation?
- How has mass production affected all Americans?

WHAT IS MASS PRODUCTION?

There were two very important advantages to Eli Whitney's method of production of muskets. First, if a musket part, such as a trigger, were to fail, it could easily be replaced with an identical part. Each part was interchangeable—it could be used in any musket. But if the trigger of a handmade musket were to break, a new trigger would have to be made to order so that it would fit that particular musket. A second advantage of Whitney's production method was that the muskets with interchangeable parts could be produced faster and at lower cost than those produced by hand.

The idea of *interchangeable parts* that Whitney developed is one of the underlying principles of mass production.

Mass production is the manufacture of large quantities of identical products in large quantities using interchangeable parts, specialized labor, and machinery.

When goods are made by hand, no two can be exactly alike. Machinery, however, can be designed to produce goods that are identical to one another. In other words, machinery made the production of interchangeable parts and tools possible.

Assembly Line

The next big step in the history of mass production was taken about 100 years after Eli Whitney developed interchangeable parts for muskets. In the early 1900s, Henry Ford first used the *assembly line* to produce the Model T automobile.

Ford's basic idea for an automobile assembly line was this. Instead of moving from one automobile to another in the course of the day, workers stood at stations on a "line." The work was brought to them.

Early 20th-Century Mass Production: (right) Assembly-line workers perform the steps to put together automobile generators; (top) finished Model T Fords roll off the conveyor belt.

Before Ford's system was put into practice, it took one worker about 20 minutes to put together a flywheel magneto for the Model T. (The magneto supplied the car's electricity. In today's cars, this is done by the battery.)

When the assembly line was introduced, the assembly of the magneto was broken down into 29 steps. These steps were performed by 29 workers spaced along a moving belt. The belt was timed so that each worker was able to complete one small task before the magneto moved on to the next worker. Within a year, the average time needed to assemble one flywheel magneto had been reduced from 20 minutes to 5. Eventually, all the steps in the manufacture of Model Ts were put on assembly lines. The results were dramatic. Whereas fewer than 11,000 Model Ts were made in 1908, that figure exploded to more than 730,000 in 1917. Meanwhile, in that period the price of a Model T dropped over 60 percent, reflecting the efficiency of the company's assembly-line production methods.

Ford's success made the Ford Motor Company the world's leading producer of automobiles. Ford became one of the richest people in the world.

Late 20th-Century Mass Production: Workers assemble computer circuit boards. How does this scene differ from the one of early mass-production assembly, on page 363?

WHY DOES MASS PRODUCTION DEPEND UPON SPECIALIZATION, THE DIVISION OF LABOR, AND AUTOMATION?

The assembly line applied two principles of economics to production: specialization and the division of labor. It also served to increase productivity by using automated machinery.

Specialization and Division of Labor

In manufacturing automobiles, no one worker assembles an entire car. Instead, each worker does only one small part of the total job. Similarly, one worker in a refrigerator factory may install thermostats while another puts on doors. This is called *specialization*.

What is true for automobiles and refrigerators also holds for manufacturing computers, television sets, airplanes, and thousands of other items. That is, production is broken down into many tasks. Each one is performed by a number of workers. When workers specialize in the production of only part of a good or service, we have a situation called the *division of labor*.

There are two important advantages to the division of labor. First, workers are more easily trained when the job they perform is limited. It is much easier to teach a group of workers how to operate one machine in a factory than to teach all the workers how to operate every machine there. If one group of workers assembles only carburetors and another group assembles only gear boxes, then only one set of skills need be taught to each group.

The second advantage to the division of labor is that each worker needs fewer skills. If one person had to produce an entire television set, he or she would need the abilities of an engineer, a cabinet maker, a mechanic, and a technician. But when these tasks are divided, a worker needs only one set of skills to perform the job.

Automation

The efforts to find more efficient methods of production have continued since the development of the assembly line in 1913. In the 1950s and 1960s, people began to speak of a revolutionary new concept in production called *automation*. This term refers to production in which machines are operated by other machines rather than by humans. A thermostat, a device that turns a machine on or off when a certain temperature is reached, is a simple example of automation.

In recent decades, the addition of computers to automated equipment has enabled machinery to perform even more tasks

Computer-Assisted Design: An engineer studies a computer display of his ideas. What economies (savings) are offered by CAD?

formerly done by humans. *Computer-assisted design* (*CAD*) refers to the use of computers and special software to assist them in the designing of products. Before the development of CAD, drafters and engineers had to spend many hours at the drafting table, drawing their designs by hand. Now, computers can prepare a perfect picture of the most complex product or any of its parts. Still another feature of computer-assisted design is that computer models can be tested even before they exist in the real world. For example, the computer can calculate how outside forces (such as wind, rain, and speed) might affect a structure.

Computer-assisted machining (*CAM*) refers to computer control of production machines. A printing press operating under instructions from a computer tape is one example of CAM. So too is a computer-directed robot used to weld automobile frames. You can see how CAD and CAM together could help to speed production of next year's model of your favorite automobile. Now if only someone could find a way to get a robot to do homework.

HOW HAS MASS PRODUCTION AFFECTED ALL AMERICANS?

The quality of life today—the way Americans live their lives—is far different from what it was a hundred years ago. People today are generally healthier and live longer, have more of the necessities

Understanding Economics

MASS PRODUCTION IN A BICYCLE COMPANY

Suppose you are the manager of a bicycle-manufacturing company. Your small factory is able to manufacture 100 bicycles every month and sell them at $90 each. It costs the firm $4,000 a month to turn out these bikes. The owners are interested in increasing their profits. So you are asked to look into the possibility of expanding the plant and bringing in modern machinery and equipment. You investigate and learn the following:

1. Expansion and modernization would increase monthly expenses to $16,000.

2. Output of bicycles would increase from 100 to 800 a month.

3. The company could sell all 800 bicycles at the old price of $90.

Would you recommend that the bicycle company expand its production? You probably would, because an increase in production would considerably increase the company's profits. Let us see why. In the small plant, it costs $4,000 to manufacture 100 bikes each month. Therefore, every bike may be said to have cost $40 because $4,000 ÷ 100 = $40. Since the selling price was $90, the company made a profit of $50 on each bike ($90 − $40 = $50), and a total monthly profit of $5,000 ($50 × 100 = $5,000).

Now let us see how the plant would do if it were to expand. With production at 800 bicycles a month and expenses at $16,000, each bicycle would cost the company $20 to produce ($16,000 ÷ 800 = $20). This would yield a profit of $70 on each bicycle ($90 − $20 = $70), and a total profit for the month of $56,000 ($70 × 800 = $56,000).

To summarize: Although enlarging the bicycle company's operations would increase its monthly costs (from $4,000 to $16,000), it would also increase its monthly production (from 100 to 800 bicycles). As a result, the production cost of each bicycle would be reduced from $40 to $20, and profits would rise from $5,000 to $56,000.

The high profits gained by the introduction of mass-production techniques serve to explain why most businesses will adopt them if they can. While costly, large-scale production enables producers to turn out many more goods at a lower cost for each item.

Figure 24.1 Mass Production in a Bicycle Factory

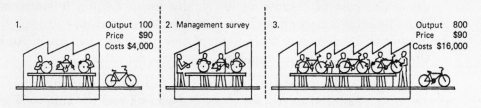

1. Output 100 / Price $90 / Costs $4,000   2. Management survey   3. Output 800 / Price $90 / Costs $16,000

What will happen to the factory's profits when it increases its output of bicycles?

and luxuries of life, and enjoy more leisure time than most Americans did in the early 1900s. Many of the reasons why our lives are different and mostly better than those of people a century ago can be credited to the advantages that followed the development of mass production.

Advantages of Mass Production

1. Productivity Gains. It costs money to produce goods. If it costs Company A $100 to produce two bicycles, each bicycle costs the firm $50 (because $100 ÷ 2 = $50). But suppose another firm, Company B, uses the latest machinery to manufacture its bicycles. Company B is able to produce four bicycles, identical to A's, for $100. That is, each bicycle costs Company B only $25 to produce ($100 ÷ 4).

When we compare the number of units of a product that are produced to the cost of producing these units, we are speaking of *productivity*. Some economists define productivity as the quantity of *output* for every unit of *input*. In our bicycle example, the input is $100. Company A's output is two bicycles, while Company B's output is four bicycles.

The principal advantage of mass-production methods is that they increase productivity. And productivity gains can benefit everyone. Productivity gains make companies more competitive. When productivity is increasing, it costs a firm less to produce each of its products. That being the case, it is possible for a company both to lower its selling prices and increase its profits. Lower prices mean that more consumers will be able to afford the product.

Sales should increase. When people buy more, their living standards rise. Workers, too, might benefit from increasing productivity, if their employers choose to share the gains with them.

2. Lower Cost of Materials, Services, and Capital. Big businesses buy in large quantities. It is an advantage to them. Suppliers usually offer discounts to businesses that place large orders. The cost of borrowing is usually lower for big businesses than it is for small ones. Banks and private investors are more willing to lend money to big companies than to little ones. And they often charge big companies lower interest rates.

3. Use of Modern Machinery and Equipment. It takes vast amounts of capital to pay for modern factories and machinery. For that reason, not all firms can afford them. But modern machines increase productivity. So those firms that can afford them are often at an advantage. They can increase their output and reduce their costs.

4. *Opportunities for Research and Development.* Businesses use scientific research to find and develop new products and production methods. But scientific research is costly. Laboratories must be built and maintained, and scientists and technicians must be paid. Only the largest firms can afford the expense of maintaining research staffs. Research can, however, bring great rewards after important discoveries are made and developed into new products or production methods.

Disadvantages of Mass Production

We have, however, paid a price for the gains made through mass production. Here are some of the disadvantages of mass production. You may be able to think of others.

1. *Enormous Capital Investment.* Mass production is very costly. The factory buildings, machinery, and other equipment of mass production must be paid for and maintained even when the demand for products declines.

Expenses that must be paid regardless of how much or how little the company earns are called *overhead* (fixed expenses). In order to pay for their overhead, companies involved in mass production must constantly seek better ways of selling their output.

2. *Threats to Personal Health and the Environment.* Factories can produce a great deal of waste. Some of this waste is released into the atmosphere in the form of smoke and gases. Liquid wastes are sometimes released intentionally or unintentionally into waterways or are allowed to seep into the soil, where they may enter the drinking water. Solid wastes are often deposited in dumps or landfills, where they may cause pollution problems underground. Sometimes solid wastes are burned, thereby contributing to air pollution.

The manner in which industries dispose of their wastes can be extremely *hazardous* (dangerous) to the environment and the public. Many chemical wastes have been linked to human cancers and chromosome damage. For that reason, the federal government now regulates the disposal of industrial wastes. Both industry and government have been studying the problem and searching for solutions.

The oil tanker *Exxon Valdez* went aground in Alaska's Prince William Sound in 1989. The tragedy resulted in the biggest oil spill in U.S. history and the destruction of vast quantities of fish, birds, and wetlands. After ten years, Exxon had paid over $2 billion just to clean up the oil spill and over $6 billion in fines and damages for that environmental disaster.

Understanding Economics

SAWMILLS ARE BUZZING AND THE ECONOMY IS HUMMING

Sawmills cut timber into boards and planks. In the past, logs were fed into huge circular saws that sliced them into lumber. Sawmills wasted a lot of wood because the trees they worked on were less than straight. There is not much that can be done about gently curved trees, because trees turn themselves toward the sun as they grow. But there is something now that can be done to get the most lumber with the least amount of waste out of curved logs.

At Willamette Industries—one of the nation's largest forest products companies—lasers scan incoming logs. The results are fed into a computer that calculates the most efficient way to cut up the logs. Then, as logs roll into the mill, 24 paired saw blades swivel and pivot to follow the curve of the tree. In no time at all, each long, not-entirely-straight log is converted to a neat stack of 2×12, 2×10, and 2×8 boards, along with a 2×6 that the saws scavenge from the narrower sides of the log. The new machines and computers enable Willamette to produce lumber with 20 percent fewer workers and 12 percent fewer trees than it needed to generate the same amount of boards ten years ago.

The introduction of new computers and machines increased productivity at Willamette. Similar productivity increases have been taking place in thousands of companies and hundreds of industries around the country. Economists tell us that the increase in productivity is helping the economy and the stock market and is raising employment levels and living standards. It also helps keep prices down.

Questions for Thought and Discussion

1. What do economists mean by "increases in productivity"?

2. How did the introduction of new machines and computers affect productivity at Willamette?

3. Explain what effects increasing productivity can have on the economy.

3. Dependence on Large-Scale Industries. Because they operate on such a large scale, mass-production industries employ large numbers of workers. The failure of a single company can result in unemployment for hundreds, thousands, or even tens of thousands of workers.

4. Many Lost Jobs. The introduction of automated production techniques sometimes means that fewer workers are needed. In 1811, British newspapers carried the story of weavers who were rampaging through textile factories. The weavers (called Luddites) were smashing the new weaving machines that had cost many of them their jobs. In more recent times, automated harvesting machines have replaced many farm workers. Robots have replaced workers on many factory assembly lines.

When people lose their jobs to machines (or "technology"), the problem is described as *technological unemployment*. While some workers who have lost a job can be retrained, losing one's job is painful. For that reason, technological unemployment is listed as one of the high costs that society must pay for the advances it makes. Because technologies keep changing, technological unemployment will continue to be a problem for workers. Perhaps every worker will have to be retrained two, three, or four times during his or her working life.

SUMMARY

Mass production is the manufacture of large quantities of identical products, using interchangeable parts, machinery, and the division of labor. Mass production enables manufacturers to produce more goods at a lower cost per unit. These gains in productivity enable many consumers and workers to live better.

Mass production has its disadvantages. The failure of an industry, or even an individual, large firm, can lead to widespread unemployment. The development of new machinery can result in technological unemployment. Industrial wastes may threaten the environment and, in turn, everyone's health.

LOOKING AHEAD

Despite the problems associated with mass production, most businesses would prefer to grow in size. One way for a business to accomplish this goal is to combine with other firms to form a larger company. In the next chapter, we will see how businesses combine. And we will learn of the problems that these combinations have created.

EXERCISES

✔ **Multiple Choice** Choose the letter of the item that best completes the statement or answers the question.

1. The assembly line changed automobile production methods because (a) workers decided what tasks they would perform during the workday (b) the parts to be worked on were brought to the

workers on a moving belt (c) workers moved from one car to the next and performed a small task on each one (d) it enabled each worker to assemble a larger portion of an entire car.

2. If a product is made with mass-production methods, it (a) will cost more to produce than if it had been produced by hand (b) is likely to cost less to set up the factory than it would to set up a shop to produce the goods by hand (c) should cost less to produce than if it had been produced by hand (d) will always be of better quality than one produced on an individual basis.

3. One advantage of the division of labor is that (a) workers can be more easily trained to perform a small number of tasks than a large number of tasks (b) workers find it more interesting to do the same small job over and over again than to complete an entire product (c) workers can do much of the production at home (d) it encourages the establishment of many small businesses rather than a few very large ones.

4. One advantage of producing goods on a very large scale is that (a) the large-scale manufacturer can come to know the workers better than a small producer can (b) overhead expenses are lower than those of small producers (c) large-scale producers do not have to borrow money, but small producers do (d) large-scale producers can usually obtain their raw materials at lower rates than small producers.

5. In 1910, the price of a Model T Ford was $950. By 1917, the average price for the same car was $360. In 1910, fewer than 19,000 Model Ts were sold. In 1917, over 730,000 were sold. What conclusion can you draw from this information? (a) The cost of living must have gone down between 1910 and 1917. (b) Henry Ford was making less money in 1917 than he was in 1910. (c) It cost the Ford Motor Company less to produce a Model T in 1917 than it did in 1910. (d) There is no relationship between the price of the Model Ts and the number sold.

6. Which of the following items is an example of an overhead expense? (a) rent on a factory (b) electricity, most of which is used to power a plant's machinery (c) raw materials used in manufacturing (d) shipping costs on goods sold. (*Hint*: Remember that overhead expenses are fixed costs, which must be paid regardless of the amount of business done.)

7. Which of the following is the best example of the use of automation? (a) a garment sewn by an operator at a sewing machine (b) a letter written by a secretary using a computer (c) an automobile painted by a computer-directed robot on an assembly line (d) a medical assistant drawing blood from a patient's arm.

✔**Matching** Match each term in Column A with its definition in Column B.

Column A

1. assembly line
2. division of labor
3. mass production
4. overhead
5. technological unemployment
6. automation
7. interchangeable parts
8. specialization

Column B

a. an expense of doing business that must be paid regardless of earnings
b. a process that involves division of labor, specialization, and machinery
c. a method of production that brings the work to the worker, rather than the worker to the work
d. the breaking down of production into a number of tasks so that each worker performs only one
e. production of a narrow range of goods
f. the concept of manufacturing using many identical units
g. a method of production in which machines operate other machines
h. the loss of jobs because machines now perform the tasks once done by workers

✔*Which Would You Choose?*

A large-scale manufacturer of kitchen appliances (refrigerators, stoves, and dishwashers) is planning to open a new factory. Three possible locations for the factory are being considered. The first of these sites is located in a rural area, the second is in a suburb, and the third is in a city. At a conference attended by the top executives of the company, the advantages and disadvantages of each site were discussed.

Ms. Backus liked the 25-acre site located in the middle of a 500-acre farm some 30 miles from the nearest town. Mrs. Martinez preferred the suburban location five miles from the city. This site was between the railroad line and the main highway leading to the city. Mr. Mott spoke in favor of the city location. This site was in the heart of the industrial district of one of the nation's largest cities.

1. List the three locations (rural, suburban, city) in the order in which you would recommend them for the site of the new appliance factory.

2. Give two reasons why you selected your first choice.

3. Explain one drawback of each of the other two sites.

✔Interpreting a Statistical Table Base your answers to the questions below on the information contained in the following table.

American Automobile Use Since 1910

Year	Passenger Car Registrations (in millions)	Passenger Cars per Thousand Persons
1910	0.458	5
1930	23.0	187
1950	40.4	266
1970	89.2	439
1990	133.7	536
1995	128.4	489
1999	132.4	482

1. Which years are illustrated in the table?

2. How many passenger cars were registered in 1930? in 1970? in the latest year shown?

3. What information is contained in the column headed "Passenger Cars per Thousand Persons"?

4. (a) What changes occurred in the ownership of automobiles in the United States during the first 80 years covered by the table?
(b) How would these changes have affected living standards?
(c) What does the information contained in the table have to do with mass production?

CHAPTER 25

Business Combinations

Key Terms

merger	vertical merger	target company
business	conglomerate	takeover
combination	merger	insider trading
monopoly	acquiring	insider
horizontal merger	company	information

Question: What do *Time* Magazine, *Fortune* Magazine, *Life* Magazine, *Sports Illustrated*, Time-Life Books, *People* Magazine, Warner Brothers Motion Pictures, Warner Brothers Records, TBS, TNT, Looney Tunes, Cartoon Network, CNN, HBO, Cinemax, America Online, CompuServe, and Netscape have in common?

Answer: (1) All were independent companies at one time.

(2) Over the years, all the companies were acquired by either AOL or Time Warner, Inc.

(3) In 2000, AOL purchased Time Warner for $165 billion and changed its name to AOL Time Warner, Inc.

When two or more companies combine into a single company, the action is called a *merger*. When AOL purchased Time Warner to form AOL Time Warner, Inc., the merger created the world's largest and most powerful company in the communications industry.

Why should an online services company such as AOL want to acquire record companies, TV stations, book publishing firms, magazines, and other media companies? Should the public be concerned about these kinds of combinations? As you read this chapter, you will learn more about business combinations. You will also learn the answers to the following questions:

- Why do some business firms combine?
- How do business firms combine?
- Why are some people concerned about mergers?

WHY DO SOME BUSINESS FIRMS COMBINE?

Business firms combine because they expect that the move will enable them to increase profits. Profits may be increased if the *business combinations* allow businesses to produce more goods at lower costs and reduce or eliminate competition.

Produce More Goods at Lower Costs

In the previous chapter, we discussed how mass-production methods enable large firms to produce goods at lower costs than small firms can. Companies that produce goods at lower cost than others in the industry can afford to lower prices and thereby take business away from their competitors.

As you know, economists use the term *productivity* to describe the efficiency with which something is produced. Productivity can be likened to the skill of a baseball player whose batting average is .350 as compared to one whose average is .200. The .350 batter may be expected to get 350 hits for every 1,000 times at bat. The .200 hitter will get only 200 hits for every 1,000 times at bat. Thus, the .350 hitter may be said to have greater productivity.

The same principle applies to industry. Workers at Company A can produce an average of 25 pocket combs per hour. Company B, which also manufactures combs, is considerably larger than Company A. Workers at Company B can produce an average of 50 pocket combs per hour. We can say that worker productivity at Company B is twice as great as productivity at Company A.

There are a number of reasons why large businesses are often more efficient than small ones.

1. Workers Assigned More Efficiently. When a retail store has branches all over town, it can transfer its experienced salespeople from one location to another as they are needed. A single store often has to keep salespeople on the payroll during slow business times so that they will be available during busy ones.

As businesses grow in size, they can afford to hire full-time specialized workers, such as accountants, advertising managers, and computer operators. The tasks that these people perform are likely to be carried out more efficiently than they would be in small businesses where most jobs are done by people who are not specialists.

2. Shared Risks. You have heard the saying, "Never put all your eggs in one basket." Why is this good advice? Because if you were to drop the basket, all the eggs might break. When a retail business opens in several locations and when a manufacturer makes a variety of products, they are "putting their eggs in several baskets." That is, they are spreading risks.

Thus, a grocery chain might find that the loss of business in one part of town has not hurt its profits because sales have picked up in another location. A manufacturer of toys, sporting goods, and tools might have a similar experience. If the demand for its tools falls off, for example, the loss may be offset by an increased demand for its toys.

3. Reduced Expenses. It is often too costly for a single store to place an ad in a local newspaper. This is not so for a firm that owns ten stores in an area. All can share the cost of the ad, and all can share in bringing the firm's name before the public.

A large chain of stores might find it profitable to buy out a manufacturer and produce its own line of goods. In this way, the goods sold by the chain could cost the chain less. For this reason, huge producers such as automobile companies have bought out firms that produce car batteries. Steel manufacturers have acquired coal mines. In these instances, the purpose was to acquire companies that produce goods that go into the making of the firm's products.

Reduce or Eliminate Competition

Normally, a restaurant will not charge for a glass of water. But just imagine what it could charge if it owned the only well in the middle of a large desert! Or imagine two small towns identical in every way. In one, there is one plumber to service the needs of the community. In the other town, there are 12 plumbers. In which town could a plumber charge more for his or her services?

In both of these examples, there was only one supplier of a product or service. In the first, there was only one seller of water; in the second, there was but one plumber. Economists describe the situation in which there is only one seller of an item or service as a *monopoly*. In both instances, the sole sellers would be able to charge a much higher price for their product or service than they could have had there been competitors. *Competition* may be defined as a state of rivalry between sellers, each of whom tries to outsell the other. The greater the rivalry, the stiffer the competition.

Because firms that have no competition are able to charge higher prices than those that must compete, some companies try to become as much like monopolies as they can. By growing ever larger in size, a business improves its chance of capturing a larger share of the *market*. (The "market" in this case refers to the total demand for a product or service.) Few companies ever gain control of an entire market. Indeed, in most instances monopolies are illegal in the United States. It is possible, however, for a company to control such a large share of the market that it can *fix* (set) prices and, in that way, increase its profits.

Thus far we have discussed only *why* many businesses have combined with other firms. The question now arises: *How* are these combinations achieved?

HOW DO BUSINESS FIRMS COMBINE?

Nowadays, most people refer to business combinations as *mergers*. When one corporation combines or merges with another, it does so by buying enough shares of the other corporation's stock to gain control of it. There are three types of mergers: horizontal, vertical, and conglomerate.

Horizontal Mergers

When a company acquires another firm that makes or sells similar products or services, we call the combination a *horizontal merger*. The acquisition of one newspaper company by another is an example of a horizontal merger.

The most important reasons why companies seek horizontal mergers are to reduce competition, acquire a larger share of the market for their goods and services, and lower certain business costs.

A horizontal merger reduces competition because the businesses that merge formerly competed against one another. For example, Sneakers Unlimited is a store located at one end of a town's business section. At the other end is Sneakers Unlimited's fiercest competitor: Soft Shoes, Inc. Sneakers Unlimited recently purchased a large percentage of the stock of Soft Shoes, Inc. The purchase enabled Sneakers Unlimited to elect its own people to Soft Shoes's board of directors and control its policies.

Since the two companies are in the same business, Sneakers's acquisition eliminated its strongest competition. From that point on, the two companies have been run by the same management. Sneakers now has retail stores in two areas of the business section. The company thus is in a position to attract more customers and increase its earnings.

The merger lowered certain business costs. Before the merger, both Sneakers Unlimited and Soft Shoes regularly placed a full-

Horizontal Merger: The Limited stores are part of a clothing and personal care conglomerate that includes Lane Bryant, Victoria's Secret, Lerner, and Bath and Body Works.

page ad in the county newspaper every Sunday. Now, instead of two pages of ads in an issue, both stores can get the same ad coverage with only one page. Advertising costs per store were cut in half. In the same way, the merged stores can now share bookkeepers, sales managers, and other personnel.

Vertical Mergers

A *vertical merger* is a merger between a company and one of its suppliers. For example, the Monster Cookie Company has become enormously successful. One of the reasons for its success is that its cookies have more chocolate in them than any of its competitors' cookies. Indeed, business has been so good that Monster Cookie recently purchased controlling interest in Chuck's Chocolate, Inc., which manufactures baking chocolate. Since chocolate is used in the production of Monster cookies, the combination of Monster Cookie with Chuck's Chocolate is a vertical merger.

The principal reason for creating a vertical merger is to reduce the costs of doing business. When USX, the nation's largest steel company, acquired an iron mine, a vertical merger was formed. Why was it called a vertical merger? Because iron ore is used in the manufacture of steel.

Figure 25.1 Types of Business Mergers

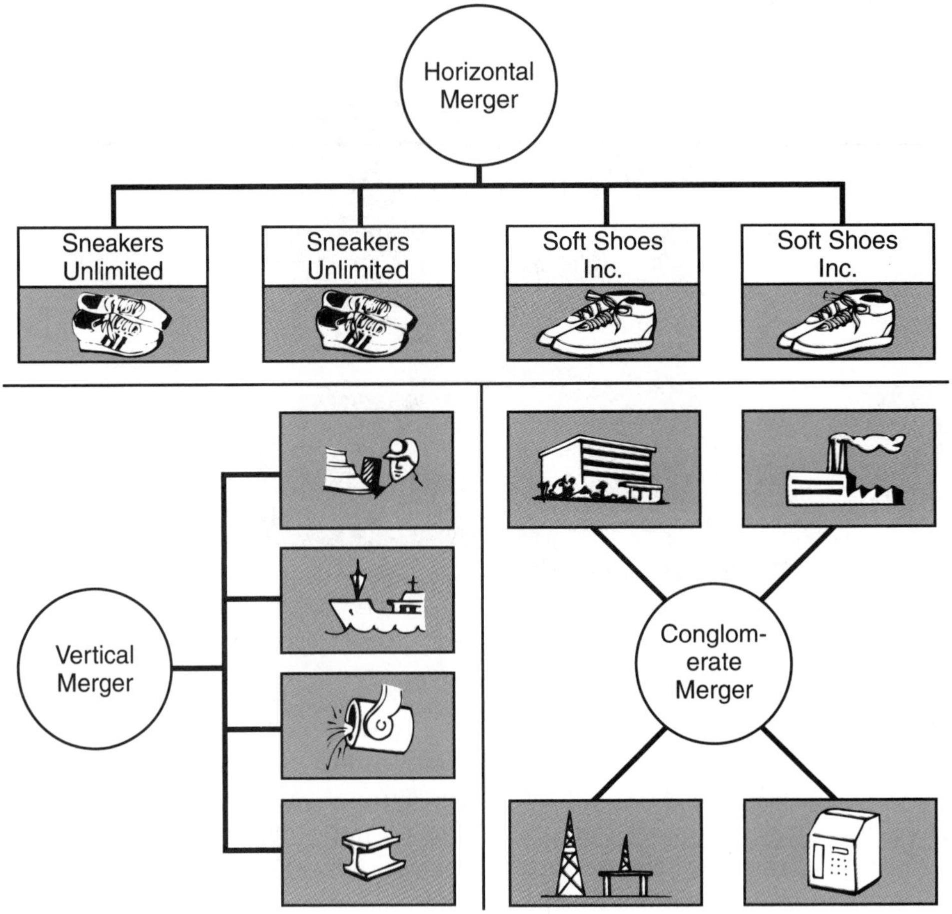

Conglomerate Mergers

A *conglomerate merger* combines companies that sell vastly different products, services, or both.

With $14.5 billion in assets, Cendant Corporation is one of the nation's larger conglomerates. Among the well-known companies combined under the Cendant logo are hotel and motel chains such as Days Inn, Ramada, Super 8, and Howard Johnson; real estate franchises like Coldwell Banker and Century 21, and financial services such as Jackson Hewitt Tax Services, as well as Long Term Preferred Care (a health-related insurance company) and Avis Rent-a-Car.

Because hotels, health insurance, real estate, financial services, and auto rental companies are hardly related, Cendant stands as a classic example of a conglomerate merger.

WHY ARE SOME PEOPLE CONCERNED ABOUT MERGERS?

Many people today are concerned about mergers because mergers may lead to monopolies. When only a few firms produce similar products, economic power may be concentrated in the hands of a few people. Americans fear concentration of power in the business world. They feel that it is unfair when the opportunity for others to enter a field is reduced or eliminated.

Americans believe in competition as a way of life. They also believe that competition is more efficient than monopoly. In a competitive market, a company succeeds by making better products at lower costs than its competitors and then selling its products to more customers.

In many industries, bigger has not always meant better. In steelmaking, new low-overhead "mini-mills" run by small, aggressive U.S. companies have been more successful than the large, multibillion-dollar steel mills built in the 1950s and 1960s. And in recent years, smaller Japanese and Korean automakers have been more efficient than the huge American auto producers.

Number of Corporate Mergers per Year

Year	Number
1970	1,351
1980	1,560
1985	1,719
1990	4,239
1994	4,383
1996	5,639
1998	9,634
2003	7,743

Mergers are costly. There are usually two companies involved in a merger: the *acquiring company* and the *target company* (the one that is being acquired). Sometimes, the company being taken over does not want to merge and will fight back. A costly struggle may result. Both companies will spend enormous sums of money to buy up the stock of the company being targeted for *takeover*. A problem caused by mergers is that those who take over companies usually pay for their purchases with borrowed funds. Often the loans are guaranteed by the parent company. This borrowing has created a mountain of debt for many companies which, sooner or later, will have to be repaid.

Some mergers involve billions of dollars. This is shown in the following table.

Recent Billion-Dollar-Plus Mergers

Acquiring Company	Target Company	Purchase Price (in billions)
America On Line	Time Warner	$181.6
Glaxo Wellcome	SmithKline	75.7
Verizon (Bell Atlantic)	GTE	65.0
Chevron	Texaco	43.0
Daimler-Benz	Chrysler	40.5
Dow Chemical	Union Carbide	11.6
Nestlé	Ralston Purina	10.3
Alcoa	Reynolds	4.8

Problems of Mergers and "Insider Trading"

Some mergers have received bad publicity because they have been associated with the illegal activity known as *insider trading*. Experts have warned that insiders can profit unfairly from advance information about corporate mergers. Those wanting to take over a company have to buy up large blocks of its stock. The increased demand pushes up the price of the shares. Then, as other investors learn of the takeover attempt, they too rush out to buy the shares of the target company, and prices rise even further.

Insiders, such as those working for the brokerage house handling the deal or for the company doing the acquiring, stand to make an easy profit from their knowledge. Such a person would simply buy shares of the target company's stock while the information was still private, and sell when the news became public and prices were rising. Profiting in this way from inside information is a violation of federal law.

Ivan F. Boesky, one of Wall Street's most successful stock traders, made nearly a billion dollars in profits in the 1980s by correctly predicting which companies were about to be taken over by others. Government investigators found that Boesky was correct so often because he had illegally obtained *insider information* about the acquisitions from people in the companies that were being acquired or those doing the buying. In 1986, Boesky was fined $100 million and sent to prison for his crime.

Despite such huge fines and prison sentences, the problem of insider trading continues. In 2000, an employee of Salomon Smith Barney—one of the nation's largest investment firms—pleaded guilty to criminal charges of insider trading. According to the Securities and Exchange Commission (SEC), the employee used information about upcoming mergers that he had gotten on the job to reap profits of nearly $2 million.

In 2001, the SEC charged insiders with having illegally used advance knowledge of the Nestlé buyout of Ralston Purina to turn a $500,000 profit. Similarly, that same year, another group of defendants were fined $581,000 for profiting from insider information about IBM's takeover of the Lotus Corporation.

SUMMARY

The acquisition, or takeover, of one corporation by another is known as a merger. One business combines with another in order to increase its productivity and profits, reduce competition, and add new products and diversify its holdings. Mergers that combine companies in the same business are horizontal mergers. Combinations of companies that could be each other's suppliers or customers are vertical mergers. Mergers that combine two or more companies in businesses that are not related to one another are called conglomerate mergers.

There are differing viewpoints about the worth of mergers. Opponents of mergers feel that the money spent to create giant new companies does not help either the U.S. economy or the public. There is also the concern that too much economic power is gained by the corporations and individuals behind the takeovers. Others disagree. They say that mergers make business more efficient and competitive.

LOOKING AHEAD

As many U.S. companies have grown in size, some lawmakers have become fearful that these companies might use their economic power to exploit the public. In the following chapter, we will learn how the government seeks to protect the public from unfair business practices.

EXERCISES

✔ **Multiple Choice** Choose the letter of the item that best completes the statement or answers the question.

1. Which one of the following is *not* a form of business combination? (a) acquisition (b) S corporation (c) conglomerate (d) merger.

2. When a business increases its productivity, the cost of producing each item will be (a) higher than before (b) lower than before (c) the same as before (d) determined by its competitors.

3. In order to avoid "putting all its eggs in one basket," a business is most likely to (a) concentrate on the production of its best product

(b) avoid growing too large (c) produce or supply a variety of goods and services (d) spend more money to improve its product.

4. A monopoly exists when (a) a company is larger than all the other companies in the industry combined (b) a company produces greater quantities of an item than any other firm (c) a company charges higher prices than anyone else for a product (d) there is only one supplier of a particular good or service.

5. Which one of the following is the best example of a conglomerate merger? (a) Five neighborhood appliance stores combine to form a chain. (b) A manufacturer of steel combines with an owner of iron mines. (c) A theater chain combines with a hotel company and a tire manufacturer. (d) A bakery merges with a flour mill.

6. Jose's Pizza Parlor, Inc., recently acquired controlling interest in Mariana's Pizza Parlor, Inc. This acquisition is called a (a) monopoly (b) vertical merger (c) conglomerate merger (d) horizontal merger.

7. Jose's Pizza Parlor, Inc., acquired the Eastern Pizza Cheese Corporation (EPCC). EPCC is a wholesale distributor of the cheese used in the making of pizza pies. The acquisition created a (a) monopoly (b) vertical merger (c) conglomerate merger (d) horizontal merger.

8. Last January, Cecilia Pye, president of the Pye Plate Company, announced that the company had acquired Young's Bicycle Rental. The Pye Plate Company manufactures dinnerware. Young's is a chain of bicycle rental stores. The acquisition of Young's Bicycles by Pye Plate is an example of a (a) monopoly (b) vertical merger (c) conglomerate merger (d) horizontal merger.

✔**Matching** Match each term in Column A with its definition in Column B.

Column A	Column B
1. productivity	a. the joining together of two or more business firms in the same business
2. monopoly	
3. competition	b. the joining together of two or more business firms in unrelated fields
4. horizontal merger	
5. conglomerate merger	c. the joining together of two or more business firms, at least one of which is a supplier of another
6. vertical merger	
7. insider trading	d. the effort of two or more firms to outsell one another in the same market
	e. a situation in which there is only one seller
	f. a measure of efficiency in turning out goods and services
	g. the buying or selling of a company's stock using private information

✔ *Critical-Thinking Questions*

The table on page 382 lists a number of recent mergers. With reference to any *one* of those mergers:

1. Identify and explain two reasons why the companies might have chosen to merge.

2. What effect, if any, might the merger have on: (a) competing firms in the industry, and (b) consumers?

✔ **Reading for Enrichment** Read the selection below and then answer the questions that follow.

Frankiedogs

Upon graduation from high school, Frankie Russo took all the money he had saved out of the bank and bought a rolling hot dog stand. He attached a colorful umbrella overhead and painted *Frankiedogs* in bright orange letters along the sides of the wagon. Frankie set his stand up in front of the local high school.

Perhaps it was the sauerkraut, maybe the spicy onions, or it may even have been the crisp French fried potatoes you got with every frankfurter—whatever it was, business was terrific. Business was so good, in fact, that whenever Frankie heard about other stand owners who were having difficulty earning a living, he would offer to buy them out. As a result, he soon owned 25 rolling hot dog carts. These, too, were fitted out with a colorful umbrella and had the trademark *Frankiedogs* painted on the sides.

Perhaps it was the sauerkraut, maybe the spicy onions, or it may even have been the crisp French fried potatoes you got with every frankfurter—whatever it was, business continued to be terrific. By the end of the next year, he owned 159 carts!

Business was so good, in fact, that Frankie went across the river into the next city and set up carts. "Why stop here?" he thought, and soon Frankiedogs and Frankiecarts were seen all over the state.

Perhaps it was the sauerkraut, maybe the spicy onions, or it may even have been the crisp French fried potatoes you got with every frankfurter—whatever it was, business continued to be terrific.

"Why stop here?" thought Frankie. He hired a personnel manager and set up a program to train people to operate his carts. He hired an advertising manager to plan his sales campaigns. "You'll be top dog, frankly, with a Frankiedog!" became a slogan known in every household.

"Why stop here?" thought Frankie. He bought out a large sausage factory, which he converted to full-time frankfurter production.

Perhaps it was the sauerkraut, maybe the spicy onions, or it may even have been the crisp French fried potatoes you got with every frankfurter—whatever it was, business continued to be terrific. Frankiedogs were the hottest selling hot dogs in the 50 states and in 17 other countries.

One day, PDQ, the nation's largest conglomerate and owners of a world championship football team, a television network, several steel mills and aircraft factories, and a host of other industrial plants, sent representatives to talk to Frankie. "We want to buy you out," they said. "We will give you $400 million for your Frankiedog business."

"I think I will retire," thought Frankie.

1. As Frankie's business grew, so did profits. Frankiedog wagons earned more for Frankie than they did for their former owners. (*a*) What *three* reasons can you think of that would explain why profits grew as Frankie added hot dog wagons? (*b*) Explain each of these reasons.

2. Why did Frankie buy a sausage factory?

3. (*a*) What kind of company bought Frankie's business? (*b*) Explain your answer. (*c*) Why do you suppose this company wanted to buy out Frankie? (*d*) Why did Frankie sell out?

CHAPTER *26*

The Government Promotes and Regulates Competition

Item: When Staples announced plans to acquire Office Depot, the Justice Department of the federal government stepped in to block the merger. Staples and Office Depot are two of the nation's three largest office supply companies. Were the merger allowed to proceed, the government explained, consumers might have to pay millions of dollars more for their office supplies.

Item: Microsoft, the world's largest software company, was found guilty of violating the nation's antitrust laws. After a long trial, a federal judge ruled that Microsoft was a monopoly. Worse yet, said the court, the company had used its "power and immense profits to harm any firm" that seriously competed with it.

Item: Two major automobile manufacturers and five St. Louis area dealerships signed agreements with the Federal Trade Commission, a government agency, to end certain advertising practices. The companies said that they would no longer omit or bury key cost information in small and sometimes unreadable print in their lease advertisements.

What do the items just mentioned have in common? In each, the government took steps to regulate or influence the way in which a company did business. First, Staples was barred from acquiring Office Depot, because doing so would have given Staples too much power in the market for office supplies. Second, the federal court ruled against Microsoft after finding that the company was trying to prevent other software companies from competing with it. Third, the Federal Trade Commission moved to make it easier for consumers to understand the terms of the automobile leases they were signing.

"But," you say, "this is supposed to be a free country. Why does the government interfere with the ways in which corporations choose to compete?" As you read this chapter, you will learn the answer to this question. You will also be able to answer these questions:

- Why is monopoly power harmful?
- Why are some monopolies legal?
- How does government promote competition?

WHY IS MONOPOLY POWER HARMFUL?

In earlier chapters, we described how the U.S. economic system is based upon *competition*. It is competition with other companies, we said, that leads businesspeople to try to please their customers. By pleasing the public, by giving it the best products at the lowest prices, a company stands to earn the greatest profits. Thus, competition encourages firms to work hard to improve their products and methods of doing business. In turn, the public benefits by having better goods and services at the lowest possible prices.

Suppose, however, that only one company sells a certain product or service. As you know, economists describe a situation in which there is but one seller as a *monopoly*. A monopolist can provide its products or services at whatever prices it wants to charge.

The same might also be true if there are just a handful of firms in an industry. A market in which there are but a few sellers is called an *oligopoly*. As in a monopoly, sellers in an oligopoly have been known to agree among themselves to set prices.

Harmful Effects of Monopoly Power

Monopolies and oligopolies wield a great deal of power over the markets for their goods and services. Sometimes, this power is harmful to the public.

Business Competition: Two fast-food restaurants on a crowded road compete for travelers' business.

1. Destroys Competition. Wealthy monopolies and oligopolies have in the past used their market power to prevent other firms from entering the field. During the early years of the 20th century, for example, the Standard Oil Company controlled about 90 percent of the gasoline industry. One reason for the company's success was its ability to destroy its competition. For example, if a competitor opened a gas station, Standard Oil responded by lowering prices at its stations in the area. Those station owners who had no financial backer could not survive. Once its competition was forced into bankruptcy, Standard Oil made up for its losses simply by raising prices.

2. Wastes Resources. When firms compete, each tries to operate with the lowest possible costs. Each wants to be able to sell its goods at the lowest possible price. Every company, large or small, will strive to get the most out of its resources. Businesspeople know that to waste scarce raw materials or fuels simply adds to the costs of doing business. So competition encourages businesses to conserve our valuable natural resources.

Monopolies are not under the same kind of pressure to conserve resources and operate efficiently. Unlike other businesses, monopolies can pass on increased costs to their customers without having to worry about being undersold by their competitors.

3. Creates Higher Prices. Prices are usually lower when there is competition. If you have ever bought food and soft drinks at a theater or stadium, you probably noticed that their prices were higher there than those in grocery stores and supermarkets. The theater and stadium vendors had a monopoly on the sale of their goods and thus charged higher prices.

4. May Not Satisfy Consumer Wants. Consumer wants are much more likely to be satisfied when there is competition. If you and a dozen friends march into the local post office and ask to buy triangle-shaped stamps, you might get a smile from the clerk. But you will not get triangular stamps. The Postal Service determines what stamps look like. On the other hand, think what would happen if you and a dozen friends asked your local pizza parlor for slices topped with bacon. You can be sure that with that kind of demand, the pizza parlor would not be long in finding a way to provide everyone who wanted them with bacon pizzas!

5. May Threaten Democratic Values. When companies become wealthy and powerful because they have little or no competition, they can use their wealth to influence government officials to favor them. Running for political office costs a great deal of money. Television and radio commercials and newspaper advertising are very expensive. Like other special interest groups, powerful monopolies have used their wealth to buy the support of elected officials. In this way, monopolies have been able to secure the enactment of laws that benefit and protect their interests.

WHY ARE SOME MONOPOLIES LEGAL?

In some instances, monopolies are considered desirable, and, therefore, have been legalized.

Patents and Copyrights

Let us pretend that you have just invented a device that will enable automobiles to run on flashlight batteries instead of gasoline. You have decided to call your invention a "Battgo." Instead of having to refill a car's tank with, say, 15 gallons of gas, a driver whose car is equipped with a Battgo will simply say to the filling station attendant, "I'll have four D-cells, please." There is not an automobile driver anywhere in the world who will not want to own such a device.

What is more, as the inventor of Battgo, you will be entitled to receive a *patent* on it. A patent is a grant issued by the federal government that gives inventors the sole right to manufacture, use, and sell their inventions. In other words, the inventor of a patented device has a legal monopoly on its manufacture and sale. After a limited number of years (usually 17), the patent will expire and everyone else will have the right to copy the invention.

Why are patents granted to inventors? The government wants to encourage new inventions and discoveries. It might have taken you years of research to invent your Battgo. And yet you continued in your efforts because you knew that if you were successful, you alone would be entitled to the rewards. Without a patent to protect you, however, it would only be a matter of time before others copied and marketed your invention.

The government also grants *copyrights* to owners of intellectual and cultural works. They give exclusive rights to authors, artists, and composers to reproduce, perform, and sell their works. Copyrights thus encourage the creation of artistic, musical, and literary works. The publishers or producers of books, magazines, newspapers, newsletters, movies, recordings, television programs, computer software, and electronic (video) games may also copyright these works.

Video game software are inventions that are copyrighted by their creators.

Natural Monopolies/Public Utilities

Most communities receive things like electricity, water, and natural gas from the *public utilities* servicing the area. Public utilities provide essential public services, and for reasons that we will soon explain, are granted a monopoly in the market that they serve.

Imagine what it would be like if say, five electric power companies served your neighborhood. In areas where the wires ran above ground, five sets of poles (one for each company) would be needed to carry them. Where the wires ran underground, five companies would have to service them. Imagine too, what things would be like if the streets had to be dug up five times as often as they are now just to maintain electric power service. Similarly, think about what might happen if water and gas service were delivered under local streets by numbers of competing companies.

It takes a huge investment to build, operate, and maintain public utilities. Nevertheless, these companies can operate at a profit if they have a monopoly because large-scale production lowers costs per unit. If there were competing companies, however, the cost to service individual households would be greater than it was when there was but one supplier. Economists describe these public utilities as *natural monopolies*. Natural monopolies occur in industries in which a single firm is more efficient and therefore more desirable than two or more competing companies.

Since competition among public utilities does not make economic sense, antitrust laws do not apply to them. Nonetheless,

Legal Monopolies—Utilities: For years, power companies like this one had a monopoly on providing power in a region.

federal, state, and/or local governments regulate public utilities to a greater extent than other kinds of enterprises.

HOW DOES THE GOVERNMENT PROMOTE COMPETITION?

Because of the many possible threats to our economy that are posed by some monopolies, government often uses its powers to (1) encourage competition in the marketplace and (2) regulate business activities. It does this through the enforcement of antitrust laws and the work of regulatory agencies.

Antitrust Laws

Laws designed to promote competition and prevent business firms from gaining monopolies are known as *antitrust laws*. The most important of the federal antitrust laws are summarized in the following table.

Federal Antitrust Laws, 1887–1950

Law	Date Enacted	Provisions
Interstate Commerce Act	1887	First federal law regulating the abuse of monopoly power. Banned certain unfair practices in the railroad industry
Sherman Antitrust Act	1890	Outlawed combinations that were "in restraint of trade"
Clayton Antitrust Act	1914	Sought to prevent the creation of monopolies by defining specific illegal practices
Federal Trade Commission Act	1914	Created the Federal Trade Commission (FTC), which has responsibility to carry out provisions of the Clayton Act
Robinson-Patman Act	1936	Protects small retailers from unfair competition by chain stores and other large-scale competitors
Celler-Kefauver Act	1950	Outlawed mergers or acquisitions that would lessen competition or create a monopoly

As the table above shows, in the past 115 years U.S. antitrust laws have outlawed monopolies, banned certain monopolistic practices, and created a federal government agency to enforce the laws. Antimonopoly laws are called antitrust laws because in the 19th century big businesses were called "trusts."

In the 1880s, Americans became aware that powerful monopolies existed in the oil, sugar, tobacco, and railroad industries. As knowledge spread of how these huge corporations had abused their power, a demand went up for the federal government to "do something about the monopolies."

Finally, in 1887, the first of the antitrust laws was passed—the Interstate Commerce Act. It was designed to regulate the nation's railroads. Three years later, in 1890, the first law affecting every business in the country was passed. This was the Sherman Antitrust Act, which declared monopolies to be illegal. The Sherman Antitrust Act was followed by the Clayton Antitrust Act in 1914. The latter closed some of the loopholes in the Sherman Act by spelling out some of the things businesses would not be allowed to do. The Federal Trade Commission Act (1914) created the Federal Trade Commission (FTC). The FTC has the responsibility of enforcing the antitrust laws. It conducts investigations and brings offending companies to court.

Still later acts have strengthened the antitrust laws. In 1936, the Robinson-Patman Act was passed. It was designed to protect small retail stores from the competition of large stores. The Celler-Kefauver Act of 1950 is also known as the Antimerger Act. It says that mergers would be illegal if it could be shown that they would "lessen competition, or . . . create a monopoly."

Is the government doing enough today to curb the power of monopolies? Some critics say it is not. If it had, there would not have been over 60,000 mergers during the last ten years. Critics also claim that the federal courts have been too "soft on monopolies." They point to a case in which Owens-Illinois purchased Brockway, Inc. Each of the companies was a major producer of glass containers. The FTC objected to the merger because it would have increased Owens's share of the market from 24 percent to 40 percent. The federal courts, however, overruled the FTC. They said that the merger would not lead to increased prices or reduced competition.

Another point that critics make is that the present laws do not cover conglomerate mergers. Conglomerates threaten competition because of their size. They can afford to take losses with low prices until they have forced their competitors out of business. Once free of competition, the conglomerates can then raise their prices to whatever level they choose. Conglomerates may also stifle competition because of their buying power. For example, a conglomerate that owns hotels, automobile rental companies, and bakeries can demand that the company from which it buys grain use its services for business travel and entertainment.

Others say that the government should keep its hands off businesses. They argue that it is contrary to the spirit of freedom and liberty for the government to tell business firms what they can

Antitrust Fervor: Public fury at the greed of the trusts was expressed in cartoons such as this one from the late 1880s. Justice "extracts" the gold (the people's money) from the dragon (Standard Oil Trust).

and cannot do. Furthermore, they say, many of the antitrust laws cost consumers money. Protecting the small, less efficient producer means that the public has to pay more for the things that it buys, claim the critics of antitrust laws.

There are, however, those who speak well of our antitrust laws. They point out that free competition still exists in the U.S. economy. Had there been no Sherman Act or Clayton Act or FTC, they argue, the likelihood is that our economy would now be in the hands of monopolies.

An Antitrust Case Study

Can you imagine a company intentionally delaying the loading of iron ore ships operated by competitors? That is what the Federal Trade Commission in 1990 charged a railroad with doing. This railroad was owned by USX, the nation's largest steel and energy corporation. Competing steelmakers said that their ships were affected. The government contended that this was a deliberate effort to restrain trade and a violation of the antitrust laws. The courts agreed. In 1994, the U.S. Supreme Court said that USX would be required to pay a total of $660 million in damages and fines to the affected firms and the government. National Steel Corporation received $110 million as its share of an antitrust judgment against the USX Corporation.

Regulatory Agencies

The government agencies that oversee the way companies in some industries do business are known as *regulatory agencies*. All public utilities and certain industries are supervised by these agencies.

1. State Public Service Commissions. Although public utilities are legal monopolies, they do not have the same freedoms enjoyed by other kinds of businesses. They cannot by themselves decide what goods or services they will provide and how much they will charge for them. Instead, the public utilities are regulated by state-run agencies known as public service commissions. These commissions issue licenses granting publicly and privately owned utilities the right to operate. They also determine the kinds of services that the utilities must provide and how much they will be permitted to charge for these services.

Why do public service commissions tell the electric power, gas, and other utilities how much they may charge for their services? Is it unfair to require that a water or telephone company get permission from the government to change its service or increase its rates when other businesses are free to take these actions on their own?

The reason utilities are regulated is that they have a monopoly over the services they provide. Other companies, such as your neighborhood appliance center, hardware store, and gasoline station, must compete in order to stay in business. Competition prevents them from taking advantage of the public. If your supermarket's prices become too high, you can take your business elsewhere. But you cannot go elsewhere if you do not like the prices charged by your electric company. Public service commissions were set up to see that public utilities use their monopoly power fairly.

2. Federal Government Agencies. Industries that have been regulated and are being regulated by federal government agencies include radio and television broadcasting, railroads, airlines, trucking, and banking. On a local basis, taxicabs, buses, and even tow trucks have been supervised by regulatory agencies.

Several of the best-known federal regulatory agencies and their functions are listed in the following table.

Some Federal Regulatory Agencies

Agency	Date Created	Function
Interstate Commerce Commission (ICC)— terminated in 1995; remaining functions picked up by Dept. of Transportation	1887	Originally created to regulate the railroads, in the 1930s its power was extended to all surface transportation.
Federal Communications Commission (FCC)	1934	Regulates radio, television, phone, telegraph, and satellite industries.
Nuclear Regulatory Commission	1974	Licenses and regulates civilian uses of nuclear energy in order to protect public health and safety, as well as the environment.

The Deregulation Movement

In the late 1970s, the U.S. economy appeared to be in trouble. For many, the source of the difficulties lay in competition from abroad. Japanese and other foreign businesses were selling their goods for less than U.S. firms. U.S. companies had difficulty competing, it was said, because of government restrictions that added to their production costs and the price at which they sold their products. The solution, it was argued, could be found in deregulation.

Deregulation is the dismantling of some or all the governmental restrictions on the operation of certain businesses. In the mid-1970s, airlines, cable television, natural gas, and electric power industries were still regulated by government agencies. Since then, there has been some deregulation in each of those industries.

Experts expected that the lifting of government restraints would result in increased competition and lower prices. As the millennium drew to a close, however, it was apparent that deregulation did not necessarily have these outcomes. We will look at three attempts at deregulation.

1. Telephone Deregulation. The Telecommunications Act of 1996 deregulated the telephone industry. As stated in its preamble, the goal of the law was: "To *promote competition* and reduce regulation in order to *secure lower prices* and higher quality services. . . ." In particular, it was expected that the new law would introduce real competition in local telephone service. After five years, few of those goals had been achieved. In 2001, 90 percent of consumers had only one choice in local telephone service. Prices of local service had not declined. Indeed, families were paying an average of 20 percent more for their telephone services than they had been paying in 1996. Meanwhile, telephone customer complaints in some regions of the country were higher than ever.

Competition for local telephone service had all but disappeared in most parts of the country because the law did not prevent some of the larger telephone companies from merging. As a result, the eight regional phone companies that existed in 1996 had been reduced to four regional carriers by 2001. Meanwhile, smaller companies that tried to enter the local telephone market could not afford to compete with their multibillion-dollar competitors.

2. Airline Deregulation. Airlines were deregulated in 1978. At the time, it was expected that deregulation would bring an increase in competition. Quite the opposite occurred. In the following decades, competition among airlines all but disappeared. Critics blamed unregulated mergers and cutthroat business practices in the airline industry for having forced over 100 carriers to close their doors. This, in turn, left large areas of the country with little or no air service. In the meantime, as the number of air carriers declined, complaints about the quality of service seemed to be on the increase.

As promised by those who fought for airline deregulation, average airfares have decreased. This has made it possible for more people than ever before to be flying to their destinations. But many travelers have to pay fares that are much higher than the average. For example, in 2001 a business traveler from Washington, D.C., to San Francisco leaving on a *Saturday* and returning the following Monday paid $543 for the flight. Were he or she to choose to spend Saturday with the family and fly out on *Sunday*, the fare would have been $2,248. Nonbusiness travelers flying from Washington, D.C., to San Francisco could do so for far less simply by buying their tickets weeks in advance of departure. Thus, it was possible that seated next to one another on the return flight from San Francisco to Washington, D.C., were three people, one of whom had spent $2,200, another $540, and another $250 for the same trip.

Increasing complaints about fares, delays, and the quality of service in air travel (as well as security concerns in light of 9/11) have led to calls for the return to regulation of the airline industry.

3. Energy Deregulation.

> . . . With only minutes of warning, sections of San Francisco, Silicon Valley, the state capital of Sacramento and a few other smaller cities went dark. . . . Traffic lights and television broadcasts blinked off, assembly lines stopped. . . . Passengers were trapped in elevators, businesses closed early, and schools dismissed students for the day. . . .

In January 2001, Californians experienced their first "rolling blackout." These were periods of an hour or two in which the power was turned off for a half million homes at a time. The blackouts were necessary because there simply was not enough electricity to go around. Something had gone terribly wrong with the deregulation of the power industry in the nation's most populous state.

In 1996, California had deregulated its electric industry. At the time, it was thought that by allowing private generating plants (both in and out of California) to compete, it would lead to lower prices. By 2000, it was obvious that deregulation was a failure. Wholesale prices of electricity increased dramatically because there were so few wholesale suppliers. But California had ordered the retailers to freeze the rates they charged their customers. With these utilities paying more for electricity than they were charging, one of the state's largest, Pacific Gas and Electric, was forced into bankruptcy.

To make matters worse, there was not enough power to go around. Consequently, in January 2001, the state introduced the first of its "rolling blackouts." Meanwhile, other states (including New York, Nevada, and Arkansas) that were planning to deregulate their power industries (or were in the process) began having second thoughts about the process.

SUMMARY

Competition in the marketplace benefits us all. It discourages waste and provides rewards for those who can sell their goods and services at the lowest prices. By contrast, monopolies often waste resources, stifle competition, raise prices, and threaten our democratic institutions.

Certain types of monopolies are thought to be in the public interest, and for that reason are legal. These include inventions (protected by patents), creative works (protected by copyright), and public utilities (regulated by public service commissions).

Government encourages competition through its antitrust laws and its regulatory agencies. The nation's antitrust laws have made the creation of monopolies and activities that interfere with competition illegal. The regulatory agencies limit the actions of certain industries and public utilities. Since the 1970s, a number of industries supervised by the regulatory agencies have been deregulated.

LOOKING AHEAD

Unit V takes us further into the role of the government in our economy. In Chapter 27, you will learn why, as the chapter says, "We are all taxpayers."

──────────────── **EXERCISES** ────────────────

✔ **Matching** Match each term in Column A with its definition in Column B.

Column A
1. oligopoly
2. public utility
3. regulatory agency
4. patent
5. antitrust law
6. copyright

Column B

a. the monopoly given to inventors to be the only persons permitted to make, use, or sell their inventions

b. an exclusive right granted to authors, artists, and composers to reproduce, perform, and sell their works

c. an industry that performs a vital public service and is regulated by the government

d. a market in which there are few sellers

e. an act of government that outlaws monopolies

f. a government organization that oversees the way companies in some industries do business

✔ *Just Suppose*

Imagine that you are the inventor of a new kind of running shoe. The unusual thing about this shoe is that it enables those who wear a pair to run 20 percent faster than they can wearing any other type of shoe. For example, if you can run a mile in ten minutes in your present shoes, you can run a mile in just eight minutes in these new shoes.

Your company is the only business firm permitted to make and sell the shoes because you hold the patent. You are now trying to decide what price to charge for the shoes. You have called a meeting of your top executives to consider the question. They have made a study and have found that the factory will be able to produce up to 50,000 pairs of running shoes a year and that each pair will cost the company about $60 to turn out. You have also invited Professor O.L. Arbiter, one of the nation's foremost authorities on business matters, to attend the meeting as adviser.

In the discussion that followed, many suggestions were made. One person said, "Let's charge $65 for each pair of shoes. At that price, we know we will sell them all and make a profit."

Another said, "That's ridiculous. We ought to charge $1,000 for each pair. There are plenty of rich people in the world who will be willing to pay that price."

Still another said, "Wait a minute. We're the only company selling these running shoes. Let's charge $5,000 a pair for them. We'll make a fortune."

The discussion went on for some time. Everyone had a different price to suggest, ranging from $65 to $5,000. Finally, it was Professor Arbiter's turn to speak. The wise professor rose and addressed the group as follows:

"I have been listening to your discussion with great interest. I do believe, however, that before you arrive at a decision on the price to charge, you ought first to conduct a study to find out how many pairs of shoes you would sell at $5,000 or $1,000 or at any other price you might think of, all the way down to $65. Remember, your objective is *profit*, not price."

Professor Arbiter had intended to remain after the meeting to answer a few questions. But the professor suddenly remembered a previous engagement and had to leave in a hurry. Here are the questions that did come up. Perhaps you can answer them for the professor.

1. What, if anything, is likely to happen to the number of pairs of running shoes sold as the price charged for them is reduced from $5,000 to $65?

2. What did Professor Arbiter mean by the statement that the company's objective was "*profit*, not price"?

3. What determines which price the company should choose for its running shoes?

4. Suppose that, as a result of the study recommended by Professor Arbiter, the following information is obtained:

At a price of	Number sold would be
$5,000	10
1,000	100
500	1,000
200	10,000
150	50,000
100	50,000
65	50,000

Which price would you recommend charging for the running shoes?

✔ *Questions for Thought and Discussion*

"Monopoly is usually good for monopolists, but bad for consumers."

1. Explain the quotation by describing one way in which monopoly "is good for monopolists" and one way in which it is "bad for consumers."

2. What has government done to limit the power of monopolies?

3. It has also been said, "There are times when monopoly is *good* for consumers." Explain this statement.

✔ *Using the Internet*

Visit the Internet to *investigate* and *report* on the status of a recent antitrust investigation. Note that the Federal Trade Commission and the Antitrust Division of the Department of Justice enforce the federal antitrust laws. You can learn more about the activities of those agencies at: <<http://www.ftc.gov/ftc/antitrust.htm>> and <<http://www.usdoj.gov/atr/>>.

Unit 5

THE ROLE OF GOVERNMENT

Taxes pay for a necessary government expense: laying new sewage lines.

The U.S. economy relies largely on private markets to provide us with our goods and services. We have seen how the desire for profits leads privately owned firms to produce the goods and services wanted by consumers, at a price they are willing to pay. The market system has given Americans one of the world's highest living standards. However, business firms and private consumers are but two of the three components of the market system. Government, or the *public sector* as it is also described, plays an important role in the U.S. system.

The Economic Role of Government

Government plays a large role in our economic system. It: (1) provides a legal system, (2) promotes competition, (3) provides public goods and services, and (4) steps in when the market system breaks down.

1. Our Legal System. Government can be helpful to our economic system. Members of government write and enforce laws, without which the economy could not function. Features like contracts, the monetary system, property rights, and the relationship between buyers and sellers—essential ingredients in every economy—are described and protected by government.

2. Promoting Competition. Competition is an essential ingredient in the market system. Without competition there is less incentive to improve goods and services and reduce costs. For that reason, government has enacted antitrust laws and other measures to protect competition.

3. Public Goods and Services. Those goods and services that might not be produced were it not for the government are called *public goods and services.* Parks, roads, lighthouses, and national defense are examples of public goods and services.

4. When the Market System Needs Help. Government steps in when the market system breaks down or is unable to deal with events. Consider, for example, a riverside furniture factory whose wastes have polluted the drinking water of a community hundreds of miles downstream. Without government help, the downstream community might have to bear the cost of purifying its water. Meanwhile the factory can price its furniture without considering the cost of water cleanup. If it costs less to pollute than not to, people and businesses will have a financial incentive to continue polluting! In those instances, it is left to government to do something to discourage the harmful effect of that economic activity. It might, for example, enact fines on polluters.

There are times when business is good and jobs are plentiful. Other times, however, the opposite may be true. There will be times when business activity around the nation is declining and unemployment is running very high. The government can take measures to *stabilize* (even out) the swings in economic activity. We will be describing these measures in this unit.

Not everyone prospers in our economy. Some people are very wealthy. Some are just comfortable. Still others do not earn enough to pay for even the necessities of life. Government has taken on the responsibility of *redistributing* wealth by taking some from those who have more than they need and transferring funds to those with less than they need.

How Large a Role Should Government Play in the Economy?

There is disagreement about how large a role government should play in our economy.

1. The Conservative View. While everyone agrees that some government participation in the economy is essential, there is considerable disagreement over how large a role that should be. Conservatives would sharply limit government's role. Conservatives believe that in most instances private markets, driven by the profit motive and competition, are better able to solve economic problems than government can. They worry about the loss of freedom that accompanies government regulation. They remind us that the expense of meeting government regulations is passed on to consumers in the form of higher prices, and that higher prices reduce everyone's living standards.

2. The Liberal View. Liberals say that society has economic goals that can only be solved by government. In their view, things like full employment, universal health care, protection of the environment, and assistance for the poor cannot be left to private enterprise and the marketplace. It is, therefore, up to government to enact and enforce the laws necessary for positive change to achieve those goals.

In Chapter 27, you will learn why federal, state, and local governments levy taxes, the kinds of taxes that are paid, and who pays them. Chapter 28 explains why it is so expensive for governments to provide all of the services that their people expect and want. You will see how governments use budgets to plan their spending, where the money comes from, and what happens when expenses exceed revenues.

Although consumers, businesses, and government hope that the U.S. economy will continue to grow, it does not always do so. Chapter 29 discusses the business cycle and how the federal government keeps track of the ups and downs of the economy. Chapter 30 explores the various economic tools that the federal government may use in order to maintain a healthy, growing economy.

CHAPTER 27

We Are All Taxpayers

Did you or any member of your family pay any taxes today? If your state or local community has a sales tax, this tax was added to the price of most purchases that you made. A tax may have been included in the price of the gasoline or the movie tickets that you or your family bought. Did someone in your family pay the rent today? If so, you can be sure that part of that payment went toward paying the tax on land or buildings that is owed to local government. And if you received your wages today, some of the money may have been held by your employer to pay your income taxes.

The author Mark Twain once said that although everybody complains about the weather, nobody does anything about it. Some of this kind of thinking seems to be true about taxes. That is, nobody likes to pay taxes. Most people complain about them. Nevertheless, taxes are a fact of life, just like the weather. Sooner or later, we all get caught in the rain. And, sooner or later, we all pay taxes.

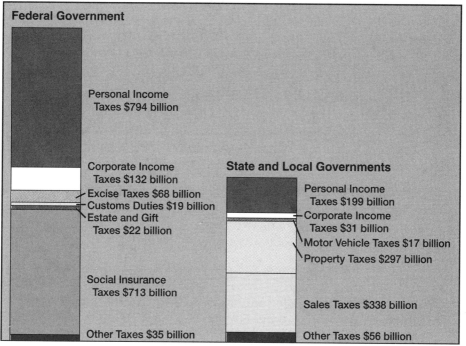

In this chapter, we will be taking a close look at the kinds of taxes we pay and the ways in which we pay them. As you read, you will learn the answers to the following questions:

- What kinds of taxes do people in the United States pay?
- Why do we pay taxes?
- How do we determine who should pay taxes?
- What effect does a tax have on taxpayers?
- Who really pays taxes?

WHAT KINDS OF TAXES DO AMERICANS PAY?

A tax is a payment to government that is required by law. People in the United States pay many different kinds of taxes. This section describes the taxes that you can expect to pay.

1. Income Taxes. An *income tax* is a tax on the earnings of individuals and corporations. The federal government, certain states, and some cities collect income taxes. Individuals pay personal income taxes. Corporations, as you know, also pay income taxes.

Figure 27.1 Taxes Collected by the Federal, State, and Local Governments, 2003

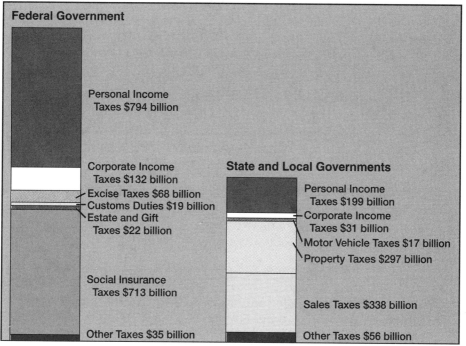

Federal Government

Personal Income
Taxes $794 billion

Corporate Income
Taxes $132 billion
Excise Taxes $68 billion
Customs Duties $19 billion
Estate and Gift
Taxes $22 billion

Social Insurance
Taxes $713 billion

Other Taxes $35 billion

State and Local Governments

Personal Income
Taxes $199 billion
Corporate Income
Taxes $31 billion
Motor Vehicle Taxes $17 billion
Property Taxes $297 billion

Sales Taxes $338 billion

Other Taxes $56 billion

2. Excise Taxes. An *excise tax* is a tax on the manufacture or sale of a specific good or service. Some states and the federal government tax such items as tobacco, alcohol, cosmetics, travel, and gasoline. Excise tax rates are different for each taxable item.

3. Sales Taxes. A *sales tax* is a levy on the selling price of most goods and services in a particular state, county, or city. The government charges one rate for a large number of items. Many states and some local governments charge a sales tax. In North Carolina, for example, most items are subject to a 6 percent sales tax. Whether you buy a pack of safety pins or an automobile, 6 percent will be added to the price as a sales tax.

For example, in Nebraska most items are subject to a state sales tax of 5 percent. In addition, many local governments have added their own 1 or 1.5 percent sales tax on top of the state's levy. Consequently, whether you buy a pack of safety pins or an automobile in Nebraska, you are likely to be charged an additional 6 or 6.5 percent in sales taxes.

4. Payroll Taxes. A business firm pays taxes based on its payroll. These are known as *payroll taxes*. The most important payroll tax is used to finance the government's Social Security program. For most jobs, a percentage of one's wages is deducted to pay the Social Security tax. In addition, the employer pays to the government an amount equal to the employee's contribution. Payment of this Social Security tax entitles one to receive a government pension when that person retires. Payroll taxes are also used to pay for social insurance programs and unemployment insurance. (These programs are discussed in more detail in Chapter 14.)

5. Property Taxes. An important source of income for local governments is the *property tax*. This tax is based upon the value of taxpayers' possessions—usually their homes and land. In some states and localities, valuable personal belongings, such as boats and automobiles, are also subject to property taxes.

6. Estate and Gift Taxes. People who inherit sizeable sums of money or who make large gifts of money to relatives have to pay taxes on these funds. These *estate taxes* and *gift taxes*, however, are not major sources of government income.

7. User Fees. Government may charge "user fees" (or more simply "fees") to those who benefit from a particular activity or are subject to regulation. The charge for admission to a state or national park is an example of a *user fee*. Similarly, you will need to pay a fee to obtain the passport required for travel abroad. About 9 percent of federal revenues, or $207 billion dollars, came from user fees in 2006.

Property Taxes: Localities levy taxes on property owners to pay for new schools.

WHY DO WE PAY TAXES?

Many people seem to believe that the only reason governments impose and collect taxes is to pay their expenses. While this is the most important reason, it is not the only one.

Pay for the Cost of Government Services

The table below illustrates what has happened to the cost of government since 1901. As you can see, federal spending in the more than 100 years since 1901 rose from $525 million to nearly $2.6 *trillion,* or 5,000 times.

To meet this huge increase, fair and efficient ways had to be found to tax the public. But the federal government has other reasons for levying taxes.

Federal Government Spending Since 1901 (in millions)

Year	Total Spent	Year	Total Spent
1901	$ 525	1960	$ 92,191
1910	694	1970	195,649
1920	6,358	1980	590,020
1930	3,320	1990	1,253,163
1940	9,468	2001	1,835,000
1950	42,562	2007	2,592,100 (est.)

Redistribute Income

Many people who are employed pay federal income taxes. This leaves them with less money than they would have had were there no income tax. Meanwhile, those entitled to receive food stamps may use them to purchase food. The funds for the food stamp program come, in part, from the federal income taxes that many employed Americans pay. Thus, one effect of the income tax is to redistribute money. It takes money from one group (those who work and earn a good income) and transfers it to another group (those who receive food stamps).

Many other government programs are designed to help people with special needs in our society. The money to pay for these programs comes, in part, from taxes. Since most taxes are paid by those who can afford to take care of themselves, these programs have the effect of taking money from people with higher incomes and passing it along to those with lower incomes. Thus, taxes tend to make the incomes of a great many people more or less equal. This is called *income redistribution.*

Aid Certain Regions and Industries

Some communities have fewer job opportunities and higher unemployment than others. By way of attracting new businesses into those areas, some state and local governments have offered tax relief. That is, in exchange for opening a plant or an office in a certain area, business firms are granted tax reductions.

The federal government has also used its power to tax to protect certain industries. It has done so by placing a tariff on certain goods brought in for sale from foreign countries. A *protective tariff* raises the price of the imported good high enough to discourage many Americans from buying it.

A few years ago, a tariff protected many U.S. furniture manufacturers from foreign competition. Depending on the kind of furniture, taxes on imported furniture ranged from 5 to 9 percent. It was estimated that more than $1 billion worth of foreign-made furniture was kept out of the United States each year. This tax on imported furniture is an example of a protective tariff because its effect is to "protect" U.S.-made goods from the competition of foreign manufacturers.

Governments may, on the other hand, levy taxes on imports simply to generate income. These are known as *revenue tariffs.*

Change Behavior

Taxes are also used in an attempt to discourage people from buying products that the government considers harmful. High excise taxes have been placed on liquor and tobacco, for example. These taxes are sometimes called *sin taxes.*

Improve the Nation's Economy

When personal and corporate taxes are increased, people and businesses have less money to spend. When these taxes are decreased, people and businesses have more to spend. There are times when it would be helpful to the economy if everyone spent less. So the government may choose to increase taxes, not because it needs the extra money, but because it wants the public to spend less. There are other times when it would be helpful if the public spent more. When the government wants to increase spending by businesses and consumers, it often reduces taxes.

HOW DO WE DETERMINE WHO SHOULD PAY TAXES?

While almost everyone will agree that taxes are necessary in a modern society, agreement breaks down over the question of *who* should be asked to pay these taxes. For example, people who do not have school-age children often resent having to pay a *school tax.* Others complain that their state income taxes are unfair because citizens in some other states pay lower state income taxes, or none at all. Two approaches to the question of who should pay taxes involve the benefits that taxpayers receive and the taxpayers' ability to pay the taxes.

Benefits-Received Principle

Certain services that are provided by government are of benefit only to a particular group. According to the *benefits-received principle* of taxation, only those who gain from a government service ought to be made to pay for it. If you never drive or ride through northern Illinois, the Northwest Tollway will be of no value to you. For those who travel this major highway, however, it is of definite value. Is it possible for the Illinois state government to require only those who use the Northwest Tollway to contribute to its cost? Yes. The state does so simply by collecting a toll from every driver who uses the road.

Suppose a new sewer line is to be installed along several residential blocks. Who should be taxed to pay for it? If we accept the benefits-received theory, our answer is that the people living on those streets ought to pay because they will benefit the most. This reasoning is frequently carried out through the use of special taxes.

Most motorists need gasoline to operate their automobiles or other motor vehicles. If the money collected from a gasoline tax were used to build and maintain roads, this tax would qualify as a benefits-received one. This is so because the money collected would be used to benefit mainly those who paid the tax (motorists).

Ability-to-Pay Principle

All taxes cannot be based on the benefits-received principle. We could hardly ask poor people to support welfare programs (which are designed to help them) with their taxes, while excusing everyone who is not poor. Besides, most government services benefit everyone. Our armed forces benefit everybody. So too do police and fire protection. The benefits-received principle does not help us decide who should pay for police and fire protection or how much each person should contribute. However, a second guideline does.

According to the *ability-to-pay principle* of taxation, people who earn more than others, or who can afford to pay more than others, should pay higher taxes. The personal income tax is an ability-to-pay tax because people with high incomes are taxed more than those with low incomes. Indeed, millions of Americans pay no income tax at all because their incomes are not high enough.

Sooner or later, as we enter the labor force and earn a weekly salary, part of our wages will go to pay federal income taxes. One widely used form for filing federal income taxes is described in the feature "Preparing an EZ Tax Return," below.

Personal Economics

PREPARING AN EZ TAX RETURN

Frank Frisella has been working after school and during vacations at Olsen's Hardware Company in Stamford, Connecticut. Last year, Frank earned a total of $9,285.

In January, Mrs. Olsen gave Frank an envelope containing a rather official-looking form.

"What's this, Mrs. Olsen?" Frank asked.

"It's your W–2 form, Frank. You'll need it when you file your federal income tax return," she replied.

"File an income tax return? I forgot that I have to do that. I wonder how much I'm going to owe in taxes." Frank sounded a little concerned.

Figure 27.2 Frank Frisella's W–2 Statement

a Control number		22222	Void ☐	For Official Use Only ▶ OMB No. 1545-0008		
b Employer identification number				1 Wages, tips, other compensation $ 9,285.00	2 Federal income tax withheld $ 995.00	
c Employer's name, address, and ZIP code				3 Social security wages $ 9,285.00	4 Social security tax withheld $ 576.00	
Olsen's Hardware Co. 26 Fairview Street Stamford, CT 06904				5 Medicare wages and tips $ 9,285.00	6 Medicare tax withheld $ 135.00	
				7 Social security tips $	8 Allocated tips $	
d Employee's social security number				9 Advance EIC payment $	10 Dependent care benefits $	
e Employee's first name and initial	Last name			11 Nonqualified plans $	12a See instructions for box 12 $	
Frank Frisella 253 Bleecker Lane Stamford, CT 06904				13 Statutory employee ☐ Retirement plan ☐ Third-party sick pay ☐ 14 Other	12b $ 12c $ 12d $	
f Employee's address and ZIP code						
15 State Employer's state ID number	16 State wages, tips, etc. $	17 State income tax $	18 Local wages, tips, etc. $	19 Local income tax $	20 Locality name	
	$	$	$	$		

Form **W-2** Wage and Tax Statement   Department of the Treasury—Internal Revenue Service

"Don't worry, Frank," Mrs. Olsen advised. "We've been deducting money for your income taxes from each paycheck. You probably won't owe the government anything more."

Every pay period, Olsen's bookkeeping department deducted a certain amount from Frank's gross salary for income, Social Security, and Medicare taxes. (Chapter 14 discusses the Social Security program.) These *deductions* are summarized in Frank's W–2 statement. (See Figure 27.2.)

Olsen's withheld $576 for Social Security, $135 for Medicare, and $995 for federal income taxes from Frank's earnings of $9,285. Frank used the income tax information to prepare his return. Let us see how he went about it.

Frank acquired a tax information booklet and several 1040EZ forms at the local post office. (Tax forms are also available on the Internet.) The booklet told Frank that he was required to file an income tax return for last year because he

had earned more than $5,000 in wages. Frank is single and has no dependents, so he will use the 1040EZ form (Figure 27.5, page 416). Here is how Frank went about the task of preparing his 1040EZ tax return. First, he read the instructions on the back of the form.

Then at the top of the front page, Frank printed his name, address, and Social Security number. Right below this section, Frank answered a question. By checking the "Yes" box, Frank told the government to place $3 of his taxes into a fund that will help pay for presidential election campaigns.

Reporting Income (on page 416)

Line 1   On line 1, Frank entered $9,285—the wages that he earned last year from Olsen's.

Line 2   Frank has a savings account at a local bank. The bank had notified Frank that he had earned $262 in interest on his account

Figure 27.3 1040 EZ Worksheet

Worksheet for dependents who checked one or both boxes on line 5 (keep a copy for your records)	Use this worksheet to figure the amount to enter on line 5 if someone can claim you (or your spouse if married filing jointly) as a dependent, even if that person chooses not to do so. To find out if someone can claim you as a dependent, use TeleTax topic 354 (see page 6).

A. Amount, if any, from line 1 on front . . . . A. __9,285__

B. Is line A more than $550?
  ☑ **Yes.** Add $250 to line A. Enter the total. ⎫ . . . . B. __9,535__
  ☐ **No.** Enter $800. ⎭

C. If **single**, enter $5,000; if **married filing jointly**, enter $10,000 . . C. __5,000__

D. Enter the **smaller** of line B or line C here. This is your standard deduction . . . . D. __5,000__

E. Exemption amount.
  • If single, enter -0-.
  • If married filing jointly and you checked—   ⎫   E. __0__
  —both boxes on line 5, enter -0-.   ⎬
  —only one box on line 5, enter $3,200.   ⎭

F. Add lines D and E. Enter the total here and on line 5 on the front . F. __5,000__

If you did not check any boxes on line 5, enter on line 5 the amount shown below that applies to you.

• Single, enter $8,200. This is the total of your standard deduction ($5,000) and your exemption ($3,200).

• Married filing jointly, enter $16,400. This is the total of your standard deduction ($10,000), your exemption ($3,200), and your spouse's exemption ($3,200).

last year. He entered $262 on line 2.

Line 3 Frank left line 3 blank since he had received no unemployment compensation.

Line 4 Frank entered the total of lines 1 and 2—$9,547—on line 4.

Line 5 Frank checked the "You" box because his parents provide for his support and claim him as a dependent on their tax return. Frank completed the worksheet (Figure 27.3) on the back of the 1040EZ form and entered the amount from line F—$5,000—on line 5.

Line 6 Frank subtracted line 5 from line 4. The difference is the income on which he must pay taxes. His *taxable income* was $4,547. He entered this amount on line 6.

Figuring the Tax

Line 7 According to Frank's W–2, Olsen's withheld $995 from his pay for federal income taxes. Frank entered this amount on line 7.

Line 8 Concerning the Earned Income Credit, Frank read a list of questions in the 1040EZ instruction booklet. He found out that he is not eligible for the earned income credit for two reasons. He is under age 25 and he is claimed as a dependent on someone else's tax returns. He left line 8 blank.

Line 9 Since line 8 was 0, adding lines 7 and 8 gave Frank $995 for line 9.

Line 10 Frank looked at the tax tables in the 1040EZ Instructions.

According to the tax tables, with taxable income of $4,547, his income tax would be $453. He entered this amount on line 10.

Refund Due or Amount Owed

Line 11   When Frank subtracted line 10 ($453) from line 9, he learned that he had overpaid his taxes by $542. He entered this amount on line 11a. The government owed Frank a refund of $542.

Line 12   Had the amount that Olsen's withheld been insufficient to cover Frank's tax bill, he would have entered the difference on line 12. In that event, Frank would have had to send a check or money order to the IRS for the amount he owed.

Signing the Return

Frank signed and dated the 1040EZ where indicated. He mailed it to the regional IRS Service Center indicated in the instructions. In a short time, Frank received his $542 refund.

Figure 27.4 Section of Federal Income Tax Table

If Form 1040EZ, line 6, is—		And you are—	
At least	But less than	Single	Married filing jointly
		Your tax is—	
4,400	4,450	443	443
4,450	4,500	448	448
4,500	4,550	453	453
4,550	4,600	458	458

Figure 27.5 Frank Frisella's 1040EZ Income Tax Return

Department of the Treasury—Internal Revenue Service

Form 1040EZ

Income Tax Return for Single and Joint Filers With No Dependents (99)

OMB No. 1545-0074

Label (See page 11.) Use the IRS label. Otherwise, please print or type.

Your first name and initial: *Frank* Last name: *Frisella*

Your social security number: 117 06 9484

If a joint return, spouse's first name and initial Last name

Spouse's social security number

Home address (number and street). If you have a P.O. box, see page 11. *253 Bleecker Lane* Apt. no.

▲ You **must** enter your SSN(s) above. ▲

City, town or post office, state, and ZIP code. If you have a foreign address, see page 11. *Stamford CT 06904*

Checking a box below will not change your tax or refund.

Presidential Election Campaign (page 12) ▶

Check here if you, or your spouse if a joint return, want $3 to go to this fund? . . . ▶ ☑ You ☐ Spouse

Income

Attach Form(s) W-2 here. Enclose, but do not attach, any payment.

1 Wages, salaries, and tips. This should be shown in box 1 of your Form(s) W-2. Attach your Form(s) W-2. — 1 — *9,285 00*

2 Taxable interest. If the total is over $1,500, you cannot use Form 1040EZ. — 2 — *262 00*

3 Unemployment compensation and Alaska Permanent Fund dividends (see page 13). — 3

4 Add lines 1, 2, and 3. This is your **adjusted gross income.** — 4 — *9,547 00*

5 If someone can claim you (or your spouse if a joint return) as a dependent, check the applicable box(es) below and enter the amount from the worksheet on back.
☑ You ☐ Spouse
If someone cannot claim you (or your spouse if a joint return), enter $8,200 if **single**; $16,400 if **married filing jointly.** See back for explanation. — 5 — *5,000 00*

6 Subtract line 5 from line 4. If line 5 is larger than line 4, enter -0-. This is your **taxable income.** ▶ 6 — *4,547 00*

Payments and tax

7 Federal income tax withheld from box 2 of your Form(s) W-2. — 7 — *995 00*

8a **Earned income credit (EIC).** — 8a

b Nontaxable combat pay election. 8b

9 Add lines 7 and 8a. These are your **total payments.** ▶ 9 — *995 00*

10 **Tax.** Use the amount on **line 6 above** to find your tax in the tax table on pages 24–32 of the booklet. Then, enter the tax from the table on this line. — 10 — *453 00*

Refund

Have it directly deposited! See page 18 and fill in 11b, 11c, and 11d.

11a If line 9 is larger than line 10, subtract line 10 from line 9. This is your **refund.** ▶ 11a — *542 00*

▶ b Routing number ▶ c Type: ☐ Checking ☐ Savings

▶ d Account number

Amount you owe

12 If line 10 is larger than line 9, subtract line 9 from line 10. This is the **amount you owe.** For details on how to pay, see page 19. ▶ 12

Third party designee

Do you want to allow another person to discuss this return with the IRS (see page 19)? ☐ **Yes.** Complete the following. ☑ **No**

Designee's name ▶ Phone no. ▶ ( ) Personal identification number (PIN) ▶

Sign here

Joint return? See page 11. Keep a copy for your records.

Under penalties of perjury, I declare that I have examined this return, and to the best of my knowledge and belief, it is true, correct, and accurately lists all amounts and sources of income I received during the tax year. Declaration of preparer (other than the taxpayer) is based on all information of which the preparer has any knowledge.

Your signature: *Frank Frisella* Date: *3/8/06* Your occupation: *Student* Daytime phone number: *(000) 647-5903*

Spouse's signature. If a joint return, **both** must sign. Date Spouse's occupation

Paid preparer's use only

Preparer's signature ▶ Date Check if self-employed ☐ Preparer's SSN or PTIN

Firm's name (or yours if self-employed), address, and ZIP code ▶ EIN Phone no. ( )

For Disclosure, Privacy Act, and Paperwork Reduction Act Notice, see page 23. Cat. No. 11329W Form **1040EZ** (2005)

WHAT EFFECT DOES A TAX HAVE ON TAXPAYERS?

Economists frequently classify taxes by the effect they have on taxpayers. Taxes may be progressive, proportional, or regressive.

Progressive Taxes

A tax that takes a larger percentage of a person's total income as that income increases is a *progressive tax*. In 2006, taxpayers earning $7,550 or less in taxable income paid 10 percent of that amount in income taxes. From $7,550 to $30,650, the tax rate was 15 percent. The remaining tax rates for that year are illustrated in the following table.

Federal Personal Income Taxes, 2006

If taxable income is: Over	But not over—	The tax is:	of the amount over—
$ 0	$ 7,550	10%	$ 0
7,550	30,650	$ 755.00 + 15%	7,550
30,650	74,200	4,220.00 + 25%	30,650
74,200	154,800	15,107.50 + 28%	74,200
154,800	336,550	37,675.50 + 33%	154,800
336,550	—	97,653.50 + 35%	336,550

While income taxes are imposed as a percentage of a taxpayer's income, not all earnings are taxed. For example, most single taxpayers could exclude $5,150 from the income they earned in 2006. What remained is known as *taxable income*, because that is the amount upon which that year's income tax is based. Since the rate increased with the taxpayers' income, the personal income tax can be described as a progressive tax.

Proportional Taxes

A tax that requires all persons to pay the same percentage of their income in taxes is a *proportional tax.* People in business for themselves pay a *self-employment tax.* The tax is computed at the rate of 15.3 percent on earnings of more than $400 and less than $76,200. Since all taxpayers pay the same 15.3 percent rate, the self-employment tax is described as a proportional tax. The effect of the tax on a variety of self-employment incomes is illustrated in the following table:

Self-Employment Tax

Taxable Income	Tax Rate (percent)	Tax Owed
$ 401	15.3	$ 61
4,000	15.3	610
8,000	15.3	1,224
16,000	15.3	2,448
32,000	15.3	4,896
64,000	15.3	9,792
72,000	15.3	11,016

Regressive Taxes

A tax that takes a larger proportion from a taxpayer with a low income than from a taxpayer with a high income is a *regressive tax.* Suppose that, like the people in the top panel of the illustration on page 419, every family in the United States had to pay a $1,000 tax. This would be a regressive tax. Why? Because $1,000 is a larger share of a low-income family's total income than it is of a high-income family's income. For example, $1,000 represents a 10 percent tax to a family with a $10,000 income. But $1,000 represents only a 5 percent tax to a family with a $20,000 income. And $1,000 represents only a 2 percent tax to a family with a $50,000 income.

The sales tax is a regressive tax. We can illustrate this as follows. Suppose that two people—call them Buyer A and Buyer B—both purchased automobiles that sold for $9,000. Both buyers paid an 8 percent sales tax, of $720. Buyer A earns $7,200 a year, while Buyer B earns $72,000. The sales tax took 10 percent of Buyer A's income, but only 1 percent of Buyer B's income. With the exception of the income tax and certain estate and gift taxes, nearly all taxes are regressive to some extent.

What kind of tax is shown in the top panel? in the bottom panel? Which tax is fairer?

WHO REALLY PAYS TAXES?

Economists distinguish between the people who pay taxes to a government and the people from whom the tax money actually comes. Economists say that people pay taxes both indirectly and directly to the government.

Indirect Taxes

If your family rents an apartment or a house, it pays a monthly rental to the owner (the landlord). The landlord must use some of this rent money to meet operating expenses. One of the expenses facing landlords is property taxes. Tenants are usually not told how much of their rent goes to property taxes. Thus, property taxes can be described as *hidden taxes*. Economists also call them indirect taxes.

An *indirect tax* is one that can be passed on, or shifted, to someone other than the person making payment to the government. In the case of the property tax, landlords pass its cost on to

Understanding Economics

THE FLAT INCOME TAX—WOULD IT BE FAIR?

While there are those who say that the income tax is the best of all federal taxes, others are critical of it. The principal argument of those favoring the income tax is that it is progressive. That is, the more one earns, the larger the percentage of their income they will have to pay in income taxes.

Critics of the income tax in its current form say that it is just too complicated for the average taxpayer to understand. They go on to say that the problem is built into the tax law as deductions, credits, incentives, and other *loopholes* (escape clauses). These loopholes enable wealthy people to reduce the taxes they pay. They do this by hiring accountants, lawyers, and other specialists to show them how to use loopholes. Less-wealthy taxpayers, unable to afford the high-priced professional help, wind up paying a larger share of the nation's tax bill.

One group of critics of the current income tax sees the solution to these problems in the *flat tax*. Unlike the progressive income tax, the flat tax is proportional. That is, the flat tax is imposed at the same rate for every level of income over a minimum amount. For example, assume that the flat tax rate were 15 percent on income above $20,000. A person earning $15,000 for the year would pay no tax since that person's income was below $20,000. One with an income of $40,000 would be liable for taxes on income above $20,000. That tax would be $3,000. ($40,000 − $20,000 = $20,000. 15 percent of $20,000 = $3,000). And a family earning $200,000 would owe $27,000 in taxes. ($200,000 − $20,000 = $180,000. 15 percent of $180,000 = $27,000.)

"What could be *simpler* than that?" argue supporters of the flat tax. With no deductions, no exemptions, no special rules as to where the income came from or how it was spent, all one needs to do to calculate one's income tax is to multiply one's taxable income by the tax rate. "And," they go on, "the more one earns, the more one pays in taxes. What could be fairer than that?"

Critics of the flat tax say that it is not such a fair tax. On the contrary, they claim, it is very unfair. It is unfair, they explain, because it would lower the tax burden on the wealthy, while at the same time increase the burden on poorer people. The problem, as they see it, is that low-income families spend a far larger proportion of their income on life's necessities (like food and rent) than do wealthier families. Thus, a family of four with an income of, say, $40,000 could well be spending 90 percent of its income ($36,000) on necessities. This would leave them with but $4,000 for luxuries. If they had to pay an income tax of $3,000, it would not leave them much for luxuries.

By contrast, the family with an income of $200,000 could be attending to its necessities on, say, 30 percent ($60,000) of its income. The taxes it paid in a flat tax system would merely reduce the amount available to them for luxuries.

The bottom line is that the flat tax takes a larger proportion of the income needed to pay for a lower income family's necessities than it does from a higher income family. For this reason, critics say the flat income tax is regressive.

tenants in the form of higher rents. A tariff is another example of an indirect tax. Although a tariff is paid to the federal government by the seller of foreign goods, this tax can be—and is—passed on to consumers in the form of higher prices for those goods.

Direct Taxes

Unlike an indirect tax, a *direct tax* is paid by taxpayers who cannot pass the cost on to others. The income tax and the sales tax are examples of direct taxes. Those who pay a direct tax know exactly when and how much they are being taxed.

Issue of Fairness

Do people care if a tax is direct or indirect, progressive or regressive? Yes, they do. Since everybody must pay taxes, most people feel they should not have to pay more than their fair share. History shows us that revolutions have been fought over the issue of unfair taxes. "Taxation without representation is tyranny!" was a rallying cry of American revolutionaries. In 1789, the people of France, too, began a revolution. There, too, the system of taxation was a major cause of discontent.

Economists today are concerned with the question of fairness in taxation. They must advise the government as to who will really be paying each tax and how the payment will affect the taxpayer. Economists must be able to identify a tax as progressive, proportional, or regressive, as indirect or direct. But, most important, they must be able to tell whether or not a tax is fair.

―――――――――――― **SUMMARY** ―――――――――――

Americans pay a variety of taxes. Those most likely to affect you directly or indirectly are the income, excise, sales, payroll, and property taxes.

We pay taxes for a number of reasons. Taxes pay the costs of running federal, state, and local governments. Taxes serve to redistribute income to people in need and help specific industries and localities. Taxes also affect the economy as a whole.

The question of how taxes should be levied is often raised. According to the benefits-received principle, those benefiting from a government service or program should be taxed to help pay for it. The ability-to-pay principle suggests that people should be taxed on a sliding scale in accordance with their incomes.

When discussing the fairness of a tax, we speak in terms of its being progressive, proportional, or regressive. A progressive tax takes a larger percentage of a high income than of a low income. A proportional tax takes the same percentage from people of all income levels. A regressive tax takes a higher percentage of a low income than of a high income.

People who pay tax bills can often shift the tax to someone else. Taxes that can be shifted in this way are called indirect, or "hidden." Taxes that cannot be shifted are known as direct taxes.

LOOKING AHEAD

Spending by the federal government in a year is about $2 trillion. The following chapter takes a look at what the government is spending this money on, how it raises the funds to meet its expenses, and how that spending affects us all.

EXERCISES

✔ **Matching** Match each term in Column A with its definition in Column B.

Column A	Column B
1. excise tax	*a.* a tax that takes a larger percentage of a low income than of a high income
2. sales tax	
3. indirect tax	*b.* the principle that those who can best afford to pay taxes should do so
4. protective tariff	
5. ability-to-pay	*c.* a tax on the manufacture or sale of a specific good or service
6. regressive tax	
7. payroll tax	*d.* a tax paid by homeowners
8. personal income tax	*e.* a tax on the earnings of corporations
	f. a local or state tax levied on a wide range of consumer items
9. progressive tax	
10. corporate income tax	*g.* an income tax on the earnings of individuals
	h. a high tax on foreign-made goods to discourage their purchase
11. property tax	
	i. a hidden tax
	j. a tax that takes a larger percentage of a high income than of a low income
	k. a tax that finances the nation's Social Security program

✔ **Multiple Choice** Choose the letter of the item that best completes the statement or answers the question.

1. Last year Jackson earned $500,000, Velez earned $50,000, and Bari earned $5,000. According to their state's tax laws, each one had to pay a tax of $500. Which one of the following terms best

describes this tax? (a) progressive (b) proportional (c) regressive (d) inexpensive.

2. Which one of the following is an example of an excise tax? (a) individual income tax (b) tax on perfume (c) corporate income tax (d) ticket of admission to Yosemite National Park.

3. Rose Chin just purchased $12 worth of school supplies. The state sales tax is 5 percent. How much did Rose have to pay for the supplies? (a) $12.60 (b) $11.40 (c) $18 (d) $6.

4. Which of the following would be an example of a property tax? (a) a tax based on the value of one's home (b) admission to Yellowstone National Park (c) a tax deducted from one's weekly wages (d) a tax added to the price of gasoline.

5. Which one of the following is the best example of the ability-to-pay principle? (a) bridge toll (b) income tax (c) sales tax (d) property tax.

6. Which one of the following is an example of a tax based on the benefits-received principle? (a) bridge toll (b) income tax (c) sales tax (d) property tax.

7. In the United States, taxes are used to accomplish all of the following *except* (a) help pay for the cost of government (b) take from the rich and give to the poor (c) determine which brands consumers buy (d) keep certain goods out of the country.

8. Brown owns an apartment house in the city. There are 50 units in the building. Brown must pay $7,200 a year in property taxes to the city. To make up for this tax, Brown has added $12 to the monthly rent on each apartment unit. For the apartment tenants, the tax is (a) an indirect tax (b) a direct tax (c) an income tax (d) a sales tax.

9. Who ultimately bears the burden of the tax in question 8? (a) the city (b) Brown (c) the tenants and Brown (d) the tenants.

10. Which one of the following is an example of a protective tariff? (a) tax on theater tickets (b) sales tax on clothing (c) bridge toll (d) tax on the importation of foreign-made cars.

✔**Understanding Graphs** Study Figure 27.1 on page 407 and then answer the following first four questions.

1. List, in their order of importance, the kinds of taxes levied by the federal government (list the biggest source first, the smallest source last).

2. List, in the order of their importance, the kinds of taxes levied by state and local governments.

3. Which taxes levied by state and local governments are *not* levied by the federal government?

4. What is the difference between a progressive tax and a regressive tax?

5. Identify *each* of the taxes listed below as either "progressive" or "regressive." Explain why you chose each label.

   Federal:
   Personal Income
   Excise
   State and Local:
   Personal Income
   Sales

6. It has been suggested that the income tax be changed so that everyone pays the same percentage of their taxable income in taxes. Suppose the tax law was changed so that everyone paid 30 percent on their taxable income. (a) How would this differ from our present income tax? (b) Which system would be fairer? Why? (c) Identify and explain *one* advantage of such a flat-tax system

CHAPTER 28

Government Spending and Budgeting

The cost of operating the federal government now comes to about $3 trillion per year. Three *trillion* (that is a 3 followed by 12 zeros) dollars is an enormous amount of money. Indeed, someone once calculated that if you could hand out a $20 bill every second of every day, it would take about 5,250 years to reach $3 trillion.

Raising and spending so much money requires months and months of planning. The results of the planning can be found in a document called the *Budget of the United States*. It is more commonly called the *federal budget*.

You have already learned how you and your family can plan your spending on the basis of your income. Like a family, the government must also budget its spending. But why does it spend so much? In this chapter, we will take a close look at how the government spends its money and why. As you read, you will learn the answers to the following questions:

- What is the federal budget?
- Why has the cost of government been increasing?
- How do governments use budgets to plan ahead?

- Is our national debt too large?
- What does a budget tell us about the economic goals of government?

WHAT IS THE FEDERAL BUDGET?

Like individual and family budgets, the federal budget is a financial plan that summarizes where its funds will be coming from, and how it intends to spend them. But since we are speaking of the United States of America, the financial plan reflected in the federal budget affects us all.

The federal budget for 2004, found on page 430, is just such a plan. It lists for example, how much the government intends to spend on each of 16 categories of items. It itemizes also how it expects to raise the more than $2 trillion called for in the budget.

The federal *budget process* (i.e., the steps that are followed in preparing a federal budget) is very time-consuming and requires the cooperation of the President of the United States and Congress.

The Budget Process: How the Government Creates a Budget

The law requires the President to submit a budget for the next fiscal year to Congress by the first Monday in February. (A *fiscal year* runs from October 1 to the following September 30.) Thus, President George W. Bush's budget for fiscal year 2004 had to be in the hands of Congress by February 2003.

But the budget transmitted to Congress by the President is only a proposal. It will now be up to Congress to review the President's suggestions. Keeping those suggestions in mind, Congress then prepares an alternative federal budget. In the course of preparing its version of the federal budget, Congress will have to decide how much the government should spend and plan how to pay for those expenditures.

Budget expenditures fall into two categories: mandatory spending and discretionary spending. *Mandatory spending*, which accounts for two-thirds of all federal expenditures, is spending authorized and required by law every year. It includes *entitlements* (benefits guaranteed to individuals because of their age, income, and other factors) like Social Security, veterans' benefits, and food stamps. It also includes interest on the national debt that the government pays to those individuals and institutions who hold federal bonds. Of course, Congress can, if it so chooses, change the laws that provide for mandatory spending.

Discretionary spending is what Congress and the President *chooses* to (but does not have to) spend during a coming fiscal year. It includes money for things like roads, defense, space exploration, and foreign aid. Discretionary spending accounts for one-third of all expenditures in the federal budget.

WHY HAS THE COST OF GOVERNMENT BEEN INCREASING?

We discussed in Chapter 27 how government spending has increased almost every year since the beginning of the 20th century. The most important reasons for this huge increase are inflation, national security, a growing population that lives longer, and environmental and social problems.

Inflation

Some of the increased cost of government is caused by inflation. As we read in Chapter 6, "a dollar is not worth a dollar anymore." That is, the value of the dollar in terms of what it could buy, or purchasing power, has been declining. In 1970, for example, the purchasing power of the dollar was six times greater than what it was in 2001. That meant that government would have to spend six times as much in 2001 as it did in 1970 to purchase the same goods and services.

National Security

In the last 100 years, the United States fought two world wars, major wars in Korea and Vietnam, as well as lesser actions in Grenada, Panama, the Persian Gulf, and Afghanistan. In addition, the government has spent enormous sums helping countries ruined by war, hunger, and other misfortune.

At one time, the people of our nation felt that the Atlantic and Pacific oceans protected us from military attack. Because of those natural barriers, we did not look upon the maintenance of peace in Europe, Asia, and Africa as a matter that concerned us. For that reason, in the years before the Spanish-American War (1898), our armed forces were tiny. In 1896, for example, our armed forces totaled a mere 42,000 people. Compare this figure to now when the U.S. armed forces number some 1.4 million men and women.

As you might expect, the nation's military buildup has been costly. Indeed, 16 cents out of every federal budget dollar was spent for national defense in 2001.

Population Growth and Longevity

The growth of the U.S. population has increased the cost of government. In 1929, there were 121 million people living in the United States. The population has since more than doubled—to about 300 million.

Another important factor in government spending is *longevity*. People have longer life spans than ever before. For that reason, a larger proportion of Americans are elderly. In 1929, about 5 percent of the American people were over 65 years of age. Now some 12 percent are over 65. The elderly receive more government services than any other age group in the population. As people live longer, more people are eligible for Social Security retirement benefits, Medicare, veterans' pensions, and surviving spouses' pensions. These payments add to the cost of government.

Greater Demands for Services

"Why doesn't the government *do* something about it?" How many times have you heard someone ask this question in connection with one of the pressing problems of the day? We expect our government to deal with many problems today: terrorism, pollution, unemployment, crime, poverty—the list is long. This attitude is relatively new in U.S. history. Before the 1930s, most Americans agreed that the less government they had the better it was. They thought that the individual, the family, charities, and businesses would be able to reduce social problems such as unemployment, poverty, and disease. Today, we look to government to do much of this work for us.

Thus far, we have been discussing the increased spending by the federal government. State and local governments have also been spending more, and for many of the same reasons that the federal government has. Fifty years ago, an all-concrete two-lane highway was considered up to date. And a high school building with separate classrooms, a library, a cafeteria, and a science lab was considered a modern school. But today's major highways have four or more lanes. A modern school contains computer and language labs. These "add-ons" cost the government more.

Environmental and Social Problems

We pay a price today for our advanced standard of living. For instance, our automobiles and factories pollute the air we breathe. Industrial wastes foul lakes, rivers, streams, and our water supply. Millions of tons of industrial and household garbage must be col-

Federal-State Cooperation: Federal and state governments share the costs of a pollution-control project. Who ultimately pays for this government activity?

lected and disposed of safely. It costs governments at all levels more money than before to deal with these *environmental problems.*

Modern times have also brought new *social problems.* Until 1920, a majority of Americans lived on farms or in rural areas. But today, three-quarters of the population lives in cities or suburbs. This concentration of large numbers of people has increased the problems of waste disposal, housing, education, transportation, and public health and safety. Efforts to meet these mounting problems cost governments far more money than before.

HOW DO GOVERNMENTS USE BUDGETS TO PLAN AHEAD?

A budget, as we learned in Chapter 15, is a plan for spending income. Budgets have two parts. One part lists the funds that are available for spending, and the other part lists how these funds are to be spent. The items to be bought and the amount to be spent for each must be listed.

Types of Budgets

Governments prepare budgets in much the same way as families do. That is, they list all the *receipts* (money coming in) that they expect for the year ahead. They also list the things that they plan to buy and the amount to be spent for each item. These amounts are the *expenditures*. Like the family budget, the finished government budget may be balanced, provide for a surplus, or result in a deficit. These budgets are described below.

Estimated Federal Budget for Fiscal Year 2007

Receipts (in billions of dollars)		Expenditures (in billions of dollars)	
Individual income taxes	$1,049	Social Security	$556
Corporation income taxes	251	Military and Defense	
Social Security	879	Department	447
Excise taxes	78	Income security	357
Estate and gift taxes	22	Interest	246
Customs duties	26	Medicare	377
Miscellaneous	132	Health	285
Total Receipts	**$2,437**	Education	88
		Transportation and Commerce	70
		Veterans benefits	66
		Natural resources and	
		environment	33
		International affairs	32
		General science, space, and	
		technology	26
		Agriculture	27
		Administration of justice	41
		General government	18
		Community and regional	
		development	15
		Total Expenditures	**$2,684**

1. Balanced Budget. A *balanced budget* is one in which receipts are exactly equal to expenditures. Many local governments (but not the federal government) are required by law to balance their budgets. They do this by calculating how much it will take to pay for their expenditures in the year to come. Taxes are then set at whatever amount is necessary to balance the budget.

Suppose that a town calculated its expenses for the following year at $1.5 million. The town earns income of $500,000 from bridge tolls, fines, and other items. The rest comes from a property tax. To balance its budget, the town has to set the property tax rate at a level that brings in $1 million.

2. Deficit Budget. A *deficit budget* is one in which expenditures are greater than income. Deficits (the difference between spending and income) must be made up out of savings and with loans. As it had in 67 out of the preceding 76 years, the federal government would end 2007 with a deficit. In that year, receipts would total $2,437 billion. Spending would come to $2,684 billion (or 2.6 trillion). This leaves a deficit of $247 billion. When the government runs a deficit, it must borrow to pay the difference between expenditures and receipts. The total value of federal government borrowing is the *national debt*. As you can see from the table on page 432, the national debt has been growing.

3. Surplus Budget. A *surplus budget* is one in which receipts are greater than expenditures. In years when it runs a surplus, a government needs to decide what to do with those funds. It could, for example, use the surplus to reduce the size of its debt. Or, it could reduce taxes. A surplus also offers the opportunity to increase government spending without raising taxes and without adding to debt.

What to do with a budgetary surplus is more often than not the subject of political controversy. This is exactly what happened in 2001 when the George W. Bush administration replaced that of President Bill Clinton. There had been a surplus in the federal budget every year since 1998. With the change of administrations, the nation debated proposals concerning the level of taxes, spending, and the national debt.

IS OUR NATIONAL DEBT TOO LARGE?

Did you know that you owe $30,024? The total amount owed by the federal government now stands at something around $8.7 trillion. $8.7 trillion averages out to roughly $30,024 for every adult, teenager, and child in the United States. But, you say, you do not have the money to pay off your part of the national debt. Since the government owes the money, let it pay it. (But the government does not have the money, and remember that *we* are the government.) Anyway, $8.7 trillion is a lot of money. Let us see what, if any, effect a debt of this size can have on us.

Size of the National Debt

When the government spends more than it earns, it must borrow to make up the difference. As you can see from reading the table on the next page, federal government debt increased from $260 billion in 1945 to $8,707 billion ($8.707 trillion) in 2004.

National Debt and Gross Domestic Product Since 1945 (in billions)

Year	National Debt	Gross Domestic Product (GDP)	Debt as a Percent of GDP
1945	$ 260.1	$ 211.9	123
1950	256.9	265.5	93
1960	290.5	505.9	57
1965	322.3	671.4	48
1970	380.9	985.6	38
1975	541.9	1,511.0	36
1980	908.5	2,644.5	34
1985	1,817.0	3,970.9	45
1990	3,206.6	5,803.2	55
1995	4,921.0	7,400.5	67
2000	5,686.3	9,872.9	58
2004	8,707.0	12,907.3	67

National debt is different from private debt. Unlike individuals or families, the federal government has an unlimited life span. Therefore, the government can go on borrowing indefinitely. People cannot. It is not the size of the debt that is important. What *is* important is the ease with which the debt can be repaid. If before you held your first job, you owed someone $5, the debt could have been a serious matter. But to someone earning $200 a week, paying back $5 should not be a problem.

One measure of the nation's earning power is its gross domestic product (GDP). You may recall from Chapter 3 that GDP is the total value of all the goods and services produced in the country in a single year. As indicated by the table, in 1945 the national debt of $260.1 billion was greater than that year's GDP. This is similar to a situation in which a family that earns $60,000 borrows $90,000 to buy a house. The $90,000 debt is greater than its annual income. But such a loan is reasonable because lenders normally give families 15 to 30 years to pay off their home mortgages.

From 1945 to 1980, the national debt as a percentage of GDP actually declined. For that reason, few economists were worried about its size. From 1980 to the mid-1990s, however, the national debt as a percentage of GDP increased. Moreover, the national debt itself increased more than five times. This caused many economists to worry that the country would lose its capacity to grow because of the need to pay interest on this huge debt.

The National Debt and Living Standards

Some people are worried about the effect of the national debt on living standards. If your family is making payments of $200 a month on a bank loan, the family has $200 less to spend. But suppose, instead, the loan is one in which a husband borrowed $1,000 from his wife, payable in five monthly installments of $200. In that instance, the $200 monthly payment does not affect the family's wealth at all. The money is simply transferred from one household member to another.

Much the same is true of the national debt. Loans that are repaid to the American people and corporations are "all in the family." Repaying that debt has no effect on total income here in the United States.

National debt that is owed to foreign individuals, businesses, and governments is another matter, however. In order to repay this debt, U.S. dollars are sent abroad. The dollars held by foreigners can eventually be used to buy U.S. goods and services. As these products leave the country, fewer goods and services are available for Americans, and the price of what remains increases.

Before 1975, only a very small percentage of the national debt was held by foreign countries. But in recent years, the percentage of debt owed abroad has been growing. For that reason, some economists worry about U.S. living standards as wealth flows out of the United States to repay the country's debts to foreign lenders.

Buying U.S. Savings Bonds

Anyone can purchase U.S. government savings bonds at a local bank or savings and loan association or on the Internet. These bonds (first discussed in Chapter 11) are certificates that guarantee the payment of interest for a specified number of years plus the return of the purchaser's original investment. People buy U.S. savings bonds because they know that the government can be counted on to make the promised payments.

Have you ever purchased a government savings bond? If you have, your purchase represented a loan to the federal government.

Bonds are a kind of IOU. The government promises to repay the sum of money it has borrowed in a year or more. Sometimes, the government sells *notes*. Notes are another form of IOU. Unlike bonds, however, notes are normally repaid in less than a year.

Dangers of a Large National Debt

Some people are troubled by the ease with which the government can add to the national debt by borrowing. Government officials discovered long ago that it is often easier to borrow in order to pay for spending programs than it is to increase taxes. For that

"BROTHER, CAN YOU SPARE A HUNDRED BILLION OR SO TOWARD THE INTEREST ON THE LAST TRILLION OR TWO?"

From whom is Uncle Sam attempting to borrow the money used to pay off the interest on the national debt? Do you think he will succeed?

FROM Herblock Through the Looking Glass (W.W. Norton, 1984). Reprinted by permission.

reason, a government often prefers to borrow to meet its expenses, even though the interest charges add to the cost of government. If the government had to balance its budget every year, critics say, it would be less likely to undertake unnecessary expenses.

Government borrowing may cause businesses that borrow to pay higher interest rates. This happens because both the government and corporations sell securities. They compete with one another for investors' money, and this competition forces interest rates up. High interest rates, it is argued, reduce private business investment because of the increased costs businesses have in borrowing money.

Government borrowing may also lead to rising prices and inflation. The more governments borrow, the more they spend. Increased spending is fine when there is an abundant supply of goods and services for sale. But if spending increases faster than the supply of goods and services, prices are forced upward.

Some economists point out that today's national debt will have to be paid off by future generations of Americans. We are still paying the costs of wars that were fought many years ago. Why, the argument continues, should people in coming decades have to pay off our debts?

WHAT DOES A BUDGET TELL US ABOUT THE ECONOMIC GOALS OF GOVERNMENT?

Concern over the nation's increasing debt led to the passage of the Balanced Budget Act of 1997. The principal goal of the act was to bring the national budget into balance by the year 2002. That objective was achieved four years ahead of schedule. For the first time in 20 years, the budget was balanced in 1998.

The federal government's budget is a reflection of the nation's goals. Let us suppose that, in a given year, the federal government spends 15 cents out of every budget dollar for *income security*—benefits paid to help the aged, disabled, and unemployed. In the next year, this spending accounts for 11 cents of every federal budget dollar. From these figures, we might infer that income security was not considered to be as important in the second year as it had been in the first year. If military spending increased, while spending for housing and agriculture was cut, this would tell us something about what the government thought of the importance of military versus housing and agricultural programs.

Each year, the media report about new federal, state, and local government budgets. Interested citizens can keep informed about the changes that are taking place in government spending at all levels. This, in turn, will give them a picture of what programs are considered more important or less important.

You and other Americans are free to object to or express agreement with the ways that governments are spending your money. By joining together with other people who share your views, you may be able to call upon governments to support the programs in which you are interested.

SUMMARY

Governments—federal, state, and local—use budgets to plan their spending programs. Some budgets provide for a surplus when spending plans are expected to cost less than anticipated income. If spending is to exceed income, the difference is called a deficit. Balanced budgets are those in which spending and income are equal.

Governments' costs have been increasing. Among the reasons are inflation, national security needs, and our growing population. Also, Americans today expect more of their governments than earlier generations did.

Budgets tell us about the goals of governments. By comparing present budgets with those of past years, we can learn which programs are increasing in importance and which ones are declining.

---------- **LOOKING AHEAD** ----------

Some times are better than others for the U.S. economy. There are periods when jobs are plentiful, wages are high, and business is booming. But during other periods, jobs are difficult to get, wages fall, and business activity slumps. The next chapter describes these economic ups and downs and explores some of the reasons why they occur.

---------- **EXERCISES** ----------

✔**Matching** Match each term in Column A with its definition in Column B.

Column A	Column B
1. balanced budget	*a.* the amount spent
	b. a spending plan in which expenditures and receipts are equal
2. deficit budget	
3. surplus	*c.* the money coming in
4. receipts	*d.* the income remaining after expenses have been met
5. expenditures	*e.* a spending plan in which expenditures are greater than receipts

✔**Multiple Choice** Choose the letter of the item that best completes the statement or answers the question.

1. Which of the following statements is true? (a) Since the end of World War II, government expenses have declined. (b) Because people's life spans are longer today than they were 50 years ago, governments do not have to spend as much as they once did to care for the sick and elderly. (c) Population growth has reduced the cost of government. (d) People now expect more of government than they did before the 1930s.

2. A government's budget is a (a) summary of the money that the government spent in past years (b) statement of government income and expenses that took place in the preceding year (c) plan of government income and expenses for the year to come (d) law to prevent the government from spending more than it takes in.

3. Your state's government has just prepared its budget for the following year. According to its plan, the state's income will be $3 billion. The state will spend $3.2 billion. (a) This is a balanced budget. (b) This is a deficit budget. (c) This is a surplus budget. (d) A state may not spend more than it takes in.

4. The government of a nearby state has just prepared its budget for the following year. According to the plan, this state expects to re-

ceive $4.5 billion in income. It plans to spend the $4.5 billion.
(a) This is a deficit budget. (b) This is a balanced budget. (c) This
is a surplus budget. (d) A state may not spend exactly the same
amount that it receives in one year.

5. In its 2007 budget, on page 430, the government planned to spend
$246 billion for *interest*. This item is the money that the govern-
ment (a) spends on the Social Security program (b) gives to the
states (c) pays to those who have bought government securities
(d) pays to needy people.

6. Which of the following calls for the largest expenditure in the 2007
federal budget? (a) military and national defense (b) interest
(c) Social Security (d) Medicare.

7. Which of the following statements describes the kind of information we can get from a government's budget? (a) The budget helps
us to understand which items a government thinks are highly important and which items it considers less important. (b) The budget
shows us how wisely the government spends its money. (c) The
budget enables us to compare wages in one country with those of
another. (d) The budget enables us to determine how democratic a
government is.

✔ Discussion Questions

1. Country A has a national debt of $500 billion. Country B has a na-
tional debt of $100 billion. Country A's national debt is 10 percent
of its gross domestic product. Country B's national debt is 40 percent of its gross domestic product. Which nation is likely to have a
easier time in repaying its debt? Why?

2. Compare the national debt in 1945 and 2004. (See the table on
page 432.) How would you account for the differences?

3. Why should it matter whether the U.S. national debt is owed to
Americans or to foreigners?

4. What effect will a deficit budget have on the national debt? What
effect will a surplus budget have?

5. Is it fair to ask future generations of Americans to pay for the debts
that we run up today? Explain your answer.

CHAPTER 29

Business Cycles: The Ups and Downs of the Economy

economic	expansion	economic
depression	recovery	indicator
Great Depression	peak	personal income
business cycle	prosperity	internal factor
recession	breadline	external factor
trough	Hooverville	

Some times are better than others for Americans and for the U.S. economy. For example:

1. June 1933. Every business day, Jack Smith got up at his usual time, dressed in his business suit, and left the house promptly at 8 A.M. He returned every evening at 7 P.M.

Jack's neighbors observed his comings and goings. But they did not know that Jack spent a lot of time sitting on a park bench. He had lost his job at a downtown department store. No other jobs were available.

Jack knew that his situation was not likely to change soon. The park benches were full of people like him—out of work, looking for jobs, waiting for something to happen.

"Imagine," he thought, "here it is the year 1933. It's been nearly four years since the Stock Market Crash. You'd think that by now someone would know how to get the country back on its feet."

2. February 1982. There were only two customers in Jeannette's Luncheonette that Thursday noontime.

"This makes a grand total of 12 customers so far this week," Jeannette thought. "It was all over when the jet engine factory laid off most of its workers in December. They were good, steady customers. Now there are just a few walk-in customers. I may as well fold up. Imagine, here it is the year 1982. You'd think that by now someone would know how to keep companies running and people working."

3. May 2000. "What are you going to do when you finish school in June?"

"I'll get a job, of course."

"What will you do?"

"Whatever I want to do! There are lots of good jobs around. All you have to do is choose a career in a growing field, get education and training, and you can go as far as you want."

In 1933, the United States was in the middle of a severe *economic depression*. This period is called the *Great Depression*. It began with the stock market collapse (the "Crash") in 1929 and lasted until 1941. The Great Depression was the worst period of business decline and unemployment in the nation's history. In 1933, 13 million people, one-quarter of all U.S. workers, were unemployed. Thousands of banks closed their doors because they were no longer able to repay their depositors. Business conditions were so bad during those years that some people predicted it would lead to the end of democracy in the United States.

The U.S. economy has improved and declined many times since the Depression. The years 1981 to 1982 were bad ones for the U.S. economy. Business activity for many firms slowed to a snail's pace. Over 9 million workers were unable to find jobs. But the business slowdown was not as bad as the one in the 1930s. By the mid-1980s, business activity was strong again, and there were many jobs. Another downturn in economic activity occurred in 1990. But in 1991, the economy reached bottom and reversed direction. The ten-year expansion that followed made it one of the longest in history. In 2001, the economy started to decline again.

Thus, in the period from the Great Depression of the 1930s to the present, the U.S. economy has had many good years and a number of bad ones. In this chapter, we will be looking at these economic ups and downs. As you read, you will learn the answers to the following questions:

- What is the business cycle?
- How do economists keep track of the business cycle?
- What causes business cycles?

WHAT IS THE BUSINESS CYCLE?

There are times when business conditions are generally poor, as they were during the years of the Great Depression and in the early 1980s and the early 1990s. But there are other times when quite the opposite is true. Business profits are high, jobs are plentiful, and consumers spend their money freely. The periodic changes in the level of the nation's business activity are called *business cycles*. One business cycle includes a period of economic expansion followed by a period of economic decline. Figure 29.1 shows the business cycles in the United States since 1914.

Phases of the Business Cycle

Like an aerial photograph of a large section of the country, this illustration gives us an overall picture of the economy. Zoom in for a closeup view, and you will see many small ups and downs, or cycles. Each cycle consists of four parts, or phases. These phases are recession, trough (or bottom), expansion (or recovery), and peak. Some cycles last only a few months, while others have lasted for years.

The phases of a business cycle are shown in the illustration on page 441 (Figure 29.2). Let us see how the economy behaves during each of the four phases of the cycle.

1. Recession. Recessions feed on themselves. During a *recession*, businesspeople spend less than they once did. Because sales are falling, businesses do what they can to reduce their spending. They lay off workers, buy less merchandise, and postpone plans to expand. When this happens, business suppliers do what they can to protect themselves. They too lay off workers and reduce spending.

As workers earn less, they spend less, and business income and profits decline still more. Businesses spend even less than before and lay off still more workers. The economy continues to slide.

2. Trough, or Bottom. Sooner or later the recession will reach the *trough*, or *bottom* of the cycle. How long it remains in the

Figure 29.1 United States Business Activity Since 1914

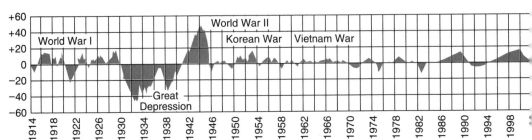

Figure 29.2 Phases of the Business Cycle

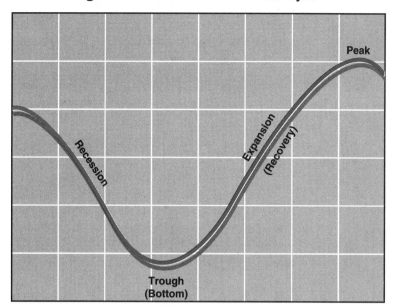

trough can vary from a matter of weeks to many months. During the 1930s, the business cycle bounced around from one bottom to another for almost ten years. That period, now remembered as "the Great Depression," was one of widespread suffering in the United States and abroad.

3. Expansion and Recovery. When business begins to improve a bit, firms will hire a few more workers and increase their orders of materials from their suppliers. Increased orders lead other firms to increase production and rehire workers. More employment leads to more consumer spending, further business activity, and still more jobs. Economists describe this upturn in the business cycle as a period of *expansion* and *recovery*.

4. Peak. At the top, or *peak*, of the business cycle, business expansion ends its upward climb. Employment, consumer spending, and production hit their highest levels. A peak, like a depression, can last for a short or long period of time. When the peak lasts for a long time, we are in a period of *prosperity*.

One of the dangers of peak periods is that of inflation. During periods of inflation, prices rise and the value of money declines. Inflation is more of a threat during peak periods because employment and earnings are at high levels. With more money in their pockets, people are willing to spend more than before. In this way, demand is increased and prices rise.

Understanding Economics

THE UNITED STATES DURING THE GREAT DEPRESSION

Business Cycle, Bottom: During the Great Depression, thousands of farm families lost their lands. Seeking work, many migrated west, to California.

What was it like to live in the United States during the Great Depression? For the unemployed, it was a time of desperation. It was nearly impossible for those out of work to find jobs. Many took to selling apples on street corners or to shining shoes. These jobs did not require much investment, and virtually anyone could do them.

One sign of the times was the ease with which courts were able to obtain jurors. In normal times, many working people called for jury duty ask to be excused from the assignment. This was not so during the Depression. The unemployed looked forward to the few dollars they received for every day of jury service.

Millions of workers had to accept wage cuts during the Depression. Therefore, even those who held on to their jobs had to learn how to get along on less.

Still another curse of the Great Depression was the large number of bank failures. Between 1930 and 1934, over 9,000 banks failed. Each bank failure resulted in the loss of depositors' savings. (Today, savings deposits are insured by the Federal Deposit Insurance Corporation, a U.S. government agency.)

There were few federal government agencies to help the needy before 1933. The philosophy at the time was that *relief* should be provided by the state and local governments and by private charities. But there were just too many needy. As a result, *breadlines* became common sights. These were long, slow-moving lines of hungry people waiting for free meals at soup kitchens. Another development was the *Hooverville*. Hoovervilles were communities of homeless people. Hoovervilles grew up on otherwise vacant land on the outskirts of major cities. The residents' shelter consisted of hand-built shacks made of anything and everything: old signboards, packing crates, and scrap metal. The Hoovervilles were named after President Herbert Hoover, whose economic policies some people blamed for creating and prolonging the Depression.

Many of the homeless wandered from place to place. "Tramps," "hoboes," "bums," and "Okies" were some of the names that more-fortunate people applied to these 1930s nomads. The name "Okies" came from Oklahoma farm families who had been forced off their land after they could no longer meet their mortgage payments.

HOW DO ECONOMISTS KEEP TRACK OF THE BUSINESS CYCLE?

For many years, economists have tried to understand why there are ups and downs in that nation's economy. They want to learn what can be done to prevent recessions and maintain prosperity. Therefore, they ask the following questions: (1) In what phase of the business cycle is our economy at the present time? (2) Where is the business cycle heading?

Economic Indicators

Economists rely on statistics called *economic indicators* to help them answer questions about the business cycle. These statistics tell about business production, the number of people who have jobs, people's earnings, and other important economic factors. Indicators help economists describe the state of the nation's economy. Here are some of the most frequently used economic indicators.

1. Gross Domestic Product (GDP). The GDP, first discussed in Chapter 3, tells the total value of all the goods and services produced in the United States in a single year. The *rate* at which GDP increases or decreases may be the most important of economic indicators because it measures the output of the entire economy. GDP declined by about 1 percent annually during the recession of 2000–2001. This was followed by a period of recovery and expansion between 2003 and 2005 as GDP grew 4 percent annually.

2. Personal Income. This figure is the total income received in one year by all families and individuals in the country. It does not include business income or government income. Economists follow personal income figures closely. They tell what to expect from consumer spending. When personal income is high, people have more money to spend, and generally do spend more.

3. Stock Market Averages. Stock prices are expressed in a variety of averages. The best known of these is the Dow Jones Industrial Average. The "Dow," as it is commonly called, is an index number based on the current prices of the stocks of a group of corporations. Those who follow the movement of the Dow do so in the hope that it will tell them something about the strength or weakness of the nation's economy, and what may be in store for the economy in the future.

4. Unemployment Rate. This figure tells us the percentage of the labor force that is unemployed at a particular time. The unemployment rate is highest during periods of recession or depression, and it declines during periods of expansion. As the table on page 445 indicates, the number of unemployed rose during the recession of 1981–1982 and again in the early 2000s. Beginning in 1993, the number of jobs in the United States increased dramatically. At the same time, the unemployment rate rose. By 2004, more than 8 million workers (nearly 6 percent of the labor force) were unemployed.

There are dozens of other economic indicators. Economists use them to draw a picture of the business cycle and to explain where the economy has been, where it is now, and where it is going.

Business Cycle, Peak: Workers assemble automobiles. When the business cycle is at its peak, most people who want jobs can find them. Which years shown in the table on page 445 might be considered peak years?

Labor Force Unemployment Since 1929 (selected years)

Year	Total labor force (millions)	Unemployed (millions)	Unemployed (percent)
1929	49.4	1.5	3.0
1933	51.8	12.8	24.7
1940	56.2	8.1	14.6
1945	53.9	1.0	1.9
1950	58.9	3.3	5.3
1960	69.6	3.8	5.4
1965	74.4	3.4	4.7
1970	82.7	4.1	4.9
1975	153.2	7.9	8.5
1980	106.9	7.6	7.1
1982	110.2	10.7	9.7
1985	115.5	8.3	7.2
1991	126.3	8.6	6.8
1994	131.0	8.0	6.1
1996	133.9	7.2	5.4
1999	139.3	5.9	4.2
2005	149.8	7.4	5.0
2007	153.0	7.0	4.5

WHAT CAUSES BUSINESS CYCLES?

In explaining why the economy moves up and down and business cycles occur, economists generally talk about factors within the economy (*internal factors*), and factors outside the economy (*external factors*). Let us take a look at each set of factors.

Internal Factors

1. Business Spending or Investment. When business firms buy new stores, factories, and equipment, this spending, or investment, adds to the income of the firms (and their employees) that supplied the stores, factories, and equipment. Business spending helps to create jobs within the companies that are expanding as well as within the firms' suppliers. Therefore, it follows that when business in general is expanding, the increased investment that accompanies expansion will help to push the business cycle to higher levels.

When business investment is declining, however, the reverse occurs. Suppliers produce less and lay off their workers. With fewer workers holding jobs, personal income and spending decrease. Other business firms then reduce the size of their operations and lay off workers. In this way, the drop in business investment pushes the business cycle downward.

2. Government Spending. Federal, state, and local governments are major spenders. When government spending increases, it adds to both business and consumer income. When government spending decreases, businesses and consumers earn less and therefore spend less.

3. Government Policies. Certain government policies affect the amount that businesses and individuals earn and spend.

When governments reduce taxes, both businesses and consumers are left with more money to spend. When governments increase taxes, consumers and businesses have less money. We can see, therefore, that government's powers to tax and spend affect how much businesses and individuals earn and spend. In this way, government policies will affect the business cycle.

The quantity of money in circulation affects prices, the value of money, and business cycle. When the money supply increases, while everything else remains the same, people have more money to spend and prices rise. When people have less money to spend, the opposite occurs. Prices fall and the value of money increases. Through the Federal Reserve System, the federal government controls the money supply. Thus, control over the money supply represents still another way in which the government affects the business cycle. (The Federal Reserve System is described in detail in Chapter 30.)

4. Consumer Spending. Consumer purchases account for some two-thirds of the nation's spending. When consumer spending increases, the increase in sales stimulates businesses and creates new jobs. When consumer spending decreases, businesses earn less and employment may fall. For these reasons, both the federal government and businesses monitor consumer spending habits very closely.

5. Psychological Factors. The way that individuals and businesses feel about the future may also affect the business cycle. Consider a family that is thinking about buying a new car. If one member is fearful of losing a job in the near future, the family is likely to postpone the purchase. But if the family believes that its income will soon be increasing, it is likely to buy the car.

Managers of a business firm often base their decisions on how they feel about the future. If the future prospects look good and the managers are optimistic, they are likely to increase the firm's spending. But if the future looks gloomy, they are likely to reduce its spending.

"I don't say he's wrong—I just don't think that's the way to report the country's leading economic indicators."

Economists use a number of economic indicators. How many can you name?

External Factors

Certain events over which no individual or group within the economy has any control can also affect the business cycle. Economists refer to these events as *external factors*. Major wars, terrorist attacks, oil embargoes, scientific and technological discoveries, bad weather, and scarce resources are examples of external factors. The spending that was necessary for the United States to fight and win World War II also served to pull the country out of the Great Depression. Recovery occurred because, in order to fight and win the war, the government had to produce massive amounts of weapons and other supplies. Increased production created many new jobs and wiped out unemployment.

When the economies of foreign nations are depressed, business activity in the United States will decline. And the oil shortages of the mid-to-late 1970s forced up the prices of many products made from petroleum, leading to inflation. Both of these factors are external.

─────────────── **SUMMARY** ───────────────

Business cycles are the periodic changes in the level of the nation's business activity. Economists have identified four phases within each cycle: expansion or recovery, peak, recession, and bottom.

Economists keep track of the business cycle by studying economic indicators. These data tell us something about the state of the economy in the past and at present and where the economy may be headed in the future.

Most economists agree that business cycles are the result of both internal and external forces. Internal forces are those involving business investment, consumer spending, government policies, and psychological factors. External forces include war, technological change, and scarcity.

─────────────── **LOOKING AHEAD** ───────────────

The next chapter explores the ways in which the government tries to limit the swings of the business cycle and to determine its direction.

─────────────── **EXERCISES** ───────────────

✔️ **Matching** Match each term in Column A with its definition in Column B.

Column A	**Column B**
1. business cycles	a. the worst period of business decline and unemployment in U.S. history
2. recession	
3. expansion	b. the lowest point of the business cycle
4. Great Depression	c. periodic changes in business activity
5. trough	d. the period of decline in a business cycle
6. economic indicator	e. a statistic that describes the state of the nation's economy
7. peak	
	f. the period of prosperity in a business cycle
	g. the period of recovery in a business cycle

✔️ **Multiple Choice** Choose the letter of the item that best completes the statement or answers the question.

Questions 1–4 are based on the illustration on page 449.

1. Which number depicts the *bottom* phase of the business cycle? (a) 1 (b) 2 (c) 3 (d) 4.

2. Which number depicts a *recession*? (a) 1 (b) 2 (c) 3 (d) 4.

3. Which number depicts the *peak* of the business cycle? (a) 1 (b) 2 (c) 3 (d) 4.

4. Which number depicts the *expansion* phase of the business cycle? (a) 1 (b) 2 (c) 3 (d) 4.

5. Which one of the following conditions would you expect to find at the bottom phase of the business cycle? (a) full employment (b) much new building (c) high unemployment (d) much business activity.

6. Which one of the following conditions would you expect to find at the peak phase of the business cycle? (a) a low rate of unemployment (b) little business activity (c) high unemployment (d) very little new building.

7. "Recessions feed on themselves." This statement means that (a) food prices fall during a recession (b) food prices rise during a recession (c) recessions are not a problem since they eventually end (d) when some businesses do poorly, their decline may cause others to do poorly also.

8. Which one of the following is an example of an economic indicator? (a) federal income tax rates (b) unemployment rates (c) crime rates (d) birth rates.

9. Which one of the following is an example of an internal economic factor? (a) the Korean War (b) business investment (c) the invention of the microcomputer (d) an increase in average rainfall around the globe.

10. Which one of the following is an example of an external economic factor? (a) terrorist attacks on the Pentagon and World Trade Center (b) consumer spending (c) government policies (d) business investment.

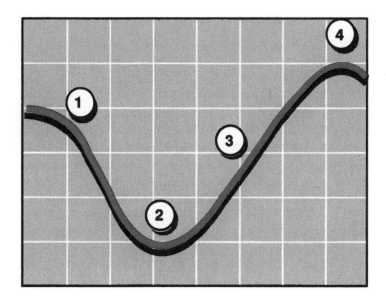

CHAPTER *30*
Economic Goals of Government

There are times when the nation's economy, like an overheated automobile, seems to stall or come close to breaking down. When that happens, recession and unemployment occur and both businesses and individuals suffer. Just as a car owner might look for the closest repair shop for help, so do our citizens look to the federal government for assistance in times of economic troubles. The economic system of the United States is described as a market economy. Individual buyers and sellers make most economic decisions in such a system, not the government. The origins of the U.S. market economy go back to the nation's beginnings. The country had survived a revolution in which it won its independence from Great Britain and its freedom from what many Americans regarded as the tyranny of British rule. By way of maintaining individual freedoms, the Constitution deliberately limited the role of government in economic affairs. Indeed, for many years Americans thought that the best way to deal with the nation's economic problems was to allow the business cycle to run its course. This policy was known as *laissez-faire* (a French phrase meaning "leave alone"). Laissez-faire is closely associated with the British economist Adam Smith, who popularized laissez-faire in his famous book, *The Wealth of Nations*, in 1776.

In applying laissez-faire to the U.S. economy, economists argued that the laws of supply and demand would keep business cycles from getting out of hand. In boom times, when jobs were plentiful and profits high, prices would rise. Eventually, rising prices would reach a point where sales would begin to slump. With sales falling, business firms would begin to lay off workers and reduce inventories. (*Inventories* are the goods held for sale by business firms.) With unemployment increasing and business spending decreasing, the business cycle would enter a decline.

When business activity was at a low point, the opposite would occur. Lower prices would stimulate sales. With wages lower than they had been, employers would hire more workers. The recession would come to an end. The key ingredient for all this to happen, according to laissez-faire theory, was a government that allowed economic activity to take place *without interference*.

Laissez-faire guided government policy until the 1930s when the Great Depression nearly destroyed the U.S. economy.

Following the Stock Market Crash of 1929, business conditions worsened. Unemployment, which had been less than 2 million in 1929, went to 4.3 million in 1930 and 8 million in 1931. Between 1920 and 1930, an average of 600 banks failed each year. Untold numbers of Americans lost their life's savings in the collapse of those banks. Meanwhile, President Hoover, who believed in the advantages of laissez-faire, assured the nation that the Depression was but a "temporary halt in prosperity." In his view, it was only a matter of time before the economy would straighten itself out.

Alas, the economy continued to decline. By 1932, unemployment had risen to 12.1 million. With business and the banking system at

Government has many "tools" to help keep the nation's economy running smoothly.

the point of collapse and one worker in four unemployed, the nation turned away from the laissez-faire policies of the Hoover administration and elected Franklin D. Roosevelt in the presidential election of 1932. Roosevelt promised to use the power of government to turn the economy around and bring the Depression to an end. The work begun by the "New Deal," as Roosevelt's economic program was called, was interrupted by U.S. participation in World War II. After the war ended, Congress formally abandoned laissez-faire by enacting the Employment Act of 1946. The act committed the U.S. government to actively promote "high levels of employment, production, and the purchasing power of the dollar."

This chapter focuses on the role of government in the economy. As you read, you will learn the answers to the following questions:

- What are our nation's economic goals?
- How does government attempt to achieve its goals?
- Why do we still have business cycles?

WHAT ARE OUR NATION'S ECONOMIC GOALS?

What kind of economic life do we want? Our nation's economic goals—as stated in the Employment Act of 1946—are full employment, economic growth, and stable prices. As we take a closer look at each goal, we will see that the goal cannot be achieved if our economy is not working well.

Full Employment

Most of us would like to live in a society in which everybody who wants a decent-paying job is able to find one. When that happens, we will have achieved the first goal, *full employment*. But full employment is not the same as no unemployment. There will always be some people seeking jobs, if only temporarily. There are always new people who are seeking to enter the labor force. Others are changing jobs for various reasons. Most economists agree that 4 or 5 percent unemployment is acceptable. Unfortunately, there have been long periods, particularly during times of recession and depression, when the rate has been much higher. Then, large numbers of workers have been unemployed for long periods of time. (See Figure 30.1 on page 454.)

Economic Growth

The nation's second economic goal is *economic growth*. Economic growth is an increase in the nation's yearly output of goods and services (its GDP). Economic growth differs from *real economic growth*. The latter term refers to an increase in the production of goods and services at a rate faster than population increase. Real economic growth makes it possible for everyone to have more than before.

Stable Prices

The nation's third economic goal is *stable prices*. In Chapters 6 and 29, we described what happens when inflation causes prices to be unstable. Inflation, you will recall, is an extended period of rising prices. (See Figure 30.2 on page 454.) It can be harmful to the economy as a whole, and to some groups in particular. You will recall, for example, that those living on fixed incomes (like the elderly) suffer because in inflationary times the cost of living increases faster than their income. Others adversely affected by inflation are creditors (lenders) because the money they lent is not worth as much today as it was at the time they made their loans.

We also learned that deflation can be harmful to businesses and the economy. Deflation is an extended period of general price decline, such as occurred during the Great Depression.

Over the years, however, economists made an interesting discovery. What they found was that some inflation, but not a lot, helped to keep the economy on an even keel. The reason for this is that there is a direct relationship between prices and employment (the number of available jobs). Studies have shown that (all other things being equal) during periods of rising prices, employers are likely to hire more workers. With available jobs on the increase, fewer workers were unemployed. On the other hand, when prices fall, employers tend to lay off workers and unemployment increases.

While rising prices (and wages) will not cause problems for a while, eventually the economy runs out of workers. When that happens, higher prices hurt sales. Businesses find it difficult to compete and, therefore, lay off workers. This adds to unemployment, and prices begin to decline. The challenge then, for those responsible for protecting the economy (especially Congress and the Federal Reserve Board) is to find a level of inflation that will keep a healthy balance between unemployment and high prices.

HOW DOES GOVERNMENT ATTEMPT TO ACHIEVE ITS GOALS?

In the previous chapter, we asked, "What causes business cycles?" Changes in spending by businesses, consumers, and government were given as major reasons why the economy moves up and

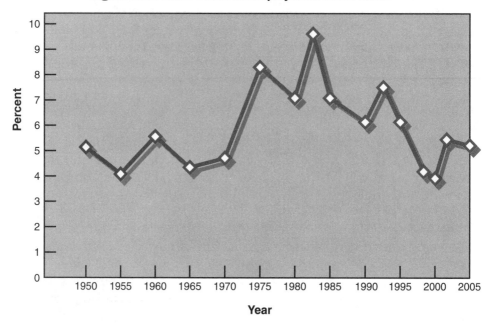

Figure 30.1 Labor Force Unemployment Since 1950

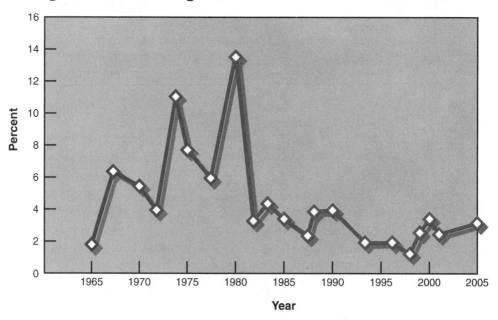

Figure 30.2 Percent Changes in the Consumer Price Index Since 1965

down. The economy is rather like a pitcher being filled with water. As long as the pitcher is not full, and as more water is added, there will be more in the pitcher to drink. But once the pitcher is full, any more water that is added will overflow and be wasted. In the same way, when employment and production are below maximum, an increase in total spending by businesses, consumers, and government will result in increased investment and employment, greater output, and stable prices. But when employment and production are already at maximum (like a pitcher that is already full), an increase in total spending cannot result in greater employment or output. What does happen is that "too many dollars chase too few goods." This condition is a cause of inflation.

Built-In Stabilizers

There are a number of economic forces in our economy that act to keep total spending from rising so high that it brings on inflation, or falling so low that it brings on a recession. These forces are known as *built-in stabilizers.*

1. Taxes. When everyone's income is rising, so too is their ability to spend. But the amount of income taxes that people pay also increases when they earn more, and this *reduces* the amount that they can spend.

2. Unemployment Insurance. Unemployment insurance is another built-in stabilizer. When unemployment increases, unemployment benefit payments also increase. Those unemployed workers who are eligible to receive such payments now have money to spend. As a result, the nation's level of consumer spending will not fall as low as it would have fallen had there been no unemployment insurance.

3. Social Security. Social Security benefit payments are another form of built-in stabilizer. As unemployment increases, older workers who are laid off from their jobs and are eligible for Social Security benefits might decide to retire. This trend opens up jobs for younger workers. Therefore, unemployment remains at reasonable levels. When the demand for workers increases, as it does during periods of prosperity, high wages and many available jobs induce some elderly workers to keep on working or to come out of retirement.

While built-in stabilizers are a help, they alone are not enough to keep the economy healthy. When the economy is sluggish (in a period of deflation) or overheated (in a period of inflation), the federal government serves as the "mechanic" to do the needed repair work. It has two major "tools" to control the ups and downs of the economy.

Monetary policy refers to programs that try to increase or decrease the level of business activity by regulating the nation's supply of money and credit.

Fiscal policy refers to the power of the federal government to tax and spend in order to achieve its goals for the economy.

In either case, whether it is using monetary policy or fiscal policy, the federal government is using its powers in order to influence total spending in the economy. Let us examine each policy more closely.

Monetary Policy

1. During Deflation or Recession. Suppose that business has been in a slump for some time. Sales in most industries have been falling. In an effort to reduce expenses, employers have been laying off workers. Unemployment, therefore, is increasing, and consumer spending is declining. Sales fall to even lower levels. This prompts businesses to cut back still further and lay off even more workers. In short, real GDP growth slows, and the business cycle now moves toward recession.

At this point, the Federal Reserve System (or "Fed") has decided to use its monetary powers to stop the decline. It will do this by increasing the amount of money and credit available. The Fed increases the supply of money and credit by allowing interest rates to fall, making it easier for banks and other lenders to make loans. When this happens, firms that previously found it too costly or too difficult to borrow will now be able to do so. Lower interest rates also make it easier for consumers to buy costly items such as appliances, automobiles, and homes. The increased money supply will enable some consumers and businesses to increase their spending. Increased spending will enable some firms to increase production and hire additional workers.

Then, as the newly hired workers and recently expanded businesses increase their buying, still more firms will expand and hire additional workers. With the economy expanding, the business cycle will now begin to turn upward.

2. During Inflation. Now let us suppose that the economy is facing another type of problem. Production, employment, and sales are at high levels. Spending by consumers and businesses increases. Prices rise. Rising prices lead workers to demand higher wages, which cause businesses to demand higher prices. This situation is what economists describe as an *inflationary cycle.*

With prices threatening to get out of hand, the Fed may decide to use its monetary powers to bring the inflation to an end. It will do this by reducing the amount of money in circulation and making it more difficult to borrow. For this purpose, the Fed will require that banks keep a larger portion of their funds on reserve, thereby leaving them with less money to lend to their customers. Less money to lend will also cause interest rates to rise. Higher interest rates make loans more costly and in that way discourage borrowing.

Understanding Economics

MONETARY POLICY AND THE FEDERAL RESERVE SYSTEM

The government's monetary policy regulates the nation's supply of money and credit. Monetary policy is the responsibility of the Board of Governors of the Federal Reserve System (or Fed). In the conduct of its monetary responsibilities, the Fed relies upon three "tools." These are (1) reserve requirements, (2) the discount rate, and (3) open-market operations.

1. Reserve Requirements. The money that banks lend to the public comes from the sums they receive from their depositors. While banks can lend most of their deposits, they cannot lend them all. Some must be kept on reserve in order to meet the needs of those who might want to withdraw their money. The size of the reserve is determined by the Board of Governors and is expressed as a percentage of total deposits. This percentage is known as the *reserve ratio.*

Suppose, for example, that a bank had deposits of $10 million and that the reserve ratio was 20 percent. How much of that amount could the bank lend? How much would it be required to keep on reserve? The bank could lend up to $8 million, while $2 million would be required to be held on reserve. (Twenty percent of $10 million equals $2 million.)

Now you can understand how the Board of Governors might use its power to set reserve requirements as a tool of monetary policy. When the board wants to tighten credit—make loans harder to obtain—it can increase the reserve ratio. It does this as part of its effort to bring down prices and fight inflation. When the board wants to expand credit—make loans easier to obtain—it can lower the reserve ratio. It does this as part of its effort to fight a recession or prevent one from occurring.

2. Discount Rate. When banks' reserves run low, they can replenish them by borrowing from the Federal Reserve bank in their district. The map on the following page shows the nation's Federal Reserve districts. The interest that banks pay for these loans is known as the *discount rate.* When the discount rate is lowered, banks can lower the interest rate that they charge on loans to their customers and still earn a profit on these transactions. When the discount rate is raised, banks will raise their rates.

In times of a recession, the Federal Reserve may choose to lower the discount rate. Then banks will be able to offer loans to the public at lower rates, thereby increasing consumer and business spending.

In inflationary times, the Federal Reserve may choose to raise the discount rate. It does so to increase the cost of bank loans, discouraging borrowing.

3. Open-Market Operations. The most important tool used by the Fed to regulate the money supply is *open-market operations.* These operations are the buying and selling of U.S. government securities such as Treasury bills and bonds. Most of these securities the government buys from or sells to banks.

When banks buy government securities from the Federal Reserve, their payments reduce the size of banks' reserves. When the Federal Reserve buys securities from banks, its payments increase banks' reserves.

In times of inflation, the Federal Reserve will sell government securities. As banks pay for the securities, their reserves are reduced. Reduced reserves leave banks with less money available for loans. Then, with the supply of available funds

Figure 30.3 The Federal Reserve System

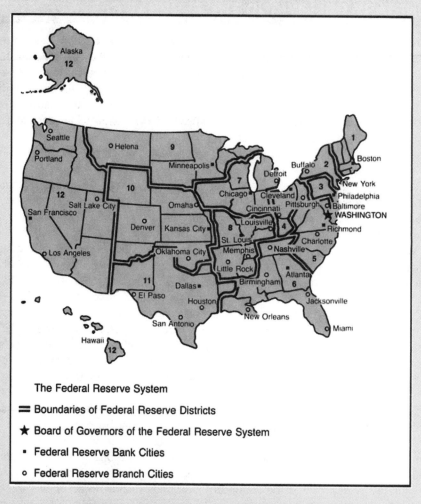

The Federal Reserve System

≡ Boundaries of Federal Reserve Districts

★ Board of Governors of the Federal Reserve System

▪ Federal Reserve Bank Cities

○ Federal Reserve Branch Cities

dwindling, the cost of borrowing (i.e., interest rates) increases. As interest rates increase, individuals and firms borrow less and spend less, business activity slows, and the inflation is brought under control.

In times of recession the opposite occurs: The Fed buys government securities. As the Fed pays for its purchases, bank reserves are increased. With more money available for loans, banks lower their interest rates as a way of attracting borrowers. Increased borrowing by consumers and businesses adds to business activity and employment, and the recession is brought to an end.

You might ask, "Why is it that banks buy and sell government securities whenever the Fed wants them to?" The reason is that the Fed makes the banks an attractive offer. That is, when buying securities, the Fed bids up prices and pays whatever it takes to reach its goals. Similarly when selling securities, the Fed will lower the price of the securities they choose to sell, as much as is necessary.

Monetary Policy and the Consumer: How may the government's policy on interest rates affect this consumer's decision about buying a new car?

Finally, the Fed may step up the level of government borrowing. When the government borrows, those who lend it the money (the general public) are left with less to spend. If you are wondering how the government gets investors to lend it money, it does so by raising its interest rates.

With less money in circulation and credit more difficult and costly to obtain, spending (the demand for goods and services) will decrease. Falling demand will serve to lower prices and bring the inflation to an end.

Fiscal Policy

The federal government has the power to tax and spend. When it uses these powers to influence the economy, it is setting fiscal policy. We saw in Chapters 27 and 28 how much the federal government collects in taxes and how much it spends in a given year. Because the income and spending of the government are so huge, they both have great impact upon the nation's economy. For example, tax increases leave us all with less to spend. Similarly, tax reductions leave us with more.

Government spending also affects our pocketbooks. When the federal government buys goods and services, payments for these purchases go directly to business firms and indirectly to their employees. The employees and the businesses, in turn, use the funds to purchase the things they want. Then the money is passed on and on through the economy. When government spending is increasing, the economy as a whole has more to spend. When government spending is decreasing, consumer incomes and spending decline.

The federal government can, and does, use its powers to tax and spend to benefit the economy. Economists call these powers the government's "fiscal tools." During periods of recession, when business activity is in decline and unemployment is rising, the government will try to use its fiscal tools to increase total spending. It does this by increasing its spending, cutting taxes, or both. Increased spending will stimulate other firms to expand their operations and hire additional workers. A tax cut will enable individuals and businesses to increase their spending and thereby promote business expansion.

If, instead, the nation is in an inflationary cycle, the federal government may use its fiscal powers to reduce total spending. It can do this by cutting its spending, increasing taxes, or both. With a reduction in government spending, individuals and businesses have less to spend. Higher taxes tend to have a similar effect. With less spending, the problem of inflation will be curbed.

Monetary and Fiscal Policy and the Business Cycle

Policy	To Combat Recession	To Combat Inflation
Monetary policy	1. Lower the reserve ratio 2. Buy government securities 3. Lower the discount rate	1. Raise the reserve ratio 2. Sell government securities 3. Raise the discount rate
Fiscal policy	1. Lower taxes 2. Increase government spending 3. Increase private spending (by built-in stabilizers)	1. Raise taxes 2. Cut government spending 3. Cut private spending (by built-in stabilizers)

WHY DO WE STILL HAVE BUSINESS CYCLES?

The table above summarizes the monetary and fiscal policies or "tools" that the federal government may use to stabilize the economy in the various phases of the business cycle. But these measures do not always work as well in the real world as they do in theory. Let us examine why this is so.

Forecasting Difficulties

Someone once said that *economic forecasting* is about as accurate as weather forecasting. As good as they are, economic indicators (discussed in Chapter 29) are only educated guesses. All too often, these data are collected after the fact—for example, when a decline in sales or an increase in prices has already begun. No one has yet discovered how to predict the economic future with 100 percent accuracy.

Political Considerations

Members of Congress often hesitate to take appropriate action out of fear of the consequences. Legislators who speak out in favor of lowering taxes will be popular among the voters. The same legislators, however, may find it hard to get reelected if they vote for higher taxes. Making cuts in government spending is another problem. Which federal program or programs should be reduced or eliminated? Voters and interest groups oppose those government spending cuts that reduce their benefits.

Variable Effectiveness

Monetary policy is more effective in restraining inflation than in curbing recession. During a period of inflation, the Federal Reserve sets high interest rates that make it difficult for business firms to borrow money. But during a period of recession, although interest rates may be low, business firms must believe that they can make additional profits by borrowing. Otherwise, they will not do so.

Fiscal policy seems to work better during a period of recession than during a period of inflation. During a period of inflation, the government should reduce federal spending. But it is politically "unhealthy" for individual members of Congress to cut back on spending programs that benefit the voters in their districts.

External Factors

Regardless of what our government tries to do, the United States is affected by economic conditions in other countries. For example, if the economies of foreign nations are depressed, business activity in the United States will be affected.

SUMMARY

The American people want their economic system to provide full employment, economic growth, and price stability. The U.S. economy, however, has its ups and downs. Built-in economic stabilizers promote total spending during periods of recession and decrease it during periods of prosperity. Among these stabilizers are federal income taxes, unemployment insurance, and Social Security benefits.

When built-in stabilizers are not effective enough to keep the economy healthy and in balance, the federal government makes use of its monetary and fiscal powers. Monetary policy refers to the strategies used by the Federal Reserve System to regulate the nation's supply of money and credit. Fiscal policy is the use of the federal government's power to tax and spend in order to regulate the level of economic activity.

During periods of recession, monetary policy tries to increase the amount of money and credit available. The purpose is to raise consumer and business spending by adding to the demand for goods and services. Fiscal policy tries to raise spending by increasing federal government spending, lowering taxes, or both.

When inflation threatens, the government may follow the opposite course. The Federal Reserve may reduce total spending by tightening the amount of money and credit available. Congress may increase taxes and reduce federal spending programs.

Monetary and fiscal policy have not eliminated recession and inflation. Economists continue to look for ways to control the swings of the business cycle.

LOOKING AHEAD

It would be hard to imagine life in the United States without the many goods and services that we purchase from other nations. Similarly, the people of other nations look to us for many things that they need for everyday living. Trade among nations has become essential to modern life. The next unit studies what economists call the global economy. The first chapter will focus on the question of why nations trade with one another.

EXERCISES

✔ **Matching** Match each term in Column A with its definition in Column B.

Column A
1. full employment
2. open-market operations
3. inflationary cycle
4. reserve ratio
5. fiscal policy
6. discount rate
7. economic growth
8. stable prices
9. monetary policy
10. built-in stabilizers

Column B
a. little or no change in the purchasing power of the dollar
b. an expansion in the output of goods and services
c. the government's use of its powers to tax and spend in order to regulate the economy
d. a situation occurring when nearly everyone looking for work is able to find a job
e. economic forces that act automatically to keep spending in balance
f. the purchase and sale of government securities by the Federal Reserve System
g. the Federal Reserve's use of its power to regulate the supply of money and credit
h. the percent of a bank's deposits that may not be loaned
i. a period of continually rising prices
j. the interest charged banks by the Federal Reserve System

✔**Interpreting a Cartoon** Study the cartoon on page 451 and then answer the following questions:

1. Who or what is represented by each of the following: the automobile, the service station, the road, and the city in the distance?

2. What do the tool kits represent?

3. How might the mechanic use the tool kits to help the auto get over a period of recession? a period of inflation?

✔ *What Would You Do If . . . ?*

Listed below are a number of economic situations that might confront the federal government. For each situation, state *one* step that might be taken *and* explain how this step would help. Use a different suggestion for each situation.

1. Prices have been increasing steadily, and the government would like to do something to slow down the inflationary cycle.

2. Unemployment has been increasing.

3. There has been a general slump in business conditions.

4. There is full employment, and prices are rising. Because of a change in the world situation, the government has increased its spending for national defense.

✔ *Using the Internet*

The Federal Reserve has a number of Websites specially created to help young people understand what it does. You will find them at:
   <<http://www.federalreserveeducation.org>>. At this site, "Fed 101" explains the workings of the Fed by focusing on five topics: history, structure, monetary policy, banking supervision, and financial services.
   Each of the 12 Federal Reserve Banks and the Board of Governors operates a Website. They are at the following addresses:
   Atlanta—<<http://www.frbatlanta.org>>
   Boston—<<http://www.bos.frb.org>>
   Chicago—<<http://www.chicagofed.org>>
   Cleveland—<<http://www.clev.frb.org>>
   Dallas—<<http://www.dallasfed.org>>
   Kansas City—<<http://www.kc.frb.org>>
   Minneapolis—<<http://www.minneapolisfed.org>>
   New York—<<http://www.ny.frb.org>>
   Philadelphia—<<http://www.phil.frb.org>>
   Richmond—<<http://www.rich.frb.org>>
   St. Louis—<<http://www.stls.frb.org>>
   San Francisco—<<http://www.frbsf.org>>
   Board of Governors—<<http://www.federalreserve.gov>>

Unit *6*

THE GLOBAL ECONOMY

International trade moves raw materials and finished goods across the globe.

Like every other nation in the world, the United States is part of the global economy. Our discussion of this worldwide economy begins with Chapter 31, which discusses international trade. In this chapter, you will find out why nations must sell their goods to other nations, and how such buying and selling benefits all nations. In Chapter 32, you will learn why governments regulate international trade, and why they often set up complicated restrictions on trade.

In Chapter 33, you will find out about the currencies (money) used by the nations of the world, and how one nation's currency is exchanged for that of another nation in order to buy and sell goods.

Chapter 34 explores the developing nations of the world. You will read about their many problems, what causes them to remain poor, and what is being done to help their economies develop.

CHAPTER *31*

International Trade

"Can you beat this? I read in my mother's union newspaper about two pairs of jeans that look alike and are on sale at Lobucks Discount Store in the mall. One pair sells for $29.95 and was made here by U.S. workers who earn $14.50 an hour. It cost the company $2.10 in labor. The other pair sells for $21.95 and was made overseas, where workers earn an average of 25 cents an hour! Those jeans cost the company only 15 cents in labor. Would you work for that? No, of course not. No American would. So what happens? U.S. firms pick up and leave the United States and set up shop in countries where labor costs are very low. Poof! There go American jobs! I think we ought to stop making it so easy for countries with low wages to sell their goods in the United States. Then U.S. companies won't be so eager to leave home."

Does this argument sound familiar? Have you heard it on television, read it in a magazine, or listened as a relative or friend said it? Do you believe that when Americans buy products made in other countries, U.S. workers lose their jobs? The fact is that if we stopped *trading* with foreign countries (that is, buying their goods and services and selling them ours), we might all be a lot worse off. As you read this chapter, you will find out why. You will also learn the answers to the following questions:

- What is the global economy?
- Why do we trade with other nations?
- Who benefits from international trade?

WHAT IS THE GLOBAL ECONOMY?

In reading this text, you have learned how the U.S. economy works. This economy is part of a worldwide economic system, or *global economy*. The global economy, as you might expect, is made up of all the buying and selling that is done by all the nations of the world. In the U.S. economy, goods and services are bought and sold across state lines. In much the same way in the global economic market, goods and services are bought and sold across the borders of nations.

Nations' Imports and Exports

The buying and selling of goods and services across nations' borders is known as *international* (or *foreign*) *trade*. *Imports* are the goods and services that individuals and businesses purchase from foreign countries. Japanese automobiles, European textiles, and Central American fruits are examples of goods imported into the United States. Imported services include flights overseas on foreign airlines and tours of foreign countries taken by U.S. travelers. *Exports* are the goods and services that individuals and businesses sell to foreign countries. The sale of machinery to Canada and the sale of wheat to Russia are two examples of U.S. exports. All nations, large or small, trade with one another in the global economy.

Imports: Tableware from Asia on sale in a New York City market. Do you and your family have many household items that were manufactured overseas?

You and your family are in contact with, and contribute to, the global economy every day. You touched the global economy this morning if you turned on a Korean-made television set or listened to a Japanese DVD player. The sugar you added to your cereal may have come from a Caribbean island nation, your coffee from Colombia or Brazil. The morning newspaper was probably printed on Canadian newsprint, with ink manufactured in Great Britain. Your hot chocolate or chocolate bar may have been made from Central African cacao beans.

Some people earn a living in international trade. Louis works for a firm in Los Angeles that sells its products to Taiwan and Indonesia. Rosa is a securities representative at the London Stock Exchange's branch office in New York City. In short, international trade can touch the lives of all of us in the products we consume, in the jobs we hold, and in the ways we spend our leisure time.

WHY DO WE TRADE WITH OTHER NATIONS?

Nations trade with one another simply because it is to their benefit to do so. Here are a few things that would happen if the United States stopped trading with other nations. (1) We would not be able to manufacture automobiles here because we would not have enough aluminum or rubber. (2) Supermarket shelves would soon be empty of chocolate, coffee, and bananas, among other items. (3) Our homes and factories would not have enough oil and gas, and our cars and planes would eventually run out of gasoline. From these examples, you can readily see that international trade is essential to the U.S. economy. Now we will look in some detail at the reasons why nations trade.

Obtain Goods We Cannot Produce Ourselves

Certain natural resources and agricultural products can be obtained only from abroad. (For examples of resources, see Figure 31.1.) All or nearly all of the bananas, coffee, cocoa, tea, and natural rubber that the U.S. consumes come from abroad. We could build greenhouses and grow tropical fruits and vegetables indoors, but the costs of growing crops this way would be much too high.

Buy Many Things at Lower Cost

Suppose that in your travels down the aisles of your supermarket you see one brand of sugar selling for 40 cents a pound and another selling for $1 a pound. If you need sugar, which brand would

Figure 31.1 U.S. Imports of Raw Materials, as a Percent of Total Used Here

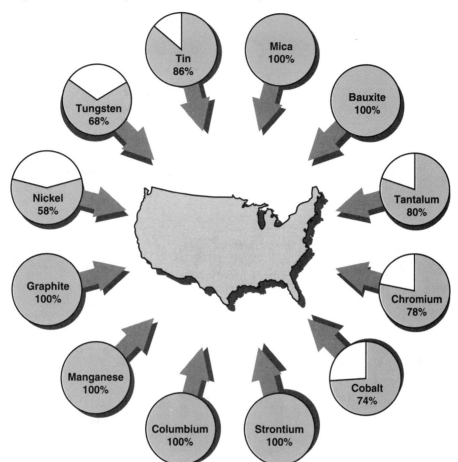

you buy? Suppose that you see two watches in a jewelry store. They look identical. One costs $60, while the other watch costs $85. Which one would you buy? Most shoppers would select the less expensive item if they are convinced that both are of equal quality. After all, why pay $1 a pound for something when you can get the same thing for 40 cents? Or $85 for a watch that you can duplicate for $60?

We import some goods from abroad for the same reason. They cost less than the same things that are produced here. Notice that we did not say that foreigners can produce everything more cheaply. No, indeed! The United States can turn out many things at lower costs than any other country. Naturally, these are the things that foreigners will buy from us. These goods and services will make up our exports.

Figure 31.2 The Ten Leading U.S. Trading Partners, 2004
(figures in billions of dollars)

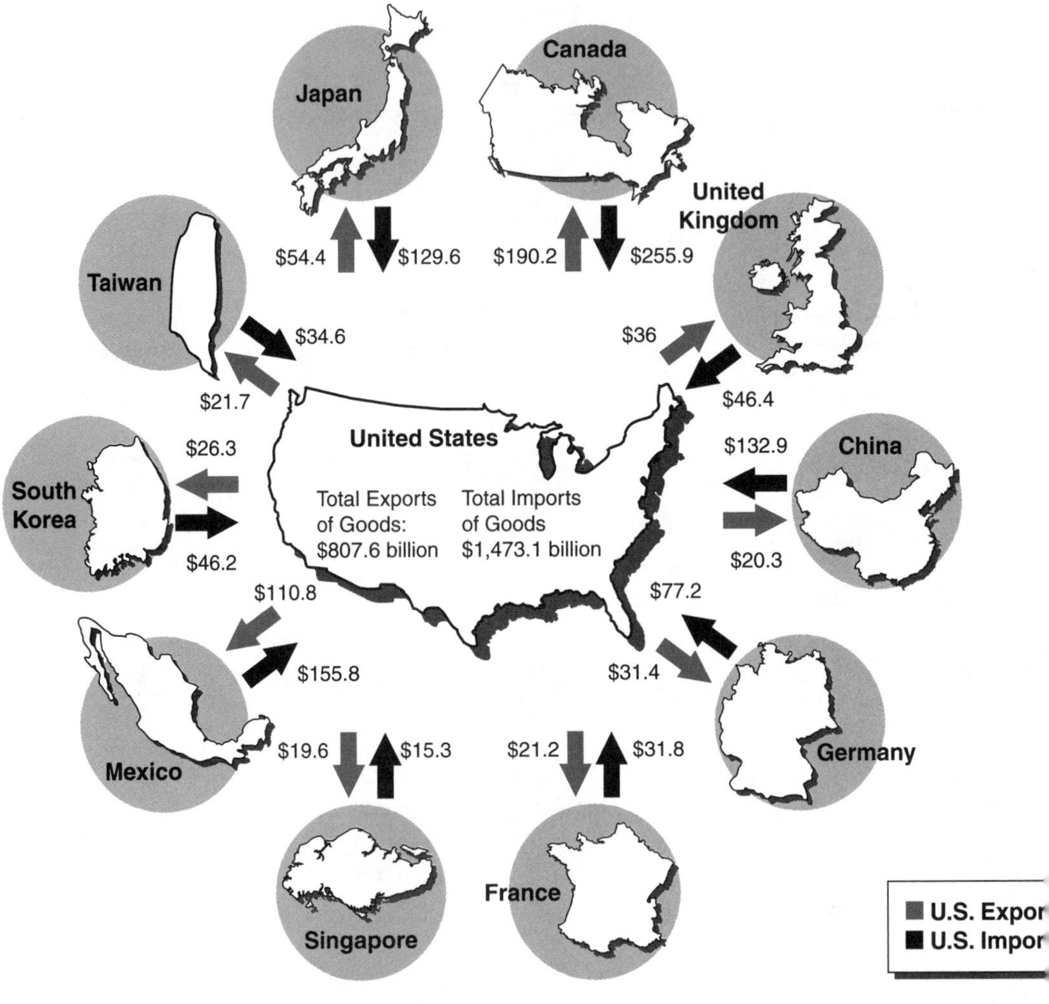

Japan $54.4 $129.6

Canada $190.2 $255.9

United Kingdom $36 $46.4

Taiwan $34.6 $21.7

China $132.9 $20.3

United States
Total Exports of Goods: $807.6 billion
Total Imports of Goods $1,473.1 billion

South Korea $26.3 $46.2

Mexico $110.8 $155.8

Germany $77.2 $31.4

Singapore $19.6 $15.3

France $21.2 $31.8

■ U.S. Expor
■ U.S. Impor

Sell Our Goods to Foreigners

When they export their goods to foreign lands, U.S. firms expect to be paid in U.S. dollars. But how do the buyers (importers) in other countries obtain dollars? When foreign firms sell goods in the United States, they are paid in U.S. dollars. Foreigners use these dollars to buy U.S. products—that is, to pay for the goods we exported to them. In other words, the dollars that Americans pay to import foreign goods enable foreigners to buy goods from us. Or, to put it more simply, *imports pay for exports*.

Raise Our Standard of Living

We have seen that imports enable Americans to buy things that they either could not have obtained or would have had to pay more money for. In other words, foreign trade enables Americans to live better. Thus, we can say that foreign trade raises living standards by making it possible for people to have more of the things they want.

Keep Our Farms and Industries Healthy

In 2004, the United States exported over $807 billion worth of goods. U.S. farmers in particular benefited from foreign trade. In a recent year, for example, some 40 percent of the nation's total farm output was sold abroad. Exports are crucial also to U.S. industries. This fact is illustrated in the following table of exports.

U.S. Exports as a Percent of Total Amount Produced Here

Products	Percent
Manufactured:	
Chemicals	24
Transportation equipment	25
Computer and electronic products	35
Office and computing machines	28
Optical instruments and lenses	21
Plastic and rubber products	17
Agricultural:	
Corn	33
Cotton	43
Soybeans	39
Wheat	47

Create Jobs for U.S. Workers

Thousands upon thousands of U.S. workers depend upon the nation's foreign trade for their jobs. For example, the airplanes flown by many foreign airlines were built in the United States by U.S. workers. Automobiles, farm machinery, movies, TV shows, computers, and hundreds of other products produced in this country are exported every year. Many other jobs owe their existence to the industries that service foreign trade. Ships and planes transporting goods to and from foreign countries have to be loaded and unloaded by U.S. dockworkers and cargo handlers. Moving goods to and from the airports and docks involves many complicated arrangements. These movements are completed by thousands of workers in the foreign trade industry.

Foreign trade also creates jobs in industries that import goods. The transportation industry would have to lay off many employees if there were no imports to be shipped around the country and across the seas. There would be no jobs at all for workers in the coffee industry, for example, if we were to stop importing coffee.

Support or Oppose Other Nations

There are times when the United States will use foreign trade *sanctions* as a means of hurting other nations. Because the U.S. government had hostile relations with Iran beginning in 1979, trade with that Middle Eastern nation was prohibited. In contrast, the U.S. government has sometimes gone out of its way to encourage the purchase of products of foreign nations friendly toward the United States.

WHO BENEFITS FROM INTERNATIONAL TRADE?

It should be clear by now that international trade can benefit all countries. Trade is a two-way street. The United States, for example, cannot simply export its goods and services to other nations. It must also import from other nations.

Suppose that each state in the nation tried to exist without trading with any of the other 49! It just could not be done. In fact, one of the reasons why in the 1780s Americans scrapped the Articles of Confederation and adopted the Constitution for the United States was to guarantee free trade among the states.

The economies of nations grow faster when the nations trade with others instead of each trying to produce by itself all of the goods and services its people need. The reasons for this growth are best understood in terms of absolute advantage, specialization, and comparative advantage.

Absolute Advantage

Some countries are rich in minerals or other natural resources. Others are not. Some have many large industries. Others do not. Some countries have warm climates and fertile soil. Others are cold and have mountainous terrain.

Geographic differences give nations certain advantages over others. Honduras's hot climate allows bananas to grow easily there. Bolivia's mineral resources enable it to dominate the tin market. Switzerland's snow-covered mountains draw thousands of skiers each year. Education and technical skills give some nations advantages over others. Skilled workers and highly developed technology explain why the United States and Japan are leading manufacturing nations.

The ability of one nation to produce certain goods and services at lower cost than another nation is known as *absolute advantage*. In other words, Honduras, Bolivia, and Switzerland have an absolute advantage over most other countries with regard to bananas, tin, and winter sports, respectively.

Specialization

Countries will often *specialize* in the production of those things in which they have an absolute advantage. Thus, Honduras specializes in producing bananas. Honduras can then trade its bananas for the goods that it wants and needs from other countries. Some nations specialize in exporting raw materials. Others specialize in exporting finished manufactured goods.

Comparative Advantage

Countries do not need to have an absolute advantage in anything in order to benefit from specialization. Consider the case of Alphaland and Betaland, for example.

The nation of Alphaland produces both aluminum and steel. If it devoted all its resources to producing aluminum, Alphaland would turn out 100 tons in five hours. If all its efforts were devoted to steel, Alphaland would produce 100 tons in six hours.

The nation of Betaland is Alphaland's neighbor and competitor. Betaland can produce 100 tons of aluminum in eight hours if all its resources are devoted to that industry. If, instead, it manufactures steel only, it can produce 100 tons in seven hours.

Time Needed to Produce 100 Tons of Aluminum and Steel

Country	Aluminum	Steel
Alphaland	5 hours	6 hours
Betaland	8 hours	7 hours

In the example, Alphaland has an absolute advantage in the production of both aluminum and steel. That is, it takes Alphaland fewer hours to produce 100 tons of both metals than Betaland. But let us compare the production of aluminum to that of steel within each country. We see that Alphaland is more efficient in the production of aluminum. This is because it takes Alphaland only five hours to produce 100 tons of aluminum as compared to six hours to produce the 100 tons of steel. Betaland is more efficient in the production of steel because it takes Betaland seven

Understanding Economics

OUTSOURCING ABROAD: THE COSTS AND BENEFITS

Terry could not get his new cell phone to work properly. He called the help number found in his instruction booklet. The technician who answered told him how to start up his phone and the problem was solved. Terry had made his call from his home in Peoria, Illinois. The technician helping him did so from an office in Bangalore, India.

ISPs (Internet service providers) provide Internet connections and services to individuals and organizations. EarthLink is an ISP with about 5 million subscribers. To assist its customers, EarthLink operates "call centers" at which requests for service and technical questions are answered. In 2004, EarthLink announced it would close its call centers and send the work to centers in India and the Philippines. (Using outside contractors to provide services to businesses is known as *outsourcing*.)

Chicago-based Radio Flyer Inc. has been manufacturing its little red wagons since the 1930s. In 2005, Radio Flyer outsourced production of its metal wagons from Chicago to China. Manufacturing of its plastic toys remained in the United States.

Many hospitals around the country outsource some of their X-ray scans over Internet lines to doctors in other states or foreign countries to read and interpret them.

The principal reason why EarthLink, Radio Flyer, and American hospitals outsourced their operations was to take advantage of the lower salaries paid to foreign workers. In 2004, for example, a typical American call-center worker earned about $20,000 plus benefits. His or her counterpart in India earned $2,500. That their firm was able to increase its profits was of little comfort to those whose jobs were lost.

The number of U.S. jobs lost has made outsourcing a controversial issue. On the one side are those arguing that the process benefits the economy as a whole. By lowering the cost of production, they say, outsourcing enables firms to keep their prices down. This benefits consumers who buy their products and services. As businesses expand, they increase spending, hire additional workers, and help the economy grow. In support of this, they cite a study that found that for every dollar spent on foreign outsourcing, the economy gains about $1.14.

Those opposed see foreign outsourcing as a threat to Americans' job security and living standards. The lower wages earned by workers abroad pressure their American counterparts to either accept lower wages or see their jobs go abroad. Critics also say that there is no guarantee that companies that increase their profits through foreign outsourcing will turn around and use those profits to support jobs in the United States.

Both sides of the controversy have called upon government to help them by either promoting international trade or restricting outsourcing. It remains to be seen which side will prevail.

hours to produce 100 tons as compared to eight hours to produce 100 tons of aluminum.

Alphaland devotes all of its energies to producing aluminum. Similarly, Betaland specializes in the production of steel. After ten hours of work, Alphaland will produce 200 tons of aluminum. In 14 hours, Betaland will have produced 200 tons of steel. Now the Alphalanders and the Betalanders can enter into a trade. Alphaland can swap 100 tons of its aluminum and receive 100 tons of steel. Betaland will give up 100 tons of steel and receive 100 tons of aluminum.

Economists explain the specialization in steel or aluminum production as an example of the law of *comparative advantage*. This law states that nations should specialize in the production of those goods and services in which they are most efficient. We can see in the table the results of the specialization and the exchange that followed.

Results of Specialization in Aluminum and Steel Production

Country	Time Worked	Quantity on Hand
Alphaland	10 hours	100 tons of aluminum produced locally and 100 tons of steel imported from Betaland
Betaland	14 hours	100 tons of aluminum imported from Alphaland and 100 tons of steel produced locally

Had they not specialized, it would have taken the Alphalanders 11 hours and the Betalanders 15 hours to produce the same amount of aluminum and steel.

SUMMARY

International trade benefits us in a number of ways. Trade enables us to obtain products that we could not produce ourselves. Our standard of living is high because of trade. Many goods and services are available at low prices. Trade keeps our farms and industries economically healthy. It creates many jobs for Americans. Trade enables foreign buyers to import U.S.-made goods and services. Imports pay for exports. Nations use the proceeds from the sale of their products abroad to finance their imports.

Differences in natural resources, population, and technology give some nations an absolute advantage in the production of certain goods and services. These nations can produce the goods and services at lower cost than other nations.

International trade enables nations to acquire more goods and services than they themselves could possibly produce. The reasons for this situation lie in two of the fundamental principles of international trade: specialization and comparative advantage. The law of comparative advantage states that nations should specialize in the production of those goods and services in which they are most efficient. These nations should export their surplus.

In this way, nations would acquire more of the things they need through imports than they could have if they had tried to produce the items.

─────────── **LOOKING AHEAD** ───────────

Despite the many advantages of foreign trade, nations often place barriers in its way. The next chapter describes the obstacles to trade in the global economy.

─────────── **EXERCISES** ───────────

✔**Matching** Match each term in Column A with its definition in Column B.

Column A	**Column B**
1. imports	*a.* an economic law urging specialization in those
2. comparative	items that can be produced most efficiently
advantage	*b.* goods and services sold to foreign buyers
3. specialization	*c.* the purchase and sale of goods and services
4. foreign trade	among nations
5. exports	*d.* a worldwide economic system
6. global economy	*e.* goods and services purchased from foreign sellers
	f. the limiting of a nation's production to items in
	which the nation has an advantage

✔ *Understanding What You Have Read*

The chapter asked the question, "Why do we trade with other nations?" In reply, we made the following points:

1. Foreign trade enables us to obtain goods that we cannot produce ourselves.

2. Foreign trade enables us to buy many things at lower cost.

3. Foreign trade enables foreigners to buy our goods.

4. Foreign trade raises our standard of living.

5. Foreign trade is important to U.S. farms and industries.

6. Foreign trade creates jobs for U.S. workers.

Listed below are statements of fact that illustrate the above points. On a separate sheet of paper, list the number of the point that is being made by each of the following statements.

a. In 2001, U.S. farmers and businesspeople sold over $730 billion worth of goods to people in other lands.

b. The United States normally imports 100 percent of the following items: cocoa, coffee, tea, bananas, carpet wool, silk, and spices.

c. Most of the goods imported into the United States last year could have been produced here.

d. America's best customers for its exports are the same countries from which it imports the most goods.

e. Exports of U.S.-made aircraft engines declined between 1982 and 1983. The number of workers employed by the aircraft engine industry also declined in the same period.

f. Television sets would be much more expensive to U.S. consumers if the United States had to produce all the sets in use in this country.

✔ **Where the United States Trades** Study the illustration on page 470 and then answer the questions below.

1. Which *five* nations of the world trade most heavily with the United States? List them in order of total value of trade (exports plus imports).

2. Why do you think that U.S. trade with Japan is greater than U.S. trade with Taiwan?

3. Why do you think that Canada is our best customer?

✔ *Imported Goods in Your Life*

On an average day, you probably come into contact with a variety of products that were made or grown abroad. Take a survey of the foreign foods and manufactured goods that you handle in one day. Create a table with the following information:

In column 1, list the imports that you came into contact with today. In column 2, tell the countries from which the imports came. In column 3, state briefly the reasons why you or your family purchased imports rather than goods that were U.S.-grown or produced.

(1) Imported Product	(2) Country or Region of Origin	(3) Reason for Purchase of Imported Item
Chocolate	South America	The bean cannot be grown in the United States.

✔ *Using the Internet*

U.S. foreign trade statistics can be found at <<http://www.census.gov>> (click on "Foreign Trade").

CHAPTER 32

Regulating International Trade

	Key Terms	
clear customs	importer	globalization
declare goods	quota	transparency
customs	subsidy	trading bloc
inspection	foreign-currency	child labor
tariff	controls	trade restriction
favorable balance	reciprocity	Luddite
of trade	most-favored	
infant industry	nation	

Bill and Pearl Backus walked quickly into the international arrivals building of the huge airport. They were eager to greet their sister, Judy. She was returning home from a visit with their grandparents on the island of Jamaica.

The clerk at the information counter explained to Bill and Pearl that although the plane had arrived, it would be a while before they could see their sister. She would first have to *clear customs*. The clerk suggested that they go to the visitor's balcony to watch what was happening.

"What does 'clearing customs' mean?" Bill asked Pearl on their way up to the balcony.

"The U.S. Bureau of Customs asks everyone entering the country from abroad to *declare* (make a list of) all the goods that they acquired in other countries and are bringing with them into this country," Pearl explained. "Customs does this for several reasons. One reason is to prevent people from bringing illegal goods into the country. Another is to find out if anything being brought in is subject to the payment of a tax. When we get to the balcony, you'll see what I mean."

Clearing Customs: Customs officer examines travelers' luggage. What kinds of foreign goods are travelers prohibited from bringing into the United States?

The scene that Pearl and Bill watched from the balcony reminded them of supermarket checkout counters. Travelers who had just arrived from abroad stood on lines with "shopping carts." Instead of holding groceries, however, the carts held their luggage.

At the head of each line stood a uniformed customs official. In some instances, the customs people asked the travelers to open their luggage to allow them to look through it. In others, they simply stamped the suitcases and boxes and sent the travelers on their way.

"There she is!" Bill exclaimed. He had spotted Judy standing in one of the lines. As he and Pearl waited, Bill could not help thinking how nice it would be if the officials could just skip all this red tape and let Judy join them right away.

As do most nations, the United States restricts the kinds and quantities of foreign goods it permits to enter the country. Some people feel that our restrictions have gone too far, while others feel that they have not gone far enough. As you read this chapter, you will learn about both sides of this controversy. You will also learn the answers to the following questions.

- Why do nations regulate international trade?
- How is international trade regulated?
- What is globalization?
- What arguments are made against globalization?
- Why do many economists support globalization?

WHY DO NATIONS REGULATE INTERNATIONAL TRADE?

Judy Backus found her return home delayed at U.S. customs. If you have ever traveled to foreign places such as Asia, Africa, Europe, or Latin America, you would have had a similar experience on your return home. Your luggage would have had to undergo some kind of *customs inspection.*

Business firms also undergo customs inspections every time they import goods from abroad. Government customs inspectors determine if the goods can legally enter the country, and if they are subject to a *tariff.* (A tariff is a tax on imports.)

The United States, like most nations, restricts the kinds and quantities of goods it will permit to enter the country. There are a number of reasons why it does this. Some reasons have to do with protecting the country from dangerous products. The average person, for example, would not be allowed to bring in illegal drugs, weapons, fresh produce, or animals. These items could be dangerous to the health of the American public or to its crops and livestock.

Sometimes, the foreign policy of the U.S. government requires that we stop all trade with certain countries. When this occurs, it becomes illegal to import any goods made by that country. It would not be possible, for example, for a U.S. firm that sells bicycles to bring into this country any bicycle made in North Korea. If Judy Backus had purchased something made in North Korea while she was visiting Jamaica, she would not have been permitted to bring it home with her.

Most of the time, nations regulate international trade for economic reasons. Since this book is about economics, we will take a closer look at those reasons.

Create a Favorable Balance of Trade

When individuals spend more than they earn, they face the possibility of running out of money. Countries face a similar situation when they import more than they export. When a nation's imports are greater than its exports, it has to make up the difference with some kind of payment. Like individuals who spend more than they earn, nations can do this for only so long.

For that reason, governments try to create a *favorable balance of trade.* This situation is one in which merchandise exports are greater than imports. Nations promote a favorable trade balance by adopting measures that increase their exports and limit their imports.

Since the mid-1970s, the United States has imported far more goods than it has exported. (See the table on page 481.) The reasons are as follows: (1) Many foreign products are attractive in this country because they cost less and are equal to or are of better quality than those made here. (2) Many U.S.-made products are not attractive overseas because they cost more or are inferior to those made in other lands. (3) Some countries have imposed restrictions on imports from the United States.

Value of U.S. Exports and Imports of Goods Since 1960
(in billions)

Year	Exports	Imports	Year	Exports	Imports
1960	$ 19.7	$ 14.8	1985	$ 215.9	$ 338.1
1968	33.6	33.0	1990	389.3	498.3
1974	98.3	103.8	1995	575.8	749.6
1980	224.3	249.8	2006	1,466.2	2,229.4

Protect Certain Industries

Most frequently, tariffs are levied to protect certain industries from *foreign competition*. A tariff makes a product more expensive to buyers than it would be if there were no tariff. For that reason, industries that are losing business to foreign imports often try to get the U.S. government to protect them with a tariff.

Opponents of tariffs believe that tariffs protect inefficient U.S. manufacturers at the expense of other Americans—consumers. These other Americans have to pay more for imported goods. The extra amount that they pay could have been used to buy more goods. Thus, their standard of living has dropped.

Prevent the Loss of Jobs

Producers in certain foreign countries can undersell U.S. manufacturers, it is argued, because their products are produced by "cheap labor" (foreign workers who earn much less than U.S. workers). U.S. producers demand trade restrictions to raise the price of goods made by the low-paid foreign workers or to prevent the goods they produce from being sold here. These restrictions will enable U.S. workers to keep their jobs and their high wages.

Protect "Infant Industries"

There was a time when the United States had very few industries of its own. In the years following the Revolution, Americans were compelled to import from Europe many of the manufactured items that they needed. Then Alexander Hamilton, the nation's first Secretary of the Treasury, proposed a tariff to protect the nation's *infant industries.* Hamilton wanted a tax on imported goods that would enable new U.S. businesses to compete with foreign ones.

Many African, Asian, and Latin American nations today find themselves in a similar position. They want to develop their own industries and become economically independent. These nations experienced a long period of economic, political, and military domination by Europe or the United States. It took many years to achieve political independence. Now these nations fear that their dependence on the industrial nations for manufactured goods will cost them some or all of their hard-won freedom. The problem of these nations is that the industrialized nations can undersell their products. Their solution is to keep competing foreign goods out of their countries until the time when their industries are mature enough to compete on their own.

HOW IS INTERNATIONAL TRADE REGULATED?

Thus far we have discussed the reasons *why* nations restrict international trade. This section describes *how* nations use tariffs, quotas, subsidies, and foreign-currency controls to achieve their goals.

Tariffs

A tariff is paid to the government by the *importer* (the person or business that purchases foreign-made goods or services and brings them into the country). Suppose, for example, that the U.S. government has placed a $20 tariff on each imported automobile tire. Let us suppose, too, that each tire ordinarily costs the importer $40. With the addition of the tariff, one tire now costs $60. Needless to say, the importer will have to pass this tax along to its customers. U.S. buyers will have to consider whether they are willing to pay the extra $20 for a foreign-made tire. If they are not, they will buy U.S.-made tires instead.

Quotas

Sometimes, the federal government places quotas on certain imports. A *quota* sets limits on the quantity or value of a good that may enter the country. For example, the U.S. government has set a quota on imported sugar. This quota limits the amount of sugar that buyers in this country can import from sugar-producing countries in one year. Once the quota has been reached, the only source of sugar for the remainder of the year must be U.S. growers. A quota on the money value of certain imported goods would set a limit on how many units are imported based on their retail costs.

Not only do customs inspectors check foreign imports that may be taxed, they look for illegal goods, such as dangerous drugs.

Subsidies

A *subsidy* is a payment by the government to firms or persons in an industry it wants to help. For example, in a recent year the Japanese government paid its rice farmers about $1 for each pound of rice they produced. This subsidy, which was ten times the world market price for rice, enabled Japanese rice farmers to stay in business. In the United States, subsidies to industries such as shipbuilding and to thousands of farmers have enabled producers to stay in otherwise unprofitable activities.

Foreign-Currency Controls

Importers need to pay for the goods they buy in foreign countries with local currencies. In payment for their exports, Indian firms expect to receive rupees; Australians, Australian dollars; and Mexicans, pesos. A national government uses *foreign-currency controls* to make it difficult, or impossible, for importers to obtain foreign currencies. For example, a government may limit the amount of foreign currencies importers may buy. In this way, a government can reduce the amount of imports entering its country.

WHAT IS GLOBALIZATION?

Ever since the publication of Adam Smith's *The Wealth of Nations* in 1776, many economists have been praising the advantages of international trade. Foreign trade, they argue, gives consumers access to a wider assortment of goods and services. Similarly, producers obtain components for their products at lower cost, and a nation's economy is given access to raw materials that are not found in that country. Meanwhile, competition from imports inspires that country's producers to improve productivity and invest in new technology.

Given its advantages, the argument continues, nations should be doing everything they can to promote international trade. Since the end of World War II, the world has been acting on this advice by reducing barriers to trade between nations. This process is called *globalization*. The most successful globalization efforts have been the *General Agreement on Tariffs and Trade (GATT)* and the *World Trade Organization (WTO)*.

GATT and the WTO

GATT, created in 1947 by the United States and 22 other countries, was based on three principles. The first principle was *reciprocity* (the idea that if one member nation lowers it tariffs, it could expect all other members to do the same). The second was the *most-favored nation* principle. This idea means that if a nation grants an especially low tariff to one country, it would be granted to all member states. The third principle was *transparency*. This idea means that "invisible barriers to trade," such as import quotas and subsidies, would be replaced by tariffs or abolished.

By 1994, GATT had grown to 117 members. That same year, the members agreed to expand the organization's scope of operations and to reform itself as the World Trade Organization (WTO).

Headquartered in Geneva, Switzerland, the WTO is an association of over 140 countries whose principal goal is the promotion of international trade. As with GATT, each WTO member agrees to treat each other equally in trading policies and to accept the principles of transparency, reciprocity, and most-favored nations in their relations with other member nations. In addition, the WTO provides a court for the settlement of disputes arising between nations.

Regional Trading Blocs

While the WTO has made considerable progress in promoting international trade, it has been slow going. By way of hastening the process, many countries have formed smaller, regional trading blocs. *Trading blocs* are groups of countries that agree to reduce tariffs and other barriers to trade among themselves. The most important of these are the *European Union*, the *North American Free Trade Agreement*, and the *Free Trade Area of the Americas*.

The European Union (EU)

Europe has long been a continent divided. Just as language, religion, or culture often differed greatly from one country to the next, so too did money, tariffs, and laws. Immigration laws kept people from moving freely from one country to another in search of economic opportunity.

Worse yet, obstacles to trade created rivalries that, on occasion, led to bloodshed and war. After the worst of these conflicts—World War II—ended in 1945, nations in Europe began to lessen economic rivalries by unifying their economies. By 1957, six European nations—France, Italy, West Germany, Belgium, the Netherlands, and Luxembourg—agreed to eliminate most of the trade barriers existing among them. The European Economic Community (*EEC* or *Common Market*, as these nations called themselves) did much to create a single market. Goods, services, people, and capital could move as freely among its members as they did within one country. Other nations became members of the Common Market over the years. Britain, Ireland, and Denmark joined in 1973. Greece was added in 1981, followed by Spain and Portugal in 1986.

Although the EEC went a long way toward removing trade barriers, many felt it had not gone far enough. What was really needed to make destructive rivalries and wars a thing of the past, they argued, was the removal of all the remaining barriers and the creation of some kind of European-wide government. Their efforts eventually led to the creation of the European Union.

In 1993, the Common Market countries meeting in Maastricht, Holland, renamed themselves the *European Union (EU)*. In 1994, the European Union grew to 15 members when Austria, Finland, and Sweden joined. European citizenship was granted to the people of each member state. Customs and immigration agreements were relaxed to allow these citizens greater freedom to live, work, and study in any of the member states. Moreover, border controls were lifted. In addition, certain governing bodies were created—the European Parliament, Court of Justice, and an investment bank. Someday, it was hoped, these agencies would provide a common government for the EU-member states.

The most dramatic steps taken by the EU were the introduction of a common currency and a central bank. The totally new currency, the euro, went into effect in 2002 in 12 of the EU nations (see page 495).

At present, the U.S. dollar is the single most important currency in the world because payment in dollars is widely accepted in international trade. But the European Union has created a market comparable in size and wealth to that of the United

States. For that reason, many predict that the euro will one day rival the U.S. dollar in the global economy.

The North American Free Trade Agreement (NAFTA)

This 1992 treaty linked the United States, Canada, and Mexico as a regional trading bloc. Under NAFTA provisions, all tariffs, quotas, and other barriers to trade were to be phased out by 2009.

NAFTA's supporters pointed to the economic benefits that were bound to result as North America from the Yukon to the Yucatan was united in a single trading unit. By removing barriers to trade, every nation stood to gain as businesses flourished, jobs increased, and living standards improved.

"Not so," said others who predicted that NAFTA was all but certain to produce job loss and/or environmental destruction in its wake. In particular, U.S. labor unions said that jobs would be lost as U.S. firms transferred their operations to Mexico, where wages were lower. At the same time, American environmental organizations were concerned that under NAFTA rules, U.S. environmental laws could not be applied to Canadian or Mexican firms.

The Free Trade Area of the Americas (FTAA)

This association of 34 nations of the Western Hemisphere has the long-term goal of creating a barrier-free trade zone from the Arctic to Argentina by December 2005. Should it succeed, FTAA would link markets of 800 million people and economies ranging from the world's largest—the United States—to some of its tiniest. Like the WTO, the FTAA has a set of rules that the members agree to follow in trading with one another, and a mechanism for settling disputes.

Many of the same arguments that were advanced against NAFTA have been expressed in opposition to FTAA. That is, that the agreement would lead to job losses in the United States and a weakening of existing environmental laws.

WHAT ARGUMENTS ARE MADE AGAINST GLOBALIZATION?

Despite the agreement among many economists as to the advantages of international trade, the efforts of both the WTO and the FTAA have generated widespread, and sometimes violent protest. At a WTO meeting in Seattle, in 1999, and again at a FTAA meeting in Quebec, Canada, in 2001, hundreds of protestors turned to the streets to demonstrate their opposition to the expansion of the global economy. While most of the demonstrations were peaceful, some were not.

1. Economic globalization threatens public health and the environment. As barriers to trade are removed, corporations can move their operations freely around the world. This enables them to escape tough pollution control laws and the taxes that pay for social and environmental programs. Making matters worse, efforts by the United States and others to require countries to protect the environment have been declared barriers to trade. Trade barriers are illegal under the WTO agreement.

2. The lowering of trade barriers by WTO, FTAA, and other treaties deprives Americans of jobs. Globalization has enabled U.S.-based corporations to move their operations to countries where wages are lower. As a result, many U.S. workers either lost their jobs or were forced to accept lower-paying jobs.

3. The WTO and FTAA promote child labor and other exploitation of workers. Critics charge that the jobs of American workers are often lost to child labor. "Child labor" refers to work by children younger than 15 that limits their physical, mental, social, or psychological development. Worldwide, an estimated 250 million children, some as young as five, are at work. As long as companies and countries are free to search for the cheapest workers and lowest standards (as they are under WTO and FTAA rules), children will suffer.

4. The lowering of trade barriers by WTO, FTAA, and other treaties ruins certain industries of some developing nations. Globalization has hurt small farmers and infant industries in some developing nations that, with no protective tariffs, can no longer compete with the large-scale agriculture and mechanized industries in other countries.

Anti-WTO protests took place in Seattle, Washington, in December 1999.

WHY DO MANY ECONOMISTS SUPPORT GLOBALIZATION?

Many economists argue that it is unwise for nations to put restrictions on foreign trade. The most important arguments are that *trade restrictions* (1) lower living standards, and (2) cause other countries to start imposing their own trade restrictions. Let us take a closer look at these arguments.

Lower Living Standards

In the late 18th century (during the early years of the Industrial Revolution in Great Britain), many jobs in the textile industry were lost when the owners brought in new machines. These machines did many of the tasks that workers had done by hand. Workers protested strongly. Some (called *Luddites*) even went so far as to break into the factories and smash the hated machines. The workers whose jobs were taken by machines suffered hardships. But the newly invented textile machines reduced the prices of many goods, thus increasing the demand for them. Far more jobs were created than had been taken away. In short, the ever-increasing output made possible by technology lowered the cost of those goods. The low cost in turn enabled more people to afford the goods, thereby creating demand for workers and raising living standards.

People who favor restrictions on international trade today are often compared to 19th-century workers who resisted the introduction of new machinery. While it is true that workers suffer when industries are put out of business by foreign competition, consumers benefit from lower prices.

The reason for the lower prices has to do with comparative advantage (discussed in Chapter 31). International trade enables countries to specialize in the production of goods and services in which they are most efficient. A country then exchanges its goods and services for the goods and services that other countries produce more efficiently. Increased efficiency prevents the waste of resources and reduces living costs. By contrast, trade restrictions *increase* these costs.

Cause More Trade Restrictions

Opponents of trade restrictions argue that when countries place tariffs and quotas on foreign trade, other countries do the same. They set up trade restrictions in retaliation. Countries whose products are kept out of U.S. markets by tariffs and quotas try to "get even" by placing similar restrictions on U.S. products. In the end, the savings that this country might gain by reducing imports are soon offset through the loss of exports. Meanwhile, consumers in both countries suffer by having to pay higher prices for goods than if there had been no trade restrictions.

The world was taught a terrible lesson about the price of trade restrictions in the 1920s. At that time, the United States and most of the other industrialized nations attempted to reduce imports by imposing record-high tariffs and quotas. Most economists now agree that those efforts were a principal cause of the Great Depression of the 1930s. (For a description of that period, see page 442.)

SUMMARY

In this chapter, we learned that nations regulate foreign trade as a way of restricting products from entering their countries and achieving certain foreign policy and economic goals. The most frequently stated economic goals of trade restriction are: to achieve a favorable balance of trade, to protect domestic industries, and to prevent the loss of jobs.

Nations regulate foreign trade in a variety of ways. Most frequently, these include one or more of the following: tariffs, quotas, subsidies, and foreign currency controls.

Those who favor globalization argue that trade restrictions waste resources, increase prices, and invite retaliation. Those opposed to globalization argue that it can threaten public health and the environment, exploit children and other groups of workers, and hurt certain U.S. industries, as well as industries in some developing nations.

LOOKING AHEAD

Paying for imports can be a complicated process. Each trading nation expects to be paid in its own currency. The next chapter describes how nations pay for imported goods and services.

EXERCISES

✔ **Understanding What You Have Read** On a separate sheet of paper, indicate whether the following statements are true or false. Write **T** if they are true and **F** if they are false.

1. Persons returning to the United States from most foreign countries must pass through customs.

2. One reason for placing a tariff on imports is to increase imports.

3. According to the "infant industry" argument, nations should levy a tariff to protect their newly developed industries.

4. One purpose of a quota is to limit imports.

5. Suppose that the tariff on an item is $1 a pound. U.S. firms make this item for sale at $10 a pound. British manufacturers can deliver the item to the United States for sale at $7 a pound. Because of the $1 tariff, Americans would probably not buy the British-made item.

6. Suppose that the tariff on the item described in question 5 is increased to $4 a pound. Americans are now likely to buy the item made by U.S. firms.

7. If the United States eliminated all tariffs, the price of imported goods would soon be likely to drop.

8. If the United States restricted the amount of Swedish money that importers could obtain, this would have no effect on our imports from Sweden.

9. Companies that export a substantial amount of their products are more likely to be in favor of restrictions on foreign trade than those firms that sell most of their products domestically (at home).

✔ **Matching** Match each term in Column A with its definition in Column B.

Column A	Column B
1. favorable balance of trade	*a.* a limit on the total amount or value of a product that may be imported
2. tariff	*b.* limits on the amount of another nation's money that an importer may buy to purchase imports
3. subsidy	
4. customs inspection	
5. "infant" industry	*c.* an excess of exports over imports
6. quota	*d.* an investigation to determine if goods entering the country are legal and if they are subject to a tariff
7. foreign-currency controls	
	e. a tax on imports
	f. an industry that is in the early stages of development in a country
	g. a government payment to support an individual, a firm, or an industry

✔ **Reading for Further Understanding** Read the selection below and then do the activities that follow.

Does Foreign Trade Put Americans Out of Work?

One argument for restricting foreign trade is that this action will protect U.S. workers from "unfair" competition by foreign workers. Most foreign workers are paid less than Americans for doing the same jobs. Foreign-made goods thus can be sold in the United States for less than the same U.S.-made products. Why, for example, should a U.S. firm that pays its employees $8 an hour have to compete with an overseas business that pays its employees only $2 an hour? The thing to do, some people believe, is to keep foreign goods out of the country with tariffs, quotas, or other devices. Then U.S. consumers will have to "buy American" (buy goods made in the United States).

Opponents of this point of view say that it is not how much workers are paid that is important in determining costs of goods but rather how much workers produce. If a foreign worker who is paid $2 an hour can produce 40 toothbrushes an hour, the brushes will cost the manufacturer 5 cents each in labor costs. But suppose that, because of modern equipment, a U.S. worker is able to turn out 400 toothbrushes an hour. At a wage of $8 an hour, this is the equivalent of only 2 cents per brush in labor costs.

Opponents of tariffs also argue that it is unfair to ask the consumer to pay the extra price that tariffs and other trade restrictions cost. When the government keeps foreign goods out of the country to protect a U.S. firm, consumers must pay the price. Efficient U.S. firms *can* compete with foreign ones. The inefficient firms ought either to improve or go out of business. If foreign goods cost less to produce than U.S. goods, the argument goes, U.S. consumers will benefit if they can buy the imports.

This, then, is the issue: **Should the government place tariffs on foreign goods in order to protect U.S. firms from foreign producers?**

1. Write a letter to the editor of your local newspaper expressing your point of view on this question. Be sure to include the reasons why you feel as you do.

2. Assume that your letter was printed and that a reader who disagreed with it wrote a reply that was also printed. Put yourself in the place of this reader and compose a letter providing arguments against the points made in your original letter.

✔ *Using the Internet*

The official Website of the WTO is <<http://www.wto.org>>, while that of the FTAA is <<http://www.ftaa-alca.org>>. The official Website of the European Union is <<http://www.europa.eu.int>>.

33

Financing International Trade

Key Terms

foreign exchange	fixed exchange	balance of
rate of exchange	rates	payments
foreign-currency	floating exchange	payments
draft	rates	
euro	competitiveness	

"This is such a colorful restaurant. Isn't it wonderful traveling to foreign places?"

"Well, I haven't traveled much. In fact, this visit to South Korea is my first trip out of the United States. But I can tell you this: I love it so far."

"Here's the check. Let's see. The total comes to . . . one thousand two hundred and fifty won each, with the tip."

"That sounds like a lot of money. How much is that in dollars?"

"Eight dollars and fifty cents."

If you have ever traveled to other countries, you know that each country you visited has its own currency. People in other countries use their currencies in exactly the same way that Americans use dollars and cents: to pay for goods and services.

Things are not so simple, however, when the buying and selling take place between nations. The problem is that sellers expect to be paid in the currency of their own country, not in that of the buyer. If you worked in a clothing store and a customer wanted to pay with bolívares (Venezuelan money) for a $150 purchase, would you accept them? Probably not. After all, how would you know what a bolívar looked like, or what it was worth? In all likelihood, you would ask your customer to exchange the bolívares for dollars before attempting to make any purchases.

In this chapter, you will learn how buyers and sellers in international trade pay for their transactions. When you have finished reading, you will be able to answer the following questions:

- What is meant by the rate of exchange?
- How does one obtain foreign exchange?
- How are exchange rates determined?
- Why should we be interested in the rate of exchange?

WHAT IS MEANT BY THE RATE OF EXCHANGE?

Take a few moments to look at the table below. From the table you will learn (1) the name of the money (or currency) used by each of the countries listed, and (2) the value of each currency in terms of dollars at a particular time.

The currencies of other nations are often referred to as *foreign exchange*. To an American, therefore, pesos and francs are two examples of foreign exchange because they are foreign currencies. To a person living in Mexico, however, dollars are a form of foreign exchange.

The price at which one nation's currency can be bought using another nation's currency is known as its *rate of exchange*, or exchange rate. For example, Swedish currency is called the krona. One Swedish krona is valued at about $.13 in U.S. money. Thus the rate of exchange is 1 krona equals $.13, or $1 equals 7.7 kronor.

Can you tell what the Venezuelan unit of currency is called? And the Swiss unit of currency? Venezuelan money is called the bolívar. Swiss money is called the franc.

What is the rate of exchange for these currencies? One bolívar is valued at about $.0005. One Swiss franc is valued at $.80.

Rate of Exchange, U.S. Dollar and Selected Foreign Currencies, June 2005

Country	Currency	U.S. Dollar Value	Country	Currency	U.S. Dollar Value
Australia	dollar	$ .76	Mexico	peso	$.09
Canada	dollar	$ .70	Poland	zloty	$.30
Europe	euro	1.23	South Korea	won	.001
Great Britain	pound	1.82	South Africa	rand	.15
India	rupee	.02	Sweden	krona	.13
Israel	shekel	.23	Switzerland	franc	.80
Japan	yen	.009	Venezuela	bolívar	.0005

Americans who travel abroad must exchange the dollars they plan to spend for the currencies of the countries that they visit. Naturally, the amount of a particular foreign currency that Americans receive for their dollars will depend upon the rate of exchange.

Imagine that through a stroke of luck you have won a trip to India. While visiting a market in New Delhi, India's capital city, you see an especially attractive pair of sandals. The shopkeeper tells you that the sandals are priced at 200 rupees. Can you afford them? This depends upon how much 200 rupees are equal to in dollars. As a tourist in India, you have already learned that the exchange rate is .02 rupee to the dollar (or $.02 equals 1 rupee). With one eye on the sandals and the other on your calculator, you determine that 200 rupees equal $4 in U.S. currency.

Businesspeople who buy and sell goods in foreign countries must also know rates of exchange of the currencies in which they are trading. A bicycle importer must know that Japanese bikes selling for 11,970 yen each will cost about $108. (11,970 × $.009 = $107.73 in U.S. currency.) Similarly, a U.S. importer has to be familiar with the dollar-peso exchange rate in order to decide whether to pay the 100 pesos asked per sweater by a Mexican exporter. (According to the table, this amount equals $9 in U.S. currency.)

HOW DOES ONE OBTAIN FOREIGN EXCHANGE?

Most U.S. commercial banks sell foreign currencies. So too do certain large tourist agencies. And in larger cities around the country, foreign currency dealers have offices where individuals can buy foreign exchange.

Americans who are planning to travel abroad often buy small amounts of foreign currencies in the United States. They do this in order to be able to make small payments when they first arrive abroad. Then after they are settled in a foreign country, travelers can obtain foreign exchange from banks and currency dealers there.

Most foreign-exchange sales involve business firms and large sums of money. U.S. importing firms that want to purchase goods from abroad usually use one of two methods of payment. In the first method, the importer buys a *foreign-currency draft*. This is a kind of check payable in a foreign currency. The importer sends the draft to the exporter in another country in payment for a shipment of goods. In the second method, the importer deposits funds in its bank in the United States. The importer's bank then advises its branch in the exporting country to make payment to the exporter using the local currency.

Understanding Economics

THE EURO

In the year 2002, the franc, mark, lira, and certain other European currencies passed into history. By that year, the people of France, Germany, Italy, and nine other nations had exchanged their money for a completely new currency, the *euro*. The adoption of a single currency by 12 of Europe's most powerful nations is the most recent and perhaps most important step toward the fulfillment of the long-held dream of economic unification. Most, but not all, of the European Union (EU) nations (Austria, Belgium, Finland, France, Germany, Greece, Ireland, Italy, Netherlands, Luxembourg, Portugal, and Spain) have adopted the new euro notes and coins. Shopkeepers in these countries no longer accept their old local currencies. How many euros did each person receive when they exchanged their currency was based on the following rates of exchange:

1 EURO EQUALED:

40.34 Belgian francs
1.96 German marks
340.75 Greek drachmas
166.39 Spanish pesetas
6.56 French francs
0.79 Irish pound
1936.27 Italian lire
40.34 Luxembourg francs
2.20 Dutch guilders
13.76 Austrian schillings
200.48 Portuguese escudos
5.95 Finnish markkaa

These euro notes have replaced the currencies of many European countries.

HOW ARE EXCHANGE RATES DETERMINED?

Perhaps you have wondered why the British pound is worth $1.82, the Venezuelan bolívar $.0005, and the Indian rupee $.02. Exchange rates may be determined in one of two ways. (1) A government decides to establish and maintain its currency at *fixed exchange rates*. (2) The value of a currency is established by *floating exchange rates*, in accordance with the laws of supply and demand. Let us take a closer look at each of these methods.

Fixed Exchange Rates

Prior to the early 1970s, most nations guaranteed to exchange their own currency for a set amount of another currency. In this way, they fixed the value of their money in terms of foreign exchange.

Americans who visited Mexico in those days knew that at the end of their trip they could step into a Mexican bank and exchange their remaining pesos at the rate of 25 to the dollar. Similarly, a French bank that had more soles (Peruvian money) than it could use would simply present its surplus to a Peruvian bank, which would exchange soles for francs at a fixed rate.

Floating Exchange Rates

By the mid-1970s, most nations allowed the value of their currencies to *float* (rise or fall) in accordance with the laws of supply and demand.

A nation's currency rises or falls in value depending on the demand for its goods and services. When the demand for a nation's products increases, more people want its currency, and the value of this currency increases. When the demand for a nation's products falls, so does the value of its currency. The bank that sells you British pounds or Japanese yen is just one of thousands of banks around the country that buy and sell foreign exchange. The prices that banks quote (such as 120 yen to the dollar) are determined by supply and demand. If the demand for Japanese goods around the world increases, so too will the demand for yen. Increasing demand will push up the cost of yen, and Americans will receive fewer yen to the dollar than before. If the demand for Japanese goods falls, the opposite will happen. Americans will be able to receive more yen for a dollar than before.

What is true for Japanese currency applies to all foreign currencies when exchange rates are allowed to float. Their prices depend on the laws of supply and demand. When the demand for the goods of a particular nation is rising, the demand for its currency will also rise. This increase in demand will increase the price of that nation's currency. When the demand for the goods of a particular nation is falling, the foreign exchange price of its currency will also fall.

WHY SHOULD WE BE INTERESTED IN THE RATE OF EXCHANGE?

Ask yourself the question, "Which Americans want to own reals (from Brazil) or rupees (from India)?" The most likely answer is Americans who expect to purchase goods from a business or a person in Brazil or India. This is the principal reason why most people want to own any foreign currency: to buy something from that country.

Since the rate of exchange is the price one pays for foreign currency, it follows that when exchange rates are rising, foreign goods (imports) will become more costly. Similarly, when exchange rates decline, these imports will become less costly. Both the rise and the fall of exchange rates could affect your standard of living.

Imported Small Electronics: What will happen to the price of these foreign-made goods if the exchange rate of the dollar rises? What will happen if the rate falls?

An electronics firm in Rochester, New York, is thinking of importing five dozen (60) cell phones from South Korea. The Korean exporter quotes a price of 2,400,000 won for the shipment. (The won is the South Korean unit of currency.) Similar U.S.-made telephones cost $40 each, or $2,400 for five dozen. The electronics firm knows that it can resell the U.S.-made telephones for $50 dollars each. At the same time, the exchange rate for the won is 1,295 to the dollar. Which telephones will it order? 2,400,000 won equals $1,853, or $31 per phone. Since $31 is less than the cost of the U.S. model, the Rochester firm purchases the Korean phones. It then resells them for $45 apiece.

How do exchange rates affect you? They help determine the price you pay for imported goods and services. Lower exchange rates mean that you will be able to buy more foreign-made goods at lower prices.

Exporting and importing firms follow exchange rates closely because these rates have a direct effect on the firms' *competitiveness* (ability to compete with others).

Is the dollar's exchange rate the same as its value (purchasing power)?

"How am I supposed to know the value of a dollar when it changes every day?"

By Lesser. From the Wall Street Journal. *By permission, Cartoon Features Syndicate.*

In the early 1980s, the value of the dollar rose to very high levels. Indeed, the dollar became so costly in terms of foreign currencies that many U.S. firms that had relied on overseas sales fell on hard times. Sales of U.S. goods abroad declined. Many U.S. factories shut down, and thousands of workers lost their jobs. Farmers too were hard hit by the rising value of the dollar because U.S. farm products became more costly to foreigners during those years. As sales of corn, wheat, and other farm products fell, many U.S. farmers were forced into bankruptcy.

These difficulties prompted the Federal Reserve System and the Treasury Department to take steps to bring down the dollar's exchange rate. In 1985, the exchange rate of the dollar began to fall. This decline made U.S. goods and farm products less costly to foreigners. As a result, U.S. exports, which had been declining, have increased substantially since the late 1980s.

We have seen that changes in the exchange rate can have a harmful effect on businesses and living standards. For that reason, the Federal Reserve System will sometimes step in to support the value of the dollar. The Fed does this by buying or selling dollars in the foreign exchange market.

For example, if the value of the dollar in terms of Swiss francs is too high, the Fed will buy up these francs. These purchases will decrease the supply of francs while increasing the supply of dollars. As a result of these actions, the price of the dollar in terms of francs will decrease, while the price of francs in terms of dollars will increase.

In following the changes in the value of the dollar, economists often look to an accounting summary of the nation's business transactions with the rest of the world. This summary is known as the balance of payments.

Understanding Economics

THE BALANCE OF PAYMENTS

The U.S. government keeps careful accounts of the nation's business transactions. One such record is called the *balance of payments*. This record is a summary of all of our nation's economic dealings with the rest of the world in one year. The table on page 500 shows the U.S. balance of payments for a recent year.

Whenever an international transaction occurs, it results in the entry of either a payment or a receipt in the balance of payments. Funds that leave the United States are recorded as *payments*. Funds that enter the United States are recorded as *receipts*.

U.S. Balance of Payments, 2004 (in billions of dollars)

Receipts	
Exports of Goods and Services	
Merchandise	$807.6
Military	13.6
Travel and Transportation	130.7
Other services	195.3
Total goods and services	$1,147.2
Income	
Net private investment[1]	$1,016.6
U.S. government receipts from abroad	6.9
Total income	$1,023.5
Total Receipts	$2,170.7

Payments	
Imports of Goods and Services	
Merchandise	$1,473.1
Military expenditures abroad	28.2
Travel and Transportation	142.2
Other services	120.8
Total goods and services	$1,764.3
Income and Investment	
Foreign investment in U.S.	$237.6
U.S. government expenditures abroad	116.8
Other	52.0
Total Income and Investment	$406.4
Total Payments	$2,170.7

[1]*Difference between U.S.-owned assets abroad and foreign-owned assets in the United States.*

Here are some examples of business transactions recorded in the balance of payments:

- A U.S. importer buys woolen sweaters in Great Britain. The transaction is recorded as a payment in our balance of payments.
- A Colombian importer buys U.S. automobiles to sell in Colombia. The payment is recorded as a receipt in our balance of payments.

- An American tourist spends $1,000 while visiting relatives in Ireland. Since this represents money leaving the United States, it is recorded as a payment in the balance of payments.
- Two Israelis fly to the United States on a U.S. airline. The money they spend for airline tickets will be recorded as a payment in our balance of payments. So too will the expenses they incur while visiting this country.

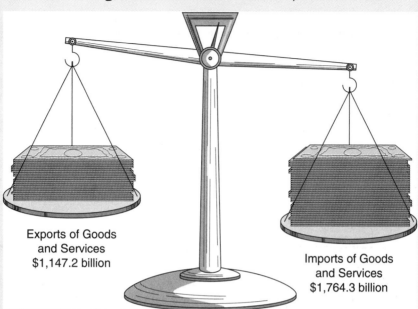

Figure 33.1 U.S. Balance of Trade, 2004

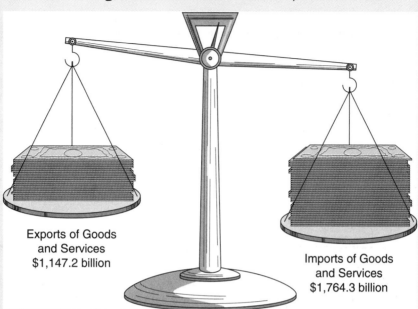

Exports of Goods
and Services
$1,147.2 billion

Imports of Goods
and Services
$1,764.3 billion

Twenty-four hours a day, seven days a week, 52 weeks of the year, payments enter and leave the country. These payments are recorded and totaled at the end of the year and make up our balance of payments.

Once all payments for the year are totaled, one of three things will be noted: (1) payments are exactly equal to receipts; (2) receipts are greater than payments abroad, thereby leaving a surplus; or (3) payments are greater than receipts from abroad, thereby leaving a deficit in our balance of payments.

As we discussed in Chapter 32, the difference between the exports and imports of goods and services is known as the balance of trade. Economists and others follow the balance of trade because of its possible effect on the value of the dollar and the level of prices.

Other things being equal, when imports of goods and services are greater than exports, the value of the dollar (in terms of foreign currencies) is likely to fall. It falls because the supply of dollars in foreign hands has increased. As the value of the dollar falls, the cost of imports will increase. Eventually, the price of goods produced at home will also increase, and, as you will recall, rising prices often signal the arrival of inflation.

On the other hand, when exports are greater than imports, the value of the dollar abroad will increase. The dollar will increase in terms of foreign currencies because of the decrease in the supply of dollars. This, in turn, will make U.S. goods more expensive to foreigners, and exports will fall. The loss of exports can be quite costly to those U.S. industries that rely heavily on overseas sales.

What to do about imbalances in exports and imports is a problem requiring the attention of economists and other specialists trained in the complexities of foreign trade.

━━━━━━━━━━━━━━━━━━ **SUMMARY** ━━━━━━━━━━━━━━━━━━

The rate of exchange is the price at which one nation's currency can be bought using another currency. Foreign currency (or foreign exchange) is bought and sold by banks and firms that specialize in the business.

At one time, nations took steps to see to it that the exchange rates of their currencies remained more or less fixed. Nowadays, most countries, including the United States, rely on floating exchange rates. These rates are determined by the forces of supply and demand.

Exchange rates affect the price we pay for imported goods and whether foreigners buy our goods. When the dollar becomes costlier in terms of other currencies, U.S. exporters find it more difficult to sell their products. When the price of the dollar falls, U.S. goods are easier to export.

━━━━━━━━━━━━━━━━━━ **LOOKING AHEAD** ━━━━━━━━━━━━━━━━━━

Three-quarters of the world's population live in developing countries. These are the poorest nations where life is often a battle against hardship, hunger, and disease. Most (but not all) of the world's developing nations are in Africa, Asia, and Latin America. What is a developing nation? Why is not every nation as developed as the United States, Canada, Japan, and Europe? You will read about these matters in the next chapter.

━━━━━━━━━━━━━━━━━━ **EXERCISES** ━━━━━━━━━━━━━━━━━━

✔ **Multiple Choice** Choose the letter of the item that best completes the statement or answers the question.

1. The rate of exchange (a) compares the exports and imports of countries (b) is the same thing as the balance of payments (c) refers to the relative value of the moneys of different nations (d) describes the speed with which imports and exports move from one place to the next.

2. The balance of payments is (a) like a budget in that it represents a plan for spending (b) a record of the nation's transactions in international trade (c) the device used to calculate the rate of exchange (d) the amount of money the United States owes to foreign countries at a particular time.

3. In the mythical kingdom of Erehwon, the basic unit of money is the rudolf. At today's exchange rate, 4 rudolfs are equal to $1. A U.S. tourist in Erehwon wishes to purchase a guidebook to the country.

The price is 6 rudolfs. How much is this in U.S. money? (a) $1.50 (b) $6 (c) $4 (d) $24.

4. Suppose the government of Erehwon wished to increase the sale of its goods abroad. Which of the following measures would be most likely to succeed? (a) Leave the exchange rate alone. (b) Change the exchange rate so that 2 rudolfs equal $1. (c) Change the exchange rate so that 1 rudolf equals $2. (d) Change the exchange rate so that 6 rudolfs equal $1.

5. When the forces of supply and demand make a nation's currency more expensive to foreigners, (a) its exports will increase because its goods will be less expensive to foreigners (b) its imports will increase because foreign goods will be less expensive (c) foreigners will find the cost of travel within the United States to be less expensive than it had been (d) there will be no effect upon imports or exports.

✔ **Matching** Match each term in Column A with its definition in Column B.

Column A	Column B
1. rate of exchange	*a.* the value of a nation's currency as determined by supply and demand
2. balance of payments	*b.* a specific value set on a nation's currency in terms of other currencies
3. floating exchange rate	*c.* the price of foreign currency
4. foreign exchange	*d.* a summary of all of a nation's transactions with the rest of the world in a year
5. fixed exchange rate	*e.* currencies of other countries

✔ *Questions for Thought and Discussion*

1. A U.S. importer of Indian goods orders a shipment of sandals from an exporter in Calcutta, India. The cost of the shipment is 6,000 rupees. After referring to the information contained in the table on page 493, (a) calculate the cost of the shipment in dollars, and (b) explain how the U.S. importer will make payment.

2. Suppose that, in a given year, sales of U.S.-made goods to Japan increase dramatically. Suppose too that, at the same time, purchases by Americans of Japanese-made goods sharply decline. How would these events affect the rate of exchange of the Japanese yen?

3. Irene and Arthur Buckley were planning a vacation in Sweden. One day, Arthur read an article in the local newspaper that described a shift in the rate of exchange of the Swedish krona.

"Look at this," he said to Irene. "The rate of exchange of the Swedish krona fell to 10 cents. Up until yesterday it was 13 cents. That has to have some effect on our trip to Sweden."

"You're right Arthur," replied Irene. "I wonder what that will be."

Explain how the fall in the price of the krona affected Americans who were vacationing in Sweden at the time.

✔ Using the Internet

If you want to use an Internet calculator of exchange rates, try either <<http://www.x-rates.com>> or <<http://www.xe.net/ucc/>>.

CHAPTER *34*
The Developing Nations

Hulga is six years old. She lives in the city of Manila, the Philippines. Hulga, her two sisters, and their mother share a one-room shack built of wood and corrugated steel. Their home has no electricity or running water. A kerosene lamp provides some light. Hulga has only a small bowl of rice for breakfast. There is usually no food for lunch. When she is lucky, Hulga has rice, some vegetables, and red fish paste for dinner.

Benito is ten years old. He lives in Rio de Janeiro, Brazil. Rio is one of the most beautiful cities in the world. But Benito lives in a poor area on the outskirts of the city. His makeshift house is much like the one Hulga lives in. Benito often goes to the fine hotels and beaches in Rio. There he finds the foreign tourists. Benito tries to earn a few coins by running errands for them. But he will also beg for money if they have no work for him.

Hussein is 26 years old. He has a car and a good job in his father's exporting business in the Saudi Arabian city of Riyadh. Each morning Hussein drives to work through the teeming crowds of workers and street vendors. He pays them little attention. Most people have enough to get by on, he tells foreign visitors. "Someday," he says, "things will be better for everyone." In his own lifetime, many of the worst conditions have been eliminated, thanks in part to the huge income his country enjoys from the sale of its oil.

The Philippines, Brazil, and Saudi Arabia are all nations that are *developing* (not yet economically developed or industrialized). They have much in common with one another. Yet each nation is different in its own way. As you read this chapter, you will learn about these similarities and differences. You will also be able to answer the following questions:

- What is a developing nation?
- How do the developing nations differ from one another?
- Why are there so many developing nations?
- How are developing nations attempting to raise their living standards?

WHAT IS A DEVELOPING NATION?

A *developing nation* is a country in the process of industrializing. While some of the world's developing nations have nearly achieved their goals, the poorest of them have a long way to go. These latter are the 48 nations that the United Nations has designated as *least developed countries*. These nations are located in Africa, Asia, Central and South America, the Caribbean, and Oceania. Most are agricultural countries with largely traditional economic systems. Afghanistan, Ethiopia, Haiti, Nepal, and Yemen are among those on the UN's list of least developed nations.

As a group, the least developed nations receive the smallest share of the world's income. Worse yet, in recent decades that share has been falling. In the 1960s, the poorest 20 percent of the world's nations received 5 percent of world income. Now they earn 3.4 percent. Compare this to the wealthiest 20 percent, which earn well over 78 percent of world income.

Americans live in a *developed nation* (one that is industrialized). Canada, Australia, New Zealand, the nations of Europe, Japan, and Israel are also developed nations. Our country's agriculture, manufacturing, and service industries are highly productive. So are similar industries in the other developed nations. Most

A Developing Nation's Economic and Social Problems: The wealthy modern section of Rio de Janeiro, Brazil, in the distance contrasts with the poverty of the neighborhood in the foreground.

of the people in the world's developed nations have better diets, medical care, and education than the people in developing nations.

Spending for public health is much lower in the developing nations than in the developed ones. So too are daily calories consumed by each person. It is not surprising that people in the developed countries can expect to live longer than people in the developing nations.

A literate person can read and write in his or her native language. Developed nations spend far more per person for education than developing ones. As a result, nearly everyone in the developed countries can read and write. But in many least developed nations, the majority do not have basic skills. The more-educated and healthier people of the developed countries can help their countries produce far more goods and services than the developing nations.

HOW DO THE DEVELOPING NATIONS DIFFER FROM ONE ANOTHER?

The developing nations are not all alike, however. They are separate nations. Each has its own strengths and weaknesses. These developing nations differ from one another in many ways: in level of development, living standards, economic and political systems, and cultural and historical background.

Level of Development

Some developing nations have greater *industrialization* (more industries) than others. For example, cars manufactured in Mexico are beginning to compete with cars made in Japan and the United States. Countries such as South Korea, Brazil, and Mexico have experienced greater industrial development than, for example, Bangladesh, Ethiopia, and Honduras.

Living Standards

When the level of a nation's industrial development rises, the nation's output increases, making more goods and services available for everyone. This means that the *living standards* of the people rise. The more industrialized developing nations, such as China and Argentina, also have longer *life expectancy*, higher *literacy rates*, and greater *energy consumption* than the least industrialized ones, such as Ethiopia.

Economic and Political Systems

Some developing nations have socialist economic systems. North Korea is an example. Others have capitalist economic systems similar to that of the United States. Brazil and Argentina are examples. Many of the developing nations, such as Syria, have one-party governments run by powerful military forces. A few, such as Jordan and Saudi Arabia, are monarchies. Many are democracies or are struggling to become democratic.

Cultural and Historical Background

In the developing nations, there are a variety of religions, languages, nationalities, beliefs, and traditions. Think back to the people we described at the beginning of this chapter. Hulga is Catholic and speaks Tagalog. Hulga's family is descended from the Malay people who settled the islands of the South Pacific. Benito,

Understanding Economics

COMPARING LEAST DEVELOPED AND DEVELOPED COUNTRIES

The table below compares six of the more dramatic differences between the world's least developed and developed countries. The results tell us something about the quality of life and other factors in the poorest of the developing nations as compared to the wealthiest, developed nations.

Least Developed and Developed Countries

	Least Developed	Developed
Life Expectancy at Birth (years)	60	78
Infant Mortality Rate (deaths per 1,000 live births)	68	6
Annual Population Growth Rate	1.2%	0.2%
Adult Literacy Rate	60%	99%
GDP Per Capita	$410	$25,730
Agriculture as a percent of GDP per capita	33%	2%

Definitions of the Data Categories

Life expectancy at birth—the average number of years that a newborn infant is expected to live.

Infant mortality rate—deaths per 1,000 live births during the first year of life.

Annual population growth rate—percentage increase of total population from one year to the next.

Adult literacy rate—the percentage of people, 15 and over, able to read and write.

GDP per capita—gross domestic product divided by the population.

Agriculture as a percent of GDP per capita—the share of the gross domestic product produced by crops, livestock, and poultry, divided by the population.

who is also Catholic, speaks Portuguese, and is descended from African slaves and the Indians of South America. Hussein and his family are Muslims who speak Arabic. They are the descendants of the nomadic peoples of the Arabian desert.

WHY ARE THERE SO MANY DEVELOPING NATIONS?

Developing nations usually have few industries, as we have said. Industrialization is the key to whether a nation is developed or not. In the developing nations, industrialization has been delayed or halted for the following reasons: clinging to traditional ways, a lack of capital, rapid population growth, and dependence on developed nations.

Traditional Ways

Traditional societies usually have traditional economies (as discussed in Chapter 2). Industrial development in such societies is delayed because it requires changes. Traditional societies usually resist changes for a number of reasons.

1. Religious Beliefs. Religions may stress the spiritual life and promise rewards in the afterlife. They may place little value on the achievements of the developed world.

2. Fear of New Farming Methods, Crops, or Equipment. Farmers often depend on each crop for their very survival. They fear that if new ways of farming fail, they will have no crops at all.

3. Attitude Toward Work and Family. Some workers are required by custom to spend large amounts of time with their families and relatives. Workers thus may be absent from their jobs for long periods.

4. Opposition of the Wealthy. Wealthy people are a small minority of the total population. As a group, the wealthy are likely to feel that economic conditions are just fine the way they are. And since the wealthy often control their countries' political life, their governments generally oppose any meaningful economic reforms, such as dividing up large farms.

Shortage of Capital

Two of the most important ingredients in economic growth are (1) modern plants and equipment and (2) the know-how to operate them. To the economist, these represent physical capital and human capital.

1. Physical Capital and Its Importance. Physical capital refers to factories, machinery, and equipment necessary to the production of goods and services. Typically, physical capital in the least developed nations is out of date and in short supply. For that reason, ways need to be found to acquire the additional plants and equipment needed to industrialize.

The process of acquiring capital is called "investment." For nations, just as for businesses and individuals, the money needed for investment comes from savings. In order to save, though, a country has to produce more than it consumes. This poses a special problem for developing nations, because they tend to produce so little that there is not much left to save.

What little surplus available in developing countries is often concentrated in the hands of a few wealthy individuals and families. Many of these wealthy people fail to invest their surplus. Instead, some of them send funds abroad for safekeeping or to make investments there. By investing in ventures in industrialized nations, they further deprive their own country of investment capital.

2. *Human Capital and Its Importance.* Modern machinery, computers, and equipment require a labor force capable of using them. The level of skills and experience of a nation's workforce is its *human capital.* But human capital requires an investment of time and money to educate and train the workforce. Here again, the high cost of education and training place developing nations at a disadvantage. Many developing nations lack good schools and training facilities.

Developing countries also have the problem of what has come to be called the *brain drain.* This term refers to the migration of skilled and educated workers to higher-paying jobs in foreign lands. The United Nations reports that 30 percent of the most highly skilled Africans (such as physicians, engineers, and university professors) are leaving their countries to live and work in foreign lands. Much the same is true for the poorer nations of Asia and Latin America. There, professionally trained specialists leave the lands of their births for employment abroad. While some among the highly skilled professionals choose to live elsewhere in search of political freedom, some others do so for economic reasons. Businesses and organizations in industrialized nations pay professionals from the developing nations much more than they can earn at home.

Rapidly Growing Populations

The developing nations' populations are growing rapidly. In many developing nations, farm and factory output cannot keep up with the rapid *population growth.* For example, if 100 baskets of food are produced to feed every 100 people, then everyone gets one basket of food. But if the population increases to 120 while food production remains the same, then there is less than one basket of food for everyone.

Population increases in the developing nations have forced many rural individuals and families to leave their homes. These farming lands can no longer support the larger populations.

People leave and move to the cities, hoping that they can find jobs. But these people do not have the skills to get good-paying jobs. They are forced to live in overcrowded slums on the fringes of the cities. Often there is no electricity. Water supplies may be contaminated. Thus, by moving to the cities, the rural poor often have merely changed the setting of their poverty. They do not add to the nation's output.

Dependence on the Developed Nations

The developing nations often look to the developed nations for capital, technical know-how, and markets for their products. Banks and other private investors have loaned money to, or have invested money in, development projects in the developing nations. But these loans often place a heavy burden of debt on them. And most of the profits earned by investment in a developing nation go to the businesses that made the investment.

The developing nations depend to some degree upon industrial nations for technical know-how. They need plant managers, tech-

Exports of rice provide income for this developing country—Myanmar. Why is it important for a nation to specialize in the production of certain goods?

nicians, scientists, and skilled workers. But only a small percentage of the world's engineers and scientists live in the developing nations. Many of their skilled workers are hired from the developed countries.

The developing nations must export some of their products to other nations in order to pay for imports. When the developed nations are experiencing prosperous times, they buy more from the developing nations. But when the developed nations are not doing well (during a recession, for example), they buy less from them. Fewer sales make it harder for developing nations to earn the income they need to pay expenses and repay debts. In the 1970s, 1980s, and 1990s, many developing nations ran up huge debts to the developed nations.

HOW ARE THE DEVELOPING NATIONS ATTEMPTING TO RAISE THEIR LIVING STANDARDS?

Economic development has more to do with a nation's ability to industrialize than with its geographic location. Industrialization requires planning, effort, and sacrifice. That is, to improve their conditions, the people in the developing nations must be willing to raise farm output, lower birthrates, build capital resources, and attract foreign investments.

Raise Agricultural Output

More than half of the people living in the developing nations are farmers. Yet they produce barely enough to feed themselves. In the United States, by contrast, less than 2 percent of the working population is in agriculture. But this small fraction of the population produces a surplus. (In Chapter 36, you will learn why U.S. farmers are trying to find ways to produce less rather than more.) The developing nations must increase *agricultural output* so that fewer farmers can produce enough to feed the population. People freed from farm work become available to do other productive work that benefits their nation's economy.

The major difference in agriculture between the developing and the developed nations involves the technology used in the developed nations: mechanized farming equipment, better seeds, crop management, insecticides, and fertilizers. But some developing nations are making positive changes. The Ivory Coast, for example, encourages agricultural development and welcomes foreign help and investment. Chinese farmers have been given more opportunities to produce and market their goods freely. Agricultural output has been increasing in many lands.

Farmers who work for themselves on their own lands tend to produce more than farm workers who labor for others. In many of the developing nations, most farm workers and holders of small plots do not own any land. One suggestion for improving farm output, then, is a government program of *land reform*. This means taking or buying lands from wealthy landlords and giving or selling them to these landless peasants.

Slow Down Population Growth

In many poor countries of Asia, Africa, and Central and South America, agricultural gains have been offset by large population increases. Responses to this problem vary. China, for example, has demanded that couples have only one child per family. Some other countries have educational programs that encourage birth control but do not mandate it. Still other countries (and many individuals) oppose efforts to control the size of families.

Steel Mill in Egypt: Small-scale industrialization adds capital resources to a developing country.

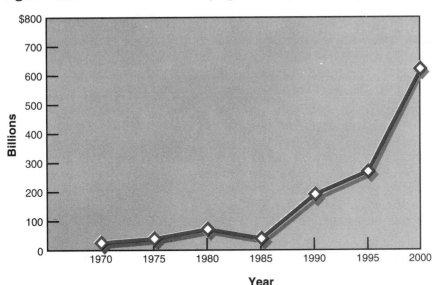

Figure 34.1 Financial Aid to Developing Nations (All Sources) Since 1970

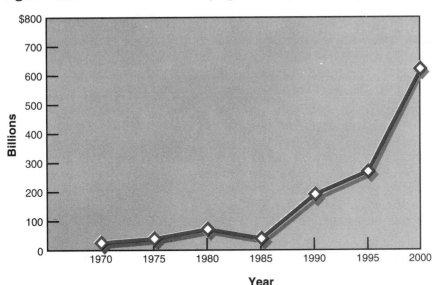

Accumulate Capital Goods and Technical Know-How

Modern production requires factories equipped with modern machinery and tools, computers, and robots. It also requires workers who understand how to use this technology. The developing nations lack enough modern equipment and people who have been trained to use it. To acquire the technology and learn the skills, they often look to outside sources.

Attract Investment and Economic Assistance

The developing nations may try to obtain money for development from private investors and banks in the developed nations, from the governments of the developed countries, and from international organizations. But there are several drawbacks to *foreign investment* and *economic assistance* in the developing nations: fears of foreign economic exploitation, the often poor record of repaying loans, and the lack of solid economic and political leadership.

Because of bad past experiences, developing nations often fear foreign control or domination of their economies. Therefore, some groups may oppose some of the suggestions given on page 517. Further, some developing nations already owe a great deal of money to foreign banks and agencies. These nations have had great difficulty in repaying what they owe. Finally, political instability (uprisings and revolutions) drives away investors who seek secure places for

Problems in Economics

DEBT AND THE LEAST DEVELOPED COUNTRIES

1. Item. In 1996, Uganda spent $3 per person for health care. But in that same year, it spent $17 per person to repay the interest on its foreign debt (the money it owed to banks and other financial institutions in other countries). Meanwhile, one-in-five Ugandan children died before the age of five from diseases that might have been prevented through greater investment in health care.

2. Item. Between 1990 and 1993, Zambia spent $37 million on primary-school education. But over the same period, it spent $1.3 billion (35 times its primary-education budget) in repayment of the nation's debt.

3. Item. In the 1990s, Tanzania spent twice as much repaying its debt as it did on administering its water supply. This happened despite the fact that: (1) more than 14 million Tanzanians lacked access to safe water, and (2) water-borne diseases were the main causes of premature death and disability in Tanzania.

Uganda, Zambia, and Tanzania are 3 of the 48 nations designated as least developed countries by the United Nations. These 48 are the world's poorest countries. Debt problems similar to those plaguing Uganda, Zambia, and Tanzania have troubled all of them. Burdened by huge debts, these countries lack the ability to modernize and raise their people's living standards.

The debt problem had its origins in the 1970s, a decade of global prosperity. Developing nations could borrow abroad at low cost and use the funds to industrialize. Because times were good, borrowing countries could sell their products and use the proceeds to repay their loans. But in 1979, a crisis in the Middle East triggered a sharp increase in oil prices and interest rates, causing a global recession. Unable to sell much of their products because of the recession, developing nations found it difficult, if not impossible, to meet debt payments.

In the fall of 1996, the International Monetary Fund (IMF) and the World Bank introduced a program to relieve the debt crisis. They called the program the Heavily Indebted Poor Countries' (HIPC) Debt Initiative. With funds from the IMF, World Bank, and several wealthy nations, existing loans were to be refinanced. That is, 1970s-era loans would be replaced with new ones at lower interest rates and longer repayment times. By 2004, it was evident that despite the billions spent over the preceding 10 years, much remained to be done to help the poor, heavily indebted countries. This was especially true in Sub-Saharan Africa, where life for many teetered on the brink of disaster (see table on page 517). Things were so bad that the *Group of Eight* (or *G8*) announced that their 2005 meeting would make the plight of the poor African nations their top priority. The G8 includes many of the world's wealthiest and most powerful nations: United States, France, Italy, Germany, United Kingdom, Russia, Canada, and Japan. The leaders of the G8 countries meet annually to discuss global problems.

As a result of the G8 meeting, it was agreed to cancel most of the debts owed by the heavily indebted poor countries. In addition, the participating nations promised to increase dollar aid to the African countries by $50 billion by 2010.

Critics of the G8 Summit said the poorest nations of Africa were largely agricultural economies that needed to sell their farm products abroad if they were ever to pay their own way. This was not possible, however, because the G8 and other wealthy nations continued to protect their own farmers from foreign competition by refusing to allow the importation of less expensive African crops.

Whatever approaches are adopted to assisst the HIPC countries, most experts agree that financial help will work only if the governments of those countries reform themselves. In too many instances, they say, loans were wasted on military hardware and/or the enrichment of the country's leaders. In one glaring example, Uganda spent $32 million of its HIPC loan to buy a jet airplane for its President.

Sub-Saharan Africa and the United States, 2004 Comparative Data

	Sub-Saharan Africa	United States
Gross National Income per capita	$500	$32,870
Life expectancy (*years*)	46	77
Fertility rate (*births per woman*)	5	2
Infant deaths (*per 1,000 live births*)	101	7
Deaths under age 5 (*per 1,000 births*)	171	8
Paved roads (*% of total*)	13	60
Adequate toilet facilities (*% urban population*)	55	100

What does the table tell us about life in Sub-Saharan Africa as compared to the United States?

their funds. Keep these limitations in mind as you examine the approaches a developing nation might take to secure financing:

1. allow foreign investors to establish businesses on their soil

2. encourage foreign firms to form partnerships with local firms

3. use earnings from exports to build schools, hospitals, and roads at home

4. accept loans from foreign banks and governments

5. accept grants and technical assistance from international benevolent organizations (such as the United Nations and the Red Cross) and foreign governments

U.S.-Owned Assembly Plant in Mexico: Why do some manufacturers in developed nations turn to developing nations for labor?

6. encourage their citizens to attend foreign schools and return home to use their skills

7. invite technicians and other skilled workers from developed nations to train their people

8. obtain loans from international organizations.

The *International Monetary Fund* (*IMF*) and the *World Bank* are other sources of help for developing countries. Both are UN agencies. The IMF makes loans to solve short-term problems. Before granting a loan, the IMF may insist that a nation seeking economic aid straighten out its economy by raising taxes or reducing expenditures.

The World Bank is the major provider of loans for development purposes. Low-interest loans are granted for periods of from 15 to 20 years. The International Development Association, a World Bank affiliate, can make interest-free loans to the least developed nations for as long as 50 years. Other agencies, such as the Asian Development Bank and the African Development Bank, make loans to nations in a particular region.

SUMMARY

A developing nation is a country that often has few industries or none at all, a low level of agricultural productivity, and low living standards. The world's least developed nations suffer most from these difficulties.

Most of the world's developing nations are located in Africa, Asia, and Central and South America.

Developing nations differ from one another in religion, ethnic background, language, history, and culture. They are also at different levels of economic development. Within each developing nation, vast differences exist among the population.

Many countries have little development because they are held back by traditional values, a lack of capital and technical skills, rapidly increasing populations, and a dependence on aid from the developed nations. In order to develop, these nations must raise their agricultural output, accumulate capital and technical skills, and reduce rapid population growth. Developing nations are getting assistance from foreign firms, investors, banks, and governments. International agencies are also aiding the developing nations.

—— LOOKING AHEAD ——

Our final unit discusses some of the major issues and problems that the United States faces. We begin by examining how the United States tries to balance the need to increase its output and create jobs with the need for a healthy environment.

—— EXERCISES ——

✔ **Matching** Match each term in Column A with its definition in Column B.

Column A	Column B
1. developing nation	*a.* the ability to read and write
2. International Monetary Fund	*b.* a measure of how much industrialization has taken place in a country
3. literacy	*c.* a program of giving farmland to peasants
4. population growth	*d.* a country that continues to do things in the same ways as in the distant past
5. developed nation	
6. level of development	*e.* a measure of the material things as well as the health, education, and life expectancy enjoyed by people in a nation
7. living standards	
8. traditional society	
9. land reform	*f.* an organization that gives loans to developing nations
	g. a country with much industrialization and high living standards
	h. an increase in the number of people
	i. a country with little or no industrialization and low living standards for most of its people

✔**Multiple Choice** Choose the letter of the item that best completes the statement or answers the question.

1. A major problem for a developing nation is most likely to be (a) low output per person (b) high living standards (c) rapid industrialization (d) low birthrate.

2. A developing nation is most likely to have (a) declining population (b) large amounts of capital (c) high farm productivity (d) widespread poverty.

3. When contrasted with a person born in a developed nation, an individual born in a developing nation can be expected to (a) have a better diet (b) live longer (c) have poorer health (d) have greater educational opportunities.

4. Developing nations are often poor because they (a) are located in Africa, Asia, and Central and South America (b) are not yet industrialized (c) constantly try new ways of doing things (d) have small populations.

5. Traditional ways, a lack of capital, and rapid population growth help to explain why (a) some developing nations are wealthy (b) developing nations are all exactly alike (c) industrialization has been delayed in many developing nations (d) no developing nation will ever become a developed one.

6. The brain drain is a problem for developing nations because it (a) deprives them of human capital (b) requires expensive plumbing fixtures (c) lures too many skilled workers into working in developing nations (d) discourages young people in developing nations from entering college.

7. One way that developing nations can get the capital they need is to (a) prohibit foreign investors from doing business in their countries (b) refuse to accept loans from foreign banks (c) turn down loans from foreign governments (d) accept help from foreign investors, banks, and governments.

8. The International Monetary Fund, the World Bank, and the International Development Association are international organizations that (a) keep track of world population growth (b) make loans to developing nations (c) limit loans and investments to nations located in certain regions (d) have refused to help the developing nations.

9. Japan is a developed nation. This fact proves that (a) only nations in Europe and North America can become developed (b) nations in Asia can become developed (c) it is easy for a nation to industrialize (d) the Japanese people are smarter than most other people.

10. Which statement is true? (a) There are more developing than developed nations in the world. (b) A relatively high percentage of the

people in developing nations are employed in manufacturing. (c) The populations in developing nations are growing more slowly than in the developed nations. (d) Per capita GDP is higher in developing nations than in developed ones.

✔ Reading for Further Understanding Read the following selection and then answer the questions that follow.

A Challenge to the Developed Nations

In the past century, many countries in Europe and North America, as well as Japan, have become immensely rich and powerful. But many of the countries in Africa, Asia, and Central and South America have stayed poor and undeveloped. Many of their people suffer from malnutrition and preventable diseases. The output of goods and services in the developed countries is ten times greater than that of the developing nations. In the developed countries, life expectancy is 15 years longer, literacy rates are almost twice as high, and 16 times as much money is spent for education than in the developing countries.

The great differences between the developed and the developing nations are well known to people everywhere. Movies and television, letters from relatives and friends, and travelers returning from abroad have opened up the wonders of the developed world to people in the world's most remote places. The poverty of much of the developing world has been seen firsthand by travelers from developed lands.

The United States and Europe have given gifts of money, food, and technical assistance to developing nations. Huge loans have been made to the developing nations. But the gap between the rich and the poor nations remains. And many developing nations have found that they could not repay the loans they received from the developed nations.

Some of the developing countries are calling for a new international economic order. This would require the developed nations to transfer trillions of dollars to the developing nations. The developing nations also want the industrialized countries to give freely of their advanced technology.

There are humanitarian reasons why those nations that have abundant food, medical supplies, and technical skills should help others that have far less. But there are also practical reasons why they should be helped. Some of these reasons are described below.

A. It is in the best interests of the industrial nations to assist the economic growth of the developing countries. The industrial nations want to sell more of their goods to the developing nations. Improving the economies of the developing nations will increase their buying power, and sales to them will increase.

Increased sales, in turn, will create more jobs for workers in the developed nations where the goods are produced.

B. Despite the remarkable advances made by science and medicine, infectious and chronic disease continues to threaten civilization. While major killers like AIDS, tuberculosis, drug abuse, and malaria are concentrated in the poor and developing nations, they also have taken many lives in developed countries, including the United States. Similarly, diseases like plague and cholera, once thought to have disappeared, have reemerged with deadly results. Here again, it has been the poorest nations of the developing world that have been hardest hit. But disease does not recognize international boundaries. When, a few years ago, the deadly Ebola virus appeared in the African nation of Zaire, it did not take long before emergency measures had to be taken in the United States to stop its spread.

International authorities including the United Nation's World Health Organization agree that poverty and disease go hand in hand. For that reason, the poorest nations suffer the most from deadly epidemics. But given the rapid growth of trade and the ease of travel between countries, it is small wonder that even the wealthiest nations are at risk when deadly illnesses strike even in the most remote lands. If for no other reason than national self-preservation, the wealthy nations need to do what they can to prevent the spread of disease by helping the world's poor to improve their living standards.

1. Should the United States and Western Europe share some of their wealth with the poorer nations? Explain.

2. Should a developed nation, such as the United States or Japan, give economic aid directly to poor nations, or should this aid be channeled through international organizations?

3. Poverty and hunger still exist in the United States. Should the United States wipe out its own problems before trying to help other countries?

4. Some developing countries have been sympathetic to terrorist organizations like the one that attacked the World Trade Center. Should the United States provide economic assistance to those countries?

✔️ *Analyzing a Table*

The next table contrasts the economies of ten countries. Study the data and answer the questions that follow.

Contrasting the Economies of Developing and Developed Nations

Country	(1) Population (millions)	(2) GDP (billions)	(3) GDP per capita	(4) Life Expectancy at birth (years)	(5) % Adults able to read and write	(6) % Urban Population with access to toilet facilities	(7) % Population with access to safe water
Angola	13	$ 3.8	$ 290	47	42.0	34	38
Australia	19	388.3	20,240	79	*	100	100
Burundi	7	0.7	110	42	46.9	60	52
Chad	8	1.5	200	48	41.0	74	27
France	59	1,438.3	24,090	77	*	100	100
Japan	127	4,519.1	35,620	81	*	100	96
Sierra Leone	5	647.0	130	39	32.0	17	28
Sweden	9	240.7	27,140	80	*	100	100
United States	283	9,601.5	34,100	77	*	100	100
Zambia	10	3.0	300	38	77.2	23	64

* = over 99%

1. Using the data contained in the table, identify the nations that would be classified as developing and those that would be classified as developed.

2. (a) Which *one* of countries listed has the greatest GDP per capita? The smallest? (b) What does *GDP per capita* tell us about the state of a nation's economy?

3. The data, contained in seven columns of this table, tells us something about the quality of life in the listed countries. (a) What do columns 4 through 7 tell us about life in France and Sweden as compared to Chad and Zambia? (b) Which column would you say was most important in demonstrating the differences between life in Japan and Sierra Leone? Why?

4. The best explanation for the differences between the *two* groups of nations is: (a) developing nations have lower rates of population growth than developed nations (b) developing nations have no raw materials with which to fuel industrial development (c) developing nations have more difficulty acquiring capital than developed countries (d) people in developing nations do not work as hard as people in developed nations.

✔ Using the Internet

To explore the subject of development further, look at the Websites of the World Bank and the United Nations: <<http://worldbank.org>> and <<http://www.undp.org>>.

Unit 7

TODAY'S ISSUES AND PROBLEMS

Cities and metropolitan areas depend upon their ability to move people and goods quickly.

In this book, you have learned what economics is all about. At the same time, you have learned how economists look at the world, and what tools they use to understand it. In this unit, you will be asked to put your new skills and understandings to use when considering the issues and problems that the United States faces today.

In Chapter 35, you will find out that economic growth is important if the United States is to remain strong, and if all Americans are to share in the nation's prosperity. But you will also learn why this growth is not easy to maintain, and how it affects the environment.

Chapter 36 discusses why the problems of U.S. farmers, who are only a small percentage of our total population, are everybody's problems. You will consider the strange fact that while people in many parts of the world do not have enough to eat, U.S. farmers have been encouraged to grow less food.

In Chapter 37, you will see what makes cities attractive to some people but not to others. You will also learn about the remedies that are being used to solve the problems facing cities today. Then in Chapter 38, you will learn about the causes of poverty and unemployment in the United States and the efforts of governments and private groups to relieve the poor and unemployed and to fight the underlying problems.

Economic Growth and the Environment

🔑 *Key Terms*

real GDP per capita	renewable resource	biodegradation
nonrenewable resource	environment	greenhouse effect
capital formation	pollution	acid rain
	recycling	

Betty and Dave invited six friends over for desert and coffee. Betty and Dave planned to bake a pie. Cutting it into eight equal slices would serve everyone very nicely.

Sally called to ask if she and Tony could join the group. What should Betty and Dave do about cutting the pie? They could cut it into ten slices instead of eight. Each person would then receive a smaller piece of the pie. Betty and Dave could also bake a larger pie. (Of course, they could suggest that Sally and Tony come over at another time.)

The United States and every other nation in the world today face a similar problem. Everyone wants "a slice of the pie"—their share of the goods and services that their nation produces. And these wants are increasing all the time: More people want a slice of the pie. And some people want "a bigger slice of the pie." What makes this problem difficult to solve is that many nations lack enough resources to "bake" a larger pie. (See Figure 35.1, on page 527.)

The world situation is even more critical. There are over a billion poor people in the world today. Their numbers are growing. It is estimated that it will cost about $100 billion a year for ten years just to provide the minimum level of nutrition, water, shelter, and energy for so many people. No doubt, we need to bake a bigger pie. That is, we need to provide more of the things that people want and need. Economists describe the process of producing an increasing supply of goods and services as economic growth.

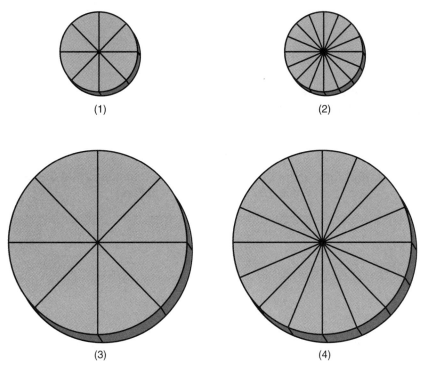

As you read this chapter, you will find out what changes are needed to increase the size of the pie. You will also learn the answers to these questions:

- What is economic growth?
- Why is economic growth important?
- What ingredients are needed for economic growth?
- Why does economic growth cause problems involving energy and the environment?

WHAT IS ECONOMIC GROWTH?

Economic growth for a nation means that it produces more goods and services each year than it did the year before. Think of Betty and Dave's pie as the nation's gross domestic product

Figure 35.1 Economic Growth, Population Growth, and GDPs

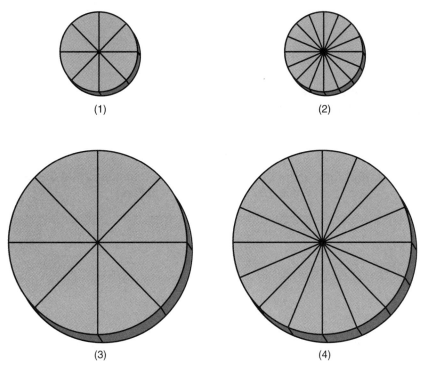

Each wedge or slice of the pie represents the portion of total goods and services (GDP) available to each person in an economy. If the GDP remains the same while the population increases (2), less will be available per capita (person) than before (1). But, when there is economic growth, the pie gets larger (3 and 4). More becomes available for each person (3). This is true even if the population increases (4).

(GDP—its output of goods and services). Then baking a larger pie represents economic growth. To give each of ten people the same quantity that each of eight people had previously been served represents economic growth of 25 percent.

The GDP of the United States is measured in dollars. In 2004, the U.S. GDP was $11,472.6 billion ($11.5 trillion). In 2005, GDP was $12,191.7 billion ($12.2 trillion). The dollar increase in GDP in one year was $719.1 billion. But how much did the *actual* (real) output of goods and services increase? To answer that question, we must know real GDP.

Real Gross Domestic Product (GDP)

Real GDP measures output in dollars that have been adjusted for price changes caused by inflation. The real GDP of the United States increased by $391.3 billion between 2004 and 2005. (See Figure 35.2, below.) Thus, economic growth did take place. Real GDP is measured in 2000 dollars.

Real GDP per Capita (Person)

The real GDP divided by the total population of the United States gives us the *real GDP per capita* (person). Real GDP per capita is a better measure of economic growth than other statistics (such as GDP or real GDP). An increase in real GDP per capita means that there is a bigger slice of the economic pie available for each person because the output per person has increased.

Figure 35.2 Real Gross Domestic Product, in Constant 2000 Dollars, Since 1975 (in trillions of dollars)

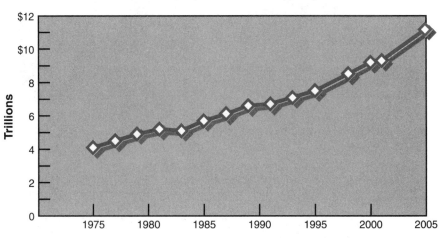

Real Gross Domestic Product per Capita Since 1990
(in 2000 Dollars)

Year	Real GDP
1990	$28,429
1993	28,940
1996	30,128
1999	33,904
2002	34,981
2005	37,590

WHY IS ECONOMIC GROWTH IMPORTANT?

Economic growth is a sign that a nation's economy is doing well. When growth is taking place, more jobs will be created, living standards will be improved, and the nation's strength will be maintained.

Creates Jobs

Economic growth puts more people to work to produce more goods and services. But if our nation's output declines, or grows slowly as the population continues to grow, fewer workers will be needed. The result will be rising unemployment.

Raises Living Standards

With more of everything to go around, each person may receive more, and *living standards* will rise. A larger portion of the nation's increased output can then be set aside to help the needy. During periods of economic growth, more money is available for hospitals, schools, roads, and sanitation systems. If there is a decline in economic growth, less money is available. Those who will be hurt most severely are those who need the most help.

Maintains National Strength

The wealth and power of the United States depend upon the country's ability to produce goods and services. A growing economy is essential to maintain and increase current levels of employment and living standards *and* to provide a surplus used to pay for a variety of programs. The United States maintains a costly defense system and spends additional billions of dollars on research. It also gives other nations both economic and military assistance. The United States could not continue spending so much *and* meeting the needs of its citizens if economic growth were to slow or halt.

WHAT INGREDIENTS ARE NEEDED FOR ECONOMIC GROWTH?

Output per person must increase if a country is to have economic growth. The following ingredients are essential to increase the output: greater productivity, more natural resources, more savings and investment, and greater demand.

Greater Productivity

As you have learned, productivity measures the efficiency of workers and places of work. For example, consider the question, how can more cars be produced? More workers could be hired. Or the same number of workers could use better equipment and techniques. The more productive method is the one that results in producing more automobiles at the lowest cost per worker. Increased productivity depends upon the tools and equipment we have to work with; the education, skills, and experience of workers and managers; and the effort we put into our work.

More Natural Resources

We need to obtain greater quantities of important natural resources (such as oil, coal, minerals, and fiber) if we are to produce more goods and services. But all natural resources are scarce, or in limited supply, to some degree or other. Some natural resources, once used, cannot be replaced. They are *nonrenewable resources*. Coal, oil, and natural gas are resources of this type. So, too, are mineral resources such as iron and bauxite (from which aluminum is produced). In many instances, too, these resources are available mostly from foreign sources. (See the table.) Other resources—such as fish, animal, and plant products—can be carefully managed and, in many cases, their supply increased over time. These are *renewable resources*.

Selected Mineral Resources Produced Mostly From Foreign Sources

Commodity	Principal Sources
arsenic	China, Chile, Mexico
bauxite	Australia, Jamaica, Guinea
columbium	Brazil, Canada, Germany
graphite	Canada, Mexico, Chile, Madagascar
manganese	South Africa, Gabon, Australia
mica	India, Belgium, Brazil
strontium	Mexico, Germany
thallium	Belgium, Canada, Mexico
thorium	France

More Savings and Investment

U.S. workers are efficient because they are healthy, educated, and highly skilled. But new, more efficient machinery and technological advances are needed if U.S. workers are to produce more with the same amount of work. Today, the average U.S. worker produces *less* than workers in Japan and several other countries. U.S. businesses must invest in new technology and more efficient machinery.

Business investment in new equipment is called *capital formation*. It is promoted when consumers set more of their income aside as savings. When people choose to save rather than spend, the funds they set aside in things like savings accounts and insurance policies add to bank and insurance company reserves. As their reserves increase, banks and insurance companies have more money available for loans to businesses and industries.

Greater Demand

Suppose Americans increase their output of goods and services—what then? Someone must purchase that output. Much of this output will be consumed in the United States. The rest, we hope, will be exported to other nations. When more U.S. goods and services are consumed at home and abroad, employment and factory production increase in the United States. Economic growth, in turn, increases.

WHY DOES ECONOMIC GROWTH CAUSE PROBLEMS INVOLVING ENERGY AND THE ENVIRONMENT?

Some individuals and groups warn Americans to slow down on growth. They fear that rapid economic growth may exhaust the world's natural resources and destroy the *environment*—the air, soil, and water that we depend upon for life. Other concerned persons are convinced that economic growth will not endanger the environment. Let us consider each point of view.

Economic Growth: Harmful Environmental Effects

Those who oppose unrestricted growth make two predictions. (1) Americans will use up many of the world's natural resources in generating an ever-increasing output. (2) At the same time, Americans will add to the pollution of the air, soil, and water.

1. Dwindling Supplies of Safe Energy. Increased output demands an increase in energy to heat and cool homes; to operate machinery, vehicles, and factories; and to produce electricity.

Current major energy sources—oil, coal, and natural gas—are limited and nonrenewable. New energy sources have not been found that are cheap, safe, and abundant. Production of nuclear power, for example, is relatively clean. But there are no guarantees against damage to the environment from disposing of nuclear waste or from experiencing a nuclear reactor accident.

2. Increased Pollution From Growth. Economic growth causes *pollution* of the environment. Homes, office buildings, factories, and motor vehicles emit exhaust fumes that poison the air. Organic wastes from homes, office buildings, and factories foul the water supply. Some businesses and government units have disposed of supplies of *toxic* (deadly) chemicals without regard to the damage they can do to soil and water.

Economic growth, it is claimed, sacrifices the heritage of future generations to meet the selfish and shortsighted interests of the present generation. There cannot be a better life—or any life—if we exhaust natural resources and destroy the environment.

Economic Growth: No Lasting Danger to the Environment

Those in favor of continued growth argue that there can be no progress without economic growth. Moreover, they claim that

© The New Yorker Collection 1989 Richter from cartoonbank.com.

"They have very strict anti-pollution laws in this state."

Should every state in the nation have the same antipollution laws?

Coal-Burning Power Plant: Using cheap, abundant fuel, this plant produces power at low cost, but creates much air pollution. Scientists are seeking low-cost, efficient ways of trapping pollutants before they escape into the atmosphere.

(1) the prospect of depleted natural resources has been over-stressed, and (2) the problems of waste disposal and pollution are being, or can be, corrected.

1. No Problem With Resources. To restrict progress and growth is of great danger to present and future generations. There is no danger that people will use up the world's resources. Synthetics are replacing metals, fibers, and oil. Trees, fish, and wildlife are renewable. "Prophets of doom" have exaggerated this danger in the past and have been proved wrong.

We will not run out of energy. Should the demand for energy outrun the supply, the supply can be increased or the demand decreased. Supply is increased by developing new energy sources: nuclear, solar, wind, and geothermal. Moreover, the demand for energy can be reduced through conservation measures such as turning out lights and lowering thermostats in winter. Demand can be reduced still further by making energy users such as automobiles, air conditioners, and refrigerators more efficient.

2. Problems of Waste Disposal Exaggerated. Technology is available, and is being developed, for removing toxic wastes such as incinerator and fuel plant emissions, containing chemicals from

Solar Collectors: Sunlight is converted into electricity at installations such as this one. While pollution-free, solar collectors are now relatively expensive to build and operate compared to conventional power-generating plants.

manufacturing processes, and reducing air pollution from factory and auto exhaust smoke. Organic waste disposal is safe and can be a source of fuel and resource recovery.

One way to reduce wastes is to reuse them. *Recycling* takes wastes such as used paper, glass, and metal and turns them into products that can be used again. Communities throughout the United States today require households and businesses to separate newspapers, glass bottles, metal cans, batteries, and plastic containers from the rest of their garbage. Instead of being used for landfill, or simply dumped or burned (which creates toxic fumes), these materials are processed so that they can be used again.

The biological and chemical sciences are providing other methods of reducing toxic wastes. Microbes are added to certain organic wastes at many sites across the nation. These specially selected microbes "eat" (break down) organic compounds and destroy the toxic substances. This process is called *biodegradation*. Someday, microbes may be able to break down inorganic compounds such as oils and tars and render them nontoxic. At this time, scientists are also using certain chemical compounds to render other chemicals harmless.

Problems in Economics

THE EFFECTS OF POLLUTION

Until fairly recently, Americans looked at the thick black smoke rising from the smokestacks of factories all across the United States as a sign of a healthy economy. The smoke meant that steel and automobiles were being produced and that workers had jobs. But now we know that thick black smoke also means pollution. We know, too, that smoke from factories is not the only pollutant. The exhaust fumes from trucks, automobiles, and planes and the smoke from millions of residential and office buildings across the United States add to air pollution.

The carbon dioxide and other gases produced by motor vehicles, power plants, and factories create many problems. It can cause dizziness and nausea. Worse still, the level of this gas in the earth's atmosphere has risen rapidly in recent decades. Scientists now fear that we are in the midst of a global warming trend. The carbon dioxide in the earth's atmosphere absorbs and holds the sun's heat and raises the earth's temperature. Scientists call this trapping of solar heat the *greenhouse effect*. Average global temperatures, it is feared, may increase by as much as 4 degrees Fahrenheit by the year 2090. Temperatures will rise still faster in the polar regions, causing the polar ice caps to melt. This will lead to rising sea levels, which can endanger the world's coastal regions and small, low-lying islands.

Acid rain is caused primarily by the emissions from motor vehicles and coal-burning factories and power plants. (See Figure 35.3, page 536.) Sulfur oxides and nitrogen oxides combine in the air with water vapor to produce acids. These chemicals combine with moisture in the atmosphere to produce rain (or snow or fog) that is highly acidic. Acid rain pollutes lakes and kills forests. It has caused billions of dollars of environmental damage, mostly in the northeastern United States, southeastern Canada, and Europe. More importantly, acid rain is a menace to public health. The American Lung Association has linked air and ground pollution caused by acid rain to respiratory problems such as asthma and emphysema.

The Clean Air Act of 1990 was enacted to improve the nation's air quality. Among other things, the legislation enabled the Environmental Protection Agency (EPA) to establish an Acid Rain Program. Its goal is to reduce emissions of sulfates and nitrates by 2010 to half of what it had been in 1980. Accordingly, the EPA has set emission limits for individual power plants nationwide.

Homes and factories are also responsible for the pollution of soil and water. Chemicals and organic wastes are the two major water pollutants. Chemicals from insecticides used in farming seep into the soil. Acid residues, dyes, and other chemical residues come from factories. Industrial pollution has killed millions of fish in many U.S. rivers, lakes, and streams. Mercury deposits in fish have caused warnings to be issued about the kinds and quantities of fish that consumers should eat.

Organic waste is caused largely by human sewage. Untreated organic waste is often dumped into the nearest body of water. As it decays, organic waste removes oxygen from the water. This suffocates fish.

Toxic wastes pollute the soil and water supplies. In the past, many factories dumped barrels of toxic chemicals into landfill areas. (See Figure 35.3.) Over

Figure 35.3 Sources of Pollution

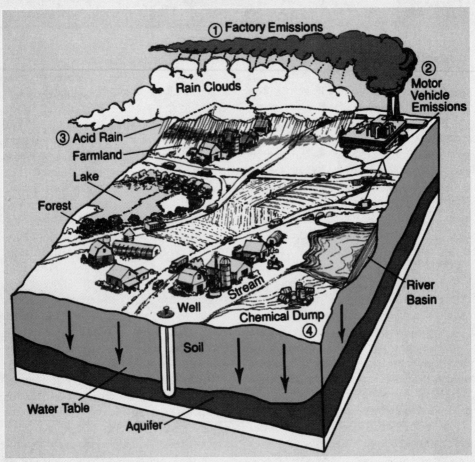

Sulfur and nitrogen oxides in factory (1) and motor vehicle (2) emissions combine with water vapor in clouds to form acid rain. (3) Farms, lakes, and forests are damaged by acid rain. Runoff from chemical dumps (4) pollutes streams and rivers, seeps into wells, and threatens underground water.

time, the chemicals leaked out and soaked into the soil and the water table. In the Love Canal area in New York State, homes were built unknowingly over one such dump site. Many residents later became ill. Most residents moved away after the dangers became known.

In 1970, over 15,000 waste sites were identified as posing hazards to human health. In 1980, Congress set up the Superfund Program to clean up these sites. The program is administered by the U.S. Environmental Protection Agency (EPA). Superfund locates, investigates, and cleans up hazardous waste sites throughout the United States. In 2001, the EPA identified some 1,226 remaining sites for clean-up. The cost of clean-up is to be paid by the people or companies responsible for contaminating the site. If those responsible cannot be identified or found, the cost will be borne by a special fund.

Questions for Thought

1. The cost of installing antipollution devices in cars and factories and meeting environmental standards is quite high. U.S. business firms already find it hard to compete with foreign companies that do not operate under strict environmental standards. For example, devices to curb auto pollution increase the price of new cars and reduce gas mileage. Are the added costs worth the probable health and environmental benefits?

2. If manufacturing companies are asked to pay the costs of controlling pollution, they will try to pass the costs on to consumers. The companies may be forced out of business if costs cannot be passed along, thus putting Americans out of work. Government may have to pay for pollution control. But, some people ask, why should American taxpayers have to pay for the environmental damage caused by private enterprise? Who should pay the costs of controlling pollution?

3. The accident at a nuclear power plant in Chernobyl, Ukraine, in 1985 directly killed 31 people and released nuclear radiation over thousands of miles. Over 100,000 people had to be evacuated from their homes because of radioactive fallout from this disaster. In 1999, a much smaller accident at a nuclear fuel processing plant in Tokaimura, Japan, killed two workers and placed over 6,000 residents of the locality in danger. It remains to be seen if there will be any long-term consequences of this event. Are the benefits of nuclear energy worth the risks? Nuclear power plants that generate electricity do not pollute the air except in an accident. An affordable alternative is to burn coal—but that, we know, causes acid rain. Can modern technology ensure that nuclear wastes, carried in trucks to special storage sites, will not be involved in a highway accident or hijacked? Can safe sites for these wastes be found? Will they be safer than the chemical dump sites? Can reactors be made foolproof so as to avoid the consequences of a nuclear accident such as those that befell Chernobyl?

Chemical Waste Dump Site: Who should pay the cost of cleaning up waste dumps such as this one if the polluters are no longer in business or do not have the funds to do so?

Problems in Economics

WILDLIFE AND THE SEARCH FOR OIL IN ALASKA

Scientists have known for many years that major oil and natural gas fields exist in northern Alaska. A hotly debated question has been whether the vast wilderness area known as the Arctic National Wildlife Refuge should be explored and developed in order to make these natural resources available to us now. Arguments in favor of such exploration point out that oil and gas are needed for the nation's continued economic growth. In addition, supporters claim, development is necessary so that the United States will be less dependent on foreign oil producers. At any time, foreign producers may raise prices or curtail supplies to suit their economic or political needs, regardless of how these actions affect the U.S. economy.

Conservationists claim, however, that building roads; drilling oil wells, and installing pipelines would damage the delicate balance of nature in the wildlife refuge. They argue that this Alaskan refuge is unique, containing plant and animal species not common elsewhere. Building roads, towns, and industries would destroy, for example, the habitat of vast herds of caribou and other creatures that live there, causing these animals to die off.

Instead of using up the nation's natural resources, the conservationists continue, why not reduce the reliance of Americans on oil? Why not build more fuel-efficient automobiles, further insulate our homes and use solar energy collecting devices and other alternate-energy sources? Since other major industrial nations have already cut back on their consumption of oil, we could do so also.

The people who favor development in Alaska claim that extracting oil and gas from the region will not do much harm to the wildlife or the land. Experience with oil and gas drilling in other areas has shown how to balance industrial needs with those of the environment. While few argue against the need to protect the environment, the question is at what cost. Over-protective regulations will hold back economic growth and progress.

In September 2001, while the nation was suffering through its first economic recession in ten years, the World Trade Center was destroyed by a terrorist attack. Both events sparked a renewal of the debate over what to do about the Arctic National Wildlife Refuge. Led by President George W. Bush, those favoring immediate drilling for oil argued that (1) Alaskan oil was needed for national defense, and (2) development would provide a needed economic stimulus and restore the economy.

At present, the United States relies on imports for more than half the oil that it consumes, and reliance on foreign oil is growing. Drilling in the wildlife refuge could increase domestic production by as much as 25 percent, supporters of drilling claimed.

Those opposed to oil development in the Arctic National Wildlife Refuge continue to argue that it is one of the last remaining unspoiled wildlife treasures. What it called for, they say, is energy conservation, not drilling in the Arctic Wildlife Refuge. For example, simply by increasing motor vehicle fuel efficiency by three miles per gallon, the country would save more oil than could be produced by the Wildlife Refuge, they claim.

What Do You Think?

1. Should we be concerned about protecting wildlife and unspoiled

Polar Bears. In 1973, the United States, Canada, Norway, Denmark, and the Soviet Union agreed by treaty to protect their polar bears. The U.S. Fish and Wildlife Service said that recent proposals to drill for oil in the Arctic National Wildlife Refuge posed a danger to polar bears and, therefore, violated the treaty.

wilderness such as the Arctic National Wildlife Refuge? Explain your answer.

2. Can conservation measures reduce much the need for importing or producing additional oil? Explain.

3. Those favoring drilling for oil in the Arctic National Wildlife Refuge ar-
gued that the project would help to fight a recession and make the country less reliant on foreign oil. Those opposed said that the environmental costs of drilling outweighed its benefits. (a) Explain the position taken by each side. (b) With which side, if either, do you agree? Explain your answer.

SUMMARY

Economic growth is an increase in a nation's gross domestic product (GDP)—its output of goods and services over a given period of time. Real GDP per capita measures output adjusted for price changes and population increases from year to year.

Growth creates jobs and improves living standards. It enables the United States to maintain its position of world leadership. The rate of economic growth—or the lack of it—tells how well the economy is doing.

The ingredients of economic growth include increases in productivity and efficiency, greater use of natural resources, increased investment, and increased demand.

Controversy has arisen over whether increased growth may be harmful or beneficial. One side argues that unchecked growth wastes our resources, pollutes the environment, and will leave a plundered land for future Americans. The other side argues that national strength and the personal well-being of all citizens depend upon growth.

─────────────── **LOOKING AHEAD** ───────────────

Increased output can be either a blessing or a curse. Farmers in the United States produce so much that they are having problems selling their output at decent prices. The problems of the farmer are discussed in the next chapter.

─────────────── **EXERCISES** ───────────────

✔**Matching** Match each term in Column A with its definition in Column B.

Column A
1. economic growth
2. real GDP
3. per capita GDP
4. acid rain
5. environment
6. renewable resources
7. nonrenewable resources
8. greenhouse effect
9. capital formation

Column B
a. precipitation with higher than normal acidity
b. an investment in new equipment
c. natural resources that cannot reproduce or renew themselves
d. an increase in a nation's output in a given period of time
e. natural resources that can reproduce or renew themselves
f. output of goods and services adjusted for price changes from year to year
g. output of a nation for a period of time divided by its population
h. the trapping of the sun's heat by gases in the air
i. the air, soil, and water that life depends upon

✔**Multiple Choice** Choose the letter of the item that best completes the statement or answers the question.

1. Economic growth measures changes in (a) population (b) money supply (c) amount of goods and services produced (d) natural resources available.

2. A decline in economic growth will probably result in (a) an increase in unemployment (b) greater productivity (c) an increase in output (d) an improvement in the standard of living.

3. If real GDP remains the same while population increases, (a) more goods and services will be available for each person (b) employment is likely to increase (c) output will increase (d) fewer goods and services will be available for each person.

4. When a nation's rate of economic growth increases, (a) fewer goods and services are available (b) the nation's economy is doing well

(c) the nation's economy is operating below capacity (d) the nation cannot afford to help other nations.

5. Economic growth requires each of the following, except (a) a reduction in demand for goods and services (b) efficiency of production (c) capital formation (d) the use of natural resources.

6. Which is an argument for limiting economic growth? (a) Jobs come first. (b) Progress should not be held back. (c) We will always find new technologies and new natural resources. (d) Future generations will have to pay the cost of today's growth.

7. Which statement about energy is true? (a) The United States produces all the energy it needs. (b) The consumption of energy by Americans is increasing. (c) The production of energy in the United States is increasing faster than its consumption. (d) The demand for energy cannot be reduced.

8. Those who argue that economic growth should be slowed down claim that (a) growth is using up the world's resources and causing pollution (b) new energy sources from the sun, wind, and water can be harnessed (c) major energy users such as automobiles can be made more efficient (d) wastes from homes and factories can be made harmless and even used for fuel.

✔ What Do You Think?

1. Energy consumption in the United States is increasing. At the same time, the country is producing less oil, a basic energy resource. Is this a problem for Americans? Explain your answer.

2. What can be done to bring a nation's energy consumption and its energy production more in balance?

3. How can the United States decrease its energy consumption?

4. How can the United States increase its energy production?

5. What role can education play in dealing with the problem of energy use and pollution?

✔ Interpreting a Graph

Base your answers to the following questions on your knowledge of economics and on the graph on page 528.

1. How is real gross domestic product measured?

2. In which year did real GDP decline from the previous year indicated?

3. In which year was real GDP highest?

4. What has been the trend in real GDP since the early 1980s?

5. If the nation's real GDP in one year was $7 trillion, and the total population was 270 million people, what was the real GDP per capita?

CHAPTER *36*

Farming in a Time of Change

Farming is the major economic activity of two-thirds of the world's people. But in many nations, farm output is too low to provide people with enough to eat. Untold millions of men, women, and children in many parts of the world go to bed hungry every night.

In the United States, the farm problem is quite different. U.S. farmers produce too much food! Consider the Nelsons, a farm family in the heart of the Midwest's farm belt.

When the Nelsons looked out their back window after the fall harvest, they saw a huge mountain of corn alongside their main barn. There was no room left in their silo to store the corn. The silo was already loaded with 60,000 bushels. The Nelsons knew they should be thinking about buying new equipment, seed, and fertilizer and planting next year's crop. But there was more corn around the country than anyone wanted or knew what to do with. The Nelsons did not know how they would find buyers.

Why should U.S. farmers be in the depths of despair when their lands produce record-level crops? And what happens when floods, hurricanes, drought, tornadoes, or insect infestation wipe out crops over vast farm areas? This chapter discusses these problems. After reading the chapter, you will be able to answer the following questions:

In addition to a large output of goods, what do farmers need in order to prosper?

- What is the miracle of U.S. farm production?
- Why are large crops a problem for U.S. farmers?
- How has the federal government tried to help farmers?

WHAT IS THE MIRACLE OF U.S. FARM PRODUCTION?

In 1850, 65 percent of all Americans who had jobs worked on farms. But today, less than 2 percent of the U.S. labor force works in *agriculture* (farming). Why? Because today's farmer is a model of productivity. One American farmer today produces enough food to feed almost 80 people. Compare this figure with one for 1850. Then, the average American farmer could produce enough for only four people. And we thought U.S. farmers were doing well just before World War II when the average farmer produced enough to feed 12 people. Farming has truly changed. How it has changed since 1950 is shown in Figure 36.1 on the next page.

Technology and Science in Agriculture

The miracle of U.S. farm production is the result of developments in *farm technology*. Compare how a farmer today harvests a crop of cotton and how it was done 50 years ago. In those days, most of the work was done by people picking cotton by hand. Today's farmer uses highly specialized machines and equipment to harvest a cotton crop. The replacement of human labor by machines is called *mechanization*.

Figure 36.1 Changes in U.S. Farming Since 1950

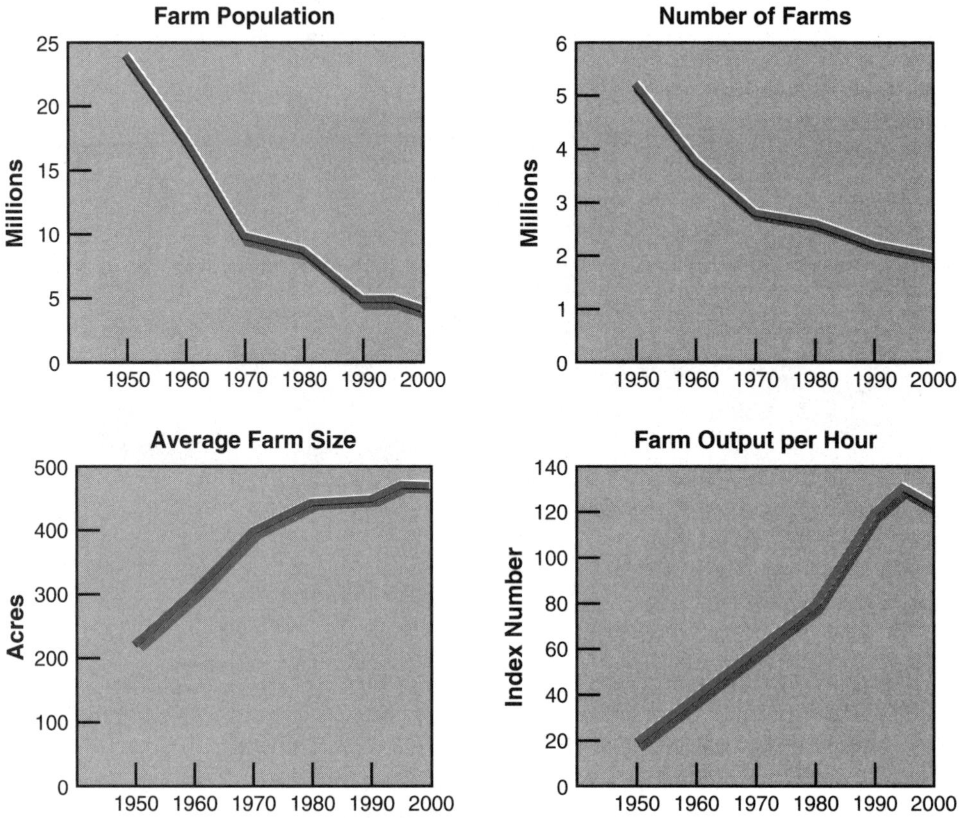

In addition to becoming mechanized, farming has been improved by the application of science to agriculture. Both the quantity and the quality of crop yields are the results of improvements in chemical fertilizers, pesticides, and seeds. Similarly, scientific knowledge has been applied to improving farm livestock. The modern farmer is often a college graduate with a degree in agricultural science or business.

Agribusiness

Although the number of farms in the United States has not changed greatly since 1970, the economic structure of farming has changed considerably. Farming has become big business. Very big business. The traditional *family farm* (of perhaps 200–300 acres worked by a husband and wife and their children) is gradually disappearing. Taking the place of small farms are large, *corporate farms.* Although a family farm can be a corporation too, most people use the term "corporate farm" to describe a big business that does farming. A large corporate farm is very often an *agribusiness* (from the words "agriculture and business"). An agribusiness may control everything from the growing of crops or raising herds to the processing, packaging, storing, and transporting of farm products. These enterprises benefit from the economies of large-scale production.

Several agribusiness corporations in the United States are very, very large. Two such corporations together control 50 percent of all grain exported from the United States; three companies together slaughter almost 80 percent of all the meat slaughtered in the United States; and four such producers control almost 90 percent of the cold cereal market in this country. Less than 2 percent of all farms account for 40 percent of the value of U.S. farm output. Most of the remaining farms earn only 15 percent of their income from farm sales.

Agribusinesses also control the processing, packaging, storing, and transporting of farm products. Farmers receive only 35 cents of every dollar that consumers spend on food.

What benefits do you think Old MacDonald expects to receive from incorporating his farm?

By Ray. From the Wall Street Journal. By Permission of Cartoon Features Syndicate.

"Old MacDonald's Farm will hereafter be known as MacDonald Enterprises Inc. . . . . However, I expect to continue to have a close relationship with each of you."

Large-Scale Wheat Farming: Increasing use of machines means that fewer workers are needed to plant, tend, and harvest crops.

WHY ARE LARGE CROPS A PROBLEM FOR U.S. FARMERS?

Agriculture is a business, and many farmers are struggling to stay in this business. U.S. farmers are caught in a bind between high costs and low incomes, between inelastic demand and inelastic supply, and between declining exports and rising imports.

High Costs

The costs of starting up and operating a farm are high. The initial investment costs include the price of farmland, barns and other storage spaces, buildings, tractors, and other equipment. Seeds, fertilizers, pesticides, and fuel are ongoing costs. Farmers often borrow large sums of money to pay off their initial investments as well as their ongoing costs. If farmers do not earn enough after the sale of their crops, they must either go more deeply into debt or leave farming. Farm debt is about $138 billion.

Low Average Income

Farm income equals the receipts from the sale of crops or livestock minus all the costs. Huge government stockpiles of *farm surplus* (unsold crops) mean that market prices for new crops are low. In the 1980s, surpluses mounted, and the income of the average farmer remained low. While farm surpluses declined in the 1990s, farm income remained low. Most farmers earn money at occupations other than farming, while still considering themselves farmers. In addition to nonfarm income earned, some farmers receive government subsidies, discussed later in this chapter. Although the average yearly net cash income of all farmers amounted to about $73,000, the average yearly net cash income from farming alone amounted to only $16,500. This last sum was below the poverty level in the United States. Keep in mind that this average income is the sum of the incomes of all farmers—farmers doing very well and farmers who lost money farming—divided by the number of farmers.

Why, then, do farmers not produce less? When auto manufacturers see that sales are falling, they lay off some workers and produce fewer cars. They may also cut prices, offer bargain accessory packages, or reduce car loan rates. When the demand for cars increases, auto workers are rehired, production is increased, and prices rise again.

Inelastic Demand and Supply

Farm products are not like cars, however. The demand for farm products is relatively inelastic. This means that a change in price will not have much effect on demand. Would your family buy twice as much bread if bread prices were reduced by half? Probably not.

Unlike the auto manufacturer, the farmer can do very little to increase or decrease the size of herds or crops until the next breeding or growing season. A rise in the price of beef will not increase the size of this year's herds. Conversely, a drop in the price of corn will not reduce the size of this year's corn crop. No one farmer can greatly influence the size of crops or herds in the United States. As a result, the supply of farm products is also inelastic. Supply will not be greatly affected by changes in price.

Because the demand for agricultural products is inelastic, low prices have not resulted in a large increase in demand for these products. And because the supply of farm products is inelastic as well, farmers have not reduced output. The result is surplus, or unsold, crops.

Declining Farm Exports, Rising Food Imports

One way to help reduce U.S. farm surpluses and increase farm income is to sell the surpluses to other countries. U.S. farmers do that. Farm exports amount to 7 percent of all U.S. exports and account for 25 cents of every dollar of U.S. farm income. But their share of the world food market has declined since the 1980s. Moreover, there has been an increase in Americans' consumption of food grown overseas.

Many countries that once were good customers for U.S. products now produce most or all of their own foods. Some even sell their surpluses in competition with U.S. farmers. Farmers in other countries have used new livestock, plants, and technology to increase their output.

The list of foods imported into the United States is long. Included are beef from Australia; pork from Canada; lamb from New Zealand; tomatoes, broccoli, and cauliflower from Mexico; olives from Portugal; apples and grapes from Chile; orange juice from Brazil; and mushrooms from Taiwan.

U.S. farm products are often overpriced in global markets. One reason has to do with the fluctuating value of the U.S. dollar in relation to other currencies. As you read in Chapter 33, when exchange rates are favorable and foreigners can buy more U.S. dollars with their currencies, then U.S. exports tend to rise. But suppose the U.S. dollar is high in comparison with the currencies of countries that compete with us for export sales—such as Canada, Australia, and Argentina. Then it is often cheaper for other nations to buy agricultural products from those competing countries than to import them from the United States.

In many cases, U.S. farm products are deliberately kept out of certain countries. Trade policies in those countries subsidize farmers and restrict imports of U.S. farm goods.

The value of U.S. agricultural exports generally increased through the 1990s, and reached $53.5 billion in 2001. However, the value of imports also increased during this period, from $22.6 billion in 1991 to $34.5 billion in 2001. The major markets for U.S. agricultural products are Canada, Mexico, and Japan. Canada and Mexico are also the leading suppliers of agricultural products to the United States, followed by Indonesia, Brazil, Italy, the Netherlands, and France.

HOW HAS THE FEDERAL GOVERNMENT TRIED TO HELP FARMERS?

The major problems that U.S. agriculture faces are chronic surpluses, low prices for farm products, increasing competition from other countries, and farm debt and failures. The federal government, through a variety of *farm-support programs*, has attempted to help U.S. farmers solve these problems or lighten farmers' burdens. Federal programs are designed to reduce farm surpluses, maintain farm income, encourage exports, and reduce farm bankruptcies. Many programs have had their supporters, but all have been criticized.

Reduce Farm Surpluses

The increasing food surpluses at home and abroad have caused farm income to decline. One federal program, therefore, attempted

Figure 36.2 Production and Exports of Corn, Soybeans, and Wheat, 2005

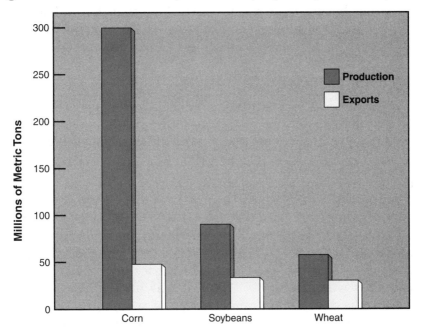

Figure 36.3 Production and Exports of Corn, Soybeans, and Wheat, as Percentages of World Total, 2005

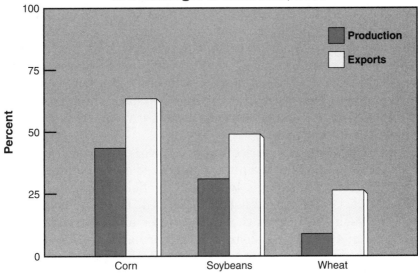

What factors account for the huge volume of U.S. exports of these crops?

to limit production. This effort would, it was hoped, reduce output and surpluses.

Under the program of *production control*, farmers were paid to leave part of their lands idle. But farmers learned how to produce as much or more on their remaining land. With the money they received, they bought more fertilizer. The land that they did not plant was, of course, the poorest land anyway. The result was overplanting on good, fertile soil. Overplanting, in turn, has eroded the soil.

Maintain Farm Income

Production controls aiming to reduce surpluses was one way to keep prices high. Another way was to fix prices at certain levels. Various programs were set up, none of which satisfied everyone.

1. Parity. A *parity price* was one that gave U.S. farmers the same purchasing power from the sale of their crops that U.S. farmers had had from the years 1910 to 1914. Those years were good ones for farmers. Suppose that from 1910 to 1914 wheat sold at 50 cents a bushel. In 1970, the cost of living was five times greater than it was from 1910 to 1914. Farmers asked that a bushel of wheat be sold for five times its 1914 cost. The parity price for a bushel of wheat thus was $2.50 (5 × $.50). At this price, farmers had the same purchasing power from the sale of wheat as U.S. farmers had had from 1910 to 1914. Parity prices were introduced by the government in 1938, and continued to 1973. Parity was replaced by market price supports and target prices.

2. Market Price Supports. To keep up farm income, the government created *market price supports* for the sale of certain agricultural goods. With market price supports, farmers may put any portion of their eligible goods in approved storage places and receive a loan from the government at a specific rate. Later, farmers may repay the loan with interest and get back their goods. Or farmers may, at the end of the loan period, give up their goods as full payment for the loan.

Here is how market price supports work. Assume that the farmer borrows $15,000 and puts in approved storage places 5,000 bushels of corn. This comes to $3 per bushel. Suppose that the market price is $3.50 per bushel. What will the farmer do? The farmer will sell the corn at the market price and receive $17,500. After repaying the $15,000 loan, the farmer has a profit of $2,500. But suppose that the market price is $2.80. What will the farmer do? The farmer gives the 5,000 bushels of corn to the government and does not have to repay the borrowed $15,000. As a result of low prices for farm products, the government has acquired in this way thousands of tons of grain, soybeans, and dairy products.

3. Target Prices. In another program, the government sets minimum or *target prices* that farmers will receive for their products. The target price is below parity and also below the expected market price. If the market price falls below the target price, farmers are paid the difference by the government. What do farmers do if the market price is higher than the target price? Farmers will, of course, sell their crops at the higher market price.

Encourage Farm Exports

Another way to increase the prices paid to farmers is to increase the demand for farm products while reducing farm surpluses. It is hoped that increased demand can be achieved by encouraging more farm exports.

One idea to bolster sagging farm exports is to give government surplus crops to food processors. For example, suppose that the processors (producers) of breakfast cereals were given surplus corn, wheat, and rice. The processors would convert these grains into cereal products. Since the food processors paid nothing for the surplus grains, they could sell the finished products—breakfast cereals—at low prices outside the United States. A second idea is to sell export crops below cost or to give away surplus U.S. crops abroad. A third proposal is to make it easier for foreign purchasers to buy U.S. farm products by granting them easy credit terms.

All of these proposals amount to subsidizing U.S. farmers. Moreover, they depart from the principle of free trade. It is feared that other nations will retaliate by doing the same thing to protect their farmers. In fact, some nations already subsidize their farmers and restrict the entry of U.S. farm products into domestic markets.

Develop New Uses for Farm Products

Petroleum (oil) is essential as a major fuel used for heating homes and offices, powering factories, and running motor vehicles. Burning oil, however, contributes to air pollution. Moreover, the growing demand for oil has made the United States partially dependent for supplies on the Middle East, a highly unstable area of the world. Therefore, the United States has been seeking alternatives to reduce our dependency on petroleum as a fuel. Ethanol fuel is one such hope.

Ethanol is a fuel manufactured from farm products such as sugarcane, corn, and other grains. It is environmentally friendly. Using ethanol as a fuel reduces the emission into the atmosphere of gases that are thought to contribute to global warming. Ethanol, however, is more expensive to produce than gasoline refined from crude oil. Brazil, the world leader in sugar production, has been making ethanol fuel since the mid-1970s, producing close

Problems in Economics

DEBATING FARM BILLS

About every five years, Congress debates and passes a farm bill. Among other provisions, each farm bill passed determines what subsidies which categories of farmers will receive.

The *farm bloc* in Congress—consisting of members of the House and Senate who represent states with a strong agricultural economy—support continuation of subsidies, quotas, and tariffs on imports. Many members of Congress from these states have farms, and they, as farmers, have personally benefited from government farm-support programs. Not every farmer has the same interests, though. The interests of dairy farmers are not the same as those of cotton, soybean, or wheat farmers. A farmer who has a large dairy herd does not like to see the price of the corn or soybean feed increase. Yet farmers of every kind favor the concept of government programs to aid farmers. Their representatives in Congress unite in the fight to continue farm-support programs.

Continuing farm subsidies, quotas, and tariffs will violate world trade agreements such as NAFTA and GATT, which require the United States to end such farm programs. The farm bloc supporters argue that though a competitive market works in theory, in the real world U.S. farmers have to compete with countries that enjoy a comparative advantage. Unlike American farmers, farmers in many developing countries do not have to deal with environmental protection laws or minimum wage laws that increase the cost of farming in the United States.

Some members of Congress have proposed transforming the farm program into a conservation program. Farmers would be paid to let their land return to a more natural state or to farm in more environmentally friendly ways. Some farm groups are in favor of this idea. But opponents say that the real purpose of the proposal is not conservation but a means for farmers to get more money from the government for doing nothing, that is, to be "non-farming farmers."

What should be the government's farm policy? The following arguments may help you decide.

Yes, Continue Government Aid

1. The farm family is important for the stability of U.S. society.

2. The food and fiber that farmers produce are essential to life.

3. All Americans have a stake in the problems facing U.S. farmers. Agriculture and its related industries employ 21 million people, more than any other single sector in the U.S. economy. Widespread farm failures may therefore affect the lives of millions of people who are not farmers.

4. Federal price supports are needed to protect farmers from unstable market prices and natural disasters. Even the most efficient farmers might be forced out of business in a few years because of falling prices, floods, or drought. Price supports have not increased food costs for U.S. consumers. Some economists believe that food prices would actually increase if price supports were to end. This increase would occur if many farmers quit farming or

stopped producing certain goods, thus forcing up their prices.

5. The federal government should allow farmers to defer or extend payments on their loans. This should help the farmers to continue operating their farms. If many farmers gave up farming, food supplies would decrease and consumer prices would rise.

6. Any system that restricts payments and penalizes efficient producers by not granting them subsidies is wrong, say the defenders of the *status quo* (the way things are now). To do so would discourage the kind of modernizing that enabled large producers to operate efficiently, and at a profit. They remind us, too, that it is the output of food and fiber provided by these giant producers that raises everyone's standard of living.

No, Stop Government Aid

1. The small family farm is a thing of the past. Forty percent of all farm sales come from farms whose annual sales run to $500,000 or more. Meanwhile, a handful of wealthy corporations are being enriched by farm subsidies of millions of dollars per farm, per year.

2. Not all farmers are in distress. Many with large farms are doing well. Price supports and acreage reductions should be eliminated. They help only large farmers and have not kept small farmers in business. In fact, 10 percent of U.S. farms getting aid receive 61 percent of all farm subsidies.

3. It is not the farmers who need government assistance—it is the people in rural areas. Some 62 million people, over one-fifth of the population, live in rural areas. Many rural people are in desperate need of better housing, education, health care, and job training.

4. It is unfair to continue giving financial help to farmers. Other small businesses also face debt problems. Furthermore, the federal debt is already much too high. Taxpayers are overburdened.

5. Price supports and loans are responsible for today's problems. Farmers have come to depend upon federal aid rather than to plan intelligently. Government price supports encourage overproduction.

6. Although farm bills were supposed to help the family farm make ends meet, in reality the wealthiest 10 percent of the 1.4 million farms benefiting from the program received 61 percent of the money. This translated to an average payment of $83,000 per year for the wealthiest 1 percent, whereas the poorest 80 percent of recipients received an average benefit of something under $1,200.

to 3.5 billion gallons a year. Blends of ethanol in fuel are sold at a number of service stations in the United States. Because of its cost, though, it is not yet in widespread use in this country. The U.S. government could promote the use of ethanol or ethanol-gasoline blends by exempting such fuels from excise taxes and subsidizing plants producing such fuels to make ethanol competitive with gasoline.

Family Farming: Knowledge of crops and animals is handed down from one generation to another.

SUMMARY

American farmers use mechanization, science, and technology to produce abundant crops with great efficiency. As a result, the number of persons engaged in farming has declined along with the number of farms. Although big corporations own only a small percentage of all U.S. farms, these farms are large business operations.

Very large crops present a problem because more is harvested than can be sold at a profit in domestic and export markets. Changes in price have little effect on the supply of or demand for farm products. This fact, together with foreign competition, makes it difficult to depend upon the free market to reduce farm surpluses.

The U.S. government helps farmers by trying to reduce farm production and maintain farm income. It does this through loans, price supports, and target prices. Farm exports have been encouraged. Low-interest loans have kept many farmers in business.

LOOKING AHEAD

Farmers and rural areas are not alone in having problems. Cities and metropolitan areas also face difficulties. The following chapter discusses some of their major problems.

———————————— **EXERCISES** ————————————

✔**Matching** Match each term in Column A with its definition in Column B.

Column A
1. parity price
2. target price
3. agribusiness
4. mechanization of agriculture
5. production controls
6. farm bloc
7. inelastic supply and demand
8. ethanol

Column B
a. attempts to reduce farm output by paying farmers not to produce or to produce less
b. a minimum price set by government that farmers will get for their crops
c. members of Congress from states where farming is very important
d. the use of machines, such as tractors, in farming
e. a price that gave farmers the same purchasing power from the sale of crops that the farmers had in a selected, earlier period
f. a fuel made from farm products
g. the conditions that exist when output and purchases are not greatly affected by small changes in price
h. a giant corporate farming and distribution company

✔**Multiple Choice** Choose the letter of the item that best completes the statement or answers the question.

1. Farming is a way of life for what percentage of the world's population? (a) 67 percent (b) 33 percent (c) 10 percent (d) 2 percent.

2. The percentage of the U.S. labor force that works in farming is (a) 25 percent (b) 12 percent (c) 5 percent (d) 2 percent.

3. According to the graphs on page 544, between 1950 and 2000 (a) the U.S. farm population declined (b) the number of U.S. farms increased (c) the average size of U.S. farms decreased (d) U.S. farm output stayed the same.

4. Suppose the prices of milk, potatoes, and bread dropped by one-third. What would your family most likely do? (a) buy one-third more of these products (b) buy one-third less of these products (c) buy about the same amount of these products and more of something else (d) substitute potatoes for bread at mealtime.

5. Farmer Smith learns that the markets are oversupplied with potatoes. But Smith has 50 acres planted in potatoes. Smith will *most likely* (a) not be able to do anything about it (b) make a lot of money this year (c) reduce the output of potatoes this season (d) raise the price for a bushel of potatoes.

6. A major purpose of production control programs was to (a) increase farm output (b) reduce farm surpluses (c) lower farm prices (d) improve agricultural efficiency.

7. The federal government buys cotton from farmers and stores it. The main purpose is to (a) maintain the price of cotton (b) lower the price of cotton (c) encourage farmers to produce more cotton (d) keep storage facilities full.

8. The main idea of this chapter is that (a) the problems of farmers in the United States are easily solved (b) farming as a whole is not as productive as most other activities (c) farmers are the only group in the United States that receives federal help (d) the basic farm problem is that output is too high, while income is too low.

✔ *Developing Economic Skills: Understanding Bar Graphs*

Study the graphs of U.S. production and export of corn, soybeans, and wheat on page 549. On a separate sheet of paper, write **T** if a statement is true and **F** if it is false. For false statements, write them so that they are true.

1. U.S. farms led the world in producing and exporting corn.

2. U.S. farmers produced more soybeans than corn.

3. Most of the corn produced in the United States was not exported.

4. The United States produced nearly twice as much corn as soybeans and wheat combined.

5. Almost one-half of the wheat produced in the United States was exported.

6. The United States exported more corn than wheat.

✔ **Reading for Further Understanding** Read the selection below and then answer the questions that follow.

The Farmer and Land, Soil, and Water

Land lost to farming is a serious problem facing the nation. Farmers are selling their lands to real estate developers. Farmlands are giving way to shopping malls, highways, industrial parks, and housing developments. At the current rate of nearly 3 million acres a year, over 100 million acres of farmland will have been converted to nonfarm uses by the year 2030.

Soil erosion is a national concern. Some farmers lose as much as 100 tons of topsoil annually. The reason for this loss is that with improvements in fertilizers, pesticides, seeds, and farm equipment, more can be produced per acre. As yields continue to rise, many farmers see little reason to spend time, effort, or money on combating soil erosion. But once the fertile topsoil is gone, hundreds of years may be needed to replenish it. Efforts are being made, though, to protect and replenish farmlands by allowing land to remain unplanted for several seasons, planting crops that enrich the soil, and by planting trees to enrich the soil and keep the soil from being washed or blown away.

Water usage affects both farmers and nonfarmers. Growing urban areas in the West compete with farms for water. Water is precious in the mountain states of the West. Colorado has built tunnels and dams to divert water from rivers in the mountainous western part of the state to the eastern region, which is the state's major farming area. People in the western part of Colorado have objected to the diversion of this water. And at the rate at which farmers in Kansas and Nebraska are using up their underground water sources to irrigate their crops, the water table there may dry up in less than 30 years.

1. To what uses has former farmland been put?

2. "Some have argued that the conversion of farmland to other uses has been for the better—others have argued that the change has been for the worse." Explain this statement.

3. Why has the problem of soil erosion increased as agricultural technology has improved?

4. Why should both farmers and nonfarmers be concerned about soil erosion?

5. Why do you suppose that the water supply is more of a concern to people in the West than in the South or East?

✔ Using the Internet

For a whole range of topics related to farming and agriculture, check the United States Department of Agriculture (USDA) comprehensive Website at <<http://www.usda.gov>>.

For international trade information, try the World Trade Organization (WTO) Website at <<http://www.wto.org/farm>>.

To find out more about farm subsidies, check the EWG Farm Subsidy Database at: <<http://www.ewg.org>>.

CHAPTER *37*

Cities: Decline and Renewal

Key Terms

city	street crime	urban
central city	slum	redevelopment
urban area	public housing	project
metropolitan area	gentrification	tax deferral
suburb	homelessness	community
inner city	affordable housing	policing
outer city	public service	regional planning
megalopolis	capital	region
tax base	improvement	household
burglary	urban renewal	

The TV newsperson stopped a young couple who were walking down North Main Street. "Hello. Would you answer a question for us on camera? You will? Good. How do you like living in this city?"

The reporter had asked the same question of several other persons, including a person getting into a taxicab. Here are some of the answers that people gave to the reporter's question:

"I hate it. I live here only because I have to. I would rather live in a small town or on a farm."

"I love it. I came to the city from a small town. Life there was dull. This is where the action is."

"It's so dirty. And I'm scared to go out alone at night."

"This city is wonderful, but I would prefer to live in a suburb where homes have lawns."

"It's O.K. It's a place to make a living. But rents are high, the traffic is awful, and cabs cost a fortune."

Perhaps you have heard these or similar comments about city life. With so many people living in cities, it is no wonder that the views about cities differ.

Cities have been around for a long time. You may have read about famous ancient cities in the Bible (Jericho and Jerusalem) or in history books (Athens and Rome). Cities have always had problems: traveling in and around the city; supplying food, water, and other essentials; providing jobs and housing; and just running the city.

In this chapter, you will read about cities and their surrounding areas. You will also learn the answers to the following questions:

- What are cities and metropolitan areas?
- How do cities and suburbs compare?
- What major problems do cities face?
- How can cities "solve" their problems?
- How can regional planning help cities?

WHAT ARE CITIES AND METROPOLITAN AREAS?

In the United States, a *city* or *central city*, as it is sometimes called, is an important town that has been given a charter by the state. This charter is similar to one given to a corporation, which you learned about in Chapter 22. Under its charter, the city governs itself within a given geographic area. Of course, a city is more than just a political and geographic area. Large numbers of people live and work in a city. City living is a way of life. Have you heard some of the many well-known songs and poems written about life in different cities?

The City

A city—also called an *urban area*—is its famous monuments, such as the Arch, the Statue of Liberty, the Golden Gate Bridge, and the Liberty Bell. A city is its entertainment centers, such as Bourbon Street and Broadway, and the crowds at the Rose Bowl or Wrigley Field. A city is shopping at Macy's, Rich's, Neiman-Marcus, or the corner deli. A city is homes, schools, parks, houses of worship, and places where people work. But a city is also vacant lots, traffic jams, and run-down neighborhoods.

Metropolitan Areas—Cities and Their Suburbs

A *metropolitan area* is a central city of 50,000 or more people plus the surrounding areas, or *suburbs*, that have close social or economic ties to that city. In some cases, as in Minneapolis-St. Paul, this involves two cities, or "twin cities." Three out of every four Americans live in metropolitan areas. The suburbs are areas just outside the official limits of the city. Many people prefer the quiet and slower pace of the suburbs to the hustle of the city. During the 1970s and 1980s, growth in metropolitan areas took place mostly in the suburbs. Central cities, with few exceptions, virtually stopped growing.

Sometimes, the oldest, most densely populated section of the central city is called the *inner city*. Most of the features of this central or inner city now also exist in areas outside the city. Many suburbs in fact have become *outer cities*. Suburban residents often do not depend upon the central city. They rarely go there. In the suburbs, they can find work, education, entertainment, and all the other services that at one time were available only in a central city.

Suburban growth sometimes looks like a series of clusters. It is easy for a person who lives in one suburb to work in a second, shop in a third, and visit friends in a fourth. The automobile and long, interconnected highways have linked the suburbs with one another. (See Figure 37.1.)

Figure 37.1 Atlanta Metropolitan Area

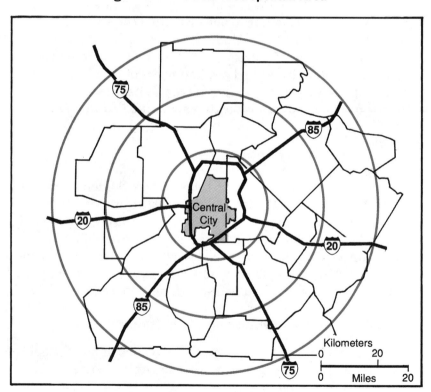

Highways connect a central city and clusters of suburbs. What public means of mass transportation are available in many large cities and metropolitan areas?

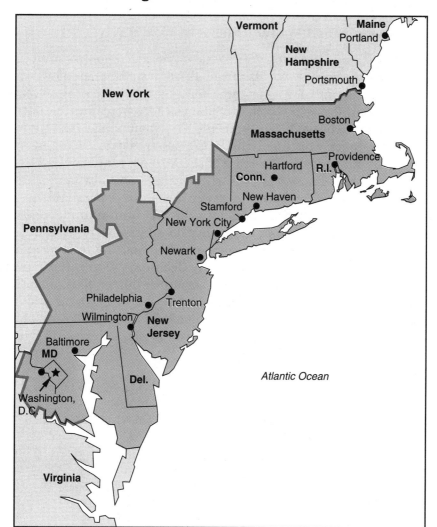

Figure 37.2 Northeast Corridor

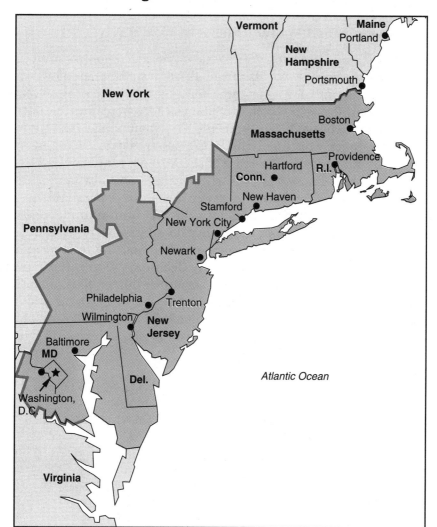

Megalopolis

Many cities and suburbs form a continuous chain of metropolitan areas. This huge chain is called a *megalopolis* ("great city"). One such area stretches up the East Coast from Arlington, Virginia, to Boston, and beyond. This area is called the Northeast Corridor. (See Figure 37.2.) It is a network of 23 interlocking metropolitan areas containing some 38 million people. A second megalopolis includes the Midwestern area from Gary, Indiana, to Milwaukee, Wisconsin. A third, in California, runs down the West Coast from San Francisco to San Diego.

HOW DO CITIES AND SUBURBS COMPARE?

Richer Suburbs and Poorer Cities

The cities and suburbs within the same metropolitan area are virtually two different worlds. They differ in income, employment, housing, and living arrangements. For example, while the poverty rate for the nation as a whole in 2004 was 12.5 percent, that of the central cities averaged 17.5 percent. That same year, the unemployment rate for workers living in the suburbs came to 5 percent, while in the cities nearly 8 percent of the workers could not find jobs.

In a recent year, average hourly earnings nationwide hovered around $16 per hour. But the earnings of the vast majority of central city workers were often only the $5.15 minimum wage or slightly higher. In the past, many city dwellers entered the workforce through jobs in manufacturing industries. Today, the number of those blue-collar jobs is rapidly declining. Often, these jobs have been replaced by low-paying service industry jobs, such as work in fast-food places, or high-paying jobs in banking and finance, advertising, and high-tech firms. The factory work once readily available in the cities has moved to the suburbs, to rural areas, or to foreign countries.

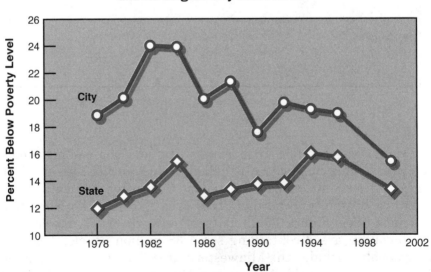

Figure 37.3 Poverty Rates in a Large Eastern State and Its Largest City Since 1978

Why do you think the poverty rate has been higher in the city?

Different Households and Families

A *household* consists of all the people who occupy a house, an apartment, or another type of living unit. A household is not necessarily the same as a family, which is a group of two or more people who are related by blood, marriage, or adoption and who live together. While the number of urban households increased in the 1970s and 1980s, the average number of people in each household has since declined. The average was 3.14 in 1970 and 2.59 in 2000.

Cities now include many elderly people living alone, single professionals without children, middle-class families with few or no children, and poor families with many children. The city child who lives in poverty is likely to have a single parent. The suburban child is more likely to live with both parents. The suburban family probably owns its home. The city family, particularly if it is poor, probably lives in a rental apartment.

Although minorities make up about 30.5 percent of the population of the United States, the minority population in many cities is a much larger percentage than the national one. Minority children represent a majority of all children in many cities.

WHAT MAJOR PROBLEMS DO CITIES FACE?

Many problems trouble U.S. cities today. Cities need great amounts of money to provide fire prevention, public safety, housing, employment assistance, schools, and other public services. In recent years, cities have found it difficult to raise the money they need to pay for all the services that people want.

Cities' Financial Problem: Less Income

The *tax base* of a city refers to all the possible sources of income for that city. As you learned in Chapter 27, the principal sources of a city's tax revenues are property taxes and sales taxes. Some cities also have income taxes. When the income from these sources declines, the tax base erodes (wears away). Then the city is in trouble.

Property taxes are usually based on the values of private homes, apartment buildings, office buildings, stores, factories, and hotels. When factories close and white-collar businesses move out of a city, they are usually not replaced by similar enterprises. This loss means that the city has lost revenues that it cannot recover. Businesses often take some of their better paid employees with them when they move out of a city. As middle-class families leave the city, neighborhoods begin to change. Houses and apartments stand empty, and owners abandon unprofitable buildings. More taxes are lost.

Businesses and families that leave a city no longer pay its taxes on retail sales, meals, and entertainment. As fewer businesspeople and travelers visit the city, tax income drops even more.

How are cities to deal with lower revenues and a reduced tax base? They may take one or more of the following paths.

1. Increase Taxes. Higher property, sales, and income taxes will be opposed by those who are obliged to pay them. Many of these taxpayers—especially businesses and middle-class people—have expressed their opposition to more taxes by voting against them at election time and/or by moving out of the city.

2. Reduce Public Services. Cuts in health, education, housing, and other public services are often favored by groups that oppose tax increases. Groups that contend government is too involved in peoples' lives also favor tax cuts. But these cuts add to the burdens of the poor, the disadvantaged, and the homeless while failing to do anything about their problems.

3. Obtain More Federal and State Funds. The federal government and the state governments are likely to provide additional funds to cities only when their own deficits are shrinking. When federal and state debts increase, programs to aid cities may be frozen or cut back.

4. Attract Businesses and Families Back to the Cities. Few, if any, disagree with this proposed solution. The proposal, however, is complicated by the problem of how to make returning to the city attractive.

Need for Special Services

Many middle-class families have left or are leaving the cities. A good number of the remaining families, or those moving into the cities, are poor, elderly, or both. Many are poor families that have young children. Many are single-parent families, and often, many have multiple problems that require city services. The poor also need more educational and vocational services.

In economic terms, those who are less in need of special city services but who are more capable of paying city taxes are leaving the cities. Those who are more in need of city services but who are less able to pay for them are increasing in number in the cities.

Police departments have gone high-tech. This officer is writing a traffic ticket on a laptop computer.

Now let us examine some of the problems and important needs that cities have.

Public Safety: Fighting Crime

Crime can happen anywhere. But most people who talk about crime in the cities are thinking of *burglaries* (thefts of personal property from people's homes) and *street crimes* (assault, armed robbery). These are crimes against other persons and property, and they are often violent.

Poor areas in cities are often breeding places for burglaries and street crimes. Illegal drugs are responsible for many crimes. Addicts often rob, steal, and murder to support their habit. Some become drug dealers and spread the drug problem into the schools. The police and courts are burdened with cases related to the sale or possession of illegal drugs or to crimes committed by people trying to get money to buy the drugs.

Housing Problems: Slums and Homelessness

There are exclusive areas in cities where apartments and homes are so expensive that only the rich can afford them. There are city areas where those with average incomes live comfortably. But in other city areas, housing exists that is run-down or hardly fit to live in. Areas that have much bad housing are called *slums.* Rats, vermin, litter, garbage, inadequate plumbing and heating, and lack of repairs are common problems in slum housing.

The people who live in slum areas are usually poor. The schools in slum areas have the highest dropout rates and the lowest academic achievement scores. The streets are often unsafe after dark. Rates of crime and drug use are higher than in other parts of the city or in the suburbs. Unemployment is also high in slum areas. Many slum residents receive some form of financial assistance. They need health and hospital services, too, but often do not have private health insurance. Thus, the city and state provide free medical services to the poor.

Slums often develop as middle-class families move to other neighborhoods or the suburbs. The housing units they vacate are filled by the poor. Private builders do not find it profitable to build new housing or to restore older, low-rent properties. Thus, city and state governments have had to find the land on which to build decent housing. But *public* (government-financed) *housing* has its opponents. People in middle-class areas often oppose public housing in their neighborhoods. Much public housing, then, is built in slum areas. The effect is to continue to keep the poor in slum areas.

Urban Street Life: A thriving inner-city neighborhood can provide many goods and services for its residents.

Urban Homeless People: What economic forces can cause homelessness? How are governments and private groups trying to help the homeless?

Many cities have attempted to rebuild older dwellings that are structurally sound. Reconstruction projects often cost less than building new housing. And they keep people in familiar neighborhoods. But much time and effort are required to reverse the trend of decades of neglect. Often, the residents of these areas are asked to contribute their time and effort in the rebuilding of the neighborhoods. Participation makes people feel that they are playing an active role in solving their problems and making their lives better.

Many Americans are homeless. They have no apartment or home to live in. They sleep in the streets, under bridges, in parks, on benches—almost anywhere they can. This problem is discussed further in the feature "Homelessness: A Growing Problem for U.S. Cities" on page 568.

Employment Problems

The employment picture in the cities has changed dramatically over the past few decades. Unskilled workers can no longer easily find employment in manufacturing. Many blue-collar jobs have gone to the suburbs or elsewhere. The number of jobs in skilled fields has been increasing. The unskilled, including high school dropouts, are unprepared for all but the lowest-paying service industry jobs in the cities. This change causes a widening of the gap between the rich and the poor in the cities.

Industries have left the cities to relocate in the suburbs, rural areas, or foreign countries where land is cheaper and taxes and

Problems in Economics

HOMELESSNESS: A GROWING PROBLEM FOR U.S. CITIES

It was a bitterly cold night. The police began their rounds to find homeless people and families and take them off the streets. But all of the family shelters were already filled. One busload of homeless people was brought to an emergency shelter in the city's welfare office. Maria and her two little girls did not have a bed or cot on which to sleep. They had to make do with a counter-top and a plastic chair in the office. Maria was given some soup and sandwiches.

Who are the homeless? Certain groups dominate their ranks. These include alcoholics, drug abusers, the mentally ill, members of minorities, single men, and families with a single, female parent. The fastest-growing group are families with children, a group that now make up about a third of the homeless population.

Another large group are the hard-core drug or alcohol abusers. Many users eventually become penniless, helpless, and then homeless. Among their group are the urban vagrants who rebel against behavioral rules imposed by the public or privately operated shelters.

A report released in 2001 by the U.S. Conference of Mayors cited the lack of *affordable housing* as the primary cause of homelessness. In the 1970s, there were twice as many affordable housing units as there were low-income households. Today, the numbers have reversed. Now we have nearly twice as many low-income families as there are affordable housing units.

Second in importance to the lack of affordable housing as a cause of homelessness, say the U.S. Mayors, has been low-paying jobs and inadequate income. That is, neither the jobs people held, nor the public assistance they received, was sufficient to enable them to afford hous-ing. If homelessness is to end, ways will have to be found to enable people to find and hold adequate-paying jobs.

Any program designed to meet the needs of the homeless costs a great deal of money. The mentally ill and drug and alcohol abusers may require long-term care. Women and children who are home-less are often the victims of domestic vio-lence. They, too, need protection, special counseling, childcare, and job training. Much of the money needed for these pro-grams comes from the federal govern-ment. States and localities contribute too. Private charities and religious groups are also doing a great deal to help provide emergency care for the homeless, and they might be asked to do more.

It is important to keep in mind that the homeless are people like us and must be helped. Can Americans sleep comfort-ably in their homes while hundreds of thousands of other Americans have no place that is decent and safe to sleep?

Questions for Thought

1. Which government, if any, should take primary responsibility for caring for the homeless: the locality where the homeless are found, the county government, the state government, or the federal government?

2. What proposals would you make for helping homeless families whose members are *not* mentally ill, alcoholic, or drug abusers?

3. Some experts believe that there has been an increase in homelessness among families whose major wage earner is out of work. How would you recommend helping this group?

labor costs are lower. Along with the industries that move out of the cities go the jobs, the incomes, and the taxes that once were collected.

Unemployment figures in cities are often misleading because they tend to show totals. They do not tell *who* is working and who is not. Uncounted are those who cannot find jobs and have stopped looking, as well as those who have turned to crime for income or survival.

Maintaining Public Services

Cities must provide many *public services*. All of these services are costly. Food, merchandise, and raw materials must be brought in on roads maintained by the cities. Finished goods must be sent out of the cities. The daily movement of people and goods often causes traffic tie-ups and wears down the streets themselves. Potholes must be filled in, roads and streets repaved, and bridges checked and repaired. The electric cables and water pipes must be serviced. Every day, city people and businesses throw away tons of cans, papers, and all sorts of trash. Cities must dispose of these and other wastes. Cities must provide pure drinking water and set standards for clean air. Most cities have a bus system; some also have a train or subway system. Maintaining all of these essential services is a never-ending job. And it is expensive.

All too often, a city neglects the maintenance of its streets, public buildings, and other properties. When money is in short supply, the city will spend only to meet its immediate needs. It will put off most *capital improvements* (repairs of tunnels, roads, bridges, and public buildings). The cost of bringing the city back up to what it was becomes overwhelming. The result is that the city becomes run-down.

Budget Items for a Typical City

Receipts	Expenses
Property taxes	Education
Sales and gross receipts taxes	Public welfare
Federal government grants	Public health and hospitals
State government grants	Police and fire
Fees for services	Parks and recreation
	Sanitation
	Public transportation and streets
	Housing
	Cultural affairs
	Water and sanitation facilities

HOW CAN CITIES "SOLVE" THEIR PROBLEMS?

Now that you know about the problems cities face, what do you think can be done about them? Read the following proposals on how to "solve" these problems. In each proposal, you will read pro and con arguments. You will be encouraged to reach your own conclusions about each proposal.

Proposal I: Cities Should Have Urban Redevelopment and Renewal Programs

This proposal involves *urban renewal*—transforming a central city area that is run-down into one that is flourishing. For example, the area between Boston's North End and its downtown financial district was once called "ghost town." Run-down housing, abandoned warehouses, and decaying wharves were common sights in this blighted section of the city. Today, the run-down housing is gone. The warehouses have been turned into apartment buildings. Waterfront promenades, parks, restaurants, and shops have replaced the abandoned wharves. Private enterprise, with help from the city of Boston, paid for all of these improvements. Private business firms, real estate companies, banks, and insurance companies invested in the *urban redevelopment projects*.

The Boston city government aided the waterfront redevelopment project in many ways. (1) The city granted *tax deferrals* that exempted the waterfront real estate developers and new businesses from paying taxes for some years. (2) The city changed some of its zoning regulations to allow new businesses to be established along the waterfront in locations previously limited to residential use. Or the cities allowed residential use of buildings or areas previously limited to commercial use. (3) The city condemned many abandoned and unused properties in the waterfront area. The city took ownership of these lands or buildings, paid their former owners a "fair" market price, and sold the properties to the waterfront developers.

Plans for redeveloping similar rundown areas in other cities are in conflict with groups of opposing beliefs and interests. Let us look at the arguments of each side.

1. Pro. Boston's waterfront redevelopment satisfies varied and conflicting interests. Instead of simply tearing down old buildings and warehouses, the developers aimed at preserving the character of old Boston. There is a mixture of housing and office buildings in the redeveloped area. In downtown Boston, laws allow people access to walks, wharves, and public areas in private buildings.

Urban Redevelopment: Begun in 1995, Boston's Central Artery-Tunnel Project, the largest urban road project in U.S. history, is scheduled for completion in 2005. When completed, it will bury underground a stretch of elevated highway now running straight through the heart of the city. Seventy-five percent of the financing for the project is coming from the federal government. The rest will come from state and private sources. When first proposed back in 1975, its cost was estimated at $300 million. By 2002, it appeared that $12.5 billion was a more realistic figure. Supporters of the project speak of underground traffic as the one thing that can save historic downtown communities. Critics focus on runaway costs and the inconveniences caused by construction.

Urban renewal aims to encourage established businesses to stay in the city and to attract new businesses to the city. In recent years, urban renewal has aimed at bringing middle-class people into an area to live by renovating the older buildings and keeping or restoring the neighborhood's traditional appearance. This latter process, called *gentrification*, often results in the poorer residents of the area not being able to afford to stay.

2. Con. In many cities, urban renewal programs and gentrification have failed to meet the needs of the poor and the lower middle class. In fact, many of those who once lived in renewal areas can no longer afford to do so. Many of those forced out of the neighborhoods are members of minority groups. Many of the businesses that have moved into the city do not hire unskilled workers. The result of urban renewal and redevelopment, then, has been to widen the gap between the rich and the poor in the cities.

With which proposal—Pro or Con—are you mostly in agreement? Explain your answer.

Proposal II: The Federal Government Should Increase Its Aid to Cities

Cities do not seem to be able to deal with all their problems by themselves. Cities lack the tax base to pay for the increasing demands for services. Federal aid to cities is not new. The federal government already pays about 90 percent of the cost of building interstate highways, which include many city streets and parkways. Federal education and job-training programs already exist, which help many city residents.

1. Pro. The federal government has the money to do the job, while the cities do not. If a city increases its property taxes to raise more money, more businesses and middle-class residents will move away. This result will only reduce the city's tax base and increase its money problems. If the city raises its sales taxes, the burden of payment will fall proportionally more on the poor—those who can least afford to pay.

Local problems do not always begin or end in the local area. Unemployment in the cities, for example, increases when the national economy is doing poorly. The national trend away from manufacturing to service industries has especially hurt minorities and other low-income workers in the cities. The flight of industries from the cities and competition from foreign countries are problems beyond the scope of any individual city.

2. Con. Federal intervention in local affairs is something we should guard against. City, regional, and state governments understand local problems better than officials in Washington, D.C. There should be fewer rather than more federal programs. The federal government is already spending too much money. Moreover, much of this spending is wasted. Federal debt must be reduced. Doing so will enable the federal government to lower its taxes. Cities and states can then raise taxes by the amount that city residents and businesses have had their federal taxes reduced. With less debt to repay, the federal government will borrow less. And when the demand for loans declines, so do interest rates. Cities and states could then borrow more cheaply at the lower interest rates.

Federal spending programs have not solved and cannot solve all or most of the cities' problems. Private aid should come from many sources: charities, foundations, businesses, religious institutions, and individuals. Americans who are able to should help other Americans in need. In many cities, business firms are becoming directly involved with schools in a variety of school-business partnerships. Private groups are building housing for people who have jobs but cannot afford to buy a house or apartment. In giving help to others, more people get involved and become part of the solution.

With which proposal—Pro or Con—are you mostly in agreement? Explain your answer.

HOW CAN REGIONAL PLANNING HELP CITIES?

It is not always practical, or even possible, to solve all of a city's or metropolitan area's problems at the local level. Many problems that seem to be local ones actually involve a much wider area. Sometimes, the area involved is an entire region. A *region* is a geographic area whose people have similar economic interests and are interested in solving a problem that they all share. A region may be part of one large state, or it may cover several states.

Planning Crosses Local Boundaries

Regional planning attempts to solve the problems that cross local or state government lines. Cities and localities in a region join together in drawing up plans to solve their shared problems so that people throughout the region benefit. Regional planning is not easy, since one group's "solution" may not please another group. Here are some regional problems, along with some possible solutions.

1. Land Use. The population in a region is increasing. Should forests and farm areas be developed for housing, industry, highways, and stores? Where should new housing developments be built: in or near a central city or in suburban areas? Where should recreation areas be located? Where should industries be located? Where should stores be located? Where and how many roads should be built?

2. Water Use. How should a region's lakes and rivers be used? For example, can the same river be used for transportation, power generation, waste removal, recreation, and drinking water? Often, a regional master plan must provide the answers.

3. Air Quality. As you learned in Chapter 35, acid rain is caused by wind-borne pollutants. It crosses state and national boundaries and destroys forests and lakes that are often hundreds of miles away from the source of the pollution. Clean air, therefore, is a goal that often requires regional cooperation. States in the Northeast have joined together to set goals for lowering carbon and sulphur dioxide emissions from autos and factories. Some areas, such as Los Angeles, have plans for reducing air pollution that require much business and public cooperation.

Problems in Economics

OUTLOOK FOR CITIES IN THE 21ST CENTURY

Not too many years ago, neighborhoods like the *South Bronx* in New York City, *Barrio Logan* in San Diego, Houston's *Fifth Ward*, and Cleveland's *Hough* were thought to be beyond help. Poverty was overwhelming, crime was out of control, business firms closed their doors, and the middle class had fled. Then during the last decades of the 20th century, a startling recovery took place. No longer feared, they and hundreds of other neighborhoods like them were transformed into places where people want to live and raise their families.

What accounts for the transformation in the 1980s and 1990s of so many formerly troubled neighborhoods? While the reasons are unclear, most experts agree that three factors were largely responsible for turning things around. These were the:

1. Growth of Neighborhood Nonprofit Groups. Community development corporations (CDCs) are nonprofit neighborhood-based organizations led by local residents. Based in low-income, inner-city communities, CDCs focus on providing things like affordable housing, economic development, and social services. Typically, this involves raising money from both private and government sources, hiring consultants, and promoting their projects. As an example of their work, CDCs in Washington, D.C., raised $26 million over a five-year period to develop 556,000 square feet of commercial, retail, and industrial space.

2. Return of Retail Stores and Other Local Businesses. When the middle class fled from neighborhoods in decline in the 1960s and 1970s, so too did many retail stores and other local businesses. Reattracting businesses into those neighborhoods was complicated because banks often refused to lend money to those living in or planning to invest in rundown communities. Things changed after Congress in 1977 enacted the Community Reinvestment Act (CRA). This law made it illegal for banks to deny loans to otherwise qualified borrowers on the basis of where they lived or where they planned to invest the money. As a result, hundreds of billions of dollars in loans were made available for the renewal of distressed neighborhoods. Many of the nation's biggest retailers found they could operate at a profit in these neighborhoods.

3. Falling Crime Rates. The rebirth of neighborhoods like the South Bronx would not have taken place were it not for a dramatic reduction in violent crime. Across the United States, neighborhoods once known for gun violence and out-in-the-open drug markets have become safer places. Urban planners and other professionals give much of the credit for the dramatic turnaround to *community policing*. It grew out of a 1994 federal law that, among other things, provides funding for cities to add 100,000 more community police officers.

Community policing takes police out of patrol cars. It assigns them instead to walk the streets and visit with schools, community centers, and local leadership. Community police officers provide a liaison between the community and the police. For example, a community police officer was assigned to a Massachusetts high school. He supervised the school grounds, taught units in certain classes, worked with an after-school "Police Academy" course, attended school events, and helped out with athletics.

Similarly, some metropolitan areas have entered into regional agreements with the surrounding suburbs in an effort to improve air quality. The Georgia Regional Transportation Authority, for example, hopes to improve the air quality of Atlanta and its surrounding communities by convincing commuters to make greater use of mass transit.

4. Economic Development and Needs. How can the natural resources of your region best be used? Should agriculture or industry be encouraged? Must industries, businesses, and homeowners pay taxes to support needs that are important to their region but outside their localities?

5. Hazardous Waste Disposal. Many states have entered into regional agreements on the disposal of hazardous wastes. They were spurred to do so by a 1986 federal law that required all the states to submit plans for disposing of these wastes. In these regional plans, the states agree where waste disposal plants will be built and how much waste from each state will be treated at each plant.

───────────────── **SUMMARY** ─────────────────

Cities are political and geographic areas. Cities are also a way of life. Suburbs are outlying cities with many of the features of the central city. A metropolitan area is a city and its surrounding suburbs. Population and jobs in the suburbs have been growing at a faster rate than in the cities. A network of interlocking metropolitan areas is called a megalopolis.

The cities and suburbs are often two different worlds. Family income is higher among suburban residents. Employment opportunities in some occupations are often better in the suburbs. Cities have a higher proportion of the elderly, the poor, minorities, and single-parent families. These groups need more services but can least afford to pay the taxes the city needs in order to provide the services. The middle class and businesses that can better afford to pay taxes have been leaving, adding to the cities' financial problems.

Major problems facing cities and metropolitan areas include street crime, drugs, inadequate housing, a shortage of jobs, and maintaining public services. As manufacturing industries have left the cities, the poor have found it more difficult to get good jobs.

In past decades, urban renewal projects sought to reverse the movement of people and businesses out of the cities. Across the nation, cities invested millions of dollars to renew blighted downtown areas. Areas that once were deserted urban wastelands now boast new businesses, residents, and cultural centers.

Proposals for solving the problems of cities and metropolitan areas, such as more urban renewal and development projects and increased federal aid, have both supporters and opponents. Regional planning attempts to solve economic problems that affect cities and localities in an area. Regional planning also attempts to bring together large areas that have similar economic problems and find solutions to benefit the entire region.

LOOKING AHEAD

Poverty and unemployment are, as you have read, closely related to the problems of metropolitan areas. These difficult problems, as you will learn in the next chapter, are national in scope and are not easily solved.

EXERCISES

✔ **Matching** Match each term in Column A with its definition in Column B.

Column A	Column B
1. city	a. a term that describes an area made up mostly of farms or small towns
2. metropolitan area	b. the area that includes a city and its surrounding suburbs
3. slum	
4. suburb	c. an important town that is given the right to govern itself by the state
5. rural	d. another name for the center or core of a city
6. urban	e. working to solve problems in an area larger than a city but smaller than a country
7. megalopolis	f. an urban area with run-down housing
8. inner city	g. a term that describes a city or metropolitan area
9. regional planning	h. a community just outside of a city
	i. a network, or chain, of metropolitan areas

✔**Multiple Choice** Choose the letter of the item that best completes the statement or answers the question.

1. The main idea of this chapter is that (a) cities are not as nice to live in as suburbs (b) the problems of cities cannot be solved (c) cities face difficult problems (d) life in the suburbs is boring.

2. Three out of every four Americans live in (a) rural areas (b) metropolitan areas (c) cities (d) suburbs.

3. The Atlanta Metropolitan Area consists of suburbs and a (a) mega-lopolis (b) central city (c) region (d) state.

4. The Northeast Corridor is an example of (a) a megalopolis (b) a central city (c) an interstate highway (d) a suburb.

5. Which statement is *true* of suburban areas today? (a) Suburban residents depend upon the city for jobs, entertainment, and essential services. (b) Median family income is lower in the suburbs than in cities. (c) More people are employed in manufacturing in the suburbs than in the cities. (d) Minorities and the elderly tend to be concentrated in the suburbs.

6. Which *one* of the following is an attempt to solve the problems of the cities? (a) urban renewal (b) flight of businesses and the middle class to the suburbs (c) deterioration of city streets and public buildings (d) increase in homelessness.

7. The decline of manufacturing industries and the increase in service jobs in the cities have resulted in (a) fewer traffic problems in the city (b) higher incomes for city workers (c) greater opportunities for high school dropouts (d) a widening of the gap between rich and poor in the cities.

8. Which *one* of the following is an argument *in favor of* urban re-newal projects? (a) Rentals in renewal areas are very high. (b) Poor people will be displaced and crowded into slums. (c) Businesses will stay and the middle class will be brought back into the city. (d) More city services will be required in renewed areas.

9. Which *one* of the following is an argument *in favor of* increased fed-eral aid to cities? (a) Federal spending has not reduced the number of high school dropouts. (b) The same urban problems often occur in many areas of the nation. (c) The people in city and state gov-ernments have better understanding of problems than the people in the federal government. (d) The federal government is already too deeply in debt.

10. Which *one* of the following supports the view that local problems do not begin or end in the local area? (a) Unemployment in the cities increases when the national economy is doing poorly. (b) Federal

aid to cities is not a new idea. (c) The federal government has the money, but the cities do not. (d) Urban renewal projects have always been successful.

✔ *Research Project*

Do library research to find out how the area you live in has changed. Get a new road map of the metropolitan area near you.

1. Identify on the map the central city or cities, the suburbs, and routes of travel connecting city and suburbs.

2. Locate unused land near a city in your area. Do you think that this land should be used for homes? schools? parks? industry? a combination of some or all of these? Tell why.

✔ *For Thought and Discussion*

1. You have learned that a metropolitan area is made up of a city and the suburbs that surround it. The middle class seems to be fleeing the cities and going to live in the suburbs. (a) What do you think middle-class people living in the suburbs owe to the city? (b) What, if anything, do you think the city owes to the suburbs that surround it?

2. Sewage and refuse from several cities up the river are carried downstream. The water is so dirty when it reaches your city that no one can go fishing or swimming in it. The river has a bad smell too. Factory chimneys in the next state pour out smoke that crosses state lines and causes acid rain and other types of air pollution. Highways cross state and city lines too. Exhaust fumes from the cars and trucks traveling along these highways also add to the air pollution in your community.

    Would you ask your city government to pass antipollution laws to protect your city? Could these laws work? How might regional planning help in this area?

3. The turnaround in many formerly troubled neighborhoods has been attributed to three interdependent factors: the growth of CDCs, return of local businesses, and falling crime rates. Explain, for example, how the return of local businesses is related to falling crime rates and how crime rates fell because local businesses returned to troubled neighborhoods.

4. The positive transformation that is discussed in the reading on pages 574–575 took place during a ten-year period of economic prosperity in the United States. How might a recession in this country affect the gains made?

✔ *How Would You Solve These Problems?*

Here are some real problems that have faced many communities. Imagine that you could do something about each problem. What would you do?

1. You live in a small suburban town. Septic tanks have begun to overflow. The seepage is polluting the water supply. Your town's engineer says that a sewage system is needed to replace all the septic tanks in town. This would be very expensive. Four nearby towns face a similar problem. Would you advise your town to build a sewage system on its own? Or would you try to get the five towns to join in the project? Explain your answers.

2. A new bridge was built across a river that separates two states. The roads and highways in the state on one side of the river are wide and modern. You live on that side. On the other side of the river, the roads are narrow and in need of repair. Each time you cross the heavily traveled bridge, you get stuck in a traffic jam on the other side.

    Explain why your state should or should not pay part of the cost for improving the roads and highways on the other side of the bridge. How might the traffic problem have been avoided?

3. Suppose that you solved problem 2. Now you find that the roads are packed with trucks, buses, and cars. When you finally get where you want to go, you cannot find a parking space. Traffic and parking are handled by the local police in each community.

    Should traffic control and parking be handled by each separate community or should regional planning be used to help this situation? Explain your answer.

✔ *Using the Internet*

You might explore how one nonprofit group is helping people living in the cities (and elsewhere) build affordable housing. Habitat for Humanity's Website is <<http://www.habitat.org>>.

Two sources of information on cities and their problems are the Website of the U.S. Department of Housing and Urban Development at <<http://www.hud.gov>> and that of the U.S. Conference of Mayors at <<http://www.usmayors.org>>.

CHAPTER *38*

Poverty and Unemployment

Things are pretty tough these days for Bob Clancy. Bob is 25 years old and has a wife and three children. Bob quit school and went to work when he was 16. He is a hard worker, but he has never earned much. His wife, Betty, is looking for a part-time job to help meet the family's expenses.

Charlie Wilson and Marty Costa both spent almost all of their working lives at a big auto plant in the Midwest. But the plant shut down two years ago, and both were laid off. Their unemployment benefits ran out after a year. Once in a while, a low-paying, temporary job turns up. Both men are applying for jobs at a new auto plant being built in another state. Meanwhile, their families are receiving income assistance and food stamps.

Christine Smith has never had a job. She dropped out of school at 16 when she became pregnant. Christine is receiving public assistance. She is going to school and is enrolled in a job-training program. She hopes to get a full-time job when she completes the program and earn enough to support herself and her son.

Mary Swenson is 73 and has been a widow for nine years. Even with Social Security payments and a small pension from her union, Mary gets by only because she spends carefully. She receives housing assistance and Medicare benefits from the government. She is proud that she does not depend on her children for support.

According to the U.S. Census Bureau, in 2004 some 37 million Americans were living in *poverty*. They lacked the income to buy the necessities of life. Can you suggest why there are so many poor people living in such a rich nation?

In most poor American families, someone works and earns an income. Therefore, just going to work does not lift one out of poverty. But poverty is often caused by unemployment. As you read this chapter, you will learn the answers to the following questions:

- How is poverty defined?
- Who are America's poor?
- Why are people unemployed?
- What is being done to reduce poverty and unemployment?

HOW IS POVERTY DEFINED?

Poverty Level

The poor are people whose cash incomes fall below a certain set cash minimum called the *poverty level*. This minimum income level is set by the federal government. It is adjusted each year to reflect changes in the cost of living, as measured by the Consumer Price Index (discussed first in Chapter 6). For example, in 1980 a family of four with an income of $8,400 or less was classified as poor. But in 2004, the same family with an income of under $19,350 was considered to be living in poverty. Many people are eligible for

Millions of Americans cannot afford private medical care. They depend on medical services paid for by government.

Figure 38.1 Americans Living Below the Poverty Level Since 1960

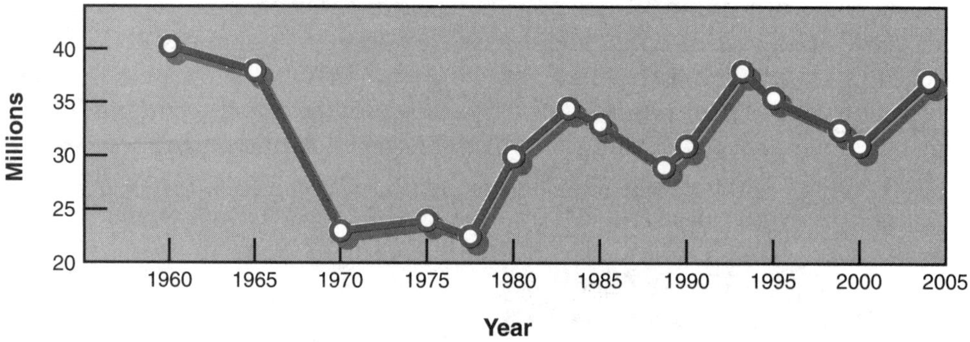

income assistance and food stamps, as well as medical care, if their incomes fall below the poverty level.

The low wages earned by some workers are a cause of poverty. The majority of poor adults in the United States hold some kind of job, often a full-time one. Despite this, their earnings are so low that even these people are below the poverty level. Thus, they are considered to be poor. Figure 38.1 shows the number of poor persons in the United States in recent decades.

Cash Income and Noncash Benefits

The official poverty level is based solely on cash income—actual money one receives from various sources, such as a job. The poverty level does not take into account the *noncash benefits* given to the poor, such as food stamps, school lunches, medical care, and housing assistance. Government benefits have an equalizing effect, it is argued. When the value of these noncash benefits is counted, some 10 percent of the people deemed as poor have risen above the poverty level.

Cash programs account for only about one-third of all government payments to the poor. Noncash programs make up the remaining two-thirds. However, some people oppose counting noncash benefits when estimating poverty. To do so, they say, lowers poverty figures and may serve as an excuse for cutting cash benefits to the poor. Two important noncash programs—food stamps and rental assistance—are discussed later in this chapter.

Poverty Rate

Thus far we have been discussing the number of Americans living below the poverty level. Reports on poverty are also given in terms of the *poverty rate*. This figure is the percentage of the total population living below the poverty level. Poverty rates over recent decades are shown in Figure 38.2.

Figure 38.2 U.S. Poverty Rates Since 1960

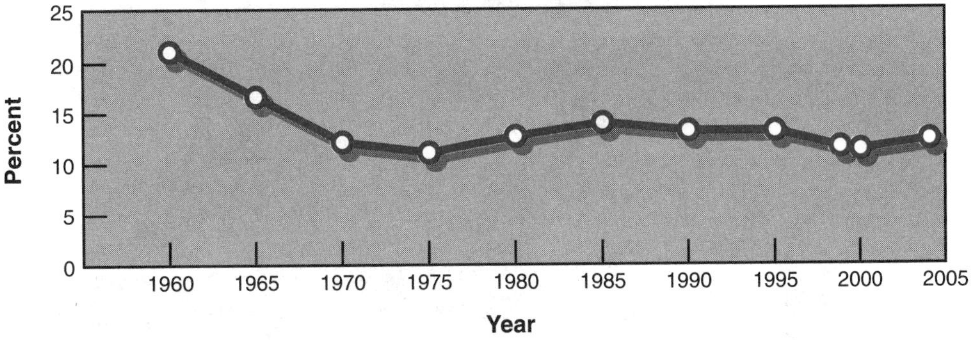

Poverty data are based on interviews with 58,000 households chosen to be representative of the entire nation's population. Armed with this information, we can now turn to the question of who are America's poor.

WHO ARE AMERICA'S POOR?

Although 12.5 percent of all Americans were considered poor in 2004, the distribution of poverty among different groups was unequal.

Minorities

Poverty affects members of many minority groups to a far greater degree than the nation as a whole. The Census Bureau, the government agency that tracks much of the data pertaining to the population, presents data for non-Hispanic whites, African Americans, Hispanics, and Asian and Pacific Islanders. According to the Census Bureau, in 2004, 16.9 million non-Hispanic whites were poor. But they represented only 8.6 percent of the total non-Hispanic white population. In contrast, the 9.0 million African-American poor were 24.7 percent of the African-American population. The 9.1 million poor Hispanics represented 21.9 percent of the Hispanic population. And the 1.2 million Asian and Pacific Islander poor represented 9.8 percent of their total population.

Children and Single-Parent Families Headed by Women

As groups, children and families headed by single women have had much higher rates of poverty than the population as a whole. Among families headed by married couples, the poverty rate was under 6.4 percent in 2004. Compare this with a poverty rate of 30.5

Single-Parent Family: Families headed by a single woman are three times more likely to be poor than families headed by couples.

percent for those headed by a single woman. At least as significant is the large percentage of children living in poverty—20.2. These and other differences are shown in the table below.

U.S. Families Living in Poverty, 2004

Type of Family	Percent
Married-couple	6.4
Non-Hispanic White	4.1
African American	9.9
Asian and Pacific Islander	6.0
Hispanic	16.4
Female householder, no spouse present	30.5
Non-Hispanic White	21.7
African American	39.5
Asian and Pacific Islander	14.4
Hispanic	39.3
Children under 18 years of age	14.3
Married couples	7.8
Female householder, no spouse	37.2

In the past, people 65 years of age and older made up the largest single group living below the poverty level. Today, the elderly as a group are no longer considered poor, although of course many individual elderly are poor. Moreover, women age 65 and over are more likely to be poor than men of that age. Retired women often suffer the effects of job and salary discrimination that they had experienced during their working years.

Why are a greater percentage of minorities and women poorer than the population as a whole? Both minorities and women still face job and salary discrimination. White men often have an easier time finding jobs than minority men and women, despite antidiscrimination laws that attempt to correct past discrimination. And even when white men, minorities, and women hold the same kinds of jobs, white men tend to earn on average higher salaries. Women who are heads of families also face the problems of raising children, holding jobs, and finding adequate child care.

A significant cause of poverty among minorities is where they live. In Chapter 37, we discussed the problems of the U.S. inner cities. Minorities are a high percentage of the population in these urban areas. Unemployment, poor education, homelessness, crime, and drug abuse are more widespread there. People who grow up in such an environment are often discouraged from obtaining a good education and getting and keeping full-time jobs.

WHY ARE PEOPLE UNEMPLOYED?

If you had a summer job and quit it at the end of August and went back to school, you would not have been considered unemployed. *You were not looking for a job.* But suppose you were out of a job and wanted to work. Then you could be classified as unemployed.

Types of Unemployment

An individual who is able and willing to work but cannot find work is considered unemployed. The *unemployment rate* is the percentage of these unemployed people in the labor force. The unemployment rate is never zero. There are always people who are between jobs. Even in an economy of "full employment," about 4 percent of the workforce will be looking for work.

Economists use the term *frictional unemployment* to describe the condition of workers who have left one job and are looking for another. Frictional unemployment is not a cause of poverty, nor is it of concern to most economists.

Unemployment that occurs because of changes in the business cycle is called *cyclical unemployment.* During a recession, the demand for goods drops. Production workers are laid off until the companies' warehouses are close to being empty and the demand for their products has increased. Workers in the service economy—which buys, distributes, and sells goods—also suffer when there is a drop in sales. As the economy improves, workers are re-hired. The number of poor, therefore, is greatest during a recession, and smallest during a booming economy.

Workers who are unemployed because their craft or trade is no longer in demand are said to be suffering the effects of *structural unemployment*. This type of unemployment has become an increasingly serious problem. The decline in manufacturing jobs and the increase in service jobs have reduced the need for mill and factory workers. These workers can often get jobs in fast-food restaurants and other low-paying places of employment. But the openings in finance, health services, and high-tech industries (discussed in Chapters 16 and 18) are usually filled by people other than those who had lost their jobs in manufacturing. People are not likely to get good-paying jobs without the education and training that are required to do them.

Structural unemployment contributes to the number of poor because the poor are mostly unskilled workers whose jobs are disappearing. Usually, however, individuals with education and skills who have lost their jobs due to structural unemployment do not remain unemployed long, particularly during a period of a booming economy.

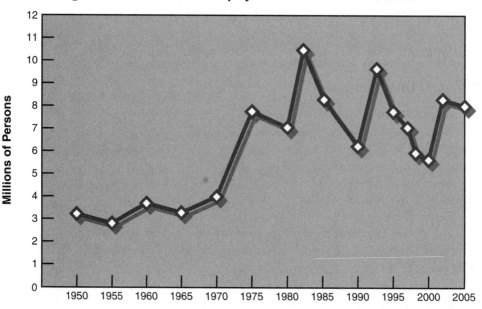

Figure 38.3 Number of Unemployed U.S. Workers Since 1950

Causes of Unemployment Among the Poor

The major reasons for unemployment among the poor are: (1) the disappearance of low-skill jobs, (2) discrimination, (3) the health of the economy, and (4) discouragement.

1. Low-Skill Jobs Have Disappeared. In this country, many low-skill factory jobs have disappeared in recent decades. Overseas companies using low-paid workers are now producing goods more cheaply than can be done here. Thus, many jobs once open to unskilled people entering the U.S. labor force have been lost. And who are the vast majority of unskilled in the United States? The poor, of course. Lacking job opportunities, unemployment increases among the poor. Not only are the poor largely unskilled. They are also among the least educated. It is difficult for unskilled, poorly educated workers to find well-paying jobs with benefits.

2. Discrimination. Minorities, women, and young people suffer higher unemployment rates than most other Americans. Why is this so? A partial answer is the discrimination in hiring discussed earlier in this chapter. Unemployment is greater among women than men. Teenagers are twice as likely to be unemployed as are adults. But African-American teenagers are the group with the highest unemployment rate.

3. The Economy. Poverty and unemployment are greatest when the economy is doing poorly and least when the economy is doing well. The reason is fairly obvious. Demand is greater for workers when business is good than when business is bad. And when the demand for workers is low, fewer jobs are available and unemployment increases. The poor are the hardest hit when the economy goes bad. This is because they have less to fall back on. They lack the savings and investments that could help tide them over until conditions improve.

4. Discouragement. The main reason people are unemployed is that they have lost their jobs. But many workers, particularly the poor who are unskilled, have become discouraged about their chances for finding jobs. They have given up looking. Minorities, particularly minority teenagers, are prominent among those who have given up looking for work. People who have dropped out of the labor force are no longer counted as unemployed. In just one year, over a million Americans said they had given up looking for work. We may conclude, therefore, that the number of unemployed is more severe than official statistics would indicate.

WHAT IS BEING DONE TO REDUCE POVERTY AND UNEMPLOYMENT?

The problem of the poor—both employed and unemployed—is with us even when the United States is enjoying a healthy economy. Thus, there is always a need for programs to meet the needs of poor people and those temporarily unemployed.

Strengthen the Economy

One of the first steps to reduce poverty and unemployment in America is to keep our economy strong. The strength of the economy has much to do with poverty and employment. The better the economy, the lower both unemployment and poverty levels. Therefore, to reduce poverty and unemployment in the United States, programs must be devised to stimulate the economy when it shows signs of weakness. The two major tools government uses to stimulate the economy are fiscal (spending and tax programs) and monetary (regulating interest rates). These tools, and government efforts to achieve full employment and economic growth, were discussed fully in Chapter 30.

Increase the Minimum Wage

Poverty, it has been noted, exists even when our economy is doing well. There are workers who do not earn enough to bring themselves above the poverty level. An individual working a 40-hour week at a minimum wage of $5.15 per hour would earn only $10,712 in a year. This amount falls below the poverty level. Many people suggest that the minimum wage be sufficiently raised to bring more workers above the poverty line. Arguments for and against raising the minimum wage were discussed in Chapter 1, pages 10–11.

Social Insurance

Social Security and unemployment insurance are the government's principal insurance programs for the nation's workforce. (They were described in Chapter 14.) Like private insurance plans, these programs provide money benefits paid out of premiums. Social Security contributions are paid by both employers and employees. The federal government pays out the benefits to workers when they retire. Unemployment premiums are paid solely by the employer, while the states pay out the benefits. Medicare, a medical benefits program for the elderly, is funded by the federal government and by the people enrolled in the program.

Public Assistance: Welfare Programs

The social insurance programs just described protect people who have made contributions to them or who have earned coverage during their working years. But what is to be done for the millions of needy people who are not covered by social insurance? Help for most of these people has been available in the form of *public assistance* or, as it is more commonly known, *welfare*.

In 1996, 15 million Americans received welfare benefits. Two-thirds of that number were children under the age of 18. In the eyes of many Americans, the welfare program itself was the main reason why so many children lived in poverty. Since its beginning in the 1930s, Aid to Families With Dependent Children (AFDC) had been the largest of the nation's welfare programs. Only single mothers were eligible for AFDC assistance. Under government rules, the more children a woman had, the more cash assistance she received. Because the jobs available to unemployed single mothers generally paid less than the package of cash assistance, food stamps, and health coverage to which they were entitled, many saw little reason to look for work. As a result, critics concluded, people in poverty, their children, and their children's children came to look upon welfare as an acceptable way of life. A term critics used to describe generations of a family being on welfare is the *cycle of dependency*. Other Americans defended AFDC and other welfare programs as necessary and humane.

Food Stamps

The federal *food stamp* program helps low-income people buy the food they need for good health. State public assistance agencies run the program through their local offices. The dollar amount of food stamps an individual or family receives will depend on the number of people in it and on how much monthly income is left after certain expenses are subtracted. Food stamps can be spent like cash at most stores that sell food. Instead of actual stamps, some households receive a special debit card that can be used in certain stores to buy needed food.

For most households, food stamps cover only part of their food budgets. Recipients must also spend some of their own cash in order to have enough food for a month. In 2001, over 18 million Americans received food stamps.

Housing Assistance

Since the Great Depression of the 1930s, the federal government has attempted to provide affordable housing to "low income" people. In the process of urban renewal, blocks of run-down housing were torn down and replaced by apartment buildings for the poor. But these public housing projects often became slums. Conditions for tenants were often unsafe, dirty, smelly, and scary. As an alternative to public housing, Congress, in the 1990s, tried to give eligible tenants the power to choose where to live. Individuals and families would receive *rent vouchers*. They could then use the vouchers to seek their own housing from private landlords. In this way, low-income tenants would not be confined to public housing.

The rent voucher program is administered by state and local units of government through a contract with the Department of Housing and Urban Development (HUD). The local government unit screens tenant applicants for eligibility, issues vouchers, contracts with landlords, inspects housing, and monitors participants for compliance with HUD regulations.

The federal government has determined that total housing expenses, including rent and utilities, should be no more than 30 percent of a tenant's income. The government subsidizes any difference in the form of a rent voucher. The amount of the voucher varies depending on the area in which the housing is sought.

Education, Training, and Counseling Programs

Many of the nation's poor are poor because they lack the education and skills for the better-paying jobs in a modern economy. Many also lack the skills to know how to find a job and, once at work, how to keep a job. They often need to learn such basic skills as getting to work on time and going to work every workday. The state and local agencies dealing with such individuals provide counseling along with their training programs. At some agencies, those receiving welfare benefits are required to work a given number of hours each week at such tasks as helping to clean parks and other public areas. This practice is known as *workfare*. Some welfare recipients are enrolled in educational programs at day or evening schools or at vocational training schools. The individual may be taught computer skills or other secretarial skills, or how to do electrical or plumbing repairs in a school environment. The most successful practice seems to be on-the-job training. Here, the individual learns the skill needed on a job while working on the job rather than in a classroom.

Self-Employment Programs

Programs to help people start their own businesses are being tried out in states across the country. In Washington State, for example, 1,000 unemployed people spent a year in a program that

Since 1964, the Job Corps has been teaching job skills to young adults age 16 to 22 in many locations across the country.

taught them skills in *self-employment* (having one's own business). To help them start businesses of their own, they received six months' worth of unemployment benefits in one lump sum (about $4,000). The results have been encouraging. A former secretary started a doll company, a welder opened his own business, and a production manager started making videotapes.

Similar self-employment programs are being tried in six other states. Some of the self-employed in these programs are former welfare recipients. Most are women. Among the businesses they have started are a restaurant, a barbecue stand, an agency for childcare workers, and a party supply shop.

Self-employment may not be the answer for everyone who is unemployed or on welfare. Running a business, you have learned, is risky. Even with training, outside help, and a small loan, it is tough to get started and make a go of it. Yet, in Pennsylvania's Self-Employment and Enterprise Development (SEED) program, 61 of the 189 people who were enrolled started businesses, two decided to go to college, and 32 found permanent full-time jobs. These results were encouraging—and far more satisfying—than collecting unemployment or welfare. For some people, self-employment may be a path to economic self-sufficiency.

Welfare Reform

In a dramatic break with past policies, Congress in 1996 reformed the nation's welfare system. It replaced Aid For Dependent Children (AFDC) with Temporary Assistance for Needy Families (TANF). The new law ended some 60 years of federal income guarantees to poor people. It replaced welfare with a work-oriented, time-limited system run largely by the states. Poor people used to receive monthly federal checks and other benefits automatically. Now they were to be given economic help only for a limited time. After the time expired, they were expected to look for a job and go to work. (Hence the word "Temporary" in TANF).

The main argument against the old welfare system had been that it trapped people in a cycle of dependency. President Bill Clinton, speaking in favor of the 1996 law, said that it would "strengthen incentives for the poor to find jobs, fend for themselves, and enjoy the self-respect that self-reliance offers." In other words, self-reliance was to replace welfare dependency.

Important Features of Welfare Reform

The 1996 law had a number of important features that made it vastly different from earlier federal laws dealing with poverty.

1. Block Grants. The federal guarantee of welfare payments directly to individuals was replaced by lump-sum payments, or "block" grants, to the states. The total yearly amount for all block grants, $16.4 billion, would remain the same until the year 2002.

2. States' Responsibility. In exchange for the block grants, the states now administer their own welfare programs in accordance with federal guidelines.

3. Work Requirements. The states must enforce the requirement that people seeking welfare or other benefits have to work (or, in some cases, go to school or enroll in a job-training program).

4. Time Limits. Individuals could receive welfare benefits for no more than five years. The heads of families receiving welfare were required to find work within two years. Failure to do so could result in a loss of family benefits.

5. Limits on Food Stamps. Adults from 18 to 50 years old with no dependent children were limited to receiving only three months of food stamps during any three-year period.

6. *Unwed Teenaged Mothers.* Unmarried teenagers with children were required to live at home and stay in school in order to be eligible for benefits.

7. *Drug Crimes.* Cash aid and food stamps were denied to anyone convicted of felony drug charges.

8. *Immigrants.* Most benefits and food stamps were denied to noncitizens (legal immigrants). Immigrants arriving after 1996 were not eligible for most other government benefits as well. States could cut off cash assistance, Medicaid, and other benefits during an immigrant's first five years in the United States. An amendment to the law in 1997 reinstated Medicaid and income supplements to some immigrants. In 1998, food stamps were restored to over 175,000 legal immigrants.

Critics of the New Welfare System

Although there was wide agreement that the welfare system needed an overhaul, the 1996 law did not please everyone. Some people thought that the law was too complex. Many of its provisions were too vague. What is defined as "work"? And what constitutes success in moving welfare recipients into jobs? Opponents questioned the wisdom of shifting responsibility for welfare from the federal government to the states. Under federal guidelines, the poor, wherever they live, are treated equally. Opponents feared that some states will neglect the poor, causing poor people to move from states providing little assistance to states providing greater help. This would place an unfair burden on those states offering more services to the poor. Localities were concerned that as people were dropped from the state welfare rolls, they would become the responsibility of local governments. Some economists argued that it was unrealistic to think that the economy would be able to match the skills of the nation's poor with the available jobs, particularly should the nation fall into recession. Immigrant groups questioned the harsh provisions that affected legal immigrants.

Despite the "naysayers," from 1996 to 2001 TANF seemed to be working as planned. Times were good, jobs were plentiful, and most families were removed from the welfare rolls. The law, you will recall, had limited help to five years. This meant that for most families still on welfare, 2001 was the end of the line. Unfortunately, 2001 also marked the beginning of an economic recession and the opening of the War on Terrorism. As jobs dried up and family benefits ran out, people feared that unless the law was

Problems in Economics

PRIVATE INITIATIVES TO FIGHT POVERTY

We have seen that there are many people and families unable to escape from poverty despite the efforts of government to improve their lot. In those circumstances, it is often left to *private initiatives*—efforts by individual citizens or groups, not by governments—to break the cycle of poverty. What follows is a description of a few of the more successful private efforts.

1. Big Brother and Big Sister Programs. Private initiatives often start very simply, with individuals trying to help others who are less fortunate. Many adults have enrolled in Big Brother and Big Sister programs and give their spare time to younger people living in poverty. A young person in poverty often does not have an adult to look up to who can give positive guidance about life, goals, and problems. A Big Brother or Big Sister often fills this need. In addition, a clear message is delivered to the young person: someone cares.

Take, for example, the experience of Lauri Jones and Mary McCartney (not their real names). Sixteen-year-old Lauri had been living in a city shelter with her mother, sister, and three brothers. They all shared one room. Mary, a 23-year-old college graduate, worked for a large securities firm. She volunteered to become Lauri's Big Sister. Lauri learned to confide about her fears and hopes to Mary. Mary listened and they talked. They went for walks together, and visited parks, museums, and department stores. Mary helped Lauri with her homework and met with a school guidance counselor to discuss Lauri's problems. Mary also helped Lauri's mother find a decent apartment in a public housing project. But Mary did more than all these things. She gave Lauri the hope and the belief that there *are* choices open to her.

2. America's Second Harvest. Poor people must eat. With that goal in mind, America's Second Harvest, a network of nonprofit food banks, provides 80 percent of the food distributed by private charities in the United States. They provide the food to privately operated food pantries, soup kitchens, and shelters. In a recent year, it helped provide food to feed some 23 million Americans.

A soup kitchen in downtown Los Angeles serves thousands of meals to the hungry of that California city.

3. Richard D. Parsons. In a commencement address delivered at Howard University, Richard D. Parsons said, "Go out in the world and try to change it. . . . You have only to believe that such power resides in you." Mr. Parsons is one who practices what he preaches.

Now Chief Executive of AOL Time Warner, Parsons was formerly President of Dime Savings Bank and chief legal counsel to the National Association for the Advancement of Colored People. He has done much to change the world in which he lives. Under his leadership, Dime Savings Bank dropped *redlining*, the illegal practice of cutting off credit to people in minority neighborhoods. He also convinced other banks to do the same. Backed by Dime Savings Bank loans, some of the most depressed neighborhoods in New York City and other cities benefited from rebuilding programs.

When, for example, it appeared that bank foreclosures and evictions might destroy the up-and-coming Jamaica Plain neighborhood of Boston, Parsons came to the rescue. "Thinking more about the community's future than the bank's bottom line," Dime Savings Bank President Parsons agreed to forgive past homeowner debts, and make new financing available for prospective homeowners and businesses in the community.

Questions for Thought

1. What is meant by the cycle of poverty? Why do you think it is very difficult to escape from this cycle?

2. List *two* kinds of private efforts, or initiatives, to reduce poverty that are discussed in the reading.

3. Where should the responsibility for reducing poverty lie—with government or with private initiatives? Explain your answer.

revised or extended, many poor people would be forced to live on the streets. Meanwhile, federal and state funds, which in normal years might be available to help the poor, were harder to come by. Tax revenues were falling and government expenses were increasing. Cities and towns across the nation were also feeling the budget crunch. Every interest group in states and localities were competing against programs to aid the poor for every available dollar.

SUMMARY

Poverty is defined in terms of cash income that falls below a minimum level set by the federal government. The poverty rate is the percentage of the total population living below the poverty level.

The groups most likely to be poor in this country are minorities, single-parent families headed by women, and children. In many poor families, someone works but does not earn enough to keep the family out of poverty. Unemployment increases the number of poor people.

An unemployed person is one who is able and willing to work but cannot find a job. Unemployment may be frictional, cyclical, or structural. Unemployment hits some groups much harder than others.

Programs to reduce poverty and unemployment provide cash payments, goods, or services. Social insurance consists of income-maintenance programs for those who have contributed to it during their working years. Welfare programs help those in need regardless of prior contributions. Work programs are designed to give education, training, and jobs to people on welfare. Self-employment programs aim to provide capital and teach business skills to persons who are unemployed or receiving welfare, if they want to start their own businesses. Federal welfare reform acts in 1996 aimed to cut the cycle of dependency.

────────────────── **EXERCISES** ──────────────────

✔ **Matching** Match each term in Column A with its definition in Column B.

Column A	Column B
1. workfare	a. public assistance programs for the needy
2. noncash income	b. programs that help poor people pay for housing
3. poverty level	c. a situation in which jobs are lost because of changes in trades or industries
4. frictional unemployment	d. the percent of the total population living below the poverty level
5. cyclical unemployment	e. benefits in the form of services, such as medical care
6. structural unemployment	f. minimum yearly income needed to stay out of poverty
7. rent voucher	g. a situation in which workers lose their jobs during a recession
8. welfare	h. a situation whereby workers are between jobs
9. poverty rate	i. a requirement that people on welfare work

✔ **Multiple Choice** Choose the letter of the item that best completes the statement or answers the question.

1. Which *one* of the following households is *most likely* to be poor? A household headed by (a) a married couple (b) a man (c) a single woman (d) an elderly person.

2. John Smith and Mary Price both earn $1,500 a month. Mary is considered poor but John is not. Which is probably a reason for this difference? (a) Mary has more people to support than John. (b) John has less education than Mary. (c) John spends his money carefully. (d) John lives in a wealthy area.

3. Which category of unemployment can best be reduced by programs to retrain workers? (a) frictional unemployment (b) cyclical unemployment (c) structural unemployment (d) seasonal unemployment.

4. Which *one* of the following is likely to affect a person's level of earnings? (a) one's sex (b) one's race (c) one's education (d) all of these.

5. According to the graph on page 582, (a) the number of people living in poverty declined from 1960 to 1970 (b) the number of people living in poverty remained unchanged from 1960 to the present (c) the number of people living in poverty was higher in 1995 than in 1960 (d) fewer people were poor in the 1980s than in the 1970s.

6. The graph on page 586 shows (a) unemployment rates (b) number of poor Americans (c) poverty rates (d) number of unemployed Americans.

7. A federal welfare reform law passed in 1996 required (a) the federal government to pay all the costs of caring for the poor (b) welfare recipients to work in order to receive benefits (c) the government to provide day care for children of all working parents (d) the government to increase assistance to all legal immigrants.

8. A major reason for the welfare reform act passed by Congress in 1996 was the view that (a) the welfare system was contributing to the cycle of dependency (b) the states could not be trusted to handle welfare programs (c) there should be no time limits to an individual receiving welfare payments (d) greater assistance should be given to immigrants and unwed mothers.

✔ Questions for Thought

Explain why you agree or disagree with each of the following statements. Refer to the text or to illustrations to prove your explanation.

1. Poverty is rapidly disappearing in this country.

2. Poverty hits some groups in society harder than others.

3. Unemployment and poverty are not related. One is not a cause of the other.

4. Most people do not want to work and support themselves.

5. Once a family goes on welfare, there is no way for it to get off.

✔ Using the Internet

Further information on poverty in the United States is available at the Census Bureau Website at: <<http://www.census.gov/hhes/www/poverty.html>>. To find out about volunteering, check out the Big Brother, Big Sister Website at <<http://www.bbbs.org>> or America's Second Harvest Website at <<http://secondharvest.volunteermatch.org>>. To find out more about the food stamp program, check the U.S. Department of Agriculture Website at <<http://www.fns.usda.gov/fsp>>.

GLOSSARY

Numbers in **boldface** refer to chapters in which the Glossary terms are first discussed.

ability-to-pay principle the belief that people who earn more than others, or who can afford to pay more than others, should pay higher taxes. **(27)**

absolute advantage the ability of one nation to produce certain goods or services at lower cost than another nation. **(31)**

acid rain precipitation of higher than normal acidity. **(35)**

acquiring company the company that purchases another company to form a merger. **(25)**

advertising paid announcements calling attention to one's product or service in the hope of attracting customers. **(8)**

affordable housing rentals and prices of apartments and houses within the income range of people with average incomes. **(37)**

agitator a negative term used to describe labor union organizers. **(19)**

agribusiness the large-scale production and distribution of agricultural goods. **(36)**

agricultural output the value of crops and livestock produced in a given period. **(34)**

annual percentage rate (APR) the percentage cost of credit on a yearly basis. **(12)**

antitrust law legislation designed to prevent business firms from gaining monopolies in their fields. **(26)**

apprenticeship program a formal training period in which an individual is taught a trade or skill by a skilled worker. **(16)**

arbitration the use of a third party, called an **arbitrator**, to make a decision that is binding on both parties in a dispute. **(20)**

assembly line production process involving bringing pieces of a product to be assembled to workers stationed along a line. **(24)**

ATM card a plastic card needed to use an automatic teller machine. **(12)**

automatic teller machine (ATM) a bank device that allows a customer to make withdrawals and deposits. **(5)**

automation the production technique of using machines to operate other machines. **(24)**

bait-and-switch an advertising technique offering a cheap product for sale with the intention of selling a more expensive product. **(8)**

balanced budget one in which receipts exactly equal expenditures. **(15)**

balance of payments a summary of all of a nation's economic dealings with the rest of the world in one year. **(33)**

balance of trade the relationship of a nation's merchandise exports to imports. **(32)**

bandwagon an advertising appeal to consumers' desire to conform. **(8)**

barter the use of goods or services instead of money as a means of exchange. **(5)**

base period a year or two whose index number is 100, to which numbers for other years are compared. **(6)**

bear an investor who believes that stock prices will decline. **(23)**

beneficiary an individual named in an insurance policy to receive insurance benefits. **(13)**

benefits-received principle the idea that only those who gain from a government service ought to pay for it. **(27)**

blacklist an illegal employer tactic of distributing lists of persons who should not be employed. **(20)**

blue-collar worker one employed in craft, manual, or operative labor. **(16)**

board of directors individuals elected by stockholders of a corporation to determine policy for the corporation. **(22)**

bond a certificate issued by a corporation or government agency in exchange for a long-term loan. **(11)**

bond fund a mutual fund that invests in different bonds. **(11)**

boycott an organized refusal of consumers to buy from a company or nation or from those who do business with that company or nation. **(20)**

brain drain the movement of experts and highly qualified individuals from one company or country to another. **(34)**

brand loyalty a consumer practice of buying a particular brand name product. **(8)**

breadline the distribution of food to needy people. **(29)**

budget a plan for dealing with future income and expenses. **(15)**

built-in stabilizer one of the economic forces in an economy that tends to keep total spending from rising so high as to bring on inflation or falling so low as to bring on recession. **(30)**

bull an investor who believes that the prices of stocks will increase. **(23)**

business association a group of businesses of the same or related type that are organized for mutual interest. **(10)**

business cycle the periodic changes in the level of a nation's business activity. **(29)**

business plan a detailed plan indicating the nature of the business, its potential market, source of funding, risks, expectations, and marketing approach. **(21)**

cancelled check one that has been paid to the final recipient and stamped so that it is no longer valid. **(5)**

capital the machines, tools, and buildings used in the production of goods and services; money. **(21)**

capital formation the accumulation of capital resources. **(35)**

capital gain the increase in the monetary value of an investment from the time of its purchase to the time of its sale. **(23)**

capitalism an economic system in which the means of production are privately owned, and the *what, how,* and *who* questions are answered by the market. **(2)**

career one's area of work over a long time. **(16)**

cash value the dollar value an individual will receive if an insurance policy is redeemed before its due date. **(13)**

central city the densely populated center of a metropolitan area; **city. (37)**

charge account a customer's account at a business to which his or her purchases are charged. **(12)**

charter a legal document issued by the state to an individual, business, or locality to act as a legal entity. **(22)**

check a written order directing a bank to pay money. **(5)**

checking account deposits in a bank allowing the depositor to make withdrawals by issuing checks against the account. **(5)**

check-off an employer's act of deducting union dues from a worker's paycheck, giving the dues to his or her union. **(20)**

child labor the employment of children below a minimum age. **(32)**

circular flow the exchange of goods, services, and payments among businesses, households, and government. **(3)**

closed corporation a corporation that does not issue stock for public purchase. **(22)**

closed shop a workplace where only members of a certain union or unions are employed. **(19)**

collateral money or items of value used to back up a loan. **(12)**

collective bargaining the negotiations between union and management representatives over salaries, benefits, and working conditions. **(20)**

collectivism community ownership of property rather than individual, private ownership. **(19)**

command economy an economic system in which the *what, how,* and *who* questions are answered by the government. **(2)**

commercial bank an institution whose principal function is to provide checking accounts and loans for business firms and individual customers. **(5)**

common stock a security that represents ownership in a corporation and entitles the owners to vote in the selection of the corporation's board of directors. **(23)**

commune a large agricultural organization that contains many villages and owns the land, buildings, animals, and equipment. **(2)**

communism an economic and political system in which all property is publicly owned, and the government makes all *what, how*, and *who* decisions. **(2)**

community policing the placement of police officers in neighborhoods on foot patrols to increase safety. **(37)**

comparable worth paying equivalent wages for work usually done by women in terms of the pay given for an occupation requiring equivalent skill and effort usually performed by men. **(18)**

comparative advantage the principle that nations should specialize in the production of those goods and services in which they are most efficient. **(31)**

comparison shopping checking prices of similar products at various sources before making purchases. **(9)**

competition a state of rivalry among sellers and among buyers for goods and services. **(3)**

competitiveness the ability to compete with others who are selling the same good or service. **(33)**

competitors two or more individuals or business firms conducting business in the same market. **(2)**

compound interest interest earned on savings and on interest previously earned. **(11)**

computer-assisted design (CAD) the use of computers and special computer software to produce designs. **(24)**

computer-assisted machining (CAM) the use of computers and computer software to operate production equipment. **(24)**

conglomerate merger the merging of companies producing unrelated products. **(25)**

conspicuous consumption buying as a means of showing one's wealth or status. **(7)**

consumer a person who buys or uses goods or services. **(1)**

Consumer Price Index (CPI) an index that measures changes in the cost of living. **(6)**

consumer sovereignty the ability of consumers to choose which goods and services are produced. **(3)**

consumption spending for consumer goods and services. **(7)**

contract a legal agreement. **(21)**

cooperative an organization of buyers or sellers whose members pool their resources as a means of operating efficiently. **(22)**

copyright a legal monopoly, granted by the government, giving exclusive rights to authors, artists, and composers to reproduce, perform, and sell their works. **(26)**

corporate bond an investment security by which a corporation promises to pay back a loan. **(23)**

corporate farm a large, mechanized farm that is organized and operates as a business corporation. **(36)**

corporate income tax a tax on net profits of incorporated businesses. **(22)**

corporation a business chartered by a state or the federal government as a legal individual and is owned by its stockholders. **(22)**

cost-push inflation rising prices caused by the generally increasing costs of doing business. **(6)**

craft union a union composed of workers in the same trade, e.g., machinists. **(19)**

credit the advance of money in exchange for a promise to repay at a specified time. **(12)**

credit history a report of an individual's past payments of loans and credit purchases. **(12)**

credit line an amount of money a bank or other business is willing to extend to a borrower. **(12)**

creditor one who lends money. **(12)**

credit union an association of people of similar interest offering members services similar to those offered by savings banks. **(5)**

currency coins and paper money issued by government and legal as a means of exchange. **(5)**

customs fees or tariffs imposed on goods entering a country. **(32)**

cycle of dependency a tendency for some families to receive welfare payments generation after generation. **(38)**

cyclical unemployment that which occurs because of changes in the business cycle. **(38)**

debit card a plastic card that may be used in the same way as a check to purchase goods and services, which are immediately charged to the individual's checking or savings account. **(5)**

deficit occurs when spending is greater than income or revenue. **(15)**

deficit budget one where the anticipated spending of government exceeds anticipated revenues. **(28)**

deflation an extended period of decline in prices. **(6)**

demand the quantity of a good or service that buyers would take at a particular price. **(4)**

demand curve a line on a graph that shows demand for a good or service at different prices. **(4)**

demand-pull inflation rising prices caused by generally increasing demand. **(6)**

deposit money placed in a bank account. **(5)**

depreciation a decline in the value of a firm's capital goods caused by use or the passage of time. **(23)**

deregulation the removal of government regulations on an industry. **(26)**

developed nation an industrialized country that has generally high living standards. **(34)**

developing nation a country that has a largely agricultural economy and is not heavily industrialized. **(34)**

direct tax one paid to the government by the person or business that is taxed; a tax that cannot be shifted. **(27)**

discount rate the interest rate charged by the Federal Reserve System to its member banks for borrowed funds. **(30)**

discretionary spending government spending that is not mandated by law from year to year. **(28)**

dividend a share of a company's profits that is issued to stockholders. **(11)**

division of labor specialization by workers in the production process. **(24)**

double taxation the taxing of a corporation's profits twice, once in the form of corporate taxes and a second time when the shareholder is taxed on dividends received. **(22)**

down payment the initial amount of money one is required to pay when buying a good or service on the installment plan. **(12)**

earnings the money a worker is paid; profits from running a business. **(16, 22)**

e-buying making purchases over the Internet. **(8)**

e-commerce the buying and selling of goods and services over the Internet. **(8)**

economic assistance grants and loans to developing countries by other countries or international agencies. **(34)**

economic depression a long period of decline in business activity. **(29)**

economic forecasting predicting how the economy will behave on the basis of specific economic data. **(30)**

economic goals the economic ends that a nation strives for, such as full employment, stable prices, and economic growth. **(3)**

economic growth the increase in output of goods and services over time. **(30)**

economic indicator a set of statistics about the performance of a sector of a nation's economy. **(29)**

economic resources the things that go into the creation of goods and services. **(1)**

economics the study of how people choose to use scarce resources to satisfy their needs and wants. **(1)**

economic system the way in which a society organizes for production. **(2)**

economist one who earns a living studying a nation's economic system or its parts. **(1)**

efficiency the achieving of maximum output with minimum input. **(4)**

elasticity of demand a ratio of changes in demand for a good or service to changes in its price. **(4)**

elasticity of supply a ratio of changes in supply of a good or service to changes in its price. **(4)**

electronic funds transfer the movement of funds from one account or bank to another electronically rather than by an actual physical delivery of these funds. **(5)**

endorsement the act of passing title of a check to another party. **(5)**

energy consumption the using up of energy. **(34)**

energy-efficiency rating a comparison of energy uses among competing products. **(10)**

entitlements government benefits guaranteed to individuals by law. **(28)**

entrepreneur one who organizes a business and assumes the risks and rewards of ownership. **(21)**

estate tax a tax imposed on inherited money or property. **(27)**

ethanol a fuel consisting of a mixture of gasoline and grain-based alcohol. **(36)**

euro the currency used as the medium of exchange in many European Union countries. **(32)**

excise tax one on the manufacture, sale or use of a specific good or service. **(27)**

expenses the money an individual or organization spends. **(21)**

exploit to take advantage of someone. **(2)**

exports the goods and services that individuals and businesses in one country sell to foreign countries. **(31)**

external factor an event that affects an economy over which individuals and governments have no control, such as the impact of a hurricane, war, or terrorism. **(29)**

fact-finding board a group called together to examine the facts in a labor-management dispute and to present findings. **(20)**

farm bloc the members of Congress representing states where farming is important and voting as a group on issues affecting farmers. **(36)**

farm-price supports federal measures to maintain at certain levels farmers' income from the sale of certain products. **(36)**

farm surplus the production of more crops or livestock than can be sold at a profit. **(36)**

farm technology the equipment, methods, and systems used in the production of crops and livestock. **(36)**

favorable balance of trade a situation in which the dollar value of merchandise exports is greater than the dollar value of imports. **(32)**

federal budget the plan of the U.S. government indicating how much money it expects to receive (**revenues**) and how much it expects to spend (**expenditures**) in a specific year. **(28)**

finance charge the interest charged on a loan and on the unpaid balance on a credit card. **(12)**

financial plan a plan of one's goals that will cost money and the means of achieving those goals. **(15)**

fiscal policy the power of the government to tax and spend in order to influence the economy. **(30)**

fiscal year any 12-month period used by a government, business, or individual for financial planning. **(28)**

five-year plan one prepared by the Soviet government to determine what and how much should be produced (and by whom) in the Soviet economy in a five-year period. **(2)**

fixed exchange rate a currency exchange rate a government sets. **(32)**

fixed expense a budget expense that does not change from month to month. **(15)**

flex time a system of allowing workers various alternatives in their working hours. **(19)**

floating exchange rate a currency exchange rate that rises and falls according to the values set in an open market. **(32)**

food stamps papers issued by the federal government to needy individuals that may be exchanged for food products according to their stated values. **(38)**

foreign exchange the currencies of other nations. **(33)**

foreign-exchange controls government regulations on the buying and selling of foreign currencies. **(32)**

foreign investments ones made by citizens and businesses of one country in other countries. **(34)**

401(k) plan a retirement plan that allows an individual to set aside and invest automatically a portion of wages and neither the savings nor any interest earned on those savings are taxed until the individual retires and withdraws the money. **(11)**

franchise a license to conduct a business using a specific brand name. **(22)**

franchisee the individual who holds a license to operate a franchise. **(22)**

franchisor the company that authorizes the use of its brand name to the franchisee to operate a specific business. **(22)**

free enterprise another name for capitalism. **(2)**

frictional unemployment a condition of being without work after leaving one job and seeking another. **(38)**

fringe benefits those that workers receive from their employer in addition to their wage or salary. **(20)**

full employment a condition that exists when all those willing and able to work can find jobs, except for those who are between jobs. **(30)**

garnish to withhold by court order all or a portion of a worker's earnings to pay that individual's debt. **(10)**

generic drug a drug identified by its chemical ingredients rather than by a brand name. **(9)**

gentrification remodeling or rebuilding an area, usually a poor neighborhood, and converting it to an area generally affordable by individuals with higher incomes than the previous inhabitants. **(37)**

gift tax a tax an individual is expected to pay on the value of gifts received. **(27)**

global economy the worldwide market in which the buying and selling of goods and services by all nations of the world take place. **(31)**

globalization the reduction of trade barriers among nations. **(32)**

goods things of value that can be seen or touched. **(1)**

goods-producing industry one that produces tangible products. **(16)**

government-support farm programs a series of legislation passed since the 1930s attempting to raise the incomes of farmers. **(36)**

greenhouse effect the trapping of solar heat caused by gases in the atmosphere. **(35)**

grievance an assertion of a union member that one or more of his or her rights under the union contract has been violated. **(20)**

gross domestic product (GDP) the total value of the goods and services produced by a nation's economy in a year. **(3)**

gross pay the amount a worker receives before deductions are taken out. **(18)**

half-truth an advertising technique whereby some information about a product is deliberately withheld. **(8)**

health insurance protection to help pay for hospital, medical, and drug costs. **(13)**

homeowner's insurance protection to cover costs of various types of potential risks to the owner of a house or apartment. **(13)**

horizontal merger the merger of two or more companies in the same business. **(25)**

household one or more people occupying the same dwelling. **(3)**

human capital the level of skills and experience of a workforce. **(34)**

human resources the people who contribute to the production of goods and services. **(1)**

illegal alien an individual who enters a country without that government's permission or who overstays the terms of one's visit. **(16)**

importer a business engaged in bringing goods from a foreign country to be sold in the domestic (home) market. **(32)**

imports the goods and services that individuals and businesses in a country purchase from foreign countries. **(31)**

impulse buying purchasing a good or service without previously planning to buy it. **(9)**

income money an individual receives from earnings or other sources. **(15)**

income redistribution taking money, usually through taxation policies, from one group of people in society and passing it along to another group. **(27)**

income security government benefits paid to help the aged, disabled, and unemployed. **(28)**

income tax a tax levied on one's earnings. **(27)**

index number a number that shows a percentage change from a number in a base year. **(6)**

indirect tax a tax that is hidden and can be passed on to someone else. **(27)**

individual retirement account (IRA) a plan one sets up to save and invest a portion of one's income for retirement. **(11)**

industrialization the process of creating more industries. **(34)**

inelastic demand/supply demand is said to be inelastic when a change in price will not have much effect on the demand for a product; supply is said to be inelastic when a change in price will have little effect on the supply of a product. **(4)**

infant industry a new business, or industry, that is in competition with established, similar industries in one or more foreign countries. **(12)**

inflation an extended period of rise in prices of goods and services. **(6)**

inflationary cycle the process whereby increased consumer demand during full employment leads to price increases, which lead to wage increases, which lead to further price increases. **(30)**

inflationary spiral the recurring of wage increases followed by price increases followed by further wage increases and price increases. **(6)**

infrastructure a country's water, transportation, and communication systems, buildings, educational system, and hospitals. **(34)**

injunction a court order not to do something. **(19)**

inner city the older, more crowded, central area of a city, often inhabited by its poorer citizens. **(37)**

input a quantity of land, labor, or capital needed to produce goods or services. **(24)**

insider trading the buying or selling of a company's securities using private information. **(25)**

installment plan a method of buying a product and making monthly or other periodic payments including interest charges. **(12)**

insurance a method of protection against financial loss by sharing the risk with others. **(13)**

insurance agent one who earns a living selling insurance policies. **(13)**

interchangeable parts a system in which individual pieces of a product are made exactly the same way and can be exchanged with one another. **(24)**

interest rate the charge for the use of borrowed money, expressed as a percent. **(12)**

internal factor something operating within the economy that causes phases of business cycles. **(29)**

interstate commerce business activity conducted across state lines. **(19)**

inventory goods and materials a business has on hand and that have not yet been sold. **(30)**

investment business spending. **(3)** the purchase of property in the hope that in time it will increase in value. **(10)**

investment bank one that places the original issues of a company's securities on the market. **(23)**

investor someone who invests his or her own money. **(23)**

job action an action short of a strike taken by a labor union to stop or slow down production. **(20)**

job outlook a forecast of the possible opportunities for employment in one or more occupations. **(16)**

jurisdictional strike one caused by a dispute between two or more unions over which one will represent certain workers. **(20)**

"keeping up with the Joneses" buying things so as to appear to be on the same economic and social level of one's friends and neighbors. **(7)**

labor force all persons 16 years of age or older who hold a job or are looking for one. **(16)**

labor laws government legislation regulating the conditions of work. **(19)**

labor union an association of workers seeking to improve wages and working conditions for its members. **(19)**

laissez-faire the view that government should not interfere with business. **(30)**

land reform measures to distribute land to landless peasants. **(34)**

Law of Demand an economic principle stating that the quantity of an item demanded will increase as prices fall and decrease as prices rise. **(4)**

Law of Supply an economic principle stating that the quantity of an item offered will increase as prices rise and decrease as prices fall. **(4)**

lawsuit a legal action taken by one individual or group against another. **(13)**

least-developed nation those that receive the smallest share of the world's income. **(34)**

lemon law legislation designed to protect consumers from unknowingly buying a defective vehicle. **(9)**

lender someone who advances money to another with the expectation of being repaid, usually with interest. **(10)**

liability insurance protection to the insured against lawsuits for injuries to other persons or damages to their property. **(13)**

life expectancy an estimate as to how long an infant will live. **(34)**

limited liability the status of a corporation that only it is responsible for a debt, not the people who own the corporation. **(22)**

limited life the status of a business that it is legally ended when one or more of the owners dies or withdraws from the business. **(21)**

liquidity the ease by which an investment can be converted into cash. **(11)**

literacy rate the percentage of a population that is able to read. **(34)**

lockout a tactic of management in a labor dispute that prevents striking workers from entering the company's property. **(20)**

longevity the life span of an individual or other entity. **(28)**

long-term goal a plan for something one may want in a year or more. **(15)**

Luddite worker opposed to the introduction of new equipment. **(32)**

luxury a desired good or service that is not necessary. **(7)**

macroeconomics the study of an economy as a whole. **(1)**

mail-order buying purchasing items advertised in catalogs received in the mail. **(8)**

mandatory spending government spending that is fixed by law from year to year. **(28)**

market the place in which or arrangement by which goods and services are bought and sold. **(2)**

marketing the skills and procedures involved in the packaging, promotion, selling, and distribution of goods. **(21)**

market price the price at which goods and services are sold. **(4)**

market system an economic system in which decisions are made as the result of the actions of buyers and sellers. **(2)**

mass production the manufacture of large quantities of identical products using interchangeable parts, assembly lines, specialization of labor, and machines. **(24)**

materialistic placing a high value on material comfort and well-being. **(7)**

maturity the date at which a bond can be redeemed at face value. **(11)**

means of production land, labor, and capital resources, which, together with entrepreneurs, enable goods and services to be produced. **(2)**

mechanization the use of machines to replace human or animal labor. **(36)**

media sources of information to the public such as newspapers, magazines, radio, TV, and the Internet. **(8)**

median a statistical point above and below which there are an equal number of values. **(18)**

mediation the use of a third party to help settle a dispute. **(20)**

medical insurance protection from the costs of hospitalization, surgery, medication, and general medical care. **(14)**

megalopolis a network of interlocking metropolitan areas. **(37)**

merger the joining of two or more companies into one. **(25)**

metropolitan area a central city of 50,000 or more people plus the surrounding settled areas. **(37)**

microeconomics the study of individual parts of an economy. **(1)**

migrant worker a laborer, generally employed on farms, who moves from place to place in search of jobs. **(16)**

minimum wage by law the lowest wage an employer may pay a worker. **(1)**

mixed economy (mixed market economy) an economic system that combines both private ownership and government ownership of the means of production. **(2)**

monetary policy the efforts by the Fed to increase or decrease the level of business activity by regulating the nation's supply of money and credit. **(6)**

monetary unit the designated currency of a country. **(5)**

money anything generally accepted in payment for goods and services. **(5)**

money market fund a mutual fund that uses the invested money of many people to buy money market notes and the notes of the federal government and large corporations. **(11)**

money market savings account a savings account where interest on the account is based on the interest rate of money market funds. **(11)**

monopoly a situation in which there is only one producer or seller of a good or service. **(25)**

most-favored nation an agreement between two nations not to impose a higher tariff on each other's imports than the lowest tariff imposed on other nations that each might trade with. **(32)**

mutual fund a business that buys the stocks and bonds of other businesses for the profit of its shareholders. **(23)**

mutual savings bank a savings bank that is owned by its depositors. **(5)**

name brand the name associated with a particular product and which distinguishes it from similar products. **(9)**

national debt the total amount of money that the federal government owes. **(28)**

natural monopoly a business in an industry in which competition would be harmful to the public or does not make economic sense. **(26)**

natural resources the things found in the world around us, such as water, land, and minerals, that are used in the production of goods. **(1)**

necessity a good or service that we cannot do without. **(7)**

no-fault insurance financial protection whereby the injured party is paid by her or his insurance company regardless of who was responsible for the loss. **(13)**

noncash benefits benefits, such as food stamps or rent vouchers that a person on welfare receives rather than the equivalent value in money. **(38)**

nonrenewable resources products from nature that, once used, cannot be replaced. **(35)**

not-for-profit corporation an institution organized as a corporation for specific purposes (such as charities, schools) and which is not supposed to make a profit. **(22)**

NOW account a checking account that pays interest. **(11)**

occupation a long-time job. **(16)**

occupational cluster a listing of a range of related occupations. **(16)**

oligopoly a market in which there are only a few sellers. **(26)**

on-the-job training learning and sharpening skills needed for a job while working on that job. **(16)**

open corporation a corporation whose stock is for sale to the general public. **(22)**

open-market operations the buying and selling of government bonds by the Fed. **(30)**

open shop a workplace in which workers are not required to join a union. **(19)**

opportunity cost one that must be given up in order to get something else; a trade-off. **(1)**

outer city a suburban area that has many characteristics of a central city. **(37)**

output the quantity of a product or service that is produced. **(18)**

overhead the cost for items such as rent, insurance, utility payments, mortgage payments, and the like that are continuing costs of doing business. **(24)**

over-the-counter drug a drug that may be purchased at a pharmacy without a doctor's prescription. **(9)**

packaging a marketing technique to increase sales of a product by giving the product a color, shape, or design that appeals to consumers. **(8)**

parity price one set by the government for farm products that gives present-day farmers the same purchasing power that farmers received during the years 1910–1914. **(36)**

partnership a business owned by two or more persons. **(21)**

passbook savings account one in which the depositor receives either a passbook or monthly statement that records deposits made to that account. **(11)**

patent a federal grant that gives inventors the sole right to manufacture, use, and sell their inventions. **(26)**

payroll taxes ones deducted directly from a worker's paycheck. **(27)**

peak a phase of the business cycle characterized by full employment, full-capacity production, and rising prices. **(29)**

personal income the total income received in a year by all families and individuals in a country. **(29)**

personal loan a loan given to a consumer by a bank. **(12)**

physical capital buildings or machinery. **(34)**

picketing the carrying of signs asking people not to buy from a business where a strike is taking place. **(20)**

piecework payment for each item produced rather than a fixed hourly sum. **(18)**

policy a contract in which an insurance company guarantees payment should the policyholder incur specified losses. **(13)**

policyholder an individual or group that pays the premium or fees to be insured by an insurance company. **(13)**

pollution physical damage to the air, water, and land. **(35)**

poverty level the minimum income level set by the government below which a person or family is considered poor. **(38)**

poverty rate the percentage of the total population living below the poverty level. **(38)**

preferred stock shares of stock that pay a fixed dividend before dividends are paid to holders of common stock. **(23)**

premium the amount of money an insured person pays regularly to maintain an insurance policy. **(13)**

prescription drug medication prescribed for a specific patient by a doctor. **(9)**

price-directed market another term for a free market, where supply and demand are allowed to determine prices. **(4)**

primary boycott the organized refusal of consumers to buy from a company being struck. **(20)**

principal the original value of a loan or deposit to which interest may be added. **(11)**

private initiative the taking of risks or actions without the help or interference of government. **(38)**

private property something of value owned by people. **(3)**

privatize the selling of a government-operated business to private individuals. **(14)**

producer one who makes a good or provides a service. **(1, 7)**

production control government regulations on how much of a product may be produced. **(36)**

productivity the quantity of output for every unit of input. **(18, 24)**

profit motive the desire of business firms to earn the greatest profits possible from the sale of goods or services. **(3)**

profits money earned from the operation of a business after expenses have been paid. **(21)**

progressive tax one that imposes a higher tax rate as an individual's income increases. **(27)**

proletariat people of the working class. **(2)**

property insurance financial protection for an insured person's property. **(13)**

property tax one on the value of the taxpayer's possessions such as a house, automobile, or other valuables. **(27)**

proportional tax one that requires all persons to pay the same percentage of their total income in taxes. **(27)**

proprietor the owner of a business. **(21)**

prosperity a phase of the business cycle characterized by a high level of business activity and high employment. **(29)**

protective tariff a tax imposed on goods coming into the country to make foreign products more expensive than domestic ones. **(27)**

proxy a transfer of a stockholder's right to vote in a corporate election to another person or group. **(22)**

public assistance government help given to needy people other than social insurance; **welfare. (38)**

public housing living units built or financed by a government entity for low-income persons. **(37)**

public property something of value owned by government. **(3)**

public relations favorable publicity for a person, firm, organization, or product. **(8)**

public sector any area of the economy that is operated by the government. **(27)**

Public Service Commission a state government agency that regulates public utilities. **(10)**

public services those provided by government, such as roads and schools. **(27)**

public utility an industry that provides an essential service, such as electric power or water. **(26)**

purchasing power a measure of what the dollar is worth compared to its worth in a past year. **(6)**

quota a limit set by the federal government on the quantity or value of a good that may enter the country from abroad. **(2)**

racketeering illegal activities by an organized criminal group. **(19)**

rate of exchange the price at which a nation's currency can be bought using another nation's currency; the **exchange rate. (33)**

real economic growth the increase in a nation's output of goods and services adjusted for price changes. **(30)**

real GDP per capita the dollar value of the output of goods and services divided by the number of people in the nation after adjusting for price changes. **(35)**

recession a phase of the business cycle characterized by a decline in spending by businesses and consumers and an increase in unemployment. **(29)**

reciprocity an agreement among nations to mutually reduce tariffs on one another's imports. **(32)**

recovery a phase of the business cycle characterized by rising employment and production. **(29)**

recycling a procedure to conserve resources by reusing consumed products in the same or another form. **(35)**

redeem to convert a note, bond, or insurance policy to the issuer for cash. **(11)**

redlining an illegal practice whereby banks refuse to grant mortgages or other loans to people living within designated areas. **(38)**

region a geographical area that may be part of one state or may cover several states. **(37)**

regional planning governmental attempts to improve economic conditions and solve problems on a regional basis. **(37)**

regressive tax a tax whose rate takes a greater percentage of one's income as income decreases. **(27)**

regulatory agency a government office set up to oversee the way companies in a designated industry do business. **(26)**

renewable resource one that can be replaced or renewed. **(35)**

renter's insurance financial protection purchased by someone who rents a house or apartment. **(13)**

rent voucher welfare assistance given to poor persons to help pay rent. **(38)**

repossess to take back a good or property for the failure of the purchaser to make required payments. **(12)**

reserve ratio the percentage of its total deposits that a bank may not lend out. **(30)**

resources the things that go into the making of goods and services: natural, human, and capital resources. **(1)**

retailer the seller of the final product to the consumer. **(3)**

revenue tariff a tax on imported products the purpose of which is to earn income (revenue) for the government. **(27)**

right-to-work law legislation that prohibits a union shop and permits workers to hold jobs without joining a union. **(19)**

rule of law the concept that no individual is above the law and that contracts are enforceable by the courts. **(3)**

sales contract a legal agreement between a buyer and a seller. **(10)**

sales tax a tax on goods or services purchased by consumers. **(27)**

savings that portion of personal or business income that is not spent. **(11)**

savings and loan association a type of bank that accepts deposits from, and makes loans to, individuals only. **(5)**

scarcity the condition resulting from the fact that there is not enough of everything to go around. **(1)**

school tax one imposed on property owners to help pay the expenses of the school system in their community. **(27)**

S-corporation a special type of small business firm that is a corporation but does not have to pay corporate income taxes. **(22)**

secured loan a loan in which the borrower pledges something of value in case the loan is not repaid. **(12)**

securities stocks and bonds. **(23)**

self-employment working for oneself; having one's own business. **(38)**

self-employment tax one imposed on persons who work as independent agents rather than as employees of someone else's business. **(27)**

seniority ranking workers according to how long they have been on the job. **(20)**

service industry one that produces a service. **(16)**

service worker one employed in a service industry. **(16)**

services things of value that can neither be seen nor touched. **(1)**

shop steward a worker in a shop who is the union's representative at the workplace. **(20)**

short-term goal something an individual wants to accomplish in a year or less. **(15)**

sin tax a tax on products, such as tobacco and alcohol, that the government considers harmful. **(27)**

skill the ability to do something that requires special training. **(16)**

slowdown a union tactic where workers continue on the job but work at a slower pace than usual. **(20)**

slum an area within the inner city characterized by poverty, high crime rates, poor education facilities and lack of decent housing. **(37)**

small claims court a local court set up to allow individuals to appear before a judge without a lawyer to press a claim involving a small amount of money. **(10)**

social insurance government insurance programs such as Social Security and unemployment insurance. **(14)**

sole proprietorship a business that is owned and run by one person. **(21)**

spam unsolicited, unwanted e-mail. **(9)**

specialization a situation in which individuals, businesses, or regions produce a narrow range of products or services. **(24)**

speculator an individual who buys and sells securities in the hope of making a quick profit. **(23)**

standard of living the quality of life that an individual or nation is accustomed to, including life span, health standards, and income level. **(3)**

stock a share in the ownership of a corporation. **(11)**

stockbroker a person who specializes in purchasing and selling securities for clients. **(23)**

stock certificate a physical document showing ownership of stock. **(22)**

stock exchange the place, or market, where securities are bought and sold. **(23)**

stockholder one who owns shares of stock and who is thus a part owner of the corporation that issued the stock. **(22)**

store brand a product that displays the name of the store in which it is sold. **(9)**

straight-life insurance a form of life insurance that also provides for forced savings and cash value. **(13)**

strike a union tactic whereby workers refuse to work. **(20)**

strikebreaker an individual who works at a place that is being struck; also **scab**. **(19)**

structural unemployment a lack of work because one's craft or industry is no longer in demand. **(38)**

subsidy a payment by the government to individuals or business firms. **(32)**

suburb a residential area outside the central city. **(37)**

supply the quantity of a good or service offered at a particular price. **(4)**

supply curve a line on a graph that shows supply of a good or service at different prices. **(4)**

surplus budget one in which anticipated revenue will be greater than anticipated expenditures. **(28)**

sweetheart contract a deal worked out between a crooked labor leader and an employer to benefit the employer at the expense of the union members who work for the employer. **(20)**

SWOT analysis a framework to evaluate a business through an analysis of its Strengths, Weaknesses, Opportunities, and Threats. **(21)**

take-home pay the amount one receives after all deductions are taken from one's paycheck. **(18)**

takeover the merging of a company with another against the wishes of the directors of the company being absorbed. **(25)**

target company a company that another company intends to take over. **(25)**

target price a minimum price set by the government that farmers will receive for their products. **(36)**

tariff a government tax on goods imported into a country. **(27)**

taxable income that which is subject to taxes. **(27)**

tax base all the possible sources of tax revenue available to a government. **(37)**

tax deferral a procedure by which a taxpayer may postpone the payment of certain taxes due. **(37)**

technological change any modification in the way machinery and equipment are used in the production of goods or services. **(19)**

technological unemployment that resulting from the displacement of workers by new technologies. **(24)**

term life insurance life insurance usually for a 1-to-5-year period that may be renewed, but at a higher premium each term. **(13)**

testimonial an advertising technique that uses the spoken or written endorsement of products by well-known personalities. **(8)**

testing organization one that tests products and attaches a mark or label of approval on those approved. **(10)**

trade-off the good or service that must be given up in order to buy another. **(1)**

trade restriction a tariff, duty, or ban on certain foreign products or on products from certain countries. **(32)**

trading the buying, selling, or exchange of goods and services. **(31)**

trading bloc a group of nations that act as a unit when trading with one another or with nonmember nations. **(32)**

traditional economic system one in which the basic economic questions are answered according to custom and things are done in the same way as they have been done for a long time. **(2)**

trough a downturn in the business cycle. **(29)**

two-tier wage a pay system under which new workers are paid at a lower scale than the more senior workers had been when they were first hired. **(20)**

unemployment the condition of being willing and able to work but unable to find a job. **(38)**

unemployment insurance a government program that pays an unemployed worker for a limited period of time a part of the salary the worker had received while working. **(14)**

unemployment rate the percentage of the workforce that is unemployed. **(38)**

union contract an agreement between a labor union and an employer concerning wages, hours, conditions of work, and benefits that the employees are entitled to. **(20)**

union organizer a person paid by a union to convince workers to join the union. **(19)**

union shop a workplace that employs only union workers. **(19)**

unit pricing the practice of marking prices in terms of cost per weight or volume. **(9)**

unlimited liability the status of a businessperson who is personally responsible for all debts incurred by her or his business. **(21)**

unlimited life the status of a business that ends when one or more of the owners leaves the business. **(22)**

unpaid balance the amount of a loan that has not yet been paid. **(12)**

unsecured loan one that has no collateral or backing if the borrower cannot pay the debt due. **(12)**

unsolicited goods those received by consumers and that have not been requested. **(9)**

urban area a populated area such as a city and its suburbs. **(37)**

urban redevelopment project a program to improve an urban area. **(37)**

urban renewal the economic rehabilitation of a rundown central city area by restoring or replacing homes, businesses, schools, and recreation areas. **(37)**

U.S. savings bond a security representing a small loan to the federal government. It promises to pay both principal and interest to the buyer of the bond many years later. **(11)**

variable expense one that may be increased or diminished and that is not necessary. **(15)**

vertical merger the combining of two or more firms where one firm produces a product or service regularly needed by the other firm. **(25)**

vocational preference test one designed to indicate the various occupations an individual might be best suited for. **(16)**

wage an hourly fee for work performed. **(4)**

wages in kind payment other than money for work performed. **(18)**

welfare government aid other than social insurance given to people in economic need. **(38)**

what, how, who the basic economic questions all societies must answer indicating what will be produced, how it will be produced, and who will get it. **(2)**

white-collar worker one employed in a clerical, professional, or management occupation. **(16)**

wholesaler a businessperson who buys from producers and sells to retailers. **(3)**

work credits a measurement of the quarters of a year that an individual has been employed so as to determine her or his Social Security benefits. **(14)**

worker mobility the relative ease or difficulty for workers to move from one area to another in search of employment. **(18)**

workers' compensation benefits paid to workers injured in accidents that happen on the job. **(14)**

workfare a law requiring welfare recipients to work or enroll in a job-training program. **(38)**

INDEX

PHOTO ACKNOWLEDGMENTS

Unit I

2: © Zausner; 5 & 6: © Jerry Howard/ Positive Images; 7: © R.W. Jones/Corbis; 8: © Joel Gordon 1983; 20: © Ulrike Welsch; 21: © Alan Carey/Image Works; 22: © Ivan Sekretarev/AP/Wide World Photos; 26: © Wolfgang Kaehler/Corbis; 29: © Holly Lee/Black Star; 36: © Robert Kaplan/ Image Works; 37: © Bob Krist/Corbis; 39 & 59: © Jerry Howard/Positive Images; 70: © Nagata/United Nations/DPI; 74: Courtesy American Express Company; 78: © Joel Gordon 1984; 79: © Arthur Tilley/Getty Images/FPG International; 82: © Alan Carey/Image Works; 92: © Mark Antman/ Image Works; 93: © Bettmann/Corbis.

Unit II

100: © Mark Lewis/Getty Images/Stone; 104 top: © Jim Kahnweiler/Positive Images; 104 middle left: © Howard Grey/ Getty Images/Stone; 104 bottom left and right: Ulrike Welsch; 105 top: © Dion Ogust/Image Works; 105 center: © David Strickler/Image Works; 105 bottom: © Ulrike Welsch; 110: © Joel Gordon 1982; 117: © Mark Antman/Image Works; 121: © Dion Ogust/Image Works; 126: © Monika Graff/Image Works; 133: © Joel Gordon 1984; 138: © Bruce Ayres/Getty Images/ Stone; 144: © Carolyn A. McKeone/Photo Researchers; 153: © Michael J. Okoniewski/ Image Works; 154: © Consumers Union of U.S., Inc. Yonkers, NY 10703-1057, a non-profit organization. Reprinted with permission from the CONSUMER REPORTS® for educational purposes only. No commercial use or photocopying permitted. Log onto www.ConsumerReports.org.; 155: © Jeff Greenberg/Visuals Unlimited; 170: © U.S. Bureau of Public Debt; 174: © Chronis Jons/Getty Images/Stone; 175: © Joel Gordon 1982; 182: © Alan Carey/Image Works; 195 top: © Dan Chidester/Image Works; 195 bottom: © Jock Pottle/Design Conceptions; 197: © Michael Krasowitz/Getty Images/FPG International; 203: © Nita Winter/Image Works; 209: © Bettmann/ Corbis; 211 top: © Nita Winter/Image Works; 211 bottom: © Bruce Ayres/Getty Images/Stone; 213: © Alan Carey/Image Works; 221 top: © Syracuse Newspapers/ Image Works; 221 bottom: © David Pratt/ Positive Images; 226: © Mary Lang/ Positive Images.

Unit III

234: © Lee F. Snyder/Photo Researchers; 239: © Bob Daemmrich/Image Works; 241: © Jane Hwang/AP/Wide World Photo; 242: © Larry Kolvoord/Image Works; 250: Courtesy of the CARPENTERS UNION, Local 247, Bruce Dennis, President, Portland Oregon; 259: Ulrike Welsch; 262: © Laima Druskis/Photo Researchers; 266: © Alan Carey/Image Works; 274 upper left: © Jack Spratt/Image Works; 274 upper right: © Joel Gordon 1982; 274 bottom left: © Alan Carey/Image Works; 274 bottom right: © David Wells/Image Works; 275 upper left: © Alan Carey/Image Works; 275 upper right: © Joel Gordon 1984; 275 bottom left: © Mark Antman/Image Works; 275 bottom right: © Peter Kornicker/ Corbis; 287: © Bettmann/Corbis; 290: © Greg Gibson/AP/Wide World Photos;

298: © Michael Smith/Newsmakers/Getty Images; 305: © Ann Heisenfelt/AP/Wide World Photos; 307: © Michael Siluk/Image Works.

Unit IV

314: © Chris Windsor/Getty Images/Stone; 320: © Matthew McVay/Stock Boston; 324: © Bettmann/Corbis; 325: © Courtesy of BET, Viacom; 326: © Courtesy of ViewSonic; 327: © Aaron Haupt/Photo Researchers; 348: Courtesy Ford Motor Company; 349: © Photo used with permission of the New York Stock Exchange; 350: © Chuck Fishman/Woodfin Camp & Associates; 363 top & bottom: Bettmann/Corbis; 364: © Richard Kalvar/Magnum Photos; 366: © Alan Carey/Image Works; 379: Paul Levesque; 389: Alan Carey/Image Works; 391: © Bob Daemmrich/Image Works; 392: © Mark Antman/Image Works; 395: © Bettmann/ Corbis.

Unit V

402: © Alan Carey/Image Works; 409: © Brad Nading/Garden City Telegram/AP/Wide World Photos; 429: © Mark Antman/Image Works; 442: © Bettmann/Corbis; 444: © Chuck Robinson/AP/Wide World Photos; 459: © Joel Gordon 1984.

Unit VI

464: © Harald Sund/The Image Bank/Getty Images; 467: © Mark Antman/Image Works; 473 top: © Ho/AP/Wide World Photo; 473 bottom: © Lou Dematteis/Image Works; 479 & 483: © Mark Antman/Image Works; 487: © Reuters Newsmedia Inc./Corbis; 495: © Stefano Bianchetti/Corbis; 497: © Paul Sakuma/AP/Wide World Photos; 512: © Richard Vogel/AP/Wide World Photos.

Unit VII

524: © Jonathan Blair/Corbis; 533: © Martin Benjamin/Image Works; 534: © Mark Antman/Image Works; 537: © Martin Benjamin/Image Works; 539: © Wayne R. Bilenduke/The Image Bank/Getty Images; 543: © Joel Gordon 1983; 546: © Grant Heilman; 554: © Yellow Dog Productions/The Image Bank/Getty Images; 565: © Jim Commentucci/Syracuse Newspapers/Image Works; 566: © Spencer Platt/Newsmakers/Getty Images; 567: © Joel Gordon 1988; 571: © Vince Streano/Corbis; 581: © John Griffin/ Image Works; 584: © Bob Daemmrich/Image Works; 591: © Bettmann/Corbis; 594: © Reed Saxon/AP/Wide World Photos.